PROBLEMS IN BIBLICAL THEOLOGY

Problems in Biblical Theology

Essays in Honor of
Rolf Knierim

Edited by

Henry T. C. Sun and Keith L. Eades
with
James M. Robinson and Garth I. Moller

WILLIAM B. EERDMANS PUBLISHING COMPANY
GRAND RAPIDS, MICHIGAN / CAMBRIDGE, U.K.

Printed in the United States of America

02 01 00 99 98 97   7 6 5 4 3 2 1

Library of Congress Cataloging-in-Publication Data

Problems in biblical theology: essays in honor of Rolf Knierim /
edited by Henry T. C. Sun . . . [et al.].

p.   cm.

Includes bibliographical references.

ISBN 0-8028-3803-0 (alk. paper)

1. Bible. O.T. — Theology. 2. Bible. O.T. — Criticism,
interpretation, etc. I. Knierim, Rolf P., 1928-   .
II. Sun, Henry T. C.

BS1192.5.P696 1997

230 — DC20   96-25403

                                                  CIP

We would like to express appreciation to Dr. J. Harold Ellens for facilitating the publication of this volume, and to several individuals, as well as to the Institute for Antiquity and Christianity and the University of Manchester Research Support Fund, for supporting its publication.

Contents

CONTENTS

Contents

Preface

The idea for this collection of essays in honor of Rolf P. Knierim was conceived in the late 1980s during a conversation between three doctoral students of the Claremont Graduate School: Keith Eades, Garth Moller, and myself. During those discussions, it became clear that were such a volume to come into existence, it would have to pay attention to the several different personae of its honoree. First and foremost, Knierim is a scholar, trained in the German tradition, whose contributions to the ongoing scholarly discussions of form criticism, tradition history, and theology have been numerous. Hence, it was decided early on that it would be necessary to invite scholars and colleagues from Europe to contribute to this Festschrift. Second, Knierim is a passionate and charismatic teacher of students, many of whom will empathize with Michael Floyd's description of himself as "both thrilled and terrified at the prospect of studying with [Knierim]." Hence, it was clear that we would have to invite all of his students — all who had completed their Ph.D.s at the time the actual invitations were sent out — to contribute an essay. Finally, Knierim served the scholarly world most visibly in his role as editor of the Forms of the Old Testament Literature commentary series, the only serious and sustained discussion of Old Testament form criticism available in English. Hence, the decision was made to invite the various commentators from this series to author a contribution to this work. Each potential contributor was asked to produce an essay in dialogue with Knierim's seminal essays on Old Testament theology which were published in *Horizons in Biblical Theology* (1984).

The response to our invitations was overwhelming. The twenty-four essays from as many scholars represent colleagues, students, and fellow commentators from Europe, North and South America, Japan, and Australia. Some of the authors have penned detailed exegetical studies. Others are concerned with theological methods and approaches from a variety of standpoints. Still others seek to relate Old Testament exegesis, theology, and hermeneutic to current interests in social scientific methods of interpretation or postmodern thought. The breadth of interests reflects something of the bursting intellectual vitality and passion which Knierim brought to the discipline. A biographical narrative written by Hildegard Knierim and a foreword by James M. Robinson provide additional insight into the historical and social context within which Knierim's work unfolded.

It now remains only to acknowledge those persons whose help made his Festschrift possible. Of the three original editors, Keith Eades (in tandem with Cynthia Eades) provided much of the computer support for the project. My thanks to them and appreciation of them know no bounds. Although Garth Moller, due to a professional relocation to another continent (!), was unable to assist in the production of the Festschrift, I gratefully acknowledge his role in the early work of inviting scholars and responding to their inquiries. Gesine Robinson and Ingrid Schaible assisted in the editing and proofreading of the contributions in German. James M. Robinson has played an essential role in gently pushing the process of publication forward, and Jon Pott and Jennifer Hoffman of William B. Eerdmans Publishing Company have greatly assisted in bringing the project to completion. And, most of all, I am profoundly indebted to those who contributed to this volume. Their eager willingness to participate in this project and to engage and advance the theological discussion is matched only by the extraordinary patience they exhibited from the time that the articles were submitted to the actual publication of the volume. It was originally planned to publish the Festschrift in December 1992, since 1992-93 was to be the year of Knierim's retirement from full-time teaching. Thus, all of the articles contained herein were completed in 1991, but unanticipated difficulties have delayed the publication of these articles until now.

HENRY T. C. SUN

Foreword

JAMES M. ROBINSON

During the first generation of the School of Theology at Claremont, of the Religion Faculty of the Claremont Graduate School, and of the Institute for Antiquity and Christianity (IAC), Rolf Knierim has been a central figure in the cluster of young scholars drawn together at Claremont, to make of a small college town an internationally known center of theological scholarship. Some five years before Knierim came, a colleague had left Claremont for Vanderbilt and Harvard Divinity School with the parting comment that Claremont was a "theological desert." Rolf Knierim is a major factor in the irrigation that over a generation turned Claremont into a theological garden.

The Old Testament had been represented at Claremont only in terms of ancient Near Eastern and Qumranian specialties. The administration was persuaded to balance the Old Testament program with an appointment in Old Testament theology. But when its normal search procedures failed to locate the kind of highly qualified person it sought, I was authorized to make inquiries in Europe. On the basis of strong recommendations by the leading German Old Testament theologians Walther Zimmerli of Göttingen and Gerhard von Rad of Heidelberg, we were able to bring as a visiting professor in 1964-65 the junior Old Testament faculty member at Heidelberg, who had published a book-length treatise on the Old Testament doctrine of sin and had been an active German Methodist pastor. The students were immediately impressed by the importance of the subject matter in his courses, first of all on the basis of the tremendous effort he was obviously making to communicate it in a foreign language with which he at first had to struggle, and then by the conviction and erudition that became hallmarks of his courses. He was promptly offered a professorship, which he then accepted after due consultation with his family and colleagues in Heidelberg, in time to begin his permanent Claremont stay early in 1966.

Already during his visiting year, plans were initiated to create around him and a few like-minded colleagues a research center modeled in part on the Göttingen Academy of Sciences — we had obtained copies of its constitution as part of the library of Walter Bauer just acquired as the core of our research library. The basic concept of the center was oriented to the fusion of the ancient Near East, the classical world of Greece and Rome, and the biblical heritage of Early Judaism and Christianity, which together formed the medieval synthesis of Christendom, out of which the modern West emerged. This concept is documented in the massive reference work *Reallexikon für Antike und Christentum*, launched by the Dölger Institut, a research center in Bonn named after the originator of the concept. This left the technical term *Antike und Christentum*, by then familiar in scholarly circles for the concept itself, still unclaimed by an institution. We hence gratefully appropriated it, so as to identify promptly in academic circles the new research center we were planning, the Institute for Antiquity and Christianity. Thus the transplanting of the erudite German tradition of theological scholarship represented by Knierim was not by accident, nor was it peripheral to the Institute, but rather fell at the very center of its initial conception.

The Old Testament Form-Critical Project directed by Knierim was one of the Institute's founding projects — one may consult the initial published announcement in *New Testament Studies* 16 (1970) 178-95, especially pages 191-93. This project, published by Eerdmans in Grand Rapids, has exceeded its initially planned dimensions to become, in effect, a multivolumed specialized Old Testament commentary. The ongoing dialogue among its editors has become *de facto* the center of Old Testament form-critical theological scholarship in America. The volumes in this series are appearing at a regular tempo as one of the more impressive accomplishments of the IAC. Knierim has brought distinction to the Institute, which in turn has provided him an intellectual home. Here his research associates working with him on the project, choice among his dozens of doctoral students over the years, have carried on the daily managing of details and copyediting to see the volumes through the press. Here members of his project have come on sabbatic leaves to work more closely with him on their own assignments. Here his work will go on, we hope far beyond his formal retirement, in the continuing direction of his project to its completion, in the advising of his many students as their *Doktorvater*, and in his own research and writing. *In multos annos!*

Abbreviations

AB	Anchor Bible
AJBI	*Annual of the Japanese Biblical Institute*
AJSL	*American Journal of Semitic Languages and Literature*
ALGHJ	Arbeiten zur Literatur und Geschichte des hellenistischen Judentums
AnBib	Analecta biblica
ANET	*Ancient Near Eastern Texts*, ed. J. B. Pritchard
AnOr	Analecta orientalia
AOAT	Alter Orient und Altes Testament
ArOr	*Archiv orientalí*
ATANT	Abhandlungen zur Theologie des Alten und Neuen Testaments
ATD	Das Alte Testament Deutsch
AusBR	*Australian Biblical Review*
AUSS	*Andrews University Seminary Studies*
BA	*Biblical Archaeologist*
BARev	*Biblical Archaeology Review*
BASOR	*Bulletin of the American Schools of Oriental Research*
BBB	Bonner biblische Beiträge
BDB	F. Brown, S. R. Driver, and C. A. Briggs, *Hebrew and English Lexicon of the Old Testament*
BFCT	Beiträge zur Förderung christlicher Theologie
BHT	Beiträge zur historischen Theologie
BibS	Biblische Studien
BJS	Brown Judaic Studies
BKAT	Biblischer Kommentar: Altes Testament

BRev	*Bible Review*
BTB	*Biblical Theology Bulletin*
BWANT	Beiträge zur Wissenschaft vom Alten und Neuen Testament
BZ	*Biblische Zeitschrift*
BZAW	Beihefte zur Zeitschrift für die alttestamentliche Wissenschaft
CAT	Commentaire de l'Ancien Testament
CBQ	*Catholic Biblical Quarterly*
CBQMS	Cathohc Biblical Quarterly — Monograph Series
CRINT	Compendia rerum iudaicarum ad novum testamentum
CTAT	*Critique textuelle de l'Ancien Testament*
DJD	Discoveries in the Judaean Desert
EBib	Etudes bibliques
EHAT	Exegetisches Handbuch zum Alten Testament
ErFor	Erträge der Forschung
EvT	*Evangelische Theologie*
ExpTim	*Expository Times*
FOTL	The Forms of the Old Testament Literature
FRLANT	Forschungen zur Religion und Literatur des Alten und Neuen Testaments
HAT	Handbuch zum Alten Testament
HBT	Horizons in Biblical Theology
HSM	Harvard Semitic Monographs
HSS	Harvard Semitic Studies
HTR	*Harvard Theological Review*
HUCA	*Hebrew Union College Annual*
IBC	Interpretation: A Bible Commentary for Preaching and Teaching
ICC	International Critical Commentary
IDB	*Interpreter's Dictionary of the Bible*
IDBSup	*Interpreter's Dictionary of the Bible, Supplementary Volume*
Int	*Interpretation*
JAAR	*Journal of the American Academy of Religion*
JANES	*Journal of the Ancient Near Eastern Society*
JBL	*Journal of Biblical Literature*
JBR	*Journal of Bible and Religion*
JJS	*Journal of Jewish Studies*
JQR	*Jewish Quarterly Review*

JR	*Journal of Religion*
JSJ	*Journal for the Study of Judaism*
JSOT	*Journal for the Study of the Old Testament*
JSOTSup	Journal for the Study of the Old Testament, Supplement Series
JSPSup	Journal for the Study of the Pseudepigrapha, Supplement Series
JSS	*Journal of Semitic Studies*
JTS	*Journal of Theological Studies*
KAI	*Kanaanäische und Aramäische Inschriften*
KAT	Kommentar zum Alten Testament
KB	L. Koehler and W. Baumgartner, *Lexicon in Veteris Testamenti Libros*
KD	*Kerygma und Dogma*
LCL	Loeb Classical Library
LTK	*Lexicon für Theologie und Kirche*
LTP	*Laval théologique et philosophique*
NCBC	New Century Bible Commentary
NICOT	New International Commentary on the Old Testament
NRT	*La nouvelle revue théologique*
OBO	Orbis biblicus et orientalis
OBT	Overtures to Biblical Theology
Or	*Orientalia*
OTL	Old Testament Library
OTS	Oudtestamentische Studiën
RB	*Revue biblique*
RevQ	*Revue de Qumran*
RGG	*Die Religion in Geschichte und Gegenwart*
SANT	Studien zum Alten und Neuen Testament
SB	Sainte bible
SBLDS	Society of Biblical Literature Dissertation Series
SBLMS	Society of Biblical Literature Monograph Series
SBS	Stuttgarter Bibelstudien
SJLA	Studies in Judaism in Late Antiquity
SSN	Studia semitica neerlandica
STDJ	Studies on the Text of the Desert of Judah
TBü	Theologische Bücherei
TD	*Theology Digest*

TDOT	*Theological Dictionary of the Old Testament*
THAT	*Theologisches Handwörterbuch zum Alten Testament*
ThLZ	*Theologische Literaturzeitung*
TOTC	Tyndale Old Testament Commentary
TQ	*Theologische Quartalschrift*
TRE	*Theologische Realenzyklopädie*
TWAT	*Theologisches Wörterbuch zum Alten Testament*
TZ	*Theologisches Zeitschrift*
USQR	*Union Seminary Quarterly Review*
VT	*Vetus Testamentum*
VTSup	Vetus Testamentum, Supplements
WBC	Word Biblical Commentary
WMANT	Wissenschaftliche Monographien zum Alten und Neuen Testament
WTJ	*Westminster Theological Journal*
ZAW	*Zeitschrift für die alttestamentliche Wissenschaft*
ZTK	*Zeitschrift für Theologie und Kirche*

Way Stations

HILDEGARD KNIERIM

Way stations are the places that catch our thoughts when they roam into the past. Each of our way stations was home to us once; they gave us shelter and a matrix to sink our roots in and grow. They are the places that let us test our capabilities and try out our skills. They are the places where we invested our energy and deposited a part of our life's span — and that probably is what draws us back.

Since I have shared some of Rolf Knierim's way stations with him, and since I know a few things about the ones I have not shared, I should like to visit them with you. As I write down the word "you," my mind sees manifold images of dear faces and my memory hears a chorus of familiar voices, and I am aware of oh so many distinguished names.

Way stations emerge from our memory rather randomly and certainly not in chronological order, so I will take the liberty of treating them in a similar manner. But you need not worry when I hop and skip here and there, because I know my way around. There is no need for much luggage either. What I ask you to take along, though, is:

a. Your own memories of Rolf Knierim, so that they can be enhanced.
b. The stories you heard him narrate, so that you can match them with their setting in life.
c. Last but not least, a smile for us fellow pilgrims.

Claremont

Let us start at the here and now, in Claremont, the neat little college town at the eastern boundary of Los Angeles County. It sits comfortably in front

1

of the foothills of massive Old Baldy (Mt. San Antonio, 10,046 ft.) and its proud companions along the San Gabriel range. The buildings of private residences and institutions for higher learning alike are tucked away under venerable trees whose branches, meeting above the streets, provide sun-shielding canopies.

"Downtown" here is lovingly called "The Village." The School of Theology, which prepares students for the ministry; the Claremont Graduate School, which provides Ph.D.s; and the Institute for Antiquity and Christianity, where the FOTL project is anchored, are the focal points of Rolf's engagement here.

Of course, some of you might privately add a cafeteria or two in appreciative recollection of the many enlightening discussions that took place there during coffee breaks.

There is yet another spot which, I hope, evokes good memories; namely, 1371 Carthage Court in the northwestern corner of Claremont. We bought the place in 1966, a house in the middle of a sunbaked stony block. We all, but especially Rolf, labored hard to turn it into an agreeable piece of property. It has also been a good home — just ask our children!

A case in point: no, no, not the snakes — but the garage! You see, in our latitude garages are usually put to better uses than merely housing the family car! So Rolf mused that ours would lend itself nicely to a playroom, with space enough for a Merklin train setup. The family agreed and cooperated in its transformation into a play area for kids of all ages! No party was complete without a tryout at the train set. Here the intelligentsia was really put to the test — and forced to cooperate! How about running a number of trains simultaneously with a dozen control switches! Stunning collisions, bewildering derailments, chaos, lighthearted restoration of order!

As time passed, the turbulence subsided and the room took on a more tranquil ambiance, that of a study. Now books, laden with knowledge, sometimes even wisdom, wait patiently side by side on the floor-to-ceiling bookshelves for their turn to be consulted. A comfortable seating arrangement provides for the professor-student encounters. It is here that Rolf tackles the problems, academic or personal, that his advisees incur. And he does that uncompromisingly, honestly, straightforwardly, with openness and fairness, analyzing the problems, giving advice, showing a possible way through, offering support and encouragement where necessary.

True, sometimes a session might have become less comfortable for the student on the receiving end, but, don't be mistaken, your problems were troubling your *Doktorvater* too. But later, with the degree completed and peers congregated in the living room or on the patio to celebrate the accomplishment, faces radiated with joy and pride! Memories of these occasions are highly treasured at 1371 Carthage Court.

Left alone, Rolf Knierim the scholar will turn to his desk to encounter The Book. His dialogues with the prophets and scholars of yore are intense and his quest to understand their writings and discover their underlying concepts is relentless.

From time to time his concentration may be diverted and his mind refreshed by a glimpse of the world outside. Oh, there is no panoramic view, no forest or lake or park. This is just a down-to-earth vegetable garden, Rolf's other hobby! Here he has knelt on every foot of ground, turned each clump of soil, held tenderly in his hand each seedling. This is where he has to replenish the humus, provide water when rain is lacking, provide protection when the sun's rays turn deadly, and harvest what his responsive charges offer him back. Here he feels the pulse of God's creation.

From November 1964 until May 1965, Rolf Knierim taught at the Southern California School of Theology as a visiting professor. He did this without previous knowledge of the English language. He was offered and accepted the Willis Fisher chair. He resumed his teaching in Heidelberg, prepared for the transition, and on March 8, 1966, entered the United States of America at Los Angeles International Airport with his wife and five children, ranging in age from twenty-one months to ten years.

Since then Rolf Knierim has supervised about thirty doctoral students to the completion of the Ph.D. About fifteen more are on their way. The numbers are constantly subject to change. He has also served as adviser to quite a few M.A. students. How many more minds beyond these he has touched and inspired in seminary classes, graduate school seminars, public lectures and clergy workshops, and in so many other ways and other countries cannot be grasped by statistics.

What a decision in 1964!

What a result in 1996!

Heidelberg

As we leave our starting point, a giant leap across the American continent and the Atlantic Ocean will be necessary to bring us to the first stopover: Heidelberg, Germany. This is Rolf Knierim's terrain. Here he lived through three phases of his life: as a student, as a pastor/assistant professor, and a *Privatdozent* (associate professor).

I feel, however, that you should have some free time for your personal encounter with this city. I hope that when we meet again you will have contracted the *genius loci* for good, with all its accompanying symptoms.

If I may suggest, take a bus to the *Kornmarkt* and continue on the cobblestone road uphill on foot. Walk slowly, watch your step, but at the same time notice the old walls on your right as they build up to the majestic castle. Take a breath here and there and delight in the scenery as it unfolds to your left. You will have a full view of it from the castle terrace: the green hills, dotted with houses surrounded by flowering gardens, sinking away toward the huddled city and its river, the Neckar. You will easily make out some distinct features among the jammed rooftops. The fortress-like building on the riverbank was built to house the Elector's horses. Now it is the Mensa. Here Rolf could trade in his food stamps for meals; food stamps for which a student had to write a seminar paper, which in turn provided the opportunity for the professor to pick out an individual from the crowd. And over there you see the slated mansard roof with the cheeky little clock tower jestingly perched on top. This is Rolf's alma mater, this is the heart of Heidelberg, the "Alte Universität," founded A.D. 1386. As you wend your way down to the city again, watch your step. I'll see you in Heidelberg at the house: in den Pfädelsäckern 36.

Come in, make yourself comfortable around the expanse of our tiled stove. This is a small house, you will notice, but it is very well designed and it had enough space for our growing family. It is also the first house we could call our own. It even had room for a study so that, in the midst of all the frolicking in the happy home, Father was able to maintain a sanctuary for his work. Here he wrote out his lectures, planned his proseminars, produced various publications for the academic arena, and wrote on vital issues for the church, in whose affairs he continued to be involved. This was a time of challenge and enhancement for Rolf. He was a member now of a faculty made up of the most prominent theologians of the time, and they appreciated him as an intellectual and accepted him as a person. And the students flocked to his classes.

Six wonderful years would pass until the lure of intellectual adventure led us to break camp and turn toward a new horizon in California.

Notable details from these years: on December 16, 1960, we moved into the house in den Pfädelsäckern 36 with our three children: Johannes, Eva, and Eberhard. Barbara and Gabriele were born during our stay there. On February 20, 1963, Rolf Knierim obtained the *Venia Legendi* (D.Habil.) from the Theological Faculty of the University of Heidelberg.

As we remain here, let me tell you about the other places in Heidelberg.

Rolf's toughest time here was certainly during our stay in the parsonage at Landhausstraße 17. Three jobs at once demanded his full-time attention: (1) he was assigned as pastor of the Methodist congregation and chaplain of the Bethanien Hospital; (2) he was personal assistant to Professor Claus Westermann, and later Gerhard von Rad; (3) he had the additional responsibility of teaching Hebrew and conducting proseminars for beginning students.

While he tackled his academic assignments with much enthusiasm, his concern for the Methodist church and its direction into the future led him more and more to assume a role of leadership there. He met with other young pastors to discuss the pressing issues, the role of women in the church among others. He wrote articles, spoke at conferences, and invited students to our dinner table for lengthy conversations. From the outset, the pastorate in Heidelberg was limited to one year. After that the bishop would have a replacement available and Rolf was granted leave to work exclusively for the university.

The first phase of Rolf Knierim's stay at "way station Heidelberg" began in 1951. He had started his academic training for the ministry at the Methodist Seminary *(Methodistisches Predigerseminar)* at Frankfurt/Main, where he could study free of charge. A friend of Rolf's parents, a wealthy shoe merchant, made the change to Heidelberg possible. This man had not forgotten the time when, as a poor and hungry little boy, he was often invited for dinner by Grandmother Knierim. He offered Rolf free room and board and enough cash to pay for the study fees and a commuter train ticket from the city of Speyer.

A summer job in Switzerland as a bricklayer brought Rolf enough hard currency to move to Heidelberg proper and share a room at Wilhelmstraße 10. His roommate was Manfred Hoffmann, now professor of church history at Candler School of Theology, Emory University, Atlanta. Further augmentation of his livelihood came from the deaconesses of Bethanien Hospital who fed the future pastor well in exchange for a meditation or a worship service here and there. Finally, and not to be forgotten: food stamps — and "care packages" from Mother and future mother-in-law.

With these mundane affairs taken care of, Rolf was free for the main task of those years, the intellectual one. How privileged he was to encounter teachers like Gerhard von Rad, Günther Bornkamm, Heinrich Bornkamm, Hans Freiherr von Campenhausen, Edmund Schlink, and Peter Brunner, to mention the most prominent ones. They unleashed Rolf Knierim's intellectual capacities and set his mind free to think, to think. This, however, was not all. The character and integrity of these teachers, many of them having emerged from years of underground activities in the Confessing Church, let them stand out as lifelong role models.

Nine months of seclusion in a little attic room at Bergheimer Landstraße, to prepare for the comprehensive final examination *(Fakulätsexamen)*, concluded Rolf's student years in Heidelberg.

On May 7, 1955, Rolf Knierim passed the *Fakultätsexamen* at the University of Heidelberg. On June 2, 1955, Rolf Knierim and Hildegard Salm were married at the Protestant church in Edenkoben an der Weinstraße by Pastor Karl Beisiegel.

Edenkoben an der Weinstraße

Now, of course, you would like to know where Edenkoben an der Weinstraße is, and I am only too happy to take you there. It is also necessary to pay a visit, because it can legitimately claim to be Rolf Knierim's second hometown.

Do you remember seeing a gentle blue mountain range to the west while standing on the Heidelberg castle terrace? These are the Haardt mountains and that is where we are heading. I would like to proceed slowly in order to have time to familiarize you with an essential part of Rolf's inner fabric and the matrix that has helped to sustain him and from which he has drawn strength and stability.

As we approach the Rhine, about to cross into the state of the Palatinate at Speyer, the compact mass of this old city's Romanesque Kaiserdom (A.D. 1032) appears looming above the trees of the riverbank. We should look into this monumental sandstone edifice, the resting place of emperors and kings. A replica of their death crown is suspended high over the altar above the crypt. A hushed quietness fills the sanctuary and draws a visitor's mind inward.

As we traverse the western half of the Rhine plain, we find ourselves in a bountiful region. Well-tended fields with a great variety of crops and stately houses along the thoroughfares of spic-and-span villages give testimony to the riches of the land and the industriousness of its people. It is hard to imagine that throughout centuries this land has been subject to fierce fighting and merciless devastation; it has been trampled on by every conceivable European army and has been tossed around between France and Germany. Out of all this, the people here have become survivors. They have their history in their blood, deeply ingrained in their being. They might hike along a forest trail and stumble upon an old Celtic earthen mound without finding anything uncommon about it. They are grateful to the Romans for bringing them the skill of wine making. They view the emperors of old and their vassal-knights as esteemed neighbors who moved away, leaving their now-ruined but nevertheless prestigious real estate as a legacy for future generations. The people come and visit and recall the history, spiced with morsels of anecdote. This is a part of the context in which Rolf Knierim lived his formative years.

As the mountains draw closer, some of these old ruins appear, the fields are replaced by the belt of vineyards that ring the foothills, and the distinctive steeples of the two churches of Edenkoben come into focus. At the eastern edge of town, we will pass the cluster of houses my clan lived in, and we will follow the one-kilometer route I took to school. As we head uphill to the middle of town and the Protestant school, can you imagine a little six-year-old boy and a little six-year-old girl with their school satchels on their backs, coming toward you!

For the moment, let's quickly turn left here to the marketplace, with the Protestant church, the linden tree, the Gothic fountain, and the statue of Ludwig I of Bavaria in civilian clothes! — who still after more than one hundred years puts his right foot forward. Up we go through a forest of chestnut trees to the king's Pompeian-style summer palace, where we can take a chair lift to the eight-hundred-year-old castle ruin on top of the mountain.

I suggest that you refresh yourself with a glass of the local wine and a plate of crusty bread and tasty sausage. While you enjoy this grandstand view over the blessed countryside and across to the blue, gentle Odenwald mountains around Heidelberg, I will bring your mind back to Rolf Knierim again.

Rolf's grandparents lived in Edenkoben and he spent all of his vacations with them; as they grew older he helped them out when need arose. During their evacuation at the beginning of World War II, the whole Knierim family found refuge here for a year. The real story, though, has a much earlier beginning. The year was 1930, when a problem arose in the Knierim household. The affordable living space became too limited for the parents of a six-year-old schoolboy, an eighteen-month-old toddler, and a newborn baby boy. So Rolf's maternal grandparents agreed to take the little toddler and care for him as long as necessary. Rolf still remembers the traumatic separation from his mother into his grandmother's arms and how he screamed. But he was in good hands; this petite, pretty woman was a darling. She always had a little smile around her mouth and her big eyes looked around, alert and friendly.

Grandfather Buchmann, however, had a different look. He appeared, especially to kids, dark and silent and was indeed a man of few words and swift actions. He worked quietly in his cobbler's workshop, but came very much alive when asked to tell stories from the time of his youth. Rolf was to stay with these two dear people until the age of seven. While attending first and second grade at the Protestant school, he met a little blonde girl. He singled himself out from the crowd of schoolchildren by accompanying her all the long way home each day after school and, in many other ways, was able to endear himself so much to her that she told him she would marry him if he became a police officer. All of which, of course, after a shift in the job description, led straight up to June 2, 1955, and an ecumenical wedding in the Protestant church in Edenkoben an der Weinstraße. After this very important event and from this dear place, we departed for our way stations in Rolf's pastorate.

Eutingen, Oeschelbronn, and Wurmberg

Eutingen, Oeschelbronn, and Wurmberg, outposts of the Methodist congregation of Pforzheim, Germany's watch and jewelry city at the northern edge of the Black Forest, were Rolf's first assignment as assistant pastor. We moved to Eutingen about four weeks after our wedding, excited and geared up to serve the church. There it was, up on a small knoll: the little chapel with a flat for the pastor above the narthex, a privilege for a young couple at a time when housing was extremely scarce. Please, do come in, we live alone on the top. Enjoy our neighbors, the birds that nest in the old trees around us, and hear them sing their joyous tunes while I tell you a little bit about the past.

Rolf's first worship service. The young pastor, full of theological learning, enthusiastically preached a sermon which would have been an utter delight for Karl Barth. Not so for the "old guard" of the congregation. Monday morning, well before breakfast, their representative appeared in our kitchen, telling the young minister that, should he dare to preach in this fashion one more time, he would remove him from the pulpit, because in forty years this congregation had not heard such things. Challenged, he could not quote anything in Rolf's sermon that was against the biblical text; as for the pulpit, the bishop appoints and recalls. As time rolled on, the people got used to the new style and appreciated it more and more.

Preaching, Bible studies, and house calls were the three staples of Rolf's ministry. It was here, in the humble environment of Black Forest villages with simple, unsophisticated, straightforward people, that the future professor developed and refined his mode of doing structure analysis for his sermons and Bible hours and, years later, the people still remembered them.

The service in three villages took all of Rolf's time and energy and there was no way for him to start working on his doctoral thesis, proposed by Professor von Rad. The bishop, who had his own plans for Rolf, understood the situation and, after a year, assigned him to a small congregation.

Let's not leave right away. I have to mention a few more things. One, which was very important for Rolf and me, was that our first child was born here, a son, and we named him Johannes Peter. The others are for the record. See, Rolf was no stranger to the faithful here. In the Methodist church a candidate for the ministry had to demonstrate his qualification by serving two years as an apprentice under a supervising pastor. At the age of twenty, Rolf came under Episcopal assignment and was stationed at Pforzheim. (His senior minister here later married us.) These practical years were physical and mental endurance tests. It was uphill and downhill, on a one-gear-only bicycle, to and from worship services, Bible classes, and youth group gatherings.

At times, they were also adventurous years. One story Rolf likes to tell is the funeral service he had to conduct with three minutes' preparation time and an old, dusty sacristy Bible to hold on to. Another story happened, if I recall correctly, at the location of Rolf's second year practicum in the Marburg/Lahn-Wetzlar area of central Germany. The incident between David and Goliath was to be dramatized by a group of schoolboys. Well, it did not go at all according to the account of The Book, but obeyed the laws of human nature with the little David ending up on the floor. Rolf, with his ever-present alertness, grasped the opportunity to point out the difference between an anointed little boy and, well, just a little boy! After the successful completion of his practicum, Rolf went on to an eagerly anticipated academic training.

8

Saarbrücken

We have to go on too. We have to cross the Rhine again and proceed west to the mountains; and farther west, in close proximity to the French border, we leave the Palatinate and enter the Saarland, another region of dispute between uneasy neighbors for a thousand years. Here we will head straight to Saarbrücken, the state's capital. This city is a total delight! Situated in the idyllic Saar valley, with its outer seams touching the French border and a citizenry conveying a joie-de-vivre attitude, one cannot but feel well here.

The Johannisplatz is a good spot to go and sit down in the shadow of the mighty Johanniskirche and in the company of busy pigeons and friendly people feeding them. The horse chestnut trees hide the house at Johassisstraße 9 where we lived. The flock Rolf had to attend to here was small. He took care of all the people's needs and problems and still had plenty of time to write his dissertation — *until* the idea crept into somebody's mind that this was a perfect time to thoroughly renovate the sanctuary! From then on, Rolf's daytime hours were filled with endless negotiations and weighty decisions, and he had to resort to the tranquillity of the night to finish his thesis, which he eventually did.

Here, in brief, is the essence of those two years in Saarbrücken. We moved to Saarbrücken in the summer of 1956. On May 12, 1957, Rolf was ordained an elder of the Methodist church at the annual conference at Pirmasens, his hometown. On August 20, 1957, our daughter Eva Elisabeth was born. On September 11, 1957, Rolf Knierim obtained his Dr. Theol., magna cum laude. Soon thereafter, a plain little postcard from Professor von Rad, inviting him to a position at the university, changed the direction of Rolf's career from the practical field of ministry in the German Methodist Church to the academic field of teaching the Old Testament at the University of Heidelberg. So, as soon as the last shovel of rubbish was hauled away, the final trace of dust carefully dabbed off, and the bishop had ceremoniously rededicated our grand little sanctuary, the Knierim family packed up their belongings and departed for Heidelberg, Landhausstraße 17.

Pirmasens

Last but not least among the way stations: Pirmasens, in the Pfalz (which is the Palatinate), Rolf Knierim's hometown. This city perches proudly on top of various hills and tries not to be squeezed too much by the narrow valleys in between. (Some of these valleys are even left alone, simply spanned by sweeping bridges of modern elegance.) The lofty twin belfries of St. Pirminius church look out over a vast expanse of woodland that rolls its green blanket with sovereign grandeur across the border and deep into the Alsace/Lorraine region of northern France.

Gnarled trees whisper their sagas as they stand guard around ancient castles or brush their branches against the timeworn outlines of giant rock formations. Little brooks meander through blooming meadows and gurgle along the roads that connect tiny hamlets. It is a hiker's and rock climber's paradise, but the climate is harsh and the soil is not suited for farming. The livelihood of the people there depends upon what the city has to offer. In Rolf's time, it had plenty to offer.

A couple of centuries ago, Pirmasens was the noted garrison of a Hessian prince who liked to play with soldiers and found delight in watching his Lange Kerle (Guard of Tall Guys) exercise. After the prince's death though, nobody was interested in the enterprise anymore, so the men lost their jobs. To fight off poverty and despair, the women took their husbands' uniforms and sewed slippers from the material and then hawked them around the vicinity. This started a shoe industry that came to boast 125 shoe factories and an international shoe fair, an industry which earned Pirmasens the reputation of Germany's shoe metropolis.

As we approach the city from Saarbrücken, the sharp westerly wind that chases the rain clouds over the high countryside will land us right before the Knierim's house, Am Mühlberg 10. They own the house thanks to the farsighted, social-minded industrialist in whose shoe factory Father Knierim worked. This industrialist had built a sizable tract of houses that his workers could afford to buy and pay off with sensible deductions from their wages.

I am sure Rolf would want you to come in, right into his parents' large spic-and-span friendly kitchen, the center of the family life. Here, Father Gottfried, a tall, wiry man with a witty sparkle in his eyes, and Mother Luise, of statuesque matriarchal appearance, were raising their four sons in the piety of the Methodist faith. The wall calendar with daily meditations printed on its leaves gives witness to the regular devotion after dinner. Beyond that, the life of the Knierim family was deeply embedded in that of the local congregation. Grandmother Knierim had been a founding member and remained a pillar throughout her life, in terms of economic support as well as an exemplary Christian lifestyle. As for Rolf, attendance at two worship services on Sundays, Bible studies and choir practice during the week, belonging to the youth group with outings and retreats in the surrounding forests, made a lasting impression on his young mind and gave him criteria for later decisions.

At the age of ten, Rolf signed up for the classical high school (*Humanistisches Gymnasium*), which meant studying Greek and Latin and reading the classics. It also meant that the humanistic quest for the True, the Beautiful, and the Good engaged itself in a dialogue with the content of the Gospel of Jesus Christ. This dialogue would never cease and formed in Rolf an honest and unmanipulative mind, gifted with an ability to think clearly.

Yes, there was a third voice coming in loud and shrill, trying to drown out both the others. It was the pathetic, pseudoreligious Zeitgeist fighting for the souls of the people, especially the young. Fortunately it was short-lived and died an ugly death. But not before it took its toll. In December 1943, Rolf's class was corporately drafted into the German air defense. The boys were between fifteen and sixteen years of age. They underwent basic training, they were taught how to handle antiaircraft guns; their formal education was also continued — somehow. The youngsters held stationary positions and suffered through saturation bombing; many schoolmates perished. They dug themselves in and for one week were eye-to-eye with General Patton's tank forces. They were perched without cover on flatbed railroad cars where they shot at fighter-bombers and were shot at by them. Way stations for growing up too soon and growing old before their time!

In the first days of March 1945, the young men were allowed to go home to await draft notices from the army. But on February 27, Pirmasens had suffered an air raid, 70 percent of the city had been reduced to ashes, and a great number of its citizens lay buried under the ruins or had perished in the raging fires. Rolf's best friend, too, was killed that night. The Knierim's house had been spared. When Rolf arrived home, no city, no mail — no draft notice!

March 21, 1945. The city was under artillery fire. Father Knierim left at night, on foot and with a little cart carrying some meager belongings. He was with the "Volkssturm," Germany's last line of defense, senior citizens and juveniles. They wanted to cross the Rhine before all bridges were blown up and join their evacuated wives and children in central Germany. Rolf, on his father's advice, left a little later with his father's bicycle. He also had in his pocket an armband of the "Volkssturm" and an army pistol. He wanted to make it to his grandparents. The road was jammed with the retreating army and the casualties of constant air attack. Rolf had to turn back. He emptied his pistol, chipping away at a milestone — child's play! Pirmasens had been taken by U.S. forces. Rolf, seeing the MPs, threw the gun away, an act which did not pass unnoticed. He was caught with his "smoking gun" lying by the wayside, and so was suspected of being a partisan; but, fortunately for Rolf, he could produce his armband, his paramilitary identification. For the rest of the day the Americans interrogated him. The last interrogator was an officer who once must have attended a *Humanistisches Gymnasium* too and could identify with a *Gymnasiast*. This American officer was an exiled German Jew, returning with the U.S. army. He sent the "suspected partisan" home.

Rolf had survived the war. The painful task of learning the truth about the previous era, to accept it and cope with it, was yet to come. It would be a task never allowed to rest, a pain never allowed to fade.

With the help of care packages from America and acquired bartering skills (e.g., shoes for potatoes) he survived the hunger years too, 1945-48. Schools resumed operation in the fall of 1946. In the summer of 1948, Rolf concluded

11

his education at the *Humanistisches Gymnasium.* He successfully passed the final exams for the diploma of maturity *(Zeugnis der Reife; Abitur).* He left Pirmasens soon afterward to pursue training for the ministry, returning to his hometown only occasionally. But he has remained a "Pirmasenser" and has never lost its distinctive inflection of the Palatinate dialect and never forgotten the unique idioms of Pirmasens.

Rolf Paul Knierim was born July 8, 1928, at Pirmasens, Germany.

This concludes our journey, revisiting the way stations of Rolf Knierim's life. I leave you to wonder which one of them impacted him most, contributing most to forming the uniqueness of his personality and to enabling the quality of his work.

Auf Wiedersehn!

Approaches to Old Testament Theology

ROLF RENDTORFF

Introductory note: It is a great privilege for me to write the introductory essay to the Festschrift for my friend Rolf Knierim on his sixty-fifth birthday. Rolf finished his doctorate in Heidelberg in 1957, the year when our teacher Gerhard von Rad published the first volume of his famous *Theologie des Alten Testaments*. In the meantime Rolf himself has become a leading voice in the discussion on Old Testament theology, in particular in the United States. My contribution will concentrate on his essays in *Horizons in Biblical Theology*, volume 6, 1 and 2, and will draw some lines back to von Rad's work.

I

In the introduction to volume 6,1 of *Horizons in Biblical Theology* Bruce C. Birch quoted some earlier books and essays lamenting that Old Testament theology was in a crisis or in an impasse. He continued, saying that "already in the late seventies there was beginning a remarkable flurry of new publication in Old Testament theology . . . these works and others seem to have signaled a new and vigorous discussion over the methods, content and prospects of Old Testament theology."[1]

Looking from a European (in particular, German) point of view, I would like to accentuate the development differently. Soon after Gerhard von Rad's *Old Testament Theology* appeared (first volume 1957, second volume 1960),[2] a

---

1. *HBT* 6,1 (1984): iii-iv.
2. G. von Rad, *Theologie des Alten Testaments*, 2 vols. (München: Kaiser, 1957/60); ET,

vivid discussion began, among others in major reviews by Friedrich Baumgärtel[3] and Walther Zimmerli[4] as well as in a number of essays and books. I would single out two main fields of discussion. A first group of contributions concentrated on the question of *Heilsgeschichte*, its theological relevance and legitimacy as well as its relation to "real" history. In this area certain battles were continued that had been fought since the early fifties with Rudolf Bultmann and others, including fundamental questions about the place and theological legitimacy of the Old Testament in Christian belief.[5]

The discussion on the second field was opened by Walther Zimmerli. In principle, he was very sympathetic with von Rad's new approach to Old Testament theology. But he raised one fundamental question: "Must not a 'theology' carry out the venture of thinking things together (das Wagnis des Zusammen-Denkens) in a much higher degree. . . ? The Old Testament has a center (eine Mitte)."[6] This was the hour of the birth of the still ongoing debate about the "center" of the Old Testament. Of course, the question as such existed much earlier, and therefore it might be appropriate to relate it back to previous discussions about the most important topics according to which an Old Testament theology should be organized.[7] But as a specific term the word "Mitte" was only used since Zimmerli's review. One of the reasons for the wide attention this question received was von Rad's brusque and angry reaction to it. In the second volume of his *Theologie* he anticipated the discussion (probably because of oral exchange) by saying, "The Old Testament has no center like the New Testament," and explaining that briefly.[8] Then his sharp rejection of the whole discussion was particularly visible in a footnote in an article from 1963, where he asked: "What's it all about with this almost *unisono* asked question about the 'unity', the 'center' of the Old Testament? Is it something so self-evident that

Old Testament Theology, 2 vols. (Edinburgh: Oliver and Boyd; New York: Harper and Row, 1962/65).

3. F. Baumgärtel, "Gerhard von Rad's 'Theologie des Alten Testaments,'" *ThLZ* 86 (1961): 801-16, 895-908.

4. W. Zimmerli, review in *VT* 13 (1963): 100-111.

5. See the collection of essays *Probleme alttestamentlicher Hermeneutik. Aufsätze zum Verstehen des Alten Testaments,* ed. C. Westermann, Theologische Bücherei 11 (München: Kaiser, 1960); ET, *Essays on Old Testament Hermeneutics* (Richmond: John Knox, 1963).

6. Zimmerli, *VT* 13, 105.

7. This is already the case with R. Smend, *Die Mitte des Alten Testaments* (Zürich: EVZ, 1970); reprinted in *Die Mitte des Alten Testaments: Gesammelte Studien, Bd. 1* (München: Kaiser, 1986), 40-84; cf. also the chapter on "The Center of the OT and OT Theology," in G. F. Hasel, *Old Testament Theology: Basic Issues in the Current Debate,* 4th ed. (Grand Rapids: Eerdmans, 1991), 139-71. Closer to the above-mentioned position is H. Graf Reventlow, *Hauptprobleme der alttestamentlichen Theologie im 20. Jahrhundert* (Darmstadt: Wissenschaftliche Buchgesellschaft, 1983), 141f.; ET, *Problems of Old Testament Theology in the Twentieth Century* (Philadelphia: Fortress, 1986), 125-33.

8. Von Rad, *Theologie des Alten Testaments,* vol. 2, 376 (4th ed., 386); ET, 362.

its proof belongs, so to speak, as a conditio sine qua non to an orderly Old Testament theology? . . . Or is this postulate less a matter of historical or theological recognition than a speculative-philosophical principle that becomes effective as an unconscious premise?"[9]

The last quotation shows von Rad's deep distrust of the whole question about a "center" of the Old Testament and of Old Testament theology. He suspects that the idea of such a center would not come from the study of the Old Testament itself but would be a premise, if even an unconscious one. Calling such an assumed premise a "speculative-philosophical principle" was a particularly sharp verdict in the framework of the dialectical theology to which von Rad belonged. Nevertheless, the question of a "center" became one of the most discussed topics in the debate around Old Testament theology in the sixties and seventies and is still going on.[10]

How is von Rad's own approach to be described? For those familiar with his previous work, the conception of his *Theologie* must have been a surprise. His most influential earlier book was *The (Formcritical) Problem of the Hexateuch* from 1938.[11] In this book he developed the well-known thesis that the "Hexateuch" was built up on the basis of the "historical creed" (Deut 26:5-9 and elsewhere) according to which the original concept of Israel's history began with the deliverance from Egypt and the settlement in the promised land. Therefore, the primeval history was only the last *Vorbau* in the development of the Hexateuch in its final form. In addition, von Rad had explained in other writings that creation never became an independent topic in Israel's religious thought but was always subordinated to salvation history. But now, his *Theologie* did not begin with the exodus but with creation. Why? Because "we have to let ourselves be guided by the sequence of events as Israel's belief saw it."[12] The subtitle of the chapter on "The Theology of the Hexateuch" reads: "The Periodization of the Canonical Salvation History by the Covenant Theology."

One could call von Rad's concept of Old Testament theology "canonical" or, at least, "canon-oriented." The guideline for the structuring of his *Theologie*

9. G. von Rad, "Offene Fragen im Umkreis einer Theologie des Alten Testaments," in *ThLZ* 88 (1963): 401-16; reprinted in *Gesammelte Studien zum Alten Testament*, vol. 2, Theologische Bücherei 48 (München: Kaiser, 1973), 289-312, n. 3a. This article was written as a reaction to Baumgärtel's review (see n. 3), but his name is not mentioned.

10. One most recent example is provided by Horst Dietrich Preuß, *Theologie des Alten Testaments*; vol. 1, *JHWHs erwählendes und verpflichtendes Handeln*; vol. 2, *Israels Weg mit JHWH* (Stuttgart: Kohlhammer, 1991/92). He defines "election" as the center of the Old Testament, describing it as follows: "'Jhwhs erwählendes Geschichtshandeln an Israel zur Gemeinschaft mit seiner Welt,' das zugleich ein dieses Volk (und die Völker) verpflichtendes Handeln ist" (29).

11. G. von Rad, *Das formgeschichtliche Problem des Hexateuchs*, BWANT 4. Folge, Heft 26 (Stuttgart: Kohlhammer, 1938); ET, *The Problem of the Hexateuch and Other Essays* (Edinburgh: Oliver and Boyd, 1965), 1-78.

12. Von Rad, *Theologie des Alten Testaments*, vol. 1, 126 (4th ed., 134); ET, 120.

is the canonical structure of the Old Testament itself. This is expressed not only by beginning the whole work with creation, but also by the division of the *Theologie* into two volumes and by their titles: "The Theology of Israel's Historical Traditions" and "The Theology of Israel's Prophetic Traditions." This division corresponds to the main parts of the canon: the first volume on the Pentateuch and the "historical books," according to the traditional Christian division; the second volume on the prophetic books. The "Writings" are included in the first volume, following the historical books according to the Christian order, under the title "Israel before Yahweh (Israel's Answer)." It is obvious that for von Rad this arrangement was not guided by a formalistic canonical principle but by theological reflections and insights, but this does not diminish its canonical character. I will come back to this later.

II

The discussion about a "center" of the Old Testament was introduced as a reaction to von Rad's *Theologie,* and even today everybody looking for or proposing a new "center" has to clarify, be it explicitly or not, his or her position to von Rad's "No" to the quest of a "center." This exemplifies that the history of recent Old Testament theology, in a sense, is to be described as that of "Old Testament Theology before and after von Rad."[13]

Previous to von Rad, it was the famous study by Walther Eichrodt[14] that ruled the field. Looking back from today, the question of how to classify this work is rather ambiguous. It belongs to the category of systematic approaches that arrange the biblical material according to a system not developed out of the texts themselves but defined from the outside. Eichrodt's forerunners and contemporaries usually took those systems from traditional Christian dogmatics, as, e.g., God-Man-Salvation, or Theology-Anthropology-Soteriology. Among Eichrodt's contemporaries this system is to be found, among others, with Ernst Sellin[15] and Ludwig Köhler.[16]

---

13. Cf. W. H. Schmidt, " 'Theologie des Alten Testaments' vor und nach Gerhard von Rad," *Verkündigung und Forschung* 17,1 (1972): 1-25; cf. also J. H. Hayes and F. Prussner, *Old Testament Theology: Its History and Development* (Atlanta: John Knox, 1985), 233: "In his theology . . . von Rad . . . inaugurated a new epoch in the study of Old Testament theology."

14. W. Eichrodt, *Theologie des Alten Testaments,* 3 vols. (Leipzig: Hinrichs, 1933-39); trans. J. A. Baker, *Theology of the Old Testament,* 2 vols., OTL (Philadelphia: Westminster, 1961/67).

15. E. Sellin, *Theologie des Alten Testaments* (Leipzig: Quelle & Meyer, 1933). Sellin published this book as the second of two volumes under the common title *Alttestamentliche Theologie auf religionsgeschichtlicher Grundlage;* the title of the first volume was *Israelitisch-jüdische Religionsgeschichte* (Leipzig: Quelle & Meyer, 1933).

16. L. Köhler, *Theologie des Alten Testaments* (Tübingen: Mohr, 1936); ET, *Old Testament Theology,* Lutterworth Library 49 (London: Lutterworth, 1957).

Eichrodt's approach is different. He explicitly refuses the traditional dogmatic scheme and declares that we "must plot our course as best we can along the lines of the OT's own dialectic that speaks about the revelation of a national God who manifests himself in his deeds as the God of the world and of the individual." This leads him to "three principal categories, within which to study the special nature of the Israelite faith in God: *God and the People, God and the World,* and *God and Man*" (ET, p. 33). Thus he found a systematic scheme within which to unfold Old Testament materials in a "cross-section method."[17]

It might be true to say: "It is to Eichrodt's credit that he broke once and for all with the traditional God-Man-Salvation arrangement, taken over from dogmatics time and again by Biblical theologians."[18] Indeed, since Eichrodt most Old Testament theologians do not use arrangements taken from the dogmatic tradition. But this does not mean that their arrangements would not be guided by certain theological convictions held by the author that are not based in the Old Testament. Eichrodt himself is a striking example. In a footnote (ET, p. 33, n. 1) he admits that he owes the idea of the three main parts to his teacher Otto Procksch. Only after his death was Procksch's *Theologie* published.[19] In fact, the second part of the book, "The World of Thought" ("Die Gedankenwelt"),[20] is arranged in three parts. But their order is different from Eichrodt's: 1. God and the world, 2. God and the people, and 3. God and man. From a theological point of view, this is a fundamental change. Procksch began with creation, whereas Eichrodt puts salvation in the first place. Obviously, this was a decision made by Eichrodt as a theologian for whom God's relation to Israel was of higher importance than God's relation to the world God created. This demonstrates the inevitable interrelation between the theology of the Old Testament and the theology of the Old Testament theologian.

Eichrodt's *Theologie* can also be classified as the climax of the systematic presentation of Old Testament theology.[21] That is why the difference between his approach and that of some of his forerunners does not seem to be too fundamental. Eichrodt, like most Old Testament theologians before him, developed a system according to which he arranged the Old Testament materials. In his particular case, this "cross-section" arrangement was rather static. Compared with later Old Testament theologies, the whole area of Israel's history as the field of God's acting is missing. The exodus from Egypt is mentioned only casually. Here one sees the influence of earlier dogmatic thinking that did not yet realize the dimension of God's acting in history as a central element of Old Testament experience and belief.

17. Cf. Hasel, 47-60 (see n. 7).
18. Hasel, 49.
19. O. Procksch, *Theologie des Alten Testaments* (Gütersloh: Bertelsmann, 1950).
20. The first part is named "The World of History" ("Die Geschichtswelt").
21. Reventlow (see n. 7), German edition, 54; ET, 49.

III

Eichrodt arranges the first part of his *Theologie*, "God and the People," according to the key word "covenant," which he calls a "central concept." Therefore there is some justification in tracing the question of the "center" of the Old Testament back to Eichrodt, even if the word "center" itself was not yet used at that time. Since Eichrodt, almost every theology has its own central concept. After the appearance of von Rad's *Theologie* the question of a center of the Old Testament advanced to an independent topic of the methodological discussion regardless of the intention of an author to write a theology himself or herself. Therefore there are now numerous, or almost innumerable, proposals for a center, a key term, a basic vantage point, or the like.[22]

To be sure, each of these proposals is carefully reflected and substantiated. Each of them makes a valid contribution to our understanding of Old Testament theology. I have to admit that many times I am impressed by a new proposal that adds a new aspect to the possible ways to look at the Old Testament as a whole, even if I do not agree that it might be the key or the center. But I have to confess that I never agree because I still believe in the truth of von Rad's "No."

In principle, this would be a reason to disagree as well with Rolf Knierim's "ultimate vantage point . . . *the universal dominion of Yahweh in justice and righteousness.*"[23] But in this case my reaction is more differentiated, mainly for two reasons. The first reason is that Knierim's vantage point is much more than only a point; it is a dynamic interaction of two important aspects, both of them covering a whole field of others: "the most universal quantitative aspect — and the qualitative aspect governing all others." This qualification of the two aspects makes it clear that they are neither endangered to lead into an *Engführung* or defile, nor are they too general as to disallow a very specific implementation. The interrelation between the two aspects opens such a wide field that indeed it seems conceivable to develop an Old Testament theology on the basis of this concept.

The other reason for my positive reaction is the universality of the concept that leads to "Yahweh's creation of and dominion over heaven and earth"[24] as "what is at issue in the Old Testament."[25] This is very unusual among the many proposals for a center of the Old Testament, because most of them are more focused on God's relation to Israel, or are less specific by calling God/YHWH the center of the Old Testament. Above I noted that von Rad also began his *Theologie* with creation, and in his later writings, in particular his book on wisdom,[26] he

---

22. Cf. Hasel, 134-71, and Reventlow, ET, 125-33 (see n. 7).

23. R. Knierim, "The Task of Old Testament Theology," *HBT* 6,1 (1984): 25-57; the quotation is from 43.

24. Ibid., 42.

25. Ibid., 43.

26. G. von Rad, *Weisheit in Israel* (Neukirchen-Vluyn: Neukirchener, 1970); ET, *Wisdom in Israel* (London: SCM; Nashville: Abingdon, 1972).

ascribed creation a central role in God's relation to humankind. Therefore it might be that the impact of our common teacher's thought led to Knierim's insights.

However, I have difficulties with the concept of "systematization." In this respect I am sympathetic to Roland Murphy's critical questions.[27] After carefully reading Knierim's answer to Murphy,[28] I want to add some remarks.

First, it is true that in all of the "some sixty" (I did not count them) Old Testament theologies published in this century certain systemic elements are to be found. The majority of them definitely have a "systemic approach." In other cases, in particular that of von Rad, I would be hesitant to use the term "approach" in this context because in his *Theologie* systemic aspects do appear here and there, but they do not provide structure to the whole. Yet I find Knierim's mention of the pre-Gabler and post-Gabler eras interesting. Gabler's point was to establish a difference between "biblical theology" and "dogmatic theology." For him, as for the majority of theologians in the following centuries, every "theology" was "systematic." But must this definition of theology be binding for biblical theology today? There was a period in Old Testament scholarship when Old Testament theology was carried out mainly in descriptive form as the history of Israel's religion. With Eichrodt and his contemporaries the pendulum swung back to a systematic approach. But this new trend did not completely cover the field, as von Rad's approach shows. On the contrary, one could compare the *Theologies* of Eichrodt and von Rad, among other aspects, from this point of view. Eichrodt's approach is strictly systematic, von Rad's is not. The latter is, as I indicated above, canon-oriented (see below).

I am far from denying that a systematic approach could be useful for one specific type of Old Testament theology. But I do not agree that Old Testament or biblical theology *eo ipso* must be systematic. I do not believe that today there is only one possible way to do Old Testament theology. As Walter Brueggemann puts it: "There is no consensus among us about what comes next. . . . It is . . . a time of experimentation in which many things may be tried."[29] Therefore we are not in a situation in which one theologian could tell another what he or she *must* do when trying to do theology. What Old Testament theology today is or could be will be defined by the presentation of books (or outlines) of an elaborated "theology" and their reception or even acceptance by Old Testament scholars and theologians. Before von Rad published his book, nobody could have expected this new kind of "theology." The same is true with Eichrodt.

This is also the question of the context, that of time as well as that of the reference group. Brueggemann mentions the "Confessing Church of the 30's"

---

27. R. E. Murphy, "A Response to 'The Task of Old Testament Theology,'" *HBT* 6,1 (1984): 65-71.

28. R. Knierim, "On the Task of Old Testament Theology: A Response to W. Harrelson, S. Towner, and R. E. Murphy," *HBT* 6,2 (1984): 91-128.

29. W. Brueggemann, "Futures in Old Testament Theology," *HBT* 6,1 (1984): 1-11; quotation, 1.

as the community of reference for von Rad's credo hypothesis.[30] I want to stress that and expand it to von Rad's insistence on the subordination of creation theology to salvation theology in 1935. He did it explicitly as a polemic against the theology of the *Deutsche Christen* who wanted to use creation theology as support for the Nazi ideology by claiming that the German *Volk* in its uniqueness was founded by creation.[31] Von Rad's later shift toward an emphasis on wisdom could also be explained in the context of changing needs and priorities. To an even greater degree this is true for his *Old Testament Theology*. Von Rad felt the need to present and to interpret in theological terms the whole new context for understanding the Old Testament that had developed in the framework of the Alt-school. Of course, one could say similar things about Eichrodt's *Theologie* by which he wanted to win back the Old Testament for theology and liberate it from the dominance of history of religion.

Thus I think we should let each other try to develop approaches to Old Testament theology, be it in the form of theses, sketches, outlines, essays on specific topics, or whatever. Again, I agree with Brueggemann that our problem is "our desire to replicate the architectural comprehensiveness of Eichrodt and von Rad," and that it is the lack of "a comprehensive paradigm that relates all the parts to each other which is immobilizing."[32] But I know that it took von Rad many, many years to arrive at the point from which he could start writing his *Theologie*. At that time he had almost nobody to talk to. So we are much better off because there is now widespread discussion on the problems of Old Testament theology. But: "There is now need for substantive proposals."[33]

IV

I want to take up one specific point that played an important role in the discussion between Knierim and Murphy. The latter raised the question whether it is possible "to speak of systematization *within* the Old Testament" and men-

---

30. Ibid., 6.

31. G. von Rad, "Das theologische Problem des alttestamentlichen Schöpfungsglaubens," in *Werden und Wesen des Alten Testament*, hg. P. Volz, F. Stummer, und J. Hempel, BZAW 66 (Berlin: Töpelmann, 1936), 138-47; reprinted in *Gesammelte Studien zum Alten Testament*, vol. 1, Theologische Bücherei 8 (München: Kaiser, 1958), 136-47; *The Problem of the Hexateuch and Other Essays*, 131-43. Cf. also R. Rendtorff, " 'Wo warst du, als ich die Erde gründete?' Schöpfung und Heilsgeschichte," in *Kanon und Theologie: Vorarbeiten zu einer Theologie des Alten Testaments* (Neukirchen-Vluyn: Neukirchener, 1991), 94-112; ET forthcoming.

32. Brueggemann, 4 (see n. 29).

33. Ibid., 7.

tioned some examples of "embryonic systematization."[34] Knierim answered with a long list of what he understands to be systematizations of different kinds in the Old Testament. In this case I am in Knierim's camp, not so much with regard to every detail of assumed systematizations but with regard to the qualification of this phenomenon. Several years ago Rudolf Smend raised the analogous question of "theology in the Old Testament," mentioning some similar phenomena.[35] I find those observations very important because they give us hints to a way Old Testament texts have been structured by different means, surface or subsurface. Murphy quotes Gerald Sheppard,[36] but Sheppard would be on Knierim's and my side, not calling this systematization embryonic but claiming to have found a very important vestige of intrinsic structuring of Old Testament texts and books.

Now the bad news: I would draw fundamentally different consequences from these observations than Knierim does. I look at those intrinsic structuring elements from a canonical point of view. They show us how texts and traditions within the Old Testament were linked to each other in many ways and on many levels leading eventually to the final form. Knierim himself formulates the program: "Of special importance, however, is the fact that larger corpora that comprise disparate genres and substantive aspects are composed under the dictate of unifying guiding ideas. They are forms of systematic unification of pluralities and diversities which must be accounted for or these corpora cannot be understood."[37] This sounds like a description of the forces acting toward the canonical shape of the texts. Particularly interesting is the emphasis that the "corpora," i.e., the present larger units or books, cannot be understood without accounting for those "unifying guiding ideas."

This leads to the question of diachronic and synchronic interpretation of the given text. Knierim demonstrates these structuring forces first of all with regard to the Pentateuch. Here I want to inquire about the role of the Pentateuchal "sources" J and P that Knierim mentions immediately before in their relation to the "redactor" R[P], which he mentions within the same brackets but is actually binding the sources together to a new unity. Obviously both represent different diachronic levels. I suppose that "R[P]" is to be related to those elements that Knierim has in mind as "compos[ing] under the dictate of unifying guiding ideas." How are these different diachronic levels to be dealt with, and how are they to be related to the synchronic reading of the text in its final shape? The same kinds of questions are to be raised with regard to the book of Isaiah where

---

34. Murphy, 68.

35. R. Smend, "Theologie im Alten Testament," *Verifikationen: Festschrift G. Ebeling zum 70. Geburtstag,* hg. E. Jüngel, J. Wallmann, und W. Werbeck (Tübingen: Mohr, 1982), 11-26; reprinted in *Die Mitte des Alten Testaments,* 40-84 (see n. 7).

36. G. Sheppard, *Wisdom as a Hermeneutical Construct,* BZAW 151 (Berlin: de Gruyter, 1980).

37. Knierim, "On the Task," 113 (see n. 28).

Knierim mentions one of the numerous recent publications on reading the sixty-six chapters as one book.[38] Here the problem of the relation of diachronic and synchronic aspects is even more complex.

Again, I agree with many of the aspects of "systematization" that Knierim is naming. But I would not take them as motivation or legitimation for my own systematizing of the Old Testament. I would rather try to follow and to understand these intrinsic activities with particular emphasis on the final results. This is not the place to enter into an exhaustive debate on a canonical reading of the Old Testament. But I believe that it was not by accident that the discussion about Old Testament theology led to this point.

Above, I labeled von Rad's theology "canonical," or at least "canon-oriented." By this differentiation I would first of all emphasize that there is no immediate relation between von Rad's *Theologie* and the recent discussion about canonical reading and interpretation of the Old Testament. I myself drew certain connections that I will try to explain briefly below. My second reason for not calling von Rad's approach "canonical" in a strict sense but rather "canon-oriented" is the fact that his own motivations and reasons for structuring his *Theologie* the way he did did not emerge from a certain theory or idea of "canon." But when he asked himself how to unfold the message (or kerygma) that became "literature" in the Old Testament he did not find any "systematic." It sounds like a contribution to our present discussion when he writes: "It becomes more and more evident to us that the structuring and literary digesting of the extremely complex tradition materials was a theological achievement of highest rate, but at the same time we are left with the confusing fact that this theological thinking was a thinking entirely without theological 'systematic.' " These authors "seemed not to feel at all the need of a theological systematic but they let themselves be guided by the sequence of the historical events."[39] This paragraph on "The Unfolding" ends with the often quoted sentence: "The most legitimate way to speak theologically about the Old Testament still is re-narration."[40]

The reader of von Rad's *Theologie* understands that for von Rad re-narration is not at all a simple matter. It is highly sophisticated because by re-narration he wants to acknowledge the high-rate theological achievement of the biblical authors. I think that at this point our present discussion can be linked with von Rad's reflections. In this context I want to interpret Knierim

38. Cf. R. Rendtorff, "The Book of Isaiah: A Complex Unity. Synchronic and Diachronic Reading," *Society of Biblical Literature 1991 Seminar Papers* (Atlanta: Scholars, 1991), 8-20.

39. Von Rad, *Theologie des Alten Testaments,* vol. 1, 121 (4th ed., 129); ET, 116.

40. Ibid., 126 (4th ed., 134). Obviously von Rad felt the need to expand this statement a bit and added in the fourth revised edition some sentences. One of them reads: "So wird sich also auch eine Theologie des Alten Testaments im rechten Nachsprechen dieser Geschichtszeugnisse zu üben haben, wenn sie die Inhalte des Alten Testaments sachgemäß erheben will" (135).

in the following way: After von Rad, and not at least by virtue of the insights we received from him, we have learned to understand a bit better the ideas and forces acting in the composition of the literary corpora in the Old Testament. In particular we understand that actually they are led by a highly differentiated systematic. Therefore we have to account for these unifying guiding ideas in order to understand the corpora themselves.

If this could be accepted, the next question would be how to unfold the theological contents of the Old Testament texts. I imagine that at this point Knierim would opt for a systematic presentation of the Old Testament ideas starting from his "ultimate vantage point." For my part, I would prefer to follow von Rad's line in a modified way as determined by our more recent insights and reflections. Here I have to come back to the question of diachronic and synchronic reading. I think that the unifying ideas described by Knierim are forcing us to pay much more attention to the later stages of the texts. With regard to the Pentateuch, von Rad himself did not even mention the "redactor" or redaction among those whose theological message has to be presented. This is particularly evident in those cases where von Rad presented the positions of the individual Pentateuchal sources about one specific topic independently from each other (e.g., in the chapter on "The Conception of Moses and his Office").[41] But we have to ask what the Pentateuch as a whole is saying about Moses. This picture surely will not be harmonized, but it will be unified in a way that makes it readable as a whole in its given context, for its contemporary readers as well as for readers of today.

It would go beyond the scope of this essay to discuss the problem of diachronic and synchronic reading in detail. I mention it because I felt that in the discussion about Old Testament theology in *Horizons in Biblical Theology* as well as in other contexts the relevance of this problem for an Old Testament theology seems to me to be underestimated, if not neglected. Just to refer again to the Pentateuch: Is it without relevance for a theological interpretation whether the so-called Yahwist (if he existed at all) wrote in the tenth century or in the sixth century B.C.E., i.e., during the time of the united kingdom or during the Babylonian exile? For me it is one of the problems I have with a purely "systematic" approach to Old Testament theology: I do not see whether and how certain main problems of Old Testament exegesis will affect the theological concepts and/or their unfolding.

V

Finally, I want to explain briefly my own ideas of how to conceive and to structure an Old Testament theology. As I indicated, first of all I want to follow

41. Ibid., 288-94 (4th ed., 302-8); ET, 284-96.

the lines of Gerhard von Rad by letting my presentation be guided by the concept of the biblical authors. Hereby I would be more "canonical" than von Rad, always taking the text in its final form as the basis for my explanation. As far as necessary I would mention, in one way or the other, divergences between different diachronical levels of the text, yet always putting the main emphasis on the meaning and message of the text in its final form.

Here I want to make two remarks with regard to canonical interpretation. First, my interest in reading the biblical text in its given form began with the shocking experience of a young scholar trained in the Wellhausen framework that the commonly accepted set of Pentateuchal theories did not work.[42] Only later I learned about the debate on "canon" beginning among American scholars and was fascinated by it. I never could see in this concept any deviation from the fundamentals of historical-critical scholarship. On the contrary, I see it as a fruitful expansion which adds the synchronic aspect to the diachronic aspect which, until then, had been exclusively dominant. Of course, this does limit the monopolistic function of diachronic analysis, and it makes things a bit more complicated, but also more interesting by the new task of raising permanently the problem of the relations of synchronic and diachronic reading of texts.

Secondly, for me this is not primarily a theological matter in the sense that only the final form of the text is of theological relevance. Therefore, I do not wish to be involved in certain kinds of theological discussions on this question. Nevertheless, sometimes I feel touched by being blamed of "fundamentalism" and the like. But I cannot see that it is more scientific in the context of historical-critical scholarship to claim that only certain hundred-year-old positions as, e.g., that of Pentateuchal "sources," are scientifically correct.[43] A canonical position as I understand it is a shift of perspective which looks at the texts from another angle and with another leading interest. Thereby I keep without qualifications to the principles of historical-critical scholarship. In a sense, my approach could be called "conservative" insofar as I am more interested in the text in its final shape than in the reconstruction of hypothetical earlier stages of the text. But to say it frankly, "exegesis" of a hypothetically reconstructed text (as, e.g., "J") that only exists in the minds of scholars who accept this hypothesis, seems to me to be a rather questionable undertaking. (To be sure, I did it myself for decades and therefore I will not blame anybody personally who continues to do so.) From my point of view, earlier stages of the text should always be interpreted as pre-stages of the text, but not as

42. Cf. R. Rendtorff, *Das überlieferungsgeschichtliche Problem des Pentateuch,* BZAW 147 (Berlin: De Gruyter, 1977); ET, *The Problem of the Process of Transmission in the Pentateuch,* JSOTSup 89 (Sheffield: JSOT, 1990).

43. Cf. R. Rendtorff, "The Paradigm is Changing: Hopes — and Fears," *Biblical Interpretation* 1 (1993): 34-53.

"texts" themselves. The "text" can only be what we have before us in its final shape.

In the books of the Pentateuch and the Former Prophets the realization of this canonical concept will be guided by the many signs and indications we find in the texts themselves, surface or subsurface, showing us how the author(s) want the reader to understand the intention and message of the text. We will have to study this aspect carefully, and I hope we will make some progress in the future.[44] With the Latter Prophets and the Writings things are less obvious so that for the moment I have to leave this question aside.[45]

This canonical way of unfolding the theological intentions of the biblical books will lead us time and again to certain topics that appear in other biblical books and therefore need to be treated beyond the framework of one individual book. Therefore I would envision as a second main part of the theology a "systematic" treatment of central topics like creation, covenant, election, law, etc. At first glance, this second part would look similar to the traditional systematic approach of Eichrodt and others. But there are two main differences. First, this would be but the second part of the book and therefore not define the general concept of the theology. Secondly, the selection of topics will be determined neither by Christian dogmatics nor by the theological reflection of the author of the theology himself, but will be deduced from the first part, from the theology of the biblical books themselves. I hope that the interplay of the two parts of the theology will give a comprehensive framework in which to deal with all aspects of Old Testament theology in an appropriate way.

VI

Some concluding remarks on two important aspects, interrelated to each other, with which I did not deal in this essay. The "Old Testament" is part of the religious traditions of two communities, the Jewish and the Christian. In both cases the community developed another set of religious writings so that the Hebrew Bible or Old Testament became but the first part of the whole corpus

---

44. As examples of how I envision the way of interpreting inner-textual connections I want to refer to some of my more recent articles: " 'Covenant' as a Structuring Concept in Genesis and Exodus," *JBL* 108 (1989): 385-93; German version: " 'Bund' als Strukturkonzept in Genesis und Exodus," in *Kanon und Theologie* (see n. 31), 123-31; "Der Text in seiner Endgestalt. überlegungen zu Exodus 19," *Ernten, was man sät. Festschrift Klaus Koch* (Neukirchen-Vluyn: Neukirchener, 1991), 459-70; "Die Geburt des Retters. Beobachtungen zur Jugendgeschichte Samuels im Rahmen der literarischen Komposition," *Storia e tradizioni di Israele: Scritti in onore di J. Alberto Soggin* (Brescia: Paideia, 1991), 205-16 (= *Kanon und Theologie*, 132-40).

45. Cf. also n. 38.

of religious traditions: the "Written Torah" in relation to the "Oral Torah" in Judaism, and the "Old Testament" in relation to the "New Testament" in Christianity. I appreciate writing this essay in a framework where theologians like Rolf Knierim are definitely clarifying a position I can agree with. Therefore I quote from the first footnote in Knierim's essay: "The proper way for the Christian tradition to submit to its standards is to recognize the Old Testament in its own right before its relationship with the New Testament is determined."[46] This is the first point, that it is of fundamental importance that the Christian Old Testament theologian first of all deals with the Old Testament in its own right. This can provide a basis for a common reading of the Old Testament or Hebrew Bible by Jewish and Christian Bible scholars.[47]

The second point is included in the first: reading and interpreting the Old Testament in its own right excludes the claim that Old Testament theology is only possible as part and parcel of "Biblical Theology" embracing both Old and New Testament. I quote again Knierim: "[T]he claim that the Old Testament is theologically significant only when it is read in light of the New Testament, or of Christ, has imperialistic implications and is theologically counterproductive."[48] Unfortunately, this "imperialistic" claim even today is time and again raised by Christian theologians, Old Testament scholars as well as New Testament scholars. Obviously this tendency is more common among German than among American theologians.[49] But I am convinced that we have to overcome this anachronistic tendency for basic theological reasons because otherwise we will never achieve an appropriate, nonimperialistic theological understanding of the Old Testament.

46. Knierim, "Task of Old Testament Theology," 53.
47. Cf. R. Brooks and J. J. Collins, eds., *Hebrew Bible or Old Testament? Studying the Bible in Judaism and Christianity* (Notre Dame: University of Notre Dame, 1990).
48. Knierim, "Task of Old Testament Theology," 52.
49. Cf. the fine paper by Werner E. Lemke, "Is Old Testament Theology an Essentially Christian Theological Discipline?" *HBT* 11,1 (1989): 59-71.

Die Erfahrung Hiobs.
"Konnektive" und "distributive" Gerechtigkeit nach dem Hiob-Buch

KLAUS BALTZER UND THOMAS KRÜGER

Die Entdeckung des "Tun-Ergehen-Zusammenhangs" als eines "impliziten Axioms" zahlreicher Texte des AT gehört zu den bedeutenden Entwicklungen der neueren atl. Wissenschaft.[1] Rolf Knierim hat neben anderen an der Rekonstruktion der Grundlinien dieses Konzeptes mitgearbeitet. Dabei hat er besonders auch seinen rechtlichen Aspekt deutlich gemacht.[2]

Als *ein,* wenn nicht *das* Thema des Hiob-Buchs[3] wird weithin die "Krise" (bzw. die kritische Auseinandersetzung mit) einer "Weisheit als Denken und Glauben im Zusammenhang von Tun und Ergehen" angesehen.[4] Die folgende Skizze möchte die Möglichkeit zur Diskussion stellen, daß es sich hierbei nicht nur um eine "Krise" der "Theorie" handelt, sondern auch um eine Problematik der sozialen "Praxis,"[5] und daß in diesem Zusammen-

---

1. Den Anstoß gab K. Koch, "Gibt es ein Vergeltungsdogma im Alten Testament?" in: *ZTK* 52 (1955) 1-42; mit anderen Beiträgen zum Thema wieder abgedruckt in: Ders. (Hg.), *Um das Prinzip der Vergeltung in Religion und Recht des Alten Testaments* (Wege der Forschung 125; Darmstadt: Wissenschaftliche Buchgesellschaft, 1972) 130-80 (danach im Folgenden zitiert).

2. R. Knierim, *Die Hauptbegriffe für Sünde im Alten Testament* (Gütersloh: Mohn, 1965) bes. 73ff.

3. Vgl. H.-P. Müller, *Das Hiobproblem* (ErFor 84; Darmstadt: Wissenschaftliche Buchgesellschaft, 1978).

4. H. D. Preuß, *Einführung in die alttestamentliche Weisheitsliteratur* (Stuttgart; Berlin; Köln; Mainz: Kohlhammer, 1987) 98. Vgl. H. H. Schmid, *Wesen und Geschichte der Weisheit* (BZAW 101; Berlin: Töpelmann, 1966) 173ff.

5. Zur Frage nach dem sozialgeschichtlichen "Hintergrund" des Hiob-Buches s. bes. F. Crüsemann, "Hiob und Kohelet; Ein Beitrag zum Verständnis des Hiobbuches" in: *Werden und Wirken des Alten Testaments: Festschrift für Claus Westermann* (Göttingen: Vandenhoeck & Ruprecht; Neukirchen-Vluyn: Neukirchener, 1980) 373-93; R. Albertz, "Der sozial-

hang im Hiob-Buch neben dem Tun-Ergehen-Zusammenhang noch weitere Aspekte der Konzeption einer "gerechten Ordnung" der Wirklichkeit kritisch beleuchtet werden. Das Hiob-Buch läßt eine enge Wechselbeziehung zwischen sozialen Erfahrungen und theologischen Konzepten erkennen. Beide werden durch die Darstellung und Reflexion der Erfahrungen "Hiobs" kommunikabel gemacht.

1. Eine exemplarische Formulierung des Konzepts eines *"Tun-Ergehen-Zusammenhangs"* bietet das Sprichwort:

"Einer gräbt eine Grube — er wird *hinein*fallen;
und einer wälzt einen Stein — er wird auf ihn *zurück*rollen."[6]

Tun und Ergehen werden hier "als ein in einem kontinuierlichen geschichtlichen Prozeß sich vollendendes, einheitliches, zielgerichtetes Geschehen sichtbar."[7] Mit seinem Handeln gegenüber seinen Mitmenschen schafft ein Mensch zugleich so etwas wie eine "Sphäre"[8] (die "Grube"), eine Art "potentielle Energie" (der "hochgerollte Stein"), die — mit zeitlicher Verzögerung und auf welchen Umwegen auch immer — schließlich auf ihn selbst zurückwirken.

Die Verbindung zwischen Tun und Ergehen kann auf unterschiedliche Weise näher bestimmt werden. "Das Tatsphärengeschehen kann . . . sowohl dynamistisch-eigengesetzlicher Qualität als auch insgesamt von Jahwe konstituiert sein."[9] Die Sozial- und Rechtsgemeinschaft kann und soll dazu beitragen, daß gute und schlechte Taten die ihnen angemessenen Folgen für den Täter haben.[10] Auf der Grundlage eines — mehr oder weniger expliziten — "consensus about what sort of acts are just and unjust"[11] behauptet *und* fordert das Konzept des Tun-Ergehen-Zusammenhangs eine "gerechte Ord-

---

geschichtliche Hintergrund des Hiobbuches und der »Babylonischen Theodizee«" in: *Die Botschaft und die Boten: Festschrift für Hans Walter Wolff zum 70. Geburtstag* (Neukirchen-Vluyn: Neukirchener, 1981) 349-72; R. Kessler, "»Ich weiß, daß mein Erlöser lebet«; Sozialgeschichtlicher Hintergrund und theologische Bedeutung der Löser-Vorstellung in Hiob 19,25," *ZTK* 89 (1992) 139-58 sowie G. Gutiérrez, *Von Gott sprechen in Unrecht und Leid — Ijob* (München: Matthias-Grünewald; Mainz: Kaiser, 1988).

6. Spr 26:27; vgl. Qoh 10:8; Sir 27:25-27; Ps 7:16f; 9:16f; 35:7f; 57:7.

7. Knierim, *Hauptbegriffe* [s.o. Anm. 2], 75.

8. Koch, "Vergeltungsdogma" [s.o. Anm. 1], 166 u. passim. Dazu kritisch Knierim, *Hauptbegriffe* [s.o. Anm. 2], 74ff.

9. Knierim, *Hauptbegriffe* [s.o. Anm. 2], 83. Vgl. etwa auch H. H. Schmid, "Schöpfung, Gerechtigkeit und Heil" in: Ders., *Altorientalische Welt in der alttestamentlichen Theologie* (Zürich: Theologischer, 1974) 9-30: 14.

10. Vgl. Knierim, *Hauptbegriffe* [s.o. Anm. 2], 77ff und z.B. F. Horst, "Recht und Religion im Bereich des Alten Testaments" in: Koch (Hg.), *Prinzip* [s.o. Anm. 1], 181-212; H. Graf Reventlow, "Sein Blut komme über sein Haupt," ebd. 412-31: 417ff.

11. J. Barton, "Natural Law and Poetic Justice in the Old Testament" in: *JTS* 30 (1979) 1-14; 13.

nung" der Wirklichkeit.[12] Sie ist als vorgegeben erfahrbar *und* muß *zugleich* durch menschliches und göttliches Handeln immer wieder neu realisiert werden.[13]

Wenn nun Hiob als ein Mann, der stets "untadelig," "rechtschaffen" und "gottesfürchtig" war und sich "vom Bösen fern" hielt (Hi 1:1, 8; 2:3), seinen Besitz und seine Nachkommen verliert (1:13-19) und noch dazu "mit bösartigem Geschwür von der Fußsohle bis zum Scheitel" geschlagen wird (2:7f), bedeutet dies eine eklatante *Störung der "gerechten Ordnung,"* wie sie der Tun-Ergehen-Zusammenhang postuliert: Hiob, der sich in seinem Verhalten allem "Schlechten" fernhielt (סר מרע *sār mērāʿ* 1:1, 8; 2:3), stürzt trotzdem ins Unglück (שחין רע *šĕḥîn rāʿ* 2:7)!

Wie diese Störung der "gerechten Ordnung" in der *sozialen "Praxis"* bewältigt werden kann, zeigt der Schluß der Rahmenerzählung des Hiob-Buchs in 42:11:[14]

> "Da kamen zu ihm alle seine Brüder und Schwestern und alle seine Bekannten von früher (כל־אחיו וכל־אחיתיו וכל־ידעיו לפנים *kol-ʾeḥâw wĕkol-ʾaḥyōtâw wĕkol-yōdĕʿâw lĕpānîm*) und aßen mit ihm Brot in seinem Haus und bezeigten ihm ihr Beileid und trösteten ihn (וינחמו אתו *waynaḥămû ʾōtô*) wegen all des Unglücks, das Jahwe über ihn gebracht hatte. Und sie gaben ihm jeder eine Kesita und einen goldenen Ring."

Die Solidarität der Verwandten und Bekannten Hiobs wirkt der Störung der "gerechten Ordnung" durch Jahwe entgegen. Im Zusammenwirken mit dem "Segen" Jahwes wird so der Tun-Ergehen-Zusammenhang wieder in Kraft gesetzt: "Und Jahwe segnete das Ende Hiobs mehr als seinen Anfang . . ." (42:12).

Das hier erkennbare Verständnis der "gerechten Ordnung" des Tun-Ergehen-Zusammenhangs entspricht in seinen Grundzügen dem Konzept der "Maʾat" als *"konnektiver Gerechtigkeit,"* wie es Jan Assmann an ägyptischen Texten des Mittleren Reiches aufgezeigt hat:

> "Maʾat verkörpert . . . das Prinzip der Solidarität, Gegenseitigkeit und Vergeltung. Vergeltung ist nach ägyptischer Auffassung — zumindest des Mittleren Reichs — . . . weder Sache eines bestrafenden und belohnenden Gottes

---

12. Vgl. H. H. Schmid, *Gerechtigkeit als Weltordnung* (BHT 40; Tübingen: Mohr [Siebeck], 1968) bes. 175ff.

13. Vgl. P. D. Miller, *Sin and Judgment in the Prophets* (SBLMS 27; Chico: Scholars, 1982), 134: "The deed-consequence relationship was probably not so much a carefully worked out theological *interpretation* of the causal nexus in human events as it was a theological *conclusion* growing out of the *experience* of that relationship (and not just by scribes and sages) which was integrated with *convictions* about the divine activity and control of human events" (Hervorhebungen von uns).

14. Übersetzung hier und im Folgenden nach F. Hesse, *Hiob* (Zürcher Bibelkommentare: Altes Testament 14: Zürich: Theologischer, 1978).

noch einer Privatinitiative der jeweils Betroffenen. Vergeltung ist aber auch nicht einer unpersönlichen Weltordnung anheimgestellt, sondern einer eminent zivilisatorischen Sozialordnung, einer Ordnung des Aneinander-Denkens und Füreinander-Handelns." — "Nur die Solidarität der Gruppe vermag den Nexus von Tun und Ergehen zu garantieren. Dieses Prinzip möchte ich die »konnektive Gerechtigkeit« nennen."[15]

Allerdings ist "das Prinzip der Solidarität und Gegenseitigkeit, wie es in den Texten des Mittleren Reichs als der Sinn der Ma'at entfaltet wird, *vertikal* gedacht"; es kommt als *"vertikale* Solidarität" im Rahmen eines hierarchisch strukturierten Sozialgefüges zum Tragen.[16] Dagegen wird in Hi 42:11 die "gerechte Ordnung" der Entsprechung von Tun und Ergehen durch Akte *"horizontaler* Solidarität" wiederhergestellt: Hiobs "Brüder," "Schwestern" und "Bekannte" haben die gleiche soziale Stellung wie er selbst.

Führt so die Rahmenerzählung des Hiob-Buchs in 42:11ff die Möglichkeit vor, Störungen der "gerechten Ordnung" des Tun-Ergehen-Zusammenhangs durch "horizontale Solidarität" sozial aufzufangen, zeigt demgegenüber der Dialogteil am Verhalten der "Freunde" Hiobs (רעי איוב *rēʿê ʾiyyôb* 2:11) auf, daß diese Ordnung durch die *Verweigerung sozialer Solidarität* tiefgreifend gefährdet werden kann: Auch Hiobs "Freunde" kommen zunächst, um ihn zu "trösten" (לנוד־לו ולנחמו *lānûd-lô ûlěnaḥămô* 2:11). Im Zuge des folgenden Gesprächs wird aber zunehmend deutlicher, daß sie ihm wirklichen "Trost" — der "reale Hilfe mit einschließt"![17] — letztlich verweigern:

"Leidige Tröster (מנחמי עמל *měnaḥămê ʿāmāl*) seid ihr alle!" (16:2)
"Wie tröstet ihr mich so nichtig (ואיך תנחמוני הבל *wěʾêk tenaḥămûnî hābel*)!" (21:34)

Angesichts dieser "Krise" der sozialen Solidarität bricht nun im Dialogteil die *theologische Frage* nach der Verantwortung Gottes für das Funktionieren des Tun-Ergehen-Zusammenhangs auf. Wenn dabei die "Freunde" Hiobs auf dem Tun-Ergehen-Zusammenhang als *vorfindlicher* Ordnung der Wirklichkeit insistieren, die sich "automatisch" oder/und durch das Wirken der Gottheit realisiert, wird daran die Fragwürdigkeit einer theologischen Konzeption einer "gerechten Weltordnung" erkennbar, die nicht (mehr) mit einer entsprechenden sozialen

---

15. J. Assmann, *Ma'at: Gerechtigkeit und Unsterblichkeit im Alten Ägypten* (München 1990) 66 und 67. Vgl. auch C.-A. Keller, "Zum sogenannten Vergeltungsglauben im Proverbienbuch," *Beiträge zur Alttestamentlichen Theologie für Walther Zimmerly zum 70. Geburtstag* (Göttingen: Vandenhoeck & Ruprecht, 1977) 223-38.

16. Assmann, a.a.O., 67 und 68; vgl. 92ff.

17. H. J. Stoebe, Art. "נחם *nḥm* pi. trösten" in: THAT II, 59-66: 62. S. auch K. Baltzer, "Liberation from Debt Slavery After the Exile in Second Isaiah and Nehemiah" in: *Ancient Israelite Religion: Essays in Honor of Frank Moore Cross* (Philadelphia: Fortress, 1987) 477-84, bes. 477.

Praxis verbunden ist — ja, die geradezu die Verweigerung praktischer Solidarität legitimieren kann:

"Bedenke doch: Wer ging je schuldlos zugrunde?
Wo kamen Rechtschaffene je um?" (4:7)

Wenn im Verlauf des Dialogs in den Reden Hiobs zunehmend deutlicher wird, daß er eine Garantie für ein seinem Tun entsprechendes Ergehen von Gott weder erwarten noch gar einklagen kann,[18] wird die Wahrnehmung der "Krise" sozialer Solidarität damit noch weiter verschärft: Gefragt ist eine soziale "Praxis," die "tröstet," nicht eine theologische "Theorie," die "vertröstet"![19]

2. Daß Hiobs Unglück (mindestens: auch) mit einem Mangel an sozialer Solidarität zu tun hat, läßt seine Klage in 19:13-19 erkennen:

"Meine Brüder ‹haben sich› von mir entfernt,
und meine Bekannten sind mir zu Fremden geworden.
Die mir nahestehen und die mir vertraut sind, die sind ausgeblieben;
es haben mich vergessen die Schutzbefohlenen meines Hauses.
Meine Sklavinnen halten mich für einen Fremden,
ein Unbekannter bin ich geworden in ihren Augen.
Rufe ich meinen Sklaven, so antwortet er nicht;
mit meinem Munde muß ich ihn anflehen.
Mein Atem ist meiner Frau widerlich,

---

18. Das wird auch durch 42:10 nicht zurückgenommen! Wenn Jahwe Hiobs "Geschick wendet," heißt dies ausweislich des sonstigen Gebrauchs der Wendung שוב שבות *šûb šĕbût* im AT gerade *nicht*, daß er Hiob ein Geschick zukommen läßt, das dieser berechtigterweise erwarten dürfte; vgl. J. M. Bracke, "*šûb šebût*: A Reappraisal" in: *ZAW* 97 (1985) 233-44. S. auch A. Cooper, "Reading and Misreading the Prologue to Job," *JSOT* 46 (1990) 67-79: 71.

19. "Trösten" ist ein Leitwort des Hiob-Buches; vgl. zu נחם *nḥm* pi. neben den bereits genannten Stellen 2:11; 16:2; 21:34 und 42:11 noch 29:25 (s.u.) und 7:13, ferner die Nomina נחמה *neḥāmâ* in 6:10 und תנחום *tanḥûm* in 15:11 und 21:2. Hiobs letztes Wort in 42:6 lautet: על־כן אמאס ונחמתי על־עפר ואפר *'al-kēn 'em'as wĕniḥamtî 'al-'āpār wā'ēper*. Ob dies als Ausdruck des "Widerrufs" und der "Reue" Hiobs "in (bzw. auf) Staub und Asche" zu verstehen ist, wie üblicherweise angenommen wird, ist fraglich. Nach I. Willi-Plein ("Heilige Schrift oder Heilige Übersetzung — Zur theologischen Relevanz hebraistischer Forschung und Lehre," *BN* 60 [1991] 48-58) wäre der Satz eher in dem Sinne zu interpretieren, daß Hiob "sich als »getröstet umgestimmt« erklärt" (52). "Es ist also zumindest erwägenswert, daß das Ijobbuch nicht auf Ijobs Reue hinausläuft, sondern auf seine Rechtfertigung, in der er schließlich Trost findet" (53; vgl. Dies., "Hiobs Widerruf? — Eine Untersuchung der Wz. נחם und ihrer erzähltechnischen Funktion im Hiobbuch" in: *I. L. Seeligmann-Jubilee-Volume* [Jerusalem: Rubinstein, 1983] 273-89). Folgt man D. Patrick ("The Translation of Job xlii 6," *VT* 26 [1976] 369-71; vgl. bereits Maimonides: s. L. J. Kaplan, "Maimonides, Dale Patrick, and Job xlii 6," *VT* 28 [1978] 356-58) und übersetzt: "Therefore I repudiate and repent in dust and ashes" (369), "that is, cease wallowing in dust and ashes" (370), könnte sich hier eine Kritik an religiösen "Selbstminderungs-Riten" andeuten (vgl. 1:20; 2:8), mit denen die Hoffnung (bzw. Vertröstung? — vgl. 22:23-30) auf ein Eingreifen Gottes verbunden ist.

31

und ich bin stinkend meinen Brüdern.
Auch die Knaben mißachten mich;
will ich mich erheben, wenden sie mir den Rücken.
Es verabscheuen mich alle Männer meines Vertrautenkreises,
und die ich liebte, haben sich gegen mich gewandt."

Neben der Verweigerung "horizontaler" Solidarität — die hier in Spannung zum (älteren?) Rahmen in 42:11ff auch den Verwandten und Bekannten Hiobs zugeschrieben wird — wird hier nun auch ein Mangel an *Solidarität in "vertikaler" Richtung* konstatiert: Auch Hiobs "Schutzbefohlene," "Sklavinnen" und "Sklaven" fangen seinen sozialen "Absturz" nicht auf!

Das dieser Klage entsprechende Gegenbild einer "gerechten Ordnung" in "vertikaler" Dimension zeichnen die Kap. 29 und 31, in denen Hiob seine soziale Stellung und sein Selbstverständnis vor dem Einbruch des Unheils darstellt: Bei seinem Auftreten verstummten selbst die führenden Persönlichkeiten (29:7-11). Seinen "Zeltgenossen" gewährte er ebenso großzügige Gastfreiheit wie durchreisenden "Fremden" (31:31f). Er achtete das Recht seiner Sklaven und Sklavinnen (31:13-15)[20] und sorgte für die *personae miserae* in seiner Umgebung: "Witwen" und "Waisen," "Elende" und "Arme" (29:11-16; 31:16-20).[21] Die soziale Stellung Hiobs als "Haupt" (ראש *rōʾš*) eines lokalen Gemeinwesens wird zusammenfassend beschrieben in 29:25:

"Ich erwählte ihren Weg und saß obenan (ואשב ראש *wěʾēšēb rōʾš*)
und thronte wie ein König (!) unter der Kriegsschar,
wie einer, der Trauernde tröstet (כאשר אבלים ינחם *kaʾăšer ʾăbēlîm yěnaḥēm*)."

Mit seiner "vertikalen Solidarität" — die hier wieder mit dem Stichwort "trösten" umschrieben wird! — sorgt Hiob für eine "gerechte Ordnung":

"Gerechtigkeit legte ich an, und sie bekleidete mich,
wie Obergewand und Turban (war) mein Recht(tun) . . .
Den Rechtsstreit Unbekannter prüfte ich.
Ich zerschmetterte die Kinnladen des Bösen
und ‹riß› den Raub aus seinen Zähnen." (29:14-17)

Hier wird ein Konzept einer "gerechten Ordnung" erkennbar, das "vertikal," genauer: "*von oben nach unten*" orientiert ist. Es schließt eine differenzierte

---

20. Die theologische Argumentation ist hier besonders bemerkenswert, weil sie die Beachtung des Rechtes mit dem gleichen Geschaffensein als Mensch verbindet: "Hat nicht mein Schöpfer auch ihn im Mutterleibe gemacht, hat nicht der Eine ‹uns› im Mutterschoß zugerüstet?" (V.15). Damit wird in der Sache die vertikale soziale Gliederung in Frage gestellt, die im Kontext als selbstverständlich vorausgesetzt ist!
21. Vgl. als Gegenstück die Vorwürfe Eliphas' in 22:6-9.

Wahrnehmung von Verantwortung in abgestuften Sozialbeziehungen ein, die vor Gott und den Menschen wahrgenommen wird. Jeder soll das bekommen, was ihm zukommt; darauf beruht der Zusammenhalt der Gemeinschaft. In Unterscheidung von der "konnektiven Gerechtigkeit" des Tun-Ergehen-Zusammenhangs könnte man diesen Aspekt der "gerechten Ordnung" als *"distributive Gerechtigkeit"* charakterisieren.[22]

Ein Ehrentitel, mit dem man Hiobs soziale Stellung und sein Ethos einer "vertikalen Solidarität" umfassend charakterisieren könnte, wäre נדיב *nādîb*, "der aus freiem Entschluß Spendende, der Edle" (HAL s.v.). Der Titel begegnet im Hiob-Buch in 12:21; 21:28 und 34:18. In 30:15 klagt Hiob über den Verlust dieser Ehrenstellung: "Wie vom Sturmwind wird mein Ansehen weggerafft (תרדף כרוח נדבתי *tirdōp kārûaḥ nĕdibātî*). . . ." Im Rahmen des in Hi 29–31 erkennbaren Konzepts einer "gerechten Ordnung" begründet die "vertikale Solidarität" des *nādîb* "von oben nach unten" die Erwartung einer entsprechenden Solidarität der von ihm Abhängigen *"von unten nach oben"*:[23]

> "Ja, wenn mich ein Ohr hörte, pries es mich glücklich,
> sah mich ein Auge, dann bezeugte es mir,
> daß ich den Elenden rettete, der um Hilfe rief,
> und die Waise, die ohne Helfer war.
> Der Segen von solchen, die dem Untergang geweiht, kam auf mich,
> und jubeln machte ich der Witwe Herz . . .
> So dachte ich: Mit meinem Nest werde ich abscheiden
> und wie der Phönix lange leben.
> Meine Wurzel ist geöffnet für das Wasser,
> und Tau nächtigt auf meinem Gezweig.
> Meine Ehre (?) wird neu bei mir bleiben,
> und mein Bogen in meiner Hand verjüngt sich (?)." (29:11-13, 18-20)

Während nun das Hiob-Buch in der vorliegenden Komposition von Rahmenerzählung und Dialog Kritik an der Verweigerung "horizontaler" Solidarität erkennen läßt, scheint es den Mangel an "vertikaler" Solidarität "von unten nach oben" nicht zu kritisieren, sondern auf *strukturelle* Ursachen zurückzuführen. Darauf deuten jedenfalls die Erfahrungen Hiobs nach seinem Abstieg von der "Spitze" des Gemeinwesens an seinen unteren Rand. Was in Kap. 29 aus der Perspektive "von oben" als "heile Welt" und "gerechte Ordnung" erschien, stellt sich "von unten" betrachtet anders dar:

---

22. Vgl. Assmann, *Ma'at* [s.o. Anm. 15], 92ff und 237ff.

23. Vgl. Keller, "Vergeltungsglauben" [s.o. Anm. 15], 234f: "Indem der Wohlhabende von seinem Reichtum zugunsten der Armen rechten Gebrauch macht, baut er sich eine Gefolgschaft von Klienten auf." — "Reichtum ist . . . dazu da, sich die Unterstützung der weniger Begüterten zu sichern und ein »big man« zu werden, Ansehen und Einfluß zu gewinnen."

"Ist nicht Frondienst des Menschen Los auf Erden,
sind seine Tage nicht wie die eines Lohnknechts?
Wie ein Sklave, der nach Schatten lechzt,
und wie ein Knecht, der auf seinen Lohn wartet,
so wurde ich beschenkt (mit) Monden des Unheils,
Nächte voll Mühsal wurden mir zugeteilt." (7:1-3)

"‹Die Übeltäter› verrücken die Grenzen;
sie rauben Herden und lassen sie (dann) weiden.
Den Esel der Waisen treiben sie fort,
nehmen das Rind der Witwe als Pfand.
Sie treiben die Armen vom Wege weg;
miteinander müssen sich verbergen die Elenden des Landes.
Siehe, (wie) Zebras in der Wüste,
so ziehen sie aus zu ihrem Tun,
indem sie nach Nahrung die Steppe durchsuchen
‹und nach› Speise für ihre Kinder.
Auf dem Felde ernten sie ‹in der Nacht›,
und den Weinberg des Bösen plündern sie aus.
Nackt übernachten sie, ohne Kleid,
und ohne Decke in der Kälte.
Vom Regenguß der Berge werden sie naß,
und ohne Schutz drücken sie sich an den Fels." (24:2-8)

Gustavo Gutiérrez sieht einen "Aspekt des Fortschritts" im Hiob-Dialog "in der Erkenntnis" Hiobs, "daß der Zufall des ungerechten Leidens nicht nur ihn alleine betrifft. Vielmehr ist dies die Situation zahlloser Armer dieser Erde, die am Straßenrand und außerhalb des Landes, das ihnen eigentlich Arbeit und Brot geben soll, mehr sterben als leben. Erschrocken stellt Ijob fest, daß sein Unglück auch das Los zahlreicher anderer ist."[24] Im Blick auf Kap. 29–31 kann man bezweifeln, ob "Hiob" wirklich zu dieser Erkenntnis mit allen Konsequenzen durchdringt. In der Tat scheint aber "der Verfasser der Schrift" seinen Lesern diese Erkenntnis nahebringen zu wollen, wenn er sich "veranlaßt [fühlt], Ijob die tiefgreifendste und grausamste Beschreibung des Elends der Armen in den Mund zu legen, die sich in der Bibel findet, und die Mächtigen heftig zu beschuldigen, die Kleinen auszubeuten und zu unterdrücken."[25]

Daß die in Kap. 29–31 erkennbare Konzeption einer "gerechten Ordnung" im Sinne einer "distributiven Gerechtigkeit" und "vertikalen Solidarität" durchaus *kritisch* zu betrachten ist, legen jedenfalls auch die Gottesreden in Kap. 38–41 nahe. In *einem* Punkt gehen sie nämlich sehr direkt auf Hiobs vorhergehende Reden ein: Sie bestreiten seine Fähigkeit, für "Recht und Ordnung" zu sorgen,

24. Gutiérrez, *Von Gott sprechen* [s.o. Anm. 5], 59.
25. Gutiérrez, a.a.O., 61.

wie er es in 29:14-17 von sich behauptete (vgl. 38:12-15; 40:9-14)![26] Wenn Hiob als Reaktion auf die (erste) Gottesrede "seine Hand auf seinen Mund legt" und verstummt (40:4f), erkennt er damit Jahwe die Stellung als "Haupt" und "König" zu, die er in 29:9f, 25 für sich selbst beanspruchte.

3. Treffen die skizzierten Überlegungen zu, so wird als *ein* Thema des Hiob-Buches die *Problematik sozialer Solidarität* erkennbar. Dabei ist zu unterscheiden zwischen "horizontaler" und "vertikaler" Solidarität. Im Blick auf die "horizontale" Solidarität zwischen sozial Gleichgestellten lassen Rahmenerzählung und Dialog Kritik an ihrer *Verweigerung* erkennen. Demgegenüber deutet sich in Dialog und Gottesreden eine kritische Sicht der sozialen *Verhältnisse* an, in deren Rahmen "vertikale" Solidarität gefordert und legitimiert wird.

Beide Dimensionen einer "gerechten Ordnung" der Wirklichkeit spielen im Hiob-Buch nun auch als Elemente der "sozio-morphen" Beschreibung der Gottesbeziehung eine Rolle: Der Dialogteil macht deutlich, daß Gott nicht als Garant eines Tun-Ergehen-Zusammenhangs im Sinne "konnektiver Gerechtigkeit" und "horizontaler Solidarität" in Anspruch genommen werden kann. An der Argumentation der "Freunde" Hiobs wird erkennbar, daß ein derartiges Gottesverständnis mit einer "Ent-Solidarisierung" auf der sozialen Ebene einhergehen und diese legitimieren kann. *Wenn* das Handeln Jahwes überhaupt in den Kategorien von "horizontaler" und "vertikaler Solidarität" erfaßbar ist, *dann* ist es — den Gottesreden entsprechend — eher als das eines "aus freiem Entschluß Spendenden, Edlen" (נדיב *nādîb*) zu beschreiben. Als Soziomorphem zur Beschreibung der Gottesbeziehung begegnet נדבה *nĕdābâ* in Hos 14:5: "Ich will ihre Abtrünnigkeit heilen, will sie aus freien Stücken lieben (אהבם נדבה *'ōhăbēm nĕdābâ*); denn mein Zorn ist von ihm gewichen."[27]

Doch lassen die Gottesreden erkennen, daß sich das Handeln Jahwes einer soziomorphen Beschreibung letztlich entzieht: Jahwe wird hier "als Kosmos schaffender Gott dargestellt, . . . der dessen chaotische Bereiche, ohne sie aufzuheben, unter Kontrolle hält." Er "hält das Chaos im Zaum, ohne es in eine langweilige, starre Ordnung zu verwandeln."[28] Jahwe steht also *über* dem Gegensatz von "Ordnung" und "Chaos." Die von ihm konstituierte *kosmische* "Ordnung" ist Bedingung der *Möglichkeit* sozialer "Ordnungen," schließt aber nicht schon ihre *Realisierung* in einer *bestimmten* Gestalt ein. Die Sorge für eine "gerechte Ordnung" der *sozialen* Wirklichkeit ist Aufgabe der Menschen!

---

26. In diese Richtung könnten auch die Aussagen in den Elihu-Reden (Kap. 32–37) deuten, die sich in Aufnahme herrschaftskritischer Traditionen des AT gegen menschliche "Hybris" wenden; vgl. 33,17; 34,18ff; 36,6ff und bereits die kritischen Bemerkungen zum Anspruch der "Alten" auf besondere "Weisheit" in 32,6ff.

27. Übersetzung von J. Jeremias, *Der Prophet Hosea* (ATD 24,1; Göttingen: Vandenhoeck & Ruprecht, 1983). Beachte die "Natur"-Terminologie in V.6ff!

28. O. Keel, *Jahwes Entgegnung an Ijob* (FRLANT 121; Göttingen: Vandenhoeck & Ruprecht, 1978) 125.

Das schließt nicht aus, daß Jahwe menschliche Bemühungen mit seinem "Segen" unterstützt (42:12), und daß er selbst in Einzelfällen zur "Wendung" einer Notlage in das Geschehen eingreift (42:10). Sein Handeln entzieht sich dann aber den Kategorien von "horizontaler" und "vertikaler Solidarität" im Rahmen einer (vermeintlich) "gerechten Ordnung" der sozialen Wirklichkeit: Die Soziomorpheme bilden als Teile eines Abstraktionsvorganges "konkrete Abstraktionen." "Die endliche Lösung Hiobs ist gerade nicht ein Tauschakt, sondern beruht auf Gottes *vorgängiger* Solidarität mit Hiob."[29] Dem käme am ehesten noch das Soziomorphem des "Lösers" (גאל *gōʾēl*) nahe (vgl. Hi 19:25-27).[30]

Die Problematik von "horizontaler" und "vertikaler" Solidarität in ihrer soziomorphen Übertragung auf die Gottesbeziehung wird noch weiter zugespitzt im Prolog des Hiob-Buches (in einer jüngeren Bearbeitung[31]?): Die Stichworte "umsonst" (חנם *ḥinnām* 1:9; 2:3)[32] und "Haut um Haut!" (2:4) behaupten für die Gottesbeziehung — wie R. Kessler es formuliert hat — eine "Alternative zwischen gleichberechtigter Warenbeziehung und der Abhängigkeit von einem Mächtigeren" — und entlarven diese Alternative im Kontext zugleich als "»satanisch« in dem doppelten Sinn, daß sie den Menschen von Gott trennt und daß sie in sich unauflösbar wird."[33]

Die Frage, ob "Hiob Gott umsonst fürchtet" (1:8), findet dann im Fortgang des vorliegenden Hiob-Buches eine mehrfache "Antwort": *sowohl* in Hiobs Festhalten an seiner Gottesbeziehung in Unterwerfung (1:21f; 2:10) *und* Protest (Kap. 3ff) — *als auch* in der Verweigerung (Kap. 4ff) *oder* Gewährung (42:11) sozialer Solidarität durch seine Bekannten und Verwandten — *als auch* in Jahwes Eingreifen zur "Wendung des Geschicks" Hiobs (42:10) *und* seiner Gewährung von "Segen" für solidarisches Verhalten im zwischenmenschlichen Bereich (42:12).

Das Hiob-Buch hält — im Sinne der rechtlichen und prophetischen Traditionen des AT — daran fest, daß Gottesbeziehung und Sozialbeziehungen — in Tun (vgl. 1:1, 8; 2:3) *und* Ergehen (vgl. 42:10-12) — nicht voneinander zu trennen sind. Indem es zugleich auch die "Transzendenz" Jahwes gegenüber der vorfindlichen sozialen Wirklichkeit mit ihren "horizontalen" und "vertikalen" Solidaritäten betont, hält es den Raum frei für eine *kritische*

---

29. Kessler, "Ich weiß" [s.o. Anm. 5], 155 Anm. 39 (Hervorhebung von uns).

30. Kessler, a.a.O., 154ff.

31. 1:6-12 (und 21b?); 2:1-10. Vgl. O. Kaiser, *Einleitung in das Alte Testament*, 5. Auf., Gütersloh: G. Mohn, 1984) 385 im Anschluß an L. Schmidt, *De Deo* (BZAW 143; Berlin; New York: de Gruyter 1976) 165ff.

32. S. dazu J. Ebach, "»Ist es ›umsonst‹, daß Hiob gottesfürchtig ist?« Lexikographische und methodologische Anmerkungen zu חנם in Hi 1,9" in: *Die Hebräische Bibel und ihre zweifache Nachgeschichte Festschrift für Rolf Rendtorff zum 65. Geburtsdag* (Neukirchen-Vluyn: Neukirchener, 1990) 319-35.

33. Kessler, "Ich weiß" [s.o. Anm. 5], 155.

Betrachtung vermeintlich "gerechter Ordnungen" — und ihre Veränderung.[34]

Diese Problemstellung und -entwicklung wird im NT aufgenommen und weitergeführt, wenn z.B. im "Gleichnis von den Arbeitern im Weinberg" der "Herr" sein Verhalten gegenüber seinen "Arbeitern" folgendermaßen verteidigt:

> "»Freund (!), ich tue dir kein Unrecht. Hattest du dich nicht auf einen Denar mit mir geeinigt? So nimm deinen Lohn und geh! Doch es ist mein Wille, diesem Letzten hier das gleiche zu geben wie dir! Sollte es mir nicht freistehen, mit meinem Eigentum zu machen, was ich will? Oder schaust du so böse drein, weil ich so gütig bin?« *So werden die Letzten Erste und die Ersten Letzte sein.*" (Mat 20:13-16)[35]

---

34. Eine kleine, aber nicht zu unterschätzende Veränderung in der sozialen Praxis Hiobs ist vielleicht darin zu sehen, daß er nach 42:15 auch seinen Töchtern "Besitzanteile unter ihren Brüdern" gibt, während er in 1:5 nur für seine Söhne "Opfer" dargebracht hatte.

35. Übersetzung von U. Wilckens, *Das Neue Testament*, 7. Aufl. (Zürich; Einsiedeln; Köln: Gütersloh: Gütersloher Verlagshaus Gerd Mohn, 1983) (Hervorhebung von uns).

Stories of Adam and Eve

DON C. BENJAMIN

The Stories of Adam and Eve (Gen 2:4b–4:2) develop from shorter creation stories which are now artistically nested one inside the other. Each investigates different questions which the ancient Near East asked about human life.[1] The theology of creation in stories like these is as important for understanding the religion of ancient Israel as is the theology of history in stories like the exodus and the settlement.[2]

The creation story follows a standard pattern. There is a sterility affidavit in the crisis, a cosmogony in the climax, and a covenant in the denouement.[3]

1. For J. O'Brien and W. Major, *In the Beginning: Creation Myths from Ancient Mesopotamia* (Chico, Calif.: Scholars, 1982), 92, the stories investigate the problem of evil; for C. Meyers, *Discovering Eve: Ancient Israelite Women in Context* (New York: Oxford University, 1988), 77-79, the pioneering values of hard work in early Israel (1250-1000 B.C.E.); for J. M. Kennedy, "Peasants in Revolt," *JSOT* 47 (1990): 3-14, the monarchy's oppression of peasants in Judah (925-587 B.C.E.). See R. P. Knierim, "Criticism of Literary Features, Form, Tradition, and Redaction," in *The Hebrew Bible and Its Modern Interpreters* (Chico, Calif.: Scholars, 1985), 146-50, 157, on tradition and anthropology in a text.

2. So R. P. Knierim, "Cosmos and History in Israel's Theology," *HBT* 3 (1981): 59-123; "The Task of Old Testament Theology," *HBT* 6,1 (1984): 25-57, in contrast to G. von Rad, *Old Testament Theology*, vol. 2 (New York: Harper and Row, 1965), 336-56, and others for whom the theology of creation in the Bible is not an expression of genuine Yahwism, or is subordinate to Israel's theology of history.

3. For E. Leach, "Levi-Straus in the Garden of Eden," in *Transactions of the New York Academy of Sciences* 23 (1961): 286-96; G. von Rad, *Old Testament Theology*, vol. 1 (New York: Harper and Row, 1962), 141-51; C. Westermann, *Genesis 1–11* (Minneapolis: Augsburg, 1984), 65; D. Jobling, "Myth and Its Limits," in *Sense of Biblical Narrative: Structural Analyses in the Hebrew Bible*, vol. 2, JSOTSup 39 (Sheffield: JSOT, 1986), 17-43, and others. Genesis 1–11 is literature, not myth — a term technically applied only to oral traditions in cultures without a sense of history. *Creation story*, here, identifies the genre which cultures with a

A sterility affidavit certifies that when the Creator set to work there was no life! Before creation everything is out of place. The Creator does not make something from nothing, but organizes chaos into cosmos. A cosmogony describes how the Creator gives birth (Gk. *agōnia*) to a world (Gk. *kosmos*). The Creator works in stages, carefully correcting and redesigning the world and its creatures. The image does not question the omnipotence and the omniscience of Yahweh, nor does it anticipate Darwin's nineteenth-century theory of evolution. It is anthropomorphic. The Creator works by trial and error because humans work by trial and error. The denouement tells how the Creator endows the new world with both the natural resources and technologies on which humans depend and the covenant whose stipulations teach them how to survive.

A Story of the Adam (Genesis 2:4b-17)

The first of the Stories of Adam and Eve is a Story of the Adam (Gen 2:4b-17). With four synonymous parallels the crisis certifies that in the beginning farming was impossible.[4] The same imagery appears in the Enuma Elish Story as it was told in Babylon between 1792 and 1750 B.C.E.

> When Yahweh Elohim began to create the heavens
> . . . and the earth,
> There were no orchards,
>   There were no fields of grain.
> There were no [planting] rains,
>   [There were no harvesting rains.]
> There was no one to work the soil,
>   [There was no soil to work.]
> Only water pouring through dikes of clay,
>   water flooding the earth. (Gen 2:4b-6, author's translation)

Grain, wine, and oil were the major farm products in the ancient Near East. What is missing is not plants and herbs (NRSV), but fields of grain, vineyards of grapes, and orchards of olive trees. Likewise, farming in Syria-Palestine depends on two periods of rainfall. What is missing is not just rain, but two rains: the rain at the end of the long, hot summer which softens the

---

sense of history develop from myth; see Knierim, "Criticism," 136-44 on form, text, and genre.

4. For Knierim ("Cosmos and History"), ". . . agriculture is that form of human activity in which the humans on earth are integrated into the cosmic life-cycle which owes its creation and ongoing existence to Yahweh" (84). "[And s]alvation-history is fulfilled in the blessing of the forever remaining annual agrarian life-cycle [Deut 26:5-11]" (98-99).

soil enough for farmers to plow and the rain near the end of the growing season which brings crops to full fruit. To prevent crop failure these twin rains must come at the right time and in the right quantity. The most colorful parallel in the sterility affidavit matches the farmer (Heb. 'ādām) with the farmland (Heb. 'ādāmâ). Land was life. Without good farmland, no farmer could survive; without good farmers, no farmland would exist.

Scholars have disagreed whether to begin the cosmogony in the Story of the Heavens and the Earth (Gen 1:1–2:4a) at Gen 1:2 or Gen 1:3.[5] Surprisingly, there has been little disagreement that the cosmogony in the Story of the Adam (Gen 1:4b–4:2) should begin in Gen 2:6. Consequently, many translations render this verse as if it describes an irrigation system parallel to the imagery in Sumer's Story of Enki, whose semen soaks the vulva of Nintu before she gives birth to the plants and animals.[6] But reading Gen 2:6 as the beginning of the cosmogony, rather than as the conclusion of the sterility affidavit, creates a literary anomaly.[7] It would be more consistent with the pattern and imagery of the standard creation story to consider these waters as destructive, not creative. They are not a cloud (Targ, Job 36:27), mist (NASB, Sir 24:3), spring (LXX), or stream (NRSV) irrigating crops, but rather a flood (JB, NEB) inundating everything in its path. The waters of chaos have different names: *chaos* (Gen 1:2), *deep* (Gen 1:2), *flood* (Gen 7:7), *yām* (Exod 14:16), *nāḥār, tĕhôm* (Gen 1:2; 7:11; 8:2), or *tiamat.* Here they are called *'ēd.* The *'ēd* do not give life, they bring death.[8] A world flooded with water is the final image in the sterility affidavit; life-giving waters appear only in the cosmogony.[9]

Yahweh's first work in the cosmogony is the *'ādām* (Gen 2:7). Some cosmogonies describe the Creator fighting with chaos, some do not. Although the Creator battles the waters of chaos in the Flood Stories (Gen 6–11) and the Exodus Stories (Exod 5–15), Yahweh in the Story of the Adam is not a warrior but an artist.[10] The image of the Creator as a potter also appears in the Story of Atrahasis as it was told in Babylon between 1646 and 1626 B.C.E.[11]

---

5. B. Otzen, "Use of Myth in Genesis," in *Myth in the Old Testament* (London: SCM, 1980), 31-39.

6. So von Rad, *Theology,* vol. 1, 148; A. J. Bledstein, "Genesis of Humans," *Judaism* 26 (1977): 189; Meyers, 84, and others, even though for G. W. Coats, *Genesis: With an Introduction to Narrative Literature,* FOTL 1 (Grand Rapids: Eerdmans, 1983), 49, it describes *pre-creation* and for Jobling, 23, ". . . the earth's water supply remains ambiguous," despite the mist.

7. O'Brien and Major, 101.

8. P. K. McCarter, "River Ordeal in Israelite Literature," *HTR* 66 (1973): 403-12.

9. M. Casalis, "The Dry and the Wet," *Semiotica* 17 (1976): 35-68.

10. For J. H. Gronbaek, "Baal's Battle with Yam," *JSOT* 33 (1985): 27-44, Gen 1:2b and Gen 2:6 originally described a violent struggle between the Creator and the waters of chaos.

11. W. G. Lambert and A. R. Millard, *Atrahasis: The Babylonian Story of the Flood with the Sumerian Flood Story by M. Civil* (Oxford: Clarendon, 1969), 5.

They entered the labor room,
    Mami the Wise and Ea the Prince.
She summoned the midwives,
    He worked the clay.
She sang the sacred song,
    He prayed the special prayer.
She finished singing,
    She pulled off fourteen pieces of clay.
She divided them into rows of seven,
    She set the birth stool between the rows.[12]

Between 10,000 and 4000 B.C.E. stone-age humans took two momentous steps toward civilization: they learned to farm and to make pottery. These inventions created a new world. Consequently, they and their descendants often thought about the Creator as a potter or a farmer. The metaphor is modified so that the techniques of the divine and human potters are similar but not identical. All potters work with two ingredients; one is firm and the other is fluid.[13] But human potters mix clay with water, while divine potters use a variety of thinners. Nintu-Mami thins her clay with blood (Atra I:229-34), Aruru uses saliva (Gilg I:30-40), and Yahweh wets the clay with only the condensation created by breathing on it (Gen 2:7).

Most translations refer to the human element as *dust*, not *clay*, and do not continue the image of the Creator as a potter from Gen 2:7a into Gen 2:7b. Consequently, they consider the divine element to be breath, not fluid (Ps 104:27-30; Job 34:14-15). Since there is no Sumerian or Babylonian parallel for breathing life into clay,[14] these interpretations parallel Egyptian art where the Creator breathes into the pharaoh's nose to authorize his coronation.[15] The parallel is attractive, but while the motif is common for a coronation, it is rarely used to describe human creation and would be the only Egyptian motif in the stories.[16] For ancient Israel, a living creature (Heb. *nepeš*) is moist, not inflated.[17]

---

12. V. H. Matthews and D. C. Benjamin, *Old Testament Parallels: Laws and Stories from the Ancient Near East* (New York and Mahwah: Paulist, 1991), 20.

13. For Casalis, 44, ". . . since dust alone cannot be fashioned, YHWH's action presupposes the addition of water to the soil's dust to obtain clay."

14. Lambert and Millard, 22.

15. W. Wifall, "Breath of His Nostrils: Gen 2:7b," *CBQ* 36 (1974): 237-40.

16. For Kennedy, 13 n. 10, the book of Lamentations (Lam 4:20) and an inscription (1421-1413 B.C.E.) in the Valley of the Nobles, where ". . . the princes of all foreign countries, . . . make supplication to the good god and . . . beg breath for their nostrils, . . . (J. A. Wilson, trans., 'Scenes of Asiatic Commerce in Theban Tombs,' in *ANET*, 1963, 249c)," are precedents for breathing humans to life.

17. But see Ps 146:4 NRSV: "When their breath [Heb. *rûaḥ*] departs, they return to the earth [Heb. *'ādāmâ*]."

It is blood, sperm, tears, and saliva which distinguish the living from the dead, the moist from the dry.

Many have used the breathing motif to explain human mortality as a radical dependence of the adam on the creator.[18] But the stories themselves explain labor and death as characteristics which result from the bond between the adam and the *'ādāmâ*, highlighted by the observations "there was no one to till the ground" (Gen 2:5) and "you are dust, and to dust you shall return" (Gen 3:19) — which create a chiasm framing or ringing them. Not only is the adam created from the *'ādāmâ*, but so are the trees from which it eats, and the animals who are its companions.[19]

To emphasize that the first creatures are extraordinary, storytellers give them special names, different from those for ordinary humans.[20] The Enuma Elish Story and the Story of Atrahasis call the people primeval *lullu;* the Story of Gilgamesh calls the first creature *enkidu.* Yahweh's first creature is an *'ādām.* Creation stories describe the differences between ordinary human beings and their predecessors in various ways. The *lullu* are fertile and immortal (Atra III:vii:1). They overpopulate and disturb the divine assembly with all the noise they make. To create ordinary human beings, the divine assembly introduces sterility, crib death, and celibacy into the world. The *enkidu* is sterile, immortal, and lazy (Ezek 28:11-19). To make it an ordinary human, the divine assembly commissions the Wise Woman (Akkad. *harimtu samhat*) to teach *enkidu* to eat bread, drink beer, wear clothes, and have sexual intercourse: to become fertile and mortal.

The Stories of Adam and Eve assume that both the *'ādām* (Gen 2:7) and the man and the woman (Gen 3:23) are immortal like the *lullu* and sterile like the *enkidu.*[21] They are living, but not fully human. The *'ādām* is a being without gender, neither male nor female.[22] The man and the woman have gender, but are

---

18. P. Trible, *God and the Rhetoric of Sexuality,* OBT (Philadelphia: Fortress, 1978), 80.

19. A. J. Hauser, "Genesis 2–3: The Theme of Intimacy and Alienation," in *Art and Meaning: Rhetoric in Biblical Literature,* ed. D. J. A. Clines, D. M. Gunn, and A. J. Hauser, JSOTSup 19 (Sheffield: University of Sheffield, 1982), 21.

20. For E. R. Leach, *Genesis as Myth and Other Essays* (London: Cape, 1969), 7-13; Y. Amit, "Biblical Utopianism," *USQR* 44 (1990): 11-17, myth posits an imaginative world unlike the world of experience to test one against the other; but for Westermann, 160-61, blessing unites the world of experience with the world in creation stories.

21. But for M. A. Knibb, "Life and Death in the Old Testament," in *The World of Ancient Israel: Sociological, Anthropological, and Political Perspectives: Essays by Members of the Society for Old Testament Study,* ed. R. E. Clements (Cambridge and New York: Cambridge University, 1989), 492-93; R. Martin-Achard, *From Death to Life* (Edinburgh: Oliver and Boyd, 1960); L. Wacheter, *Der Tod im Alten Testament,* Arbeiten zur Theologie 2 (Stuttgart: Calwer, 1967); Westermann, the adam was never immortal.

22. For Trible, 80; Meyers, 81-82; D. Rosenberg and H. Bloom, *Book of J* (New York: Grove Weidenfeld, 1990); and others, the adam is not sexual or a male creature, but neuter, an earthling or earth creature. For S. S. Lanser, "[Feminist] Criticism in the Garden," *Semeia*

sterile. The first truly human beings in the story are Adam and Eve (Gen 4:1-2). Only they have names; only they have children; only they work the land.[23]

The world Yahweh creates for the adam is called *ēden* (Gen 2:8). Romanticism in the eighteenth century branded the city as an unfit environment for humans. For Blake, Wordsworth, Coleridge, Byron, Shelley, and Keats, a city could never be a paradise. Their exaltation of human life in the open continues to evoke condemnations of urban life.

> . . . the city . . . [is] a parasite. She absolutely cannot live in and by herself. . . . Like a vampire, it preys on the true living creation, alive in its connection with the Creator. The city is dead, made of dead things for dead people. She can herself neither produce nor maintain anything whatever. . . . the city is an enormous man-eater. She does not renew herself from within, but by a constant supply of fresh blood from outside.
>
> . . . she spoils peasant values with remarkable virtuosity. . . . The very character of the city, in the economic field or the intellectual, artistic, or humanitarian, is to receive from outside, to consume, and to produce things without value or meaning, usable only inside the city and to her gain.[24]

The Romantic perspective has had an enduring effect on biblical interpretation. Consequently, many interpreters describe *ēden* as an unspoiled wilderness.[25] But in creation stories there is no naturalism or primitivism.[26] The untamed wilderness is unfit for humans who are created to live in cities, not in the great outdoors. The people primeval are wild and barbaric until the Wise tutor them in the arts (Sum. *mes*) of sexual intercourse, government, city building, trades, skills, and crafts.[27] Therefore, it is more likely that the Eden in the Story of the Adam is a

---

41 (1988): 67-84, all characters in a story have gender. According to speech-act theory, there is "no marking, no context, to lead readers to make a new inference about the meaning of *hā'ādām*" (72); therefore, the Adam is male. For Jobling, 30-41, ". . . the primal human is . . . male. The word *'dm* . . . continues to be used . . . for the man as opposed to the woman (2.25). . . . The agricultural work of the *'dm* (2.15) is specifically *male* work in 3.17-19. The body from which the woman is taken is . . . male (the alternative is that it became male during the operation!). The logic of the issue is, of course, all on Trible's side. Maleness is meaningless before sexual differentiation. The originality of maleness over femaleness is affirmed in the text against logic, but it is affirmed." For Kennedy, 13 n. 11, the adam is a peasant as defined by N. Gottwald, *The Hebrew Bible: A Socio-Literary Introduction* (Philadelphia: Fortress, 1985), 329.

23. For Meyers, 82, each character in Genesis 2–3, not just those in Gen 4:1-2, have names.

24. J. Ellul, *Meaning of the City* (Grand Rapids: Eerdmans, 1970), 150-51.

25. Meyers, 82-83, and others.

26. D. C. Benjamin, *Deuteronomy and City Life* (Lanham, Md.: UPA, 1983), 39-90.

27. S. N. Kramer, *From the Tablets of Sumer: Twenty-Five Firsts in Man's Recorded History* (Indian Hills, Colo.: Falcon's Wing, 1956), 91-93; Lambert and Millard, 18-19; O'Brien and Major, 73-74.

landscaped garden or urban masterpiece than an undeveloped wilderness or a geological wonder.[28] Like the chaos it replaces, Eden is described in parallels reflecting the order, balance, and abundance "in the day the Lord God made the earth and the heavens" (Gen 2:4b). It is built from pairs or twins. There are two of everything: two trees, two sets of rivers, two kinds of gold, two kinds of gems.[29]

The covenant which closes the story gives Eden to the adam and decrees it will survive in this new world by eating the fruit from every tree but the tree of the knowledge of good and evil. The apple tree (Lat. *pyrus malus*) was virtually unknown in the ancient Near East. It is the quince tree (Heb. *tappûaḥ*) with its apple-shaped and yellow-colored fruit whose shade, beauty, fragrance, and taste are so popular in the Bible (Cant 2:3-5; 7:9; 8:5; Joel 1:12; Prov 25:11). At some point audiences identified a fantasy from the Song of Songs (Cant 8:5) with the Stories of Adam and Eve, and the tree of the knowledge of good and evil became known as an apple tree.

The intention of the covenant in the denouement is not to restrict and tempt.[30] In the biblical world the Creator does not use law to trap and test, but to teach people how to survive. Not only do we resent laws in general today, but we consider prohibitions which order us not to do something worse than commandments which order us to do something. In the Bible, however, saying something positively is neither grammatically nor morally better than saying something negatively. The balance and repetition in parallelism make it an effective teaching technique. Parallelism here also recognizes that every decision is really two decisions: a decision to do something and a decision not to do something. Every yes has a corresponding no. Overlooking the no-consequences of a yes-decision courts failure.

A Story of Adam and the Animals (Gen 2:18-20a)

The second of the Stories of Adam and Eve is a Story of Adam and the Animals (Gen 2:18-20a). The crisis affirms that everything around the adam is twinned

28. For M. Hutter, "Adam als Gartner und Konig (Gen 2, 8.15)," *CBQ* 36 (1974): 237-40, monarchs built monumental urban gardens as symbols of the fertility which their rule brought to the state.

29. So S. N. Kramer, *Sumerian Mythology: A Study of Spiritual and Literary Achievement in the Third Millennium B.C.* (Philadelphia: American Philosophical Society, 1944), 33; Coats, 52, but for Amit, 15, ". . . gold, bdellium and onyx stone were not to be found inside the garden." For Leach, *Genesis as Myth*, 13-15, *oppositions* or twins are the framework from which prehistoric cultures construct their myths.

30. For Coats, 53, and C. Westermann, *Genesis Accounts of Creation* (Philadelphia: Fortress, 1964), 260-62, the prohibition introduces a negative character into the story. In Ps 81:8 (MT); Ezek 3:16-21; Deut 4:34, and others Yahweh *tempts* (NRSV), but not with a covenant. Yahweh *tempers metal* (Heb. *bāḥan*) to make it strong, not to see if it is weak.

and thriving, but the adam is alone and infertile. Gender and, therefore, truly human life is missing.[31] So, once again Yahweh sculpts animals from clay. By covenant the Creator gives the animals to the adam, who takes legal possession of the gifts by naming them. The Creator's humorous search for an animal partner for the adam fails and, like the denouement of the Story of the Adam, leaves the crisis only partially resolved.[32]

A Story of the Man and the Woman (Genesis 2:20b-24)

The creation story pattern appears for a third time in a Story of the Man and the Woman (Gen 2:20b-24).[33] The crisis reiterates there is still no helper (NRSV), no partner (NAB, NASV), no helpmeet (KJV) for the adam. *Helper* (Heb. *ʿēzer*) is not a patronizing term in the Bible; in fact, it is one of Yahweh's titles (Exod 18:4; Deut 33:7; Pss 33:20; 121:1-2).[34]

To begin the cosmogony, the Creator puts the adam to sleep. In the ancient world, no one may see God and live (Exod 33:20). This sleep (Heb. *tardēmâ*) is not rest but a unique state which allows the Creator to work unobserved and protects the adam from harm (Gen 15:12; Job 4:13; 33:15).[35] Although the Creator fashions both the adam and the animals from clay, the raw material for the woman is a rib. The technique is not sexist, indicating she is inferior.[36] The adam and the animals are new creations, the man and the woman are re-creations. The Creator redesigns the adam into a *man* (Heb. *ʾîš*) and a *woman* (Heb. *ʾiššâ*). Furthermore, Mesopotamian creation stories regularly play on the words *rib* and *living* because both are spelled *ti* in Sumerian.[37] The God mother is *Nin-tu* or *Nin-ti,* which means both *Life Giver*

---

31. Trible, 80.

32. For Y. T. Radday, "Humour in Names," in *On Humour and the Comic in the Hebrew Bible,* JSOTSup 23 (Sheffield: Almond, 1990), 59-97, the description of Eden is humorous, but Yahweh's search for a companion for the adam is not.

33. For Coats, 53, and W. H. Schmidt, *Die Schopfungsgeschichte der Priesterschrift,* WMANT 17 (Neukirchen-Vluyn: Neukirchener, 1973), 203; P. Humbert, *Etudes sur le recit du paradis et de la chute dans la Genese* (Neuchâtel: Secrétariat de l'Université, 1940), 48-81, garden (Heb. *gan*) stories and soil (Heb. *ʾādāmâ*) stories were originally distinct.

34. A. Laffey, *Introduction to the Old Testament: A Feminist Perspective* (Philadelphia: Fortress, 1988), 24, among others.

35. For O'Brien and Major, 102, and Meyers, 84, this sleep is sterility; for Gnostics it is the darkness with which the Creator disables humans until the serpent enlightens them with *gnōsis;* see H. Jonas, *The Gnostic Religion: The Message of the Alien God and the Beginnings of Christianity,* 2nd rev. ed. (Boston: Beacon, 1963), 68-73.

36. P. Trible, "Depatriarchalizing in Biblical Interpretation," *JAAR* 41 (1973): 37.

37. T. H. Gaster, *Myth and Legend and Custom in the Old Testament* (New York: Harper and Row, 1975), 21-23.

and *Rib Lady*.[38] The same wordplay appears in the Stories of Adam and Eve (Gen 2:21-22; 3:20). The puns create a similarity in the sounds of the two words, but not necessarily any parallelism in meaning.[39]

To celebrate the woman's creation, the man sings a hymn (Gen 2:23). He is not naming or taking possession of the woman here in the way he names and takes possession of the animals and birds (Gen 2:19-20). In the first episode the language is legal, in the second it is liturgical. Like hymns in the book of Psalms, the man's words praise Yahweh for a work of creation.[40]

The story comes to a close with a covenant decreeing the establishment of the social institution of marriage. The word for marriage does not appear in the story itself.[41] But the Creator proceeds with the woman to the man, as a father brings his daughter to her groom (Gen 29:23), and marriage is a social institution like many of those which covenants regularly inaugurate in the denouement of a standard creation story.[42]

Before the Story of the Man and the Woman became an episode in the Stories of Adam and Eve, their characters would have been fully human and capable of reproduction. Consequently, for many the work the Creator begins in Gen 2:4b is completed in Gen 2:25, rather than Gen 4:2.[43] That development, however, now takes place in the following story. Therefore, even though they are now distinguished from one another by gender, the man and the woman remain people primeval, still immortal and still infertile.

A Story of Eve and the Serpent (Genesis 2:25–4:2)

The Story of Eve and the Serpent which concludes this series of Stories of Adam and Eve is superb (Gen 2:25–4:2). The last verse in Genesis 2 and the first verse

38. O'Brien and Major, 102.

39. So E. A. Speiser, *Genesis*, AB (Garden City, New York: Doubleday, 1964), 18; Laffey, 24-25; and Hauser, 24, for whom *rib* (Heb. *'eṣem*) and *companion* (Heb. *'ēzer*) are also puns.

40. For commentators cited by A. Tosato, "On Genesis 2:24," *CBQ* 52 (1990): 390 n. 4, naming connotes juridical authority (Num 32:38; 2 Kgs 23:24; 24:17; 2 Chr 36:4); for Hauser, 22-23, it refers to the man's thorough scrutiny of the animals to discern for himself a companion. But the liturgical character of naming here was recognized by O. Eissfeldt, *The Old Testament: An Introduction* (London: Basil Blackwell, 1965), 65, who classified it as a *saying* ". . . which accompanied the vicissitudes of individual life . . . betrothal, wedding and divorce. The joy of the bridegroom is to be heard in the words with which man greets the woman formed from his rib (Gen 2:23)." See also H. W. Wolff, *Anthropology of the Old Testament* (Philadelphia: Fortress, 1974), 159.

41. For Tosato, 389-409, Gen 2:24 is a gloss prohibiting the mixed and polygamous marriages common in Judah during the exile (587-537 B.C.E.), which converts the focus from sexuality to marriage.

42. Hauser, 23.

43. So von Rad, *Theology*, vol. 1, 139-60, and others.

in Genesis 3 are joined by a play on the words *naked* (Gen 2:25) and *cunning* (Gen 3:1). The man and the woman have no clothes (Heb. *ʿārûmmîm*) and the serpent has no rivals (Heb. *ʿārûm*). Both contain the same three Hebrew letters: ע, *ʿayin;* ר, *resh;* and מ, *mem.* By describing the man and the woman as naked, storytellers indicate that they are not ordinary human beings; they are people primeval, more divine than human (Gilg ii:28).[44]

The serpent in this story is also hardly an ordinary reptile. It talks. The talking serpent (Gen 3:1) and the teaching tree (Gen 3:6-7) are examples of fable which gives plants and animals anthropomorphic or human characteristics.[45] And even though the extraordinary title "more subtle than any other wild animal that the Lord God had made" (Gen 3:1) identifies the serpent as a creature, she still plays the role of a member of the divine assembly just as the satan does in the book of Job (Job 1:1–2:13).[46]

Sometime after 300 B.C.E., both biblical and nonbiblical traditions began identifying the serpent as the devil (Wis 2:24; Rev 12:9; 20:2) and the woman as a temptress. The best-known Christian interpretation of Genesis 1–11 considers them to be stories about sin or original sin, which tell how God created a perfect world for humans (Gen 1–2). Nonetheless, they sinned (Gen 3), setting in motion a chain reaction of sins (Gen 4–5), which eventually destroyed God's once-perfect world (Gen 6–11). Subsequently, every human born into this now-imperfect world was born sinful or alienated from God, even without having personally sinned.[47] To re-create a perfect world, God introduced religion, the faith of Abraham and Sarah (Gen 12). Now, humans could overcome their alienation from God by entering a religion and rejecting the radical sinfulness of the world around them.

Neither the Hebrew Bible nor the Gospels refer to original sin. The first reference to the woman as evil does not appear until after 180 B.C.E. in the book

44. So A. J. Williams "Relationship of Genesis 3:20 to the Serpent," *ZAW* 89 (1977): 371. See Pss 104:1-2; 8:5; S. P. Brock, "Clothing Metaphors as a Means of Theological Expression," in *Typus, Symbol, Allegorie bei den östlichen Vätern und ihren Parallelen im Mittelalter* (Regensburg: Pustet, 1982), 11-40; J. Schneider, "Anthropology of Cloth," *Annual Review of Anthropology* 16 (1987): 409-48; for O'Brien and Major, 92, and most others, ". . . the couple's nakedness and lack of shame underscore their goodness and sexual openness."

45. M. A. Beavis, "Parable and Fable," *CBQ* 52 (1990): 473-98; A. M. Vater Solomon, "Fable," in *Saga, Legend, Tale, Novella, Fable: Narrative Forms in Old Testament Literature*, ed. G. W. Coats, JSOTSup 35 (Sheffield: JSOT, 1985), 114-32.

46. For Kennedy, 9, the serpent personifies ". . . fomenters of peasant unrest . . . amorphous entities that live in the nooks and crannies of life." For Laffey, 23, "serpent is feminine in Hebrew," which may, if it were correct, link the serpent to the wise woman who appears in the book of Proverbs and the Story of Gilgamesh. But the grammatical forms of *nāḥāš* and *rōbēṣ* and the verbs and modifiers used with them in the story are, in fact, masculine.

47. K. Rahner and H. Vorgrimler, *Theological Dictionary* (New York: Herder and Herder, 1965), 329-31; R. P. McBrien, *Catholicism* (Minneapolis: Winston, 1980), 162-68.

of Sirach from the Septuagint used by Greek-speaking Jews in Egypt.[48] It was never part of the Hebrew Bible used by Aramaic-speaking Jews in Syria-Palestine.

> Do not be ensnared by a woman's beauty,
>> Do not desire a woman's possessions.
> There is quarreling, disobedience and a loss of face,
>> When a wife supports her husband.
> A dejected mind, a gloomy face,
>> A broken heart are caused by a bad wife.
> Powerless hands and weak knees are the result of a wife
>> Who does not make her husband happy.
> From a woman, sin had its beginning,
>> Because of a woman, we all die.
> Allow water no outlet,
>> Give a bad wife no voice.
> If your wife does not obey,
>> Divorce her. (Sir 25:21-26, author's translation)

The Books of Adam and Eve and the Apocalypse of Moses, which were popular, nonbiblical books in the Jewish community around 100 B.C.E., share Ben Sira's portrayal. By 100 C.E., the New Testament had canonized the image of Eve as the *Mother of Sin and Death* and in 382 C.E. Jerome's Latin translation of the Bible distributed it throughout the Christian world.[49]

> . . . This erroneous view has a long history, dating from late antiquity to our own time. The author of I Timothy [1 Tim 2:11-14] connects woman's inferiority in his own society to Adam and Eve. . . . In fact, all the New Testament writers who explain woman's subordination to man refer either directly or indirectly to Eve's later creation.
>
> In subsequent ages, writers continued to use this same kind of logic to explain their own social views. Gregory Nazianzus (about 380 A.D.), for instance, called Eve "a deadly delight." But perhaps the most influential shaper of the myth was John Milton in the seventeenth century. Milton's massive and majestic *Paradise Lost* has so overshadowed the simple biblical story that even today we remember his portraits of Eve and Satan when we think we are remembering the Yahwist's account.[50]

48. J. Levison, "Is Eve to Blame: A Contextual Analysis of Sirach 25:24," *CBQ* 47 (1985): 617-23.
49. B. J. Malina, "Some Observations on the Origin of Sin in Judaism and St. Paul," *CBQ* 31 (1969): 18-34; Meyers, 72-77.
50. For O'Brien and Major, 94-95: "Milton . . . intended to remain faithful to the Bible, but his hierarchical world view led him to assume that every creature had its proper place in an elaborately descending order from God . . . to angels, men, women, animals, plants,

The original sin reading of the Stories of Adam and Eve developed from a commentary on 1 Cor 15:20-28 and Rom 5:12-23 by Augustine (354-430), who became a bishop near the ancient city of Carthage in today's Tunisia, North Africa. He was an influential teacher or father in the early Christian church. The Council of Trent (1542-63) in modern Italy officially adopted his teaching.[51]

Prior to Augustine, readings of the Stories of Adam and Eve stressed that human beings are free to choose good or evil; Augustine, on the other hand, stressed that human beings are slaves to sin, whose emancipation requires not only faith and baptism but a commitment to asceticism, especially celibacy.[52] The teaching is certainly quite negative, but its corollaries are quite positive, which may account for its enduring popularity. For example, everyone is free to accept or reject a god, who does not impose grace or salvation on anyone.[53] His interpretation was more than theological reflection, it was a constitution for the political order of his day. Government is an indispensable defense against the forces sin has unleashed in human nature. He drafted the concordat which united the church and the Roman Empire and served as the basis for all subsequent societies with an established religion.

Although biblical scholars generally concurred with Augustine's commentary, some noted it was anomalous.

> . . . "sin" is very seldom spoken of in theoretical and theological terms. The Old Testament is chock-full of references to sins which have been committed at some particular place, at some particular time, and by some particular person. But we seldom find theological reflection on "sin" as a religious phenomenon of the utmost complexity. . . .
>
> In contrast with this, the Jahwist's great harmartiology in Gen. iii-xi about the way in which sin broke in and spread like an avalanche is undoubtedly

---

and finally non-living creatures. Even within human society, this hierarchy was necessary. Rulers of the state were God's deputies on earth, and husbands were his deputies in the family. . . . Consequently, Eve is expected to follow the 'right reason' of Adam, her 'head,' and her duties consist of studying 'household good' and promoting 'good works in her Husband' (*Paradise Lost* 9.233). For Milton, then, Adam and Eve are both created 'in God's image' as in Genesis 1:27, but Eve is less in God's image (8.540ff.) and Adam's 'perfection far excelled Hers in all real dignity' (10.150-51). Thus, despite the redemptive role that Milton's Eve plays in the final books of the epic, she is subordinated to Adam far more radically than in the original story."

51. Denzinger, *Enchiridion Symbolorum: Definitionum et Declarationum de Rebus Fidei et Morum* (Barcelona: Herder, 1960), #787-92; Paul III called the Council of Trent in 1542. War postponed it until 1545; it met intermittently until 1563. See W. Walker, *History of the Christian Church* (New York: Scribner, 1970), 339.

52. G. G. Harpham, *Ascetic Imperative in Philosophy, Art, and Criticism* (Berkeley: University of California, 1988).

53. B. L. Nassif, "Toward a 'Catholic' Understanding of St Augustine's View of Original Sin," *USQR* 39 (1984): 287-99.

something exceptional; for never again did Israel speak in such universal terms of sin as exemplified in standardized models, and yet at the same time in such great detail.[54]

Nevertheless, for many today, the Story of Eve and the Serpent still introduces a ". . . *discordant element . . . the wily serpent entices, the woman disobeys, and the man passively follows suit.*"[55] One sociologist observed that, even though she is both Jewish and a feminist, the dominant culture in which she was reared convinced her that Eve is a criminal character.[56] She is created after the adam, from the adam, and as the adam's helper, and she is named by the adam; she is seduced by the serpent and then seduces the man.[57] The sad legacy of this long tradition of interpretation is the gruesome theological anthropology which views women as condemned to agonizing deliveries as a sentence for seducing men to whom they are intellectually and morally inferior.[58]

Nonetheless, a reassessment of Augustine's reading is taking place in more than one area of study. There are scholars of classical antiquity researching the Greco-Roman attitudes toward sexuality, moral freedom, and human value in Augustine's world.[59] There are feminist scholars working to reduce the impact of sexism on the interpretation of women's roles in the Bible.[60] Today, a religiously conservative male scholar can propose that the original sin is not the woman's conspiracy against the Creator, but the man's perjury in denying his own guilt.[61] And two literary critics can argue that the Stories of Adam and Eve have nothing to do with a fall, but only with an arbitrary and disproportionate punishment.[62] But perhaps the most compelling arguments for revising Augustine are emerging from the world of the Bible itself.

Serpent characters in the ancient Near East are not just adversaries, they are also helpers.[63] Both are cunning or wise. As adversaries serpents take away

54. Von Rad, *Theology,* 154.
55. O'Brien and Major (emphasis added), 93. For R. C. Culley, "Action Sequences in Genesis 2–3," *Semeia* 18 (1980): 25-33, Augustine's analysis is still defensible even with a contemporary method of biblical analysis like structuralism. But see Jobling, 20-22.
56. N. Dotan, "Forbidden Fruits and Sorrow: Eve and the Sociology of Knowledge," *Journal of Pastoral Counseling* 21 (1986): 105-18.
57. P. J. Milne, "Eve and Adam — Is a Feminist Reading Possible?" *BRev* 6 (1988): 13ff.
58. Trible, *God and the Rhetoric of Sexuality,* 73.
59. E. Pagels, "Politics of Paradise," in *Adam, Eve, and the Serpent: Gen 1–3,* Occasional Papers 3 (Claremont: Institute for Antiquity and Christianity, 1988), 98-126; M. R. Miles, "Adam and Eve and Augustine," *Christianity and Crisis* 48 (1988): 347-49.
60. L. M. Russell, ed., *Feminist Interpretation of the Bible* (Philadelphia: Westminster, 1985); Trible, *God and the Rhetoric of Sexuality,* 72-143; Meyers, 72-121; Milne.
61. B. J. Leonard, "Forgiving Eve," *Christian Century* 101 (1984): 1038-40.
62. Rosenberg and Bloom.
63. K. R. Joines, "Serpent in Gen 3," *ZAW* 87 (1975): 1-11.

life; as helpers they renew it. Adversary serpents trick protagonists into trading away their youth; helpers teach them the secret of eternal youth.

In Egypt, the wadjet or uraeus is a helper serpent who rides on the forehead of pharaohs, protecting them from their enemies. The serpent swallowing its own tail is Egypt's official symbol of immortality, and the coiled serpent represents the *ma'at* laws which govern the universe. Ordinary Egyptians carried snakeskin to help them make good decisions. In the Mesopotamian Story of Adapa, the serpent Ningishzida tries to help Adapa by offering him the bread and water of life which would make him immortal. In Syria-Palestine, serpents — like sexual organs, water, bulls, and doves — symbolize human fertility.

Apophis is Egypt's adversary serpent who waits to swallow the sun as it sets. In Mesopotamia, the serpent in the Story of Gilgamesh tricks Gilgamesh out of the plant which would make him immortal, and Tiamat in the Enuma Elish Story is the sea serpent who tries to trick the divine assembly into giving her control of the cosmos.

The character of the serpent in the Story of Eve and the Serpent is more a helper than an adversary.[64] The serpent is informed and questioning, not malicious. It is subtle or cunning like a sage pondering the age-old questions of life and death. The serpent knows the Creator's decree. It walks in the garden at this point in the story just as Yahweh will walk in the garden later. And neither the man nor the woman fears the serpent when they meet, but they talk quite openly.

Today, readers are more familiar with the animal who is benign rather than threatening from children's stories. Children's stories construct a universe where everything can change and anything can happen.[65] The protagonist has been abandoned or cast out. Whether due to evil or accident, the child dwells in dark, lonely surroundings until help arrives through the agency of a benevolent and powerful animal character. The serpent in the Stories of Adam and Eve is not so much a character who kidnaps the man and the woman from their home in Eden, but rather a helper who leads them from sterility in the epoch primeval to fertility on the human plane.[66]

---

64. Coats, *Genesis*, 54.

65. B. Bettelheim, *The Uses of Enchantment: The Meaning and Importance of Fairy Tales* (New York: Vintage, 1976, repr. 1989).

66. For Gnostics, the serpent is a redeemer whose *gnōsis* delivers the man and the woman from the Creator holding them hostage in the garden. Jesus is the serpent or the fruit of the tree or cross, and they are *Ophites* (Gk. *ophis*) or *Naasenes* (Heb. *nāḥāš*) — disciples of the Serpent; see Jonas, 92-94; I. S. Gilhus, "The Gnostic Demiurge: The Agnostic Trickster," *Religion: Journal of Religion and Religions* 14 (1984): 301-11. Similarly, Jobling, 22-27, uses V. Propp, *Morphology of the Folktale*, 2nd rev. ed. (Austin: University of Texas, 1968), to consider "Yahweh . . . in the role of [a] villain, [who] steals the man from the earth to work his own private domain (the garden)."

The serpent and the woman speak of delicate subjects using socially acceptable metaphors. Eating and knowing are euphemisms for having sexual intercourse and conceiving a child. Semitic vocabulary for having sexual intercourse, learning, eating, farming, fighting, and sacrificing can overlap (Gilg I:iv:16ff.; Canticles). When the serpent asks the woman, "Did God say, 'You shall not eat from any tree in the garden'?" it means: "Are you fertile?" When it says: ". . . when you eat of it your eyes will be opened, . . . knowing good and evil," it means: "You will become fertile."[67] Just as the word *life* is ambivalent in the discussion between the woman and the serpent, so is the word *death*. The woman will not be summarily executed for eating of the fruit of the tree. In exchange for the ability to bear children, she will labor and eventually die. The serpent and the woman discuss whether humans should be mortal or immortal, fertile or infertile.[68] The serpent does not offer immortality to the man and the woman. They are already immortal when the story begins. And the serpent does not steal immortality from them. It simply convinces them to exchange their immortality for fertility by pointing out that the wise know what is good and what is bad. They realize that human life, which is good, requires suffering, which is bad.[69] It teaches them that they must labor to have children and a harvest.

Unlike the previous stories, this one has the man and the woman share in the Creator's work of making them fully human. As in many creation stories, there is tension between the Creator and the people primeval. The tension leads to changes in creation, but it is too simple to reduce that tension to raw human disobedience. Truly human life results not simply from a grand divine plan but from the interaction, the cooperation, the tension between the Creator and the first creatures. People primeval become human, not because of their disobedience, but because of their intimacy with and imitation of the Creator.[70] Here the tensions lead to the creation of a world in which Adam and Eve can have children, who can herd and farm the land.

67. So H. Gunkel, *Genesis* (Göttingen: Vandenhoeck & Ruprecht, 1910), 18; R. Gordis, "The Knowledge of Good and Evil in the Old Testament and Qumran Scrolls," *JBL* 76 (1957): 123-38; Speiser, 25; I. Engnell, " 'Knowledge' and 'Life' in the Creation Story," in *Wisdom in Israel and the Ancient Near East*, VTSup 3 (Leiden: Brill, 1960), 103-19; O'Brien and Major, 102. For von Rad, *Theology*, 155; Westermann, *Genesis 1–11*, 241, the knowledge is general, not specific; for W. M. Clark, "A Legal Background to the Yahwist's Use of 'God and Evil' in Genesis 2–3," *JBL* 88 (1969): 266-78; for Kennedy, 6-7, it is political.

68. J. D. Crossan, "Response to White: Felix Culpa and Foenix Culprit," *Semeia* 18 (1980): 109-10.

69. R. M. Davidson, "Theology of Sexuality in the Beginning," *AUSS* 26 (1988): 121-31; for Jobling, 29-39, in the old world of the adam there is only a single, male, autochthonous, immortal, and ignorant creature, without companions or animals, who farms effortlessly; in the new world of Adam and Eve, there is a society of sexually reproductive, mortal, and knowledgeable men and women who laboriously hunt, farm, and herd.

70. But see Hauser, 20-36.

The serpent chooses to speak with the woman, not because she is gullible, but because women play a more important role than men in human reproduction, which is the subject of the conversation. Tellers also take advantage of at least two other motifs by having the serpent and the woman speak with one another. With only a slight change in pronunciation, the same word can mean either a female serpent or the woman Eve (Heb. *ḥawwâ*). The pun emphasizes the reciprocity between the serpent, who understands fertility, and the woman, who must decide whether or not to become fertile. And the selection of the woman to instruct the man in the ritual of intercourse in the Story of Eve and the Serpent recalls the commissioning of the wise woman in the Story of Gilgamesh (Gilg I:3-4; 2:3) to tutor *enkidu* in the facts of life.

In contrast to the remarkably universal postbiblical interpretation of Eve, the original storytellers regarded Eve as an important (Gen 3:1), wise (Gen 3:2-3), and self-sacrificing (Gen 3:16) woman, whom they honored as *Mother of All Living* (Gen 3:20). The woman shows her intelligence in the accuracy with which she quotes Yahweh's decree. She shows her moral integrity in the strictness with which she interprets the decree by extending it from a prohibition against eating the fruit of the tree to touching it. She shows her generosity in making the choice to bear children, even though it demands labor.

On the basis of her discussion with the serpent about the quality of their life primeval, she decides to lay down her life in order to create life. The woman is willing to create, to die, and so, by implication, is the man. The woman goes to the man, not to seduce him, but simply because she has discovered the technique of sexual intercourse by which she can conceive a child.[71]

It is common enough to read the denouement of the story as a curse or criminal sentence.[72] It is an understandable human reaction to consider the labor of having a child or working a field as a curse or a sentence, and there is certainly legal language in the text itself. But this reading unnecessarily imposes a criminal character on the story as a whole.

Neither syntax nor legal anthropology definitively identifies Gen 3:13-19 as a prescriptive and promulgated law, on the one hand, or an adjudicatory judgment and court verdict on the other.[73] None of the technical terms for

---

71. Jobling, 34, and others cite ". . . a deeply rooted biblical pattern [1 Kgs 15,26] in which the instigators of sin are more negatively assessed, and more severely punished, than the sinners themselves . . ." in characterizing the woman as seducing the man.

72. So O'Brien and Major, 94; Coats, *Genesis*, 56-57; Westermann, *Genesis Accounts*, 95, and others.

73. For R. P. Knierim, "The Problem of Ancient Israel's Prescriptive Legal Traditions," in *Semeia* 45 (1989): 7-25, ". . . the death formula, . . . is to be translated 'he belongs to (the sphere of) death' . . . and not, as usual, 'he shall surely be put to death' . . . "; for E. Gestenberger, *Wesen und Herkunft des 'apodiktischen Rechts,'* WMANT 20 (Neukirchen-Vluyn: Neukirchener, 1965), prohibitions reflect an ethical, rather than a legal tradition.

crime or sin is applied to actions of the serpent, the woman, or the man,[74] and only the serpent and the soil are cursed (Heb. *'ārûr*); the man and the woman are not.[75] And ancient Israel sees much more of the Creator in portrayals of Yahweh as a judge such as this than its interpreters.[76]

The intention of the story is not to punish but to create by persuading its listeners that the blessings of fertility are worth the labor. By farming and childbearing the man and the woman, and subsequently all humans, imitate the Creator, even though human creativity demands labor and divine creativity does not.[77] Labor marks humans as different from God, not disobedient to God. For humans, the ecstasy of giving life to another human being in birth or to the earth in farming demands the agony of labor. The Creator here is more a midwife than a judge.[78] The midwife does not impose labor pain upon a mother as a sentence for conceiving a child, she interprets it and all the consequences of parenthood.[79] Similarly, Yahweh enlists the serpent and the soil to tutor the couple in the consequences of their new role as co-creators.

Between 2113 and 2096 B.C.E., Ur-Nammu authorized the first legal code which divided society into classes, and applied uniform principles of justice to a wide range of social institutions. The Code of Ur-Nammu established an enduring legal tradition to which the covenant in the Story of Eve and the Serpent belongs. The Creator explains the principles which will apply to the relationships of three major classes of society in the new world which the woman and the man have inaugurated.

The serpent's choice to counsel the man and the woman to become human has consequences on her relationship, and the relationship of all the animals, with humans. Snakes were a menacing aspect of daily life in Syria-Palestine. Poisonous snakes and barren soil were reminders of the labor which human creativity demands. As an etiology the story explains why snakes crawl and why they strike at humans. The explanations teach simple lessons. Crawling is a punishment for snakes and snakebites are a punishment for humans. Like all punishments they are painful, but something can be learned from them. Eti-

---

74. See R. P. Knierim, *Die Hauptbegriffe für Sunde im Alten Testament* (Gütersloh: Mohn, 1965), and in *THAT*, 2 vols. (München: Kaiser, 1971-76).

75. Coats, *Genesis*, 56; Laffey, 25, and others.

76. Knierim, "Cosmos and History," 99-101: ". . . Yahweh is seen as the Lord-creator of the world, and not only as the Lord-judge of history. . . . Israel's theology of universal justice . . . is itself anchored in her theology of the just and righteous order of the world."

77. Von Rad, *Theology*, 142-43.

78. D. C. Benjamin, "Israel's God as Mother and Midwife," *BTB* 19 (1989): 115-20.

79. Similarly for C. Westermann, *Basic Forms of Prophetic Speech* (Philadelphia: Westminster, 1967), 129-68, and G. M. Tucker, "Prophecy and the Prophetic Literature," in *The Hebrew Bible and Its Modern Interpreters*, 336, a prophetic judgment announces the future; it does not predict it; see also D. C. Benjamin, "Anthropology of Prophecy," *BTB* 21 (1991): 135-44.

ologies by no means struggle with the profound questions which are the main subject of creation stories. Nonetheless they are popular in every culture as a way of teaching how to turn human curiosity into a learning experience.[80] The Creator assigns the serpent the continuing task of reminding humans of the suffering which creativity demands. Having undertaken to educate the people primeval from sterility to fertility, the Creator now points out to her that the task is far from easy and far from over.

The woman's choice to create has consequences on her relationship to her children. She will be able to give birth, but not without effort. But if the woman actually made a choice, why does she seemingly deny it (Gen 3:13)? Refusing to take responsibility for the choice may simply be a demur. She has acted courageously, but in the world of the Bible it would be inappropriate for her to brag about what she has done. So, she simply says it was nothing. But the woman's response to Yahweh may also reflect a basic question about life. *Did humans freely choose to become fertile and mortal or were they tricked?* The woman's response raises the question to which the stories as a whole provide an answer. They want their audiences to regard fertility as a freely chosen blessing and to embrace the asceticism of laying down their lives by childbearing and farming.

Another objection to the characterization of Eve as having made an heroic choice is the long-standing tradition of interpretation which emphasizes the negative consequences her actions have on her relationship to her man (Gen 3:14-16). As it now stands, the woman seems sentenced to be subordinate to the man.[81] But originally this consequence may have applied to the serpent, not to the woman. A parallel from the Stories of Cain and Abel (Gen 4:7) may provide a clue both to the original meaning and position of Gen 3:16b.[82]

> The Lord said to Cain . . .
> . . . sin [Heb. *rōbēṣ*] is lurking at the door;
>   its desire is for you [Heb. *tēšûqâ*],
> but you must master it. (Gen 4:6-7)

---

80. P. J. Van Dyk, "Function of So-called Etiological Elements in Narratives," *ZAW* 102 (1990): 19-33; F. W. Golka, "Aetiologies in the Old Testament," *VT* 26 (1976): 410-28; *VT* 27 (1977): 36-47.

81. Davidson, 123-26, lists five traditions of interpretation: God created the woman subordinate, but after the fall subordination either (1) becomes painful (2) or becomes a support-system during labor. God created the woman equal, but after the fall either (3) the woman subordinates herself, (4) God re-creates her as subordinate, or (5) God reaffirms her equality (Heb. *māšal*) to argue Gen 3:16 is an antithetical parallel balancing the curse of subordination with the blessing of having the man as a support; for M. H. Pope, *Song of Songs*, AB (Garden City: Doubleday, 1977), 643; Trible, *God and the Rhetoric of Sexuality*, 144-65, the Song describes the sexual equality assumed in Gen 2:4b–3:15.

82. But see U. Cassuto, *A Commentary on the Book of Genesis*, 2 vols. (Jerusalem: Magnes, 1961), 1:212-13.

Both *rōbēṣ* (Gen 4:7) and *nāḥāš* (Gen 3:14) mean a *serpent* which lurks around doorways to strike out (Heb. *tēšûqâ*) at those who enter and leave. The subjects of the two verses are synonymous and the verbs in both are identical. Rather than consider one to refer to a woman's urge to have sexual intercourse and the other to a snake's instinct to strike at anyone who threatens it, it may be better to read both as referring to a snake's instinct to strike, and move Gen 3:16b ahead of Gen 3:16a. Just as the serpent in the Stories of Cain and Abel stalks Cain, the serpent in the Story of Eve and the Serpent stalks Eve's children.

> The Lord God said to the serpent, . . .
> You and the woman will be enemies,
> > Your children will kill her children.
> Her child will stomp on your head,
> > Your child will strike at its heel.
> Your instinct will be to strike at humans,
> > Even though they will master you.
> To the woman he said,
> I will greatly increase your pangs in childbearing;
> > In pain you shall bring forth children.
> > > (Gen 3:14-16, author's translation)

The man's choice to create has consequences on his relationship to the land. He will be able to bring in a harvest, but not without effort. Although the Stories of Adam and Eve begin with a sterility affidavit which clearly observes that the essentials for agriculture are missing, the Story of Eve and the Serpent tells only her story.[83] Nonetheless, storytellers assume that the man goes through a similar process of discovery to become fertile. His story now appears in the Stories of Cain and Abel (Gen 4:3–5:31).[84]

Most interpreters end the Stories of Adam and Eve at Gen 3:24.

> . . . despite complexities in structure that point to a tradition history, the story ends where the plot intends it to end. The man violated the law of obedience placed on him by God. His punishment is death on that very day. And that happens, despite delays, despite signs of God's grace (if any should be there). The basic structure thus unfolds on two pillars: the creation of paradise and the loss of paradise. The second pillar can be understood under the structural pattern of sin and judgment. The judgment, despite man's continued life, is

---

83. For Jobling, 22, ". . . it is the *man's* fate alone which is at issue in 2.16-17, . . . though the serpent and the woman will be involved in the curses, only the man will be expelled from the garden in 3.22-24."

84. For Jobling, 27, the original intention of the stories is "a man to till the earth, . . . [which] has been overtaken or 'upstaged' by other themes — especially the theological theme of the fall, and . . . the social theme of marriage . . . "; for Hauser, 26, the plural verbs in Gen 3:1-6 address both the man and the woman.

death. Alienation from the source of his life, opposition from that which gives him life, is the order he has to live in or die in.[85]

But the work which Yahweh began (Gen 2:7) is completed only when Adam and Eve give birth to Cain and Abel (Gen 4:1-2).[86] In the Story of the Adam, only Yahweh farms; the adam simply tends (Gen 2:15). Whereas in the Story of Eve and the Serpent, the man actually farms (Gen 3:23).[87] A creation story never ends one world without inaugurating another. Eden is closed, but the East is open (Gen 3:24; 4:16).[88] The story celebrates Eve in the same way that the Story of Atrahasis celebrates Nintu-Mami. Both carry the title *Mother of All* (Atra I:245-46; Gen 3:20); Nintu-Mami gives birth to seven sets of twins, Eve gives birth to two sons;[89] Nintu-Mami celebrates her delivery by singing, "You commanded me a task — I have completed it" (Atra I:237-38); Eve sings to celebrate her sons, whom she names *Cain* (dominant or strong as iron) and *Abel* (recessive or fragile as a breath of air) (Eccl 1:14).[90]

I have gotten a man with the help of the Lord!
    Yahweh gave me a task! I have completed it!
I have created,
    Just as Yahweh created! (Gen 4:1, author's translation)[91]

---

85. Coats, *Genesis*, 57.

86. For Propp, *Morphology of the Folktale,* folk stories move from a crisis which disrupts the order necessary for life to disorder in the climax before reestablishing an enriched life-support system in the denouement celebrated with a marriage. The new world of the denouement is always better, never worse, than the old world destroyed in the crisis. As Eissfeldt, 129, points out, traditions for dividing these creation stories differ. For example, "[t]he end . . . of the paradise and fall stories (Gen. iii,24) is separated from the beginning of the Cain narrative (iv,1) only by a 'closed' *parasha* whereas the conclusion of the first section, namely the expulsion from paradise in iii,22-4, is separated from the preceding section by an 'open' *parasha;* this has the effect of closely linking material which does not really belong together, and of separating material which really forms one continuous whole. Here the chapter division is better."

87. For Coats, *Genesis*, 51-53; Amit, 16, the adam in Gen 2:4b-17 actually farms.

88. See H. J. Kraus, "Schopfung und Weltvollendung," in *Biblische Theologische Aufsätze* (Neukirchen: Neukirchener, 1972), 151-78, and others.

89. Although Cain and Abel are generally considered brothers, not twins, the story itself describes Eve as conceiving only once, but delivering twice (Gen 4:1-2); see N. J. Cohen, "Two That Are One: Sibling Rivalry in Genesis," *Judaism* 32 (1983): 331-42.

90. Eissfeldt, 65; Borger, "Gen iv,i," *VT* 9 (1959): 85-86.

91. "I have created [Heb. *qānîtî*] a man, just as [Heb. *'et*] Yahweh created!" better translates Gen 4:1b than "I have produced [Heb. *qānîtî*] a man with the help of [Heb. *'et*] the Lord" (NRSV). The verb *I have gotten* (Heb. *qānîtî*) regularly identifies Yahweh as creator. For example, Yahweh is the *creator* (Heb. *qōnēh*) of heaven and earth (Gen 14:19-22). Likewise, Deut 32:6 asks: "Is Yahweh not the father who created you [Heb. *qānekā*]?" Although the syntax in Deut 32:6 is masculine, its connotations are feminine, identifying the labor of a birth mother or midwife. Similar connotations appears in Prov 8:22: "Yahweh begot [Heb.

Eve's hymn summarizes what the Stories of Adam and Eve teach. She is as delighted that she has learned how to use her power to create as the man was delighted in Yahweh's creation of her (Gen 2:23). She sees the successful birth of a child as a divine work.

The Stories of Adam and Eve are part of an ancient quest to understand human life. Does immortality or creativity better define human life? The search is positive and inspiring, not cynical or complaining. They ponder both the life of God and the life of the people primeval to better understand human life. For them, God is immortal and fertile; God lives forever and God creates. The people primeval, on the other hand, are immortal but infertile; they live forever but cannot create. Ordinary humans, finally, are mortal but can create.

The tellers of the Stories of Adam and Eve were not utopian dreamers. Their investigation of the assets and liabilities of both immortality and fertility is brutally realistic. The immortal life of the people primeval was certainly enjoyable but not completely satisfying; human creativity is godlike but painful. Childbirth is agonizing and farming exhausting. Nonetheless, the stories conclude that humans are most like God when they create, not when they live forever.

---

qānānî] me . . . ," and Ps 139:13: ". . . you have formed [Heb. qānîtā] my inmost being; you have knit me in my mother's womb."

The Qumran Scrolls and Old Testament Theology

GEORGE J. BROOKE

I. Introduction

The purpose of this study is to show how the Qumran scrolls, through their very existence and because of their contents, both highlight the problems that beset anyone who tries to engage in the task of Old Testament theology and offer some clues as to how that task might be approached.[1] The scrolls created a great stir when they first came to light. In addition to what could become known concerning the history of early Palestinian Judaism, for Old Testament scholars excitement lay especially in what might be learned of the history of the biblical text; for New Testament scholars interest lay particularly in what might be discovered about Jewish eschatology, especially messianism, in a period approximately contemporary with Jesus himself.[2] Among other matters, the slow progress in publishing all the scrolls has resulted in scholars recently engaged in biblical studies conclud-

---

1. It is a privilege to offer this study to honor Rolf Knierim, from whom I learned both skills in attention to detail and also many methodological insights.

The term Qumran refers simply to the place where the various manuscripts were found; in the study which follows I define which texts may reflect the ideology of the community resident there.

2. For the history of the biblical text see especially the summary collection of essays in F. M. Cross and S. Talmon, eds., *Qumran and the History of the Biblical Text* (Cambridge: Harvard, 1975). For the scrolls and the New Testament little new has been attempted since the collections of essays in K. Stendahl, ed., *The Scrolls and the New Testament* (London: SCM Press, 1958); M. Black, ed., *The Scrolls and Christianity*, SPCK Theological Collections 11 (London: SPCK, 1969); J. Murphy-O'Connor, ed., *Paul and Qumran* (London: Chapman, 1968); J. H. Charlesworth, ed., *John and Qumran* (London: Chapman, 1972); the suitability of the 1990 reissue of the last two has been justifiably questioned by F. García Martínez in his review in *JSJ* 22 (1991): 125-26.

ing frustratingly that there was little or nothing new that could be learned from the scrolls that had not already been covered in a mass of learned studies;[3] all that was necessary was a cursory nod in the direction of the scrolls and the summary findings of the first generation of investigators, then one was free to return to some narrower specialist biblical concern.[4] Biblical theologians have been particularly prone to this attitude to the scrolls, because of the natural assumption that the primary, even sole, object of their discourses was the canon; all other literary works could be deemed secondary. But the evidence of the scrolls will not go away and should be taken into account in the questioning and honing of the task of Old Testament theologians. In any case, since 1991, when access to unpublished manuscripts was permitted, the situation has changed: the scrolls are due to come back into the limelight.[5]

Within the discipline of Old Testament theology there has long been a tension between two approaches.[6] On the one hand are those who have attempted to make sense of the whole Old Testament, even the whole Christian Bible, on the basis of acknowledging the status of the collection as canon[7] and

---

3. For a list of the bibliographies of the hundreds of specialist scrolls studies see J. A. Fitzmyer, *The Dead Sea Scrolls: Major Publications and Tools for Study*, SBLSDS 20 (Atlanta: Scholars Press, 1990), 97-98. J. Strugnell has recently argued that the opportunities for a large amount of new work to be done on the scrolls published to 1987 has been sidestepped by most scholars ("The Qumran Scrolls: A Report on Work in Progress," in *Jewish Civilization in the Hellenistic-Roman Period*, ed. S. Talmon, JSPSup 10 [Sheffield: JSOT Press, 1991], 105-6); notable exceptions are the studies of E. Peuch, "Quelques aspects de la restauration du Rouleau des Hymnes (1QH)," *JJS* 39 (1988): 38-55, and "Un hymne essénien en partie retrouvé et les Béatitudes: 1QH V 12–VI 18 (= col. XIII–XIV 7) et 4QBéat.," *RevQ* 13 (1988): 59-89, and A. Steudel, "Der Midrasch zur Eschatologie aus der Qumrangemeinde (4Q-MidrEschat[a.b])" (Dissertation, Göttingen, 1990).

4. This nod toward the scrolls is visible in the way the endpapers of some of the Hermeneia series of commentaries contain photographs of the relevant Qumran manuscript, but the commentary remains based on the MT.

5. The history of the debate about the process of publication of the scrolls and the scholarly pressure applied, especially recently, can be found in many places, e.g., in a series of articles in *BARev* (13/5 [1985], 13/6 [1987], 15/3 [1989], 15/4 [1989], 15/5 [1989], 15/6 [1989], 16/2 [1990], 16/4 [1990], 16/5 [1990], 17/1 [1991], 17/2 [1991]), in Z. J. Kapera, "The Unfortunate Story of the Qumran Cave Four," *Qumran Cave IV and MMT: Special Report*, ed. Z. J. Kapera, *Qumran Chronicle* 1/2-3 (1990-91): 5-53; in J. A. Sanders, "Dead Sea Scrolls Access: A New Reality," *Folio* 11/3 (1991): 1-4; and in "Dead Sea Scrolls Published," *Bulletin of the Institute for Antiquity and Christianity* 18/4 (1991): 4-7.

6. Rolf Knierim himself has described something of this tension from his own perspective in "Cosmos and History in Israel's Theology," *HBT* 6 (1984): 25-57. Part of the vast literature includes R. E. Clements, *A Century of Old Testament Study* (Guilford: Lutterworth, 1976), 118-40; H. G. Reventlow, *Problems of Old Testament Theology in the Twentieth Century* (London: SCM, 1985); J. H. Hayes and F. C. Prussner, *Old Testament Theology: Its History and Development* (London: SCM, 1985); R. J. Coggins, *Introducing the Old Testament* (London: Oxford University, 1990), 145-57.

7. On the problems of the various meanings of the term "canon" see J. Barr, *Holy*

then proceeding to locate its central motif, its ideological kernel, the common denominator shared by its various parts.[8] On the other hand are those who, while acknowledging that the extent of the canon gives them their material, have attempted to pay somewhat closer attention to the findings of historical-critical research and so have organized their systematization of the Old Testament around a historical reconstruction which the texts themselves may imply; this historical approach naturally tends to be more permissive of the pluralism and variety within the Old Testament itself. More recently some have attempted to find a third way, almost combining the canonical and historical approaches, by paying attention both to the traditions which make up any particular Old Testament book (its prehistory and composition) and its effect on and subsequent treatment within the believing communities which accorded it some status. The very existence of the Dead Sea Scrolls, but the Qumran scrolls in particular, sheds light in several ways on all these approaches within the discipline of so-called Old Testament theology.

II. The Existence of the Scrolls and Old Testament Theology: Canon and Text

To begin with, the Qumran scrolls highlight dramatically the problem of the definition of the canon. Many modern writers point to the end of the first century C.E. for the delimitation of the Jewish canon (Hebrew Bible),[9] but since Old Testament theology has largely been the preserve of Protestant (especially German) scholars over the last two hundred years, the actual working assumption has generally been that it is the Hebrew canon as established within Protestantism since the Reformation which is the subject matter ripe for theological systematization. Before the scrolls were discovered, it was obvious that this was a pragmatic but problematic definition, for it effectively excluded a mass of material held variously in authoritative, even possibly

---

Scripture: Canon, Authority, Criticism (Oxford: Clarendon, 1983), 49-126; also E. C. Ulrich, "The Canonical Process, Textual Criticism, and Later Stages in the Composition of the Bible," *"Sha'arei Talmon" Studies in the Bible, Qumran, and the Ancient Near East Presented to Shemaryahu Talmon*, ed. M. Fishbane and E. Tov (Winona Lake: Eisenbrauns, 1992), 267-76.

8. What this unitive approach to the Bible owes to the influence of Barth is helpfully and summarily described, e.g., by J. Rogerson, "The Old Testament," in J. Rogerson, C. Rowland, and B. Lindars, *The Study and Use of the Bible* (Basingstoke: Marshall, Morgan and Scott, 1989), 139-42.

9. Though a putative Council of Jamnia cannot be held responsible for anything (see most recently D. E. Aune, "On the Origins of the 'Council of Javneh' Myth," *JBL* 110 [1991]: 491-93), it is still the case that the earliest enumerations for the biblical books are from the first few decades after the fall of the temple: Josephus, *Ag. Ap.* 1.37-42 (22 books), and 4 Ezra 14:45 (24 books).

canonical, esteem by the early churches and by not a few contemporary Christians. But the working assumption concerning the extent of the canon was based upon another; namely, that the Protestant Old Testament contained not simply all the Hebrew scriptures that had survived but all that had existed in the early second temple period and before. Though manifestly historically false, this assumption about the precanonical antiquity of the canon seemed to be confirmed by the attitudes of late second-temple-period authors such as Ben Sira. Furthermore, it seemed as if text critics could confirm the antiquity of the Hebrew texts, and thus their status, through their ability to isolate the causes of variants and errors in the manuscript and versional evidence: for example, all major variants in the LXX were considered to be the responsibility of the Greek translators and did not witness to a plurality of Hebrew texts. On such bases the Old Testament canon in its Hebrew text form as acknowledged at the time of the Reformation could be understood as both singularly representative and coherent.

The problem of the definition of the canon which the existence of the scrolls highlights is precisely in the area of the relationship of precanonical authoritative texts to the contents of the canon itself. In relation to the extent of the canon, the existence of actual manuscripts from the mid–second temple period discloses something of the breadth of literature available in Palestine for the literate élite. The matter of canon is thus not a straightforward matter of inclusivity, but a reflection of a determined policy of exclusivity, exercised by some dominant group.[10] The large number of pseudepigrapha demonstrates how some authors or groups went about trying to establish their writings as authoritative. The problem is posed even in the New Testament, where there is evidence that some early Jewish Christians assigned authoritative status to texts such as *Enoch* (Jude 14-15).[11] If it is clearly acknowledged that the definition of the extent of the canon is a particular feature of domineering forms of both Judaism and Christianity, especially from the period immediately following the fall of the second temple, then the use of such definitions today for forming a systematic appreciation of the texts is at worst somewhat arbitrary, at best little more than an intriguing attempt at discovering what might have been in the minds of some of those involved in delimiting the canon with a view to making that relevant in some way for today's reader.

10. As argued, e.g., by M. Smith, *Palestinian Parties and Politics That Shaped the Old Testament,* 2nd ed. (London: SCM Press, 1987), 1-10.

11. See R. J. Bauckham, "James, 1 and 2 Peter, Jude," *It Is Written: Scripture Citing Scripture: Essays in Honour of Barnabas Lindars SSF,* ed. D. A. Carson and H. G. M. Williamson (Cambridge: University, 1988), 303-6, and his *Jude and the Relatives of Jesus in the Early Church* (Edinburgh: T & T Clark, 1990), 137-39, 210-17. The extant parts of the text of *1 Enoch* 10:9 in 4QEn[c] 1 i 15-17 (J. T. Milik, *The Books of Enoch: Aramaic Fragments of Qumrân Cave 4* [Oxford: Clarendon, 1976], 184-86) show that the quotation in Jude is an exegetically adjusted text; *Enoch* thus had a living authority.

Those who would wish to discover what may be the central or controlling motif of the biblical material may play down the problem of identifying the criteria (and their sociopolitical significance) lying behind the definition of the canon through asserting that it is the center, about which there was widespread agreement over an extended period, which can justifiably form the base material for any theological systematization. This center is located within the threefold categorization of texts known from the second century B.C.E. onward. In this respect appeal can be made to the prologue of Ben Sira, which speaks three times of the law, the prophets, and the other books, or to a text like Luke 24:44, which mentions the law of Moses, the prophets, and the psalms, to show that over a period of three hundred years or more, the very period which begins the epoch of Jewish and Christian self-definitions, there was a widespread under-standing of what categories of texts were authoritative.[12] Although we know of groups who operated on a more restricted canon, the manuscripts from Qum-ran suggest that for one or more groups the number of texts with authority exceeded the later delimitations. The delimitation of the canon is a matter of excluding as well as of including various writings. The fluidity in the number of authoritative texts for various Jewish groups in the second temple period shows how historically arbitrary is the canon adopted by Old Testament theo-logians.

It needs to be made clear that it is not just a question of insisting that the whole breadth of Jewish literature should be taken into account in defining how modern theological statements about the canonical texts should be historically nuanced. Rather, in the precanonical period various Jewish groups had varying collections of authoritative texts and through the status accorded these writings the use and form of the books which were later to become canonical for the rabbis were variously influenced. From an angle other than the text-critical it is thus clear that the writings which are later to be included in the canon are passed on in particular contexts of scribal activity which sometimes lead to their significant modification. It is impossible as yet to identify any uniform perspec-tive as the hallmark of the scribal traditores of the biblical texts found in the Qumran caves, but analysis of each manuscript in turn discloses something of the viewpoint of its copyist(s).

The overall theological outlook of the group to be linked with the Qumran site (say, in the first century B.C.E.) might be measured by the number of manu-scripts to have survived there of any particular work and by the references in any

12. It is best to understand Ben Sira's prologue as referring to three categories of texts; see H. M. Orlinsky, "Some Terms in the Prologue to Ben Sira and the Hebrew Canon," *JBL* 110 (1991): 483-90. 4 Ezra 14:45 notes that in addition to the twenty-four scriptural books there are seventy books written last for the wise among the people. Note also the somewhat different remarks on the formation of the prophetic canon in the second temple period by J. Barton, *Oracles of God: Perceptions of Ancient Prophecy in Israel after the Exile* (London: Darton, Longman and Todd, 1986).

texts to other texts deemed as authoritative.[13] Alongside the large number of copies of Deuteronomy, Isaiah, and the Psalms can be put the similarly large numbers for copies of works like *Jubilees, Enoch,* the *Serek Ha-yahad,* and the so-called MMT.[14] Furthermore, though an argument from silence, the absence or near absence of certain texts later included in the canon needs to be noted: Esther, Ezra-Nehemiah, 1 and 2 Chronicles.[15] In addition, some texts which are generally agreed to be closely associated with the ideology of the community at Qumran speak of other writings in a way which assigns them some authority: the references to the "Book of the Divisions of Times into Their Jubilees and Weeks" in CD 16:3-4[16] and to a saying of Levi introduced in a standard and suitably authoritative way in CD 4:15-16,[17] the possible allusion to a second law in 4QCat[a] 1-4:13-14,[18]

13. See the analysis of the number of biblical manuscripts in G. Vermes, *The Dead Sea Scrolls: Qumran in Perspective,* 2nd ed. (London: SCM, 1982), 200-203. Note also conversely H. Stegemann's comment that among other things the relative paucity of copies of the *Temple Scroll* at Qumran suggests that that text was only of antiquarian interest there: "nobody cited it as an authority; none of the books written at Qumran mentioned its existence; no copy of it was to be found in the main library of the group, hidden in Qumran's cave 4" ("The Literary Composition of the Temple Scroll and Its Status at Qumran," *Temple Scroll Studies,* ed. G. J. Brooke, JSPSup 7 [Sheffield: JSOT, 1989], 143).

14. For *Jubilees* see J. C. VanderKam, *Textual and Historical Studies in the Book of Jubilees,* HSM 14 (Missoula: Scholars Press, 1977); M. Kister, "Newly Identified Fragments of the Book of Jubilees: Jub. 23:21-23, 30-31," *RevQ* 12 (1985-87): 529-36; J. C. VanderKam and J. T. Milik, "The First *Jubilees* Manuscript from Qumran Cave 4: A Preliminary Publication," *JBL* 110 (1991): 243-70.

For *Enoch* see Milik, *The Books of Enoch.*

For the *Serek ha-Yahad* see J. T. Milik, "Review" of P. Wernberg-Møller, *The Manual of Discipline Translated and Annotated,* STDJ 1 (Leiden: Brill, 1957), *RB* 67 (1960): 410-16; G. Vermes, "Preliminary Remarks on Unpublished Fragments of the Community Rule from Qumran Cave 4," *JJS* 42 (1991): 250-55.

For 4QMMT see F. García-Martínez, "Lista de MSS procedentes de Qumran," *Henoch* 11 (1989): 205.

15. On the likely absence of Ezra-Nehemiah and Chronicles from Qumran see the intriguing suggestions of G. Garbini, *History and Ideology in Ancient Israel* (London: SCM, 1988), esp. 209 n. 60.

16. Identified with the *Book of Jubilees* by most scholars: e.g., C. Rabin, *The Zadokite Documents* (Oxford: Clarendon Press, 1958), 75. The relevant section of CD 16:3-4 is also present in 4QD[c] 2 ii 5 and 4QD[e] 10 ii 17 (J. T. Milik's work represented now in B.-Z. Wacholder and M. Abegg, *A Preliminary Edition of the Unpublished Dead Sea Scrolls* [Washington: Biblical Archaeology Society, 1991], 42, 45).

17. On the identification of the quotation see J. C. Greenfield, "The Words of Levi Son of Jacob in Damascus Document IV,15-19," *RevQ* 13 (1988): 319-22. The passage is not extant in the surviving fragments of 4QD.

18. This second law has been identified with the *Temple Scroll:* Y. Yadin, *The Temple Scroll: The Hidden Law of the Dead Sea Sect* (London: Weidenfeld and Nicolson, 1985), 226-28. In agreement with other scholars A. Steudel ("Midrasch zur Eschatologie," 121, 171) argues most recently that the phrase is best translated as "das ist wiederum das Buch der Thora/that is the book of the Law again."

and the mentions of a Book of Hagu/Hagi (CD 10:6; 13:2; 14:7-8; 1QSa 1:7).[19] Furthermore, in 11QPs[a] so-called apocryphal psalms are juxtaposed with psalms now present in the canonical psalter.[20]

The Qumran scrolls show that it is not just the extent of the canon which is problematic, but also the form of its text. Though we may be able to see that in Palestine in the late second temple period there was a gradual shift in some circles (even evident in some of the Qumran biblical manuscripts) toward standardizing the form of the text along the lines of what became the dominant Hebrew text-type in the Tannaitic period and thereafter, there is a widespread pluriformity of text types among the so-called biblical texts, so much so that it may be preferable in several instances to talk of individual texts rather than of types.[21] Since many of these manuscripts have yet to be published with even preliminary analysis, and since the precise form of the text is not a subject upon which Jewish and Christian writers of the classical period dwell when discussing the canonical status of biblical books, Old Testament theologians cannot be held entirely to blame for not taking this more obviously into account. However, unless such theologians acknowledge the somewhat arbitrary, though pragmatic, nature of their stance, it is becoming increasingly difficult to maintain that the Protestant ordering of the MT should remain the sole basis for theological approaches to the various books.

For the texts which are close to the core of any collection of authoritative materials for Palestinian Jews of the late second temple period, the Qumran scrolls have made it easy for scholars to draw attention to the existence of multiple Hebrew editions. Recently E. C. Ulrich has elegantly summarized something of the significance of double editions of various biblical books: for Exodus the text of 4QpaleoExod[m] is a secondary edition compared with the MT and LXX; for 1 Samuel the Qumran Samuel manuscripts let us see that whereas in 1 Samuel 1–2 the MT may be the earlier form and the *Vorlage* of the LXX a secondary edition, in 1 Samuel 17–18 it is the other way round; for Jeremiah the scrolls support the conclusion that the LXX displays an earlier edition of the entire book and the MT an expanded second edition; and for Daniel 4–6 the MT and the Old Greek exhibit two different editions of chapters

---

19. Though this may be an apocryphal work, it may be no more than a euphemism for the Torah, as is maintained by L. H. Schiffman, *The Eschatological Community of the Dead Sea Scrolls*, SBLMS 38 (Atlanta: Scholars Press, 1989), 15. CD 10:6 is matched by 4QD[b] 17 iii 4 (Milik/Wacholder/Abegg, 18); CD 13:2 is not extant in 4QD; CD 14:7-8 is matched in 4QD[d] 11 ii 12 (Milik/Wacholder/Abegg, 34).

20. See J. A. Sanders, *The Dead Sea Psalms Scroll* (Ithaca: Cornell University, 1967), 10-14. The significant point is that in all the various psalms in this scroll the tetragrammaton is written consistently in paleo-Hebrew.

21. See E. Tov, "Hebrew Biblical Manuscripts from the Judaean Desert: Their Contribution to Textual Criticism," *JJS* 39 (1988): 28-32; reprinted in a slightly revised form in *Jewish Civilization in the Hellenistic-Roman Period*, 126-32.

4–6, both apparently being secondary.[22] The proper acknowledgment of such information radically relativizes the status of any text. In most cases a pure or original (or "inspired") form slips beyond the grasp of the theologian or historian. It becomes natural to insist that theological analysis must be based on the final form of the text as we have it,[23] but then the question remains concerning whose theological perspective is being investigated on the basis of such a final form.

Although all this undermines the understanding of the value of the biblical text for those modern interpreters who consider it from an idealistic (or conservative) standpoint, for others it suggests much more realistically that texts can never be viewed in a vacuum apart from the communities whose members composed them and the communities which subsequently copied and preserved them for a wide variety of reasons. And so it must be acknowledged that the literary remains from the hundreds of years between the exodus and the fall of the first temple are a very slender basis for establishing the religion(s) of Israel in that period and its (their) central theological insights. Here the evidence from Qumran is a very valuable historical control, for we have the literary remains of a community or communities which can be suitably dated and assessed; in that community, which undoubtedly was literate in a nonexemplary fashion, there is a very great variety of opinion, so much so that only recently have scholars begun to attempt to clarify it.

Some might say that this is to overstate the case, but an example of the kind of problem for theological assessment of the Old Testament can be found in 4QGenExod[a] for Gen 22:14. The relevant fragment of the manuscript reads *]l[h]ym yr'h 'šr y'[mr*. Since the combination of letters *yr'h 'šr y'mr* occurs only in Gen 22:14 in the whole MT, the identification of the biblical passage is not seriously in doubt. However, as J. R. Davila has pointed out,[24] all the ancient witnesses attest YHWH for the *'lhym* of 4QGenExod[a]. Although several scholars have detected a difficulty with YHWH in Gen 22:14, without textual support all emendations, however plausible and ingenious, have looked like scholarly tampering with the text. 4QGenExod[a] now provides textual support for all those who have reckoned that the whole pericope should be construed as consistently Elohistic (whatever that may imply). Some large and significant issues remain to be sorted out: the original reading, the place of composition of the pericope, the theological ethos of the original composer, the date of the change, and the relationship between Gen 22:1-19 (in some form) and 2 Chr 3:1. For those

---

22. Ulrich, 276-87.

23. Working with the final form of the text is one of the fundamental principles of the "Forms of the Old Testament Literature" project under the overall editorship of Rolf Knierim and G. M. Tucker.

24. "The Name of God at Moriah: An Unpublished Fragment from 4QGenExod[a]," *JBL* 110 (1991): 577-82.

wanting to work theologically only with the final form of the text as in the MT, the problems can be glossed over, but for anyone with an historical perspective, the final MT form can no longer be understood adequately, even correctly, without some clear justification of its particular reading in this place for the divine epithet and all that goes with it.

A further intriguing example is visible in 11QpaleoLev frg. I:1-2, a place in the manuscript where there seems to have been deliberate scribal alteration to the text involving an assimilation with another passage in Leviticus. There are many instances of assimilation in manuscripts,[25] but few where the process can be clearly seen to be deliberate. That such was the case in 11QpaleoLev I:1-2 is apparent because the scribe has actually marked off the passage which he has included by means of a parenthesis.[26] His text of Lev 18:27 now reads: "for all of] these abominations they did [{they did these things and I abhorred them and I have said t]o you, You shall inherit[ ]their 1[a]nd} the men of the land who were befo[re you and it became de]filed, the land." In this way the two passages on sexual defilement (Lev 18:6-25 and 20:10-22) are inextricably linked and, if more of the manuscript had survived, we might have found other harmonistic assimilations in the presentation of the text of Leviticus 18.[27] Again, those who are concerned to make theology out of the MT alone will find no difficulty in rejecting the parenthetical reading of 11QpaleoLev I, but they may well end up providing a theologically harmonized interpretation of the passages on sexual immorality, just as the scribe of 11QpaleoLev has done. Those whose concern is more historically oriented will see in the scribal handling of Lev 18:27 an appealing example of how one traditor in his particular situation was attempting to show something of the significance of the text as he passed it on. This scribal adjustment is not an error, but a deliberate updating and improvement of the text. There are many other examples of this taking place, all of which show how in precanonical times a text could remain authoritative and relevant in successive generations, not as a static object of veneration but as part of a lively scribal interpretative tradition.

This brief description of a few matters from the Qumran literary evidence shows that the extent of the canon and the form of its text need to be taken into account by those who would engage in the task of Old Testament theology. More precisely the existence of the scrolls declares that the task of Old Testament theology, if it is to be connected in any way with historical realities, can only ever be done in relation to particular communities. The scrolls provide an

25. See E. Tov, "The Nature and Background of Harmonizations in Biblical Manuscripts," *JSOT* 31 (1985): 3-29.

26. The text of this section of 11QpaleoLev can be found in D. N. Freedman and K. A. Mathews, *The Paleo-Hebrew Leviticus Scroll* (Winona Lake: Eisenbrauns, 1985), 36 (plate 3, p. 103).

27. As in 11QT[a] 66:11-17.

opportunity and a challenge to those theologians who remain concerned to ground their theological analysis in historical-critical exegesis and the socioreligious setting and function of texts.

III. The Contents of the Scrolls and Old Testament Theology: Cultic Integration

Turning from the questions which the existence of the scrolls pose for the theologian of the Old Testament to honing the theologian's task on the basis of their content, it is important to preface any remarks with a word of caution concerning the nature of the manuscripts from the eleven caves at Qumran as a collection. Among the scrolls it is easy enough to identify what, somewhat anachronistically, we might call biblical texts. While some may contain readings reflecting a particular viewpoint, it is impossible to locate anything in the variants which could fairly be labeled narrowly or distinctively sectarian.[28] A second group of texts are those which seem to use certain technical terms more or less consistently and which may be held to represent the viewpoint of the community or communities which produced them and passed them on. Among these texts would be placed those that use the term *yahad* in a particular way.[29] The third group of texts, that is, the rest, is more difficult to assess. The question remains whether, together with the second group, these other nonbiblical texts reflect a coherent perspective, whether some of them have been preserved in the caves for purely antiquarian purposes, or whether they actually form a more heterogeneous collection, perhaps from Jerusalem, of the spread of literature available in late second-temple-period Palestine.

Given the conclusion that it is necessary for theological analysis to be done in relation to particular communities, it is appropriate to focus a few comments about what the Old Testament theologian might attempt to describe by addressing some matters which arise primarily out of the texts that are most closely associated with the so-called Qumran community. Since it is theology with which we are concerned, it is appropriate to begin with the understanding of God. There has been considerable interest in the dualisms implied in some texts: these involve angelology (angel of darkness/angel of truth), society (sons of light/men of the lot of Belial), and ethics (spirit of truth/spirit of falsehood). But there is no corresponding theological ontological dualism. In fact, the very same pericope which

---

28. There is no evidence in 4QpaleoExod^m for the distinctive Samaritan readings in the Exodus Decalogue pericope.

29. Some scholars even call the community that resided at Qumran the *Yahad* so as to avoid committing themselves on whether the group there is to be associated with the Essene movement in some way: e.g., S. Talmon, "Between the Bible and the Mishna," *The World of Qumran from Within* (Jerusalem: Magnes, 1989), 16-19.

contains the most dualistic expressions is prefaced with an insistence on the singular origin of all things from God: "from the God of knowledge comes all that is and shall be. . . . The laws of *[mšpty]* all things are in his hand."[30]

Yet, despite this clear monotheistic assertion, the angelology of some texts suggests that both in thought and in experience there was the need for some form of qualification. The *Songs of the Sabbath Sacrifice*, which may or may not be a narrowly sectarian text,[31] contain numerous designations for heavenly beings. Of particular note are the uses of *'ēlîm* and *'ēlôhîm*, often in various combinations, such as *'ēlēy 'ôr* and *'ēlôhēy ḥayyim*.[32] Particularly frequent in the Sabbath Songs is the designation *'ēlēy da'at*, which may be a counterpart to the overarching epithet of God as *'el haddē'ôt* (1QS 3:15). This correspondence gives the impression that for the traditores of these texts it was clear that the highly significant epithets for angels in Pss 29:1 and 89:7 *(bny 'lym)* and Dan 11:36 *('l 'lym)* demonstrated that it was through the angelic beings that God could be experienced as active. Several uses of *'lwhym* in the *Sabbath Songs* are ambiguous but in expressions such as *kwl 'lwhym* and *mlk 'lwhym* there is some unequivocal evidence for the use of *'lwhym* of angels, as also in the use of Ps 82:1 in 11QMelch 2:10 of Melchizedek. What God desired, the angels carried out; when the angelic Melchizedek acts as judge, he does so as God's agent.

This developed angelology is commonly supposed to protect the transcendence of God,[33] sometimes a protectiveness that is read as Israel's near loss of the sense of the divine altogether. But that is to tell only half the story. Alongside the transcendent origin of all things needs to be put the life and raison d'être of the believing communities. A text like the *Songs of the Sabbath Sacrifice* shows that when the community is aligned suitably with the purposes of God, particularly as those are expressed in the Torah as correctly understood and practiced, then in its worship it will be aligned with or even participating in the worship of the angels whose primary function is the praise of God.[34]

---

30. 1QS 3:15-4:26. See W. H. Brownlee, "The Ineffable Name of God," *BASOR* 226 (1977): 39-46. 1QS 3:15-18 and 4:18-26 beautifully sum up how Israel's God is concerned with cosmos and history, and qualitatively with righteousness, matters which Knierim sees as programmatic for the suitable theological reading of Old Testament texts: R. Knierim, "Cosmos and History," 63-73, and "The Task of Old Testament Theology," *HBT* 6,1 (1984): 42-43.

31. C. Newsom concludes cautiously that "the scroll of the Sabbath Shirot is a product of the Qumran community": *Songs of the Sabbath Sacrifice: A Critical Edition,* HSS 27 (Atlanta: Scholars, 1985), 4.

32. *'ēlôhey ḥayyim* seems to be reflected in the particular designation for God which Josephus ascribes to the Essenes: "At the beginning and at the end they bless God as the giver of life (χορηγὸν τῆς ζωῆς)" (*War* 2.131).

33. See the classic statement on angelology made by W. Eichrodt: "it served in the first place to illustrate the exaltedness of Yahweh" (*Theology of the Old Testament,* vol. 2 [London: SCM, 1967], 200).

34. Newsom, 23-38.

This is the case even though the group asserting this may well not be active in any way in the dominant location of God's presence, the temple. In fact, the community may have considered itself to be an anticipation of the place of God's worship which God himself would one day create;[35] this would be like a return to Eden.[36]

This sense of the presence of the reality of God in the worship, especially the sabbath worship,[37] of the community has important implications for the debate within the discipline of Old Testament theology concerning whether creation or history should be seen as the dominant ideological perspective controlling the literary materials, both in themselves and in their analysis.[38] The functional definition of God which features so prominently in 1QS 3:15, "from the God of knowledge comes all that is and will be," contains both elements. God is the creator of all things not just as the prime mover, but as one who remains responsible for all that will be. The community's view of the future, essentially its eschatology, is an expectation both of a future defeat of Belial and all those of his lot and one which expects that such a victory will restore all things to their original purposes which were visible in Eden and will be made manifest in the heavenly temple which is to be built precisely according to the divine blueprint.

The assessment of these juxtaposed motifs, of cosmos and eschatology, of creation and history, has been present in recent decades both in the debate about the proper focus of Old Testament theology and in scholarly considerations of apocalyptic. The rediscovery of cosmology in apocalyptic has been in large measure the result of a careful analysis of the various subgenres which make up the texts that might be grouped together under the overarching umbrella of "descriptions of visions or auditions framed in a narrative." The two principal subcategories have now been recognized as cosmological and eschatological.[39]

---

35. As is the most likely interpretation of 4QFlor: G. J. Brooke, *Exegesis at Qumran: 4QFlorilegium in Its Jewish Context* (Sheffield: JSOT, 1985), 184-87; D. Dimant, "4QFlorilegium and the Idea of the Community as Temple," *Hellenica et Judaica: Hommage à Valentin Nikiprowetzky*, ed. A. Caquot, M. Hadas-Lebel, and J. Riaud (Leuven: Peeters, 1986), 176-80, 188-89.

36. M. O. Wise thinks this return will take place in two stages, the first man-made, the second divinely created. For him *mqdš 'dm,* "the temple of Adam," in 4QFlor corresponds with the first stage: see M. O. Wise, "4QFlorilegium and the Temple of Adam," *RevQ* 15 (1991-92): 103-32.

37. This particular keeping of the sabbath through worship is distinctively Qumranian and is the clearest way that law and cult are woven together, that cyclic cosmic time and history are combined, in the self-understanding of the community; cf. Knierim, "Cosmos and History," 80-85.

38. See Knierim, "Cosmos and History," 59-74.

39. E.g., J. J. Collins labels these two basic generic categories "the 'historical' apocalypses" and "otherworldly journeys": *Daniel: With an Introduction to Apocalyptic Literature,* FOTL 20 (Grand Rapids: Eerdmans, 1984), 6-19.

Though some apocalypses proper may stress one or the other, they are commonly represented together. Thus, for all that Enoch has visions of the heavens and is thus introduced to the makeup of the cosmos, he is also shown how judgment and justice are being and will be worked out. Though the Qumran community is falsely labeled apocalyptic, the combination of interwoven cosmological and eschatological perspectives is very important in its self-definition.

The self-definition of the community does not rest in its being persecuted by the Jerusalem hierarchy. The date and extent of such persecution is very debatable in any case. Rather, the community's self-definition seems to depend on its determination to order its life to provide for worship according to its understanding of the purposes of God discernible in the ordering of nature which have been engraved in a statute for ever (*khwq hrwt l'd*; 1QS 10:6). The hymnic material at the end of 1QS makes it clear that the following of the appointed times as reflected in the seasons of the years is the underlying assumption behind all that has been said earlier in the *Serek* about joining the community and living out one's life as a member of it. It is the determination to accept the calendar of 364 days as most clearly reflecting how God has made himself known in the order of nature which affects everything else in the community's organization and practice of the Law. This calendar is not based, as is commonly assumed, solely on the sun; it is not a straightforward solar calendar. Rather, it is based in the first place in the unit of seven days, the week, which is the period of the ordering of creation (hence six is significant) and a day of rest (sabbath). The annual calendar is organized as fifty-two weeks of seven days. The pericope on David's compositions in 11QPs^a 27:3-11 makes this clear: David wrote "songs to sing before the altar over the whole-burnt perpetual offering every day, for all the days of the year, 364; and for the offerings of the Sabbaths, 52 songs."[40]

Furthermore, this fifty-two-week calendar paid very close attention to the moon's phases. The *Mishmerot* texts emphasize this bluntly.[41] Though there are many details yet to be interpreted correctly, especially concerning how the system of intercalation was applied, it seems likely that the twenty-four priestly courses of 1 Chr 24:7-18 were assigned in rotation so that in a six-year cycle they would return to their original positions.[42] There is no attempt to turn the twenty-four courses into twenty-six so that the whole system might fit together more readily. Rather, perhaps because twelve (and its multiples) was also a

40. Sanders, *Dead Sea Psalms Scroll*, 87.

41. See S. Talmon and I. Knohl, "A Calendrical Scroll from Qumran Cave IV," presented at the Third International Colloquium on the Dead Sea Scrolls, Mogilany, Poland, August 1991; J. T. Milik's preliminary work is represented in Wacholder and Abegg, 60-95, 104-118.

42. Knierim's comments on creation as cyclic cosmic time are significant in this respect too: "Cosmos and History," 80-85.

significant number for the community as for others,[43] a system was devised which allowed for twenty-four courses to service fifty-two weeks, a system whose benefits prevented any one course from claiming any particular preeminence as the one always on duty at a particular festival. It is possible that here there is a good example of an authoritative priestly text not being altered because it could be seen to fit the overall chronometric perspective of the community.

The effect of following the 364-day calendar is that the sabbath never coincides with the principal days of any festival nor with the first day of any month. At one stroke all the problems that beset some forms of Judaism over which prescriptions take precedence when there is a clash with the sabbath are avoided. The natural order engraved in statute has not been revealed in order to show conflict with some other law. God's purposes, when appreciated aright, are consistent in themselves. The scribal attitude which is reflected in the process of the harmonization of legal materials is the precise counterpart to these assumptions concerning the coherence and consistency of what can be known about God from the Torah and the natural order of creation.

An effect of allocating the priestly courses in rotation is that according to the calendric information at the end of 4QS^e the total calendar rotates every six jubilee periods (294 years).[44] The practice of the annual cycle very quickly leads to chronometric calculations beyond the weekly and annual unit. The hymnic section at the end of 1QS makes this clear: "the seasons of years to their weeks and at the beginning of their weeks to the season of release (drwr)." Beyond the week of years it is the jubilee cycle that dominates the periodization of history. This plays a part in how the history of the past was viewed and recounted. Above all such jubilee periodization is visible in the Book of Jubilees itself, but it is also apparent in the so-called Psalms of Joshua.[45]

Just as the past is understood in jubilee cycles, so is the future. 6Q12 talks of what will happen "after the jubilees." Above all in 11QMelch at the end of the tenth jubilee period there is atonement for all the sons of light and the men of the lot of Melchizedek; this is the Day of Atonement at which Melchizedek seems to preside, certainly as the agent of God's judgment, probably also as a heavenly high priest who can "proclaim to them liberty, forgiving them the wrong-doings of all their iniquities." For all that some of the details are unclear, it remains plain that the climax of the tenth jubilee on the Day of Atonement involves the celebratory release which is based in the right ordering of worship. Cosmology and eschatology come together.

This cosmological and eschatological self-understanding is expressed pre-

43. J. M. Baumgarten, "The Duodecimal Courts of Qumran, the Apocalypse, and the Sanhedrin," JBL 95 (1976): 59-78; reprinted in Studies in Qumran Law, SJLA 24 (Leiden: Brill, 1977), 145-71.

44. Wacholder and Abegg, 96.

45. C. A. Newsom, "The 'Psalms of Joshua' from Qumran Cave 4," JJS 39 (1988): 56-73; see esp. 4Q379 frg. 12, 1.5 on the jubilee reckoning for the entry into Canaan.

dominantly and practically in the application of the Torah in worship. The Qumran handling of the tradition falls precisely within the tension of the matrix which historians of the late second temple period have often represented in terms of the temple and the law.[46] This arena of cultic practice also becomes a focus for defining the different groups of humanity. Just as the eschatological battles will be led by priests and those who are set in battle order are as pure as those admitted to the temple precincts, so the eschatological sanctuary will not be polluted by any unqualified people. Thus in 1QM 7:4-6 one reads that "no man who is lame, or blind, or crippled or afflicted with a lasting bodily blemish or smitten with a bodily impurity, none of these shall march out to war with them," and that "no man shall go down with them on the day of battle who is impure because of his fount, for the holy angels shall be with their hosts." In a corresponding manner in 4QFlor 1:3-4 one reads of the exclusion of the Ammonite, the Moabite, the bastard, the stranger, and the proselyte from the future sanctuary. The reasons for the exclusions are very similar in both cases. In 1QM it is because the "holy angels shall be with their hosts"; in 4QFlor because "his holy ones are there." The justification in part for the application of Deuteronomy 23 to the eschatological activities of the community rests in the presence of angels.

The community's attitude to the will of God as disclosed in the natural ordering of things in weeks and years is the basis for their own closer self-definition in relation to the rest of Israel, including renegade members of the early community. The opening pages of the *Damascus Document* make it clear in a repetitive fashion that the community of that text, perhaps a predecessor of the Qumran community, differentiated itself from others who were considered to have transgressed the covenant and violated the precept (*ḥwq*; CD 1:20; 2:6).[47] In the third introductory exhortation the reader is told that the Watchers fell because they did not keep the commandments (*mṣwt*; CD 2:18) of God; and the rest of Israel has sadly also been led astray. These general categorizations are not given specific justification until the end of this third introductory exhortation. The first time the reader is given specific criteria of differentiation regarding the content of the commandments (*mṣwt*; CD 3:12) the hidden things are involved, namely, "His holy sabbaths and his glorious feasts, the testimonies of his righteousness, and the ways of his truth and the desires of his will which a man must do in order to live" (CD 3:14-16).[48] The

---

46. As most clearly presented by J. Maier, *Zwischen den Testamenten: Geschichte und Religion in der Zeit des Zweiten Tempels*, NEG (Würzburg: Echter, 1990), 212-35.

47. In a way not dissimilar to its usage in CD, Knierim says of *ḥwq* that "when used in connection with the creation and existence of the world [it] comes close to being the Hebrew word itself for world-order" ("Cosmos and History," 87).

48. It is noteworthy that the reading of the traditions according to CD is not unlike that of K. Koch, "Wort und Einheit des Schöpfergottes in Memphis und Jerusalem," *ZTK* 62 (1965): 251-93; quoted approvingly by Knierim, "Cosmos and History," 71-72. Perhaps it is

three nets of Belial which will undoubtedly ensnare the rest of Israel, because they are three kinds of righteousness in disguise, are fornication, riches, and the profanation of the temple. Again the natural order and the moral order correspond in the right ordering of the cult, the way of worship.[49]

According to the *Damascus Document* this differentiation between the community and the rest of Israel is a matter well in the past with ongoing significance. According to 1QpHab 11:2-8 this differentiation is a matter of the more recent history of the community: the Wicked Priest has pursued the Teacher of Righteousness on the Day of Atonement. According to a text like 4QFlor this differentiation will be the hallmark of the community in the future. Since some kind of observance of the sabbath, though not necessarily liturgical worship on that day, was common to all Jews in the late second temple period, the basis of this differentiation in the sabbath is not in itself sectarian, even though the practice of the sabbath by the communities of CD and 1QS may have been distinctive.

In making sense of the worldview of the people of the communities reflected in texts like the *Manual of Discipline* and the *Damascus Document*, it is important to note the broader bases upon which their outlook was built. The significance of these communities and their texts cannot be dismissed through labeling them as narrowly sectarian. Rather, they present a significant reading of earlier traditions, as significant in their own ways as the approximately contemporary readings of those same traditions by the communities whose literary deposit is the New Testament.

This study has tried to show in a very brief compass that the theological outlook of the 1QS and CD communities was based on attitudes to tradition and the created order which were mindful of the consistency of God in himself and in his activity in the world. The ordering of the cosmos in weeks, months, years, weeks of years, and jubilee periods provides for a periodization of history which allows one to see who in the past lived their lives according to God's precepts and who in the present is not being led astray, and to estimate when those who keep to the correct application of the commandments will be vindicated. The historical, especially eschatological outlook of the communities depends upon their knowledge of the God who creates and sustains the cosmos.

The cognitive dissonance that may result from their having a minority perspective in late second-temple-period Judaism, and unfulfilled expectations, is accommodated through the sense of the proximity of the creator God through his angelic agents. Since the principal function of angels is to praise God, so the

---

not too much to say that a careful reading of some of these early Jewish texts can provide suitable insights into how the earlier traditions may best be handled theologically.

49. This is akin to what Knierim has argued for on the basis of Genesis 1 in another context: "the cosmic order itself reflects the ongoing presence of creation. It remains loyal to its origin. This ongoing presence of creation is therefore, an ultimate presence" ("Cosmos and History," 81).

lifestyle of the members of the community is dominated not by the living out of divine action in the world, even though they consider themselves to be the elect, but by Torah-based worship in which the histories of the world, Israel, and the community are integrated under the dominant perspective of the divinely ordered cosmos. All is oriented toward God as universal creator and based in a wider field of thought than ever came to be the contents of the canon.

IV. Conclusion

The lessons here for the practice of Old Testament theology are manifold. There should be nothing controversial about stating that if Old Testament theology is to claim any historical validity, then the texts which form its basis cannot be studied apart from particular sociopolitical and religious contexts. Sound exegesis, the basis of sound theological extrapolation, will always try to take account of such contexts. The theological bases of the worldviews of the individuals and groups belonging to those contexts cannot be definitively derived solely from the canonical texts; even the theological principles of those who determined the final extent of the canon cannot be derived solely from those texts. More obviously, the validity of any community's theological worldview cannot be verified from the texts alone. In addition, in respect to the later canonical books the preservation of a wide range of earlier textual forms of those books provides some clues as to the motivation of various scribes in reflecting the overall coherence of how the created order is reflected in the Torah; the authority of the traditions lay in the very fact that they needed to be reworked, interpreted, and updated, not in the veneration of any particular form of the text as providing the hermeneutical key for giving meaning to present experience.

In the scrolls from Qumran, especially those that can be most readily associated with the viewpoint of the community there, we have a glimpse of the religious perspectives of a particular Jewish group which was attempting to make sense of the world and to give meaning to its experience in light of some basic theological assumptions. Before the temple was destroyed and before the extent of the canon was delimited, this group had already put into practice a lifestyle based on received lively traditions, a lifestyle which tried to integrate Torah and cult, creation and history, cosmology and eschatology. In the light of that attempt Old Testament theologians might find guidelines for their task of describing in a unitive and coherent fashion the relationship between God and the world, especially as that may be summed up in the prayer and praise of a believing community of any period. The criteria for discerning the validity both of that worship and of its theological description may be the absence of idolatry and the determination to avoid the nets of Belial.

Structure Analysis and the Art of Exegesis
(1 Samuel 16:14–18:30)

ANTONY F. CAMPBELL, S.J.

The Holy Grail of biblical interpretation should be the meaning of a text: the best insight the interpreter can offer, after all the acumen of scholarship has been brought to bear, as to what the text is doing or saying.[1] Like the Grail itself, meaning proves elusive to those who engage in its quest. It is easy to make archaeological, geographical, and historical comments or to note critical and linguistic issues. It is quite another question to lay bare one's conviction as to a text's meaning. The process tends to lay bare the interpreter's being.[2]

Gerhard von Rad noted long ago that, although we have a vast panoply of exegetical weaponry to bring to bear upon the biblical text, when exegetes ask what, with all its details, the text is saying they generally find themselves alone. "It would be a great mistake to regard this establishment of the meaning of a text, which is the final stage and crown of exposition, as something simple,

---

1. I appreciate Frederick W. Locke's comment in a study of the Grail legend: "Only when the ultimate significance of the Grail has been uncovered will the complexity of the work yield, revealing that center of unity which is at the heart of every artistic creation" (*The Quest for the Holy Grail: A Literary Study of a Thirteenth-Century French Romance* [Stanford: Stanford University, 1960], 12).

2. It is not appropriate to go into the many discussions of what is meant by "meaning." Our context should make clear that it is not paraphrase or description of the text; it is not a mass of facts about the text, even facts grammatical and syntactical. Meaning is the interpretative experience emerging out of the encounter between the reader and the text. Meaning can be spoken of as a function of the text: what the text says or does. Or it can be spoken of as a function of the reader: what is said or done to the reader by the text. It is necessarily the outcome of the conjunction of both forces, reader and text and their worlds, involving the baggage that both bring to the encounter.

a thing which dawns as it were automatically on the expositor's mind."[3] The meaning of a text should be the Holy Grail of exegesis, which is the art of interpretation.

Rolf Knierim, the jubilarian we celebrate in this volume, is a first-rate teacher, with remarkable gifts for uncovering the meaning of a text. It is a common phenomenon that graduate students regard their senior professors as great teachers and revered figures. Knierim's remarkable talents as a teacher, however, are well known to his friends and associates; by any standard, Rolf Knierim is an extremely good teacher.

One of the tools that Knierim uses most powerfully to introduce students to a text, to involve them in it and enthrall them with it, is what he calls "structure analysis." As used by him, structure analysis is peculiar to Knierim and "The Forms of the Old Testament Literature" project he initiated with Gene Tucker. Apparently similar analyses are frequently used; often they have not been crafted along the specific guidelines which are critical to Knierim's understanding of the art. In such cases, we occasionally have little more than glorified tables of contents. Structure analysis is a key to Knierim's approach to texts and their interpretation.

It is a source of regret that Knierim has never written a descriptive analysis of his approach with a full unfolding of its theoretical underpinnings. This Festschrift provides the occasion for a poor substitute: an analysis of the approach by a former student. In doing so, we are not straying too far from the central focus of this volume, for it is the way that his structure analyses take Knierim into the text that allows him to bring rich theological lode out of it.

The reason for offering this analysis is not simply to honor the jubilarian. Rather, Knierim's concept of structure analysis has an important role to play in the methodology of interpretation. It is a starting point for getting into a text; it is a summary point for verifying and validating an interpretation. Life is short and academics are busy people; we often do not have the time to take a text apart with painstakingly meticulous care before we tell a class or an audience what it is all about. I cannot speak for all who have been schooled in the art of structure analysis, but for myself I know that if I deal with a text which I have not subjected to structure analysis, I am selling the text short and working at a predominantly superficial level. Similarly, when I have put an enormous amount of time and effort into the study of a text, if I have not pulled it together in a structure analysis, then I have not yet put the final crown on the text's interpretation.

As a starting point, the methodological contribution of Knierim's structure analysis is to provide a relatively neutral way into the text. While this may seem so basic as to be banal, it is not. In most manuals of exegesis, e.g., the first step to be taken is text criticism. Without having established a text, any task of

---

3. G. von Rad, *Old Testament Theology,* vol. 2 (New York: Harper and Row, 1965), 416.

interpretation would be premature. But no text criticism can take place without some idea of the nature of the text under study, what might make sense in such a text and what can be expected of such a text. The expectations in a legal text are not identical with those in a narrative text.

As a summary point, the methodological contribution of Knierim's structure analysis is to check that every element of the text has been accounted for. For an interpretation to claim adequacy and validity, it must at least account for the majority of elements and signals in the text it interprets. It is relatively easy to produce a fine-sounding interpretation of a text, if we discreetly ignore those parts of the text which do not fit our understanding. Of course, none of us reading this would do such a thing, but we may notice it occasionally in the work of others. A structure analysis does not allow us to do this unawares. It forces us to name the form or function of every element in the text, within its context. By obliging us to write out the verse numbers in sequence down the right-hand side of the page, it brings to our attention aspects we may have too conveniently overlooked.

Basics of the Approach

Structure analysis, as advocated by Rolf Knierim, focuses directly on the text. First of all, it has to be identified: as text, where does it start and where does it end? Second, what are the major building blocks of its construction: does it have an introduction, a conclusion, and what are the principal constituents of the body of the text? Third, how do these building blocks relate to each other within the text to shape its meaning?

The primary difference between a Knierim structure analysis and a table of contents is that the former normally focuses on form and the latter on content. This focus does not take us prematurely into the form-critical arena. Its concern is not yet with the form of the text as a whole, but rather with the form of the elements which make up that whole. Some examples may help.

- Introduction is a statement about form.
     Persons, places, and times are matters of content.
- Exhortation is a statement about form.
     "Importance of keeping the law" is a statement about content.
- Motivation is a statement about form.
     "Promise of prosperity and peace" is a statement about content.
- Prohibition is a statement about form.
     "Against lying and stealing" is a statement about content.
- Conclusion is a statement about form.
     "Death of the king" is a statement about content.

78

Not everything can be expressed in the language of form, and often form needs to be specified with content. The issue is one of focus and priority; the focus is on form, and form gets priority. "Promise of prosperity and peace" can be a statement of form; this verse is in the form of a promise. Where the promise of prosperity and peace is understood to reinforce an exhortation to live wisely and well, it is primarily a motivation; its content is a promise. On occasion content is the most concise label available for recording a formal observation in a structure analysis. It should seldom be content for its own sake.

Interrelatedness — how the building blocks relate to each other to shape the text's meaning — is an essential element of analysis. Aristotle's remark in the *Poetics* is still valid: all works of literature have a beginning, a middle, and an end. What functions as introduction and what contribution does it make to the shape of the text? What does the end bring into focus and what aspects of the text does it leave aside?[4] How does the middle move to enable the beginning to reach an end, a lack to be satisfied, an imbalance to be brought into balance?

These building blocks in a text can be described by a variety of metaphors. The reality is not a matter of scientific analysis but of intuitive perception. "Focus" is an optical metaphor; "conceptualization" takes it into a more abstract level. Both seek to grasp the structure of a text by how it may be seen and understood. "Act" and "scene" are dramatic metaphors. They correlate major blocks with subordinate ones, as acts in a play are subdivided into scenes. "Take" is a similar metaphor from cinema or television. A take is an uninterrupted piece of photography; it therefore has some sort of inherent unity. Whatever metaphors are used for description, the aim is to visualize and name how the parts of the text fit together to form a whole.

One way of envisaging this task is to think of it as recapturing the outline that was in the author's mind. A storyteller, e.g., has to have a sense of where a story will begin, how it will unfold, and where it will end. The main actions will be grouped in clusters, for ease of memory. The details can be left to the imagination of the moment, as the telling proceeds. While this approach is appealing, it is methodologically dangerous. It must be true that storytellers organized their material in their minds, so that the bold outline was clear and the details could take care of themselves in due course. Methodologically, however, we must remain aware that we do not have access to the storyteller's mind, only to the storyteller's text. Our concern has to be for the structure in the text, not the structure outlined in the storyteller's mind. Similarly, our concern has to be for the meaning in the storyteller's text, not the meaning in the storyteller's mind. What is out of reach is out of reach — the storyteller. What is within our reach is the text in all the manifold complexity of its signals.

---

4. E.g., in the sacrifice of Isaac the first ending (Gen 22:14, 19) focuses on God's providing and leaves aside issues of sacrifice; it focuses on Abraham's return to Beersheba and leaves aside the fate of Isaac as well as any implications for the life of Abraham.

The phrase quoted earlier (n. 1 above) — "that center of unity which is at the heart of every artistic creation" — can be understood with "creation" interpreted as process or as product. As process, the center of unity would be the driving purpose that was in the author's mind. It is better understood as product, where the artistic creation is the text and the center of unity is to be found in the text itself.

Practical Illustration

As a process, structure analysis will vary, with different texts having different requirements and different interpreters having different skills. Rather than attempt an abstract and global presentation of the concept — difficult to do and difficult to follow — it may help more to use a specific text as a practical illustration. Given that structure analysis follows a concentric rather than a linear approach, a certain amount of repetition is inevitable. On balance, it should not be harmful.

The first temptation of anyone beginning the process of structure analysis is to list in sequence the component elements of the text. This is precisely what a table of contents does; it is precisely what a structure analysis should not do.

Invariably, in narrative, the constitutive blocks of a text are grouped in twos or threes rather than sixes or sevens. Beginning, middle, and end is a threesome. The folkloric triad is a threesome; it is somehow natural for things to come in threes. Hence the French proverb "Jamais deux sans trois" — never two without a third. Proverbs reminds us that three can be expanded into four; "Three things are too wonderful for me; four I do not understand" (Prov 30:18). When our assessment of a text stretches to five blocks, we may begin to suspect that a higher grouping or a different grouping has escaped our notice. A number beyond four is not impossible, simply suspect. Two of course is not only the natural binary division of left and right, front and back, raw and cooked; it is also the primary structure of Hebrew poetry — the division of a line into two versets, or sometimes three. The first verset will often be expressed in general terms, while the second verset is more concrete and more specific.[5] A similar movement is often visible in Hebrew narrative; a general statement, for example, is followed by its unfolding in concrete detail. Narrative movement may often be structured in pairs: a command is followed by the report of compliance; acts are followed by their consequences, and so on.

Once this tendency toward groupings of two and three has been recognized, attention to the focus of interest in the movement of a text will frequently reveal groupings and structure within a superficially purely sequential text. In

5. See, e.g., Robert Alter, *The Art of Biblical Poetry* (New York: Basic Books, 1985).

such ways, meaning emerges from unordered fact. It is not a matter of imposing an order on a text; it is a matter of reflecting whether there is such an order in a text. There is no hard-and-fast commitment to twos and threes, simply a predilection for them.[6]

The Process of Structural Discovery

There is no hard-and-fast procedure for creating a structure analysis. One of the beauties of the beast is its freedom from mechanical method. Others might proceed in other ways. In my experience, the following steps are usually central.

Establishing the limits of the unit constituting a text
Establishing the limits of the major blocks within the text
Analyzing the elements and their relationship within each block
Analyzing the relationships of the blocks to the whole
Establishing an initial hypothesis as to the meaning of the text

As noted, an abstract description is difficult to give and difficult to follow. I will use the story of David's single combat with the Philistine as a practical illustration of what structure analysis involves and offers.[7]

Establishing the Limits of the Unit Constituting a Text

The first task in analyzing a text is to discover where it begins and where it ends. Often an instinctive form-critical judgment will operate here. Beginning and end may not be identifiable without knowing what "it" is. What "it" is, of course, is always a form-critical judgment. "It" is the text to be analyzed. Its beginning and end may depend on the sort of text it is. Often the decision about beginning and end can be made on basically syntactical grounds; at other times, matters of theme and content, even narrative plot or literary form may have a role to play. The question is: What is the text? What is its extent?

6. No one has ever said that seven and eight are not significant numbers, so potential factors for order. The body of Amos 1–2 in the present text is structured around a sequence of eight, to be understood as seven plus one: Damascus, Gaza, Tyre, Edom, Ammon, Moab, Judah, and Israel. If Judah is omitted as a later addition, we have a sequence of seven. If Tyre and Edom are also regarded as secondary, the original sequence is reduced to five. A prophetic collection, of course, need not be bound by the same conventions as narrative.

7. The text refers to David's opponent throughout as "the Philistine." It mentions the name Goliath twice only (17:4, 23); in verse 23, in particular, the proper name seems intrusive in the text. Hence my preference for conforming to the text and referring to the Philistine.

The story of David and the Philistine is a good example of the subtleties involved. If we think of the text simply as a battle story, the battle story begins in 1 Sam 17:1. The Philistine champion is introduced in 17:4-7; David is introduced in 17:12-15. The battle story ends with 17:52-54, the pursuit of the fleeing foe and the taking of plunder.

Two oddities may attract our attention, however. First, the Philistine has been shouting his challenge morning and evening for forty days (v. 16). It is, therefore, very odd that all Israel should be reported to have fled from him in fear when they saw him (v. 24). Such fearful flight can hardly have happened twice a day for forty days or have erupted only on the first and fortieth day. Second, when David is summoned by Saul, there are no introductions, no questions asked about David's identity; David speaks up and addresses Saul (v. 32). Only later, in a segment that is situated outside the frame of the battle story, as Saul sees David going out against the Philistine, does Saul ask Abner, "Whose son is this young man?" (v. 55). Abner does not know.

Another segment associated with this identification scene (17:55-58) has Jonathan form an instant friendship with David, solemnize it with a covenant, and celebrate it in an exchange of garments — and David is so successful that he is given an army command (18:1-5). The focus has moved from the little group on the battlefield to a far wider view of space and time.

Finally, in yet another segment, David is said to be playing the lyre for Saul, who is troubled by an evil spirit; it is noted as common practice, "as he did day by day" (18:10). There is no introduction to this practice in chapter 18. This might not matter, except that there is an introduction to it in chapter 16. Possibly the story may have to be extended back to at least 16:14.

It is possible that it may have to be extended forward too. In the battle story, as the Philistine's challenge is discussed, the Israelite troops assure David that "The king will greatly enrich the man who kills him, and will give him his daughter and make his family free in Israel" (17:25). There is no talk subsequently of David's family being made free, but twice the issue of David's marriage to a daughter of Saul is taken up and developed (18:17-19, 20-29).

Tentatively, it is worth considering that the limits of the text may extend from 16:14 to 18:30.

Our primary focus is less the clarification of the story of David and the Philistine than the clarification of the process of structure analysis. My concern is with a holistic interpretation of the text and the contribution of structure analysis to this task. The discussion, in commentaries and elsewhere, of the issues and details of 1 Sam 16:14–18:30 cannot be debated in the space available to us. Almost all are well known; it is a text where few stones have been left unturned. What is significant is the context the interpreter creates within which these details are understood. The valuable collection of studies and discussion by D. Barthélemy, D. W. Gooding, J. Lust, and E. Tov points to the difficulties of finding agreement across differing interests.[8] Room remains for more insight into the text, more options for understanding, more possibilities for meaning.

In this paper, my interest is in exploring a structure analysis of the text, while assuming intelligent compilers and giving weight to the involvement of tradition and the creative liberty of the ancient storyteller. Of course, if the substantial compilation of the text were demonstrably late, the proposals advanced here might require nuancing in the light of our understanding of the circles responsible. The need to shape scripture and preserve tradition might take precedence over the creative activity of storytellers. Discussing all the options would, again, extend this paper unreasonably.

Establishing the Limits of the Major Blocks within the Text

The second task in analyzing a text is to discover where the major constitutive blocks within it begin and end. As part of a text there may be framing blocks such as introduction, body of the text, and conclusion. Such framing structures may seem simple, but they are often significant. Within the body of the text, there will be the blocks which are the load-bearing pillars of the text's center. The task of identifying these requires attention to the movement of the text through plot or its equivalent and to the syntactical signals embedded in the text for our guidance.

Movement through the text will vary according to the nature of the text. In a series of laws, each law might be a single block or several laws together might constitute a block. In a narrative text, the blocks are likely to correspond with aspects of the plot or its equivalent. They may be large or as small as a single sentence; they are unlikely to be numerous. Syntactical links seldom extend across major blocks. So a block will begin with its own subject and verb; pronouns and pronominal suffixes will find their antecedents within their own block. The syntactical signals can be varied; the message they send is that a new block begins or ends here.

We might look, e.g., at the blocks in 1 Sam 16:14 to 18:30. Something new is signaled in 16:14: the spirit of the LORD has departed from Saul and he is tormented by an evil spirit from the LORD.[9] Saul's need for attention is identified

---

8. D. Barthélemy, D. W. Gooding, J. Lust, and E. Tov, *The Story of David and Goliath: Textual and Literary Criticism,* OBO 73 (Fribourg, Suisse: Editions Universitaires, 1986). A unitary view is defended by Gooding against traditional analyses (esp. 55-86). See also R. Polzin, *A Literary Study of the Deuteronomic History,* part 2, *Samuel and the Deuteronomist* (San Francisco: Harper and Row, 1989), 152-81.

9. Those who do not have access to the Hebrew text must always remember that English conjunctions such as "and," "but," "if," "then," "when," and others usually represent the one principal Hebrew conjunction "wě-"; translation depends on context. In the NRSV, 16:14 begins with "Now"; 16:15 begins with "And." Both times, the Hebrew has the same

by his servants, a remedy is proposed, David is hired as lyre-player to soothe Saul, and Saul's need is satisfied. The block is 16:14-23. Within the block, it is noted that David became Saul's armor-bearer. There is no reference back to 16:1-13 that might require its association with this text. The thematic link is from 16:1-13 to 16:14-23 and what follows, not the reverse. 16:1-13 has potential to illuminate the following text; but it remains in the background, it is not spelled out.

With 17:1, a new block clearly begins. The principals are new: the Philistines on one side, Saul and the Israelites on the other. The location is new: Ephes-dammim and Elah. The topic is new: battle. So far, so good. Determining where this block ends is more difficult. There is a temptation to close it at 17:11, because of the evident new beginning in verse 12. Against this, verses 1-11 have set the scene for a battle between Israel and the Philistines and the battle has hardly been begun, much less brought to a narrative conclusion. So 17:12 probably begins a sub-block rather than a major block. Once this is agreed to, the major block must extend to 17:54 where the battle story is brought to a conclusion. The block is 17:1-54.

The next block is larger than it appears at first sight. It might first seem to be constituted by 17:55-58. But the Hebrew of 18:1 begins: "When he had finished speaking to Saul. . . ." Although David is mentioned later in the sentence, this "he" depends on 17:58 for the identification of its subject. The next move seems to be to extend the block to 18:5. Here again 18:6 begins: "As they were coming home. . . ." This syntactical link exists at the level of the present text. An earlier independent text might have begun: "When David returned . . . "; but the present text does not begin that way. While 17:55–18:9 might look to be the appropriate block in the present text, the opening of 18:10 — "The next day" — ties it into what precedes, as well as the thematic association with jealousy. The block, at the level of the present text, has to be 17:55–18:11. It comprises Saul's becoming aware of David's identity, the friendship with Jonathan, Saul's heir, and the emergence of Saul's jealousy toward David.

The time lines in this block are complicated. The first part overlaps with the battle story; Saul's first question is put to Abner as David goes out against the Philistine (17:55). In the middle, the report surveys enough time for sustained success to be established on David's part (18:5). The issue of Saul's jealousy brings us back to the return from battle and the day following that return.

The next block is 18:12-16. It stands out for its shift in focus, standing outside the detailed narrative as comment. It makes statements and then substantiates them. It deals with the major players: Saul, David, and all Israel and Judah.

---

conjunction, *"wĕ-"*; the context, however, is different. In narrative prose, almost every Hebrew sentence begins with this conjunction, *"wĕ-."* Conclusion: when working with a translation, conjunctions cannot be relied on for structure analysis unless they have been checked against the Hebrew.

The remaining text, 18:17-30, comprises two episodes about Saul's daughters being offered to David in marriage. At first sight they appear syntactically independent, one a short notice about Merab and the other an anecdote about Michal. In the present text, however, they are linked by the second's reference back to the first: "Therefore Saul said to David a second time" (v. 21). Once viewed as a block, the thematic unity is clear: Saul used the promise of his daughters in marriage as a snare to have David killed. Saul's attempts to kill David continue in the subsequent narrative and become increasingly direct. They drive David first from Saul's court, then from Saul's kingdom. What focuses these two stories as a block is the issue of the marriage to Saul's daughters. What closes off this final block is the narrative irony of verse 30. Using his daughters as bait, Saul has twice tried to create a situation in which the Philistines kill David. Saul fails. This narrative ends on the note that as often as the Philistines came out to battle, David had more success than Saul's followers. Saul tried to have the Philistines kill David. David turned out to be extremely good at killing Philistines. David succeeds.

It is time for a rudimentary structure analysis:

I. Introduction of David to court of Saul
II. Story of battle
III. Introduction of David to court of Saul
IV. Saul's jealousy toward David

Such an analysis may be expressed in a triple structure, but the dual introduction of David to Saul's court remains.

I. Prelude to battle: introduction of David to court of Saul
II. Story of battle
III. Aftermath of battle
  A. Introduction of David to court of Saul
  B. Saul's jealousy toward David

The shape of a narrative is stirring here, but the repeated "introduction of David to court of Saul" is a clear signal that the present text is not straightforward. An examination of the interrelationships within the blocks may be the best procedure to discover where the meaning of this text lies.

Analyzing the Elements and Their Relationship within Each Block

1 Sam 16:14-23. The movement of the text is straightforward: a problem exists which needs to be remedied. Saul is tormented by an evil spirit. Music is recommended and a musician is sought. David, a skillful player of the lyre, is identified and summoned to Saul's service.

On its own, the passage is complete. It exhibits the classic movement of story: from an imbalance which needs to be corrected to the establishment of equilibrium. Certain elements point further. The evil spirit which torments Saul is "from the LORD"; worse still, the spirit of the LORD is said to have departed from Saul. Something is amiss in the kingdom. Secondly, as has been widely noted, the description of David, unnamed, goes beyond the requirements of a lyre-player. Six pairs of words describe six courtly attributes: musically skilled, sufficiently well-off, militarily trained, able speaker, good presence, and divinely favored (the LORD with him). Such qualities seem more in keeping with the court of David than with Saul's. Finally, David is not only to be Saul's musician; he is also given the role of Saul's armor-bearer.

In brief, the structural elements are:

   I. Need: description of Saul's plight   v. 14
  II. Remedy: proposal to seek a lyre-player   vv. 15-16
 III. Outcome: successful — David enters Saul's service   vv. 17-23

1 Sam 17:1-54. Here the elements are more complex. The block opens with an introduction which sets the scene for battle between the Philistines and Israel. Specifically a challenge is issued to settle the battle by single combat. Saul has been established as king over Israel because of his demonstrated ability to deliver Israel in time of trouble.[10] Such is the role of a king. This should be Saul's moment. But the spirit of the LORD has departed from Saul (16:14). The future movement of the narrative has to be uncertain.

Instead of proceeding with Israel's response to the Philistine challenge, the narrative turns to the figure of David. It situates him within his family in Bethlehem, refers to the three eldest sons at the war, and through the device of paying a visit to them brings David on to the scene in time to hear the challenge to single combat. All Israel flees and the soldiers begin to discuss what might be in it for the Israelite who kills the Philistine. The response is almost that of standard folktale: half of the kingdom and the hand of the king's daughter in marriage. The victor is assured of great wealth, the hand of the king's daughter, and honored status for his family. David is instantly interested and verifies the possibility. His eldest brother comes on the scene for a brief and bitter exchange. David leaves him to continue questioning as before. Finally he comes before Saul.

It is clear that David is to play a dramatic role in this story. On the level of literary unity, this flashback to the ancestral home in Bethlehem might serve to give a sense of local color and a trace of the human touch to the man so

---

10. Cf. 1 Samuel 11. In 1 Sam 9:16, Saul's anointing is specifically with a view to saving Israel from the Philistines. On traditio-historical grounds, I would prefer not to appeal to 9:16 here.

soon to be Israel's hero. The narrative is aware that David was in service at the court of Saul, but it makes the flashback possible by having David return home regularly. We might object that Saul's armor-bearer should be by the king's side in preparation for a major battle with the Philistines. We might also recognize that a gifted storyteller would probably have little difficulty in making such an absence plausible.

A gifted storyteller may make plausible what appears to be a difficult text. This assertion rests on a basic assumption: that often the biblical text may not be the end product of a narrator's art — a polished gem or the verbatim mirror of a performance — but the basis from which a narrator's performance began. There is not space to develop this here.[11] However, there is a serious question as to "whether all our biblical texts are the final product of literary output or whether some of them are intended as the starting point from which literary output is produced."[12] If the question is answered affirmatively, then we must take into account the potential a storyteller might develop from a text that at first sight seems difficult or disjointed.[13]

The flashback has its problems, however. The Philistine is portrayed uttering his challenge twice a day for forty days (17:16). David is chatting with his brothers when the Philistine repeats his challenge. The narrative continues: "All the Israelites, when they saw the man, fled from him and were very much afraid" (17:24). This is odd behavior in response to a ceremonial challenge which was being proclaimed twice daily for forty days. Had the Israelites advanced toward the Philistine lines and fled in panic for forty days, morning and evening? It would tax a storyteller's skills to make this plausible. An isolated panic by the Israelites would be just as hard to portray as credible. There is a difficulty here.

There is also a difficulty in deciding whether the next section, within this block, begins with 17:31 or 32. With the focus on David's words, verse 31 could be taken as a conclusion: David has got what he wants, an audience with the king. David's words to Saul then burst into the narrative baldly and bluntly. To avoid this, verse 31 could be seen as the introduction to David's audience with Saul. While this is satisfactory for the context of chapter 17 alone, we have begun our text at 16:14. David is Saul's armor-bearer and could be expected to report to his king once this critical challenge has occurred. Verse 31 has to be the conclusion to the portrayal of David's ambition and David's speech has to begin baldly and bluntly.

Despite this, it is odd that Saul, who has sent for David, has nothing to say to him. Instead it is David who initiates the conversation. His words to Saul

---

11. See A. F. Campbell, "The Reported Story: Midway between Oral Performance and Literary Art," *Semeia* 46 (1989): 77-85, and A. F. Campbell and M. A. O'Brien, *Sources of the Pentateuch: Texts, Introductions, Annotations* (Minneapolis: Fortress, 1993), 203-11.

12. Campbell and O'Brien, 208.

13. E.g., see the treatment of Gen 37:21-35 in Campbell and O'Brien, 231-35.

refer directly back either to 17:11, where "Saul and all Israel . . . were dismayed and greatly afraid," or to 17:24, where "All the Israelites . . . were very much afraid." Summoned to the royal presence (v. 31), it would have been arrogant and presumptuous of David to assume Saul's fear. In the present text, Saul's fear is mentioned in verse 11, when David was not present to witness it. It is not mentioned in verse 24, when David was present, perhaps because David while on the battlefield was not in Saul's presence.

We might want to argue that Saul's fear is not central, since the Hebrew text in 17:32 does not refer to Saul specifically — "Let no one's heart fail because of him." The Greek, however, has specific reference to "the heart of my lord." Even with the more discreet and diplomatic Hebrew version, Saul cannot be taken out of the picture. As king, it is his role here to show courage and exercise command. The initiative given to David in the story is an initiative that belongs to Saul, that Saul should have taken. Saul's silence after he has sent for David (v. 31) is odd. A skilled storyteller would have little difficulty using it to highlight the king's fear. At this point in the story the focus is on the contrast between Saul and David.

David is eager to fight the Philistine; Saul is reluctant to let him. Saul's reluctance is not spelled out beyond David's inexperience (youth). Within the context of contrast between the two figures, Saul is paralyzed by unkingly fear. Within the context of the Philistine challenge, Saul may be rightly unwilling to risk the fate of all Israel on the fighting skills of an untested David. The text is silent. No better warrior is named. David protests that it is the LORD who will give him victory. Saul concedes: "Go, and may the LORD be with you" (v. 37).

David's trust in God is brought out in the next two episodes. It is implicit in the symbolism of his refusing the offer of Saul's armor. It is explicit in the speeches exchanged with the Philistines. It is common to tie the rejection of Saul's armor to David's small size, being a boy. Three sources contribute to this image of David: his description as Jesse's eighth and youngest son (16:11-12); the comment by Saul that he is no match for the Philistine (17:33); and the Philistine's disdain (17:42).[14] While there are different traditions at work here, none specifies the size of the youngest son or his absence of military training. The inexperience of the recent recruit and his good looks and lack of impressive equipment can account for all three occurrences.

---

14. The NRSV prejudices the interpretation in translating one and the same Hebrew root in verse 33 by "just a boy" for David and by "from his youth" for the Philistine. In verse 42, it reverts to "only a youth." The qualifiers "just" and "only" are from the interpretation; they are not specified by the text. The precise meaning of the Hebrew *na'ar* is determined by its context. It can be used of an infant (1 Sam 1:22), a young soldier (2 Sam 2:12-17), or a royal overseer (1 Kgs 11:28) — see A. F. Campbell, *The Study Companion to Old Testament Literature* (Collegeville: Liturgical Press, 1989/92), 209. The plain meaning in this context is that David is now what the Philistine was at the start of his military career: a young and untried soldier.

This "small boy" interpretation is in stark contrast with David's self-description in verses 34-35 — fast enough to overtake a marauding predator, strong enough to kill it, and with reflexes good enough to grab it by the jaw. In earlier text, Saul is described as head and shoulders taller than any soldier in Israel (1 Sam 10:23); the offer of Saul's armor to a "small boy" would be narrative nonsense. In the present text, David has been appointed Saul's armor-bearer; a "small boy" does not get the armor-bearer's job. The rejection of Saul's armor is best read symbolically, in conjunction with the exchange of speeches. In rejecting the armor, David turns aside from "the sword and spear" that are not the LORD's instruments (v. 47). In the exchange of speeches, David emphasizes that his trust is explicitly in the LORD.

For a storyteller who wants to exploit it, there is irony here. A big man in Saul's armor has no chance against the giant Philistine. A fast, light-armed slinger, with good reflexes, is militarily Israel's best chance against the big champion. David is the perfect pick.[15] As the speeches are exchanged, David has a stick in his hand and the Philistine focuses on it in his contempt (v. 43). Presumably, the sling in the other hand is behind David's back. The longer the speeches go on, the closer David can get while the Philistine's shield is still on his shield-bearer's arm (v. 41). The closer David gets, the surer his shot will be. All he needs is cool nerves and good luck — and that is where trust in the LORD comes in.

This discussion has taken us a long way from the structural concerns that are central to this paper. It is necessary as an attempt to free the text from the numerous presuppositions that beset it. It is time to move on.

With the preliminaries to battle out of the way, the narrative moves swiftly to the single combat itself. The two antagonists move toward each other and, with a single shot from his sling, David drops his opponent to the ground. The death of the Philistine raises a difficulty, however. According to verse 50, David killed his man with the sling-stone; quite explicitly, the Philistine is dead and there is no sword in David's hand. According to verse 51, to the contrary, David killed his man with the Philistine's own sword; just as explicitly, David drew the Philistine's sword and killed him with it, and then he cut off the Philistine's head. It is not easy to reconcile these two views of the final act of combat.

The final act of the battle story, of course, is the pursuit and plunder. David is reported to have brought the Philistine's head to Jerusalem, at that time a Jebusite city not under Israelite control. Maybe this is an anachronism read back into the text. More likely the meaning is symbolic. The note that

---

15. For some readers, the issue here can be confused by the American usage of slingshot for "a forked stick with an elastic band attached for shooting small stones" (Webster's). In British usage, these are called catapults (Oxford). Confusion with the ancient catapult, used as a siege weapon against walled towns, would be most misleading. The sling — which was "whirled round to discharge its missile by centrifugal force" (Webster's) — was as much a military weapon in ancient Israel as the sword and spear. It was accurate (Judg 20:16); it was standard military equipment subject to normal procurement (2 Chr 26:14).

David brought the Philistine's head to Jerusalem serves as a reminder that it was the Philistine's head that brought David to Jerusalem. David's triumph over this Philistine champion is at the cost of Saul's royal destiny. This deed is symptomatic of David's destiny which will bring him to the throne over all Israel in Jerusalem.

Structurally, what we have seen might be expressed as follows.

I. Introduction	vv. 1-23
A. The battle scene	vv. 1-3
B. The Philistine and his challenge	vv. 4-11
C. David and the challenge	vv. 12-23
II. Complication: David's response to the challenge	vv. 24-40
A. Before the soldiers: what profit is there for David?	vv. 24-31
B. Before the king: what David can do with faith	vv. 32-40
III. Resolution: the single combat	vv. 41-54
A. Preliminaries: exchange of speeches	vv. 41-47
B. Climax: combat and death of the Philistine	vv. 48-51a
C. Conclusion: pursuit and plunder	vv. 51b-54

This analysis, however, rides roughshod over a number of signals in the text. An adequate interpretation should be able to account for the signals in the text within a coherent horizon, all things being equal. The clearest mark of inadequate interpretation is that it leaves significant signals unheeded.

In this case, the signals are:

  i. The triple uneasiness engendered by David's movement to and from court and home (v. 15), by the twice daily challenge over forty days (v. 16), and by the panicked flight of all the Israelites as late in the piece as the fortieth day (v. 24).

  ii. A certain ambiguity in the portrayal of David. Before all the soldiers, he appears inspired by ambition (vv. 25-31). Before the king, he appears inspired by faith in God (vv. 32-40). Situated between these two portrayals is Saul's summoning of David and David's initiative in the conversation. While we have seen that a competent storyteller could well blend these into a harmonious narrative, we note that the text itself does not achieve this harmony.

  iii. There is a dual portrayal of the Philistine's death, killed once by the sling-stone and killed once by his own sword (vv. 50-51).

1 Sam 17:55–18:11. As we have noted already, this block comprises Saul's becoming aware of David's identity, the friendship with Jonathan, David's reputation as a commander, and the emergence of Saul's jealousy toward David; the time lines are complicated.

Abner, the army commander, appears as a new figure in the narrative.[16] The question Saul puts to him is puzzling. Its literal meaning is: whose son is this young man? Yet recently in the narrative Saul was talking to David and did not ask the question (17:31-39); earlier in the narrative David found favor in Saul's sight and was engaged as armor-bearer and lyre-player, by royal command sent to his father Jesse (16:19-22). When David is finally brought before Saul (17:57-58), the information that Saul elicits is information that in the narrative he has known since David's arrival at the court or that at least he might have asked before permitting David to accept the Philistine's challenge. The literal meaning is difficult. The question remains open whether a different understanding can throw light on the question.[17]

The next section within the block does not shed light directly on the point of Saul's question. A deep and committed friendship between David and Jonathan is reported. It could have been triggered by the appearance on the scene of this newcomer; it could equally have been triggered by the heroic achievement of the recently appointed armor-bearer. Saul's action in keeping David at court (18:2) could report the engagement of a newcomer; it could equally report the termination of David's freedom to go back and forth to his father's house (cf. 17:15).[18] Even the transfer of Jonathan's gear to David is open to two interpretations: either Jonathan's equipping the newly arrived slinger or the sign of his new friendship for the young armor-bearer. A storyteller could clarify these ambiguities. The text does not.

The report of David's success (18:5) extends well beyond the record of Jonathan's friendship offered to David. David is given a command, which meets with the approval of Saul's troops. A considerable period of time is in view. The exercise of command, the gaining of success, and the winning of the soldiers' approval are all part of David's establishing a reputation, once he is taken into Saul's court.

The final section in this block returns to the time period associated with the Philistine battle. The song of the women greeting the returning warriors angers Saul and provokes Saul's jealousy. A whole new horizon is suddenly created by Saul's angry rhetoric: "What more can he have but the kingdom?" (18:8).

The jealousy which started by stirring within Saul's mind is promptly brought on to the stage of the external world. The evil spirit from God which

16. Abner is first named in the summary of Saul's household, 1 Sam 14:50-51. After his role here, he reappears at Saul's side in 1 Sam 20:25 and 26:5, 7, 14-15. Later he leads the house of Saul against David, until his apparent peace mission ends in his assassination by Joab.

17. We remember that the literal meaning of David's taking the Philistine's head to the foreign city of Jerusalem made no sense. On a symbolic level, it could be a pointer to the significance of this victory — it began David's move to kingship over Israel in Jerusalem.

18. See Polzin, 171-76.

has so far tormented and disempowered Saul now moves him to the folly of destroying Israel's deliverer. Twice Saul seeks to spear David; twice David eludes him.

The structure of the block in its literal sense is as follows.

I.	Introduction of David to Saul: identity	17:55-58
II.	Incorporation of David into Saul's court	18:1-6a
	A. Jonathan's devotion to David	v. 1
	B. Saul's engagement of David	v. 2
	C. Jonathan's demonstration of friendship	vv. 3-4
III.	Establishment of David's reputation as a commander	v. 5
IV.	Conclusion: onset of Saul's jealousy	vv. 6-11
	A. In Saul's mind	vv. 6-9
	B. In Saul's action	vv. 10-11

1 Sam 18:12-16. This is a fascinating block of text. It opens with theological interpretation of the situation, moves to narrative report, and concludes with comments on each of the three players in the contest for royal power in Israel. First, Saul's fear of David is noted and theologically interpreted: because the LORD was with David but had departed from Saul. Then the text notes Saul's action as a result of his fear: he removes David from the court and gives him a senior command. Saul has made two errors. He has removed the source of his own healing. He has put David in a position where he will enhance his reputation and transform Saul's fears for his kingdom into political reality.

The final three verses of the block sum up the situation. David is successful, because the LORD is with him. Saul is fearful, because of David's success. All Israel and Judah love David, because of his military leadership. The issue of military leadership is repeated in almost identical language in 2 Sam 5:2.[19] The narrative is clear that the kingship is on the line.

The structural representation is as follows.

I.	Theological comment on the situation	v. 12
II.	Report of consequent action	v. 13
	A. Taken by Saul	v. 13a
	B. Achieved by David	v. 13b
III.	Summary comment	vv. 14-16
	A. Concerning David	v. 14
	B. Concerning Saul	v. 15
	C. Concerning all Israel and Judah	v. 16

19. It is "went out and came in before them" *(qal)* in 1 Sam 18:16. It is "led out and brought in Israel" *(hiphil)* in 2 Sam 5:2. Unfortunately, the NRSV does not catch this echo as effectively as it might.

1 Sam 18:17-30. The final block takes up the issue of marriage to the king's daughter, which was part of the reward the soldiers assured David would come with victory. As a conclusion to this narrative, the royal marriage is no longer the victor's reward. Saul wants David dead and is willing to use his daughters as bait in the process.

Merab is first offered as a wife, not for the past victory but on condition of future valor. The initiative is Saul's. His thought is simple — let the Philistines kill David for me: "I will not raise a hand against him; let the Philistines deal with him" (18:17). In due course, Merab is given to another.

The second time, Michal makes it easy for Saul. She falls in love with David. This time the story is more complex and Saul negotiates through intermediaries. This time Saul is also trickier. He asks for a marriage present that ought give the Philistines every opportunity to kill David for him — he asks for one hundred Philistine foreskins. David delivers. The marriage occurs. Saul's fear turns to hostility. David's success increases.

The structural representation can be briefly noted.

I.	First attempt to eliminate David: Merab	vv. 17-19
II.	Second attempt to eliminate David: Michal	vv. 20-29
III.	Conclusion: David's success increases	v. 30

Analyzing the Relationships of the Blocks to the Whole

The task that lies before us at this stage is the most challenging in the process of interpretation. Now that the blocks have been established and their components analyzed, the data are available to determine the overall shape of the text. It is now time to put the pieces together. We are rather like someone doing a jigsaw puzzle. The box has been emptied, the pieces have been counted and sorted according to the major components of the picture where they might belong; then the picture has to be assembled.

Earlier, we established a broad preliminary structure.

I. Prelude to battle: introduction of David to court of Saul
II. Story of battle
III. Aftermath of battle
    A. Introduction of David to court of Saul
    B. Saul's jealousy toward David

The study of the elements within each block has not changed this basic perception. The difficulty of the double introduction of David into Saul's court remains. Rather than being lessened, the difficulty has increased because further signs of duality have emerged in the course of closer study.

To recapitulate, the difficulties are:

a. David's going back and forth appears to harmonize two introductory sections (17:15).
b. The Philistine's repetition of his challenge twice a day for forty days seems a similar harmonization (17:16).
c. Israel's flight and panic after forty days appears forced (17:24).
d. Ambiguity in the portrayal of David before and after his meeting with Saul (17:25-30, 32-37).
e. Saul's silence after sending for David (17:31-32).
f. Duality in the report of the Philistine's death (17:50-51).
g. Saul's sudden and belated interest in David's identity (17:55-58).

In analyzing the relationship of the blocks in this narrative to the whole narrative, these difficulties pose a primary question. Can we find the most satisfactory meaning in relating the blocks to each other in a single narrative sequence? Or can we find meaning more satisfactorily in some other way of relating these blocks?

Since part of the problem is the existence of two introductions of David to the court of Saul, an obvious solution is to eliminate the first one from the story. If the text begins with 17:1, the difficulty may be thought to disappear. Unfortunately it does not. First, Saul's interest in David's identity, at the moment when David is on his way out to meet the Philistine, remains odd; it would seem appropriate when they spoke together earlier in the story. Second, the other pointers to duality, noted above as c, d, e, and f, remain as obstacles to a single narrative sequence. If the forty days is set aside as a later harmonization, the Philistine's challenge and Israel's fear are still reported as two pairs of events, first in 17:10-11 and then in 17:23-24 — although verses 23-24 might be seen as a repetition meant to bring the flashback up-to-date with the main story. The other difficulties remain: the ambiguous portrayal of David, Saul's silence, and the manner of the Philistine's death. Further-more, if 16:14-23 is not part of the narrative, the context for Saul's fear about the loss of his kingdom is changed (18:8, 14-16). With 16:14-23, Saul's kingdom is at risk because the spirit of the LORD has departed from him (16:14).

Another approach offered is to eliminate the second introduction. Effec-tively, this is what Robert Polzin does. For him, Saul's question to David — "Whose son are you, young man?" — is not about identity but about loyalty. "Saul's question carries with it a threat of coercion, for Saul thereby asks David formally to renounce Jesse's paternity in favor of his own. . . . The king recog-nizes how necessary it is that David give his full allegiance to him by renouncing Jesse's paternal hold over him. . . . As for David, his straightforward answer carries with it a refusal to respond as Saul would have wished, and the chapter ends on a note of defiance that will necessitate Saul's immediate and coercive reaction. . . ."[20] So there is no longer a second introduction of David; instead there is the issue of loyalty and permanence at Saul's court.

Unfortunately, this interpretation flies in the face of the plain sense of the words. Of course a polite reply can communicate veiled defiance — but hardly here. Can all of the weight of Saul's demand for exclusive loyalty be expressed in so ambiguous a form? How is it to be projected back to make sense of the earlier question to Abner — is Abner being asked where David's loyalties lie? Hebrew has adequate words for dealing with matters of choice and loyalty. They are absent here. In order to achieve sequential coherence in the narrative, the exchange is being asked to mean what it does not say. Texts can do that; in this text, in my judgment, it is not plausible.

How, then, can a meaningful relationship be established between the component blocks of 1 Sam 16:14–18:30? The earlier references to duality point to the simple solution of two or more traditions. Nevertheless, the same question remains: can a meaningful relationship be established between the component traditions of 1 Sam 16:14–18:30? The appeal to sources or traditions does not answer the question of the meaningfulness we can discern in the present text.

If a single sequential narrative seems to be excluded, there is another option to be considered. Earlier, we discussed the possibility that at least some of our biblical texts are best understood as "the basis from which a narrator's performance began" (above, p. 87). If so, a biblical text might well offer a gifted storyteller more than one way of telling a story. Where two or more stories were traditional, the text — as the basis for a narrator's performance — might well include key aspects of both stories, or tell one in its entirety and include key aspects of the other. In my judgment, this possibility makes eminent sense in the case of 1 Sam 16:14–18:30.

Before presenting the structure analysis which attempts to summarize these observations, one aspect needs to be emphasized. Anyone familiar with the differ-

---

20. Polzin, 175. I admire Polzin's passion for the present text and I have learned much from him. Here, however, I have to differ. Polzin celebrates the quality of repetition as a central characteristic in this story (pp. 163-64). But such signals are set in the text to generate meaning, and the meaningfulness of much of this repetition needs to be made clear. Similarly the artfulness of segments of the narrative, indicated by Polzin (pp. 164-67), is to be expected of good storytelling. What needs to be shown is how these various gems of the narrator's art combine to form an artful whole.

D. W. Gooding takes another tack, seeing the text focusing on the identity of David's father so that his family may be free in Israel (cf. 17:25; *Story of David and Goliath*, 60). In our context, this still creates difficulty for a unitary text. Saul is given Jesse's name before he is given David's (16:18). Apart from this, Gooding's view remains problematic since the family is honored through David alone, without reference to Jesse — if these attempts on David's life are to be considered honors. Note that the reward was not promised by Saul but talked about by the soldiers.

ences between the Greek and Hebrew manuscripts[21] in this text will be aware that the division within the following structure does not correspond completely with the difference in the text traditions. The structure has been driven by the present Masoretic Text of the Hebrew Bible; it has not been driven by concern for the earlier textual versions. By and large, the main story mirrors the text common to both Hebrew and Greek text traditions; the variant sections reflect material that is found in the Hebrew but not in the Greek. However, the structure below includes in the main story the following verses that are not part of the text common to both traditions, i.e., that are not found in the Greek: 17:41, 48b; 18:6a*, 10-11, 12b, as well as 17:50 (noted as a variant). On the other hand, the structure includes in the variant story 18:20-29a, which is part of the text common to both Greek and Hebrew traditions (except for 18:21b). In the present text, the marriage stories in 18:17-30 are associated with the variant story through the assurance given David of the gift of the king's daughter for the man who kills this Philistine (17:25-26). Saul's realization in 18:28 that the LORD is with David, a main-story theme, is too commonplace to carry weight against the marriage interest.

What this structure analysis identifies are the relationships discernible within the present biblical text. How these relate to the sources which may have been used to compile the present text is a question for source criticism (see below). It is part of the exegetical process. But it should be subordinate to the interpretation of the present text as a whole. What this structure analysis makes surprisingly clear is that the present text is more than and different from the sum of its component parts. The usual process of exegesis, beginning with text criticism and source criticism, will miss this reality by the simple fact of the process. To this degree, the process is prejudicial. Structure analysis, as process, is a relatively neutral way into the text.

The structure of the text, then, unfolds as follows.

I. Main story: opening	16:14–17:11
A. Introduction: coming of David to the court of Saul	16:14-23
1. Need: Saul's plight	v. 14
2. Remedy: lyre-player	vv. 15-16
3. Outcome: David's entry into Saul's service	vv. 17-23
B. Story of battle	17:1-54*
1. Introduction: the battle scene	vv. 1-3
2. Challenge and single combat	vv. 4-51*
a. The challenge	vv. 4-40*
1) Challenge from the Philistine	vv. 4-10
2) Response from Israel	vv. 11-40*
a) From Saul and all Israel: fear	v. 11

21. See E. Tov, "The David and Goliath Saga: How a Biblical Editor Combined the Two Versions," *Bible Review* 2,4 (1986): 34-41, with a graphic presentation on 37-38.

IA. Variant story: opening	*vv. 12-31*
A. David and the Philistine challenge	*vv. 12-23*
B. David's response to the challenge	*vv. 24-30*
C. Saul summons David	*v. 31*
II. Main story: continuation —	vv. 32-54
b) From David: courage	vv. 32-40
b. The single combat	vv. 41-51a
1) Pre-battle speeches	vv. 41-47
2) Battle proper	vv. 48-51
a) The approach	v. 48
b) Victory to David by the sling	v. 49
c) Death of the Philistine	vv. 50-51
(1) Version 1: no sword	v. 50
(2) Version 2: Philistine's sword	v. 51a
3. Conclusion: pursuit and plunder	vv. 51b-54
IIA. Variant story: coming of David to the court of Saul	*17:55–18:5*
A. Introduction of David to Saul	*17:55-58*
B. Incorporation of David into Saul's circle	*18:1-5*
1. Jonathan's devotion to David	*v. 1*
2. David's entry into Saul's service	*v. 2*
3. Jonathan's demonstration of friendship	*vv. 3-4*
C. Reputation of David as a commander	*v. 5*
III. Main story: conclusion	vv. 6-16
A. Onset of Saul's jealousy	vv. 6-13
1. Influenced by the song of the women	vv. 6-9
2. Influenced by an evil spirit	vv. 10-11
3. Influenced by fear	vv. 12-13
B. Concluding summary comment	vv. 14-16
1. Concerning David	v. 14
2. Concerning Saul	v. 15
3. Concerning all Israel and Judah	v. 16
IIIA. Variant story: conclusion	*vv. 17-30*
A. First attempt to eliminate David: Merab	*vv. 17-19*
B. Second attempt to eliminate David: Michal	*vv. 20-29*
C. Conclusion: David's success increases	*v. 30*

This is not a normal structure analysis by Knierim's standards. I am not sure whether he would approve the paralleling of I-II-III by IA-IIA-IIIA. Normal structure analyses flow in a smooth consecutive sequence; but this is not a normal text. I did not envisage such a structure when I began this article. My only justification is the claim that this structure was forced on me by the text — to my surprise.

The Roman numerals I-II-III and IA-IIA-IIIA do not represent the narrative flow within the text as a whole; rather, they indicate the major blocks of each story in the text. This is particularly clear for the heading "II. Main story: continuation — " which, within its own story, comes between two contiguous verses portraying the responses from Israel to the Philistine's challenge (17:11 and 32). The narrative sequence within each story is begun at the levels of A-B-C. Note, e.g., "A. Introduction" and "B. Story of battle" under the over-arching heading "I. Main story: opening."

This is a good example of the difference between "a text" and "the text." Where we have a coherent unified narrative, to the best of our knowledge of the ancient Israelite conventions, we have "a text" — e.g., the main story here. When, as here, the coherent unified narrative has been augmented by enhance-ments or variant versions, etc., that disrupt the unity and flow of that narrative, we do not have "a text." We have "the text" — the present biblical text. Here, "the text" is structured at the level I-II-III and IA-IIA-IIIA. The levels A-B-C and beyond structure what is either "a text" (the main story) or key elements of "a text" (the variant story). It is a mistake to assume that "the text" always constitutes "a text" — at least in the sense used here.[22]

A couple of points need noting. First, the structure analysis presents the component elements of the text in their relation to each other and to the whole so that what we might call the text's skeletal structure emerges, which inter-pretation must clothe with the flesh of meaning. The analysis has not been represented in comprehensive detail or with full attention to aspects of form. Nevertheless, the skeletal structure is clear.

The main story has its three parts: introduction, story of battle, and conclusion. The elements within these are clear. For the introduction: need, remedy, and outcome; for the story of battle: the battle scene, challenge and single combat, and pursuit and plunder; for the conclusion: onset of Saul's jealousy and summary comment. Within each of these, the component elements are identified where appropriate.

The variant story is incorporated at three nodal points. The main story has David come to the court of Saul as lyre-player and armor-bearer. The first variant has David come to the battle from his father's farm, hear the Philistine's challenge, and explore the possibilities that it opens for David. The second variant offers a different view of how David came to the court of Saul: his introduction to Saul after killing the Philistine, his incorporation into Saul's circle, and the establishment of his reputation as a commander. The third variant offers two accounts of Saul's attempt to eliminate David using his daughters as bait.

As presented, there is not a continuity between these three blocks of text.

22. For further discussion of the concepts of "a text" and "the text," see A. F. Campbell, "Past History and Present Text: The Clash of Classical and Post-critical Approaches to Biblical Text," *AusBR* 39 (1991): 1-18.

There is a gap between David's response to the challenge (vv. 24-30) and his introduction to Saul (v. 55). We may assume that a storyteller would have no difficulty filling such a gap. What we do not know is whether the storyteller would choose to have David summoned to Saul. The inquiry about David's identity suggests not, so that David would have been depicted moving against the Philistine without a commission from Saul. In this scenario, 17:31 becomes a bridging verse without structural significance. There is a second gap between the establishment of David's reputation as a successful commander and the attempts by Saul to have him killed. Again, we may assume such a gap is easily filled by a storyteller.

It is worth noting how small observations control the analysis of structure. The pursuit and plunder (17:51b-54) is not the conclusion to the single combat. It returns to the wider perspective of the battle scene, with all the Philistines and the Israelites. The reputation of David as a commander (18:5) is not part of his incorporation into Saul's circle. Its purview is far wider in terms of time and people involved. Accurate structure analysis, like responsible interpretation, is built on close observation of the text in its form and content, its grammar and syntax, and its interrelatedness.

Second, the text manifests both unity and duality. Any claim to the meaning of the text must account both for its unity and its duality.

Establishing an Initial Hypothesis as to the Meaning of the Text

What is the basic conceptualization that underpins the text? What meaning for the text can we generate which makes best sense of the features revealed by the structure analysis?

How do we account for the unity and duality which is so striking a feature of this text? In my judgment, this is best done by seeing this text not as the final product of literary output but as a starting point from which literary output is produced. The text is not conceptualized as a performed or polished story. It is rather the basis from which a storyteller's performance might begin. The justification for this view is the presence in the text of two story lines, one relatively complete, the other with significant gaps. While both stories reflect the same event, they deal with it quite differently. The event which powers the two stories is David's single combat with a Philistine champion.

The two stories could have been preserved separately; this happens elsewhere in the Davidic traditions. Duality would reign. The interweaving of the two indicates a desire to retain both traditions and a concern for their unity. The concern for unity makes good sense if the story of David's fight with the Philistine was widely seen as the charismatic point of departure for his rise to being Israel's king. The unity of the event must be maintained, while differing views of how it took place are preserved. In one view, David's charisma is fueled by faith, within the context of God's activity; in the other, it is driven by the coincidence of opportunity and ambition.

The main story opens with David coming to Saul's court to soothe the troubled king, because the spirit of the LORD has departed from Saul. It concludes with Saul's jealousy and fear for his kingdom and with the narrator's summary comment which points to David's ultimate leadership over all Israel and Judah. A glance at the structure analysis shows that the response to the Philistine challenge is twofold.

a) From Saul and all Israel: fear   v. 11

b) From David: courage   v. 32

In the present text, these are separated by the variant story's introduction. In the main story, the verses stand side by side. In the main story, Saul and David stood side by side — the king and his armor-bearer. In the main story, Saul's unkingly cowardice and David's kingly courage stand in stark contrast. The contrast is pursued in what follows. The Philistine is portrayed sharing Saul's view of David — to Saul's shame, narratively speaking. The contrast reaches its peak in the summary comment: the dispirited Saul is in awe of the successful David, who is admired as leader by all Israel and Judah.

This main story lays out in microcosm the path by which the much more extensive Story of David's Rise leads David to kingship over Israel and Judah.[23] David, who trusts in the LORD (17:37), succeeds in all his undertakings because the LORD is with him (16:18 and 18:14).

The variant story is set in a different context. The youngest son comes from the family farm to visit his three elder brothers who are in service with Saul's army. He hears the Philistine's challenge and is assured that fame and fortune will go to the soldier who kills the challenger. When he has slain the Philistine with a well-placed stone from his sling, he is summoned before Saul. He is rewarded with a place at court, the friendship of the crown prince, and a significant military command. Finally, the variant story takes up the theme of marriage to the king's daughter, an assurance given earlier by the soldiers (17:25). However, the promise of marriage has become Saul's attempt to eliminate David, now seen as a rival. A hero to the end, David triumphs over the snares set by Saul and Saul is confirmed in fear.

The variant story takes David's path to the throne and tells of its beginning in a folktale in which the youngest son seized the opportunity to distinguish himself, win a place at court, and gain the hand of the king's daughter in marriage. The note of Saul's hostility and fear allows the folktale to lead into the well-known traditions of the struggle between Saul and David for power in Israel.

23. See A. F. Campbell, "From Philistine to Throne (1 Sam 16:14–18:16)," *AusBR* 34 (1986): 35-41.

The text, as we have it, offers a storyteller the option of telling one version or the other or, perhaps, of combining elements from both. For example, a flashback technique could be used to combine the opening of the main story (16:14–17:11) with the start of the variant story (17:12-23). The storyteller has two versions to choose from for the Philistine's death. If verse 50 is selected, perhaps for theological reasons, part of the plundering will need to include the severing of the giant's head, with a view to either verse 54 or verse 57. Similarly, the storyteller has three motifs to choose from in depicting the onset of Saul's jealousy; a choice might be made, or all three might be exploited. The same can be said of the offers of Merab and Michal in marriage.

On the other hand, we may assume that a storyteller would not select contradictory elements from the text. If the main story's account of David's coming to the court of Saul is used (16:14-23), the variant version would have to be omitted (17:55–18:5). David's ambition in the variant story (17:25-30) would not sit well alongside the portrayal of David's faith in the main story (17:32-37).

It may seem that we are requiring too much of an ancient storyteller, apparently asked to be aware of the results of modern analytic exegesis. It is my assumption that Israel's storytellers were familiar with their repertoire and recognized automatically what we moderns have to labor to discover. We come to the text as a unity and laboriously discover its duality. They, on the other hand, were familiar with both storytelling traditions; presumably, they would have had little difficulty identifying their respective traits.

Conclusion

The process of structure analysis, as we have explored it in this example, has been principally at the preliminary level. The analysis has served as a relatively neutral tool to open up the text for interpretation. The text has merely been opened up. It is now ready for exploration with all the tools and insights that modern exegesis brings to the interpretative process.

Text-critical study can now be done while being aware of the function of each part of the text within the whole. In some cases, this can be highly significant for text-critical decisions.[24]

Source-critical (or literary-critical) study not only can examine the identification of main and variant stories in the analysis, but will go further to examine the textual traditions and their relevance for understanding the sources

---

24. In this area, for this text, see particularly the work of Barthélemy, Gooding, Lust, and Tov in *The Story of David and Goliath*. The close association between text and source/literary criticism recurs through the final reflections (pp. 121-54).

of this text. As we pointed out above, the analysis of the present text does not correspond 100 percent with the division into textual traditions. The text is more than its component sources. Study of the interplay of sources and final text can illuminate the text's meaning and its possible functions for a storyteller.

Form-critical study can assess the present text as compilation and go beyond to study the traditions which have been incorporated into it or are associated with it. Attention to the bridging verses, in conjunction with redaction criticism, may sharpen our focus on the nature of the compiled text.

Tradition history can situate the text in its place in Israel's literature. Where does the material come from? What are its links to traditions not included in this text? What is the correlation between the main story and the Story of David's Rise? Where does the variant story fit in the Davidic traditions? What other associations can be traced?

Redaction criticism may be concerned for the bridging verses, in particular 17:15, 16, 31. Is there any evidence that enables us to know whether they were part of the original compilation or were added later? The implications of this question are important for understanding the nature of the compilation. Equally, redaction criticism will be sensitive to the possibility of later theological touches or observations, such as 18:5 or 12b, for example.

As these areas are being explored, the initial hypothesis as to the meaning of the text is constantly challenged or confirmed. Space does not allow a detailed presentation here; an outline will have to do.

In my judgment, the horizon most appropriate for finding meaning in this text is not that of a unified narrative composition. The nature of the materials found in the text suggests a focus on the unity of the combat story as a significant event, coupled with the expression of two different optics for viewing this event.

The central focus of the text is David's emergence into public prominence through his victory over the Philistine challenger at a climactic point in the Israel-Philistine conflict.

The main story associates David's prominence from the outset with the issue of kingship (16:14; 18:9). This story is set within a major theological interpretation of political developments. Its opening statement is that the spirit of the LORD has departed from Saul. Its central image is less the triumphant slinger and the prostrate Philistine than the dispirited and fearful Saul compared with the courageous and spirited David. The point of the story is that David came to power in Israel because he stepped into the vacuum left by Saul's failure of nerve in the critical area of Israel's survival against the Philistines. David's success is theologically interpreted as the LORD's being with him when Israel was bereft of royal deliverance. It depicts in microcosm what is painted with a broad brush in the Story of David's Rise. This is a story of royal failure and divine favor.

Right or wrong, this is a tendentious interpretation of the process that brought David to power. It was not shared throughout Israel (cf. the views of

Shimei ben Gera, 2 Sam 16:5-8). Perhaps that is why the variant story is also preserved, with its key elements incorporated into the text.

In the variant story, the central issue is still David's rise to prominence. However, God's guidance and even Saul's failure are pushed firmly into the background. David seizes opportunity when it is offered. David comes on the scene in time to hear the Philistine's challenge. He realizes that an agile slinger is more than a match for the lumbering infantryman. He sees his chance and grasps it. Without the comment in 17:11 and perhaps with no report of David's coming into Saul's presence, the king's paralyzed fear is swallowed up in the general statement that all the Israelites were very much afraid (17:24). In the text we have identified as the variant story, the LORD's favor is left unmentioned until 18:28.[25] This is a story of singular chance swiftly seized.

Prophetic circles will later claim that David's rise to power was triggered by their prophetic anointing (16:1-13).[26] The two traditions in 1 Sam 16:14–18:30 have as their common focus that David's prominence in Israel began with his victory over a Philistine champion. The main story, associating the combat with the Story of David's Rise, depicts a flawed and abandoned Saul and a divinely favored David. It is highly compatible with the prophetic view in 16:1-13. Far less compatible with the prophetic claim is the variant story, with its portrayal of an ambitious young man seizing on a window of opportunity, although it too could be used to begin a different version of David's rise to power. Israel kept both these traditions alive, while remembering that both bore on one and the same moment of human experience.

Finally, when all this work has been done, the structure analysis can be revisited. After playing its initial role as a starting point, and providing a framework and control point during subsequent study, it can play its final role as a summary point. If we fill out the analysis for ourselves in detail, single element by single element, we will know whether we have found a coherent horizon within which all the signals of the text can be situated, interpreted, and given meaning. If successful, we will have good grounds to claim that we have found "that center of unity which is at the heart of every artistic creation." The complexity of the work will have yielded up an adequate and responsible meaning.

---

25. In the separation according to textual traditions, 18:28 belongs with the main story, leaving the variant story fully secular.

26. See, e.g., A. F. Campbell, *Of Prophets and Kings: A Late Ninth-Century Document (1 Samuel 1–2 Kings 10)*, CBQMS 17 (Washington, D.C.: Catholic Biblical Association of America, 1986).

Festival Ideology in Chronicles[1]

SIMON J. DE VRIES

1-2 Chronicles, composed in the Persian dependency of Yehud sometime during the fourth century B.C.E., is a work that exhibits an inordinately large variety of formal genres and set phrases or formulas. I have discovered that it contains also a number of special schemata which together provide most of the narrative framework for the history of the kings from Solomon to Zedekiah. These are: (1) a schema of dynastic endangerment, featuring the tension between the fulfillment of the dynastic promise and an insatiable blood lust among the Omride Baalists and their Judahite in-laws;[2] (2) a schema of revelational appearances, which is a pattern in which the bearers of revelation offer assurance and encouragement to good kings and threaten wrath on bad kings, or on good kings doing bad; (3) a schema of reward and retribution, featuring a repeated cycle of virtue and reward, apostasy and punishment; and (4) a festival schema, a pattern for the religious festivals held by several exemplary kings and following this sequence: date, identification of participants, description of ritual, and a celebration of rejoicing. I wish to take the present opportunity for enlarging upon what I have said about this fourth schema in my 1989 FOTL commentary.

---

1. Short sections from S. J. De Vries, *1-2 Chronicles,* FOTL 11 (Grand Rapids: Eerdmans, 1989), 102-5, 113, 119-20, 275-77, have been included in this article by permission of the publishers.
2. Cf. S. J. De Vries, "The Schema of Dynastic Endangerment in Chronicles," *Proceedings, Eastern Great Lakes and Midwest Biblical Societies* 7 (1987): 59-77.

I. The Festival Schema

In my article "Moses and David as Cult Founders in Chronicles,"[3] I argued that David completely overshadows Moses as the guarantor of proper religion in the period of the rebuilt temple. The ideological program of the Chronicler identifies David as the prototypical figure of the *Urzeit* rather than of an *Endzeit* yet to come. However, the Davidic kings have no special cultic function in Chronicles. Numerous references to kings making sacrifices (e.g., in 1 Chr 21:28) must be understood to mean that they presented the sacrificial animals while the priests carried out the actual ritual. The Chronicler has much to say about regulations for priests and Levites, but nothing whatever for the king. All the same, the king is given an august place of importance as the founder, patron, and supervisor of temple and ritual. We think especially of David and Solomon, of Asa and Jehoshaphat, of Hezekiah and Josiah.

The temple dominates the entire book of 1-2 Chronicles. David prepares for it and Solomon builds it. Early Israel's cult objects and cult traditions are drawn into it: ark, tabernacle or tent of meeting, altar of the holocaust, Mount Moriah. Solomon dedicates the temple; Ahaz defiles it; Joash, Hezekiah, and Josiah repair it and cleanse it; Nebuchadnezzar destroys it. The Chronicler allows others (Ezra 3:8ff.; 6:14ff.) to tell how it was rebuilt after the return from exile, but the very way in which he specifies the temple duties of the Levites and other orders shows that it surely existed in his time. He is also concerned to imply that the temple could again and again be repaired and reconsecrated or defiled and destroyed. The religious festivals, including the Passover, were now pilgrim feasts and were celebrated at the Jerusalem temple. Attendance at these festivals was motivated by sincere piety and always resulted in profound and universal rejoicing.[4]

The obvious Hezekiah/Josiah versus David/Solomon typology is intended to put attendance at the Passover festival on an equal plane with honor to the temple itself; by telling of two successive Passovers, the Chronicler shows his postexilic contemporaries that this is the premier sacral time, and the temple the premier holy place, for Ideal Israel to realize its unity and worship Yahweh as its one god.

The Passover feasts of Hezekiah and Josiah, together with the Weeks (*šābuʿôt*) festival of Asa, are based structurally on Solomon's Tabernacles festival, which happens also to be the feast for the dedication of the temple. Sukkoth or Tabernacles had always been a feast of special joy for the Israelites. 2 Chr 5:3

---

3. S. J. De Vries, "Moses and David as Cult Founders in Chronicles," *JBL* 107 (1988): 619-39.

4. Neh 7:73–8:18; 12:43 combine elements of the festival schema, but without the clear patterning of Chronicles. This is one among a number of weighty considerations against common authorship for Ezra-Nehemiah and Chronicles.

modifies the prescribed festival calendar in such a way as to bring "all the men of Israel," i.e., males prepared for the festival, to Jerusalem "at the feast that is in the seventh month," but this must mean that they came ahead of time, prepared for Tabernacles, because 2 Chr 7:8 reports that the dedication ceremonies led directly into a "feast for seven days," explained in the following verse as being for "the dedication of the altar,[5] seven days," after which "the feast [*heḥāg;* cf. 5:3]" was kept another seven days (successively rather than contemporaneously), after which the "eighth day" came for a "solemn assembly [*'ăṣeret;* cf. Lev 23:36]." This brings the narrative to "the twenty-third day of the seventh month" (v. 10), the regular time for concluding Tabernacles.

Figure 1 shows how the five passages that exhibit the festival schema compare with one another. From this outline it may be seen that (1) the opening notice, (2) the identification of the participants, (3) an account of the ceremonies, and (4) the notice of a joyful celebration at the end are features of these narratives. The identification of the participants includes a notice of purification in three passages but is omitted in 2 Chronicles 7 and 35. Structurally, this is meant as part of (2) above rather than (3), for the notice of purification precedes the identification of the participants in two passages, 2 Chronicles 15 and 29. In chapter 30, where it follows the identification of the participants, it appears both before and after the notice of date. The elements of purification and of participants precede the notice of date in 2 Chronicles 15 and 30, but an initial place for the date is made secure by attention to its position in the text that is the obvious model of all the others: 2 Chronicles 7 (par. 1 Kgs 8). Thus, we see that in the deployment of this schema, rigidity of order has given way to a fluidity that is expressive of a creative freedom on the Chronicler's part.

This freedom is seen also in his narrative development pertaining to the various ceremonies. In 2 Chronicles 7 and 35 this occupies but a single verse, being restricted to a notice that the ceremony in question was held, along with a statement that the duration of the festival was in compliance with the regulation. In 2 Chronicles 15 this element is fleshed out to include information about the covenant oath. In chapter 29, fifteen verses are given over to the enumeration of intricate details, but this is because this is also a rededication festival. In chapter 30, containing the account of Hezekiah's actual Passover, a statement of procedures is expanded by interpretive elements concerning the attitude of king and people.

---

5. It is evident that the Chronicler intends the phrase *kî ḥănukkat hammizbēaḥ 'āśû* as a comprehensive summary of the entire dedication ceremony (cf. 7:5b par. 1 Kgs 8:63b, where the verb *ḥnk* has as its object *'et-bêt YHWH/hā'ĕlōhîm*, not the altar in itself; cf. 1 Kgs 8:64b par. 2 Chr 7:7b). The dedicatory declaration that the Chronicler puts in David's mouth in 1 Chr 22:1 places "the house *[bêt]* of Yahweh" and "the altar of burnt offering for Israel" in close parallelism. Cf. the special notice concerning the altar in 2 Chr 4:1 (without a counterpart in Kings).

Figure 1. Passages Exhibiting the Festival Schema

2 Chr 7	2 Chr 15	2 Chr 29	2 Chr 30	2 Chr 35
(Solomon)	(Asa)	(Hezekiah)	(Hezekiah)	(Josiah)
Dedication (= Tabernacles)	Covenant renewal (= Weeks)	Rededication	Passover/ Mazzoth	Passover/ Mazzoth
Seventh month	Third month	First month	Second Month	First Month
	Purification, 8			
	Participants, 9		Participants, 1-13a	
			Purification, 14	
Date, 8a (5:3)	Date, 10	Date, 3a, 17	Date, 15a (2, 13)	Date, 1
Participants, 8b				
		Purification, 3b-19	Purification, 15b-20	
		Participants, 20		
				Preparations, 2-16
Ceremonies, 9	Ceremonies, 11-14	Ceremonies, 21-35	Ceremonies, 21-24	Ceremonies, 17-18
1) Dedication 7 days			1) Mazzoth	Mazzoth 7 days
2) Feast 7 days			2) Feast 7 days	
Date, 10aα				Date, 19
Dismissal, 10aβ				
Celebration, 10b	Celebration, 15	Celebration, 36	Celebration, 25-26	
			Dismissal, 27	

This last passage is especially noteworthy because it endeavors to replicate the seven days of feasting from chapter 7. The Chronicler seems especially anxious here to legitimize Hezekiah's second-month Passover and the novelty of a second seven-day festival by drawing forward the element of celebration. Thus verse 21 states that the proper Mazzoth ceremony for the first seven days was held *bĕśimḥâ gĕdôlâ*, "with great rejoicing," and verse 23 states that the second seven-day ceremony was kept with rejoicing (*śimḥâ*). This turns the concluding element of celebration, verses 25-26, into a resumptive summary, with the operative verb *wayyiśmĕḥû*, "and they rejoiced," foremost in verse 25 and the verbal clause *wattĕhî śimḥâ-gĕdôlâ bîrûśālāyim*, "and there was great joy in Jerusalem," foremost in verse 26. A statement of incomparability appears in each of the two Passover accounts, but in chapter 30 this is part of the celebration notice (v. 26), while it is part of the description of ceremonies in 35:18. Only the Josiah account lacks the element of celebration.

It does not seem venturesome to suggest that the Chronicler shaped his narratives of festival ritual from his observation of, and participation in, the temple services as they were actually observed in his own time. During the postexilic period the same four elements would have retained their paramount importance: (1) a proper date; (2) ritual preparation of the participants and rites of purification for the holy precincts; (3) the ceremonies and rituals proper to the respective festivals; and (4) the holy joy that would come upon all worshipers both during and following the feast. The Chronicler was almost certainly a Levite, perhaps even a member of the guild of singers. He would himself have been a devout and happy worshiper.

In addition to this element of personal interest and experience, the Chronicler found what were to him historical sources in Kings that referred in one way or another to the festival liturgy: specifically, the account of Solomon's dedication of the temple in 1 Kings 8 and the brief notice of Josiah's Passover in 2 Kgs 23:21-23. For Asa and Hezekiah no such notice had been preserved, yet the Chronicler did find in 1 Kgs 15:12-15 and 2 Kgs 18:4 notices of these kings' cultic reforms focusing on the temple. These were evidently stimulus enough to set him to speculating about important festival observances during the reigns of these two kings to parallel those of Solomon and Josiah.

II. The Festivals of Solomon and Asa

2 Chronicles reproduces most of the account in Kings concerning Solomon's dedication of the temple, making only minor modifications. The Chronicler might possibly not have thought of Solomon's dedication ceremony in terms of festival ideology had it not been for the fact that 1 Kgs 8:2 expressly makes this association in its statement that the dedication assembly took place "at the feast in the month Ethanim, which is the seventh month." Early Israel held only one feast in the seventh month, and that was Booths or Tabernacles (Lev 23:33-38, 39-42; Num 29:7-39). This statement stands near the beginning of the narrative about Solomon, and its effect is to identify that king's dedication festival as a shadow feast of Tabernacles. That this is the intent of the Kings account is made clear by the concluding notice in 1 Kgs 8:65-66: "So Solomon held the feast at that time, and all Israel with him. . . . On the eighth day he sent the people away." The Chronicler equates the dedication festival with Tabernacles, therefore, because of what he found in Kings.

The report about a Weeks festival during Asa's reign in 2 Chr 15:8-15 is drawn up mainly out of the Chronicler's own imagination. As has been said, all he had to go on was 1 Kgs 15:12-15. Here in the account of the successive reigns of the Davidic kings was his earliest opportunity to expand upon the Solomon typology[6] with respect to the festival cult. The report about Asa's zeal in cultic reform perhaps set him thinking about expanding the model of the Solomon account with a parallel narrative concerning a new religious festival.

This time it would be Weeks or *šābu'ôt*, held in Jerusalem during the third month. The day of the month is not mentioned, but that this is the festival intended is made clear from the elaborate punning in verses 14-15, based on the vocable *šb'*, "swear an oath." It may also be that the Chronicler was influenced by the "sevens" in the Solomon account (2 Chr 7:8-9). To draw up a cohesive narrative based on these loose associations, the Chronicler had to look closely in his inventory of Asa traditions — whatever they may have been — to find a suitable foundation. He had only the concluding epitome to a quasi–holy war narrative involving a certain Zerah (14:8-14 [Eng. 9-15]), which he detached from the narrative proper in order to insert it into a report concerning the actual festival (15:9-15). The epitomizing statement is in 15:11: "They sacrificed to Yahweh on that day from the spoil which they brought, seven hundred oxen and seven thousand sheep."[7] The Chronicler seized this occasion to compare Asa with Jehoiada and Josiah, who likewise held covenant ceremonies characterized by the zeal and ardor of the participants (2 Chr 23:3, 16-17; 34:31-33).[8] Not only were all present required to seek *(drš)* Yahweh "with all their heart and with all their soul" (2 Chr 15:12), but they were even threatened with execution if they should refuse to swear a solemn oath to do so (v. 13).

Somehow the Chronicler has contrived to make everything else in this context subservient to this festival report: the report of Asa's religious and military preparations in 14:2-7 (Eng. 3-8); the battle report of 14:8-14 (Eng. 9-15); the revelation through Azariah, 15:1-7; the cultic purge and summoning of worshipers in 15:8-9; and, at the end, further information about cultic reforms drawn from 1 Kgs 15:13-15. In the midst of all this the festival schema still stands out. The narrative first takes note of the participants and the purification (vv. 8-9); this is followed by the date (v. 10), the ceremonies (vv. 11-14), and the joyful celebration (v. 15) in proper sequence.

One should take special note of the fact that the Chronicler has managed to work into this narrative a notice that Asa "repaired the altar of Yahweh that

---

6. Cf. R. L. Braun, "Solomonic Apologetic in Chronicles," *JBL* 92 (1973): 503-16.

7. Cf. S. J. De Vries, *Yesterday, Today, and Tomorrow* (Grand Rapids: Eerdmans; London: SPCK, 1975), 96-97. The "sevens" are probably intended as part of the punning upon *šb'*.

8. Cf. M. Weinfeld, "Pentecost as a Festival of the Giving of the Law," *Immanuel* 8 (1978): 11. In 2 Chr 19:10 Hezekiah announces his intent to "make a covenant with Yahweh" even though there is no report of his carrying out this intention (see below).

was in front of the vestibule of Yahweh's temple" (15:8b). Why the altar needed repair is not mentioned. The motif of repairing or rebuilding the temple and its appurtenances is a regular feature in the "preparation" element in the festival schema (2 Chr 4; 15:8b; 29:3; 34:10-13). We may assume that this is employed as a perpetual parenesis for the postexilic community for whom Chronicles was being written.

III. Hezekiah's Rededication and Passover/Mazzoth Festivals

For the report of Hezekiah's two festivals, which are really one, the Chronicler may have had some fragments of narrative tradition at his disposal, and certainly he made good use of current cultic tradition. Nevertheless, the greater part of what he has written in 2 Chronicles 29–30 is self-conceived and programmatic.

The most notable novelties in this account are the rededication of the temple in the first month and the Passover/Mazzoth festival in the second month. Inasmuch as 2 Kings says nothing of Hezekiah in connection with a Passover celebration, while the Chronicler follows 2 Kings in recording a first-month Passover for Josiah, one has to query why he felt compelled to tell about it here, unless it be that, having established Hezekiah as the cleanser and rededicator of the temple, he also felt the need to show how the rededicated temple was used. With Hezekiah (otherwise than with Josiah), it is the temple cleansing and rededication that are of prime importance. When he goes on to tell about Josiah, he will dutifully record a proper Passover celebration, but then it will serve his major interest to memorialize Josiah as the king who reestablished the law and the covenant. Thus the Chronicler's typology will be: (1) Hezekiah, rededicator of the temple; (2) Josiah, renewer of the law. These are each images that the Chronicler wishes to attach to the symbol of kingship as it survived into the postexilic period.

There is, beyond doubt, a solid historical foundation for the image of Hezekiah as rededicator of the temple, already firmly fixed in the brief account in 2 Kings. The Chronicler has reproduced 2 Kgs 18:2-3, but rather than repeat the statement about cultic reforms in 18:4, the encomium of 18:5, and glowing testimony of 18:6-7a, he brings in all new material at 2 Chr 29:3–31:21 to show the same thing in his own way. This is mainly in narrative form, but its description is meant as prescription; in other words, to be copied by contemporaries and by generations to come.

The Chronicler gives a large role to the priests and Levites, especially to the latter since they were to be responsible at all times and in all situations for enforcing the king's ordinances. The Chronicler holds fast to the theory that regal authority underlies the cult. This is why he has Hezekiah give the command, not only for the work of cleansing the sanctuary, but for moving from one step to

110

another within the ritual celebration. The king must always be at least symbolically present to represent authority and to personify the unity of God's people.

The notation in 2 Chr 29:3 that Hezekiah began his reforms by opening and repairing the temple doors "in the first year of his reign, in the first month," certainly means Nisan, universally the beginning of the spring new year in postexilic times and also the proper accession month for a new king. The Chronicler intends to accomplish two things: (1) to put Hezekiah to work at reform as early as possible after the reign of his wicked father, Ahaz; and (2) to fill up the time between the first and the sixteenth day of this month with cleansing operations (v. 17), allowing a festival of cleansing and rededication to occur on the sixteenth (vv. 20ff). This enables the Chronicler to accomplish a third purpose; viz., to provide a rationale for celebrating Passover on the fourteenth day of the second month rather than the first (30:2, 15), for too many days would have already been spent in the cleansing operation to allow the Passover to be kept at its proper time as specified in Exod 12:1ff.

We are faced here with a conundrum: was it the tradition of a sixteen-day cleansing that was first in place, or the tradition of a second-month Passover? We must not overlook that (1) 35:1-19 takes considerable pains to describe the details of Josiah's Passover in the correct month — the first — suggesting that the Chronicler did after all consider the first month to be correct; and (2) that the dedication festival described in chapter 30, at the end of the cleansing period, is to be recognized as primary in the Chronicler's interest, demanding priority over a routine celebration of the Passover. The motif of rebuilding the temple, modeled after the image of its construction and dedication by Solomon, is the primary element, while the image of a festival celebration, added to conform to the Solomon and Asa accounts, is typical but incidental.[9]

Though it is about a dedication ceremony, 2 Chr 29:1-36 has the four regular elements of the festival schema: the notice of date (v. 3); the identification and purification of the participants (vv. 4-19); a description of the ceremonies (vv. 20-35); and a notice of joyful celebration (v. 36). A conclusion that may be drawn from this is that the Chronicler is already making Hezekiah emulate Solomon in repeating the dedication of the temple, giving this event the added dimension of a shadow Passover similar to the shadow festival of Tabernacles superimposed upon Solomon's feast of dedication. This is a clue that the Chronicler may have been thinking of Hezekiah's second-month Passover as entirely symbolic. Nevertheless, he seems to be glad to have a later opportunity for correcting a false impression by telling of Josiah's first-month Passover.[10]

---

9. All the same, the fact that the Chronicler is quite willing at this point to adjust a cultic rule to suit the convenience of his narrative reveals an unsuspected level of latitudinarianism on the part of one who was probably involved in the ritual of the postexilic temple.

10. Since he intends these kings' respective Passovers to serve as models for the postexilic cult, he cannot allow the question of a correct calendar to be regarded as a matter of indifference; see below.

Hezekiah's charge given to the Levites in 29:5 is to "sanctify yourselves" (cf. 29:31; 30:15, 24) and Yahweh's temple, removing all its uncleanness (niddâ). The need for this is explicated both in general and in specific complaints introduced by kî in verses 6-7.[11] He confesses that "our fathers" — meaning Ahaz specifically but including all previous sinners among royalty as well as laity — have done maʿal, "outrageous behavior" (cf. 26:18), making themselves like the elders of Ezek 8:16, turning their faces away from Yahweh while giving him their backside (ʿōrep) instead. This is Hezekiah's general complaint. His specific charges are introduced by the word gam: (1) they have shut the temple gates; (2) they have put out the lamps; (3) they have neglected the incense; and (4) they have abandoned the burnt offering. The result has been divine wrath (qeṣep) which has manifested itself in two ways: (1) Judah and Jerusalem have become a laughingstock and (2) the fathers have died by the sword while their sons, daughters, and wives have been taken away captive (cf. 2 Chr 36:17). The only remedy is to "make" (i.e., renew) Yahweh's covenant, thus turning away the wrath (29:10). Because we find no narrative of an actual covenant ceremony following this, we assume that Hezekiah is thinking of righteous acts as tantamount to covenant renewal.

The Levites, with the priests, obeyed. Corresponding to a two-stage removal of uncleanness is a two-stage time schedule (v. 17), which is strange not only in allowing eight days equally for each precinct of the temple area, but particularly in the fact that the area "up to the porch [ʾûlām]," the proper domain of the Levites, was finished first, and then the temple itself, assigned to the priests. According to this, the Levites took eight days to cleanse the courts and then had to carry away for another eight days the "uncleanness" that the priests had found in the temple. From this we gather that the Levites worked twice as long as the priests. However, this is meant not as an image of the former showing subservience by performing a more menial service, but of the priests actually being under Levitical supervision, beginning their special task only when the Levites were ready for them to begin. The report to the king in verses 18-19 has to be taken as spoken by the leading Levites on behalf of all the workers, Levitical and priestly.

An entirely new move is signaled in verse 20 in the clause "And king Hezekiah started out,"[12] meaning that the king now takes his part in the action. All of verses 20-35a is concerned with the offering of dedicatory sacrifices. First there are two sorts of official sacrifices (vv. 20-29); next there is congregational singing (v. 30); finally, there are spontaneous lay offerings (vv. 31-35a). Among

---

11. K. Galling, Die Bücher der Chronik, Esra, Nehemia, ATD (Göttingen: Vandenhoeck & Ruprecht, 1954), in loco, discards verse 6 as a gloss without realizing that this is in fact the Chronicler's own judgmental interpretation about what is going on.

12. Not "rose early" as in RSV because no time-sequence is implied; cf. Jehoshaphat, 20:20.

the official sacrifices, over which the king has direct authority, there are two kinds: sin offerings to atone for the people's guilt and whole burnt offerings for praise.[13]

We must pay particular attention to places in the account where the king intervenes. In addition to verse 21b, this occurs at verses 27, 30, and 31. In the last three verses the king's command *('mr)* carries the action further. Both verse 21b and verse 24b ought to be taken as asides — explaining the action in progress. However, verse 25 has to be a secondary expansion, and for the following reasons: (1) it has the only introductory verb (hiph.) without the regular subject, Hezekiah; (2) the addition of Nathan and Gad to David (cf. v. 27) as authorities, without explicit theological rationale, is suspicious; (3) the qal of *'md* at the beginning of verse 26 can be identified as the likely takeoff point for this expansion, with its initial *'md* hiph.; and (4) verse 25b (*kî bĕyad YHWH hammiṣwâ bĕyad nēbî'âw*, "for the command was by Yahweh's hand by the hand of his prophets") is awkwardly phrased and transparently artificial.

The whole burnt offerings mentioned in verse 24b are meant to follow next in sequence after the sin offerings; the Levites are not nearly so prominent if we acknowledge that this half-verse may be another secondary expansion. A new section begins with the statement in verse 26 that the Levites and priests were stationed in their assigned places with David's instruments and trumpets[14] in hand; emphasis is on the loud sound of these instruments as the burnt offerings were being sacrificed (vv. 27-28). According to verses 28-30, the congregation *(qāhāl)* bows down in worship three times over: (1) while the sacrifice is being offered, (2) at its conclusion, and (3) while the Levites are singing praise songs.

In verse 30 it is the king and the princes who call for these praise psalms, but in verse 31 it is Hezekiah alone who calls the laity to voluntary offerings of their own. That something dramatically new is coming is signaled by the word *'attâ,* "so now." The king makes the astounding declaration that the people have ordained themselves *(millē'tem yedkem),* hence are now invited to present their

---

13. The interpretation of H. G. M. Williamson in *1 and 2 Chronicles,* NCBC (Grand Rapids: Eerdmans; London: Marshall, Morgan and Scott, 1982), *in loco,* is that these acts took place simultaneously. The impression that this might have been so may come from the fact that the Aaronite priests are commanded in verse 21a to offer up (*'lh* hiph.) upon the altar (no object being given). This would involve the assumption that this refers back to at least some of the victims that had been brought according to verse 21a, *lĕhaṭṭā't,* "to make atonement." We must choose either of two possibilities: (1) that the best and largest of the animals were reserved for the *'ôlâ* sacrifice that was to follow — this reference being therefore proleptic — or (2) that Williamson is correct in stating that both kinds of sacrificing went on simultaneously. While either interpretation is theoretically possible, the latter is less likely. Both in consideration of the orderliness of the Chronicler's habit of mind and of what we might logically expect in an actual service, it is hard to believe that the Chronicler intended simultaneity.

14. Cf. 1 Chr 15:16-24.

zĕbāḥîm and *tôdôt*, "sacrifices" and "thank offerings."[15] In verse 31b they do just that; and afterward anyone who is truly *nādîb lēb*, "willing of heart" (cf. 1 Chr 29:6), presents his own special burnt offering. To demonstrate the magnitude of this voluntary outpouring of gifts, the Chronicler next tallies the bulls, rams, and lambs that are offered.[16] Finally comes a section, verses 34-35a, that states that the Levites have to hustle to help the priests handle these numerous sacrifices, showing that theirs was the greater zeal for Yahweh's service.

Deliberate Solomon typology emerges clearly in the summary conclusion of verse 35b, *wattikkôn 'ăbôdat bêt-YHWH*, "so was completed the ritual of Yahweh's temple";[17] one should compare this with the statement concerning Solomon's work at 2 Chr 8:16. Chapter 29 is rounded off in verse 36 by the fourth element of the festival schema, telling how the king and people rejoiced. This joy is not sentimental but theological: "because of what God had done for the people" (v. 36a), explained by the cryptic statement (v. 36b), "for the thing came about suddenly *[pit'ōm]*." Perhaps the Chronicler adds this as an apologia for the confusion in festival chronology that this emphasis on the temple's rededication has occasioned.

We turn now to 2 Chronicles 30, which tells about the actual Passover festival. As has been suggested, the Chronicler's main reason for this additional narration is its omission at what should have been the regular time for it during the first month. The fact that 2 Kings knows nothing of it makes it virtually certain that the Chronicler is creating it out of his imagination. But this is not the only inconcinnity produced by the Chronicler's intrusion; scholars have been particularly perturbed about the way in which he shifts between Passover and Mazzoth nomenclature and practice, as well as by the addition of an extra seven-day feast in verses 23ff. This is particularly vexing because Josiah's Passover celebration in chapter 35 will include only a single seven-day celebration.[18]

Before we enter into a detailed analysis of chapter 30, we need to point out that the Chronicler's second feast (vv. 23-24) is essentially a rather bizarre application of a typological numeral seven, for which he seems to have special fascination. In the five passages under study, all but 2 Chronicles 15 specify a period of seven days for the festival ritual, but here in chapter 30 there is both a regular seven-day Mazzoth festival and a second seven days of the same or an additional festival. The Chronicler borrows this additional seven, it would seem, from chapter 7, which mentions a normal seven-day festival for Tabernacles in verse 8, but then in verse 9, following the mention of the eighth-day *'ăṣāret*, takes the conflation of dedication and Tabernacles to mean that a separate

15. Lev 7:2.
16. Cf. 1 Chr 26:20, 26; 28:12; 2 Chr 31:12; 35:13.
17. Not "Thus the service of the house of the LORD was restored," RSV.
18. On the problem of the Passover/Mazzoth, here and in chapter 35, one should consult the judicious observations of Williamson in his commentary, pp. 361-65.

114

festival was held for an additional seven days. Modern interpreters, observing the degree to which the Chronicler on occasion allows himself to be dominated by extraneous models and motifs, will of course be especially skeptical about the historicity of this item.

In chapter 30 the Chronicler tells about a combined Passover/Mazzoth festival. Verses 15-18a describe the ceremony for the Passover and verses 21 and 22b describe the ceremony for the Mazzoth. What once appeared to have been separate ceremonies were each ordained in Exod 12:1-13 and 14-20 to begin on the same day, and the one always suggests and implies the other. This is how we must understand the mention of the Passover alone in verses 1, 2, and 5, for it includes the second; but it is strange that the introductory statement in verse 13 mentions only Mazzoth even though the sequel describes both rituals.

The most remarkable thing is, of course, that this combined Passover/Mazzoth festival was to be celebrated in the second rather than the first month. We have discussed a probable reason for this shift. The P legislation at Num 9:6-11 makes express provision for a possible change from the first to the second month under very special circumstances, and even though the circumstances here are different from those envisioned in Numbers 9, we can scarcely doubt that the Chronicler is taking advantage of this ambivalence in the received tradition.[19]

If we keep in mind that verse 1 is an introductory summary for the whole, we will avoid the RSV's misleading "for" (wanting in Hebrew) and the pluperfect tense in verse 2, as well as any impression that the sending of the couriers in verse 6 may be a doublet to the charge given in verse 1.[20] A joint decision is made regarding the impossibility of keeping the Passover *bā'ēt hahî*, "at this time,"[21] the reason being that it is now 16/I and too late for the traditional start on 14/I. Avoiding a straightforward reason for the shift to a new date, the Chronicler substitutes two that are altogether facetious and unconvincing (v. 3). These are offered in parallel grounding clauses with *kî*: (1) there are not enough sanctified priests[22] and (2) not enough laypeople have yet arrived in Jerusalem

19. Cf. J. R. Shaver, "Torah and the Chronicler's History Book" (Dissertation, Notre Dame, 1983), 158-64; published as *Torah and the Chronicler's History Book*, BJS 196 (Atlanta: Scholars, 1989).

20. Verse 1 intends to say that the invitation was "to all Israel," including specifically Judah, and was written in letters for Ephraim and Manasseh (the Chronicler's term for the remnant of northern Israel). This is phrased differently in verse 6, but it means the same. The late practice of sending letters suggests special concern, urgency, and authority.

21. Not "in its time" (RSV); the expression as the Chronicler uses it does not imply that there was one proper time, only that there is a problem in coordinating the two. Although he makes the king the supreme authority in cultic matters, the Chronicler sees the need for the consent of the officials and the entire assembly in order to avoid the appearance of any arbitrariness in such a weighty matter.

22. Insinuating an item of antipriestly critique, as seen elsewhere in this passage in the dominance of the Levites over the priests wherever the two act together.

(cf. Num 9:9-12). Hence the decree is to invite "all Israel,"[23] requiring a pilgrimage from however far away. A new grounding clause in verse 5b seems as facetious as the Chronicler's previous reasons: *kî lō' lārōb 'āśû kakkātûb,* "for they had not done it in large numbers as prescribed."[24]

The actual feast is introduced in verse 13 with the statement that *'am-rab,* "a great people," came; it was in fact a *qāhāl lārōb mĕ'ōd,* "an exceedingly large congregation." Immediately the assembled congregation got busy throwing more of Ahaz's altars (of which there seems to have been a conveniently large supply) into Kidron (v. 14). Next came the matter of the ritual uncleanness of the participants. We know that this was a serious problem for the returned exiles (cf. Hag 2:12-14; Zech 3:1-9; 5:5-11), and it occupies all of verses 15-20. Following a casual notice about killing the Passover lamb, the Chronicler notes that the priests and Levites needed to be shamed into becoming ritually clean before they would be fit to bring the burnt offerings. When they did so, each group of clergy were allowed to take their assigned positions. The Levites were to hand over the sacrificial blood to the priests for sprinkling on the altar (cf. 29:22; 35:11).[25] This is explained in verse 17, which tells that many worshipers were not ritually clean, making their Passover victims ritually unclean as well, apparently forcing the Levites to do the work of killing in order to hand their blood to the priests.

The king's prayer in verse 18 is a remarkable one. Hezekiah asks God to pardon every ritual transgression, if only the worshiper seeks *(drš),* i.e., worships, the ancestral god. One who reads this can scarcely believe that the Chronicler was a sterile ritualist. Still less did he believe that Yahweh is a god who holds rigidly to rules: "And Yahweh listened to Hezekiah and healed the people" (v. 20). No wonder, then, that the *bĕnê yiśrā'ēl* (the Chronicler's inclusive term for "Israelites") were able to keep the Mazzoth feast with great gladness, and that the clergy praised Yahweh continuously and with all their might (v. 21).[26] Verse 22a has Hezekiah praising the Levites for their skill, and 22b tells about the actual ritual of feasting, sacrificing, and giving thanks.

Then comes the second festival week, the special celebration commonly agreed upon (vv. 23-24; cf. v. 2). A grounding clause provides its justification: the added capabilities offered by the large number of available sacrificial victims and the increased number of sanctified priests. In telling of the unparalleled rejoicing that resulted, the Chronicler first identifies the four distinct groups

23. "From Beersheba to Dan" is the Chronicler's peculiar way of resetting the old phrase, reflecting his southern bias (cf. 1 Chr 21:1).

24. According to 2 Kgs 23:22, Israel had not kept the Passover since the days of the judges!

25. See T. Willi, "Thora in den biblischen Chronikbüchern," *Judaica* 36 (1980): 102ff., 148ff.

26. Reading *bĕkol-'ōz* for MT *biklê-'ōz;* cf. BHS[mg]. M. Buttenweiser, *JBL* 45 (1926): 156-58, offered a fanciful argument that *kĕlê* is a technical word for a special type of song, and that *'ōz lĕYHWH* was the name of the song that was sung.

who are present: (1) Judah's own congregation; (2) the priests and Levites; (3) the congregation of Israel; and (4) *haggērîm habbā'îm mē'ereṣ yiśrā'ēl,* "the sojourners coming out of the land of Israel,"[27] along with those who have settled *(hayyôšēbîm)* in Judah.

Following this listing, the Chronicler goes on to compare Hezekiah with Solomon, stating that his festival was the greatest occasion for rejoicing since that king's time. The final act is mentioned in verse 27a: the priests and Levites[28] arise to bless the people. A closing word about divine transcendence states that the people's prayer came to God's holy habitation in heaven (v. 27b). Afterward "all Israel" go out to destroy intrusive altars throughout their respective territories, and then return home (31:1).

We see that in chapter 30 the Chronicler has made even greater use of Solomonic typology than in chapter 29. Hezekiah is identified not only as a descendant of Solomon but as a veritable new Solomon. The Chronicler is not at all interested in that king's fame for wisdom (a construct of the wisdom tradition). He does make some use of the tradition regarding Solomon's fabulous riches in verse 24, where he tells of Hezekiah's generous gifts of sacrificial victims, but that too is not central for him. The main element of Solomon typology as the Chronicler sees it is that great king's work of building and dedicating the temple. Much space has been previously given in this book (2 Chron 2–8) to that role. For the Chronicler it is not the wisdom or the riches of Solomon that survive, but his temple. It remains in the Chronicler's own time as the object of his greatest concern.

But there are still more items of Solomonic ideology in chapter 30. In verse 9 Hezekiah's couriers echo Solomon's dedicatory prayer in their repetition of the promise of return for any who repent (cf. 6:36-39). Also, the encomium of 30:26 makes the express comparison with Solomon: "Since the time of Solomon the son of David, king of Israel, there had been nothing like it in Jerusalem." In the summary for Hezekiah's reign in 31:20-21, the Chronicler will go on to laud this king for doing the same good things that Solomon had done: work for the service of God's house, keep the law and commandments, seek God with all his heart.

We should not forget the point made earlier about the special emphasis placed in 2 Chronicles 30 upon the element of gladness. The Chronicler's characterization of the worshipers as motivated by gratitude is an implicit enjoinment to the same attitude in the hearts of his contemporaries.

27. The expression *'ereṣ yiśrā'ēl* occurs in 1 Chr 22:2; 2 Chr 2:16; and 34:7; cf. H. G. M. Williamson, *Israel in the Books of Chronicles* (Cambridge: Cambridge University Press, 1977), 123. Exod 12:48-49 permits sojourners to partake of Passover/Mazzoth by submitting to circumcision.

28. It is significant that the Levites bless alongside the priests. On the possibility that "the priests the Levites," i.e., "the Levitical priests," may be original in this text, see G. von Rad, *Das Geschichtsbild des chronistischen Werkes,* BWANT 3 (Stuttgart: Kohlhammer, 1930), 87.

According to verse 20, Yahweh listened to Hezekiah's plea that would-be worshipers should be pardoned for any possible ritual uncleanness. We know that the wish to be cleansed of sin in spite of previous offenses is a frequent theme in postexilic literature (cf. Jer 31:31-34; Zech 5:5-11; Neh 9; Dan 9; and the penitential psalms). It is especially out of gratitude for Yahweh's uncalculating mercy that Hezekiah's fellow worshipers now gladly keep the Mazzoth festival and gladly observe the additional feast, for their joy is greater than any since the time of Solomon.

Details about the sacrificial system and the festivals mentioned in these two chapters may be traced to, or at least correlated with, specific passages in the Pentateuch. This shows that the latter was at least roughly equivalent in content to what is cited as the "law of Moses" in this book, the only apparent exception being the reference in 30:16 to a Mosaic ordinance that is not found in the Pentateuch. This is important incidental evidence that there was still an element of uncontrolled oral tradition for what Moses' law was and of what it required. A further novelty is the claim in 29:15 and 30:12 that the king's decree regarding matters of ritual had the authority of special revelation from God, reproducing David's claim in 1 Chr 28:19 that his plan for the temple had been written by the hand of Yahweh, just as the plan for the tabernacle had been given to Moses.[29]

IV. Josiah's Reforms and Passover

In his introductory summary for Josiah at 2 Chr 34:1-2, the Chronicler repeats the theological evaluation given in 2 Kgs 22:1-2 to the effect that this king "did right in Yahweh's eyes and walked in the ways of David his father [cf. for Hezekiah, 29:2], and did not turn aside to the right or to the left." This is a description of absolute rectitude especially suitable for the king who is reported to have done the most to establish the authority of the law. As has been mentioned, it was for this, more than for an institution of ritual, that Josiah was memorialized by the Chronicler.

The Chronicler proceeds to tell of Josiah's cultic reforms in 34:3-7. Two things are notable about this report. First, the chronology is set forward in comparison with that of 2 Kings, from the eighteenth year to the twelfth year of Josiah's reign, and the reforms as an event are also placed forward within the overall narration, severing them completely from the story of the finding of the lawbook. The Chronicler's description of the reforms is in fact a mere para-

---

29. This explains why most of the examples of an "authorization formula" go back to Moses for authority while examples of a "regulation formula" go back to David (comparing 30:16 with 29:25, 27), as explained in De Vries, "Moses and David," 619-39.

phrase of the lengthy and detailed account of reform found in 2 Kgs 23:4-20, where undoubtedly it is meant to be prescriptive for the deuteronomistic reform as a continuing program.

Before this reform could begin, spiritual maturity must have come to evidence in the reformer's own person. Thus the Chronicler informs us (v. 3a) that already in Josiah's eighth year of reign, when he was sixteen and just developing into manhood, he began to seek "the god of David his father,"[30] and verse 3b states that in Josiah's twelfth year he began to purge idols from the land. Summarizing details from 2 Kings, the Chronicler mentions that Josiah first purged Judah and Jerusalem, destroying all relics of Baal worship. He does not neglect to insert the rather astounding note that Josiah also burnt on their own altars the bones of the priests who had served the country shrines in Samaria. He goes on to tell that Josiah also extended his purge to "cities" in the dependent territories of Manasseh, Ephraim, and Simeon, going on "as far as Naphtali," in which Josiah apparently enjoyed only partial control.[31]

The age of Josiah when he began this reform has been much discussed because it affects the chronology of his reign. There have been advocates for the Chronicler's twelfth year over against the Deuteronomist's eighteenth year, which would be 622-21 B.C.E., with attempts to relate the earlier figure to known events in the late Assyrian empire; but since no direct correlation is possible, there seems to be no reason to discard the date in 2 Kings as correct. On the other hand, something of the Chronicler's design may be discerned. A rule in interpreting Chronicles is that ideological *Tendenz* and historicity are in inverse proportion to each other. The Chronicler apparently wants to depict Josiah as a lifelong reformer, beginning as early as possible, seeking to undo the great evil that remained from the reigns of his grandfather Manasseh and his father Amon. This new date may in fact have special theological significance, for elsewhere in Chronicles dating at the beginning of a particular king's reign regularly stands as a sign of divine approval; cf. 2 Chr 17:7 for Jehoshaphat and 2 Chr 29:3 for Hezekiah.

We observe that the Chronicler does in any event preserve the Deuteronomist's eighteenth year for the finding of the lawbook (34:8, from 2 Kgs 22:3). This means to say that Josiah was already six years into the work of purging before the lawbook was found, making his purges the precondition rather than the consequence of the finding of the book. In the Chronicler's view, Josiah knows that it is his duty to cleanse the land of idolatry entirely without any special lawbook. One should note also that the purge that the Chronicler allows

---

30. "The god of David his father" is Israel's God as personally known and worshiped by David as a founder of Israel's nation and cult. The Chronicler does not employ here his usual term, "the god of your fathers," meaning the ancestral god, which might carry the insinuation of a return to covenant morality when Josiah had not, in fact, forsaken it.

31. *Běhar bōtêhem śābîb* is an apparent corruption in the MT; cf. the RSV, BHS[mg].

to follow the discovery and reading of the lawbook is only summarily noted in 34:33a, in striking contrast to the extensive account in 2 Kgs 23:1-25. It is to be understood only as an extension and continuation of the independent reform that this pious young king had already begun.

As the Chronicler tells it, when Josiah receives Huldah's message about the lawbook, he does everything to show repentance (vv. 29-30). He offers inclusive terminology to describe the company of those who listened to the reading. We take special note of the fact that the "prophets" (2 Kgs 23:2) have now become "Levites" (2 Chr 34:30). Another change is in the designation of the book itself, which is now called "the book of the covenant" in anticipation of the covenant-renewal ceremony that immediately follows (vv. 31-32).

Some kind of ritual is involved in this ceremony of covenant renewal, for there is a special place for the king to stand (contrast original material elsewhere in Chronicles, which never attempts to regulate the ritual for the king's participation). In actuality, the Chronicler is not at all interested in Josiah's participation in this ritual because he does not truly regard this king, in contrast to Hezekiah, as a legitimizer of ritual. What interests him in this brief notice are the agreements that Josiah makes: to walk after Yahweh, to keep the commandments with heart and soul, and to perform the words of this covenant book. A regal policy is immediately activated to remove all the *tôʿēbôt*, "abominations"; cf. 33:2 (Ahaz). This removal was to be *mikkol hāʾărāṣôt ʾăšer libnê yiśrāʾēl*, "from all the lands belonging to the Israelites" — probably an idealistic reimaging of Solomon's vast realm since the plural of *ʾereṣ* can hardly mean "territorial holdings" in a local sense. By this purge Josiah removes every temptation, so that "all that were found in Israel" (cf. v. 32) are obliged to serve Yahweh as their god. Doom was inevitable upon this place, i.e., shrine, but during Josiah's own reign "they did not turn away from Yahweh their ancestral god" (v. 33).

In spite of this special interpretation of Josiah's covenant, the priority given in Chronicles to purifying the land puts the finding of the lawbook in an entirely different light than that of Kings. There nothing is said of Josiah's "beginning to purge" in his twelfth year; the reader is to suppose that the evil example of Amon continued to affect the people and perhaps Josiah himself, which would account for Josiah's great alarm at hearing the book read and the vigor of his far-reaching measures. Not so according to the Chronicler, for Josiah is himself well prepared ("While he was yet a boy he began to seek Yahweh," 34:3), and so are the people, all of whose intrusive idols, except apparently the *tôʿēbôt* mentioned in verse 33, have been removed prior to any repairs on the temple.

The fact that the Levites are given supervision also over this work underscores the impression that cultic purification is Josiah's paramount concern in the Chronicler's interpretation. In preaching to his own contemporaries, the Chronicler interprets Huldah's threat upon "this place and its inhabitants" (v. 24) as a continuing warning that the curses of the lawbook still stand. The forefathers of Israel before the exile had piled up such a vast measure of wrath that any further apostasy in the present generation might provoke an even greater measure of Yahweh's anger.

We turn now to chapter 35. It is clear that Josiah's Passover celebration reported in this chapter must be understood against the Chronicler's ideology concerning Josiah's reform.

There are two main lines of evidence that this chapter is not a literary unity but has received expansions from a parallel account.[32] One is that in verse 4 and again in verse 10 the vocable *kwn*, "prepare," refers to assigning liturgical stations and roles to the priests and Levites in preparation for the religious ceremony, whereas in verses 6, 14 (bis), 15 it clearly refers to preparing and distributing the sacrificial victims. Since the burnt offerings are mentioned in verse 16 as part of the Passover ritual and are covered by the clause *wattikkôn kol-'ăbôdat YHWH*, "so all the service of Yahweh was prepared," this verse should also be listed with the latter group of occurrences. The second item of evidence is the fact that the time designative in verse 16, *bayyôm hahû'*, "on that day," marks this verse as the epitomizing conclusion to a narrative pericope, whereas verse 17 uses the parallel temporal phrase *bā'ēt hahî'*, "at that time," in a similar function. The two phrases are never found together in an original pericope. One should observe further that the summarizing statement in this verse duplicates at least in part the clause "and they killed the Passover lamb" in verse 11; also that verse 17 refers to the feast of Mazzoth, not mentioned elsewhere in this context, while failing to make any reference to the sacrifices that are so prominent in verses 12ff.

The original narration is in 35:1-5, 10, 17-19, a brief account in which Josiah instructs the priests and Levites, and each group of clergy then makes ready according to the king's command, so that everyone present celebrates the Passover "at that time" (i.e., on the date mentioned in v. 1) together with the following seven-day feast of Mazzoth. This original narrative has an introductory summary in verse 1 and concludes with an encomium in verse 18 and a chronological statement in verse 19 that places all that happens between 34:8 and 35:18 within the same short time frame. All the remaining material in chapter 35 (vv. 6-9, 11-18) is secondary.[33] The fact that verse 18 parallels 2 Kgs

---

32. See pp. 412-16 in my commentary; also De Vries, *Yesterday, Today, and Tomorrow*, 72-73. Galling, *ATD in loco*, identifies verses 7-10 as secondary; T. Willi, *Die Chronik als Auslegung. Untersuchungen zur literarischen Gestaltung der historischen Überlieferung Israels*, FRLANT 106 (Göttingen: Vandenhoeck & Ruprecht, 1972), 197, 200, omits verses 2-6, 9-10.

33. That it concludes with a formal epitome in verse 18 (with the parallel temporal formula, *bayyôm hahû'*), makes it almost certain that it was once an independent and complete narrative. It began with identifying Josiah as the speaker of verse 6, followed this with a list of contributors, including a fantastic tally of victims (vv. 7-9), then went on to describe the sacrificial ritual with the following feast (vv. 11-13) and to specify the groups of clergy who were served (vv. 14-15), ending in the epitomizing statement of verse 16 to

23:22, and that verse 19 duplicates 2 Kgs 23:23, shows that it is the Chronicler himself who supplies the original verses, and that he does so according to his usual method of utilizing his source materials. We also see that 2 Kgs 23:21, the command that connects the Passover with the finding of the lawbook, finds its counterpart in 2 Chr 35:1; thus all that Kings has provided concerning Josiah's Passover is utilized in this original strand of 2 Chronicles 35.

We must briefly review the content of 35:1-18 as a conflate account. In verse 1 Josiah's "making a Passover" is meant as an introductory summary, "they killed" being proleptic to verse 17. The Chronicler mentions 14/I as the date, and there is no question here similar to that faced in 30:2, 13. Verses 2-5 commence the narration proper, with appropriate discourse. The Levites are identified in verse 3 as the sanctified teachers of "all Israel," a position to which they had been appointed by Jehoshaphat according to 17:7-9.[34] "Bearing the ark" is meant metaphorically; although the Levites had brought the ark into David's tent-shrine (1 Chr 15:14, 26), according to 2 Chr 5:7ff. it had been the priests who had actually placed this cult object inside Solomon's temple. The present duty of the Levites would be therefore to "serve Yahweh your god and his people Israel" (cf. 1 Chr 16:4). The special authority for this command is cited in a "regulation formula" that alludes to 1 Chronicles 23–26 as a "writing" authorized by David and to 2 Chr 8:14 as a "writing" of Solomon.[35]

Verse 5 is a new command in which the king tells the Levites to "stand," i.e., take a preassigned liturgical position and assume a specified ritual role in order to represent the respective ancestral families. Here the original material breaks off.

There are special problems in verses 6-9, 11-15. Verse 6, beginning the secondary account, has a command to slaughter victims (cf. 30:17) — carried out in verse 11 — and then to prepare (*kwn* hiph.) the flesh for the fellow clergy. For this the authority of Moses is cited (authorization formula), as in 30:16. Verses 7-15 continue the secondary narrative, integrating original material in verse 10. Verse 11 states that the priests sprinkled the blood at the same time the Levites were flaying the victims, in contrast to 30:16b, where it is stated that the priests sprinkled the blood which the Levites provided.[36] Verse 13 disagrees with Exod 12:8-9 and follows Deut 16:7 in stating that the flesh was not roasted

---

the effect that "King Josiah's" command had been carried out. The large-scale offering of bulls and additional sheep in this version in combination with the proper Passover ritual of the slaying of the lamb is suggested also in 30:15, but it has no counterpart in 35:15, 10, 17-19. The original version is concerned primarily with the proper instruction and ritual preparation of the clergy, while the secondary version is concerned with identifying rich contributors and specifying the beneficiaries.

34. Cf. von Rad, 96-98.

35. For further discussion of this point, see De Vries, "Moses and David," 639.

36. Both reports are ambiguous about how much the Levites were allowed to do; but if the Levites were allowed to flay the victims, one would assume that they also did the killing.

but boiled. In verse 16, *wattikkôn kol-'ăbôdat YHWH* is neither a repetition of verses 11-15 nor a contradiction of verse 10, but the concluding epitome of this secondary version.

According to verse 17, which introduces the concluding epitome of the original version, Josiah makes no special effort, like that of Hezekiah in 30:1-9, to summon great numbers of worshipers from afar; rather, his Passover was just for "the people of Israel who were present." A technique used in 30:25 is reproduced here; four separate groups take part: (1) Josiah, (2) the priests and Levites, (3) those from all Judah and Israel who happened to be present, and (4) the Jerusalemites themselves.[37] Though the details differ, the mentality of the same writer is clearly in evidence.

If we allow the encomium of verse 18 to serve in the place of the usual celebration element, all four standard elements of the Chronicler's festival schema are present. With the addition of the expansions from the secondary account, the second (participants/purification) and third (ceremonies) elements of the schema are brought to greater prominence, but the structure remains the same. We may be quite certain that the Chronicler as well as his epigone intended this account of Josiah's Passover to serve as a model for the perpetual celebration of this high holy feast *'ad-'ôlām,* "unto perpetuity."

In the course of historical development, the Passover had only gradually been merged with the Mazzoth festival. The two had been held together as a family festival from their initial combination until the time of the exile. In Deut 16:5-6 the combined festival is called a "Passover sacrifice" and is brought to the central shrine, Jerusalem. As we have seen, Kings makes no mention of a Passover festival for Hezekiah, but states in 2 Kgs 23:21-23 that Josiah did keep a Passover, making no mention either of the Mazzoth observance or of additional sacrifices. In 2 Chronicles 30 the Mazzoth ritual is not only joined to the Passover but becomes the main part of the entire festival. 2 Chronicles 35, on the other hand, models itself on the 2 Kings parallel in virtually ignoring the Mazzoth element, and its original version is instructively silent regarding special sacrifices.

There can be little doubt but that the aim of this last passage is to attribute to Josiah a correct liturgical calendar over against Hezekiah's highly suspicious celebration in the second month. This the Chronicler himself realizes — perhaps from a fresh reading of 2 Kings — needs to be corrected if it is not to give a wrong example. In his original account at 35:1 this is made emphatic, and at verse 17 it is underscored by an emphatic time-identifier, *bā'ēt hahî'.* Furthermore, the Chronicler allows Josiah to get a foot up on Hezekiah by comparing his religious zeal to that of all the kings going back to Samuel, not just to that of those going back to Solomon, as in 30:26. Finally, by including the dating formula from 2 Kgs 23:23 in verse 19 the Chronicler effectively makes the

---

37. Cf. Williamson, *Israel,* 12-13.

Passover observance an integral part of cultic reform. This is, to be sure, a pattern that pertains also to Hezekiah, whose purification rites recounted in chapter 29 preceded the festival celebration of chapter 30, showing that there can be no true celebration without ritual cleansing.

The secondary version in 2 Chronicles 35 reflects a period somewhat later than that of the Chronicler, a time when public sacrifices had come to expand markedly the private and familial aspects of the original ritual. Inasmuch as one of the secondary verses (15) refers to the Asaphite singers in an order of precedence that reflects Gese's tradition A, dated to ca. 350,[38] it is probable that this expansion comes from approximately that date. It is nevertheless not appreciably later than the original composition.

Conclusion

We have seen that the Chronicler seized every opportunity to describe one or another of the high feast days held under the auspices of a "good" king, the chief of whom was Solomon himself. The narratives of these festivals are not just description, but prescription. We may be quite certain that Josiah's Passover, the last of the series, reflects the Passover celebration as it was ideally held in the Chronicler's own time and as he intended it to be celebrated in the future.[39] It was important for the Chronicler to ensure the prestige and authority of David and his most worthy successors in order to ensure the legitimation of this festival.[40] The Israel that had come out of the exile needed continual and renewed purification, just as the damaged and desecrated temple required rebuilding and reconsecration. In the Chronicler's time the parallel dangers of the people's corruption and of the temple's desecration remained as tangible threats. The parenetic purpose of 1-2 Chronicles as a whole is to warn against these perils and to help the ideal Israel for whom it was written become all that they were ordained to be.

---

38. H. Gese, "Zur Geschichte der Kultsänger am zweiten Tempel," *Abraham unser Vater. Juden und Christen im Gespräch über die Bibel*, ed. O. Betz, M. Hengel, and P. Schmidt, Festschrift for O. Michel (Leiden: Brill, 1963), 222-24. Cf. D. L. Petersen, *Late Israelite Prophecy: Studies in Deutero-Prophetic Literature and in Chronicles*, SBLMS 23 (Missoula: Scholars, 1977), 86, identifying a significant "tradition shift."

39. The secondary expansion reflects a further shift in contemporary liturgical practice; see above.

40. "The idealized figure of David in 1-2 Chronicles belongs . . . not to the eschaton but to the *Urzeit*. . . . Even though Moses and the Mosaic tradition would continue in honor, it is the David who ordained the Levites . . . who brought the worship of Yahweh to its highest perfection and its true fulfilment" (De Vries, "Moses and David," 639).

Cosmos and History in Zechariah's View of the Restoration (Zechariah 1:7–6:15)

MICHAEL H. FLOYD

> Because the world is round it turns me on.
>
> *John Lennon and Paul McCartney*

In my first encounter with Rolf Knierim, as a new graduate student who was both thrilled and terrified at the prospect of studying with him, he converted me to his general slant on form criticism by explaining, in animated discussion over steak sandwiches and beer, how he thought the discipline was in need of a reformation.[1] One of his main points was that the texts themselves, by their very nature, call into question some of the methodological principles that form critics have generally assumed to be axiomatic. My heart was strangely warmed by this conversation, and ever since then I have remained impressed by Knierim's striking capacity to do biblical interpretation, so as to let the texts themselves call into question the conventional assumptions with which we approach them.

This capacity is notably evident in his article "Cosmos and History in Israel's Theology," in which Knierim brings some brute textual facts into confrontation with our recent historicist tendency to downplay the significance of creation as a primary, overarching category in biblical theology.[2] His essay makes it impossible to presuppose any longer that in the Old Testament, as a general rule, "time rather than space, history rather than cosmology, is the central concern."[3] Knierim points to the necessity of examining how cosmic

---

1. The main themes of our conversation were later programmatically articulated in R. Knierim, "Old Testament Form Criticism Reconsidered," *Int* 27 (1973): 435-68.
2. R. Knierim, "Cosmos and History in Israel's Theology," *HBT* 3 (1981): 59-123.
3. B. Anderson, *Creation versus Chaos* (New York: Association, 1967), 110.

and historical processes are related in certain key texts, and thereby opens up the possibility of reading other texts along similar lines. In homage to him I would here like to examine the relationship between cosmos and history in Zech 1:7–6:15, a text that has generally been approached with rather narrowly defined historical questions concerning the main events of the Judean restoration.[4] In light of the insights from Knierim's seminal essay this passage may gain a fresh reading.

In order to do this, it will be necessary to utilize an exegetical method somewhat different from the one that has often been employed in historical criticism. Much of the historical-critical work on such prophetic texts is still characterized by the separation of the individual units of prophetic discourse from one another, and hence the dissolution of their arrangement within their present literary context, so that they can be rearranged and read in relation to a chronologically ordered course of events.[5] The very method itself thus pre-

---

4. Recent commentaries on this passage include: S. Amsler, *Aggée, Zacharie 1–8*, CAT 11c (Neuchatel and Paris: Delachaux & Niestle, 1981); J. G. Baldwin, *Haggai, Zechariah, Malachi*, TOTC (London: Tyndale; Downers Grove: Inter-Varsity, 1972); W. A. M. Beuken, *Haggai-Sacharja 1–8*, SSN 10 (Assen: Van Gorcum, 1967); T. Chary, *Aggée-Zacharie, Malachie*, SB (Paris: Gabalda, 1969); M. Delcor, *Zacharie*, SB[PC] 8,1 (Paris: Letouzey & Ane, 1961); K. Elliger, *Das Buch der zwölf Kleinen Propheten II*, 3rd ed., ATD 25 (Göttingen: Vandenhoeck & Ruprecht, 1956); F. Horst, *Die Zwölf Kleinen Propheten. Nahum bis Maleachi*, 2nd ed., HAT 1,14 (Tübingen: Mohr, 1954); C. L. Meyers and E. M. Meyers, *Haggai, Zechariah 1–8*, AB 25B (Garden City: Doubleday, 1987); D. L. Petersen, *Haggai and Zechariah 1–8*, OTL (Philadelphia: Westminster, 1984); and W. Rudolph, *Haggai — Sacharja 1–8 — Sacharja 9–14 — Maleachi*, KAT 13,4 (Gütersloh: Mohn, 1976). Other studies include P. R. Ackroyd, *Exile and Restoration*, OTL (Philadelphia: Westminster, 1968), 171-217; also P. Hanson, *The Dawn of Apocalyptic* (Philadelphia: Fortress, 1975), 240-62.

More specialized studies of this part of Zechariah 1–8 include: M. Bič, *Die Nachtgesichte des Sacharja*, BibS[N] 42 (Neukirchen: Neukirchener, 1964); C. Jeremias, *Die Nachtgesichte des Sacharja*, FRLANT 117 (Göttingen: Vandenhoeck & Ruprecht, 1977); A. Petitjean, *Les Oracles du Proto-Zacharie*, EBib (Paris: Librairie Lecoffie, J. Gabalda, 1969); L. Rignell, *Die Nachtgesichte des Sacharja* (Lund: Gleerup, 1950); D. J. W. Rothstein, *Die Nachtgesichte des Sacharja*, BWANT 8 (Leipzig: Hinrichs, 1910); H.-G. Schötter, *Gott inmitten seines Volkes: Die Neuordnung des Gottesvolkes nach Zacharja 1–6*, Trierer theologische Studien 43 (Trier: Paulinus-Verlag, 1987); and K. Seybold, *Bilder zum Tempelbau: Die Visionen des Propheten Sacharja*, SBS 70 (Stuttgart: KBW, 1974).

5. With regard to 1:7–6:15 there has been a tendency not only to separate the individual units of prophetic discourse from one another, but also to separate the nonvisionary oracular material, including 1:14-17; 2:10-17 (Eng. 2:6-13); 3:8-10; 4:6aβ-10a; and 6:9-15, from the surrounding visionary material (e.g., A. Petitjean, *Oracles*). In the case of 2:10-17 (Eng. 2:6-13) and 6:9-15, which constitute nonvisionary textual units, the distinction is at least pertinent, though the presupposition that the visionary material is somehow more primary is dubious. The excision of the oracular materials in 1:14-17; 3:8-10; and 4:6aβ-10a from the vision reports that contain them is purely arbitrary and unwarranted, however. The vision report genre typically contains some explication of the symbolic figures that are visualized by the prophetic recipient of the vision (S. Amsler, "La parole visionnaire des prophètes," *VT* 31 [1981]: 359-63), and this frequently takes the form of an oracular speech (e.g., Amos

---

supposes that the historical significance of prophetic texts, conceived in terms of how they reflect the course of human events, is their primary dimension of meaning. The cosmic significance of the texts, conceived in terms of what they may say about natural or superhuman realities in relation to the human social world, is thus by definition relegated to a secondary or subordinate status, if not lost sight of altogether.

If our search for what Zech 1:7–6:15 has to say about cosmos and history is not to be prejudiced from the outset, we must therefore employ a somewhat different method. This is not to say that our approach will be either ahistorical or uncritical. The composition of a text is after all an event that, like any other event, is open to historical investigation. Such investigation, to whatever extent may be feasible, is an essential part of understanding any ancient text. The method to be employed here will thus involve the dating of the various units of prophetic discourse, as well as the dating of the whole passage. It will also, however, allow for the possibility that the present compositional arrangement of these textual units may have some significance in its own right, even if it is nonchronological, and for the possibility that such an arrangement may disclose a meaning concerned with cosmic realities extending beyond the human social world. This kind of meaning may well have conceptual priority over other things that the text has to say, even if it comes to expression relatively late in the text's literary development. In other words, our interpretation will be based on the structural interrelation of the individual units of discourse in the final form of the text, as well as the conceptual principles that account for their coherence on this level.

Zech 1:7–6:15 is the second of the three major sections of chapters 1–8, each of which is marked off by an introduction in which an unidentified narrator describes the prophet's reception of a revelation on a particular date (1:7; cf. 1:1 and 7:1). The main body of this section (1:8–6:15) is contrastingly expressed in the first-person style of an autobiographical report. In the main body the prophet narrates in his own words a series of revelations that he has received, most of which are visions.[6] There is a definite narrative sequence, consisting of two episodes (1:6–3:10 and 4:1–6:15), but in each episode the sequence is subjected to a jarring interruption (2:10-17 and 4:6aβ-10a, respectively). In order to ascertain the significance of these interruptions it is first

---

8:1-3; 9:1-4; Jer 1:11-16; 24:1-10; Ezek 37:1-14; etc.). There is thus no a priori reason to suppose that 1:14-17 did not originally belong together with 1:8-13, or that 3:8-10 did not originally belong together with 3:1-7, or even that 4:6aβ-10a did not originally fit within 4:1-6aα + 10b-14 — though 4:6aβ-10a is obviously in some sense intrusive (see below, pp. 131-32).

6. Scholars have thus tended to see the basic structure of this passage in terms of a vision cycle, into which nonvisionary materials have been inserted. The function of such nonvisionary units as 2:10-17 (Eng. 2:6-13) and 6:9-15 in the final compositional form has thus gone largely unexamined.

necessary to examine more closely the way in which the narrative sequence is established.

The patterned use of formulaic language provides a telling indication of how the narration is organized. The first episode begins with the most basic variant of the vision report formula, using ראה, "to see," in its qal perfect form (1:8). The vision report that is thus introduced (1:8-17) continues until 2:1. There the idiomatic phrase נשא עינים, "to lift up the eyes," in *waw*-consecutive qal imperfect is combined with the recurrence of ראה, now in *waw*-consecutive qal imperfect. This indicates a shift in the field of perception and hence a transition to a second vision report (2:1-4).[7] Within this unit there occurs yet another variant of the vision report formula, using ראה in its *waw*-consecutive hiphil imperfect (ויראני יהוה, "And Yahweh caused me to see"), which here (2:3) serves to signal the appearance of new images within the same scene. Another shift in the field of perception and the concomitant transition to a third vision report (2:5-9) is indicated by a repetition in 2:5 of the same phraseology that marks the beginning of the second report in 2:1, i.e., the combination of נשא עינים and ראה in *waw*-consecutive imperfect. This formulaic language links these three vision reports together in a series, describing several tableaux that the prophet perceived successively in a continuous bout of visionary activity. The brief but deft descriptive stroke in 1:8, which indicates that the prophet saw things הלילה, "at night," thus sets the stage for this entire series of visions. The prophet envisions three scenes, consisting of various images that shine luminously out of the dark, all of which are explicated for him in one way or another by an interpreter angel who emerges from the scene.

The visionary activity obviously comes to an end at 2:10, as the narration is interrupted by a prophetic exhortation that extends through 2:17. Though the prophetic voice no longer speaks in a reporting mode, it is still heard in an oracular first-person style. Otherwise the scene goes blank. The narrative representation of the prophet's seeing luminous images in the dark is abandoned altogether, and the character of the interpreter angel — whose role has heretofore been defined exclusively in terms of this perceptual phenomenon — thus disappears.

It is important to note, however, that the exhortation in 2:10-17 does not break the narrative sequence altogether, but remains contained within it. This is indicated by the way the description of visionary activity resumes at 3:1. Here there is another instance of the hiphil variant of the vision report formula, like the one that occurs in 2:3, but without any explicit subject (ויראני). Narrative continuity is indicated formally by the *waw*-consecutive imperfect verb and

---

7. There is a discrepancy at this point between MT and most English versions with respect to the enumeration of chapter and verse. 2:1-4 MT = 1:18-21 Eng.; 2:5-9 MT = 2:1-5 Eng.; and, as already indicated above, 2:10-17 MT = 2:6-13 Eng. Subsequent citations are all according to MT.

materially by the fact that the reader must refer back to the emphatic repetition of the divine name in the immediately preceding unit (nine times in 2:10-17), as well as back to the initial occurrence of the same variant of the formula in 2:3, in order to identify Yahweh as the subject of the verb. Though the formulaic expression in 3:1 clearly shows a return to the same sort of visionary activity that is described in 1:8–2:9, there is no indication that this happens under the same conditions. On the one hand there is nothing to suggest that in 3:1-10 night has given way to day, but on the other hand there is also nothing to suggest that the scene described in this unit appears to the prophet from out of the darkness. In addition the interpreter angel remains absent or at least anonymous, since neither his characteristic role nor his characteristic epithet (הדבר בי, "the one who spoke with me") is ascribed to any of the angelic figures in this unit.

The first episode can thus be defined as an extended vision report (1:8–3:10) in which a prophetic exhortation (2:10-17) serves to demarcate visionary activity that involves both seeing in the dark and interacting with the interpreter angel (1:8–2:9) from visionary activity that does not explicitly involve either of these phenomena (3:1-10). The vision that is described in 3:1-10 thus stands in relation to the three visions that are described in 1:8–2:9 as their outcome, but it is an outcome that cannot be understood as such on the basis of the three previous visions alone. One must heed what the exhortation in 2:10-17 has to say in order to understand how the visions of 1:8–2:9 lead up to and eventuate in the vision in 3:1-10.

The commencement of a second episode (4:1–6:15) in the continuing narration is specifically indicated by the description of a return to the kind of visionary activity with which the first episode began. In 4:1 the interpreter angel is explicitly said to come again (וישב, "and he returned"), after having vanished from the scene at 2:10, and the representation of the prophet's seeing in the dark is resumed. With regard to the latter it is not reiterated here that the prophet saw something הלילה, "at night" (1:8), but a similar idea is instead expressed metaphorically by likening the prophet's being primed for further revelation to his being roused from sleep. Since sleep usually happens at night, being roused from sleep to see something is tantamount to seeing it in the dark.[8]

As in the first episode, the nature of the narrative continuity is indicated by the patterned use of the formulaic language with which each unit is intro-

8. Commentators have attempted to relate the prophetic visionary experience described in Zechariah with dreaming (see most recently S. Niditch, *The Symbolic Vision in Biblical Tradition*, HSM 30 [Chico, Calif.: Scholars, 1983], 12-19; also Petersen, 111-12). The narrative description in 4:1, however, compares the reception of revelation to waking up. Since one goes to sleep in order to dream, this is hardly the metaphor one would choose to describe a revelation imparted through a dream. Such language points instead to a state of altered consciousness that stands in relation to the normal waking state much as the normal waking state stands in relation to sleep, i.e., it points to a state of heightened awareness.

duced. Various forms of the vision report formula in the first four units indicate a series of vision reports: 4:1-14; 5:1-4; 5:5-11; and 6:1-8. Each is linked to the preceding unit by beginning with *waw*-consecutive imperfect verbs, and the idiomatic phrase נשׂא עינים, "to lift the eyes," describes each shift in the field of perception that marks the transition to another vision report. The night vision phenomenon thus continues until 6:9, where the introductory prophetic word formula (ויהי דבר יהוה אלי, "and the word of Yahweh came to me") begins to report a kind of revelation that is not visionary. In 4:1–6:8 the action of the interpreter angel not only begins the episode as a whole (4:1-2) but also begins another unit (5:5), thus constituting two scenes. When the prophet takes the lead, he is explicitly said to be doing so again (note שׂוב in both 5:1 and 6:1), which, in conjunction with the use of the same terminology in 4:1 to describe the interpreter angel's return, underscores the fact that 4:1–6:15 stands in relation to 1:8–3:10 as a second episode.

In the first episode the interruption (2:10-17) comes between vision reports (2:5-9 and 3:1-10), but in the second episode the interruption (4:6aβ-10a) comes right in the middle of one (4:1-6aα + 10b-14). In the first episode the interruption is in the form of a single oracle, but here it consists of two (4:6aβ-7 and 4:8-10a).[9] They are both interpolated into the narrative at the point where the interpreter angel begins to answer the prophet's question concerning the image he has just seen, but each is integrated into the surrounding vision report in a rather different way. Though the first oracle (4:6aβ-7) appears to interrupt what the interpreter angel is about to say to the prophet, it has no narrative introduction of its own, but only a heading (v. 6aβ). With respect to content 4:6aβ-7 is somewhat incongruous in relation to its context. With respect to form, however, it creates and fills an ellipsis between the narrative introduction to the interpreter angel's reply to the prophet and the quotation of the reply itself: "Then he said to me, 'This is the word of Yahweh to Zerubbabel . . . these seven are the eyes of Yahweh. . . .'" It thus remains firmly contained within the direct discourse structure and does not totally disrupt the prophet's account of his vision. Unlike the first oracle, the second (4:8-10a) has its own narrative introduction based on the prophetic word formula (ויהי דבר יהוה אלי). Thus it constitutes an aside on the part of the narrator, in which he briefly abandons the report of his visionary experience before resuming it in verse 10b. Such intrusions into the narrative continuity of the vision report certainly leave the reader wondering what these two oracles could possibly have to do with the meaning of the image that the prophet has seen, as well as what each has to do with the other, but this may be precisely the point.

The second episode can thus be defined as an extended report of a revelation, which begins in a visionary mode with a series of four night visions

---

9. This is the general consensus, but Amsler sees three: verses 6aβ, 7, and 8-10a (*Aggée, Zacharie 1–8*, 92-95).

(4:1–6:8) but then in conclusion shifts to a nonvisionary mode (6:9-15). Two oracles interrupt at the same point in the first vision report of the series (4:1-14), each posing in its own way at the very outset a complicating issue for the unfolding narrative development of the episode as a whole. The first oracle (4:6aβ-7) stands in relation to the narrative continuity of the vision report that surrounds it exactly as the oracle in 2:10-17 stands in relation to the narrative continuity of the first episode as a whole (1:8–3:10). It disrupts but does not sunder the narration, in order to present in nonnarrative form some information that is essential for understanding how the plot unfolds. The second oracle (4:8-10a) stands in relation to the narrative continuity of the vision report that surrounds it exactly as the oracle in 6:9-15 stands in relation to the narrative continuity of the second episode as a whole (4:1–6:15). Just as the formulaic introduction to 4:8-10a indicates a breaking away from the surrounding account of a visionary revelation, in order to bring in an account of a somewhat different kind of revelation, so the same formulaic introduction to 6:9-15 indicates a breaking away from the preceding account of four visionary revelations, in order to conclude with an account of a similarly somewhat different kind of revelation. The oracle in 4:6aβ-7 thus stops to tell the reader something that is important in order to understand the explanation that the interpreter angel is about to give in 4:6aα, and finally manages to give in 6:10b. The immediately ensuing, thematically related oracle in 4:8-10a then more forcefully interjects a complication into the first four visions of the second episode, which is finally resolved only in the concluding, nonvisionary report of a revelation (6:9-15).

This description of the compositional form of Zech 1:7–6:15 may be summarized in the following outline of its structure:

I. Narrative introduction	1:7
A. Date citation	1:7a
B. Prophetic word formula	1:7b
II. Main body: report of prophetic revelation	1:8–6:15
A. First episode	1:8–3:10
1. Narration begun: series of three night vision reports	1:8–2:9
a. First vision	1:8-17
b. Second vision	2:1-4
c. Third vision	2:5-9
2. Narration interrupted: exhortation	2:10-17
3. Narration resumed: concluding vision report	3:1-10
B. Second episode	4:1–6:15
1. Series of four night vision reports in two scenes	4:1–6:8
a. First scene	4:1–5:4
1) Narrative introduction	4:1
2) Pair of visions	4:2–5:4
a) First vision	4:2-14

On the basis of this overview of how the various parts of this section of Zechariah are structured into their final compositional form, we can delve into the content of the various units of prophetic discourse that make up the composition. A full exegesis of each unit is beyond the scope of this essay. In line with our primary concern with cosmos and history, we will instead build upon Knierim's observation that the biblical concept of the cosmos is basically defined in terms of the relationship between heaven and earth, and focus on how this relationship informs each unit.[10]

The first episode's first vision (1:8-17) describes a change of heart on Yahweh's part, from anger toward his people to compassion for them. This takes place in heaven, but it impinges rather directly on earthly affairs. Yahweh has dispatched cosmic forces, envisioned as a kind of celestial cavalry corps, to transform the international situation. The world is thus getting settled (והנה כל הארץ ישבת ושקטת; 1:11b, NRSV "and lo, the whole earth remains at peace"), but there is as yet only one manifestation of this change as far as Judah is concerned: Yahweh has returned to Jerusalem (שבתי ברחמים לירושלם; 1:16aα, NRSV "I have returned to Jerusalem with compassion"). This portends, however, Judah's full restoration and recovery of their status as Yahweh's elect.

The first episode's second vision (2:1-4) reiterates from an international rather than a heavenly perspective that Judah's restoration is occurring at a turning point in world history. In the former epoch the imperial powers, represented by four horns (קרנות), have characteristically ruled by brute force, through such policies as mass deportation, and thus have scattered Yahweh's

---

10. Knierim, "Cosmos and History," 76-80.

people. In the new epoch, however, the imperial powers, represented by four artisans (חרשים), are shown by Yahweh to have a more creative capacity for ruling in a more humane way. They are thus overthrowing the old order and creating a new one, of which the restored Judah will be an integral part.

The first episode's third vision (2:5-9) reiterates from the down-to-earth local perspective of an ordinary human being that Judah's restoration involves Jerusalem's full recovery of its socioeconomic viability (cf. 1:16b-17a). The image of the surveyor with his tools suggests that measurable progress along these lines is already evident, and he is advised that further progress does not entail a city wall. Yahweh is creating conditions under which a wall is no longer militarily or socioeconomically necessary.

The exhortation (2:10-17) that interrupts this series of visions is addressed to all the earth in general (כל בשׂר, lit. "all flesh," v. 17; NRSV "all people," v. 13), and to the exiles in particular (ציון, "Zion," vv. 11a, 14a), in an appeal for each to make an appropriate response to Yahweh's heavenly initiative. Yahweh once scattered his people in an action comparable to dispersing his cosmic forces (represented by ארבע רוחות השמים, v. 10b; NRSV "the four winds of heaven," v. 6b), and he has now initiated from his heavenly dwelling a reversal of this process. All the earth is to stand in silent awe (הס, v. 17; NRSV "Be silent," v. 13), as the exiles flee from the place where chaos threatens to break out (ארץ צפון, v. 10a; NRSV "the land of the north," v. 6a) and return with joy to Jerusalem.[11] This reversal will bring about a change in Judah's international status, so that they will cease to have their resources confiscated by the imperial system and will instead come to benefit from the resources that the imperial system has confiscated from their former captors (vv. 12-13a). This change in international status, from being plundered to becoming plunderers, is not a recovery of national identity, however. The identity of Yahweh's people will no longer be determined on the basis of nationality but will encompass people from many nations (גוים רבים; v. 15a).

In the final scene of the first episode (3:1-10), as the narration of visionary activity resumes, the perspective shifts to a very heavenly one, though a human being is the center of attention. Joshua, the high priest, stands in the midst of the divine council, and the angelic prosecutor (הסטן) presses the issue of the impurity incurred by his family's living in exile. The question is whether this disqualifies Joshua from heading a cult that can legitimately atone for the people's sins and legitimately represent Yahweh's heavenly kingship. Yahweh dismisses the case because Joshua, as a descendant of a priestly line that antedated Jerusalem's destruction by the Babylonians, establishes some continuity between the old preexilic royal sanctuary and the restored sacrificial

---

11. On צפון as the locus of incipient chaos see B. S. Childs, "The Enemy from the North and the Chaos Tradition," *JBL* 78 (1959): 187-98; also R. J. Clifford, *The Cosmic Mountain in Canaan and the Old Testament*, HSM 4 (Cambridge: Harvard, 1972), 57-79.

cult.[12] Joshua is thus declared clean and given the prerogative of ruling (דין) the temple so as to represent the rule of the heavenly council (vv. 6-7). He is also provided by Yahweh with a couple of omens to authenticate his legitimacy in the eyes of his associates: a messianic counterpart (צמח; NRSV "the Branch," v. 8b) and a divinely inscribed stone that betokens his capacity to effect atonement (v. 9).

The two visions that make up the first scene of the second episode (4:1-14 and 5:1-4) have in common the motif of worldwide movement (כל הארץ). In the first case it is the eyes of Yahweh (עיני יהוה), represented by the seven lights of the golden lampstand, that survey (שוט) the whole earth (4:10b). In the second case it is the flying scroll (מגלה עפה) that goes forth (יצא) as a curse (אלה) over the whole earth (5:1b, 3a). The interposition of the two oracles in 4:6aβ-7 and 4:8-10a associates this movement with the temple in general, and more specifically with Zerubbabel's role as temple builder. This scene thus graphically depicts the significance and implications of Zerubbabel's temple rebuilding project in terms of its constituting an earthly center point from which various manifestations of Yahweh's heavenly actions emanate.

The lampstand, as a temple furnishing that symbolizes Yahweh's eyes, identifies the sanctuary as the central place in which the heavenly creator's capacity to oversee all the earth becomes manifest. The vision goes on to suggest that this symbolic function of the temple entails its being jointly supervised by the two בני היצהר (NRSV "anointed ones"). In relation to this earthly localized manifestation of Yahweh's kingship, the temple's coregents occupy a human position that corresponds to the role of the angelic attendants closest to Yahweh's heavenly throne (cf. 6:5). It is in this sense that Joshua, the high priest, and Zerubbabel, the governor, both stand beside the heavenly king (עמדים על אדון כל הארץ; 4:14b).

In contrast with the earthbound sanctuary lampstand, the scroll flies (5:1). It represents a divinely animated expression of the covenant tradition in documentary form. In this guise the covenant ideals are disseminated worldwide and become operative among the people through the power of the divine curse. In the form of a Torah scroll the knowledge and power of the covenant are extended, so that its scope and force can hardly be limited to whatever political form Judah may assume. As the earthly representation of Yahweh's heavenly rule, the restored royal sanctuary in Jerusalem becomes the cultic focal point, toward which all his people must orient themselves. Their identity as Yahweh's people, however, cannot be reduced to membership in Judah's body politic, for the covenant now extends beyond such geopolitical bounds to encompass the whole earth.

The two visions that make up the second scene of the second episode (5:5-11 and 6:1-8) have in common the motif of movement toward Babylon.

12. Meyers and Meyers, 187.

The focus thus shifts away from the center and its emanations to developments on the periphery. The vision of the ephah satirizes the establishment of a temple anywhere away from the central sanctuary in Jerusalem.[13] The ephah is an ironic inversion of all that the lampstand (4:1-14) and the scroll (5:1-4) both represent. It is in the process of becoming, like the lampstand, a cult object standing in a temple (v. 11). Unlike the lampstand, however, it holds nothing beneficial — but rather wickedness (רשעה) personified. Like the scroll, the ephah flies. The scroll, however, moves and takes effect (as the curse) through its own supernatural power. The ephah is so weighed down by the force required to contain wickedness that it can only get off the ground with the unnatural help of the two harpies. A communal identity based on such an idolatrous cult object, located outside the pale of Jerusalem, cannot counteract the effects of the exile. A cult in Shinar, the site from which Yahweh scattered primeval humanity (Gen 9:2), would only aggravate the assimilative scattering of his own people.

The vision of the four chariots (6:1-8) puts Jerusalem's claim of exclusive cultic legitimacy in a broader context. The chariots represent cosmic forces that are identified with the winds stationed (מהתיצב) beside the Lord of all the earth (v. 5b). These forces of Yahweh are thus the heavenly counterparts of the two similarly positioned earthly בני היצר in 4:14. They move against a mythic backdrop defined in terms of two bronze mountains (הרי נחשת), from between which they initially emerge (v. 1). The names of these mountains are mythic toponyms, as well as geographic terms that indicate points of the compass in relation to Judah and Jerusalem. Two chariots go north to צפון, the place from which chaos threatens to break out (cf. Isa 14:31; 41:25; Jer 1:14; 6:22; etc.), while one chariot goes south to תימן, the place from which Yahweh comes to defend his people against their foes (also called פארן and סיני; cf. Deut 33:1 and Hab 3:3).[14] One or all of the chariots are subsequently dispatched to go patrol (התהלך) the earth (vv. 6-7).

This particular campaign thus entails the involvement of Yahweh's forces

---

13. This reading of the vision of the ephah (5:5-11) is considerably different from the conventional interpretation given by most scholars, according to which its main theme is the removal of Judah's guilt. Here there is only room enough to state my position, without making much of a case for it. I hope to present a more detailed argument elsewhere.

14. See n. 11 above; see further Clifford, 107-31. Some have questioned MT's mentioning only three chariots in the description of the maneuvers, and on the basis of LXX have supposed that all four are explicitly mentioned. This is perhaps warranted on textual grounds, though the relationship between the Greek and Hebrew versions of 6:6 is not at all clear. In any case, however, the movements of the chariots are clearly not directed toward all four points of the compass, as some have supposed. If MT is followed, two head north while one heads south, and then all four (collectively designated as האמצים; NRSV "the steeds") come and request Yahweh's permission to reconnoiter the earth (6:7a). If LXX is followed, two chariots head north while one heads south, and the remaining chariot then comes and requests Yahweh's permission to reconnoiter the earth. Either way the initial movement is along the north-south axis, and not along the east-west axis as well.

on several fronts. He is mostly concerned with quelling the tendency toward chaos that threatens to break out from the north and engulf the whole world. At the same time he is also concerned, but to a somewhat lesser extent, with the deliverance of his own people on the southern front. Because he is not content to pursue these combined initiatives on the heavenly level alone, he also sends his forces to oversee their taking effect on the earthly level. The emphasis, however, is clearly on the confrontation with chaos on the northern front. This is where Yahweh's creative energy has been most forcefully expressed (v. 8), and this is thus the place from which the resulting new world order emerges.[15] This fact does not keep the focus of Yahweh's people on the north alone, however (i.e., on Babylon; cf. 2:10-11). Yahweh's simultaneous action to deliver them creates for them the impetus to look southward toward Jerusalem as well, and to focus also upon developments there, where the effects of divine activity on both fronts are manifest in the restoration.

In the conclusion of the second episode (6:9-15) the prophetic narrator abandons the visionary mode and reports instead his reception of a command to perform a symbolic action. He is to solicit silver and gold from some returned exiles, make one or more crowns from their donations, and perform a kind of coronation ceremony involving Joshua, the high priest.[16] The crown(s) will finally be placed in the temple, to commemorate the donors' contribution to the restoration effort (v. 14). Though Joshua is the one to be crowned, this act has significance in terms of the royal prerogatives that are thereby symbolically bestowed upon his counterpart, Zerubbabel. Though a messianic title (צמח, "the Branch," v. 12b) and a certain regal preeminence both pertain to Zerubbabel's position, it is only by virtue of the high priest's cooperative counsel and his command of the temple cult that the governorship can claim to have such significance. It is Zerubbabel's association with the reincarnation of the Davidic temple, as its builder and patron, that makes his provincial administration kingly in any real sense. And it is only the complementarity of the governor with the high priest that makes them together capable of humanly representing the kingdom of heaven.

15. The phrase הניחו את רוחי (6:8b) can be understood by way of analogy with its closet phraseological counterpart, namely, the expression נוח חמה in Ezekiel (5:13; 16:42; 24:13; 21:22). There the hiphil of נוח means something like "give vent to," so that the expression means "vent anger." Here the verb itself has a similar sense, but both the object and the overall context are different. The phrase means "vent my Spirit," signifying an expression of Yahweh's creative force rather than of his anger.

16. The form עטרות, "crowns," is well attested in 6:11, but in 6:14 it is spelled defectively as עטרת and combined with a singular verb, which suggests that the original reading of 6:14 may have been a feminine singular form of the word (cf. LXX). This makes the question of whether one or more crowns are involved a rather vexed one. Even if two or more crowns are involved, however, there is little warrant for supposing that the symbolic action of the prophet entails the crowning of both Zerubbabel and Joshua. Only the crowning of Joshua is commanded.

From this survey of the units that make up 1:8–6:15 it is obvious that the relationship between heaven and earth informs, in various ways and to various degrees, every one of them. This dominant theme is in large part what the story is all about. To grasp how this theme is developed one must thus grasp how the story unfolds and come to some understanding of the principle on which the narrative progression is based. The question of whether it is chronologically ordered arises, not just because of some modern preoccupation with historicity, but in the nature of the case. Many narratives do progress in chronological order, and this possibility is suggested here by the citation of a date in the introduction to this whole section (1:7). The revelation reported in 1:8–6:15 is thereby situated on "the twenty-fourth day of the eleventh month (i.e., the month of Shebat) in the second year of Darius." The narration thus somehow relates every one of its units to this point in the course of human events. The question is how.

The prophecies that make up the first episode appear to have originated at various times. Two of them, 2:1-4 and 2:10-17, directly reflect the Persians' innovations in foreign policy, which favored the adaptation rather than the eradication of local traditions in accord with imperial aims. This ended the type of imperial domination that entailed Judah's being scattered (זרה, 2:4) and plundered (שׁלל, 2:12-13). Both could thus have come from a time as early as Cyrus's overthrow of Babylon, or from any subsequent time during his reign (ca. 539-529 B.C.E.). They might also have come from a later time, however, early in the reign of Darius (ca. 521). Persian hegemony through Cyrus's innovative foreign policy was then reaffirmed, as Darius put down the rebellion that had broken out on the untimely death of Cyrus's son, Cambyses.[17]

Two other prophecies from the first episode, 1:8-17 and 3:1-10, reflect a time somewhat later in the reign of Darius (ca. 520), when regular sacrificial worship was being resumed on the temple site in Jerusalem, even though the temple itself had not yet been rebuilt (Ezra 3:1-6). This resumption of sacrifices would have been the concrete sign of Yahweh's renewed presence in Jerusalem, to which the vision report in 1:8-17 explicitly refers (1:16a), as well as the development that raised concretely the issue of Joshua's priestly legitimacy, with which the vision report in 3:1-10 is principally concerned. The remaining prophecy from the first episode, 2:5-9, reflects a time when the restoration had moved beyond its initial preoccupation with reinstating the cult to address other socioeconomic aspects of the city's urban redevelopment. This is difficult to date with any precision, but the question of whether a wall was necessary for Jerusalem's defense and socioeconomic viability would probably not have arisen until the resumption of a regular cultic life brought the population there to a certain threshold, sometime after 520.

---

17. For a general sketch of this period and the historiographical problems that affect our understanding of it, see G. Widengren, "The Persian Period," in *Israelite and Judean History*, ed. J. H. Hayes and J. M. Miller, OTL (Philadelphia: Westminster, 1977), 489-538.

The prophecies of the second episode are all related to the activity with which the two intrusive oracles in 4:6aβ-7 and 4:8-10a are concerned, namely, Zerubbabel's temple rebuilding project. The first (4:6aβ-7) foretells Zerubbabel's overcoming great obstacles to lay the foundation again; and the second (4:8-10a) describes his having done so, as it foretells his bringing the construction to completion.[18] The other prophecies that constitute the narrative sequence of the second episode, 4:1-6aα + 4:10b-14; 5:1-4; 5:5-11; 6:1-8; and 6:9-15, are all concerned in some way with what it means to restore the old royal sanctuary. They identify the Jerusalem temple, under the joint leadership of Joshua and Zerubbabel, as the place where the symbolization of Yahweh's heavenly rule over all the earth is centered, whose exclusive legitimacy in this regard is universally acknowledged by a worldwide Torah-reading covenant community, even as it is recognized that the chief locus of Yahweh's involvement in earthly affairs lies elsewhere. The prophecies of the second episode thus come from around the time when Zerubbabel's project was in the works, ca. 520-516.

From even such a cursory dating of the prophecies in 1:8–6:15, it is obvious that the narrative sequence in which they appear is not ordered chronologically. This is particularly evident in the first episode, where prophecies that specifically reflect developments occurring well after the returnees' resettlement in the land (1:8-17 and 2:5-9) precede rather than follow other prophecies that generally reflect the circumstances of the exiles' departure from Babylon and arrival in Jerusalem (2:1-4 and 2:10-17). In view of this kaleidoscopically shifting temporal perspective the narrative sequence can hardly be correlated with the course of earthly events.

It is ordered instead by progressive shifts in cosmic spatial perspective. Every unit deals in some way with the correspondence between things that happen in the heavenly realm of divine beings and things that happen in the earthly realm of human beings, but each unit describes this correspondence from a different vantage point. In the first episode there is a progression from what might be called the juncture of heaven and earth in 1:8-17, down to the international dimension of earthly affairs in 2:1-4, further down to the local dimension of earthly affairs in 2:5-9, back up to the juncture of heaven and earth in 2:10-17, and finally on up into heaven itself in 3:1-10. In the first episode the narrative thus moves from heaven down to earth, and then back up to heaven. In the second episode this pattern is reversed. In 4:1-14 the correspondence between heaven and earth is viewed from the earthly vantage point of the temple precincts. The perspective shifts in 5:1-4 and 5:5-11 to a superter-

---

18. This reading of 4:6aβ-7 follows those interpretations based on the work of R. Ellis (*Foundation Deposits in Ancient Mesopotamia*, Yale Near Eastern Researches 2 [New Haven: Yale, 1968]), which view verse 7b, and particularly the phrase הוֹצִיא אֶת הָאֶבֶן הָרֹאשָׁה, as a reference to a temple refoundation ceremony. See Petersen, 239-42; also Meyers and Meyers, 246-49.

restrial but not quite heavenly one (בין הארץ ובין השמים; NRSV "between earth and sky," 5:9b); then in 6:1-8 it moves upward to the juncture of heaven and earth; and finally in 6:9-15 it comes back down to the earthly Jerusalem. In the second episode the narrative thus moves from earth up to heaven, and then back down to earth.[19]

The first episode is concerned with the Judean restoration as a whole, viewing it as a heavenly initiative that develops through interaction with its down-to-earth effects. The restoration is portrayed, not as a linear sequence of events, but as a historical process with various aspects that in its totality constitutes the earthly result and representation of a great revolution in the heavenly cosmic cycle. The cosmic cycle recapitulates creation, moving from the threat of chaos to an innovative reordering of the world within the limits established in the beginning.[20] As the world is reordered, Judah is renewed in a form that is in some ways continuous with its past existence and in some ways discontinuous.

The second episode is in contrast concerned with just one part of the restoration process, the rebuilding of the temple itself. This project is viewed as an earthly local development that, because it constitutes a response to a heavenly initiative, has vast cosmic implications. The rebuilding of the temple is associated with a particular phase of the cosmic cycle that recapitulates Yahweh's creation of the world through combat with chaos. This is the phase in which he brings his power to bear from down south, as he destroys the forces of chaos coming from the north, in order to save his own people. The temple restored by Zerubbabel, when seen in this context, becomes the definitive sign of Judah's salvation, which also points beyond Yahweh's acting for the sake of his people to his acting for the sake of the whole world.

On the date cited in 1:7 the realization of Zerubbabel's plans was questionable. By the eleventh month of Darius's second year the process of return and resettlement had been going on for about twenty years, but the initial attempts to rebuild the temple had not met with any success. Only a few months earlier Zerubbabel and Joshua had managed to reinstigate this project, despite many

---

19. Petersen has noticed this sequencing principle with respect to the progression of the three-vision series in 1:8–2:9 (p. 172), but he has not extended the analysis of cosmic perspective any further. Meyers and Meyers similarly analyze what they call the cosmic "purview," but only of the visions (pp. liv-lvii).

20. B. Halpern has similarly observed that "Zechariah's night vision . . . assumes the form of a combat cycle" ("The Ritual Background of Zechariah's Temple Song," *CBQ* 40 [1978]: 189), but he describes the correspondences with the mythic background in altogether different terms.

I am here using the term *cosmic cycle* in roughly the same sense as Knierim ("Cosmos and History," 80-85). This phrase is not meant to describe a kind of endless, static repetition of the same events over and over, but rather the recapitulation of archetypal events according to a mythic pattern in a dynamic, transformational process.

obstacles, with the construction of an altar and the resumption of sacrifices in anticipation of soon laying the foundation and eventually completing the entire structure (Ezra 3:1-13; cf. 5:13-16).[21] In the process they were confronted with the question of whether this project would ever be finished.

The compositional design of this passage addresses this question by rhetorically positioning the audience at a particular point in the intersection of human history with the heavenly cosmic cycle. The introduction in 1:7 temporally locates the audience from the outset at a particular point in earthly time that corresponds with a particular point in the cosmic process described by the unfolding narrative sequence of 1:8–6:15, namely, the beginning of the second episode. The date cited in 1:7 falls around the time when the conditions described in 4:8-10b obtain, i.e., Zerubbabel has managed to get the temple foundation laid, but its completion still remains questionable.[22]

The third-person narrator in 1:7 thus puts the audience in a particular relationship with the account of the first-person narrator in 1:8–6:15. The audience is placed at that point in the first-person account when the first episode's prophecies regarding the exiles' return and Jerusalem's rehabilitation either have been fulfilled, or are at least well on their way to fulfillment, but the second episode's prophecies regarding the temple and its completion under Zerubbabel have just barely begun to be fulfilled, and have rather doubtful prospects. By reading the story from this particular point of reference, the audience is led to realize that the prophet's overall interpretation of the restoration's cosmic significance, expressed in the first episode, has already been authenticated in the actual course of events. His more specific interpretation of its temple rebuilding phase and its cosmic significance, expressed in the second episode, will thus turn out to be true, and can therefore be believed (2:13b, 15b; 4:9b; 6:15aα). The audience is meant to give its assent and to support the project that Zerubbabel has begun, because the significance that is claimed for it in the second episode fits the shape of the new world order that Yahweh is shown to be configuring in the first episode.

It is generally maintained that the prophecies in 4:6aβ-7 and 4:8-10a were inserted relatively late into an already existing cycle of Zechariah's night visions.[23] In view of the way 1:7–6:15 is structured overall, however, just the

---

21. A. Gelston, "The Foundations of the Second Temple," *VT* 16 (1966): 232-35.

22. The reconstruction of an absolute chronology for this period is of course a very complicated and tenuous affair (G. Widengren, "Persian Period"). It is perhaps debatable from the standpoint of modern historiographical canons whether the temple refoundation ceremony foretold in 4:6aβ-7 and described in Ezra 3:8-13 had actually come to pass by the date cited in 1:7. The reference in 4:9a to Zerubbabel's refoundation of the temple as a past event shows, however, that from the standpoint of whoever put the text in its final form this was indeed the case.

23. Beuken (pp. 260-74) and Petitjean (p. 267), however, both argue for an original vision report containing various parts of both 4:6aβ-10a and 4:1-6aα + 10b-14.

opposite seems more likely. The problem posed by the people's failure to believe in 4:8-10a, despite the fulfillment of 4:6aβ-7, seems precisely the problem that the composition of this whole section of Zechariah, including the sequencing of both the visionary and the nonvisionary prophecies, is designed to address. The way in which these two nonvisionary prophecies are related to the visionary narration that surrounds them is stylistically consistent and all of a piece with the way in which the nonvisionary prophecies in 2:10-17 and 6:9-15 are related to the visionary narration that forms their context.[24] It is therefore probable that the pair of prophecies in 4:6aβ-10a constituted the redactional starting point, around which the other prophetic materials of various kinds and from various times were arranged into their present compositional form.

The prophetic insight expressed through such a redactional work was the product of retrospective reflection upon the prophetic insights previously expressed in the individual units themselves. The redactor could have been Zechariah himself, attempting to discern and express the cumulative significance of some of his own earlier work; or it could have been someone else, attempting to reinterpret the significance of revelations reported by Zechariah for a new and different situation. The redaction could have been done before the completion of the temple by Zerubbabel (ca. 516), in which case the composition would have functioned as an inducement to support this project. It could also have been done sometime afterward, however, in which case the composition would have functioned to review some of Zechariah's prophecies concerning various aspects of the restoration, from the standpoint of the time in which the issue of their credibility came decisively to a head. In any case the audience who reads this text in the wake of the temple's completion is imaginatively put back into the time when this eventuality seemed doubtful, and thus enabled to recapitulate the process of its being foretold and coming to pass, so that they can come to understand the ultimate significance of the old royal sanctuary's having been rebuilt.

According to the first episode the whole process of the restoration culminates in the rebuilding of the temple. Insofar as the process tends toward that goal, it signifies the reconstitution of Judah as Yahweh's elect, but not the regaining of their national identity. The restoration of Judah is an integral part of the larger process, in which Yahweh's heavenly initiative brings about a new world order under the Persians, making social identity no longer a matter of locality alone. This leaves unresolved the issue of how Judah, without a national identity and hence without a king, could continue to represent on earth the reality of Yahweh's heavenly rule.

This issue is posed sharply by the plot complication in 2:10-17, and finally resolved by the denouement in 3:1-10. There it is shown that a legitimate high

---

24. See pp. 133-35 above. Such observations as Halpern's, that the interruptions in 4:6aβ-10a are "unparalleled" and "stylistically intolerable" (p. 189), are thus quite mistaken.

priest, heading up the administration of the restored sacrificial cult, can serve as the human representative of Yahweh's divine kingship over creation. By associating with the temple where this high priest presides, Zerubbabel, as its builder and patron, can attain to a messianic title (i.e., צמח, "the Branch," 3:8b). The high priest and governor together can thus represent under the conditions of the new age all that the monarchy represented in ages past.

The second episode deals again with this same issue. It is posed from the outset by the two oracles in 4:6aβ-10a, introducing into the middle of the lampstand vision (4:1-14) a complication that gets resolved only in the last scene (6:9-15). Because temple building is typically a royal role, there is a kind of inner contradiction in the claim that Zerubbabel, who is not a king, is the divinely designated director of the project.[25] The unfolding plot of the second episode develops the theme of Jerusalem's being recentered and decentered within the overall scheme of things, in order to work this contradiction out.

On the one hand the rebuilt temple makes Jerusalem the only place where Yahweh dwells in the midst of his people, and the only place where the symbolization of his heavenly rule over all creation is centered. On the other hand, however, Jerusalem is definitely not the point at which Yahweh's heavenly initiatives impinge most directly and most forcefully upon world affairs. Yahweh's salvific creation of a worldwide covenant community, whose identity is focused on the restored royal sanctuary in Jerusalem, can only be understood as part of the larger process through which Yahweh, as creator of heaven and earth, reverses the threat of chaos to make the earth generally more just. Because this reordering of the world involves the salvation of Yahweh's people, it can conversely be seen by all as Yahweh's work. The restored temple is the earthly sign of this divine creativity, but the earthly effects of such creativity are largely realized by other means and largely located elsewhere.

This idea of the temple's significance, as the main sign but not the main site of Yahweh's activity in the world, becomes the conceptual basis for defining the kind of messianic significance that the provincial leadership can have, though there is now no king. The final scene (6:9-15) reiterates that the dyarchy of governor and high priest enjoys a kind of messianic status by virtue of their being jointly associated with the restored royal sanctuary, a messianic status that pertains to the governorship but is rooted in the high priesthood. Together they constitute the chief earthly sign of Yahweh's heavenly agency, but they are not his chief earthly agents. He also has a whole host of heavenly forces, as well as his human prophets (cf. 2:12a), through which he works to see that his will is done on earth as it is in heaven.

This is somewhat different from preexilic concepts of messianic status that tend to see the Davidic king as a direct representation of Yahweh's cosmic reign and an overt participant in his divine activity throughout creation. Ps 89,

25. A. S. Kapelrud, "Temple-Building, a Task for Gods and Kings," *Or* 32 (1963): 52-62.

e.g., describes the king as Yahweh's adopted son (vv. 27-28), whose earthly rule is a direct extension of Yahweh's combat with chaos (v. 26). The loss of the kingship thus tears a gaping hole in the fabric of creation, and the concomitant complaint raises the issue of whether this tear can ever be mended, particularly when the royal piece of the fabric remains missing (vv. 47, 50). Zech 1:7–6:15 is, as it were, a reply to this complaint. It affirms that the kingdom of heaven can be humanly represented in a form somewhat different from the Davidic monarchy. The correspondence between heaven and earth that was broken in the loss of the monarchy can therefore be reestablished in a somewhat different way. Zechariah's view of the temple and its leadership is in the final analysis compelling because it acknowledges the end of Judah's existence as a nation and yet promises the opportunity for Judah's preexilic worldview to regain much of its familiar shape.

Zech 1:7–6:15 is clearly a text that has something to say on the subject of cosmos and history. With respect to the Judean restoration it affirms not only that Yahweh liberated his people from the condition of exile, thereby transforming the basis of their social identity, but also that Yahweh did this precisely in his capacity as the liberating creator of the whole world. As Knierim has observed, one of the main issues that arises from such an affirmation is the question of whether Yahweh renews the world for the sake of his elect, or whether he renews his elect for the sake of the world.[26]

As far as the text in question is concerned, these alternatives seem not to be mutually exclusive. Though this text obviously focuses on Judah, and on a rather exclusive redefinition of their identity as Yahweh's people, it does not do so at the expense of the rest of the world. Because the identity of Yahweh's people is redefined in international rather than national terms, people from many nations can identify with this group; and the role of Yahweh's people is to signal to the rest of the world that Yahweh is covertly active among them all, for the good of all. Yahweh's salvation of his own people is an integral part of the process through which he renews the whole world, and his salvific intention for all creation is made manifest through his people. The prospect of salvation may be all the more palpable to those who explicitly recognize what Yahweh is doing; but because Yahweh's activity encompasses the whole world, this prospect is also shared by many who do not explicitly recognize what he is doing. In other words, this text suggests the possibility of defining the identity of God's people in terms that are very particularistic, while at the same time making membership open to all, and envisioning God's salvation in terms that are virtually universalistic. This is only possible, however, when human history is seen to emerge from and interact with the divinely animated cosmic process of creation — as it is in this text.

26. Knierim, "Cosmos and History," 108-9.

Zechariah's view of the restoration posed for postexilic Jews the issue of whether they, as the people of God, would historically define their identity and their role in world affairs in accord with Yahweh's renewal of the cosmic cycle. This is now perhaps an even more crucial issue for the communities of faith that stand both in continuity and in discontinuity with second temple Judaism. Knierim has rightly pointed out that the possibility of wrecking the global ecosystem now makes it all the more urgent for both theology and faith to seek and articulate the meaning of creation, and to make this the measure of our common life.

In making such an observation Knierim discloses a telling and typical characteristic of nearly all his scholarly work. He exemplifies the kind of academic discipline that is intellectually and analytically rigorous, while at the same time socially aware and engaged. For this influence, and for all else that he has taught us, I am deeply grateful; and to him I dedicate these remarks with respect and affection.[27]

27. I would like to thank Professor Roy Melugin for his constructive response to earlier drafts of this essay.

Der befreiende Gott: Zum Standort lateinamerikanischer Theologie

ERHARD S. GERSTENBERGER

1. Vom hermeneutischen Ansatz

1.1 Rolf Knierim hat sicherlich Recht, wenn er mit großer Beharrlichkeit nach einer theologischen Leitlinie fragt, welche die Pluralität theologischer Aussagen im Alten Testament (und in der ganzen Bibel) zu ordnen vermag. Er baut sein Interpretationsmodell auf der theologisch prallen Aussage von "Jahwes universaler Herrschaft in Gerechtigkeit und Recht"[1] auf. Damit ist Wesentliches über das Verständnis Gottes gesagt. Die fundamentale Gottesbestimmung wird aber nicht weiter hinterfragt, ebensowenig wie der Weg dorthin. Ihr "Sitz im Leben" steht nicht mehr zur Debatte. Beleuchtet man "Herrschaft in Gerechtigkeit und Recht" aus einer Dritt-Welt-Perspektive, dann kann sehr leicht der Verdacht aufkommen, daß die "Herrschaft Gottes" — dem jeweiligen Autor unbewußt — ein echtes Produkt der westlichen Industriewelt darstellt. Denn die Lage der Dritten und Vierten Welt ist so katastrophal, daß keine auch noch so vorläufig konzipierte "Herrschaft" einen Ausweg verspricht, sondern nur noch die grundlegende und schnelle Veränderung aller Zustände. Darum muß die Befreiungstheologie (ähnlich verhält es sich aus analogen Gründen mit der feministischen Theologie) auf grundlegende Umwandlung der bestehenden Verhältnisse setzen. Sie darf sich nicht mit irgendetwas Etabliertem, Beherrschbaren, zufriedengeben. Das Chaos ist nicht regierbar, es sei denn, es werde zuvor revolutionär verwandelt. Natürlich erweist sich auch die Vorstellung eines befreienden Gottes als zeit- und ortsbedingt, genau wie das Konzept des gerechten Gottes. Es ist aber gerade die Aufgabe einer ökumenisch weiten Theologie, die Begrenztheiten der regionalen und schichtenspezifischen (auch der geschlechts-,

---

1. Rolf Knierim, "The Task of Old Testament Theology," *HBT* 6,1 (1984) 43.

kultur- und rassegebundenen) Theologien zu erkennen und die partikularen Erkenntnisse und Bekenntnisse miteinander ins Gespräch zu bringen. Dazu soll auch der gegenwärtige Beitrag zur Ehrengabe für einen verdienten, geachteten und befreundeten Alttestamentler dienen.

1.2 Wie kommen die unterschiedlichen theologischen Konzepte der ersten und der dritten Welt zustande? Theologinnen und Theologen der Industriewelt verstehen die theologische Arbeit als Reflexion über die biblische Botschaft, als geistige Auseinandersetzung mit Lehräußerungen, als notwendige Systematisierung widerstreitender Aussagen.[2] Angestrebt wird ein in sich stimmiges Gebäude von Lehrmeinungen über Gott, Mensch und Welt, das auch geeignet ist, die bestehenden Kirchen (und in weiterem Sinne die sie umgebenden, westlichen Gesellschaften) zu legitimieren und in ihrem Auftrag zu motivieren und zu tragen. Theologie ist eine kritische und konstruktive Wissenschaft, welche aber de facto bestehende Verhältnisse wenn nicht ausdrücklich heilig spricht, dann doch in den Grundzügen voll bejaht und weiterentwickeln will. Lateinamerikanische Theologie hingegen geht von dem Neuen und Umwälzenden, von der Praxis der Menschlichkeit, aus, die ständig unter uns passiert und leicht mit dem Wirken Gottes und dem gekommenen Gottesreich identifiziert werden kann. Da bewegen sich Christen gegen den Strom und gegen das bedrückende Establishment. Da wird lebenschaffende Liebe in einer Welt des Todes und des Elends wirksam. Da entsteht gegen jede Vernunft Gemeinschaft und Solidarität unter den Leidenden, d.h. Kirche Jesu Christi.[3] Über diese Ereignisse und Taten beginnen Menschen zu staunen und nachzudenken. Das ist die Geburtsstunde von Theologie. Theologie ist nicht Reflexion über geistige Sachverhalte und Aporien, sondern Nachdenken über Taten Gottes, Ereignisse, die anders sind als die normale Alltagswirklichkeit. Theologie der Befreiung speist sich aus der Wirklichkeit und Wahrnehmbarkeit neuen Lebens in einer von Grund auf erneuerungsbedürftigen Welt.[4]

1.3 Die Theologien der industriellen Welt sind fest im Gehäuse von Uni-

---

2. Vgl. jedes beliebige, europäische Lehrbuch christlicher, systematischer Theologie. Es fällt auf, daß selbst so ökumenisch offene theologische Entwürfe wie die von Dietrich Bonhoeffer oder Jürgen Moltmann in Lateinamerika kritisch aus der nicht-industriellen Perspektive gelesen werden, vgl. Gustavo Gutiérrez, A força histórica dos pobres (unten Anm. 8), 314-28; José Míguez Bonino, La fe en busca de eficacia (unten Anm. 6).

3. Zu den sogenannten "Basisgemeinschaften" in Lateinamerika gibt es eine unübersehbare Literatur, vgl. z.B. Faustino Luiz Couto Teixeira, Cumunidades eclesiais de base (Petrópolis: Vozes, 1988); Clodovis Boff, Comunidade eclesial — comunidade política (Petrópolis: Vozes, 1978).

4. Befreiungstheologen/Innen werden nicht müde, die "Ekklesiogenese" als den Ausgangspunkt für alle theologische Reflexion darzustellen, vgl. Leonardo Boff, A fé na periferia do mundo (Petrópolis: Vozes, 1983); Gustavo Gutiérrez, Teología de la liberación (Salamanca: Sígueme, 1972); Ronaldo Muñoz, Nueva conciencia de la iglesia en America Latina (Salamanca: Sígueme, 1974). Vgl. aber auch den weiteren, die wahre Menschlichkeit einschließenden Begriff von Befreiung bei Hugo Assmann (unten Anm. 17).

versitäten, Akademien und Predigerseminaren verankert. Sie haben ihre Referenzrahmen in der Welt der Gebildeten, und seien es auch die Gebildeten unter ihren Verächtern (Schleiermacher). Sozialgeschichtlich betrachtet ist die Theologie der sogenannten westlichen Welt in der Eliteschicht zu Hause. Sie teilt darum die Vorzüge und Mängel dieser Elite. Die Befreiungstheologie in Lateinamerika lebt — wenn sie denn echt ist — wie ein Fisch im Wasser des Volkes. Dort geschieht ja das Wunder des neuen Lebens, darum ist dort, in der großen Masse der Verlorenen und Verdammten, der eigentliche Haftpunkt für das Nachdenken über Gott.[5] Die enge Bindung an die arme Volksmehrheit hat ihre Vorzüge und Nachteile, wie sollte das anders sein. Sie ist in jedem Fall eine andere Ausgangsposition für das theologische Nachdenken. Von dem anderen Ausgangspunkt her muß man in Lateinamerika auch zu anderen Sichtweisen und Ergebnissen kommen. Klar, daß im Vordergrund dieser Theologie aus dem Volk heraus die aktuellen und materiellen Probleme stehen, nicht die geschichtlichen, kulturellen, abstrakt theologischen und hochgeistigen Fragen. Theologie hat es mit diesem Leben hier und jetzt zu tun. Von da aus greift sie möglicherweise auch in die geistigen Auseinandersetzungen der Zeit ein, nicht umgekehrt.

1.4 Westliche, den Industriemächten verbundene Theologinnen und Theologen lieben es, die historische Wahrheit in entfernten Weltgegenden aufzusuchen, kritisch zu analysieren und deskriptiv darzustellen. Dann wenden sie sich gerne den hermeneutischen Fragen zu, versuchen, ihren Standort oder ihr Vorverständnis zu bestimmen, um schließlich die Übertragungsarbeit von damals nach heute in Angriff zu nehmen. Die Dolmetscherarbeit ist schwer und entsagungsvoll und muß selbstverständlich von hochqualifizierten Fachkräften geleistet oder vorbereitet werden. Lateinamerikanische Theologinnen und Theologen beginnen ihre theologische Arbeit in der notvollen Gegenwart. Sie wissen, daß jede menschliche Aussage kontext- und interessengebunden ist. Darum wollen sie zuerst die eigene Ausgangsposition — und die der theologischen Lehrer, Mahner und ex-cathedra-Redner — klären. Ein gesundes Mißtrauen gegen jede theologische Behauptung ist so lange nötig, bis die hermeneutische (einschließlich der sozialen und wirtschaftlichen) Plattform des Sprechers oder der Sprecherin ermittelt ist. Die eigene Verwurzelung in der Weltwirklichkeit muß natürlich ebenso kritisch betrachtet werden.[6]

1.5 Aus der hermeneutischen Standortbestimmung ergibt sich ein allgemein verbindlicher methodischer Ansatz. Theologie kann nie im luftleeren

---

5. Vgl. Frantz Fanon, *Les damnés de la terre* (Paris: F. Maspero, 1961); José J. Queiroz (Hg.), *A igreja dos pobres na America Latina* (São Paulo: Brasiliense, 1980); Julio de Santa Ana, *A igreja e o desafio dos pobres* (Petrópolis: Vozes, 1980); Leonardo Boff, *Do lugar do pobre* (Petrópolis: Vozes, 1984).

6. Vgl. Juan Luis Segundo, *Libertação da teologia* (São Paulo: Loyola, 1978); José Míguez Bonino, *La fé en busca de eficacia* (Salamanca: Sígueme, 1977).

Raum betrieben werden. Sie ist ja nachlaufende Reflexion über das neue Leben in einer todessüchtigen Welt. Darum ist der erste Schritt jeder theologischen, auch jeder exegetischen!, Arbeit die Analyse der Wirklichkeiten, in denen Rede von Gott stattgefunden hat oder stattfinden soll. Aus der lateinamerikanischen Erfahrung heraus ist die alles überragende Dominante der heutigen Menschheitsexistenz das Unverhältnis der Lebenschancen in Nord und Süd. Die seit der Kolonialzeit gewachsenen Machtverhältnisse erlauben einer Minderheit der Weltbevölkerung (etwa 30%) den Verzehr von mehr als 2/3 aller Güter, die auf der Erde produziert werden.[7] Außerdem beuten die Machthaber die Ressourcen der ganzen Erde rücksichtslos aus und zerstören bedenkenlos die Lebenssphäre. Dieser globale Hintergrund und die regional verschiedenen Folgen unterdrückerischer Wirtschaftspolitik müssen als Folie für alles theologische Reden bewußt werden.

1.6 Theologie geschieht zuerst und vor allem auf der Seite der Opfer, weil Gott sich nach Ausweis der biblischen Zeugnisse zuerst und vor allem um die Opfer kümmert. Die lateinamerikanischen Theologinnen und Theologen werden also konsequent in die Parteilichkeit mit den leidenden, unter unmenschlichen Bedingungen vegetierenden Massen hineingeführt (vorzugsweise Option für die Armen).[8] Der Referenzrahmen ihres Denkens und Handelns ist ein menschlicher, politischer, leidenschaftlich parteilicher. "Befreiung" ist das einzig legitime Ziel einer Kirche und Theologie, die sich dem Handeln Gottes und Jesu Christi verpflichtet weiß. "Befreiung" signalisiert menschenwürdige Lebensverhältnisse für alle Menschen und Bewahrung der Schöpfung vor selbstmörderischer Zerstörung. Der erstrebte Zustand ist der des "Reiches Gottes", und jede bruchstückhafte Verwirklichung von Gerechtigkeit, Menschenwürde und Umweltschutz ist ein kleiner Schritt in Richtung auf dieses gottgewollte Reich.[9]

1.7 Trotz aller Parteinahme für die Opfer der Weltbeherrscher bleibt der Blick der Befreiungstheologen/Innen auf das Ganze gerichtet. Es geht um das universale Überleben, es geht um die gesamte Menschheit und die ganze Schöpfung. Die Erde ist nicht mehr teilbar. Aus der Perspektive eines versklavten Kontinents mit seiner gnadenlos ausgebeuteten Bevölkerungsmehrheit sieht der Globus natürlich anders aus als aus der Sicht der Industrienationen. Vielleicht muß man in einem "Entwicklungsland" (welcher Euphemismus!) gelebt haben, um die Positionen dort überhaupt verstehen zu können. Wenn Lateinamerikaner/Innen von den saturierten und an der "Überentwicklung" leidenden Minderheiten reden (und wir Mitarbeiter/Innen und Leser/Innen dieser Fest-

---

7. Vgl. Franz Hinkelammert, *Las armas idológicas de la muerte* (San José: DEI, 1981).

8. Jorge Pixley und Clodovis Boff, *Opção pelos pobres* (Petrópolis: Vozes, 1987); Gustavo Gutiérrez, *A força histórica dos pobres* (orig. Lima, 1979; Petrópolis: Vozes, 1981).

9. J. Severino Croatto, *Exodus, A Hermeneutics of Freedom* (Maryknoll: Orbis, 1981); F.L.C. Teixeira, a.a.O. (oben Anm. 3).

schrift gehören überwiegend in diese Gruppe), dann klassifizieren sie ihre Peiniger nicht als Feinde (vgl. Ps 109), sondern als Mitmenschen, die an ihrer Stelle vom Leid der Übersättigung befreit werden müssen.[10]

2. Gottesvorstellungen in Lateinamerika

Beim Aufbruch der christlichen Kirche und Theologie in Lateinamerika hat die Bibel eine nicht zu unterschätzende Rolle gespielt. Augenöffnende Bibellektüre und aktuelle Erfahrung von Liebe und Gemeinschaft im Elend haben sich dabei wechselseitig befruchtet. Der die ungerechte Welt verändernde und die Menschen befreiende Gott wird zur zentralen theologischen Vorstellung.[11]

2.1 Der Gott der Bibel erscheint in Lateinamerika nicht herrscherlich und dynastiebegünstigend, sondern menschennah, freundlich, zornig gegen die Mächtigen. Er ist ein Gott zum Anfassen, ein Gott der menschliches Leid sieht und dem Kleinsten hilft. Hat er nicht den Menschen nach seinem eigenen Bild geschaffen? Hat er sich nicht in Bundesschlüssen mit dem unbedeutenden Volk Israel verschwistert? Sind nicht seine Propheten gegen das Unrecht aufgestanden? Hat nicht sein Sohn das Schicksal eines Verachteten und Verurteilten auf sich genommen? Dieser Gott leidet nicht unter philosophischer Blässe. Er ist Teil des Alltags und der Menschenwelt. Die Vereinbarkeit der biblischen Gottesvorstellungen mit heutigen wissenschaftlichen Erkenntnissen ist kein Problem. Die Übertragbarkeit der Rede vom Gott Israels auf unsere von tödlichen Konflikten geplagte eine, nicht mehr spaltbare, universale Welt wird nicht diskutiert. Es zählt allein das befreiende Wissen um den Gott, der real in dieser Welt von Gewalttat und Hunger erfahrbar ist, der sich auch quälend entzieht, aber doch immer wieder präsent ist und die radikale Umwandlung der Welt in sein "Reich" vorantreiben will. Jeder Gottesdienst, jeder durchgestandene Streik oder Landkonflikt, jede kleine Errungenschaft der Gemeinschaft sind Beweis des Geistes und der Kraft Gottes, sie sind Zeugnis von seiner Menschlichkeit.[12]

2.2 Der universale Gott, der in den menschlichen und mitmenschlichen Beziehungen direkt erfahrbar wird, will die volle Mitwirkung des Menschen in seiner Schöpfung. Das mag protestantischen Ohren verdächtig katholisch klingen, ist sicherlich auch der katholischen Lehrtradition entnommen. Doch gewinnt die Lehre im Lebensvollzug einen neuen Sinn. Denn so ohnmächtig

---

10. Vgl. Paulo Freire, *Pädagogik der Unterdrückten* (Stuttgart: Kreuz Verlag, 1971).

11. Vgl. Jon Sobrino, *Cristologia a partir da América Latina* (orig. Mexico, 1976; Petrópolis: Vozes 1983); analog geschieht der Perspektivenwechsel in der feministischen Theologie, vgl. Sally McFague, *Models of God* (Philadelphia: Fortress, 1987).

12. Vgl. Leonardo Boff, *Jesus Cristo libertador* (Petrópolis: Vozes, 1972); Erhard S. Gerstenberger, "Deus libertador," in: derselbe (Hg.), *Deus no Antigo Testamento* (São Paulo: Associação de Seminários Teológicos Evangélicos, 1981) 11-29.

die Entrechteten in Lateinamerika auch sind, werden sie einmal von dem befreienden Glauben angesteckt, dann wächst ihr Selbstvertrauen. Befreiende Verkündigung des Evangeliums bedeutet ja, den Opfern der Unterdrückung, denen Ichbewußtsein und Menschenwürde geraubt worden sind, einen aufrechten Gang zu ermöglichen. Aus dieser Wieder-Anerkennung der Verachteten als Menschen folgt unmittelbar ihre Beteiligung (participação) an den für sie wichtigen Entscheidungsprozessen. Und theologisch gesehen: Gott will, daß alle Menschen das Haupt frei erheben können. Er will ihre gleichberechtigte Zusammenarbeit in Basisgemeinschaften. Er erkennt und braucht sie als Mitarbeiter in seinem Welterhaltungs- und Friedensplan. Die lateinamerikanische Erfahrung der Kooperation mit Gott findet ihre Entsprechung in zahlreichen biblischen Zeugnissen von menschlich-göttlicher Zusammenarbeit und Auseinandersetzung.

2.3 Die alttestamentliche Rede von Gott besteht bei näherem Zusehen aus einer Kette von sich wandelnden, z.T. sehr unterschiedlichen Gottesvorstellungen. Befreiungstheologen/Innen stehen nicht unter dem Druck, alle Einzeltheologien harmonisieren zu müssen. Sie erkennen die verschiedenen Gesellschaftsformationen, denen spezifische Gottesbilder entsprechen, neben- und nacheinander an. Was Mühe bereitet, ist die Rede von Gott, die offensichtlich den Mächtigen um seiner selbst willen begünstigt. Deboras Kriegergott ist in Lateinamerika völlig akzeptabel, denn er kämpft für die unterdrückten Bauern und gegen die ausbeuterischen, kanaanäischen Stadtkönige. Aber Davids und Salomos imperialer Gott, in dessen Namen auch Fronarbeit geschieht und das Bauernlegen sanktioniert wird, muß verdächtig erscheinen. Er gilt in Lateinamerikas Basisgemeinden als der von höfischen Cliquen (Beamten, Priestern, Großgrundbesitzern) instrumentalisierte Gott. Ihm muß man die Gefolgschaft verweigern. Der wahre Gott hält den Schwachen durch alle wechselnden Gesellschaftsformationen hindurch die Treue. Gott ist ein Gott der "kleinen Leute", nein, der Unterlegenen und Bedrohten, denen die Lebensmöglichkeiten geraubt werden. Mit ihnen baut er sein Reich. Von ihnen aus oder: über sie, durch ihre Vermittlung (das ist eine Umkehrung der sonst in der Geschichtsbetrachtung geltenden Maßstäbe) ist er sekundär auch der Gott der Reichen und Herrschenden. Über dieses Kriterium systematischer Theologie müßte man reden und gegebenenfalls im ökumenischen Rahmen streiten.

2.4 Auf der Linie der präferentiellen Option für die Armen liegt ein anderes theologisches Kriterium, welches in Lateinamerika als Scheidemaß zwischen richtigen und falschen Gottesaussagen gilt und das uns in den etablierten Industrieländern dubios vorkommt. Die Lateinamerikaner/Innen lassen es nicht bei der Solidarität und dem Leiden Gottes mit den Armen bewenden. Sie finden in der Bibel einen Gott der militanten Liebe, der für die Entrechteten das Schwert zieht und damit im Prinzip die revolutionäre Gewaltanwendung erlaubt. Der berühmte Gott des Exodus steht in Lateinamerika hoch im Kurs — in unseren Breiten fristet er ein Schattendasein. Er läßt die Verfolger ersaufen, er vernichtet, wer sich seinem Volk in den Weg stellt. Gewalt, theologisch legitimiert? Wir wissen leidvoll, wie sich Tyrannen und Ausbeuter den Schein des Rechts verschaffen, um zu morden und zu unterdrücken. Auch an dieser Stelle ist die ökumenische Auseinandersetzung dringend erforderlich.[13]

2.5 Zunehmend kommen auch in Lateinamerika kritische Gedanken zum eigenen Gottesverständnis zur Sprache. Die grauenvolle Ausbeutung der Bevölkerungsmehrheiten durch (christliche!) Minderheiten und das entgegenwirkende Handeln Gottes ist der einzig mögliche Ausgangspunkt für die theologische Reflexion auf dem kolonialisierten Kontinent. Aber enthält nicht auch die Befreiungstheologie (noch) Elemente der Unterdrückung? Wenn Bevölkerungsteile weiter marginalisiert werden (Indianer), wenn Frauen immer noch als nachgeordnet behandelt werden, wenn neue Herrschaftsstrukturen in der Basisbewegung entstehen? In der Tat ist alles menschliche Streben anfällig für Überheblichkeit und Mißbrauch. Selbst die schönste Theologie ist nicht davor gefeit. Es macht die Befreiungstheologen/Innen so sympathisch, daß sie entschieden ihren Standpunkt vertreten, aber bereit sind, Schwächen zu erkennen und zu diskutieren.

3. Befreiende, theologische Praxis

Kirche entsteht in den Gemeinden, aus dem Volk. Da, wo sich Menschen um die Bibel versammeln, das Leben aus dem Evangelium von Jesus Christus gestalten wollen, da ist Kirche. In Lateinamerika spricht man häufig von der "Ekklesiogenese", der Geburt der Kirche im armen, benachteiligten Volk.[14] Erst in zweiter Linie entsteht Theologie. Denn Theologie ist nach dem Verständnis der Mitglieder von Basisgemeinschaften das Nachdenken über Gottes Handeln in dieser Welt. Weil aber Gott erst handeln muß, bevor wir darüber nachdenken, kommt Theologie immer an zweiter Stelle. Und weil Gott in den Basisgemeinden handelt, entsteht aus der Basisbewegung in den christlichen Kirchen eine neue, sehr ökumenisch gestimmte Theologie.

3.1 Befreiungstheologie geschieht ganz bewußt auf dem Boden der Basisgemeinden und in kritischer Selbstbesinnung auf diesen Ursprungsort. Eine ganz wesentliche Entdeckung der Befreiungstheologen ist, wie gesagt: Es gibt gar keine abstrakte theologische Reflexion. Die traditionelle Theologie, besonders die europäische, hat immer behauptet, allgemeine, für alle Menschen gültige Wahrheiten zu sagen. Insgeheim waren es aber die Wahrheiten, die den europäischen Interessen nützten, die die Ungerechtigkeiten des Kolonialismus

---

13. Vgl. Walter Altmann, *In Christus Befreiung erfahren*, Vortrag 1987; derselbe, Teologia da libertação, *Estudos Teológicos* [São Leopoldo] 19,1 (1979) 27-35.
14. Vgl. oben Anm. 4.

und Imperialismus, des Rassismus und der raffgierigen, westlichen Weltwirtschaft geflissentlich übersahen und verdrängten. Die Industrienationen predigten in aller Welt die Liebe Gottes für alle Menschen, aber nur abstrakt. Sie verschwiegen, daß Politik und Wirtschaft einseitig für das Wohl der Nordhalbkugel ausgenutzt werden, die Menschen der Südhalbkugel in tiefstes Elend stürzen und darum schlicht Sünde sind. Befreiungstheologie hält es vom Evangelium Jesu Christi her geboten, das Christentum von den Ärmsten dieser Welt her, oder doch zumindest unter Einschluß der "Verdammten dieser Erde" zu leben und zu planen. Darum begeben Befreiungstheologen sich gern in die ärmsten Basisgemeinden. Sie leben dort mindestens zeitweise, und sie scheuen sich nicht, das arme Volk als Gesprächspartner und Lehrmeister anzunehmen. (Carlos Mesters schrieb einen erschütternden, auch selbstkritischen Erlebnisbericht über seinen pastoralen Besuch in einem gottvergessenen Dorf.[15]) Wie könnte das anders sein, wo doch Gott selbst unter den Elenden wirkt, seine Gemeinde sammelt, seine Wunder der Liebe, Versöhnung, Auferbauung tut?

3.2 Die Bibel spielt nicht nur im praktischen Leben der Basisgemeinden eine große Rolle, sondern auch für die theologischen "Nachdenker". Was ist das für ein seltsames, wunderbares Buch, das über Jahrtausende hinweg Anregung, Hilfestellung, Inspiration gibt? Es enthält die gesammelten Zeugnisse der leidenden Gemeinde, des Volkes Gottes. Die Bibel ist nicht ein dogmatisches Werk einer Lehrkommission, noch das akademische Erzeugnis von Rabbis und Professoren. Ihre Erzählungen, Gebete, Lieder, Gebote, Reflexionen sind direkt aus dem Leben und Gottesdienst der früheren Gemeinden gegriffen. Sie sind uns Glaubensbeispiele einer vergangenen Zeit, die wir beherzt in unserer anderen Zeit bedenken sollten. Befreiungstheologen sind sich bewußt, daß die Verhältnisse heute andere sind als damals. Darum sind sie vorsichtiger als die Bibelleserinnen und Bibelleser in den Basisgruppen, wenn es darum geht, die biblischen Geschichten und Sachverhalte auf uns zu beziehen. Sie befürworten eine gründliche Analyse unserer eigenen Gegenwart im Licht und im Dialog mit der biblischen Botschaft.[16] Einige sagen auch, daß die Bibel unmöglich auf unsere heutigen Probleme antworten kann.[17] Kurz: Es hat sich in Lateinamerika eine neue Weise der Bibellektüre herausgebildet, die eng mit dem gelebten Evangelium in den Basisgruppen zusammenhängt.[18]

3.3 Bei allem Nachdenken über Gott und seine Gemeinde und in der

15. Carlos Mesters, *Seis dias nos porões da humanidade* (Petrópolis: Vozes, 1977).

16. Vgl. Carlos Mesters, *Por trás das palavras*, Bd. 1 (Petrópolis: Vozes, 1974); derselbe, *Flor sem defesa* (Petrópolis: Vozes, 1983); derselbe, *Vom Leben zur Bibel, von der Bibel zum Leben*, 2 Bde. (Mainz und München: Grünewald u. Kaiser, 1983).

17. Hugo Assmann, *Teologia desde la praxis de la liberación* (Salamanca: Sígueme, 1976).

18. Vgl. Ernesto Cardenal, *Das Evangelium der Bauern von Solentiname*, 2 Bd. (Wuppertal: Jugenddienst, 1976 u. 1980); Carlos Mesters, Pablo Richard u.a., *A Bíblia como memória dos pobres* (Estudios Bíblicos 1: Petrópolis: Vozes, 1984); Carlos Mesters, Milton Schwantes u.a., *Leitura popular da Bíblia* (RIBLA 1; São Paulo: Metodista et al., 1988).

befreienden Praxis geht es zentral um die Erlösung und Wiederherstellung des ganzen Menschen. Traditionelle Theologie verkündet oft eine Teilerlösung der Seele oder des wiedererstandenen Geistleibes im künftigen Reich Gottes. Befreiungstheologen behaupten, die biblische Botschaft wolle nicht auf das Jenseits vertrösten und den irdischen Leib, die gute Schöpfung Gottes einfach abtun. Sie meinen, die alttestamentliche Botschaft, die noch gar keine Auferstehung kennt und die sehr diesseitige Predigt Jesu selbst seien starke Beweise dafür, daß Gott nicht nur die geistige Existenz retten und heiligen will. Für sie sind Menschenwürde, soziale Gerechtigkeit, Bewahrung der Schöpfung untrennbar und unaufgebbar in den Heilsplan Gottes mit dieser Erde hineingebunden. Bischof Pedro Casaldaliga dichtete ein sehr populäres Lied für die landlosen Arbeiter:

> Wir sind Menschen, Gottes Volk sind wir,
> wir brauchen Land auf der Erde,
> im Himmel haben wir schon ein Feld.

Das ganze irdische Leben mit allen seinen politischen, wirtschaftlichen, kulturellen Verhältnissen ist Schauplatz des Wirkens Gottes. Darum muß es voll in die Überlegungen zur Befreiung und Erlösung der Menschen einbezogen werden. Befreiungstheologen nehmen darum zu den Vorgängen in Weltwirtschaft und Weltpolitik aus der Sicht der ausgebeuteten Drittweltsklaven eindeutig Stellung. Sie plädieren, an die industrielle Welt gewandt, für eine Befreiung auch der Reichen dieser Erde. Die Befreiung der Armen kann ja gar nicht anders geschehen als durch eine Bekehrung der Reichen. Das ist nicht durch Spendenaktionen, sondern nur durch eine Umstrukturierung der gesamten Weltgesellschaft möglich.

3.4 Kirche und Ökumene gewinnen in der Befreiungstheologie ganz andere Konturen als in der herkömmlichen christlichen Lehre. Der Grund ist klar: Aus der Sicht jener Theologen, die von der untersten gesellschaftlichen Schicht her Gott und die Welt verstehen wollen, steht die traditionelle Kirche nicht gut da. Sie hat doch durch Jahrhunderte die Interessen der Eliten vertreten. Sie hat (immer natürlich mit Ausnahmen) Reichtum, Macht und Ehre der Gesellschaft mehr gesucht als die Armut Jesu und das Leiden der vielen Entrechteten dieser Erde. Auch die starke Bindung an die eigene Konfession wird hauptsächlich als Schutzmaßnahme zur Förderung der eigenen Sicherheit verstanden. Das traditionelle Christentum, gleich welcher Konfession, ist nach Meinung der Befreiungstheologen eher eine vielgestaltige Gesellschaft zur eigenen Selbsterhaltung und Glorifizierung, als ein Instrument Gottes zur Rettung der verlorenen Welt. Als solches Instrument wollen sie aber die echte Kirche, d.h. die Basisgemeinden, verstehen. Die Gemeinde sei eben nicht um ihrer selbst willen geschaffen, sondern um der leidenden Menschheit willen. Die Kirche habe sich ständig an die Welt hinzugeben, anstatt sie beherrschen zu wollen. Wenn die Rücksichten auf die eigene Existenz wegfallen, kann auch ökumenische Weite eintreten. Es ist erstaunlich, mit welcher Gelassenheit Christen und Christinnen in den Basisgemeinden und Theologen, die ihnen nahestehen, die konfessionelle Vielfalt und kirchliche Gegensätzlichkeit betrachten. Sie breiten die Arme aus für alle, die sich an Jesus Christus orientieren wollen, und sie sind darüberhinaus bereit, mit allen Menschen guten Willens zur Besserung der irdischen Verhältnisse zusammenzuarbeiten.

3.5 Klingt das nicht wiederum alles sehr katholisch? Wo bleiben die typisch evangelischen Lehrinhalte? Gelegentlich versuchen die wenigen Lutheraner des Kontinents, vom Kern des Luthertums her Stellung zu beziehen zu den Anliegen der Basisgemeinden und der Befreiungstheologie. Ebenso gibt es methodistische, anglikanische, presbyterianische Stimmen in der theologischen Debatte.[19] Bei der Lehre von der Schrift und den Sakramenten, von der Kirche und dem Reich Gottes und an vielen anderen Punkten besteht keine schwerwiegende Differenz zu dem, was in den Basisgemeinden geglaubt und gelebt wird. Aber in der Rechtfertigungslehre könnte sich ein konfliktträchtiger Punkt herauskristallisieren. Hatte nicht Luther immer wieder mit Nachdruck darauf gepocht, daß der Mensch "aus Gnade gerecht wird, durch den Glauben, und nicht durch Werke"? Und fordert die Befreiungstheologie nicht geradezu den aktiven Einsatz von Gemeinden und Einzelpersonen zur Rettung der Menschen, zur Herbeiführung einer heilsamen, gerechten Weltordnung nach dem Willen Gottes? Sicher, wer hier einen Gegensatz sehen will, kann das tun. Dennoch sagen protestantische Theologen, daß ein Scheinproblem vorliege. Auch Luther wollte durch die Verkündigung der Rechtfertigung allein aus dem Glauben doch nicht verhindern, daß Menschen sich mit voller Kraft für die Welt und die anderen Menschen einsetzen. Im Gegenteil. Er wollte ihnen die volle Glaubenskraft für einen solchen Einsatz geben, indem er ihnen zusicherte, daß die Gnade Gottes schon vor der Hingabe wirksam ist, daß darum die selbstquälerische, lähmende Ungewißheit über das Einverständnis Gottes gegenstandlos ist und der Christ freudig und ungehemmt von Schuldkomplexen oder Minderwertigkeitsgefühlen sich in den Dienst Gottes stellen kann. Recht verstanden befreit die Rechtfertigungslehre zum unbekümmerten, den ganzen Menschen umfassenden und tragenden Mittun (ohne Lohnabhängigkeit!) im Erlösungswerk Jesu Christi.[20]

3.6 Das Hauptanliegen der Befreiungstheologie, die sich von den wirklich existierenden Basisgemeinden herleitet, kann man auch mit der Bitte des Vaterunsers beschreiben: "Dein Reich komme". Befreiungstheologie ist eine hoffnungsvoll in die Zukunft blickende Theologie. Sie erkennt das Wirken

---

19. Vgl. José Miguez Bonino (oben Anm. 6); Rubem A. Alves, *Protestantismo e repressão* (São Paulo: Ática, 1979); derselbe, *Dogmatismo e tolerância* (São Paulo: Paulinas, 1982).

20. Vgl. das Sonderheft der Zeitschrift *Estudos Teológicos* [São Leopoldo], 1990: *Releitura da teologia de Lutero em contexto do Terceiro Mundo*, mit Beiträgen von Albérico Baeske, Naozumi Eto, Ricardo Pietrantonio, Prasanna K. Samuel, Devasahayam W. Jesudoss, Philip Moila, Walter Altmann.

Gottes in der gegenwärtigen Geschichte, sie sieht sein gütiges, mitleidvolles Gesicht überall in unserer Welt. Sie entdeckt in den Basisbewegungen die Zeichen der nahenden Gottesherrschaft und der Veränderung aller bestehenden Verhältnisse. Das ist kein Fortschrittsglaube, wie wir ihn seit dem 19. Jahrhundert pflegen: "Es wird schon irgendwie besser werden!" Es ist die von einem tiefen Glauben gegen jeden Augenschein getragene Gewißheit, daß die total korrupte, von Machtbegier und Gewinnsucht beherrschte, verkehrte Welt doch Gottes Schöpfung bleibt und durch Liebe repariert werden kann. Statt vieler textlicher Belege nur zwei kleine Meditationen von Dom Helder Camara:

> Dieses verschwollene Gesicht,
> schmutzig
> schweißbedeckt
> gezeichnet von Stürzen oder Schlägen —
> ist es das Gesicht
> eines Trinkers, eines Bettlers,
> oder stehen wir gar auf dem
> Kalvarienberg
> und blicken dem Gottessohn
> ins heilige Antlitz?[21]

Und der andere Text, gleichfalls aus dem kleinen Bändchen entnommen, dessen Titel Bände spricht: "Mach aus mir einen Regenbogen":

> Hefte dein Ohr an den Boden
> und merk auf die Geräusche ringsum.
> Es überwiegt das Scharren
> unruhiger, erregter Schritte,
> furchtsamer Schritte im Dunkeln,
> von bitteren, zornigen Schritten.
> Noch kein Hall
> von ersten Schritten der Hoffnung.
> Presse dein Ohr noch fester an den Boden.
> Halte den Atem an.
> Streck deine Fühler aus:
> der Meister naht.
> Es kann sein, daß Er nicht
> zur glücklichen Stunde kommt,
> sondern zur harten Stunde
> zweifelnder und schwieriger Schritte.[22]

21. Helder Camara, *Mach aus mir einen Regenbogen* (orig. Zürich, 1980; Graz: Styria, 1981) 83.
22. Helder Camara, a.a.O. 67.

4. Befreiung im Alten Testament

Wenn wir ein Gespräch über die Kontinente hinweg beginnen wollen, dann müssen wir auch die biblische Tradition hören, welche die christliche Rede von Gott angestoßen hat und die auch in den unterschiedlichen Situationen der heutigen christlichen Lebenspraxis als Triebkraft und Korrektiv bereitsteht. Die Grundzüge der lateinamerikanischen und der westlich-industriellen Theologien müßten anhand der alten Zeugnisse überprüft werden. Wir können uns jetzt nur auf einen schmalen Ausschnitt der relevanten Zeugnisse einlassen.

4.1 Jede Interpretation von Texten, besonders von antiken Texten, geht von Grundannahmen aus, die wir hier nicht entfalten können aber wenigstens andeuten müssen. Die uns im hebräischen Kanon vorliegenden Textzeugnisse stammen aus einer sehr fernen Zeit und Kultur. Sie spiegeln die geschichtlichen und gesellschaftlichen Ereignisse und Strukturen, welche das Volk Israel und die frühjüdische Gemeinde gestaltet, erlebt und erlitten hat, und zwar im Verlauf mehrerer Jahrhunderte (die äußersten zeitlichen Grenzen der in den Texten bezeugten Glaubensgeschichte liegen bei 1200 und 200 v.Chr.). Wir müssen uns bewußt sein, daß die Zeitumstände und Gesellschaftsstrukturen damals nicht die unseren waren. Andererseits sind in den so verschiedenen Gegebenheiten allgemein-menschliche Glaubenserfahrungen gemacht worden, die weiterwirkten und für uns heute nicht nur dialogfähig, sondern notwendig zu berücksichtigende Positionen sind. Denn wir haben unsere geschichtlichen und theologischen Wurzeln in jenen fernen Zeiten. Doch dürfen wir unter keinen Umständen die Zeugnisse der Alten einfach als Normen für uns verstehen. Dringend erforderlich ist das Gespräch mit den damaligen Zeugen. Jedes Kopieren ihrer Glaubenserkenntnisse oder Normsetzungen würde unsere eigene Zeit und Gesellschaft vergewaltigen.

4.2 Das uns interessierende und von uns aus der heutigen Weltlage heraus konzipierte Thema "Befreiung" kommt im Alten Testament in mindestens drei Überlieferungskreisen zum Ausdruck. Klassisch geworden und an vorderster Stelle heute im Blickfeld ist das alttestamentliche Thema "Herausführung aus Ägypten", wie es in Ex 1-15 dargestellt ist. Diesem Grundtext sind natürlich die entsprechenden Parallelstellen aus dem Deuteronomium, den Psalmen und Prophetenbüchern, aber auch die Wiederaufnahme der Herausführungsthematik im Buch Deuterojesaja (Jes 40–55) an die Seite zu stellen. Die Rettung aus Ägypten und die Heimführung aus der babylonischen Gefangenschaft gehören für manche alttestamentlichen Zeitgenossen eng zusammen. Aber die geschichtlichen Rettungstaten Jahwes für Israel (wir müssen in diesem Zusammenhang auch an die Richterzeit erinnern!) sind durchaus nicht die einzigen Zeugnisse für "Befreiungserfahrungen" in Israel. Hinzu kommt das weite Gebiet der israelitischen Sozialgesetzgebung. Die ethischen Normen, welche uns im hebräischen Kanon erhalten sind — bruchstückhaft, wie ich meine — zeigen nicht nur eine außerordentlich starke Sensibilität für gesellschaftliche Randgruppen, z.B. Witwen, Waisen, Ausländer, sondern enthalten geradezu Befreiungsgesetze: Die hebräischen Schuldsklaven, die bei den Gläubigern oder für sie ihre Schulden abarbeiten mußten, sollten periodisch alle sieben Jahre in die Freiheit entlassen und ihre Schulden getilgt werden (Ex 21,1-11; Lev 25,39-41; Dt 15,12-17; Jer 34,8-16). Und da ist ein dritter Komplex von Textzeugnissen verstreut hauptsächlich über die prophetischen Schriften: Israel und besonders die Stadt Jerusalem mit Zionsberg und Tempel wird in der Zukunft eine wunderbare Befreiung von Krieg und Gewalt, Krankheit und Schuld, Hunger und Elend erleben (vgl. Jes 60–62; Sach 8–9; 14; Ps 46; 48; 76). Ich zitiere nur einen Text dieser letzten Gruppe, weil er auch in der lateinamerikanischen Befreiungstheologie eine große Rolle spielt:

> Der Geist des Herrn Jahwe ist auf mir, denn Jahwe hat mich gesalbt.
> Er hat mich gesandt, den Elenden gute Botschaft zu bringen, die
>   zerbrochenen Herzen zu verbinden,
> zu verkündigen den Gefangenen die Freiheit, den Gebundenen, daß sie
>   frei und ledig sein sollen;
> zu verkündigen ein gnädiges Jahr von Jahwe und einen Tag der Vergeltung
>   unseres Gottes,
> zu trösten alle Trauernden. (Jes 61,1-2)

Wir werden uns ein wenig auf die Herausführung aus Ägypten konzentrieren, aber die beiden anderen Themenkomplexe im Auge behalten.

4.3 Die Herausbildung und Darstellung der drei alttestamentlichen Befreiungstraditionen sind zeitbedingt und spezifisch für das Volk, das seine Glaubenserfahrungen mit Jahwe gemacht hat. Wir bemerken es sofort, wenn wir zum Vergleich die Befreiungsbereiche danebenhalten, welche uns in unserer Situation am meisten interessieren müssen: Politisch und wirtschaftlich Abhängige, Frauen, rassische und religiöse Minderheiten, homophile Menschen, Alte, Behinderte usw. suchen in der heutigen Welt und unter den gegenwärtigen Bedingungen Anerkennung, Gleichberechtigung, Freiheit. Schon diese sehr unterschiedlichen Gruppen decken sich nicht oder nur sehr mittelbar mit der Volk der Israeliten, das aus der Herrschaft des Pharaonenreiches ausbrach, mit den Schuldsklaven oder den Einwohnern des zukünftigen Jerusalems. Es sind heute anders strukturierte Gruppen, die aufgrund anderer Normvorstellungen und völlig verschiedener Freiheitserwartungen handeln.

4.4 Welche Vorstellungen von Rettung vermitteln uns die Erzählungen von der Herausführung des Volkes Israel aus Ägypten? Historisch-kritisch gesehen ist die Exoduserzählung ein späteres Volksepos, das die Ursprünge Israels erklären soll. Wir wissen, daß in der geschichtlichen Wirklichkeit höchstens ein kleiner Trupp von "Prä"-Israeliten, oft die Mose-Schar genannt, der Fronarbeit der Pharaonen am unteren Nil entkommen ist.[23] Dieses historische Ereignis, das ins 12.Jahrhundert v.Chr. fallen mag, wurde nach langer, kreativer Überlieferung in viel späterer Zeit zu der heute vorhandenen, wunderbaren Geschichte von Moses Kindheit, seiner Berufung, den zehn Plagen, welche die Ägypter zermürbten, dem Auszugspassa und dem siegreichen Durchzug durch das Schilfmeer ausgestaltet. Aber in dieser Endform und als Glaubenszeugnis der späteren Gemeinde betrachtet: Was haben die Exoduszeugnisse des Alten Testaments zu sagen? Ich greife ohne Anspruch auf Vollständigkeit einige wichtige Punkte heraus.[24]

4.4.1 Die Handlungen der Exoduserzählungen verlaufen in einem Dreieck, das aus Jahwe, Mose und dem Volk Israel besteht. Der Pharao mit seinen Beamten, Zauberern und Militärs ist der Gegenspieler der drei erstgenannten Aktanten. Er bleibt außen vor: Das wesentliche Geschehen wird zwischen den drei Hauptakteuren ausgemacht, die — ganz im Gegensatz zu jeder geschichtlichen Erfahrung — politisch und wirtschaftlich völlig unterlegen sind, aber trotzdem die entscheidende Macht in der Hand haben. Sie zwingen den Tyrannen in die Knie.

4.4.2 Die Freiheit, die Israel gegeben und von Mose und seiner Schar auch erkämpft wird, besteht in erster Linie in der Selbstbestimmung einer Gruppe, die Sklavenarbeit tut. Die Fronarbeit hört auf. Die Hebräer entkommen der Peitsche der Aufseher, dem Hunger und den unmenschlichen Lebens- und Arbeitsverhältnissen im Tyrannenland. Die Freiheit der Prä-Israeliten und die von der späteren Gemeinde ersehnte Freiheit hat also ganz deutlich soziale und wirtschaftliche Züge.

4.4.3 Die Freiheit ist aber auch Freiheit der Kultausübung. Jedenfalls spielt das Motiv des "Opfer für Jahwe in der Wüste" bei den Auszugsverhandlungen eine große Rolle (vgl. Ex 3,18; 5,1-4). Dieses Motiv ist deutlich aus späterer Sicht gestaltet: Israel muß erst konstituiert sein, bevor es Jahwe anbeten kann. Und Israel wird nach der Exodusgeschichte erst am Sinai konstituiert, nach unserer geschichtlichen Kenntnis erst im Lande Kanaan. Weiter ist die Zuständigkeit Jahwes für die Wüstenregionen südlich des Landes Kanaan vorausgesetzt. Um diesem Gott Opfer zu bringen, muß das Volk an seinen Wohnsitz wandern (vgl. noch 1 Kön 19: Elia zieht zum Gottesberg). Freie Kultausübung schließt also die Bewegungsfreiheit im Lande Kanaan mit ein.

4.4.4 Eigentümlicherweise ist die Freiheit nicht nur durch den bösen Gegenspieler, den Weltherrscher Ägyptens, bedroht, sondern auch durch das Volk Israel selbst. Der Bericht sieht von Anfang an Unglauben und Widerspenstigkeit der zu Rettenden voraus (Ex 4,1-17). Im Verlauf der Exodusgeschichte

23. Vgl. z.B. Herbert Donner, *Geschichte des Volkes Israel und seiner Nachbarn in Grundzügen*, Bd. 1 (Göttingen: Vandenhoeck, 1984) 84-107; Jorge Pixley, *A história de Israel a partir dos pobres* (Petrópolis: Vozes, 1989).

24. Vgl. Jorge Pixley, *Êxodo* (São Paulo: Paulinas, 1987).

entladen sich mancherlei Widerstände in Rebellionen gegen Mose und dessen Befreiergott Jahwe (vgl. Ex 16f u.ö.). Freiheit ist also auch — und nicht zuletzt! — von innen bedroht.

4.4.5 Die theologische Aussage ruht, wie schon durch das Dreieck der Akteure angedeutet, auf der Gewißheit, daß Jahwe sein Volk Israel vor anderen Völkern, Reichen und Gruppen auserwählt hat. In Ex 19,4-6:

> Ihr habt gesehen, was ich mit den Ägyptern getan habe und wie ich euch getragen habe auf Adlerflügeln und euch zu mir gebracht. Werdet ihr nun meiner Stimme gehorchen und meinen Bund halten, so sollt ihr mein Eigentum sein vor allen Völkern; denn die ganze Erde ist mein. Und ihr sollt mir ein Königreich von Priestern und ein heiliges Volk sein.

Diese programmatische Erklärung ist der geheime Hintergrund auch schon der Auszugserzählungen Ex 1–15. Um sie dreht sich das ganze Buch Exodus, ohne sie konnte die Sammlung von Geschichten und Gesetzen gar nicht zustandekommen. Dieses Erwählungsbewußtsein ist wahrscheinlich eine späte Frucht in der altisraelitischen Tradition, also eher exilisch-nachexilisch als vor dem Exil entstanden. Ein solches Selbstbewußtsein muß geschichtlich verstanden und kann nicht absolut gesetzt werden. Befreiung des Volkes Israel bedeutet also: In der Rückschau erkennt Israel die Flucht einer kleinen Gruppe von Prä-Israeliten aus Ägypten als die konstitutive Befreiungstat des Berggottes Jahwe und gestaltet dieses Ereignis zu einem konfessionellen Epos der frühen jüdischen Gemeinde aus. Viele andere Völker haben vergleichbare Anfangsmythen, welche die Existenz der Gemeinschaft erklären und ihr Identitätsgefühl artikulieren und stärken. Die Navajos z.B. erzählen, ihr Volk sei in der Urzeit aus der Unterwelt heraufgeführt und in das heilige Land der vier Götterberge (heute nur noch annähernd mit dem Navajo-Reservat in Arizona/Neu Mexiko deckungsgleich) gebracht worden.[25]

4.4.6 Die Befreiungsgeschichte Israels ist also aus unserer heutigen Sicht ein wichtiges Zeugnis für das Selbstverständnis der frühen jüdischen Bekenntnisgemeinschaft. Aber es ist nicht das normative, ein für allemal gültige Modell der Befreiung. Dazu ist es viel zu partikular, geschichtlich bedingt, kurz: zeitlich und menschlich. Wir haben keine ewiggültigen Denk- oder Glaubensmuster in der Bibel, nur jeweils geschichts- und gesellschaftsbezogene Aussagen, die in ihrer Bedingtheit erkannt und ernstgenommen werden müssen. Als solche aber haben sie in der jüdisch-christlichen Tradition eine ungeheure Wirkungsgeschichte entfaltet. Viele Völker und Gruppen haben sich als das Volk des

---

25. Vgl. Paul G. Zolbrod, *Diné bahané. The Navajo Creation Story* (Albuquerque: University of New Mexico, 1984). Den geschichtlich-anthropologischen Hintergrund vermitteln Clyde Kluckhohn und Dorothea Leighton, *The Navaho* (orig. 1946; Garden City: Doubleday, 1962) und Ruth M. Underhill, *Red Man's Religion* (Chicago: University of Chicago, 1965).

Exodus verstanden, z.T. die Auswanderer nach Nordamerika, die Buren in Süd-afrika, die Nachkommen der Sklaven in den USA. Der Negro-spiritual "Let my people go" ist ein eindrucksvoller Beweis für die Identifizierung mit der Mose-schar in Ägypten. Auch diese Identifizierungen müssen kritisch analysiert wer-den, weil heutzutage eine universale Befreiungstheologie nötig ist, die nieman-den prinzipiell ausschließt.

4.5 Wir haben zu fragen, was die beiden anderen Überlieferungskomplexe von "Befreiung", die wir im Alten Testament finden, über die Befreiungser-zählungen hinaus für unser Thema beisteuern.

4.5.1 Die Freilassung von Schuldsklaven und die allgemeine Solidarität mit den Randgruppen der Gesellschaft (Witwen, Waisen, Fremde, Behinderte) in den Gesetzestexten gehören als Traditionsmotiv nicht zu den eine Gemein-schaft konstituierenden Überlieferungen. Vielmehr setzen Rechtsvorschriften immer eine bestehende Gemeinschaft voraus. Sie versuchen, das Leben in der Gemeinschaft nach den Grundwerten von Gerechtigkeit und Billigkeit zu or-ganisieren. Die alttestamentliche Gesetzgebung besonders der Spätzeit geht dabei von einer grundsätzlichen Gleichheit aller Israeliten vor Jahwe aus. Das Bild des Vaters Jahwe, der für seine Söhne (manchmal: Söhne und Töchter! Vgl. Hos 11,1-7; Jes 63,7–64,11; Joel 3,1-2) sorgt, impliziert zumindest eine familiäre — wenn auch nicht eine in unserem Sinne demokratische — Gleichbehand-lung. Befreiung ist in den Gesetzestexten des Alten Testaments also nicht als die Konstituierung einer neuen, freien Gemeinschaft zu verstehen, sondern als die je und dann Unrecht korrigierenden Handlungen von gesetzgeberischen Körperschaften und Regierungen (vgl. Jer 34). Solche befreienden Urteile und Handlungen sind begründet im Gemeinschaftsethos, das wir auch als religiöse, konfessionelle und ethnische Solidarität miteinander beschreiben können.

4.5.2 Die "prophetischen" Zukunftsansagen eines befreiten Jerusalems, in dem kein Unheil mehr existiert, gehören wiederum zu einer anderen Zeit und einem anderen Erwartungshorizont. Sie sind offensichtlich vor dem Hinter-grund schlimmer Erfahrungen mit den erhofften Befreiungen gesellschaftlich-politischer Art zu verstehen. Wo die Hoffnung auf mehr Gerechtigkeit, Menschlichkeit und Liebe immer wieder frustriert wird, da baut sich ein Hoffnungspotential auf, das über die aktuell erfahrene Geschichte hinausreicht. Nicht, daß alttestamentliche Theologen sich schnell und vorbehaltlos auf ein himmlisches Jenseits geworfen hätten, in dem die irdischen Fehler aufgehoben wären. Nein, alttestamentliche Zukunftshoffnung ist in der Regel sehr irdisch und realistisch. Aber sie bleibt in den prophetischen Ansagen der Jerusalemer Freiheit doch ein utopischer Zukunftsverweis.

> So spricht Jahwe Zebaoth: Es sollen hinfort wieder sitzen auf den Plätzen
> Jerusalems alte Männer und Frauen, jeder mit seinem Stock in der Hand vor
> hohem Alter, und die Plätze der Stadt sollen voll sein von Knaben und
> Mädchen, die dort spielen. (Sach 8,4f)

Siehe, ich will Jerusalem zur Wonne machen und sein Volk zur Freude, und ich will fröhlich sein über Jerusalem und mich freuen über mein Volk. Man soll in ihm nicht mehr hören die Stimme des Weinens noch die Stimme des Klagens. Es sollen keine Kinder mehr da sein, die nur einige Tage leben, oder Alte, die ihre Jahre nicht erfüllen, sondern als Knabe gilt, wer hundert Jahre alt stirbt, und wer die hundert Jahre nicht erreicht, gilt als verflucht. (Jes 65,18-20; des weiteren: Die Arbeit bringt Frucht und die Gesamtsituation ist paradiesisch: bis hin zum Stroh fressenden Löwen)

Es gibt Stellen im Alten Testament, in denen nicht nur der befriedete Endzustand, die heilvolle Gottesstadt, thematisiert wird, sondern auch der Befreiungskampf selbst. Die Völker stürmen gegen die Wohnung Gottes an, sie werden zuschanden. Sie rennen sich mit aller ihrer überlegenen Bewaffnung die Köpfe ein (vg. 2 Kön 18; Ps 48; Sach 14). Je später diese Visionen verfaßt sind, desto mehr nehmen sie den Charakter von endzeitlichen Schlachten an. Wichtig erscheint mir, daß die Zukunftsschau der Befreiung aufgeladen ist mit Sehnsüchten, welche die Erfahrungswirklichkeit weit übersteigen. Befreiung wird in den absoluten Kategorien des Reiches Gottes gedacht, ausgemalt, vielleicht auch im Gottesdienst und in der Gemeinschaft vorweggenommen.

4.6 Wenigstens am Rande erwähnen muß ich noch die Befreiung, die im Neuen Testament um und durch Christus bezeugt wird, und die im Alten Testament eine merkwürdige Vorabbildung im leidenden Gottesknecht hat (Jes 40–53: die dort enthaltenen Gottesknechtslieder).[26] Befreiung ist hier personalisiert. Nicht in der Gestalt eines mächtigen Befreiers, wie sie noch in den Retterfiguren des Richterbuches oder dem Eroberer Cyrus (Jes 45; 48) auftritt, sondern eben in dem mißhandelten, ohnmächtigen Knecht, der die Schuld der Zeitgenossen trägt:

> Er war verachtet, von allen verlassen,
> ein Mensch voller Schmerzen und Krankheit.
> Man sah ihn nicht mehr an,
> so verachtet war er. Auch wir haben ihn nicht gemocht.
> Doch er nahm auf sich unsere Krankheit;
> er litt unsere Schmerzen.
> Wir dachten, er sei von Gott geschlagen,
> von ihm bestraft und erniedrigt.
> Nein, wegen unserer Schuld ist er verwundet,
> wegen unserer Sünden ganz zerschlagen.
> Er bekam die Schläge, damit wir frei ausgingen;
> er wurde verwundet, damit wir gesund werden konnten. (Jes 53,3-5)

---

26. In der lateinamerikanischen Exegese wird die Verbindung des Gottesknechtes mit der Gestalt Jesu Christi stark betont, vgl. Carlos Mesters, *Missão do povo que sofre* (Petrópolis: Vozes, 1981).

Das Geheimnis dieser Befreiung liegt in der Stellvertretung. Doch sollten wir uns hüten, aus den Gottesknechtsliedern die Distanziertheit des nicht betroffenen Beobachters herauslesen zu wollen. Vielmehr scheint gerade in der Identifikation mit dem Opfer und mitten im Leiden die Befreiung des Volkes oder der Gemeinde vonstatten zu gehen.

4.7 Wir sehen: Im Alten Testament gibt es mindestens drei oder vier Modelle der Befreiung, die je ihre eigenen Charakteristiken haben, weil sie aus verschiedenen Überlieferungsströmen und geschichtlichen wie gesellschaftlichen Situationen stammen. Es geht nicht an, "das Thema Befreiung" abstrakt und pauschal abzuhandeln. Wir müssen genauer hinsehen, um welche Befreiung zu welcher Zeit, an welchem Ort und für welche Gruppen oder Gemeinschaften es sich handelt. Alle vier kurz aufgezeigten Befreiungskonzepte mögen sich ursprünglich auf Israel, spezieller, auf die frühjüdische, d.h. nachexilische Gemeinde beziehen. Das könnte der gemeinsame Nenner sein, der für uns den geschichtlichen Abstand deutlich macht. Wir sind nicht Israel. Wir sind nicht frühjüdische Gemeinde. Aber wir sind durch die lückenlose Traditionsgeschichte mit den Befreiungsmodellen der Bibel verbunden. Darum dürfen und müssen wir uns mit ihnen auseinandersetzen. Und es ist heilsam, erst gar nicht das uniforme Bild einer einzigen biblischen "Befreiung" zu entwerfen, sondern von Anfang an auf die unterschiedlichen Dimensionen und Strukturen der Befreiung hinzuweisen.

5. Das ökumenische Gespräch

Sind die Kontinente und Lebensumstände zu weit voneinander entfernt, als daß Bibelexegeten/Innen noch miteinander reden könnten? Manchmal scheint es so. Begegnungen finden selten statt und sind durch Sprachbarrieren erschwert.[27] Das eine und gemeinsame Schicksal der Welt zwingt aber dazu, auf allen Ebenen das nichtdiskriminierende Gespräch zu suchen. Die vielfachen Ansätze im Gedenkjahr der "Entdeckung" und Eroberung müßten massiv weiterentwickelt werden. In der Bibelinterpretation, die eine außerordentlich wichtige Rolle auch im Zeitalter der Entdeckungen gespielt hat,[28] wird es heute darum gehen, die eigenen Ausgangspunkte und das gemeinsame Ziel des Weges klar zu erkennen und im Wissen um die Relativität der Sichtweisen und im Hören aufeinander zu definieren. Dann kann es wirklich zu Begegnungen, fruchtbaren Auseinandersetzungen und zum Fortschreiten in der richtigen Richtung kommen.

27. Rolf Knierim hat selbst eine Reise nach Brasilien unternommen (1989) und pflegt ständigen Kontakt mit lateinamerikanischen Fachleuten.
28. Vgl. Sérgio Buarque de Holanda, *Visão do paraiso*, 2.Aufl. (São Paulo: Univ. de São Paulo, 1969); Vitorino Magalhaes Godinho, *Mito e mercadoria, utopia e prática de navegar* (Lissabon/Rio de Janeiro: DIFEL, 1990).

5.1 In der Tat ist die Bestimmung des jeweils eigenen Ausgangspunktes eine elementare, die Möglichkeit des Dialogs vorentscheidende Aufgabe. Wer meint, es gebe nur eine, absolute Perspektive und einen, ausschließlichen Weg zur Wahrheit, der setzt sich und seine gesellschaftliche Ordnung zum Maßstab aller Dinge. Wir kommen von verschiedenen Seiten der geschichtlichen Entwicklung, wir sind Täter und Opfer, die sich bei der Lektüre der Bibel treffen. Lateinamerikaner/Innen (unter ihnen durchaus nicht nur Opfer!) sind in der Regel den Europäern und Amerikanern durch ihre Leidenserfahrungen oder Leidensanschauungen weit voraus. Sie sehen grundsätzlich die Notwendigkeit einer hermeneutischen Ortsbeschreibung ein. Die nüchterne Selbsteinschätzung im Rahmen der universalen Welt fällt ihnen relativ leichter als den durch Wohlstand und altes, koloniales Herrschaftsdenken verblendeten Erstweltlern. Aufgrund der imperialen Geschichte, die in Europa ihren Ausgang nahm, halten Exegeten/Innen der sogenannten Ersten Welt unbewußt ihren partikularen, interessengebundenen Standort für den archimedischen Punkt, von dem aus Bibel und Welt verstanden werden müßten.[29] Viel, vielleicht alles, wäre gewonnen, wenn wir, die Bibelleser/Innen und -forscher/Innen aus der industriellen und der agrarischen Welt unsere Konzepte von "Gerechtigkeit, Frieden und Bewahrung der Schöpfung" relativieren und vergleichen könnten.[30] Die einzig wahren Ausgangspositionen, die in kolonialen und imperialen Kirchen zu den bekannten alten Missionsstrategien[31] geführt hatten, sind immer Herrschaftsbastionen gewesen. In der heutigen, ökumenischen Bibelexegese brauchen wir zuerst das Eingeständnis, daß unser eigener, axiomatischer Grundansatz — ganz gleich, wie er inhaltlich oder methodisch definiert sei — relativ, weil geschichtlich und gesellschaftlich konditioniert ist. Wir haben unseren Standort nicht als "Ist-Aussage", sondern als "Ich/wir sehe(n) das so" — Aussage zu formulieren und von vornherein alle Dominanzansprüche aufzugeben.

5.2 Die Relativität und Interessenverflochtenheit der eigenen Erkenntnis ist theologisch gut sichtbar zu machen durch den Hinweis auf den einen, universalen, absoluten Gott und die jeweils geschichtliche Konkretheit, Vorläufigkeit und Weltlichkeit seiner Offenbarung. Der Monotheismus und die

---

29. Vgl. Erhard S. Gerstenberger, "Der Realitätsbezug alttestamentlicher Exegese," *Congress Volume, Salamanca, 1983* (VTSup 36: Leiden: Brill, 1985) 132-44.

30. Die Verhandlungen und Konferenzen, die unter diesem wahrhaft konziliaren Welt — Thema abgehalten wurden, haben die enormen Schwierigkeiten des Nord — Süddialogs offenbart. Ermutigend ist allein die Erkenntnis, daß der Zwang zum weltweiten Grundsatzgespräch weithin eingesehen wird. Vgl. auch die Auseinandersetzungen vor und auf dem Umweltgipfel in Rio de Janeiro, Juni 1992!

31. Vgl. die in Lateinamerika, hauptsächlich durch den katholischen Indianer-Missions-Rat (CIMI) erarbeitete neue Praxis der Mission: Carlos Brandão u.a., *Inculturação e libertação*, 2. Aufl. (São Paulo: Paulinas, 1986). Sehr aufschlußreich sind auch die Berichte des Ehepaares Lori Altmann und Roberto Zwetsch, die sieben Jahre beim Volk der Kulina in Acre lebten.

christliche Offenbarungslehre sind ja fürchterlich mißbraucht worden, solange Kirchen und Christen daraus für sich selbst einen Besitz- und Alleinvertretungsanspruch auf die göttliche Wahrheit ableiteten. Aus der Einheit und Ausschließlichkeit Gottes wie aus der Tatsache seiner Selbstmitteilung durch menschliche Vermittlung kann nie die Einzigkeit und das Privileg der Gottesdiener, sondern höchstens die Konkretheit und Beschränktheit ihrer Erkenntnis, die gleichen Rechte aller anderen Menschen und die Dienstbereitschaft der Glaubenden geschlossen werden. Wer das Umfassende und Absolute erahnt, der kann doch nicht überheblich werden, sondern wird sich seiner Erbärmlichkeit bewußt. Das ist in manchen biblischen Texten der Fall, in anderen nicht. Aber die Einsicht gilt auch für die biblischen Zeugen: Wo immer sie Herrschaftsansprüche über die "Ungläubigen", "Heiden", "Gegner" anmelden, sind sie theologisch auf dem Holzweg. Der eine Gott — wenn er denn der eine und einzige ist — hat viele gleichberechtigte Kinder. Sie alle sind in ihrer Unvollkommenheit gottunmittelbar und haben auf ihre Weise teil an der Liebe und am Leben, die von Gott kommen. Bei der Bibelinterpretation ist jedes Kind mitspracheberechtigt, und jedes wird aus seiner Erfahrung Wesentliches zum Verständnis der Botschaft von "Gerechtigkeit und Frieden" beisteuern können.[32]

5.3 In der Praxis läßt sich die Relativität der Positionen am besten dadurch erkennen, daß Positionswechsel versucht werden. Befreiungstheologen halten es für unerläßlich, das Leben der Armen und Ärmsten aus der unmittelbaren Nähe und in Solidarität mit ihnen kennenzulernen. Darum verbinden sie oft ihre akademische Lehrtätigkeit mit der pastoralen Praxis. Sie suchen die favelas auf und leben mit den Verelendeten. Aber auch der gedankliche Versuch eines Rollenwechsels ist nicht zu unterschätzen. Was sagt ein gegebener Bibeltext unter der Voraussetzung, daß ich chronisch Hunger leiden müßte? Wie sieht ein Lateinamerikaner den Europäer, dessen gesicherter Lohn bei gleicher Tätigkeit mindestens die zehnfache Kaufkraft hat? Der soziale Status und das Einkommen beeinflussen unsere Bibellektüre. Ein physischer Wechsel in eine Drittweltsituation (oder ins Obdachlosen-, Asylanten-, Arbeitslosenmilieu hierzulande) läßt es wie Schuppen von unseren Augen fallen. Der krasse Perspektivunterschied zwischen Besitzenden (und deswegen vielleicht psychisch stark Belasteten und Gestreßten) und den Elenden dieser Welt (die möglicherweise viel gelassener und hoffnungsvoller sind) macht auch die Relativität der Bibelauslegung verständlich.

5.4 Mit der partikularen Standortbestimmung ergibt sich ein konditioniertes Bild von der Welt und ihrem Zustand im ganzen und im einzelnen. Auch

32. Eindrucksvoll ist, mit welcher Geduld Befreiungstheologen/Innen auf die Stimme des Volkes hören können. Es gibt eine ausgeprägte Literaturgattung in den Basisgemeinden, die der Stimme der untersten sozialen Schichten bei der Bibelauslegung Raum gibt. Vgl. *Os estudios bíblicos de um lavrador* (Tempo e Presença Suppl. 25; Rio de Janeiro: Tempo e Presença, 1979).

Gott und Mensch werden durch die kulturelle, soziale, wirtschaftliche Brille gesehen. Bewohner der Industrieländer finden die herrschenden Zustände — was das eigene Leben angeht — durchweg erträglich und sicherungswert. Alle reden von schlimmen Dingen und Gefahren, dort, bei den "anderen", aber alle möchten ihren Wohlstand behalten und vermehren. In Lateinamerika liegt die Tatsache auf der Hand: So darf es nicht weitergehen! Während die Erste Welt den Frieden und die Gerechtigkeit beschwört, die in Wirklichkeit nicht vorhanden sind, wissen die hungernden Massen, daß die Menschheit schon in den Abgrund gestürzt ist. Die Industriewelt meint, durch leichte Reformen, die ihr selbst nichts abverlangen, alle Gefahren wenden zu können. Lateinamerikas Theologen/Innen können nur in apokalyptischen Paradigmen denken. Gibt es Berührungspunkte? Der sogenannte Westen ist nach dem Untergang des realen Sozialismus in der äußersten Gefahr, sich selbst zu betrügen. Das eigene System hat sich als überlegen und darum scheinbar als gut und gerecht erwiesen.[33] Die Einsicht, daß das westliche, marktwirtschaftliche System nur einer sehr begrenzten Minderheit gute Lebensqualität verschafft, und das auf Kosten der darbenden Mehrheit, müßte eigentlich den Siegerstolz dämpfen und zu einer realistischeren Einschätzung der Weltlage führen. Weil wir die Bibelauslegung in unsere Welt hinein vollziehen, ist der konzeptionelle Hintergrund außerordentlich wichtig. Die Beurteilung der Welt kann dann gelingen, wenn wir die Erfahrungen aus allen Kontinenten, Volksgruppen und sozialen Schichten zusammenschauen und kritisch aneinander messen. (Die ökologische Katastrophe und die Bevölkerungsexplosion sind besonders in den Industrieländern gefürchtete Entwicklungen; doch auch hier sind die Ursachen nicht einseitig bei einer Partei zu suchen).

5.5 Das "Mißtrauen" (suspeita) gegen interessengebundene Axiome ist ein grundlegendes hermeneutisches Prinzip.[34] Es soll dazu anleiten, die unreflektierten Grundprinzipien der eigenen (und aller anderen) Interpretationsansätze offenzulegen. Nur wenn dies geschieht, kann ein echtes, weiterführendes Gespräch zustandekommen. Das Anfangsmißtrauen gilt aber auch gegenüber den biblischen Zeugen. Sie waren selbst interessegebundene Menschen, die von partikularen Positionen aus dachten und argumentierten. Also müssen auch ihre Grundanschauungen und Sichtweisen der Kritik unterzogen werden. Es geht nicht an, biblische Aussagen zu enthistorisieren und als solche zu glorifizieren. Wir müssen z.B. Positionen der Schwäche und des Hasses (vgl. Ps 137,8f), des militärischen Zynismus (vgl. 2 Sam 8,2; Jes 63,1-6) oder von Allmachtsphantasien (vgl. Ps 2,9-12)[35] beim Namen nennen. Biblische Zeugnisse sind

---

33. Vgl. Francis Fukuyama, *Das Ende der Geschichte* (Stuttgart: Klett, 1992).

34. Vgl. Juan Luis Segundo, *Libertação da teologia* (oben Anm. 6); Elisabeth Schüssler Fiorenza, *Bread, not Stone* (Boston: Beacon, 1984).

35. Vgl. Erhard S. Gerstenberger, *Psalms: Part 1 with an Introduction to Cultic Poetry,* FOTL 14,1 (Grand Rapids: Eerdmans, 1988) 44-49 (zu Psalm 2).

zeit-, orts- und interessegebunden, darum sind sie bis in die wichtigsten theologischen Vorstellungen hinein unterschiedlich, ja, widersprüchlich. Das Problem der richtigen Auslegungskriterien stellt sich aber für die lateinamerikanische Exegese anders als für uns. Wir suchen den gemeinsamen begrifflichen
Nenner in den biblischen Zeugnissen.[36] In Lateinamerika geht man auf die
analogen sozialen Situationen zu. Wo die Bibel von Unterdrückung und aus der
Sicht der Elenden von der bevorstehenden Befreiung redet — und das geschieht
dank der Leidensgeschichte Israels in den allermeisten Texten —, da ist das
wahre Wort Gottes für uns. Der Auslegungsmaßstab ist mithin der gegenwärtigen Weltsituation entnommen.[37] Aber das gilt genauso für die begrifflichen
Harmonisierungen der alttestamentlichen Aussagen. Einwenden kann man
gegen die lateinamerikanische Befreiungshermeneutik, daß Unterdrückung und
Befreiung in der Antike ganz andere Dimensionen hatten als in der industriellen
und postmodernen Welt. Dazu ist das ökumenische Gespräch zwischen den
Kontinenten und mit den Bibeltexten wichtig.

5.6 Es kann nach allem Gesagten nicht darum gehen, irgendeinen hermeneutischen Ansatz als den allein wahren auszugeben. Die Pluralität der Erfahrungen, Situationen und Interessen bedingt in der Gegenwart (das gilt mu-
tatis mutandis auch für die Antike) unterschiedliche und konfliktgeladene
Auslegungsansätze und -modelle. Interessengruppierungen mannigfacher Art
stehen dahinter. Das ökumenische Gespräch aller, die sich auf die Bibel als eines
Urdokuments des Glaubens beziehen, darf und muß geführt werden, weil Gott
diese Welt noch nicht ganz dem Untergang übergeben hat. Daß es hier und da
geführt wird, nicht zuletzt in Claremont unter aktiver Beteiligung Rolf Knierims,
ist ein Zeichen der Hoffnung.

36. Vgl. Gerhard S. Hasel, *Old Testament Theology,* 2. Aufl. (Grand Rapids: Eerdmans,
1975); Manfred Oeming, *Gesamtbiblische Theologien der Gegenwart,* 2. Aufl. (Stuttgart:
Kohlhammer, 1987).

37. Vgl. das sehr eindrucksvolle Plädoyer J. Severino Croattos für die notwendige
"Eisegese": *Exodus, A Hermeneutics of Freedom* (o. Anm. 9), 2: "When a word expresses the
meaning of an event, it is giving meaning to the event. There is nothing paradoxical in this;
it is rather the very essence of every moment of interpretation. Exegesis is eisegesis, and
anybody who claims to be doing only the former is, wittingly or unwittingly, engaged in
ideological subterfuge. Not even the physical sciences are exempt from this principle."

Sin, Purification, and Group Process

K. C. HANSON

This essay, offered to honor Professor Rolf P. Knierim, combines several issues about which I have learned much from his lectures and writings: sin, Leviticus, Jeremiah, hermeneutics, and setting in life. Those acquainted with his work will recognize his insights and concerns throughout. In fact, two of the texts addressed below, Leviticus 4 and Jeremiah 7, were covered in Knierim lectures and seminars in my first year of graduate study. His exegeses of these texts form the foundation for my analysis. What I am attempting here is to combine the form-critical, tradition-historical, theological approaches with cultural anthropology as well as learn something from the juxtaposition of these texts.

The central hermeneutical question is: How do we listen to, make use of, and appropriate biblical texts? This question arises because we are separated from the communities of the texts in terms of time, space, language, and literary tradition. Modern interpretative methods have all emerged in order to bridge these gaps: history, historical geography, linguistics, literary criticism, redaction criticism, form criticism, tradition history. But only in recent years has the *cultural* chasm been addressed in a systematic way.

The social scientific methods of cultural anthropology, macro-sociology, and social psychology have only recently been systematically employed for the interpretation of ancient texts.[1] But certainly we must recognize the contribu-

---

1. For bibliographies and overviews see, e.g., J. H. Elliott, "Social Scientific Criticism of the New Testament and its Social World," *Semeia* 35 (1986): 1-34, and D. J. Harrington, "Second Testament Exegesis and the Social Sciences: A Bibliography," *BTB* 18 (1988): 77-85; J. W. Flanagan, *David's Social Drama: A Hologram of Israel's Early Iron Age*, JSOTSup 73 (Sheffield: Almond, 1988).

tions which Gunkel, Mowinckel, and Pedersen (among others) made in pointing us in that direction.

When modern, Western readers of the Bible encounter texts which refer to the culpability of *groups,* those texts are naturally jarring and disorienting if taken seriously: "How could God hold *me* accountable for something my parents, religious leaders, or government officials did?" The same is true of the individual's responsibility to the group for deviance: "My sins are between God and me, and no one else." Even the Roman Catholic tradition of the confessional retains anonymity. The reason this disorientation arises (or should) is that Western culture socializes its members toward an individualistic understanding of human experience.

A team of sociologists examining American individualism observes:

> Individualism lies at the very core of American culture. . . . We believe in the dignity, indeed the sacredness, of the individual. Anything that would violate our right to think for ourselves, judge for ourselves, make our own decisions, live our lives as we see fit, is not only morally wrong, it is sacrilegious.[2]

My concern here is to analyze biblical texts from different settings in life which address the issue of sin and the means to remedy it in terms of *group process* as opposed to individualistically. This requires an examination of how individuals are oriented to groups, how social structures are perceived as facilitating or not facilitating the values of the group, and how deviance ("sin") is addressed and remedied.

The texts analyzed here represent two basic approaches: "structure" and "counter-structure." By "structure" I mean a symbol system which supports the dominant culture: its social structures and values; the expected behavior is *conformity.* "Counter-structure" is thus an alternative symbol system offered by a subgroup embedded within a larger culture; and the expected behavior is either *innovation* (creating new means to realize the goals of the dominant society) or *rebellion* (rejecting the dominant society's means and ends, and substituting new ones).[3]

Dyadic Personality

As Clifford Geertz (a field anthropologist who has worked in Indonesia and Morocco) has pointed out, the modern, Western conception of an individual,

2. R. N. Bellah et al., *Habits of the Heart: Individualism and Commitment in American Life* (New York: Harper and Row, 1985), 142.

3. B. J. Malina, *Christian Origins and Cultural Anthropology: Practical Models for Biblical Interpretation* (Atlanta: John Knox, 1986), 125-26.

as a bounded, unique, more or less integrated motivational and cognitive universe, a dynamic center of awareness, emotion, judgment and action organized into a distinctive whole and set contrastively both against other such wholes and against its social and natural background, is, however incorrigible it may seem to us, a rather peculiar idea within the context of the world's cultures.[4]

In addressing the understanding of the individual and the group, two primary paths have been followed by biblical scholars. The first is to dismiss any gap between cultural understandings of individual and group. The interpretative problems which confront the modern reader, argues Bultmann, are linguistic meanings, historical possibilities, and existential appropriation.[5] Thus Bultmann is keen to avoid linguistic misunderstandings, anachronisms, and inauthentic actualizations. But he is unfortunately not so aware of the ethnocentric assumptions which his existential interpretation involves. As Stendahl points out, this assumes an unbroken continuity between first-century Christians and modern, Western Christians in their understandings of "existence," and thus the nature of individuals.[6]

Another approach is to admit the disjunctures and to interpret them in terms of "primitive mentalities." The discussions of "corporate personality," "corporate representation," "corporate responsibility," and "psychical unity" were given currency by Pedersen,[7] Robinson,[8] Johnson,[9] and Knierim.[10] They followed the lead, directly or indirectly, of the French anthropologist Levy-Bruhl[11] down this path; for example:

> in Israelite thought, as in that of the so-called "primitive" peoples of our own day, there is a vivid sense of what has been called "corporate personality." In other words, the individual is regarded as a centre of power which extends

4. C. Geertz, *Local Knowledge: Further Essays in Interpretive Anthropology* (New York: Basic Books, 1983), 59.

5. R. Bultmann, "The Problem of Hermeneutics," in *The New Testament and Mythology and Other Essays* (Philadelphia: Fortress, 1984), 86-88.

6. K. Stendahl, "The Apostle Paul and the Introspective Conscience of the West," in *Paul among Jews and Gentiles and Other Essays* (Philadelphia: Fortress, 1976).

7. J. Pedersen, *Israel: Its Life and Culture,* 2 vols. (London: Oxford University, 1926).

8. H. W. Robinson, *Corporate Personality in Ancient Israel,* rev. ed. (Philadelphia: Fortress, 1980); original articles 1936-37.

9. A. R. Johnson, *The One and the Many in the Israelite Conception of God,* 2nd ed. (Cardiff: University of Wales, 1961); *The Vitality of the Individual in the Thought of Ancient Israel,* 2nd ed. (Cardiff: University of Wales, 1964); *Sacral Kingship in Ancient Israel,* 2nd ed. (Cardiff: University of Wales, 1967).

10. R. P. Knierim, *Die Hauptbegriffe für Sünde im Alten Testament* (Gütersloh: Gütersloher Verlagshaus Gerd Mohn, 1965), 97-111.

11. L. Levy-Bruhl, *Primitive Mentality* (London: G. Allen and Unwin, 1923); *How Primitives Think* (London: G. Allen and Unwin, 1926).

far beyond the contour of the body and mingles with that of the family and the family property, and the tribe and the tribal possessions, or the nation and the national inheritance, to form a psychical whole; and, what is more, such a psychical whole has an extension in time as well as space, so that the mystic bond which unites society may be conceived retrospectively as regards its ancestors and prospectively with regard to future generations.[12]

It is clear that these authors are appropriately sensitive to a very real distinction between the perspective of the biblical texts and the modern, Western reader. And I would agree with much of what Johnson says here. The question becomes: is their interpretative model of the phenomena and their definition of terms adequate? As Porter,[13] Rogerson,[14] and Tucker[15] have pointed out, several problems emerge in continuing to use these formulations and this model: (1) the ambiguity in definition and usage of these terms, (2) the suitability of alternative explanations for some of the texts which require no such concepts, (3) the renunciation by Levy-Bruhl in his later works of some of his earlier conclusions (such as "pre-logical thinking"), (4) the misleading chronological typology of a simplistic linear progression toward individual moral responsibility, and (5) basing conclusions upon Levy-Bruhl's weak methodological procedures. For a critique of Levy-Bruhl's methodology, see Rogerson.[16]

If neither an ethnocentric view of existential continuity (per Bultmann) nor a formulation based upon theories of "primitive mentalities" (per Levy-Bruhl and Robinson) is admitted, is there a viable alternative? Malina has offered an interpretation of individual and group in the New Testament based upon contemporary anthropological studies.[17] Ancient Mediterranean societies have in common with other traditional, honor-shame cultures (ancient and modern) a different understanding of individual and group. The term modern anthropologists employ for this is "dyadic personality" (from the Greek for "pair"). Rather than a primitive mentality, dyadic personality is a term which identifies a mode of socialization.

---

12. Johnson, *Sacral Kingship in Ancient Israel*, 2-3.

13. J. R. Porter, "The Legal Aspects of the Concept of 'Corporate Personality,' in the Old Testament," *VT* 15 (1965): 361-80; "Biblical Classics III: Johs. Pedersen, *Israel*," *ExpTim* 90 (1978): 36-40.

14. J. W. Rogerson, "The Hebrew Conception of Corporate Personality: A Reexamination," in *Anthropological Approaches to the Old Testament*, ed. B. Lang, Issues in Religion and Theology 8 (Philadelphia: Fortress, 1985); original article 1970.

15. G. M. Tucker, "Introduction" to Robinson, *Corporate Personality in Ancient Israel.*

16. J. W. Rogerson, *Anthropology and the Old Testament* (Atlanta: John Knox, 1978), 53-59; "Hebrew Conception of Corporate Personality," 51-52.

17. B. J. Malina, "Individual and the Community — Personality in the Social World of Early Christianity," *BTB* 9 (1979): 126-38; *The New Testament World: Insights from Cultural Anthropology* (Atlanta: John Knox, 1981), 51-70.

A dyadic personality is defined "as a distinctive whole *set in relation* to other wholes and *set within* a given social and natural background. Every individual is perceived as embedded in some other, in a sequence of embeddedness, so to say."[18] Moreover, the dyadic personality emphasizes social over psychological perspective: how one is perceived in the group is what is important, rather than personal introspection. Identity is a product of interactive relationships rather than individualistic ego-formation. Perhaps the most convenient way to see how modern, Western individualism compares to dyadism is to reproduce selective portions of the comparative list in Malina and Neyrey:

The U.S. View	The Mediterranean View
Emphasis on autonomy and individualism . . .	Emphasis on sociality and group orientation . . .
Emphasis on rights and the right to experiment and change individually and socially.	Emphasis on duty and loyalty with the obligation to remain in one's group(s) and abide by its decisions.
Preference for majoritarian decision making, with the willingness to abide by the will of the majority.	Preference for consensual decision making, with dissatisfaction should one be omitted from the consensual process of one's peers.
Respect for efficiency, ability, success.	Respect for hierarchy, seniority, family.
Quality of life assessed in terms of individual success, achievement, self-actualization, self-respect.	Quality of life assessed in terms of family/group success, achievement, respect of others for the group.
Quality of work life judged by a task's challenge to the individual and the intrinsic needs of the individual that it meets.	Quality of work life judged by degree to which a job allows the individual to fulfill obligations to the family/groups.
Avoiding guilt, either internalized or applied by another for some infraction, is a fundamental concern.	Avoiding being shamed by others, and thus maintaining one's family's/group's honor, is a fundamental concern.
Preserving self-respect is basic.	Preserving face, i.e., respect from one's reference groups, is basic.

18. Malina, "Individual and the Community," 128; author's emphasis.

Children learn to think of themselves as "I."	Children learn to think of themselves as "we."
A person-based culture: there are relatively overlapping social roles for males and females, with no explicit sexual division of labor. Yet dominant values are those of males . . .	A gender-based culture: a sexual division of labor with no overlapping roles. . . . Dominant values are those of males with females embedded or encysted in males.[19]

Malina notes that the various ancient Mediterranean cultures agree in this dyadism at a high level of abstraction; but differences do exist. Their specific articulations of personality perception are quite distinctive:

> Greek and Roman philosophers and their followers talked of the makeup of man in terms of body and soul, in terms of intellect, will, and conscience, in terms of virtues and vices that fazed one's immortal soul. Such ideas and terminology are absent from the biblical writings.[20]

This leads Malina to employ de Geradon's threefold model of personality, representative of Semitic discourse, to analyze biblical perceptions of personality: the "zone of emotion-fused thought" (eyes, heart, etc., and their activities); "zone of self-expressive speech" (mouth, ears, tongue, etc., and their activities); and "zone of purposeful action" (hands, feet, etc., and their actions).[21] The usefulness of this model derives from the fact that the biblical texts (Old Testament, Apocrypha, and New Testament) employ metaphors of the body to symbolize human behavior from the outside, rather than introspectively (e.g., Prov 6:16-19; Sir 17:2-19; Matt 13:13-17).

Group and Grid

Malina fits the model of dyadic personality into the larger matrix of cultural scripts. The analysis of societies or their subgroups in terms of their cultural scripts employing two variables — group and grid — was begun by Mary Douglas[22] and has been applied to the New Testament by several scholars: e.g.,

19. B. J. Malina and J. H. Neyrey, *Calling Jesus Names: The Social Value of Labels in Matthew*, Social Facets (Sonoma, Calif.: Polebridge, 1988), 145-49.

20. Malina, *New Testament World*, 60.

21. B. de Geradon, "L'homme a l'image de Dieu," *NRT* 80 (1958): 683-95; Malina, *New Testament World*, 60-67.

22. M. Douglas, *Natural Symbols: Explorations in Cosmology*, 1st ed. (New York: Vintage, 1973).

Malina,[23] White,[24] Neyrey,[25] and Atkins.[26] These analyses have demonstrated that Douglas's model is an effective tool for determining the orientation of social units. While this model results in a "snapshot" of different groups, this can be complemented with an analysis of how differing locations can result in conflict between groups.

Brief definitions of the key terms will suffice here. For fuller definitions and analysis see Malina.[27] *Group* identifies the continuum from "strong" to "weak" group commitments and expectations: relative pressure to conform to group norms, and personal identity derived from group membership or individual experience. The biblical texts are virtually all products of "strong group" societies, with the notable exception of the gospel of John.[28] This means that ancient Israelite, Judean, and Christian groups all exerted pressure on their members to conform, and members understood their identity in terms of their group embeddedness. The high value which the dominant U.S. culture ascribes to individuality identifies it as "weak group." Weak group does not mean that Americans do not belong to groups or make no commitments to them. It does mean that individual rights supersede those of the group; tolerance is expected for shifting from one group to another (e.g., marriage, school, company, neighborhood, parish); and the individual is expected to develop a unique, self-expressive personality, and seek personal goals.

Grid refers to high and low degrees of match between values and experience, and the effectiveness of the social structures to facilitate its values. The society's symbol system is perceived as effective or noneffective in giving meaning and bringing order to the group's experiences. Groups which assume a substantial agreement between values, social structures, and experience can be termed "high grid." Those which discern a gap between their values and the ability to achieve them by means of the existing structures are "low grid." It is the diversity of grid that is critical in interpreting the differences between the texts addressed below.

This results in four quadrants, each embodying different cultural scripts which exemplify those locations (see Fig. 1 on p. 174).

Douglas[29] identified the features of each script, and Malina refined the

23. B. Malina, *The Gospel of John in Sociolinguistic Perspective*, ed. H. Waetjen, Forty-eighth Colloquy of the Center for Hermeneutical Studies (Berkeley: Center for Hermeneutical Studies, 1985); *Christian Origins*.

24. L. J. White, "Grid and Group in Matthew's Community: The Righteousness/Honor Code in the Sermon on the Mount," *Semeia* 35 (1986): 61-90.

25. J. H. Neyrey, *An Ideology of Revolt: John's Christology in Social Science Perspective* (Philadelphia: Fortress, 1988).

26. R. A. Atkins, Jr., *Egalitarian Community: Ethnography and Exegesis* (Tuscaloosa: University of Alabama, 1991).

27. *Christian Origins*.

28. See Malina, *Gospel of John*; Neyrey, *Ideology of Revolt*.

29. Douglas, *Natural Symbols*.

Figure 1. Group and Grid

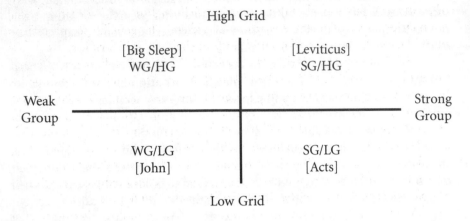

High Grid

[Big Sleep] WG/HG	[Leviticus] SG/HG

Weak Group   Strong Group

WG/LG [John]	SG/LG [Acts]

Low Grid

definitions and organized them for easier comparison: purity, rite, personal identity, body, sin, cosmology, and suffering and misfortune.[30] (Malina's definitions are followed here, even though he is not cited at every step.) The Bible includes texts which are products of three of these quadrants, and U.S. society provides the fourth; some examples will make the point. "Strong group/high grid" characterizes the Jerusalem priesthood and the book of Leviticus. Judean prophetic groups and the book of Jeremiah are representative of "strong group/low grid"; the same is true of early Christian groups and Luke-Acts. "Weak group/low grid" describes Johannine Christians and the gospel of John. And dominant U.S. society and Raymond Chandler's *The Big Sleep* are examples of "weak group/high grid."

With these four quadrants in mind (the abbreviations of SG/HG, etc., will be used in the subsequent discussion), we can proceed by focusing on four of the script features: purity, rite, personal identity, and sin. These are the features with the most direct relevance to the topic at hand. They will be analyzed for each of four texts from different settings.

Leviticus 4–5

As a product of a SG/HG subgroup (the Jerusalem priesthood of the second temple), the book of Leviticus demonstrates a vigorous concern for purity and well-defined rites to effect it. "Purity and pollution" is the system of properly situating people, places, times, acts, and objects. Purity codes embody a culture's

---

30. Malina, *Christian Origins*, 14-15, 20-27.

understanding of clean and unclean, sacred and profane, proper and deviant; and they further rank the members of each category into hierarchies — levels of purity and pollution.[31] Purity rites are instituted in order to define social boundaries and sustain the structures of society. The general perspective on purity forms the backdrop for an analysis of the Levitical sacrifices.

The "sin offering" (Heb. *ḥaṭṭāʾt;* Lev 4:1–5:13) and "culpability offering" (*ʾāšām;* Lev 5:14–6:7 [MT 5:14-26]) regulations are a complex collection which has gone through extensive editing as part of the larger sacrificial regulations in Leviticus 1–7. This is made clear by the mixture of terminology (5:6-7), the repeated "supplements" (5:1-6 + 7-10 + 11-13), and the duplication of topics (Lev 4:27-35//5:14-19). It is supplemented with instructions for priests eating these sacrifices in Lev 6:17-23 (Eng. 6:24-30) and 7:1-10. The Levitical regulations were probably given final written form in the postexilic, second temple period (after 515 B.C.E.), even if many of the rituals date from the first temple period.

A basic difference between a "sin offering" and a "culpability offering" is that the former relates exclusively to inadvertent, accidental, or unwitting acts of defilement. The latter is of two types: for inadvertent sin (5:14-19) and for knowing sin (5:20-26 [Eng. 6:1-7]); it requires restitution and reparations. Due to the ambiguity and a certain amount of overlap between them, scholars are not agreed as to the precise distinctions or tradition histories of the sin and culpability offerings; for a discussion of different views, see de Vaux,[32] Kellermann,[33] and Knierim.[34] An analysis of the "sin offering" will suffice for the subsequent comparisons.

The legislation is articulated as a Yahweh speech to Moses. It is structured in the following way:

Leviticus 4:1–5:13

I. Introductory speech formula	4:1
II. Speech proper	4:2–5:13
A. Commissioning formula	v. 2a
B. Regulation	vv. 2b-35
1. Basic case: inadvertent sin	v. 2b
2. Specifications (by offenders and sacrifice)	vv. 3-35
a. Anointed priest: young bull	vv. 3-12
b. Whole community: young bull	vv. 13-21

---

31. See especially the Holiness Code in Leviticus 17–26; M. Douglas, *Purity and Danger: An Analysis of the Concepts of Pollution and Taboo* (London: Routledge and Kegan Paul, 1966); Malina, *New Testament World,* 122-52; and J. H. Neyrey, "Unclean, Common, Polluted, and Taboo: A Short Reading Guide," *Forum* 4,4 (1988): 72-82.

32. R. de Vaux, *Ancient Israel* (New York: McGraw-Hill, 1961), 420-21.

33. D. Kellermann, "'asham," in *TDOT,* vol. 1, 431-35.

34. Knierim, 55-112; "*ʾāšām*" and "*ḥṭʾ*" in *THAT.*

One can readily see that every group and individual has a responsibility to guard carefully against pollution. The unwitting acts of sin are polluting, despite a lack of intentionality. And whether an individual *or* a group has acted wrongfully, communal consequences follow (see Num 16:20-24). As Knierim points out, *ḥṭ'* is a critical, evaluative, disqualifying term; it has the character of a juridical sentence which objectively pronounces a verdict on a *deed*.[35]

Everyone is not equal in terms of sin. Priests and leaders can be singled out for special responsibility and sacrifices, over against the community or ordinary individuals. The sequence of required sacrifices (4:3-35) indicates a progression of descending pollution consequences: larger to smaller, and male to female. The exceptions for the economically disadvantaged (5:7-13) also indicate a descending scale: from more to less expensive, and animate to inanimate. The species, gender, value, and animation of sacrifices, then, symbolically correspond to the status of the offenders.

The sin of a single priest is on par with a sin by the whole community, and both cases require the same sacrifice: a young bull. As a representative of the whole community, the sin of a prince is singled out as more polluting than an ordinary individual's, but less polluting than a priest's or the community's, thus requiring a lesser sacrifice: a male goat. The sin of a layperson requires the least potent sacrifice: a female goat or lamb, two turtledoves or pigeons, or one-tenth ephah of flour. That male animals are depicted as having more potent ritual effect in the priestly regulations than females is demonstrable from the extremely sacred sacrifices of the Day of Atonement in Leviticus 16: a bull, two male goats, and a ram.

These rituals result in forgiveness for the offenders (Lev 4:20, 26, 31, 35;

35. Pp. 58-60.

5:10, 13), although it is not specified in the case of the priest. But lest one give an individualistic interpretation to even the sacrifices for the individual, it should be noted that the consequences of such a sin offering were communal. An individual's sin not only incurs personal culpability, it pollutes the sanctuary. Milgrom has demonstrated that the differences in the rituals for the various offenders correspond to the extent to which they have polluted the sanctuary; thus the atonement is *of* the sanctuary, and *for/on behalf of* the offenders. The further the penetration of the culpable party into the sanctuary, the greater the pollution. The sacrifice for the whole community parallels that for the priest because the priests are part of the community. The sin offering functions "as a ritual detergent for purging the sanctuary."[36] Blood is sprinkled before the veil and on the inner altar for the priest and community (4:5-7, 16-18), on the outer altar for a prince or an individual (4:25, 30).

Focusing on the second case here (II.B.2.b. above; Lev 4:13-21), the inadvertent sin of the whole community, will provide a means for comparison to the prophetic materials and Acts. Noth argues that this section pertains to communal culpability for an individual's sins.[37] At least three possible situations, however, could be covered by this legislation: (1) an individual's sin results in communal pollution (per Noth; e.g., Josh 7:1-26); (2) a subgroup within Israel (a family or village) brings communal guilt on all Israel (e.g., 2 Sam 21:1-14); or (3) the whole community (or a substantial portion of it) incurs guilt (e.g., 2 Chr 36:15-21). Since a separate sacrifice relates to an individual's sin (4:27-35), Noth's suggestion is the least likely of the three.

As a regulation, the "sin of inadvertence" cannot take effect unless someone (unspecified) informs the group of its wrongdoing (4:14a). Lev 4:13-21, then, provides a "priestly *torah*" (instruction) to remedy such situations. It provides the answers to a whole series of questions. A question/answer format will highlight the issues:

Q: If such an act occurs and is made public, what are its identifying marks?
A: It is "inadvertent," "hidden," and "forbidden by Yahweh" (4:13a-c).
Q: What is the result of inadvertent sin?
A: "Culpability" (4:13d).
Q: What is the ritual process required for purification?
A: The assembly should bring a young bull as a "sin offering" (4:14); the elders act as representatives (4:15); and the blood ritual is carried out by a priest (4:16-21).
Q: And what is the result of the ritual process?
A: "Atonement": by the priest (of the sanctuary), for the assembly; and "forgiveness" for the offenders (4:20).

36. J. Milgrom, "Sacrifices and Offerings," *IDBSup*, 766.
37. M. Noth, *Leviticus*, rev. ed., OTL (Philadelphia: Westminster, 1977), 40-41.

All of the script features indicate that Leviticus 4–5 embodies an SG/HG perspective. In terms of *purity*, it exhibits a strong concern: *'šm*, "culpability"; *ḥṭ'*, "sin"; *ṭhr*, "pure"; *ṭm'*, "polluted"; *kpr*, "atone." Precise procedures for purification are instituted: formal presentation of sacrifice, laying hands on sacrifice, killing the bull, blood ritual, and fat burning. And finally, these regulations maintain the social unit before Yahweh: atonement and forgiveness.

In terms of *rite*, the larger program of Leviticus 1–7 depicts a society of fixed rites which cover a broad spectrum of circumstances. Those rites symbolize the internal classification system of the group: priest/community/prince/individual; inner altar/outer altar; bull/goat/lamb/turtledoves/pigeons/flour; male/female animals. The ritual symbols are effective in all contexts: the sacrifices can be reduced for the poor, but no one is exempted. And a permanent sacred space is assumed: while the "tent of meeting" of the wilderness is described in the narration of Leviticus (4:14-18), the structure and function of the Jerusalem temple are assumed.

The sense of *personal identity* in Leviticus 4–5 is dyadic: the sin of any of Israel's members results in communal implications, and an entire group can incur guilt. The social roles are clearly articulated, enduring, and internalized: Leviticus sees clear social roles for the priests and "princes" as leaders over the community (4:3-12, 22-26), and these are lifetime roles. The individual is subservient to, but not in conflict with, society: Leviticus sees no social conflict inherent in the hierarchy, including the distinction between the economically poor and the rest of society (5:7-13); and the individual has group responsibilities (4:27–5:13).

The understanding of *sin* in this text is fundamentally the violation of formal rules. The focus is directed to behavior rather than to internal states of being: *'āśâ*, "do, commit" (4:13). Rites are effective in counteracting sin: the effects of the sacrifice and blood ritual are atonement and forgiveness (4:20). And the individual is responsible for deviance: the priest, prince, or layperson (4:3, 22, 27).

Jeremiah 7 and 26

The prophetic corpus recounts repeated "summonses to repentance" addressed to the communities of Israel and Judah. Raitt has identified the basic form of these summonses.[38] I would only note that Raitt's identification of "admonition" must be expanded: either "admonition" (negative), or "exhortation" (positive), or both (parenesis) may be employed:

38. T. M. Raitt, "The Prophetic Summons to Repentance," *ZAW* 83 (1971): 30-49, esp. 33-36.

I. Appeal
    A. Messenger formula
    B. Vocative
    C. Parenesis
        1. Admonition
        2. Exhortation
II. Motivation
    A. Promise
    B. Accusation
    C. Threat

Raitt summarizes the perspective of these summonses as: "1. The people must repent in order to avoid doom"; "2. Doom is proclaimed to incite repentance"; "3. Failure to repent is made a basis for the certain approach of doom"; and "4. Doom is inevitable."[39]

The significance of Raitt's identification and analysis of this genre is to push beyond earlier studies[40] which subsumed this form to Oracles of Disaster or Oracles of Deliverance and denied that it had its own form and tradition history and could be analyzed independently of the oracles. Note that the genre appears in narrative contexts: e.g., 2 Kgs 17:13; 2 Chr 30:6-9; and Neh 1:8-9. A recognition of this form highlights the issue of repentance in the prophetic message.

Scholars have long recognized that Jeremiah 7 and 26 are two accounts of the same prophecy, delivered in 609 B.C.E.: one emphasizing the speech (7) and the other the narrative (26).[41] The *literary* unit of the "temple speech" is 7:1–8:3, since the commissioning formula in 8:4 marks a new unit. But this text is formally a compilation of several, originally separate, units collected around the common theme of cultic impropriety: 7:1-15; 7:16-20; 7:21-28; 7:29-34; and 8:1-3. Moreover, since 7:13-15 assumes that Jeremiah received a negative response to the speech, it may be an appendix to 7:1-12; Holladay thinks Jeremiah added them himself after Jehoiakim's burning of the scroll.[42]

The contents of the final form of 7:1–8:3 will be examined here, not because they were delivered in the same oral address (they are different form-critical units), but because they all speak to the issue at hand: inadvertent sin of the group and its remedy. Holladay argues that all of these units include genuine Jeremiah material (with the exception of 8:1-3, which is an exilic

---

39. Raitt, 47.

40. E.g., H. W. Wolff, "Das Thema 'Umkehr' in der alttestamentlichen Prophetie," *ZTK* 48 (1951): 129-48; C. Westermann, *Basic Forms of Prophetic Speech* (Philadelphia: Westminster, 1967).

41. See, e.g., W. L. Holladay, *Jeremiah 1: A Commentary on the Book of the Prophet Jeremiah Chapters 1–25*, Hermeneia (Philadelphia: Fortress, 1986), 239-40.

42. Holladay, 248.

addition), even if they come from different periods;[43] Overholt thinks 7:16–8:3 is a commentary on the temple sermon of 7:1-15;[44] and Carroll thinks virtually all of 7:1–8:3 is an exilic composition of the deuteronomistic school.[45] Whatever one determines about the amount of material that originates with Jeremiah himself as opposed to later editors, the different parts of 7:1–8:3 do focus on the same general topic and share the same social perspective.[46]

The historical setting of Jeremiah's temple speech is the decade prior to the Babylonian invasion of Judah in 598/7 B.C.E.: Jer 26:1 dates it ca. 609. One should keep in mind several salient factors about the Judeans whom Jeremiah addresses. King Josiah, who had promulgated the political and cultic reforms in line with deuteronomic theology (ca. 621), had died in battle in 609 (2 Kgs 23:29). The Judeans anointed his son, Jehoahaz, in his place; but he lasted only three months (2 Kgs 23:30-31). Pharaoh Neco (who had defeated Josiah) imprisoned Jehoahaz and replaced him with his brother, Eliakim (renamed Jehoiakim), and exacted vassal tribute from Judah (2 Kgs 23:33-35). Despite their defeat by the Egyptians, Judah still had a Davidic king, and the temple was left unharmed. This probably only added fuel to the Judean "Zion theology" which hailed Jerusalem as impenetrable, and Yahweh's holy abode (e.g., Pss 48; 68; 78; Isa 14:28-32). Jeremiah attacks this theology as misplaced, delusional, and dangerous ideology.

The form-critical structure of the Yahweh speeches outlined here is based upon an adaptation of Knierim's analysis[47] of 7:1-15:

Jeremiah 7:1–8:3

I. Report formula	7:1
II. Series of Yahweh Speeches	7:2–8:3
A. First Yahweh word: to "all the men of Judah"	7:2-15
1. Series of commissions: stand, proclaim, say	v. 2a
2. Content	vv. 2b-15
a. Announcement of Yahweh word	vv. 2b-3a
1) Call to attention (with vocative)	v. 2b
2) Messenger formula	v. 3a
b. Yahweh word proper	vv. 3b-15

43. Holladay, 234-72.
44. T. W. Overholt, "Jeremiah," *Harper's Bible Commentary*, ed. J. L. Mays et al. (San Francisco: Harper, 1988), 615.
45. R. P. Carroll, *From Chaos to Covenant: Prophecy in the Book of Jeremiah* (New York: Crossroad, 1981), 84-95.
46. See W. Brueggemann, *To Pluck Up, to Tear Down: A Commentary on the Book of Jeremiah 1–25* (Grand Rapids: Eerdmans, 1988), 74-81.
47. R. P. Knierim, "Jeremiah," lectures given at the School of Theology at Claremont, California, February-April 1975.

This structure reveals the similarities and differences of formal structure between the units, the repetition of forms, the building to a climax of "sanction/threat," and the alternation of addressees. But more importantly for our purposes here, it identifies the location of the offenses (accusations; and sometimes implied in parenesis), the remedies (exhortations and admonitions), the consequences of compliance (promises), and the consequences of noncompliance (sanctions/threats). The next step is to relate these forms to the content:

1. Offenses
   a. Trust in deceptive words (7:4)
   b. Robbery, murder, etc., followed by a declaration of deliverance (7:8-11)
   c. Nonresponsiveness to Yahweh's call (7:13, 28b)
   d. Illicit family cults (7:17-18)
   e. Pollution of the temple (7:30)
   f. Child sacrifice at Topheth (7:31)
   g. Astral cults (8:1-2)
2. Remedies
   a. Amend ways (7:3b, 5a)
   b. Do not trust "deceptive words" (7:4)
   c. Execute justice, with specifications (7:5b-6)
      1) Not oppressing the alien, fatherless, widow (7:6a)
      2) Not shedding innocent blood in the temple (7:6b)
      3) Not going after other gods (7:6c)
3. Consequences of noncompliance
   a. Destruction of temple (7:14)
   b. Cast out — exile (7:15; 8:3)
   c. Yahweh's "burning" anger on: temple, humans, beasts, land (7:20)
   d. Death for inhabitants and devastation of the land (7:32-34)
   e. Disinterment of Jerusalemite corpses: kings, princes, priests, prophets, (commoner) Jerusalemites (8:1-3)

What sort of cultural script does this set of speeches embody? It is clear that, as far as Jeremiah is concerned, the Judean social structures no longer facilitate the achievement of values: the people of Judah and Jerusalem trust their liturgies and rites to purify them (7:4, 10), but they are only under an illusion of purity, due to their social and cultic corruption. That they do not perceive their actions or theology as sin, but as piety, identifies this as "inadvertent sin" as defined in Lev 4:13. And Jeremiah's prophetic announcement serves the function of exposing their acts as sin (Lev 4:14). This mismatch of values and experience which Jeremiah announces represents an SG/LG perspective. Thus the prophet and the group(s) for whom he speaks view the larger culture with contempt. That this conflict of grids was clearly perceived by Jeremiah's audience is made clear in Jeremiah 26 when the authorities arrest and try him; but he does gain some popular support.

Malina's description of prophets in general, and Paul in particular, in relation to horizontal and vertical relationships and sin, opens up the dynamics of Jer 7:1–8:3:

In a Jewish context the task of the leader known as prophet was to make known and articulate the specific will of God in and for some here-and-now situation so as to influence and persuade the members of the group (not outsiders) to adopt a given perspective or follow a given line of conduct that would be in conformity with God's good pleasure. The goal is to please God and simultaneously realize the culture's core value. What characterizes Paul's implementation of this leadership role, at least insofar as his letters attest, is his ability to articulate the problems faced by the group, such as the strong group/low grid problem of pervading negative influence which Paul calls "Sin," to set out a culturally plausible and realistic solution to those problems, to fend off possible objections, and thus to win commitment or emotional anchorage from group members to the new sets of symbols that he presents.[48]

The *purity* concerns of the SG/LG script are just as strong as those of the SG/HG. The difference is that LG groups perceive that both the social and physical body are under attack: the land lacks justice (7:5-7), the temple has become a "den of robbers" (7:11), sacrifices to other gods go on in the streets (7:17-18). They are totally corrupt, as all three "zones" demonstrate their disobedience (7:24): "ear" (zone of self-expressive speech), "walk" (zone of purposeful action), and "heart" (zone of emotion-fused thought). They have defiled the sanctuary (7:30). Furthermore, purification rites will no longer produce the desired effects; in fact, Yahweh never ordered their sacrificial system in the first place (7:21-23)!

In terms of *rites*, these Jeremiah speeches have little to say that is positive. The LG script alerts the reader to expect rites to focus on group boundaries, but the only positive reference is to mourning rites: cutting hair and crying out (7:29). With regard to fluid sacred spaces, Jeremiah contends that Yahweh himself destroyed the Yahweh-sanctuary in Shiloh, and he would do the same in Jerusalem (7:12-15).

Personal identity for LG is located in group membership, not in the internalization of roles, which are confused. This means that roles are not permanent and enduring, as they are assumed in HG groups (this aspect does not appear here). A distinction is made between appearance and internal states: while the words of the people seem pious (7:4, 10), they are corrupt (7:5-10). And dyadic personality is assumed; Jeremiah treats collective guilt and collective punishment: "all the Judeans who enter these gates to worship Yahweh" (7:2), "the children of Judah" (7:30), the imperatives are all plural (e.g., 7:5), and the temple will be destroyed and the people cast out as a group (7:12-15).

The sense of *sin* in the LG script is one of deviance. Jeremiah makes it clear that he sees the Judeans as deviants, manifested in their disobedience to

---

48. Malina, *Christian Origins*, 134.

Yahweh's voice, and pursuing illegitimate ends (7:13, 19, 24-28, 30-31). Evil is lodged in both the individual and the society: they commit abominations (7:10), are corrupt like the Israelites (7:12), and have evil hearts (7:24). Sin resembles a disease which derives from the social structure.

In a critique of the prophets, Carroll argues that the concept of communal repentance is without substance. He contends that the prophets were misguided to expect any such thing since the idea of an entire population quickly changing its behavior patterns is ludicrous.[49] The problem with Carroll's critique is that it assumes an individualist rather than a dyadic personality for the ancient Israelites and Judeans. And it further fails to take into account the clear assumption of group culpability in legal and narrative texts. I would suggest that the prophetic LG perspective is radical in its expectations for structural shake-up. Given the references to group culpability and purification in other texts, the goal seems to be: get the group representatives (king, princes, priests, elders) to recognize a structural problem and induce them to "repent" and lead the people in a new direction (e.g., Josiah's reforms following 621 B.C.E.; 2 Kgs 23:1-25). Both Lev 4:13-21 and Jer 26:1-19 demonstrate the fundamental role of group representatives.

For Jeremiah, more sacrifice (i.e., conformity to the structure) is not the remedy of Judah's offenses. The only corrective is a total reorientation of society. This he summarizes in two phrases: "amend your ways" (7:3b, 5a), and "execute/do/perform justice between an individual and his neighbor" (7:5b). But what would this look like? The prophet goes on to specify three categories of behavior in 7:6 which require special attention: oppression of the socially marginal (widows, fatherless, aliens), shedding innocent blood (see Jer 2:34), and pursuing other gods. In terms of modern categories these represent examples of social policy, criminal behavior, and state religion. Thus Jeremiah does not concentrate on formal rules (i.e., citing laws) but appeals to the Judeans to correct their horizontal and vertical relationships. This puts the prophet's "counter-structure" in conflict with the "structure" of the temple and political authorities.

Since the authorities represent an HG perspective, they would view the sacrifices (like those described in Lev 4–5) as efficacious to purify from sin. Jeremiah challenges not just a particular act as sinful, however, but the whole structure of the cult and Judean society (contra Deut 12). Jeremiah and his audience would not disagree about values (e.g., justice), but about the social structure's ability to facilitate those values. Thus Jeremiah is not "counter-cultural," but is "counter-structural." The prophetic message is that Yahweh will pull down the structures: the temple will be destroyed (7:12-14), the people will lose the land (7:15) and the whole country will be ravaged (7:20), and the leadership will be killed along with the population (8:1). As Knierim

49. Carroll, 80-83.

points out: "The pattern of 'If you amend your ways . . . I will forgive you' stands not at the beginning of God's relationship with his people, but at the end — in which they have rejected his salvation and life throughout their history."[50]

The conflict is played out in the narrative of Jeremiah 26. The priests and temple prophets (backed by the crowd) accuse Jeremiah, and they arrest him as a dangerous deviant (26:8, 11). At the trial the rural elders step forward in his defense, citing a precedent for Jeremiah's prophecy in Micah of Moresheth, a century before (26:17-19). The support of the rural elders confirms that the prophet is not just a lone individual, but gives voice to the concerns of a social group which supports his LG perspective. The princes (backed by the crowd, which has switched sides) determine that Jeremiah does not deserve the death penalty (26:16). The conflict between Jeremiah and the priests and institutional prophets is thus only momentarily resolved: the princes allow Jeremiah his say without penalty. But on the other hand, they give no indication of heeding the prophet's message. Wilson suggests, however, that Jer 36:14-19 does indicate that Jeremiah's message of disaster was taken seriously by some of the political leaders.[51]

As Overholt has shown, one of Jeremiah's fundamental themes is "falsehood" (Heb. *šeqer*), focused on three objects: false security, the falsehood of idolatry, and false prophets.[52] In Jer 7:1–8:3 the first two of these are addressed. The prophet's message was that the Jerusalem temple had become an ideological symbol of protection, which has led the Judeans to a false sense of security: they "trust in deceptive *[šeqer]* words to no avail" (Jer 7:8). This is the essence of the LG perspective and critique: the social structures will not lead to the desired goals — security and relationship with Yahweh (7:3, 5-7).

Acts 2

The "Pentecost Speech" in Acts 2 has received intensive scrutiny in this century (see, e.g., Zehnle).[53] A few commentators notwithstanding, scholars have concluded that Peter's speech (like the other Acts speeches) is the literary construct of Luke rather than a stenographic transcription of an oral

---

50. Knierim, "Jeremiah" lectures, 1975.

51. R. R. Wilson, *Prophecy and Society in Ancient Israel* (Philadelphia: Fortress, 1980), 247.

52. T. W. Overholt, *The Threat of Falsehood: A Study in the Theology of the Book of Jeremiah,* Studies in Biblical Theology 2, 16 (Naperville: Alec R. Allenson, 1970), 1-23.

53. See, e.g., R. F. Zehnle, *Peter's Pentecost Discourse: Tradition and Lukan Reinterpretation in Peter's Speeches of Acts 2 and 3,* SBLMS 15 (Nashville: Abingdon, 1971).

address.[54] I take this text, then, as Luke's understanding of the earliest community's proclamation in Jerusalem. The following is my form-critical outline of the speech.

Acts 2:1-42

I. Epiphany Report .... vv. 1-13
  A. Introduction: time and space .... v. 1
  B. Report proper .... v. 2
    1. Spirit manifestations among Jewish Christians .... vv. 2-4
    2. Jewish response .... vv. 5-13
      a. Description .... vv. 5-7a
      b. Quotations .... vv. 7b-13
II. Dialogue .... vv. 14-40
  A. Peter .... vv. 14-36
    1. Introductory speech formula .... v. 14a
    2. Speech proper .... vv. 14b-36
      a. Interpretation of Spirit manifestation .... vv. 14b-21
        1) Introductory address and call to attention .... v. 14b
        2) Interpretation proper .... vv. 15-21
          a) Stated negatively: not drunk .... v. 15
          b) Stated positively: prophetic fulfillment .... vv. 16-21
            (1) Interpretative rubric .... v. 16
            (2) Quotation of Joel 2:28-32 .... vv. 17-21
      b. Interpretation of Jesus' ministry, crucifixion,
        resurrection, and exaltation .... vv. 22-36
        1) Introductory address and call to attention .... v. 22a
        2) Interpretation proper .... vv. 22b-36
          a) Attestation of Jesus' works .... v. 22b
          b) First indictment of crowd: crucifixion .... v. 23
          c) Attestation of Jesus' resurrection and
            exaltation .... vv. 24-36a
          d) Second indictment of crowd .... v. 36b
  B. Crowd .... v. 37
    1. Introductory description: cut to the heart .... v. 37a
    2. Speech proper: question — what shall we do? .... v. 37b
  C. Peter .... vv. 38-40
    1. Introductory speech formula .... v. 38a
    2. Speech proper: summons to repentance .... vv. 38b-39

---

54. See M. Dibelius, "The Speeches in Acts and Ancient Historiography," in *Studies in the Acts of the Apostles,* ed. H. Greeven (London: SCM, 1956); E. Haenchen, *The Acts of the Apostles: A Commentary* (Philadelphia: Westminster, 1971).

a. Exhortation	v. 38b-d
1) Twofold exhortation proper	v. 38b-c
a) Repent	v. 38b
b) Be baptized	v. 38c
2) Reason: forgiveness of sins	v. 38d
b. Promise	vv. 38e-39
1) Promise proper	v. 38e
2) Explanation: generational and geographical inclusion	v. 39
3. Summarizing formula	v. 40a
4. Speech proper: concluding exhortation — be delivered	v. 40b
III. Compliance Report	vv. 41-42
A. Immediate response: transformation ritual (baptism)	v. 41
B. Ongoing response: loyalty	v. 42
1. To apostle's teaching	v. 42a
2. To fellowship	v. 42b
3. To breaking of bread	v. 42c
4. To prayers	v. 42d

For comparison to the other texts, the central concern is 2:22-40. While Peter's address has been called a "sermon" or a "missionary speech," these designations miss the mark, since they are too generalized. These genres fail to take into account the importance of the indictments, the summons to repentance, and the text's connections to earlier paradigms of purification. In terms of genre this speech is a "prophetic call to repentance."

The issues may again be cast in a question/answer format. In fact, the "apostolic torah" (2:38-40) is a direct response to the question posed by the crowd (2:37b). And the question from the crowd is prompted by the two indictments made by Peter (2:23, 36b).

Q: What is the nature of the offense?
A: "This Jesus . . . you crucified and killed by the hands of lawless men" (2:23, 36).
Q: What is the ritual process required for purification (2:37)?
A: "Repent and be baptized every one of you in the name of Jesus Christ . . ." (2:38a).
Q: What is the result of the ritual process?
A: ". . . the forgiveness of your sins and you will receive the gift of the Holy Spirit" (2:38b); "be delivered from this wicked generation" (2:40).

This may be interpreted in terms of "inadvertent sin" (Lev 4:1–5:13; Jer 7:1–8:3; 1QS 8–9). The indictments Peter makes in the speech are addressed not to all people, or even to all Jews. They are addressed to the Judean and

Diaspora Jews in Jerusalem who actively or passively participated in Jesus' death. By extension, Luke understands the initiation ritual as offered to all (Acts 2:39). Thus, like Jeremiah, Peter functions in the story as the one who brings inadvertent sin to the attention of the community (see Lev 4:14a). That the crucifixion is understood by the characters as *sin* (and not merely an unfortunate situation) is clear from the crowd's reaction (Acts 2:37b) and Peter's call for repentance (2:38). That it is understood as *inadvertent* sin is demonstrated in this case by the description of the crowd as surprised and dismayed: "cut to the heart" (2:37). And that it is understood as *communal* sin is indicated by the communal referent ("all the house of Israel," 2:36a), the crowd's question ("Brethren, what shall *we* do?" 2:37b), and from Peter's response with plural forms (even though obscured in English): "repent" (2:38b), "your sins" (2:38d), "you shall receive" (2:38e), "you and your children" (2:39), "be delivered" (2:40b).

Like Jeremiah and the Community Rule from Qumran (1QS), Acts represents an SG/LG perspective. The early Christians were LG in terms of the Roman Empire and the Judean establishment. Christian values were not facilitated by Roman law, the Jerusalem temple-cult, or the Jewish synagogue.

The *purity* concern of Acts 2 is manifested in the treatment of repentance, sins, and deliverance (2:38, 40b). But the purification rites of the strong group (the Jerusalem temple rites) are ineffective in treating the pollution at hand. Forgiveness is offered to those who go through a new purificatory transformation ritual: baptism.[55]

LG subgroups can be expected to focus their *rites* upon group boundaries. Thus baptism relates at one and the same time to purification and community definition. Indeed, the "gift of the Holy Spirit," whatever its specific contours, must be connected to community formation (2:41-42). While the culpability Peter identifies is communal, and the community is addressed, the act of baptism is for the individual who responds and enters the new community: "let each of you be baptized" (2:38). The rite is not efficacious for those who do not choose to participate.

Personal identity in LG perspective is located in group membership, not in the internalization of roles, which are confused. Thus Luke describes the Jews and proselytes present at Pentecost in terms of their geographical region (2:9-11). Appearances are deceptive in this quadrant: Jesus was crucified as a criminal, but God made him "Lord and Christ" (2:36); the Romans, who appear to epitomize law, are "lawless men" (2:23); and the Jews who were in Jerusalem for religious reasons are culpable for the death of God's chosen emissary. As

55. See M. McVann, "Rituals of Status Transformation in Luke-Acts: The Case of Jesus the Prophet," in *The Social World of Luke-Acts: Models for Interpretation*, ed. J. H. Neyrey (Peabody, Mass.: Hendrickson, 1991), 333-60.

already noted, Acts 2 assumes a communal culpability and thus a dyadic view of personality.

Sin in Acts 2 is both individual and communal, and it is polluting (2:23, 36b, 40b). While formal rules may be important, internal states take precedence: Peter refers to repentance as the presupposition to baptism (2:38b-c). That is, a correspondence between the internal and external is called for.

It needs to be clear that baptism in Acts 2 is an initiation *ritual,* transporting the initiant from outside to inside the Christian community; it is thus a boundary-establishing ritual.[56] But it is also understood as a purification ritual (see also 1 Pet 3:21). It does not treat the ongoing issue of repeatable *ceremonies* of boundary-crossing from polluted to purified for those *within* the Christian community, as do those of Leviticus, the Manual of Discipline, and the Mishnah tractate Mikvaoth. The use of meal and community exclusion (and restitution) found in Matthew, Paul, and the deutero-Pauline literature seems to parallel that of the Community Rule (Matt 18:15-17; 1 Cor 5:1-13; 2 Cor 2:5-11; 2 Thess 3:14-15).

Summary and Conclusions

In order for modern readers to understand ancient Judean and Christian texts which address the culpability of groups, they must grasp several things: "dyadic personality" in traditional cultures, the differences between "high grid" and "low grid" cultural scripts, the differences between purity codes, and the conflict which may result from the differences in grid location.

While all three of the texts addressed here represent a strong group perspective, only Leviticus 4 is high grid, and thus socially "structural." Jeremiah 7 and Acts 2 are both low grid, and socially "counter-structural." Because the three texts derive from different social quadrants, their cultural scripts are not only different but highlight the conflict of perspectives. Jeremiah and Acts, though spanning a seven-hundred-year history, both provide a different negative response to the Jerusalem cult: Jeremiah attacks it frontally, Acts provides an alternative community and social structure. Leviticus 4 is in the form of regulations, Jeremiah 7 is the report of prophetic speeches, and Acts 2 is cast as an apostolic speech embodying a call to repentance. The similarities and differences between the three texts are summarized below:

---

56. W. A. Meeks, *The First Urban Christians: The Social World of the Apostle Paul* (New Haven: Yale, 1983), 102.

Sin and Purification — Two Paradigms

Texts	Social Location	Offender/s	Offense	Remedy	Result of Compliance	Result of Non-compliance
Leviticus 4:13-21	SG/HG	whole congregation of Israel	inadvertent sin: general	sin offering	atonement and forgiveness	culpability
Jeremiah 7:1–8:13	SG/LG	all Judeans	inadvertent sin: no justice, other gods, cultic pollution	repentance, obedience, justice	Yahweh diverts destruction of Jerusalem	destruction of temple and exile
Acts 2:1-42	SG/LG	whole house of Israel	inadvertent sin: crucifixion of Jesus	repentance and baptism	forgiveness, gift of Spirit, deliverance	(unstated)

One of the conclusions I would draw from the foregoing analysis is that individuals and subgroups in the SG/HG quadrant may eventually "drop" in grid when their values are no longer facilitated by the HG social structures. That drop in grid usually results in an antagonism toward the HG dominant society. It may eventually solidify into alternative structures to accommodate their different perspectives, such as those of the Essenes and the Jewish Christians. Acts 2 provides a paradigmatic text to examine counter-structural purity codes and rituals.

Another aspect of this drop in grid is that either a single event or a combination of events precipitates it. If the redactors of Jeremiah are accurate in identifying 609 B.C.E. as the date of Jeremiah's "temple sermon," then the coronation of Jehoiakim as Judean king by the Egyptians appears to have been the event which led to Jeremiah's attack on the cult. He attacked a variety of cultic and ethical pollutions, but the new social situation brought about the "critical mass."

The earliest Christians in Judea and Galilee certainly saw themselves as a faction of Judaism, and not a distinct religion. But Acts 2 makes clear an issue which pervades the early Christian writings: the death of Jesus and his vindication by God were the critical events which resulted in the formation of new communities. On the one hand these Christians continued to go to synagogues (Acts 9:20; 13:5; 14:1), meet at the Jerusalem temple (2:46; 5:42; 21:26), and employ the Septuagint as their Bible (e.g., 2:17-22, 25-28, 34-35; 4:25-26). But they developed their own initiation ritual (baptism), ceremony of solidarity (Lord's Supper), foundation stories (Gospels), and leadership (pastor-teachers, evangelists, prophets, apostles). Several points of contention emerged between Christian Jews and the rest of Judaism: a focus on Jesus' death and vindication, acceptance of Gentiles, open table-fellowship, and a break with conservative Torah interpretation. Eventually they were thrown out of the synagogues.[57]

Two hermeneutical questions emerge from this social analysis. The first is: as modern Westerners reading the biblical texts (and thus weak group), how do we appropriate, make use of, and listen to texts which are strong group in social orientation? I would suggest that they are challenges to our easy sacralizing (if not deification) of individualism. Christian community calls for an inclusiveness, a commitment to sharing, and a global concern which takes us beyond our own families and cliques.

The second is: how do we, in a high grid orientation, handle texts from the low grid? Rather than easily identifying with the prophet, or the early Christians in their challenge of the sacrificial cult as empty and ineffective, we too are called into question. Our economic, political, and religious structures, hierarchies, and purity codes can just as easily become delusional ideologies and ineffective in accomplishing their stated goals as the Jerusalem cult did. To use Barth's phrase, they can become "the *dysangelion*, 'bad news.'"[58]

57. See John 9:34; 12:42; 16:2; J. L. Martyn, *History and Theology in the Fourth Gospel,* rev. ed. (Nashville: Abingdon, 1979), 37-62; Neyrey, *Ideology of Revolt,* 35.
58. K. Barth, *Introduction to Evangelical Theology* (New York: Holt, Rinehart and Winston, 1963), 11.

Ganzheitsdenken in the Book of Ruth[1]

ROBERT L. HUBBARD, JR.

This essay pursues a topic to which Rolf Knierim first introduced me long ago, the relationship between law and dynamism in the Old Testament's view of reality.[2] His own ground-breaking study of Hebrew words for sin had unearthed *Ganzheitsdenken* ("totality-thinking") as the foundation of the Old Testament's worldview.[3] He showed *Ganzheitsdenken* to be a holistic worldview which encompassed two epistemological perspectives which scholars previously had viewed as competing worldviews; namely, Koch's concept of *Tatsphäredenken* (the idea that acts automatically produce their corresponding consequences) and Horst's emphasis on legal thought.[4] Subsequent scholar-

---

1. Happy sixty-fifth birthday, Rolf! With the highest respect and deepest feeling, I congratulate you on reaching this milestone. As Wellhausen once said of Vatke, from you "I have learned most and best." Thanks for all you have done for me personally and professionally over the last two decades. Pam joins me in wishing you and Hildegard God's richest blessings in the years ahead.

2. Eventually, that introduction led to my "Dynamistic and Legal Language in Complaint Psalms" (Dissertation, Claremont Graduate School, 1980); cf. also my "Dynamistic and Legal Processes in Psalm 7," *ZAW* 94 (1982): 267-68.

3. R. Knierim, *Die Hauptbegriffe für Sünde im Alten Testament* (Gütersloh: Mohn, 1965), 73-112; cf. its role in his articles in *THAT*, vol. 1, 81-84 (אָוֶן), 251-57 (אָשָׁם), 541-49 (חֵטְא); vol. 2, 223-28 (עָוֹל), 243-49 (עָוֹן), 488-95 (פֶּשַׁע), 869-72 (שָׁגָג). For a summary of his view, see Hubbard, "Dynamistic and Legal Language," 41-46.

4. Cf. K. Koch, "Gibt es ein Vergeltungsdogma im Alten Testament?" *ZTK* 52 (1955): 1-42; reprinted in J. L. Crenshaw, *Theodicy in the Old Testament* (Philadelphia: Fortress, 1983), 57-87; F. Horst, "Recht und Religion im Bereich des Alten Testaments," *EvT* 16 (1956): 49-75; reprinted in *Gottes Recht. Gesammelte Studien zum Recht im Alten Testament*, TBü 12 (Munich: Chr. Kaiser, 1961), 260-91. For the larger discussion, see Hubbard, "Dynamistic and Legal Language," 1-41 (with bibliography).

192

ship has pursued the subject in various Old Testament traditions,[5] but only Otto has examined its influence on Israel's narrative literature.[6] The present study proposes to examine the role *Ganzheitsdenken,* including law and dynamism, plays in another narrative, the book of Ruth. Besides following up Knierim's earlier research, it also takes up his recent challenge that Old Testament theologians show how the Old Testament's competing theologies relate to each other.[7]

Before beginning, however, I must define some key terminology to be used. By "law" I mean the system of obligations and procedures which govern relationships with fellow humans and with God in ancient Israel.[8] The system includes duties and legal processes articulated in formal legal legislation, whether civil or cultic, and those which a society informally assumes to be obligatory. The term "dynamism," by contrast, describes the theory that acts automatically release power which causes their corresponding consequences.[9] Texts reflect the operation of dynamism in three ways: first, when they report someone's wish or prayer that another party receive an outcome commensurate with some prior or anticipated action; second, when they report how a deed produced a subsequent result whose occurrence is traceable to the original deed; and third, when they use words whose range of meanings encompasses both an act and its resulting consequence.[10]

---

5. Cf. H. Gese, *Lehre und Wirklichkeit in der Alten Weisheit* (Tübingen: Mohr-Siebeck, 1958), 33-50; H. H. Schmid, *Wesen und Geschichte der Weisheit,* BZAW 101 (Berlin: Töpelmann, 1966), 146-64; *Gerechtigkeit als Weltordnung,* BHT 40 (Tübingen: Mohr-Siebeck, 1968), 144-86; J. Gammie, "The Theology of Retribution in the Book of Deuteronomy," *CBQ* 32 (1970): 1-12; W. S. Towner, "Retribution Theology in the Apocalyptic Setting," *USQR* 26 (1971): 203-14; J. K. Kuntz, "The Retribution Motif in Psalmic Wisdom," *ZAW* 89 (1977): 223-33; J. A. Burger, "The Law of Yahweh, the Fear of Yahweh, and Retribution in the Wisdom Psalms," *Old Testament Essays* 2/3 (1989): 75-95.

6. E. Otto, "Die 'synthetische Lebensauffassung' in der frühköniglichen Novellistik Israels," *ZTK* 74 (1977): 371-400, examined the influence of dynamism in the "Succession Narrative" and the Joseph story.

7. R. Knierim, "The Task of Old Testament Theology," *HBT* 6,1 (1984): 25-57.

8. For what follows, cf. Hubbard, "Dynamistic and Legal Language," 1 n. 1.

9. Because "dynamism" and its synonyms "the dynamic" or "the dynamistic process" imply the release of "power" by an act, I prefer them to Koch's "Tatsphäredenken." For the term *dynamism,* see J. Haekel, "Dynamismus. I. Religionswissenschaftlich," *LTK,* vol. 3, 618-19; N. Söderblom and C.-M. Edsman, "Macht. I. Religionsgeschichtlich," *RGG,* 3rd ed., vol. 4, 564-57.

10. E.g., the word רעה designates both an "evil (act)" and the "misfortune" which results; cf. KB, vol. 4, 1177-79; K. Hj. Fahlgren, "Die Gegensätze von ṣedaqā im Alten Testament," in *Um das Prinzip der Vergeltung in Religion und Recht des Alten Testaments,* ed. K. Koch, Wege der Forschung 125 (Darmstadt: Wissenschaftliche Buchgesellschaft, 1972), 122-29; H. J. Stoebe, "רעע," *THAT,* vol. 2, 794-803.

I

Two statements which reflect the operation of dynamism occur in the book of Ruth. The first is the wish that widowed Naomi gives her daughters-in-law, Ruth and Orpah (1:8). Naomi has begun her sad return trip to Judah accompanied by the two younger women (vv. 6-7). En route, she pauses to urge them to go back to Moab, supporting her plea with this wish:

יעשׂ יהוה עמכם חסד כאשׁר עשׂיתם עם־המתים ועמדי[11]

May Yahweh treat you as kindly as you have treated the dead and me.[12]

For our purposes, several things are striking about this brief statement. First, these are the first words which Naomi speaks in the book. Up to now, the narrator has reported the poor woman's surprising string of bitter misfortunes — famine, exile, and grief (vv. 1-5). As is well known, dialogues between characters are the most prominent literary feature of this delightful story, serving both to advance the plot and to interpret its events.[13] Thus, in the context of the whole book, Naomi's words take on programmatic significance.

Second, the statement implies that unfilled obligations remained between Naomi and the women. Evidently, the formula עשׂה חסד עם ("treat [someone] kindly") was a formal way of bringing a relationship to an end.[14] By invoking that traditional phrase of farewell, Naomi accomplished two things: on the one hand, she relieved her daughters-in-law of any further obligation toward herself, thereby freeing them to return home; on the other hand, she passed on to Yahweh the obligation to repay their kindness because she was powerless to do so herself. Third, and most important, in essence the wish asks that Yahweh repay the kindness the women have done with an appropriate kindness of his own. Yahweh is to "do kindness with" them (עשׂה חסד עם) because that is what they have "done with" (עשׂה עם) her and "the dead." The word כאשׁר ("as, like") underscores that Yahweh's future kindness will somehow correspond to theirs.[15]

---

11. Reading the Qere jussive (ya'aś).

12. The translation and subsequent remarks follow R. L. Hubbard, Jr., *The Book of Ruth*, NICOT (Grand Rapids: Eerdmans, 1988), 98, 103-5. Unless otherwise indicated, all translations below are my own.

13. For a study of the plot, see B. Green, "The Plot of the Biblical Story of Ruth," *JSOT* 23 (1982): 55-68.

14. Cf. 2 Sam 2:6; 15:20 (emended after the LXX); K. Sakenfeld, *The Meaning of Hesed in the Hebrew Bible: A New Inquiry,* HSM 17 (Missoula: Scholars Press, 1978), 107-11.

15. Cf. P. Trible, "Two Women in a Man's World," *Soundings* 59 (1976): 255: "At the heart of Naomi's poem are these female foreigners as models for Yahweh. They show the deity a more excellent way. Once again levels of opposites meet and crisscross: the past loyalty of human beings (foreign women, at that) is a paradigm for the future kindness of the divine being."

Specifically, what had they done? Presumably, the reference is to their self-sacrificial devotion to Naomi after the death of their husbands (cf. 2:11). That devotion was particularly remarkable if one assumes that the death of their mates had relieved the widows of all such social duties and freed them to remarry (cf. v. 9).[16] The point is, however, that Naomi petitioned Yahweh to reward their actions — in dynamistic terms, to give the kind actions of the women their equivalent kind consequences. In verse 9, she clarifies the shape of those consequences: Naomi wants Yahweh to find second husbands for her two companions. Thematically, of course, this is significant for the entire book. It hints that the theme of a widow's finding a husband will play an important role in subsequent events (cf. 3:1-2, 18; 4:13). More important, this implies that, should a remarriage occur, the reader should view it as the fulfillment of Naomi's wish, that is, as the consequence of the earlier kindness of the young women.

Why is appeal made to Yahweh in this case, and what is his assumed role here? To appeal to Yahweh for חסד is entirely appropriate since the Old Testament often pictures Yahweh as a God of whom חסד is an important character trait and, hence, who commonly does חסד for his people.[17] Further, Naomi's appeal to Yahweh to connect act and consequence assumes the common Old Testament view that Yahweh is the guarantor of the act-consequence connection.[18] Thus, on behalf of the two women, Naomi avails herself of those well-known aspects of Yahweh's character and role. It also implies that, should such a connection occur later in the story, the reader should regard it as an act of Yahweh. As for Yahweh's role, the text gives evidence that Naomi appeals to Yahweh, not as Israel's covenant partner, but as creation's cosmic ruler.[19] Naomi's petition for חסד seems to have a cosmic rather than a covenant basis. To this point, neither Orpah nor Ruth is a member of Israel's covenant community. Indeed, Naomi's later plea that Ruth follow Orpah and "go back to her people and her god" (1:15) implies that they still worship the Moabite god Chemosh.[20]

Thus, Naomi's wish for Yahweh to do them חסד presupposes that Yahweh repays even non-Israelites for their חסד. In turn, that seems to share the Old Testament's common assumption that חסד forms a constituent element of the universe's underlying world order, an order over which Yahweh presides and of

16. For suggestions on how their חסד could affect the dead, see Hubbard, *Ruth,* 104.

17. Gen 24:12, 14; Exod 20:5-6; 34:6; Deut 5:10; 7:9, 12; 1 Kgs 3:6 (= 2 Chr 1:8); Jer 9:23; 32:18; Ps 18:51 (= 2 Sam 22:51); 25:10; 103:8; Job 10:12; et al.; H. J. Stoebe, "חסד," *THAT*, vol. 1, 612-18; H.-J. Zobel, "חסד," *TDOT*, vol. 5, 54-58.

18. It might also assume that such a connection would not happen automatically without divine intervention or that it might be slow in coming.

19. What follows draws on R. L. Hubbard, Jr., "The Go'el in Ancient Israel: Theological Reflections on an Israelite Institution," *Bulletin for Biblical Research* 1 (1992): 16.

20. As further evidence, consider that in 1:20-21 Naomi's appeal is to Shaddai, i.e., to Yahweh as cosmic ruler; cf. Hubbard, "The Go'el in Ancient Israel," 16-17.

which Israel's own ideal life of חסד (cf. Mic 6:8) offers a unique expression.[21] If human evil threw that cosmic order out of balance, Israel believed that Yahweh would intervene to restore it to its prior homeostasis of שלום. By the same token, if human good (e.g., חסד) conformed to its order, Israel assumed that Yahweh would likewise intervene, not to restore order, but to reward the good. In sum, Naomi's appeal rests on a cosmic basis — the belief that Yahweh would reward חסד in his role as overseer of cosmic world order. By implication, the audience is to read any remarriage by Ruth or Orpah later in the story as the answer to Naomi's prayer given by Yahweh in his role as cosmic ruler.

II

The second example in Ruth which reflects belief in dynamism comes from the mouth of Boaz, Naomi's prominent Bethlehemite in-law.[22] During his first-ever meeting with Ruth, he voices a wish similar to Naomi's that Yahweh act on Ruth's behalf. As we shall see, like Naomi's wish in 1:8-9, it also casts a programmatic interpretive shadow over the story's subsequent events. He says (2:12):

ישלם יהוה פעלך
ותהי משׂכרתך שׁלמה
מעם יהוה אלהי ישׂראל
אשׁר־באת לחסות תחת־כנפיו

> May Yahweh repay your action,
>> and may your wages be paid in full
> from Yahweh, the God of Israel,
>> under whose wings you have come to seek refuge.

The statement consists of four somewhat parallel lines which, though technically not "poetry," read with poetic rhythm.[23] In fact, as Segert notes, its seemingly

---

21. Cf. Gen 21:23; Josh 2:12, 14; Judg 8:35; Ps 33:5-9; Prov 3:3; 11:17; et al. For discussion of the "life of חסד," see E. F. Campbell, Jr., *Ruth*, AB 7 (Garden City: Doubleday, 1975), 29-30; Hubbard, *Ruth*, 72-74.

22. Cf. 2:1, reading the Ketib מְיֻדָּע ("friend") over the Qere מוֹדָע ("relative"); so also Campbell, 87-88; J. M. Sasson, *Ruth: A New Translation with a Philological Commentary and a Formalist-Folklorist Interpretation* (Baltimore: Johns Hopkins, 1979), 39; contra P. Joüon, *Ruth* (Rome: Pontifical Biblical Institute, 1953), 46; W. Rudolph, *Das Buch Ruth, Das Hohelied, Die Klagelieder* 2, KAT (Gütersloh: Mohn, 1962), 46; E. Würthwein, *Ruth* 2, HAT 18 (Tübingen: Mohr-Siebeck, 1969), 13. For a discussion of Naomi's relationship to Boaz, see Hubbard, *Ruth*, 132-33.

23. Concerning the poetic form, see J. M. Myers, *The Linguistic and Literary Form of the Book of Ruth* (Leiden: Brill, 1955), 36, 41.

poetic form probably derives from its literary nature as a kind of saying.[24] Our primary interest, however, lies with the statement's first two cola, lines strikingly framed with a kind of semantic and thematic inclusio by words derived from the root שלם.[25] Careful attention to the language of those two lines confirms my contention that the dynamistic worldview underlies this statement.

The first line, ישלם יהוה פעלך ("May Yahweh repay your action"), is a short form of a formula which appears elsewhere as "May Yahweh repay [ל, "to"] X according to [כ] his/her/your/their good/evil deed."[26] Grammatically, both long and short forms share the same basic sentence ("May Yahweh repay"). At its heart lies the piel verb ישלם which linguistically derives from the stative verb שלם, "to be complete, whole."[27] The piel here has the well-known factitive sense, denoting an action which causes the root's stative sense to come about.[28] Literally, then, the basic sentence means "May Yahweh complete/make whole . . . ," that is, either to bring about the final completion of an action begun earlier, or to restore something presently incomplete to its previous state of completeness.[29] Given its contextual usage as an economic term, however, one usually renders שלם piel "to repay, compensate."[30] Hence, it portrays that completion as a repayment or compensation disbursed by Yahweh himself.

Beyond the basic sentence, the present short form differs significantly from the long one. Only the short form completes that sentence with an impersonal direct object ("your action") rather than a personal indirect object ("to X"). Further, the short form omits the long form's standard of reward ("according to . . ."), the phrase which describes the action for which repayment is due "X." Thus, while the long form cites the prior action as a standard or guide to which the reward should

---

24. S. Segert, "Vorarbeiten zur Hebräischen Metrik," *ArOr* 25 (1957): 192-93, 194-95, calls it a "benediction" *(Segensspruch)* after O. Eissfeldt, *The Old Testament: An Introduction,* trans. P. R. Ackroyd (Oxford: Basil Blackwell, 1965), 56-87. Cf. also Segert's critique (190-200) of the view that the lines are actually poetry.

25. Note also the metaphonic sound wordplay (so Sasson, 52). For the grammatical contrasts between the two cola, see A. Berlin, *The Dynamics of Biblical Parallelism* (Bloomington: Indiana University Press, 1985), 40, 55.

26. Campbell, 99; 2 Sam 3:39; Jer 25:14; 50:29; cf. Deut 7:10; Jer 32:18.

27. KB, vol. 4, 1419-20; BDB, 1022.

28. B. K. Waltke and M. O'Connor, *An Introduction to Biblical Hebrew Syntax* (Winona Lake: Eisenbrauns, 1990), 349 (§20.2m), 372 (§22.4d), 400 (§24.2a, n. 18); S. A. Ryder II, *The D-Stem in Western Semitic* (The Hague: Mouton, 1974), 94, 97-104; E. Jenni, *Das hebräische Pi'el: Syntaktisch-semasiologische Untersuchung einer Verbalform im Alten Testament* (Zürich: EVZ, 1968), 20-21.

29. E.g., 1 Kgs 9:25 (שלם־הבית, "he finished the temple"). Cf. W. Eisenbeis, *Wurzel šlm im Alten Testament,* BZAW 113 (Berlin: De Gruyter, 1969), 322.

30. E.g., Joel 2:25; Exod 21:37; 2 Kgs 4:7; Ps 37:21; J. Scharbert, "ŠLM im Alten Testament," in *Um das Prinzip der Vergeltung,* 313-14; cf. G. Gerleman, "שלם," *THAT,* vol. 2, 933: "Die Grundbedeutung von šlm pi. 'eine zustehende Gegenleistung erstatten' ist jedoch klar ersichtlich, auch wenn Jahwe als Vergelter dasteht, z.B. Jes 57:18; Jo 2:25; Hi 8:6; 41:3; Ruth 2:12. An diesen Stellen hat das Vergelten Jahwes den Charakter eines Schadenersatzes. . . ."

somehow compare, in the short form the prior action directly receives it. In other words, in the present case the recipient of the completion/repayment is not actually the doer of the action (i.e., Ruth) but the action itself. This assumes, of course, that some prior action on Ruth's part has earned her some sort of repayment from Yahweh. That is what is incomplete: Ruth has "worked" but not been paid for it. Hence, her "work" is "incomplete"; it has not reached its proper end.

To what does פעל ("deed, act") refer here? As is well known, the noun פעל has three main meanings. It describes the actual doing of something ("action," "behavior"; Deut 33:11; Jer 25:14), the result of that action ("deed," "work"; 2 Sam 23:20; Isa 59:6; Ps 104:23), and what the deed gained ("reward," "profit"; Jer 22:13; Job 7:2).[31] In the present context, verse 11 clarifies the specific sense of פעל in use here. Boaz first refers broadly to "all that [Ruth] did [עשית] for your mother-in-law after the death of your husband," then specifies how "you left your father and mother and your native land behind and came to a people with whom you have had few dealings before." In other words, he has in mind not just a single deed but a series of actions commencing with her husband's death and concluding with the present moment. He views Ruth's פעל as a totality — her entire pattern of conduct during that entire period.[32] The point is that, in Boaz's view, her "action" is incomplete because it remains unrewarded. He therefore asks Yahweh to complete it by rewarding Ruth. He asks Yahweh to connect an appropriate consequence with her earlier acts.[33]

The second colon, ותהי משכרתך שלמה מעם יהוה ("and may your wages be paid in full from Yahweh"), continues the economic terminology of its parallel. At its heart is the basic sentence היה + a subject + a predicate adjective + the prepositional phrase מעם יהוה ("X is/may be Y from Yahweh").[34] Here היה is in the jussive mood with משכרת ("wages") as its subject and שלמה ("complete, whole") as its predicate adjective. The word משכרת ("wages") is a collective feminine noun which occurs elsewhere only three times, all in reports about Jacob's salary disputes with Laban (Gen 29:15; 31:7, 41).[35] As a predicate adjective

---

31. J. Vollmer, "פעל," THAT, vol. 2, 463; KB, vol. 3, 896; cf. G. Fohrer, "Zweifache Aspekte hebräischer Wörter," in Studien zu alttestamentlichen Texten und Theman (1966-1972), BZAW 155 (Berlin: De Gruyter, 1981), 208.

32. Cf. KB, vol. 3, 896 ("Verhalten").

33. The presence of פעל here presents an intriguing alternative interpretation. In two contexts it means "wages" (Job 7:2; Jer 22:13; cf. the similar sense of its female cognate in Lev 19:13; Prov 10:16; 11:18; Ezek 29:20; Isa 49:4); cf. BDB, 821; KB, vol. 3, 896-97. Hence, the phrase שלם פעל piel might mean "to pay wages," making the present statement even more parallel to the following one.

34. This sentence structure is without an exact parallel in the Old Testament. For the closest parallels with מעם יהוה, see 1 Kgs 2:33 (ל + subj. + היה; cf. Isa 8:18); 1 Kgs 12:15 and 2 Chr 10:15 (subj. + היה); cf. Ps 121:2 (nominal sentence); Isa 28:29 (with יצא); Isa 29:6 (with פקד ni.); Gen 41:32 (נכון הדבר מעם האלהים); cf. BDB, 768-69.

35. Its presence here confirms our reading of the preceding colon as an economic statement. Its masculine cognate שכר means "wages" (Gen 30:28, 32, 33; 31:8) and, more

198

modifying "wages," here שְׁלֵמָה ("complete, whole") must mean "(paid) in full."[36] Semantically, it parallels its cognate יְשַׁלֵּם (cf. our remarks above).

As for the prepositional phrase מֵעִם יְהוָה, a close look at the contexts in which it occurs yields two significant observations. First, it usually appears in contexts which involve key turning points in someone's destiny. Second, its contexts often describe Yahweh's hidden or unexpected activity. So, e.g., rather than suffer the disaster of Joab's bloodguilt, "from Yahweh" David's dynasty will enjoy eternal blessing (1 Kgs 2:33). Also, "from Yahweh" Rehoboam turned a deaf ear to northern protests, thereby setting in motion events which produced the divided kingdom and fulfilled Ahijah of Shiloh's prophecy (1 Kgs 12:15; 2 Chr 10:15).[37] And "from Yahweh" will come his sudden obliteration of Jerusalem's attackers, thereby relieving her awful siege (Isa 29:6). In sum, the phrase's wider associations raise reader expectations that, if Boaz's words come true, their fulfillment will involve either Yahweh's hidden activity or something unanticipated. As with Naomi's programmatic statement, so this one by Boaz raises reader expectations that his words might indeed come true.

Why would Boaz appeal for Yahweh to act? What role of Yahweh do these two cola presuppose? With Naomi in 1:8-9, Boaz clearly shares the common Old Testament assumption that Yahweh is the true guardian of dynamism, that is, that Yahweh repays good (and evil) human deeds.[38] That Yahweh is the subject of שׁלם piel ("to repay, compensate") in more than one-third of its occurrences gives that assumption added credence. So, given Israel's theology about Yahweh, an appeal to him for reward makes very good sense. Further, it also seems likely that, like Naomi, Boaz files his appeal with Yahweh because only Yahweh has the resources sufficient to repay Ruth's devotion. While one cannot calculate the value of Ruth's actions, their remarkable character would seem to entitle her to large "wages." If so, what imaginable human resource could pay her off in full?

Most important, Boaz assumes that no one else but Yahweh owes Ruth her "wages." That, in turn, seems to imply that Ruth's devotion actually was work done for Yahweh — or at least that it was of such great interest to him

---

figuratively, "reward" (Gen 15:1; 30:18). It also occurs in parallelism with the feminine cognate of פֹּעַל (Isa 40:10; 62:11; Ezek 29:19-20; et al.).

36. Cf. Scharbert, 303; Eisenbeis, 349-50. Elsewhere שְׁלֵמָה pictures honest (i.e., whole) weights (Deut 25:14; Prov 11:1) and both hewn (i.e., finished) and unhewn (i.e., whole) stones (Deut 27:6; Josh 8:31; 1 Kgs 6:7); cf. 2 Chr 8:16.

37. Cf. Isa 28:29, which affirms how Yahweh teaches farmers wise farming; Gen 41:32, where מֵעִם הָאֱלֹהִים came two dreams which announced God's irreversible secret plans for Egypt. See also Isa 8:18; Ps 121:2.

38. E.g., Jer 25:14; Ps 28:4; Job 34:11; Prov 24:12; cf. Isa 1:31, where a man's evil פֹּעַל sowed the seeds of his downfall; Phil 4:18-19; Gerleman, *THAT*, vol. 2, 933, who also says, "Explizit oder implizit ist Jahwe der eigentliche Garant des Tun-Ergehen-Zusammenhangs. Daß Gott vergilt heisst, daß er belohnt oder straft."

that he would honor it anyway. That is why Boaz asks Yahweh to pay off Ruth's overdue wages fully as if he were somehow in debt to her (cf. Prov 19:17). Finally, the petition assumes that, without Yahweh's help, the connection of her acts (פעל) with their proper consequences (מֹשכרת) might not occur. At least, there is some doubt in Boaz's mind on the subject. In sum, like Naomi, Boaz passes to Yahweh the responsibility for the substantial recompense to which Ruth is entitled. Though one might credit this transfer of responsibility to Boaz's unwillingness to act, it is more likely due to his perceived inability to do so.

As for Yahweh's role, verse 12b identifies him as "the God of Israel under whose wings you have come to seek refuge." In the Old Testament, both the title "God of Israel" (אלהי ישֹראל) and the idiom חסה תחת כנפים ("to seek refuge under [someone's] wings") are most at home in cultic contexts.[39] Thus, if Naomi invoked Yahweh as cosmic ruler, here Boaz invokes him as the covenant God whom Israel worships and whose powerful, outstretched "wings" protect Ruth. Boaz implies that, since Ruth has "entered" (באת) Yahweh's protective realm (i.e., joined his worshiping community), she may expect to experience his personal watchcare. In sum, Boaz's appeal is to Yahweh as Israel's covenant God, the one who guards his people.

In conclusion, we must observe the important footnote to 2:12 which appears in 3:9 where Ruth proposes marriage to Boaz at the threshing floor. In reply, Boaz praises Ruth as worthy of Yahweh's blessing (3:10):

ברוכה את ליהוה בתי היטבת חסדך האחרון מן־הראשון
לבלתי־לכת אחרי הבחורים אם־דל ואם־שיר

> Blessed are you by Yahweh, my daughter! In this last kind act, you have even exceeded your earlier one by not offering yourself to the choice young men whether poor or rich.

According to Boaz, Ruth is praiseworthy because her "last kind act" (האחרון חסדך) has outdone her "earlier one." With a sizable consensus, I take the latter as an allusion to Boaz's own remark about Ruth's פעל in 2:11.[40] Given the present context, "last kind act" refers to verse 9 — to Ruth's commitment to provide Naomi an heir by marriage to a kinsman-redeemer such as Boaz.[41] That she

---

39. Hubbard, *Ruth*, 167-68. For the former, see Josh 7:19; Judg 5:3; 21:3; 1 Sam 6:3; 1 Kgs 8:17, 20; et al.; cf. W. Schmidt, "אלהים," *THAT*, vol. 1, 161; H. Ringgren, "אלהים," *TDOT*, vol. 1, 277-79; for the latter, see Ps 57:2; 61:5; 91:4; E. Gerstenberger, "חסה," *THAT*, vol. 1, 622-23.

40. Joüon, 74; Rudolph, 56; G. Gerleman, *Ruth. Das Hohelied* 2, BKAT 18 (Neukirchen-Vluyn: Neukirchener, 1981), 32; et al. Alternatively, both Sasson (84) and A. Berlin (*The Poetics and Interpretation of Biblical Narrative* [Sheffield: Almond, 1983], 90) believe it simply refers to Ruth's desire for an ordinary husband. For another (in my view, improbable) interpretation, see Sakenfeld, 43.

41. Sasson, 84; Joüon; Rudolph; Gerleman, *Ruth*; et al.

bypassed "the choice young men" for Boaz of her own free will (v. 10) made her commitment to Naomi especially remarkable.

Several implications flow from this comment by Boaz. First, it implies, on the one hand, that he regarded Ruth's earlier פעל as חסד, and, on the other, that her חסד formed the basis for his appeal that Yahweh repay Ruth (2:12). That means that the latter appeal rests on the same foundation as the earlier plea by Naomi (1:8-9). Second, since the last "kindness" has outdone the earlier one, one for which payment was already due, Boaz's praise implies that Ruth may expect additional wages beyond those which Yahweh already "owed" her. In other words, if Boaz is right, Ruth has quite a sizable "paycheck" coming! The precise contours of that paycheck emerge in the following discussion of the consequences which Ruth experiences later in the story.

III

Many commentators observe the positive reversal of fortunes which the story reports for Ruth and Naomi.[42] Indeed, literarily the two texts just discussed create reader anticipation of such reversals and assurance that they come from Yahweh. The following chart summarizes the main actions of Ruth and what I take to be their corresponding results in the story:

Ruth's Actions	The Results
Sacrifice of second marriage (1:8-14)	Marriage to Boaz (4:11, 13)[43]
Exclusive devotion to Yahweh (1:16)	Refuge under Yahweh's wings (2:12b)[44]
Leaving of Moabite family/homeland (1:16; 2:11)[45]	Integration into Israel[46]

42. Conveniently, see Hubbard, *Ruth*, 63-65; cf. D. F. Rauber, "The Book of Ruth," in *Literary Interpretations of Biblical Narratives*, ed. K. Gros Louis et al. (Nashville: Abingdon, 1974), 163-76.

43. This, of course, supplied the "resting place" (מנחה) for which Naomi wished (1:8-9).

44. For more on this, see below.

45. Since ancient Semites buried their dead in family graves, I regard Ruth's commitment to burial with Naomi (1:17) as an extension of her abandonment of her Moabite family.

46. By "integration," I mean Ruth's rise from the status of "foreigner" (נכריה; 2:10) and "maidservant" (שפחה; 2:13) — including her inclusion in Boaz's people (2:8-23) —

Plan to glean (2:2)	Plentiful food (2:8-23; 3:15-17)
Gō'ēl-marriage to preserve Elimelech's family line (3:9-10)	Her own family line (4:21-22)
	"Founding mother" of David's dynasty (4:11-12, 17)

In my view, a careful reading of the story supports the above correspondences.[47] Several constitute direct answers to the programmatic petitions of Naomi and Boaz discussed above (1:8-9; 2:12). So, Ruth's marriage to Boaz rewarded her sacrifice of a second marriage (i.e., her refusal to obey Naomi's command to go back to Moab in hopes of remarrying). That marriage answered Naomi's petition that Yahweh repay Ruth's (and Orpah's) kindness with new husbands. That Ruth also voluntarily cut all her familial and ethnic ties to Moab resulted in her becoming a full member of the family of Boaz and the people of Israel. That result also answered Boaz's wish that Yahweh repay Ruth's devotion to Naomi. For cutting her religious ties and devoting herself exclusively to Yahweh, the story rewards her with refuge under Yahweh's wings. Similarly, the continuing supply of food which Ruth and Naomi enjoyed resulted from Ruth's initiative to go gleaning in nearby fields.[48] Finally, her decision to provide Naomi an heir to preserve Elimelech's family line led to her having her own family line in Israel.

Observe, however, that the chart has one result without an antecedent, corresponding prior action. This item derives from the observation that Ruth later gains national fame as David's great-grandmother. Granted, the story itself nowhere specifically makes that claim. Rather, it is an inference to be drawn from the connection the narrative apparently makes between the blessings of the crowd (4:11-12) and the descent of David from Ruth and Boaz (4:17b). Briefly, let us follow that connection beginning with the crowd's cry at the end of the legal proceedings (4:11-12):

> May the Lord grant the wife about to enter your house to be like Rachel and Leah, the two who built the house of Israel, so you may prosper in Ephrathah

---

through "marriageable maiden" (אמה; 3:9) to worthy "wife" of Boaz (אשה, 4:11; cf. 3:11). In sum, through this process she regains both a family (i.e., that of Boaz) and a homeland (i.e., she attains full membership in Israel).

47. I have omitted one act of Ruth, her gift of a "son" to Naomi (4:14-16), because it is my own interpretation and without a supporting scholarly consensus. In my view (see *Ruth*, 263-66), Ruth voluntarily gave Naomi her son to care for, thereby making him Naomi's "son" in more than just the abstract legal sense of heir. Cf. also Sasson's thesis (158-61) that the birth episode (4:13-17) actually derives from two originally separate episodes; but cf. my critique (*Ruth*, 263 n. 1).

48. In context, the stable food supply also formed part of Yahweh's "wages" for Ruth's devotion.

and enjoy fame in Bethlehem. Also, may your house be like the house of Perez, whom Tamar bore to Judah, from the descendants which the Lord may give you from this young woman.

Strikingly, they invoke the names of Rachel and Leah, Israel's founding mothers, and Tamar, mother of Perez, the founder of Judah's leading clan. One must not miss the significance of their invocation of those famous ancestral names: it represents a subtle shift in the story's focus of attention. Up to now, the narrative's main concern has been with the problem of finding an heir for Elimelech. Literarily, that concern reaches its conclusion in two places — in Boaz's declaration that his marriage to Ruth intends to provide Elimelech with an heir (4:10), and in the episode in which Naomi finally receives that heir (4:14-17a). The crowd's wishes, however, make no mention of an heir for Elimelech and the survival of his family line. Instead, they conjure up visions of great national leaders descending from the union of Ruth and Boaz. They also implicitly wish for Ruth a future national notoriety similar to that enjoyed by Rachel, Leah, and Tamar.

Now, in my view, the wishes literarily prepare the reader for the story's concluding surprise, the unexpected revelation that King David descends from Ruth and Boaz (4:17b, 18-22).[49] If so, they confirm that Ruth did indeed attain the national notoriety which the crowd wished for her. In fact, the very existence of the book of Ruth itself bears witness to her fame in Israel. The question is, however, from which of Ruth's prior actions does this result? The story reports nothing even remotely comparable to it. It says nothing about Ruth's sacrificing either actual or anticipated fame in Moab in order to migrate with Naomi to Judah. Hence, unlike several of the other results, her fame does not substitute for something she gave up or lost.[50] Thus, one might argue that Ruth's lasting reputation flows from earlier actions which the book views as especially noteworthy — her embracing of Yahweh (1:16), her willing choice of a gōʾēl-marriage (3:9), or both. In other words, it amounts to a rewarding outcome which the book presupposes to be commensurate with either or both of them and in addition to the results which the chart lists above for them.

Several considerations undermine this view, however. The book seems to portray both deeds as rewarded through other, more equivalent ways. For example, consider how the book understands the "refuge" to which Ruth has come and which I take as the result of her devotion to Yahweh. Above, we noted that Yahweh's "wings of refuge" connoted the realm where she may experience

---

49. Cf. the thesis of S. B. Parker, "The Marriage Blessing in Israelite and Ugaritic Literature," *JBL* 95 (1976): 23-30, that the reference to Perez in 4:12 depends on the genealogy (4:18-22); cf. also Sasson, 156-57, 181-84. For a critique of Parker's suggestion, see S. Rummel, "Narrative Structures in the Ugaritic Texts," in *Ras Shamra Parallels*, vol. 3, ed. S. Rummel, AnOr 51 (Rome: Pontifical Biblical Institute, 1981), 324-32.

50. E.g., by giving up a possible second marriage, her familial and ethnic roots, her Moabite god, and an ordinary marriage in favor of one to Boaz.

his protective watchcare. The story, however, pictures Boaz as the means through whom Yahweh puts that protection into effect. Most representative of this idea is the wordplay on כנף which Ruth invokes in 3:9. By recalling Boaz's reference to Yahweh's protective "wings" (כנף) in 2:12, her plea for Boaz to spread his "garment-edge" (כנף) over her implies that Boaz's marital protection of Ruth would actually implement Yahweh's protection of her.[51] Once the narrative makes that connection, it forces the reader to view all of Boaz's subsequent activity on Ruth's behalf bifocally, that is, as both the care of Boaz and of Yahweh at the same time. Thus, the book implies that, besides replacing Ruth's prospective marriage in Moab, the marriage of Boaz and Ruth also provided the "refuge" of Yahweh which rewarded her devotion to him. If so, there is no reason to read Ruth's later fame as the consequence of that devotion.

As for Ruth's decision to provide Naomi an heir by marrying a gōʾēl, the fact that Ruth obtains her own family line by doing so seems to be its appropriate consequence. By contrast, her later notoriety is due, not to the existence of that family line itself, but to the fact that it turns out to be a specifically historic, royal one. On the other hand, even if one concedes that Ruth's fame flows from either or both of those earlier acts, the fact remains that the consequence exceeds what one would expect within the book's framework of dynamism. Indeed, that is precisely my thesis — that Ruth's national fame amounts to a kind of unexpected "bonus" payment which goes beyond the expectations of dynamism. If so, that implies something important about the narrator's theology of retribution. On the one hand, the writer assumes the traditional view of dynamism — i.e., that Yahweh appropriately rewards those who please him. On the other hand, the writer also believes that Yahweh may in some cases actually repay deeds with consequences which, though related to them, exceed the original deed. He may reward beyond what one might regard as "normal" expectations.

In sum, the story portrays Ruth as enjoying the positive consequences of her acts. At the same time, it seems to suggest that one of Ruth's rewards actually exceeds what one might expect from her previous deeds. Theologically, this implies that Yahweh, like Boaz in chapter 2, may himself pour generosity on someone who, like Ruth, especially pleases him.

IV

Two final subjects await treatment to round out our grasp of *Ganzheitsdenken* in Ruth. First, we must probe the relationship between law and dynamism in

---

51. Campbell, 29, 138. Cf. L. Morris, "Ruth," in A. Cundall and L. Morris, *Judges and Ruth*, TOTC (Downers Grove: InterVarsity, 1968), 290: "Ruth had put herself under Yahweh's 'wing' when she came to Judah. Now she seeks also to put herself under that of Boaz."

the book (i.e., how law contributes to the connection of acts and con-sequences).[52] Second, we must discuss how Yahweh relates to both law and dynamism in the book. As is well known, the book of Ruth reflects the influence of Israelite legal customs concerning inheritance, redemption (גאלה), and the marriage of a childless widow. This is not the place to rehearse the important scholarly discussion on aspects of law which its pages have generated.[53] Rather, our focus will fall upon the two customs which drive the book's plot, those of gleaning and the *gō'ēl* or kinsman-redeemer.[54]

Old Testament law clearly sanctioned the practice of gleaning as Yahweh's way of providing food for poor Israelites (Lev 19:9-10; 23:22; Deut 24:19-22). Ruth decides to take advantage of the custom in order to provide food for her and Naomi (2:2). More important, her initiative advances the book's plot by providing the occasion for Ruth and Boaz to meet for the first time (2:2-4). The rest of the story directly flows out of their initial "chance" meeting. Now, as noted above, Ruth's act of gleaning produced a happy, surprising result, namely, the provision of abundant food for her and Naomi (v. 17). It also put her in touch with Boaz, whose obvious "favor" not only reciprocated her devotion to Naomi but boded well for possible future benefits. In sum, the legally sanctioned gleaning practice is, on the one hand, an act which ends in an appropriate consequence, and, on the other hand, it forges a relationship of favor which both rewards Ruth for past deeds and lays a foundation for later narrative developments.

The roots of the *gō'ēl* custom lie in Israelite family law which, like gleaning, enjoys the sanction of Old Testament legal texts.[55] As is well known, however, elsewhere the Old Testament neither mentions nor legislates the specific case which the book of Ruth relates — the provision by a *gō'ēl* of an heir for a deceased relative. On the other hand, there are good reasons for accepting the book's assumption that the present case also enjoys legal sanction in Israel.[56] Like gleaning, the *gō'ēl*-duty plays a crucial role in the story's plot. It underlies Ruth's proposal of marriage to Boaz (3:9) and his introduction of an unexpected complication — the existence of a closer relative who must waive his prior legal

---

52. In my view, the story does not involve the reverse alternative, the implementation of law through dynamism. The reason is that the legal process in Ruth 4 is administrative, not criminal; cf. Hubbard, *Ruth*, 231.

53. For a review and assessment, see Hubbard, *Ruth*, 48-63.

54. For use of *g'l* and *gō'ēl*, see J. J. Stamm, "גאל," *THAT*, vol. 1, 384-87; H. Ringgren, "גאל," *TDOT*, vol. 2, 351-52.

55. Lev 25:25-30, 47-55; cf. Leviticus 27; Num 35:12, 19-27; Deut 19:6, 12; Josh 20:2-3, 5, 9; Ringgren, *TDOT*, vol. 1, 351-52; Stamm, *TDOT*, vol. 1, 384-85.

56. See my discussion (*Ruth*, 48-52), noting especially the denial that the union of Ruth and Boaz involves a levirate marriage (cf. Gen 38; Deut 25:5-10). Cf. T. and D. Thompson, "Some Legal Problems in the Book of Ruth," *VT* 18 (1968): 83-84, who observe that reports of actual legal activities like Ruth 4:1-12 in fact provide better evidence of Israel's actual legal practices than do legal instructions.

right to serve as *gō'ēl* before Boaz can marry Ruth (3:12-13).[57] That complication, in turn, motivates Boaz's legal discussion with the other kinsman at the
city gate about who will serve as *gō'ēl* in the matter (4:1-8).

Most important, however, the legal process at the gate both directly brings
about consequences and opens the way for other consequences to follow. First,
it is the legal process which gives Boaz the right as *gō'ēl* to marry Ruth (vv. 7-8).
Further, it grants their marriage official legal standing in the community of
Bethlehem (vv. 9-11a). Second, through the marriage, the legal process
completes Ruth's full integration into Israel. The term אִשָּׁה ("wife"; 4:11, 13)
and the comparison of Ruth to Rachel, Leah, and Tamar (vv. 11-12) suggest
that in marriage Ruth achieved some sort of Israelite "citizenship," however
Israel understood that concept. Her status as "wife" replaced her earlier stand-
ings as "foreigner" (נכריה; 2:10) and "Moabitess" (מואביה; 1:22; 2:2, 6, 21; 4:5,
10). This, in turn, brought to completion the process begun by her renunciation
of her ethnic roots, her embracing of Israel, and her seeking of refuge in Yahweh
(1:15-16; 2:11-12). Finally, the marriage leads to the birth of Obed and the
entire family line which descends from Ruth and Boaz (4:17b, 21-22). As noted
above, that line is the "wage" Ruth earned for choosing a marriage to benefit
Naomi rather than herself.[58]

How does the book understand Yahweh's involvement in both law and
dynamism? To answer that question requires us to survey Yahweh's involvement in the story as a whole. Theologically, recent commentators observe
that the book portrays Yahweh's involvement as hidden and indirect, almost
as if he were totally absent from the story.[59] During the legal process, e.g.,
no one even mentions his name until the crowd concludes the scene by calling
upon Yahweh to bless the newlyweds. At other key points, characters also
invoke his name in wishes, oaths, and blessings.[60] Such invocations subtly
keep an awareness of his presence and possible involvement in events alive
in the audience, despite the absence of direct divine interventions. Further,
as Hals observes, the narrator even resorts to a kind of "underplaying for
effect" — that is, intentionally *not* reporting God's activity at crucial junc-
tures in order to make the audience all the more aware of it.[61] Literarily, the

57. For this scene's legal complexities and various scholarly views, see Hubbard, *Ruth*,
51-62.
58. The book presupposes that Obed carries on the lines of both Elimelech and Boaz.
For the possible legal basis for this dual heirship, see Hubbard, *Ruth,* 62-63.
59. Cf. R. M. Hals, *The Theology of the Book of Ruth* (Philadelphia: Fortress, 1969),
3-19; W. S. Prinsloo, "The Theology of the Book of Ruth," *VT* 30 (1980): 340-41; Campbell,
28-32; Gerleman, *Ruth,* 9-10; Hubbard, *Ruth,* 66-71. Contrast Sasson, 44-45; idem, "Divine
Providence or Human Plan?" *Interpretation* 30 (1976): 415-19.
60. Besides texts discussed above (1:8-9; 2:12; 4:11-12), cf. 1:13, 17, 20-21; 2:4, 20;
3:13; 4:14.
61. Hals, 12. The two most significant examples are Ruth's "lucky" arrival at Boaz's
field (2:3) and the descent of David from Ruth and Boaz (4:17b).

effect is to heighten audience awareness of his possible presence and to hint at his participation in the plot.[62]

As for God's direct action, the story reports only two occasions of divine intervention, his gift of food to end the introductory famine (1:1, 6) and his gift of conception to Ruth (4:13). Of the two, only in the latter did Yahweh directly connect a human act with its proper consequence.[63] Theologically, that intervention clearly underscores one crucial limitation of law. Following the courtroom scene, the narrator briefly reports that the newlyweds sexually consummate their marriage and that Ruth gives birth to a son (4:13). Between the reports of lovemaking and birth, however, the writer interposes a theological statement, namely, that "Yahweh gave her [Ruth] conception." The statement affirms that Ruth's pregnancy results, not from human sexual relations, but from a divine gift.[64] Ruth's conception derives, not from law — i.e., from legally sanctioned conjugal relations — but from divine intervention. In other words, the law may legitimate a marriage, but it cannot produce children — only Yahweh can do that (4:13b). Only he can establish a family line for Ruth and cause David's descent from it.

Theologically, this implies two things: first, that human conception ultimately belongs to Yahweh's exclusive province; second, that such divine intervention hints at a great destiny awaiting the child to be born.[65] In sum, in this story the legal process serves as a kind of dynamistic midwife, both connecting appropriate consequences to earlier actions and setting up a legally sanctioned context in which other consequences may occur. With one consequence (i.e., pregnancy), however, Yahweh reserves the right to give it as a gift.

Does this mean, however, that the book does not perceive God to be involved in the other connections? Do they happen simply because of the operation of dynamism without divine involvement? At this point one must grasp the full hermeneutical significance of the oft-overlooked declaration by Naomi's friends (4:14):

ברוך יהוה אשר לא השבית לך גאל היום

Praised be Yahweh who has not left you without a kinsman-redeemer today. . . !

62. Cf. Trible, 260 ("Within human luck is divine intentionality").
63. Though it does not form an act-consequence connection, the gift of food sets in motion an important chain of events — Naomi's (and Ruth's) return to Bethlehem (1:7, 19) and the two meetings of Ruth and Boaz (chaps. 2, 3). If God did not actually cause the latter events to occur, the food-gift at least implied his indirect causality.
64. Note that the verb ויתן recalls the blessing which the crowd heaped on Ruth (cf. יתן, v. 11b), implying that Ruth's pregnancy marked Yahweh's answer to their wish for fertility.
65. Such divine intervention in conception is typical of birth narratives involving Israel's tribal ancestors (Gen 21:1-2; 25:21; 29:31; 30:17, 22, 23) or some of her great leaders (Judg 13 [Samson]; 1 Sam 1:19-20 [Samuel]).

In context, Ruth's newborn son is the kinsman-redeemer in this verse, the only Old Testament text in which *gō'ēl* refers to an infant.[66] Coming on the heels of verse 13, it certainly affirms what the narrator reports — that Yahweh had provided the newborn. More important, in my view, it offers a brief, comprehensive theological commentary on Yahweh's involvement in the entire course of events which preceded his conception and birth.[67] It implies that divine guidance lay behind everything from Ruth's migration to Judah (chap. 1), through her meetings with Boaz in the field (chap. 2) and at the threshing floor (chap. 3), to Boaz's legal dialogue at the city gate (4:1-12) and the pair's marital consummation (4:13). Thus, the women regard all those apparently human actions also as Yahweh's actions.

In sum, though presenting Yahweh's involvement in the story as "behind the scenes," in the end the book gives him all the credit.[68] For our purposes, this means that the book understands Yahweh as the one who connects all the acts with their corresponding consequences, including those joined through or as the result of the legal process. Though the book reports only two moments of direct divine intervention, by praising him in the end for everything, it in effect affirms that his intervention lies behind the story's whole chain of events.

V

In a 1984 article, Knierim remarked that Israel's "dynamistic understanding of reality" represented "an understanding of causality, widely presupposed in the Old Testament . . . without which many texts simply cannot be understood."[69] The present paper argues that the book of Ruth reflects the influence of that same understanding of reality. In my view, that understanding undergirds two programmatic appeals by Naomi and Boaz that Yahweh reward Ruth for her actions, both of which raise reader expectations of an eventual turnaround in the story. Thus, when the story later reports the realization of those expectations — i.e., the connection of acts and consequences — we rightly read them as the answers to those appeals.

As for Israelite law, it plays a dual role in the story. On the one hand, it directly brings about two consequences, Ruth's marriage to Boaz and her full

---

66. Cf. 4:15, which specifies that Ruth has born him; Sasson, 162-64; Gerleman, *Ruth*, 37; Campbell, 164 (conceding, however, that it could be Yahweh); et al.; contra J. A. Bewer, "The Goël in Ruth 4:14, 15," *AJSL* 20 (1903-4): 202-6, who believes it refers to Boaz; and H.-F. Richter, "Zum Levirat im Buch Ruth," *ZAW* 95 (1983): 125, who suggests that a copyist wrongly substituted *gō'ēl* for an original *bêt* ("house").

67. Cf. Hubbard, "The Go'el in Ancient Israel," 18.

68. This, of course, assumes that the women also voice the narrator's opinion.

69. R. Knierim, "On the Task of Old Testament Theology," *HBT* 6 (1984): 118.

integration into Israel. In turn, from the marriage two important further consequences result, the birth of Obed as Elimelech's replacement heir and the beginning of a new family line for Boaz and Ruth. On the other hand, besides directly realizing consequences, law also gives legal sanction to the actions which yielded those further consequences. So, it legally supported Ruth's plan to glean, the plan from which followed not only the provision of food for her and Naomi but Ruth's contact with Boaz, her future husband. At the same, however, the story shows one limit of law; i.e., that its sanction cannot bring about one expected consequence, Ruth's conception of a child. In the story, Yahweh reserves the right to give that as a gift and thereby stamps the newborn Obed with Yahweh's sign of destiny.

Strikingly, the story reports one result which seems to lack any antecedent act, Ruth's fame as founding mother of the Davidic dynasty. Theologically, this implies that Yahweh is not bound to conform to the dictates of dynamism but has the freedom to transcend it. This means that he can, on the one hand, give rewards which generously exceed the expectations of dynamism and, on the other hand, give rewards of his own free will and not in response to a prior action.

What is Yahweh's relationship to law and dynamism in Ruth? Clearly, the book portrays Yahweh as the one who oversees the operation of dynamism, i.e., who connects acts and consequences. He is the one to whom Naomi, Boaz, the crowd at the gate, and Naomi's neighbors appeal for rewards (1:8-9; 2:12; 4:11-12, 14). He is the one who works behind the scenes, within the actions of the human characters, to bring about the consequences which serve his purposes. Whether through human schemes or legal means, he is at work — hence, the book gives him the ultimate credit for the results. At the same time, the book emphasizes the participation of the human characters in the process of dynamism. They are neither puppets manipulated by Yahweh's hidden hands nor bystanders gawking at the unfolding plot from the sidelines. Rather, Yahweh oversees and implements dynamism through their actions. That is why in the end the women praise not only Yahweh but Ruth (4:14-15) — and why someone wrote this story down and why others incorporated it into their canon. In sum, the book of Ruth models the divine-human relationship as a cooperative venture — God working through his people to reward them and to achieve his larger purposes.

The Language of Prophecy:
Thoughts on the Macrosyntax of the
děbar YHWH and Its Semantic Implications
in the Deuteronomistic History

KLAUS KOCH

1. The Present Controversy

Prophetism is the outstanding representation of the religion of ancient Israel. Already in the view of the New Testament authors the prophet is the preeminent proclaimer of God's word and God's will during the time of the old covenant (Eph 2:20f.; cf. Matt 24:34; Acts 3:25; Rom 1:2). Even today there is a broad consensus among biblical scholars that the prophetic movement and its new formulation of the implications of the Yahweh-religion was decisive for the distinctive features of that religion, for its consequent advance toward a monotheistic creed and the development of a strict ethic of human solidarity.

Although the distinctive traces of the thinking and preaching of these curious men are recognizable in the foundations of both Christianity and Judaism, it is rather difficult to clear up the exact intentions and ideas of figures such as Amos and Isaiah, as well as of the other authors and redactors of the prophetic books collected in the canon. Many issues are controversial today. Was the aim of the reform prophets of the eighth century to issue a call for repentance or to announce unconditional doom? Was the starting point of their prophecies the inspiration of a horrible picture of an unavoidable coming disaster or the critique of contemporary society? What role did the hope of restoration after the coming catastrophe play? Were such expectations introduced only by later redactors or were they already present in the speeches of Amos and Isaiah? An adequate understanding of these and other important issues is crucial not only for historical reconstruction but also for the application of the prophetic message to the problems of theology and the church today. But how can one actualize the prophetic *děbar YHWH* if there is no convincing comprehension of its exact significance?

Since Hermann Gunkel's revolutionary breakthrough,[1] the conviction has arisen that in spite of the existence of large prophetic books the great figures of the prophetic movement in Israel were originally inspired speakers and not primarily literary authors. This astonishing statement is confirmed by the prevalence of prophetic utterances consisting of small units with clear-cut structures in both the prophetic books themselves and in the narratives about prophetic activities in the historical books. Hence Gunkel distinguished some special genres of prophetic speech and considered them the right basis for the proper understanding of the convictions and intentions of these great men of God.

In common-day language the use of genres is often not easy to determine because of the flexibility of every language and the possible vagueness of intention. But, as a rule, the more authoritative or performative the speaker wants to be, the clearer the profile of the employed genre becomes. Nowadays a prayer or a sermon in the context of Sunday morning worship certainly exhibits a more elaborate structure than a trivial conversation among friends. The prophetic speeches of Old Testament literature claim an exceptional significance as proclaiming the very word of God, and so they require a distinct profile recognizable by their contemporary audience.

To the extent that exegetes are concerned with form-critical observations, there is a certain consensus, reaching back to Wolff's study,[2] that the most frequent genre of prophetic speech is a presentation of the *dĕbar YHWH* with two clearly distinct parts. The first is related to the present, sometimes also to the past, and is mostly concerned with indefensible social or cultic conditions originating in human unfaithfulness and sin. The second part — sometimes, though rarely, preceding the part just mentioned — predicts future events in connection with divine intervention and against the background of the prevailing situation. Occasionally a third part is added, usually introduced by a *kî*-clause, which sounds like a concluding characterization.[3] But this last portion may be lacking because it need not belong to the regular pattern of the genre (cf. the critical questions of Knierim).[4]

It is obvious that the part concerning the future in this prophetic genre, which may be termed the prophecy in the narrower sense, is in every extant case directly related to the presupposed circumstances mentioned in the part concerned with the present and therefore called the *Begründung* by Wolff. This

1. H. Gunkel, *Die Propheten* (Göttingen: Vandenhoeck & Ruprecht, 1917).

2. H. W. Wolff, "Die Begründungen der prophetischen Heils- und Unheilssprüch," *ZAW* 52 (1934): 1-22 = *Gesammelte Studien zum Alten Testament*, TBü 22 (München: Kaiser, 1964), 9-35.

3. K. Koch, *The Growth of the Biblical Tradition* (New York: Charles Scribner's Sons, 1969), 212.

4. R. Knierim, "Criticism of Literary Features, Form, Tradition, and Redaction," in *The Hebrew Bible and Its Modern Interpreters*, ed. D. A. Knight and G. M. Tucker (Chico, Calif.: Scholars, 1985), 123-65, see 141f.

observation marks an important issue in the understanding of this kind of prophecy in Israel. The inspired speaker is by no means a mere soothsayer but delivers divine arguments about why the future must come in just this way and in no other. But what then is the underlying concept of God's relation to the people and their history? How is the prophetic task to be defined within this context?

In spite of a certain accord among scholars regarding the bipartite structure of the dominant prophetic genre, there is no unanimity concerning its proper meaning.[5] Reconstructing a rather speculative history of this genre, Gunkel supposed it to be a secondary combination of two originally independent genres, a *Scheltwort* (reproach), insofar as negative phenomena are mentioned, and a *Drohwort* (threat) predicting the future. Similarly, he considered oracles of salvation to be comprised of a *Mahnwort* (exhortation) and a *Verheißung* (promise), also previously two separate genres.

Westermann has presented a quite different approach.[6] He takes the bipartite utterances as an original unity. In his opinion this pattern is taken over from the forms of speech used in legal procedures and reflects a *Gerichtswort* (judgment speech). The first part consists of the *Anklage* (accusation), and the second corresponds to the *Gerichtsankündigung* (sentence). Although no example of the profane use of this kind of speech exists, Westermann's interpretation is taken for granted by many colleagues in the German-speaking scholarly world. It fits in very well with the primary understanding of God as a transcendent judge which prevails in the theology of Western Christianity.

Mention should also be made of the attempt of some scholars to locate the origin of the genre in a covenant cult, but they have not found many adherents (cf. the survey of Tucker).[7]

My own suggestion[8] is based on two observations: (1) the bipartite structure is already attested in some of the Mari prophecies, and (2) it is also rather common in diplomatic messenger speeches between human sovereigns. The obvious conclusion is that a typical type of northwest Semitic oracular speech was adopted by the prophets of Israel. It then developed in such a way that in the course of time two subgenres were generated, one concerning reproach and doom, the other relating to divine *ṣĕdāqâ* and salvation. In every instance the dominant genre of prophetic speech must be interpreted in itself. There is no trace of any larger analogy deriving from the judicial or cultic sphere.

In recent years Rolf Knierim[9] has raised some critical questions con-

5. Knierim, 140-41; G. M. Tucker, "Prophecy and the Prophetic Literature," in *The Hebrew Bible and Its Modern Interpreters*, 325-68, see 336f.
6. C. Westermann, *Grundformen prophetischer Rede* (München: Kaiser, 1960); ET, *Basic Forms of Prophetic Speech* (Philadelphia: Westminster, 1967).
7. Tucker, "Prophecy and the Prophetic Literature," 338f.
8. K. Koch, *Was ist Formgeschichte?* (Neukirchen-Vluyn: Neukirchener, 1964), §18.
9. Knierim, 140-44.

cerning my statements on "prophecy proper." Nevertheless, he stresses that "the further clarification of this issue is certainly one of the most important tasks immediately ahead."[10] Taking up the challenge, I will attempt to achieve some further clarification. But rather than offering a further analysis of the one chapter discussed by us,[11] I will broaden the basis of comparison and examine the macrosyntactical elements of all the prophecies proper that are recorded in the books of the deuteronomistic history. To advance the definition of the genre and its semantic implications, it may be helpful to collect the relevant examples in a relatively large but nonetheless well-rounded literary complex.

There are two primary reasons for selecting this body of literature. The prophetic books properly so called, though containing more numerous and more profound examples of the genre, have been more extensively subjected to the process of successive adaptation and redaction than have the historical books, and so the original structure of the small units is more likely to have been altered in them. Also, the deuteronomistic writers do not understand themselves as prophets. Their respect for prophetism was enormous, but they look at it from the perspective of those outside the movement. Therefore, their transmission of the *děbar YHWH* is strictly bound to the commonly known markers of that kind of speech, whereas a charismatic person within the movement may be more flexible and free in the choice of expressions.

2. Messenger Formula and Messenger Speech

The best criterion for selecting relevant examples seems to be the beginning of a quotation with the stereotypical sentence "Thus has Yahweh spoken" within the narrative. What follows appears as a divine word transmitted by a charismatic speaker. Because the similar expression "Thus has N. N. spoken" is used about a dozen times in these books referring to a communication from one person to another person of high standing and which is transmitted by a special functionary, the term "messenger formula" has become common for the introductory *kô 'āmar* (KA) formula. How significant is this kind of introduction? Does it indicate the beginning of a distinct genre, as Westermann[12] and many others have maintained but as Rendtorff[13] has contested? The answer will be important for elucidating the deuteronomistic understand-

---

10. Knierim, 144.

11. 2 Kings 1; Koch, *Formgeschichte*, §15; *Was ist Formgeschichte?* 5th ed. (Neukirchen-Vluyn: Neukirchener, 1989), 291-95; Knierim, "Criticism," 140-44.

12. Westermann, 71-81.

13. See 171f. in R. Rendtorff, "Botenformel und Botenspruch," *ZAW* 74 (1962): 165-77 = *Gesammelte Studien zum alten Testament,* TBü 57 (München: Kaiser, 1975), 243-55.

ing of prophetism and probably also for the self-understanding of the prophets themselves.

Now there are some examples of official, profane messages where after the KA-formula only a short command or an ultimatum follows (1 Kgs 2:30; 20:3; 22:27; 2 Kgs 1:11 [9:18f.]), sometimes substantiated by a *kî*-clause (2 Kgs 18:29; cf. Num 22:16f.). Where, however, a longer speech is recorded, it is distinctly divided into two parts, one referring to the existing circumstances and the relationship between sender and receiver, the other — usually indicated by the particle *wĕ῾attâ* — continuing with further actions or developments of both parties (Judg 11:15-27; 2 Kgs 18:19-25; [19:3f.]; cf. Gen 32:4-6; 45:9; Num 22:5f.). As a rule the difference between the short and the long type of speech depends on the status of the two parties. If the receiver is of lower status than the sender, only a short sentence is appropriate. If both are of equal rank, the use of more sophisticated formulations is required. Regarding this last type, Westermann's contention that a special genre which he calls the *Botenspruch* (messenger speech) exists[14] is certainly justified.

In "prophetic" utterances the same difference regarding the sequence after the KA-formula can be observed. There are some cases where the sentence "Thus has Yahweh spoken" does not precede a longer speech but only a short command (1 Kgs 12:24; 2 Kgs 4:43; 20:1), an ultimatum (2 Sam 24:12), a response to a human request (1 Kgs 20:14; 2 Kgs 7:1), an explanation of a symbolic action (1 Kgs 22:11), or information about a divine word directed to a foreign king (2 Kgs 19:20). These examples are generally neglected in the following analysis. They are, however, taken into consideration if that kind of short remark or call is accompanied by a special statement (e.g., 1 Sam 10:17-19; 15:2-3).

But in about a dozen places the divine word introduced by *kô ᾽āmar YHWH* is followed by an elaborate two-stage speech structured similarly to the above-mentioned profane genre. Regarding these texts Westermann is correct in seeing a prophetic messenger speech and in viewing the prophet as an authoritative speaker of the word of God. Regarding the books of Joshua-2 Kings, however, there is no balance in the use of this genre. In Joshua and Judges only a few irregular examples occur. Josh 7:13-15 exhibits a demand for a cultic action introduced by a KA-sentence. Joshua 24 presents the same situation, although here the sentence is preceded by a long historical survey. Judg 6:8-10 refers only to a divine speech and the disobedience of the people in former days. In 1 Samuel there is only one example of a real messenger speech, and in 2 Samuel there are two; whereas in the books of Kings the examples are numerous. This distribution is certainly due to the different sources of the deuteronomistic writings, i.e., to the history of prophetism. Nonetheless, the

14. Westermann, 71-82.

basic features in the use of the genre persist throughout Samuel and Kings, as the synopsis below demonstrates.

Although Westermann has stressed the relationship of the dominant prophetic manner of speaking to the official messenger speeches and the messenger function of the prophets, he suddenly replaces the term *prophetischer Botenspruch* (prophetic messenger speech) with *Gerichtsrede* (judgment speech) in his monograph. In his opinion the prophet is first and foremost a functionary of a heavenly law court and of a supreme divine judge. Westermann justifies the transition in terminology on the basis of three texts which he only partially quotes, two of which belong to the deuteronomistic history (1 Kgs 21:17-19; 2 Kgs 1:3-4; further Amos 7:16-17).[15] But does his conception really originate in form-critical observations or is it the result of a step in a different direction? Has a presumed content become so prominent as to cause a disregard for the verbal expressions and surface structure of the texts? To arrive at convincing results it is necessary to look at all examples of a possible genre within the literary corpus.

3. Macrosyntactical Elements in Quotations of Prophetic Speeches

In the following synopsis (Fig. 1) all examples of an elaborate prophecy in the books in question are listed. The columns display the outstanding characteristics structuring each utterance as a whole. Because of the limitation of space only a few markers which I consider significant could be selected. Others would perhaps emphasize different phenomena.

Besides the introduction of a divine word by "Thus has Yahweh spoken" there is another formula, "The word of Yahweh happened to N. N.," *wayĕhî dĕbar YHWH-'el,* which marks direct quotations. But it relates to a private oracle, to an address directed to the prophet himself and not to an outside audience (1 Kgs 17:28; 18:1; 19:9; 21:28). Often it hints at the manner in which the official prophecy is to be announced, so the KA-formula may follow in the next sentence (2 Sam 7:4; 24:11; 1 Kgs 12:22f.; 13:20; 21:17f.; cf. 2 Kgs 20:4). In 1 Kgs 6:11 the *wayĕhî*-formula stands before an exhortation to King Solomon. The only exception is 1 Kgs 16:1-4, where that sentence is the only one in connection with a prophecy to a northern king. A similar expression, "Hear the word of Yahweh," is the superscription of a prophetic prediction (2 Kgs 20:16f.; cf. further 2 Kgs 7:1). In 1 Sam 13:13-14 a special case occurs because Samuel utters a prediction in his own words, speaking of God in the third person. All these exceptional speeches are neglected in the synopsis.

15. Westermann, 93.

Type	Text	KA	AC + Narr		Question		ועתה	לכן	KA	הנה + part	ו + AC	לא + impf	imper	כי
			pos	crit	pos	crit								
-	(Josh 24)	+	+				+						+	
(D)	Judg 6:8-10	+	+	+										
D/S	1 Sam 2:27ff	+	+		+	+	+	+		+	+	+		
-	(10:18f)	+	+	+			+						+	
-	(15:2-3)	+	+				(+)						+	
S	2 Sam 7:5-7	+	+			+								
	7:8-16	+	+				+				+	+		
D	12:7-10	+	+			+	+					+		+
	12:11-12							+		+	+			+
D/S	1 Kgs 11:31ff								+	+	+	+		
D	13:2-3								+	+	+			
D	13:21f	+		+								+		
D	14:7-16	+	+	+				+		+	+		+	+
S	17:14								+		+			
S	20:13	+			+					+	+			(+)
S	20:28	+	+								+			(+)
D	20:42	+		+							+			
D	21:19	+				+			+		(+)			
D	21:20-26			(+)						+	+			
D	2 Kgs 1:3-4				+		+	+				+		+
D	1:6	+			+		+					+		+
D	1:16	+		+	+		+					+		+
S	2:21	+	+									+		
S	(3:16)								+					(+)
	3:17-19								+		+	+		
S	9:6-10	+	+								+			
	9:12	+	+											
S	19:6-7	+								+	+			
D/S	19:32-33							+	+			+	+		
S	20:5-6	+	+								+	+		
D	21:11-15			+				+	+	+	+			
D	22:15									+				+	
	22:16-17			+						+	+	+	+		(v. 17)
	22:18-20	+	+						+	+	+	+		

Figure 1. Synopsis of the Macrosyntax of Prophetic Speeches: Joshua–2 Kings

216

4. Explanation of the Synopsis

Type announces whether future disaster (D) or future salvation (S) is predicted. The information in this column does not refer to the macrosyntax but only to the content (according to modern interpretations), but it is added because many exegetes currently assume that such a difference suggests two separate genres.

Text lists all comprehensive prophetic speeches introduced by the so-called messenger formula.

KA = *kô 'āmar YHWH,* the messenger formula. It normally appears before the first part of the speech, which describes former and present circumstances. Frequently only the second, predictive part of the prophetic utterance is recorded. In such cases the formula is placed before this portion. In a few texts the formula appears twice (1 Kgs 21:19f.; 2 Kgs 22:15f.). In 1 Sam 2:30; 2 Kgs 19:33; 22:19 *ně'um YHWH* is added in the second part.

AC stands for afformative conjugation (= perfect). In the context of prophetic utterances it characterizes the present relationship between the divine and the human partner of the speech. Where this section is more extensive, references to the past in the narrative tense (= consecutive imperfect) may be added. The indication of the situation contains positive statements generally pertaining to divine activities or critical ones condemning human behavior. The initial sentence may be preceded by *ya'an 'ăšer* (1 Kgs 11:33; 13:20; 14:7; etc.).

Questions in a rhetorical manner are sometimes used instead of statements. With the exception of 1 Kgs 20:13, their aim is critique and reproach.

ועתה and לכן precede the second part in nearly half of the texts, announcing the turning point of the speech, the transition from the present situation to further developments. The first particle belongs also to profane, official messenger speeches. The second one seems to be a prophetic innovation.

הנה with a following participle marks the beginning of the prediction proper in half of the examples. The corresponding sentence refers to a divine condemning or rescuing action setting in motion further consequences which are formulated by the *copula* and *AC* (*waw* perfect).

לא with imperfect (*impf* = preformative conjugation) represents another way of formulating the prediction. It resembles the prohibitive commandments in Hebrew and may have a kind of apodictic character. In only a few instances does it occur in conjunction with a preceding *hinnê* sentence.

Imperative as command to the human addressee appears sometimes instead of a prediction.

כי sentences, where they occur, conclude the quotation and refer to the present state of the relationship and motivate the speech as a whole. This kind of concluding characterization[16] may be neglected for present purposes since it does not seem to play a decisive role within the deuteronomistic books.

16. K. Koch, *Growth of the Biblical Tradition,* 212.

5. Preliminary Results

As indicated above, the synopsis could not register all syntactical details of every prophetic utterance recounted in the deuteronomistic history. Nonetheless, I have tried to take into account the most significant features, especially the decisive markers of beginnings and transitions. The common order of these elements is followed; a few texts exhibit some rearrangements which could not be indicated. A greater deficiency is the neglect of the framing context which certainly also influences the speeches in question. But here only the corpus of direct speeches could be considered. Yet, even so, certain reflections on the prophetic logic are possible.

Wherever prophetic speeches are quoted, the pattern of language is rather stereotyped compared with other speeches of human protagonists or with the genre of the surrounding narrative. Apparently the authors are compelled to formulate every prophetic transmission of divine words in this solemn way. It seems that the use of the formulas in question, the linking particles, and the changes of tense all have semantic significance. How can this significance be determined? Given the preliminary character of the current study, only a synchronic view is appropriate, even if tradition-historical considerations may be necessary at a later stage of investigation.

Regarding the surface structure of these texts some consequences are rather obvious.

1. Contrary to the common opinion among exegetes, no difference can be detected between predictions of coming disaster and predictions of future salvation. The popular division between so-called judgment speeches (*Gerichtsworte*) and salvation oracles (*Heilsworte*), especially stressed by Westermann,[17] seems to have no basis in the Hebrew text of the books in question.

2. Although in Samuel and Kings most of the prophetic utterances are addressed to individuals, there is no structural distinction between divine words to individual persons and those to the people as a whole (cf. 2 Kgs 22:16-17 and vv. 18-20) or even a speech to objects such as an altar (1 Kgs 13:2-3).

3. In most cases two parts of the divine word are clearly discernible. First, the present state of affairs between God and the addressee is described. Then follows a second part relating to the future aspects of human life and dependent on the conditions mentioned in the first part. Hence, the prophets are not conceived as pure soothsayers, revealing what will happen by chance in days to come, but rather as "futurologists." Their God extrapolates the necessity of salvation or condemnation from the course of a divine-human metahistory. The emphasis of the utterance lies in nearly every case on the second, predictive part.

4. In half of the cases this future part is formulated with a negated imperfect (preformative conjugation) in an "apodictic" manner. Such sentences

17. In *Grundformen prophetischer Rede.*

218

indicate that the normal course of events will be unequivocally stopped (2 Sam 12:10; 1 Kgs 13:22; 2 Kgs 2:21; 3:17; 19:32; cf. the command of 1 Kgs 12:24) or that it will continue irreversibly against all expectations (2 Sam 7:10; 1 Kgs 17:14; 2 Kgs 19:6, 16). No divine intervention as such is explicitly mentioned, although God's activity is beyond doubt in this regard.

5. Another possible formulation of the second section uses the particle *hinnê*, "behold," and continues first with a divine action expressed by a participle and then with further specifications employing finite verbs, as a rule the copula and the perfect tense (afformative conjugation). In three instances God utters a very general prediction, "behold, I am bringing evil" *(hinĕnî mēbî' rā'â)*, which is followed by special announcements (2 Sam 12:11; 1 Kgs 14:10; 2 Kgs 21:12). In two other cases he pronounces a single action with far-reaching consequences (2 Kgs 19:7; 20:5). The text of 1 Kgs 13:2 connects *hinnê* with a subject other than God, referring to the decisive human agent of the divine will. The introduction of the future developments with *hinnê* and a nominal clause expresses the immediate divine reaction, which then appears to be simultaneous with the sin of humans.

6. In spite of the deuteronomistic conviction of a warning task for the prophets and their exhortative aim ("Turn from your evil ways," 2 Kgs 17:13-14), there are seldom admonitions within the quoted speeches. The predicted future knows no alternative. Only an appendix sometimes opens up additional aspects that are contingent on human behavior (1 Kgs 11:38).

7. There is no relationship to any juridical genre. Some of the questions of the first part do in fact reproach the addressee, but any kind of accusation before a third party or a court of law is lacking and the characteristic features of the second part have no parallels in a public verdict. No judge in Israel could have started his pronouncement of sentence with "Behold, I am bringing evil upon you"! It may be worth noting that there is no reference to any divine commandment. The argumentation does not proceed in terms of law and judgment.

8. In some of the more elaborate examples the bridge from the present circumstances to the future is built by *talio*, by catastrophes exactly corresponding to the manner of the wrongdoing. David has wrongly taken the wife of another man and unjustly used the sword; hence, taking the wives of David and using the sword against his house will be the future response (2 Sam 12).[18] Ahab's bloodshed calls for bloodshed regarding his own family (1 Kgs 21).[19] But the decisive point is the special conception of God and of the divine word underlying these speeches. This last issue requires further consideration which goes beyond the mere observation of formulas and includes some of the prominent elements of the content.

18. Cf. Koch, *Die Profeten*, 2. Auf., Bd. 1 (Stuttgart; Berlin; Köln; Mainz: Kohlhammer, 1987), 30-33; ET, *The Prophets*, vol. 1 (Philadelphia: Fortress, 1982), 19-22.
19. Cf. Koch, *Profeten*, 45; *Prophets*, 34f.

6. The Function of the Divine Word

What conception of deity corresponds to the deuteronomistic presentation of prophetic speeches? Some intimations in this direction may be formulated.

1. The *děbar YHWH* uttered by a charismatic speaker announces a forth-coming divine intervention in the course of history, be it the history of an individual or of a nation. For example, God will give victory to an Israelite king (1 Kgs 20:13, 28) or send a disturbing spirit to a foreign one (2 Kgs 19:7), grant a kingdom or take it away (1 Kgs 11:31). God may intend to remove a priestly class (1 Sam 2:31) or to destroy a dynasty (1 Kgs 14:10; 21:21) or even the holy city of Jerusalem (2 Kgs 21:13). God gives women and takes them away (2 Sam 12:8, 11), he may heal an individual from disease (2 Kgs 20:5) or gather a person to the grave (2 Kgs 22:20).

2. What the prophet announces in this way is usually totally unexpected for the audience. It implies a sudden turn in the normal chain of events, either salvific or catastrophic. But it is nevertheless a logical consequence of the disturbed circumstances. The prophet puts forth why God is obliged to act in the manner predicted. The particle *lākēn*, "therefore," at the transition from the present to the future portion of the speech informs the listener that the coming events — unexpected though they may be — are rooted in a divine extrapolation of the prevailing circumstances. God himself is engaged in the course of the history of the people and their land. He represents the other, invisible side of reality which is the basic reality of all existence and therefore the determining force of metahistory. Where evil and crime occur he will immediately cause the backlash: "Behold, I am bringing evil upon him" (2 Sam 12:11; 1 Kgs 14:10; 21:21; 2 Kgs 21:12; 22:16). Yet in spite of many predictions of doom and disaster, God's final intention is salvation for his elected people. The rules of the divine guidance of history and the numerous divine interventions have been obvious since the days of the exodus. God is constantly concerned about the necessary institutions of Israel such as priesthood and kingship (Judg 6:8-10; 1 Sam 2:27ff.; 2 Sam 7:5-16; 1 Kgs 11:31ff.).

3. Within the course of metahistory the *děbar YHWH* plays an important role. The prophecies are not merely information about coming events; they are the very means to produce them. Von Rad[20] has emphasized how much the fulfillment of such speeches determined the course of Israelite history according to the deuteronomistic view in the books of Kings. If Yahweh has spoken, the coming realization is included; there is no need for a further divine intervention. Yahweh has only to establish *(hēqîm)* the secret dynamics which are encompassed in the *dābār*. Hence, God is not conceived as a judge who requires a

---

20. G. von Rad, "Die deuteronomistische Geschichtstheologie in den Königsbüchern," *Deuteronomium-Studien,* FRLANT, NF 40 (Göttingen: Vandenhoeck & Ruprecht, 1947), 52-64 = *Gesammelte Studien zum Alten Testament,* TBü 8 (München: Kaiser, 1958), 189-204.

police force and jailers. No terminology of verdict and punishment appears. But the *dābār* may be a product of divine anger which means nothing else than God's severe reaction against a defiled world.

In the foregoing considerations I have attempted to demonstrate that the sober study of the surface structure of Hebrew prophecies may open our eyes to some essential issues concerning Old Testament prophetism. Much remains to be done in this field. But we will gain deeper insights only if we take into account the special way of thinking characteristic of the ancient Hebrews and if we try to avoid the hasty application of Western categories.

Again and again Rolf Knierim has discussed the methodological questions of biblical exegesis in an outstanding manner. In a convincing manner he stresses the significance of the generic structures of biblical language, only "detectable in the surface texts."[21] My considerations attempt to pursue that way and to present a further contribution to a friend and colleague in a surely ongoing discussion.[22]

21. Knierim, 142.
22. I would like to thank Dwight R. Daniels for improving my English style.

Letting Rival Gods Be Rivals: Biblical Theology in a Postmodern Age[1]

BURKE O. LONG

Once, when Mesha, king of Moab, refused to pay the taxes of vassalage to his overlord, King Jehoram of Israel, YHWH and YHWH's prophet Elisha were drawn into Jehoram's efforts to retain control of Moabite territory (2 Kgs 3:4-27). Not because of Jehoram, as the narrator reported Elisha's words, but out of respect for the Judean king Jehoshaphat, Elisha would consult God on behalf of this military mission. An unambiguous prophecy of victory followed: "He [YHWH] will give Moab into your hand" (v. 18). But when the moment of final triumph for Israel arrived, the king of Moab offered up his firstborn son as a burnt offering. Immediately, "a great wrath [קצף גדול] came upon Israel," and the troops withdrew to their own land (vv. 26-27).

Was it the wrath of Chemosh, god of Moab, that broke out upon the troops? Or the fearful punishment of YHWH, which would be the usual referent of qeṣep?[2] Or did a dispiriting panic of ambiguous origin send the soldiers into retreat? The narrator (or redactor) does not say. This lack of a clear statement about YHWH triumphant — or rather, the unspoken possibility that a Moabite god effectively denied Israel the victory — greatly disturbed subsequent readers, ancient and modern alike, who could give no credence to a divinity that rivaled the exclusive power of YHWH. As Mordechai Cogan and Hayim Tadmor succinctly expressed the problem: "The equivocal

---

1. I am very pleased to dedicate these reflections to Rolf Knierim, whose works on form criticism and theology have not only been exemplary of their kind, but have unfailingly stimulated forthright dialogue and scholarly engagement.

2. Num 17:11; 18:5; Josh 22:20; Deut 29:27; Isa 60:10; Jer 21:5; 50:13; 2 Chr 29:8. See *TWAT,* vol. 7, 95-103.

'wrath' might have satisfied the ancient editor, but it has been an embarrassment to all his readers."[3]

From very earliest times, translators and critical commentators, interpreters all, sought to alleviate their discomfort. The Mesha (Moabite) inscription helps us understand why, for on that stele a Moabite scribe enumerated Mesha's successes with conventions of theological historiography that are virtually indistinguishable in underlying outlook from those used in Israel, save for the god in question.[4] Affliction of Moab is attributable to Chemosh's anger (line 5), and upturns in her fortune, specifically the king's conquest of city-states, fold into metaphors of immanence: "Chemosh dwelt there (in the conquered city)" (ll. 9, 33). Some of Mesha's conquests take place at the behest of Chemosh, and afterwards the king offers the spoils of war to his god (ll. 14-16; cf. 32). While commemorating Mesha's piety and the establishment of a sanctuary to Chemosh (l. 3), the inscription construes human history as an arena of divine action, and divinely directed royal deed.

> "Go, take Nebo from Israel!" And I went by night and fought against it from dawn until midday. And I took it and slew them all — seven thousand men (warriors) . . . [men?], and women and [. . .] and maidens, for to Ashtar-Chemosh I had devoted it to (sacrificial) destruction. And I took from there the [. . .] of Yahweh and I dragged them before Chemosh. And the king of Israel (had) built Jahaz, and he dwelt there while fighting against me. But Chemosh drove him out before me and I took it. From Moab I took two hundred men, everyone a leader (?). And I led them against Jahaz and took it, to attach it to Dibon.[5]

If something like this ideology is implied in the arresting equivocation of 2 Kgs 3:26-27, then we may sense the claims and counterclaims that could be made in Israel on behalf of rival gods.

At the hands of various translators and interpreters, even before the discovery of the Mesha inscription, the Moabite god was killed off. He was dismissed by the privileged claims of exclusivist and absolutist YHWH monotheism, or simply effaced, not so much in the text itself as in *readings* of the text that insisted on overcoming the plainness of its ambiguity. One common stratagem rested on ideological principle: the biblical narrator cannot have referred to the effective power of a non-Israelite god; how could such a non-biblical belief have been put forth, or been allowed to stand in the Bible or in the great historiography spanning Joshua through 2 Kings? The canonical voice

---

3. M. Cogan and H. Tadmor, *II Kings*, AB 11 (New York: Doubleday, 1988), 52.

4. Donner and Röllig, *KAI* #181.

5. Lines 14-21. See also lines 32-34. See K. A. D. Smelik, "King Mesha's Inscription: Between History and Fiction," in Smelik, *Converting the Past: Studies in Ancient Israelite and Moabite Historiography*, OTS 28 (Leiden: Brill, 1992), 59-92.

of exclusivist Yahweh devotion, the narratival perspective which measured history by its alignment with this God's demands, was simply too strong. Thus "great wrath" must have been associated with *Israel's* God or with a *human* condition among Israel's troops. The logic inexorably demanded that Chemosh, or the mere possibility of Chemosh, be displaced in the narrative. The Greek translators spoke of μετάμελος μέγας, a change of heart or a "great repentance" that came upon Israel; this apparently influenced Josephus, who wrote that the Israelite kings were "moved by a feeling of humanity and compassion" (παθόντες ἀνθρώπινόν τι καὶ ἐλεεινόν) and so left off the siege.[6] The Vulgate translated "great indignation" *(et facta est indignatio magna in Israel)*.[7] Qimḥi and Gersonides, joining 2 Kgs 3:26 with Amos 2:1, attributed *qeṣep gādôl* to the king of Edom, who, although an ally of the Israelites in the narrative, turned against them because his son had been taken captive by Mesha in an earlier battle.[8]

Many historically oriented critics followed similar strategies of displacement. The "great wrath" denoted the anger of Israel's own troops[9] or their "dismay" at the sight before them.[10] Others explained *qeṣep gādôl* as Israelite abhorrence of human sacrifice.[11] With this, displacement is joined to ideological delegitimation, for the horror which gripped the soldiers, imply the commentators, was rooted in their (and our) ethical and religious superiority. Human sacrifice was after all prohibited in this more advanced culture of Israel and denounced by the dominant voices in the biblical tradition.[12]

When linguistic considerations are woven into such notions of privileged ethical and theological truth, the resulting rhetoric not only displaces a potential rival to Yahweh but effectively strips him of cognitive or emotional appeal. This double move may be readily observed in many modern commentaries. For

6. Josephus, *Jewish Antiquities* 9:42-43. The translator in the Loeb edition, Ralph Marcus, had no difficulty in thinking the biblical writer attributed the outcome to the "anger" of the Moabite god (Josephus, *Jewish Antiquities*, LCL 6 [Cambridge: Harvard, 1937], 25).

7. See further comments in J. Montgomery, *The Books of Kings*, ICC (Edinburgh: T. & T. Clark, 1951), 364.

8. Cited by Cogan and Tadmor, 48, paraphrasing Qimḥi and Gersonides from מקראות גדולות.

9. O. Thenius, *Die Bücher der Könige*, 2nd ed. (Leipzig: Hirzel, 1873), 284.

10. J. Gray, *I and II Kings: A Commentary*, 2nd ed., OTL (Philadelphia: Westminster, 1970), 490.

11. H. Schweitzer, *Elischa in den Kriegen. Literaturwissenschaftliche Untersuchung von 2 Kön 3; 6:8-23; 6:24–7:20*, SANT 37 (München: Kösel, 1974), 168; E. Würthwein, *Die Bücher der Könige*, ATD 11 (Göttingen: Vandenhoeck & Ruprecht, 1977/84), 284; A. Graeme Auld, *I and II Kings* (Philadelphia: Westminster, 1986), 159; B. Margalit, "Why Mesha King of Moab Sacrificed His Oldest Son," *BARev* 12/6 (1986): 62-63, 76.

12. See especially Würthwein, 284, whose perspective blends easily with that of the DtrH in its condemnation of non-Israelite practices: "Der Erzähler scheint sagen zu wollen, daß angesichts des unerhörten und in Israel streng verpönten Menschenopfers irrationaler 'Zorn' über das Heer kam und Israel veranlaßte, aus dem Land abzuziehen, in dem solcher Greuel geschah."

example, A. Šanda supposed that an original reference to Chemosh had been effaced by a Yahwistic redactor. Since he "no longer recognized the reality of heathen gods as had the naively thinking original author," this redactor protected and proclaimed the elevated monotheism of Israel. Šanda's language is formally descriptive, embodying the emotional distance of a "scientific" historian. Yet his own ideological perspective seems indistinguishable from that which he attributes to an ancient redactor. It is Šanda after all who gives evaluative tone to this constructed literary history, and thus shows his approval of the hypothetical redactor's point of view. "*Heathen* gods" and "*naively* thinking" imply the absolutist dichotomy of one theology triumphant over another, and a vague rationalistic norm of cultural progress.[13]

James Montgomery encoded similar values within his comment on the biblical text, but without speaking of literary history. He thought it not at all necessary to assume that "the wrath of Chemosh" was once in the text, but then went on to remove any possibility that it *could* have been, or at least that such a "primitive implication" of the textual ambiguity could have lasted very long in the canonical environment. In any case — he now reverses ground and disambiguates the text — *qeṣep gādôl* refers to a "panic fear" which fell upon the Israelites, who "lost all heart in sight of the gruesome act." Then, as though to remove any trace of sympathy for these pagan-leaning soldiers, whose "superstitious fears . . . must have been much more alive in a land that was not their God's," Montgomery judges them by another text now made normative for the occasion: "The contrast between panic fear [what the soldiers were said to experience] and true religion appears in Ex. 15:16."[14] Thus "panic fear" in the soldiers takes the place of Chemosh in the narrative, which, even if it should be considered, belongs to a "primitive implication." Even the soldier's dread, as though this emotion in a biblical character might give some power to Chemosh, is relegated to "superstitious fear."

Some more recent commentators emphasize literary rather than historical features of the received text of 2 Kings, but continue the ancient strategies of displacement. T. R. Hobbs, e.g., acknowledged the uncertain referent of *qeṣep gādôl* but immediately offered two alternatives for limiting its meaning, neither of which involved Chemosh as subject: either the battle suddenly went against the Israelites or they withdrew "in disgust" (presumably at the human sacrifice).[15] Furthermore, as though still contending with a Chemosh exiled from the text, Hobbs located the reason for Jehoram's defeat in exclusively Yahwistic

---

13. "R erkannte aber das Existenzrecht der Heidengötter nicht mehr an wie der diesbezüglich noch naiv denkende ursprüngliche Verfasser. Darum drehte er die Phrasen so, daß wenigstens die Erwähnung des Kemoš wegfiel." A. Šanda, *Die Bücher der Könige II*, EHAT 9 (Münster: Aschendorf, 1911-12), 24.

14. Montgomery, 364.

15. T. R. Hobbs, *2 Kings*, WBC (Waco: Word Books, 1985), 38.

authorial intention. Whatever the "great wrath" might suggest (and we have been given only two choices), Jehoram's abortive mission illustrates the deuteronomistic principle that apostasy brings defeat. Thus, as written, the story expresses the narrator's final judgment on this king who, from the beginning, was condemned for his apostate ways (3:13; cf. 3:2-3).

Also emphasizing literary matters, Richard Nelson more resolutely permitted textual ambiguity to stand. It is up to the reader to say what the "wrath" was that saved the day for Moab.[16] But owing to his explicitly stated goal "to open up Kings for the preaching and teaching of the Christian Church" (p. 3), Nelson understandably was determined to remove Chemosh from the narrative or, at the very least, diminish any possibility that a biblical writer could have suggested that Chemosh matched Yahweh's power. First of all, the "puzzle of national defeat" invites mystification. The narrative, writes Nelson, "takes the reader deep into the mystery of God's will and the control of history." This is a statement of principle which obscures the ideological clash hidden within textual ambiguity. Chemosh at the outset is crippled, left with only the *appearance* of power. While allowing that the Moabites would have insisted that it was a "great wrath" from Chemosh that had afflicted the enemy troops, their claim makes no ultimate difference, Nelson asserts. No difference to whom? Presumably a reader, ancient or modern, who has constructed from the canonical traditions, or applied to them, a unified ideological perspective. For such a reader, the deuteronomistic historian had already demonstrated who is really God in 1 Kings 18, and the overall plot of 1-2 Kings made clear that Yahweh alone controls events for all peoples, including alien armies and foreign kings who "perform Yahweh's will for good or ill." So why the silence of the narrator addressing a friendly, sympathetic audience, but faced in 3:27 with a suggestion of ideological deviance? Nelson returns to his first premise: "Perhaps this text is hinting that even foreign gods like Chemosh" can be "a tool for the purposes of the one true God."[17] Thus the problem enshrined in textual ambiguity evaporates by theological premise into a unitary hierarchy of power, into a gesture toward Yahweh's supremacy over all gods. Nelson's addition of the adjective "true" removes the slight whiff of henotheism from his suggestion. The text, now clarified for Christian sensibilities, is implicitly aligned with texts redolent of exalted monotheism: Isa 44:6-8, 23-28; 45:1-17. If not quite displaced, Chemosh is certainly relegated to a lower order, and, finally, delegitimated altogether.

I have taken the trouble to analyze these representative treatments of 2 Kgs 3:26-27 to illustrate how powerful, widespread, and persistent has been the covert impulse to remove ideological embarrassment when faced with a text which can challenge dominant voices of exclusivist monotheism. In effect, these

16. R. Nelson, *First and Second Kings*, IBC (Atlanta: John Knox, 1987), 169.
17. Ibid., 169-70.

readers refuse the ambiguity which the biblical narrative obstinately permits. In substance, we see exegetes practicing the craft of biblical theology, even though not all these interpreters would claim to be theologians or even that they were offering theological exegesis. In the end, these readers aim to precipitate from a cloudy solution the crystalline verities of Israel's one God, *the* God of Judaism and Christianity.

Despite all such efforts, we are left with a narrative that suggests unrelieved conflict, a text of ruptures and disjunctions, a story which presents a fictive world in which opposing ideological commitments compete for preeminence.[18] The writer or redactor or narrator — in this text such modernist authorial *personae* may be subsumed into one implied presence — recounts Moab's rebellion and its suppression. And yet, if one does not immediately defend ideological conformity or Yahwistic supremacy, it is questionable whether the victory was complete, and if not, why Yahweh failed to provide the means to victory. The allied kings in their own ways dispute the matter. Jehoram, e.g., thinks of himself as a victim of Yahweh's election, not at all destined to prevail in the conflict (v. 10). By shrinking prophesied victory to indeterminate outcome, especially in a way that creates space for Chemosh, the narrator seems to equivocate, or rather, the mode of telling the tale undermines any simplistic appropriation of it — unless, of course, the ambiguity be clarified in the reading.

If one refuses a strategy of reading for conceptual, thematic, or ideological unity, the biblical narrative then may suggest itself as a metaphor for today's hermeneutical situation. The story evokes a world of unresolved ideological conflict, objectivist claims opposing one another for the last word about what is really true, what powers are actually at work. Some readers engage that conflict even while suppressing or trying to overcome its discomforting implications. Others accept contestatory indeterminacy as a fact of human existence.

Our times present us with plenty of old-fashioned conflict among beliefs, each typically assumed to mirror more or less exactly the substance of objective reality. Yet a new party has entered the contest today, a belief about beliefs which is more disturbing than the familiar combatants who cross their convictions like flint-hard swords. Statements about the nature of things, about values, about religion, about monotheism or polytheism, so the argument goes, are *readings* of reality. Not at all beyond time, such statements are ever changing interpretative, i.e., linguistic, constructs arising from the social orders in which people live and work out their psycho-philosophical-practical orientation to the world. In this view, *all* statements of truth are radically historical; none may, or should, claim universal privilege owing to a reputed status beyond the historical limitations of rival statements because all affirmations of truth and value

18. See the full treatment in B. Long, *2 Kings*, FOTL 10 (Grand Rapids: Eerdmans, 1991), 39-48.

are rooted in dynamic, timebound circumstances of human society. Statements or assumptions taken to represent "things as they really are" are more like social transactions: they begin in preference and belief, grow into social consensus, and decay into curiosities as new formulations take their place.[19]

Translating all this into the world of biblical criticism and biblical theology, we may note that the discord which characterizes biblical studies today reflects in part such a change in foundational orientation. Many scholars (exactly how many I would like to know) are choosing philosophical assumptions to guide their work that are fundamentally at odds with the epistemological and metaphysical convictions that have nourished most post-Enlightenment, "scientific" biblical criticism.

Despite their varying methods of interpretation, the modernist historical critics wish to discipline a reader's energies and competence so as to locate the meaning of the Bible within a determined historical and social world. The originary literary act may be imagined as belonging to an author and document (source and textual criticism), an editor (redaction criticism), a societal institution (form criticism), or a community whose members show canonical intention (canon criticism). Insofar as such authorial *personae* are taken to set the norms of our reading, they are vested with prescriptive power, with authority that is distinct from, or external to, the process of interpretation.

Moreover, when theology is invoked as the aim of exegesis, such interpretations naturally involve a metaphysics and epistemology of transcendence. In granting special privilege to any of these authorial constructs, and implicating historical inquiry in the process, biblical scholars defer to a theological axiom: revelation — in this case, the monotheistic revelation of a Judaism or a Christianity — came definitively to human beings at a single moment (or several moments) in the past and was deposited essentially *in* text, where it awaits discovery by readers of historical-critical competence. By investigating those moments, one grants authority to human vehicles through whom revelation flowed and applies the corrective rod of objective historical knowledge to errant teachings, inappropriate anachronizing, and other sorts of supposed misunderstandings in our own day. At the end of this path of objectivist authority stands God — in this case, the *one* God — who wears various garments: holy inspira-

---

19. These claims about the status of belief are among the many features of our late-twentieth-century culture, which has, for better or worse, been described as "postmodern." Although awkward, and still meeting with resistance, the term has now been widely accepted. Ihab Hassan (*The Postmodern Turn: Essays in Postmodern Theory and Culture* [Columbus: Ohio State University, 1987]) provides a very useful assessment of the phenomena, not to make a consolidating statement on the matter (that would violate his postmodern convictions), but rather to review a range of typical postmodern questions. A popular and on the whole responsible treatment of postmodernism in its broad cultural dimensions may be found in Walter T. Anderson, *Reality Isn't What It Used to Be* (New York/San Francisco: Harper, 1991).

tion, or inerrancy of Scripture, or God invoked as Torah, or God as Holy Spirit Logos-made-flesh. By whatever name, this external force guides true understanding. Hidden in all this discussion is the assumption that human language is a perfectible instrument with which to state objective truth.

In our late twentieth century, some literary theorists, philosophers, and social scientists imagine a quite different and fundamentally this-worldly setting for texts, interpretation, and meaning. They assume, with Nietzsche, that every human situation is a product of human history, though we may be convinced that some notions or ways of behaving in the world may "naturally" mirror unchanging reality. Such convictions about the "naturalness" of human ways, so the argument goes, prevent us from treating particular views, habits, institutions, and values as contingent creations. There was a time when they did not exist, and there can be a time when they no longer will exist.

With this turn away from objectivist ontology and its confident grasp of ideal general Truth has come a fascination with fundamentally linguistic processes through which human beings construct their "truths," their senses of reality from within limited psychosocial contexts. Such a swerve toward reader, whether it be the reader of a literary text, a social phenomenon, or of the natural world, assumes that our relation to the "is-ness" of the world is not positive knowledge, but a hermeneutical construct.[20] Put another way, the claim is that both the "world" and the observing, reflecting "self" are constituted as "real" by linguistic constructs.

From this vantage point, which, according to the theory, is not fixed but is itself enmeshed in hermeneutics, one may account for the pluralistic republic wherein scholars of the humanities, including biblical critics, dwell nowadays. A labyrinth of methodological allegiances yielding pluriform and sometimes contradictory interpretations is encouraged, celebrated, deconstructed, and constructed all over again. And the harsh light of "revisionary" criticism[21] exposes special interests which readers vest in methods to secure readerly competence.

This postmodern swerve toward reader undermines the modernist (in one form, the historical-critical) comfort of believing that some external authority, or a grasp of "objective truth," however approximate, assures the "correctness" of any particular reading, or even theory of reading. The result is open ideological conflict, in its benign as well as destructive forms. Thus, discussions shift from adjudicating ultimate truth — this seems to be the aim of ideologi-

20. See Elizabeth Freund, *The Return of the Reader* (London/New York: Methuen, 1987), 5; Peter Berger and Thomas Luckmann, *The Social Construction of Reality: A Treatise in the Sociology of Knowledge* (Garden City: Doubleday, 1966); and Ferdinand de Saussure, *Course in General Linguistics*, trans. Wade Baskin (New York: Philosophical Library, 1959).

21. Geoffrey Hartman, *Criticism in the Wilderness: The Study of Literature Today* (New Haven: Yale, 1980).

cally charged will-to-dominance — to the ethical, social, and political implications of *holding* certain things to be true.

This change in foundational orientation of course reflects massive social changes that have occurred in our late twentieth century, but it also offers theoretical understanding for such changes, including a willingness to decanonize all totalizing postures and conventions of social and intellectual authority. Such a postmodern temperament, in all its dialectical qualities and relationship to the past, also entails negotiating newly discomforting and yet exhilarating passages for the future: choosing fracture and fractiousness over consensus; substituting fragments of difference for coherent identities; writing (or rewriting) small histories of the overlooked and forgotten (or suppressed); opening up and exploring the fissures of grander narratives that typically authorize values and worldviews of whole cultures and peoples; exchanging comfortable certainties for disquieting ambiguities. Ihab Hassan put the matter very well:

> from the "death of God" to the "death of the author" and "death of the father," from the derision of authority to revision of the curriculum, we decanonize culture, demystify knowledge, deconstruct the languages of power, desire, deceit. Derision and revision are versions of subversions, of which the most baleful example is the rampant terrorism of our time. But "subversion" may take other, more benevolent, forms such as minority movements or the feminization of culture, which also require decanonization.[22]

Looked at with a dash of such "postmodernist" persuasions, the narrative about Elisha, the kings, and thwarted prophecy-fulfillment victory over the Moabites presents a postmodern-like picture. Or more accurately, we may now sight the narrative through a postmodern glass. Opposed convictions about the crucial events so jostle one another that even the omniscient narrator, who along with later theologically vested readers claims to represent *the* view of God, cannot escape suspicion cast upon *all* totalizing claims.

In this context, we may ask how biblical theology, that disciplined disambiguation of the textually textured eternal verities of God, might carry itself in a world of postmodernist predilections. One option, of course, would be to continue the modernist blend of historical criticism and confessional theology evident in the work of recent biblical commentators, and in the continuing flow of specifically theological monographs.[23] John Collins proposes a refinement of this choice. While breaking with more confessional modes of biblical theology that are to his mind incompatible with historical criticism, Collins reclaims biblical theology as an enterprise disciplined by thorough and consistent appli-

22. Hassan, 169.
23. See, e.g., G. F. Hasel, *Old Testament Theology: Basic Issues in the Current Debate* (Grand Rapids: Eerdmans, 4th ed., 1991); H. D. Preuss, *Theologie des Alten Testaments,* Band 1 und 2 (Stuttgart: Kohlhammer, 1991, 1992).

cation of historical criticism. Biblical theology should be "an open-ended and critical inquiry into the meaning and function of God-language," done not simply out of antiquarian concerns (as though *any* historical project could be *merely* antiquarian), but to "clarify the meaning and truth-claims of what was thought and believed from a modern critical perspective. . . ."[24]

The program recently advocated by Rolf Knierim marks a milestone within this tradition since it builds a bridge between the diversities of historical description and the *ahistorical* conceptual categories on which systematic philosophers and theologians have chosen to rely.[25] For Knierim, the pluralism of theologies in the Bible is a problem. (He has in mind not theologies of rival gods, as might be suggested by my reading of 2 Kgs 3, but diverse ways of speaking about Israel's God.) An untidy residue of the historical process, this pluralism threatens to atomize the unitary substance of biblical theology. It endangers a fundamental *desideratum* of the theologian to understand the Bible "as a whole" and to understand it correctly (p. 25). What is the solution? Impose order on the disorderly, overcome the messiness of history, achieve truth. One must examine systematically (as opposed to historically) "various themes and *theologoumena* under theologically valid priorities." That means, among other things, establishing "legitimate priorities" by identifying those substantive theological claims which are fundamental (encompassing, universal) in the Bible, and therefore normative for all other elements in the hierarchical scheme. As a second step, a biblical theologian would then "assess individually exegeted messages, kerygmata, and/or theologies of the Old Testament" in the light of this system of evaluative priorities.[26] The task of the theologian is thus neither "descriptive nor confessional. It is systematic." The resulting Old Testament theology, then,

> systematizes the plurality of theologies analyzed by exegesis, and summarily described in the conclusions or appendices to exegetical works, under theological priorities discerned from within the Old Testament, and it provides the criteria for the accountability of what ought to be confessed.[27]

Obviously, Knierim cannot easily engage a postmodern temperament through his program. I do not know that he would even wish to do so. I can hardly imagine a better example of modernism, that broad cultural river out of which postmodernism came and from which it continues, even in opposition, to derive essential nourishment. Nor can I imagine better ground from which to view the unstable fault lines between modernism and postmodernism.

24. John Collins, "Is a Critical Biblical Theology Possible?" in William Propp et al., *The Hebrew Bible and Its Interpreters* (Winona Lake: Eisenbrauns, 1990), 9, 14.
25. R. Knierim, "The Task of Old Testament Theology," *HBT* 6,1 (1984): 25-57.
26. Ibid., 31-45.
27. Ibid., 47.

Knierim exhibits deeply held interests in normativity and hierarchy, not only in the concern to establish "valid" criteria to evaluate theological claims, but in the favored status he accords ahistorical categories of reason, the implicit ontology and epistemology of philosophical idealism; postmodernists tend to distrust hierarchy, to decanonize conventional "givens," to challenge, e.g., any imperialistic privileges accorded philosophical idealism. Knierim seems driven to systematize and adjudicate objectivist truth; a postmodernist, as a matter of temperament and principle, might seek to expose fissures in grand systems, unmask the element of subjective choice in the objective truths of systems makers, challenge the ethics and politics of truth-mastery, and build critical discourse out of difference rather than unanimity. Knierim takes theological pluralism to be problematic and dangerous; postmodern thinkers, artists, scholars, and critics might abhor attempts to *overcome* ambiguity, preferring to revel in indeterminacies of many kinds.[28]

It seems clear that other biblical scholars are beginning to explore postmodernist ways of practicing their craft. They are contributing to a breakdown of singular notions of theology and of biblical criticism. Perhaps more important, and more in the spirit of postmodern culture, is that scholars nowadays more readily accept approaches to the field that are not simply variant tracks within historically oriented paradigms, but modes of criticism predicated upon fundamentally different philosophical assumptions.

Such a shift in values is perhaps unprecedented.[29] I do not wish to overstate the case. Yet it seems that, increasingly, the practice of scholarly criticism resembles a darting and weaving ballet — two figures, bound as one while moving as two, rhythmic and arhythmic coordination/discoordination — a dialectical dance of momentary clarifications. Frequently absent is the Great Clarifier, unchallenged and unchallengeable Consensus. And when this Absence attempts to become Presence, the politics of postmodernism, the centripetal and centrifugal assertions of differences that demand recognition and acceptance, drive the dance forward.

How will biblical theologians dance the postmodern dance? I suppose however poststructuralist, feminist, African-American, deconstructionist, and any number of other against-the-center and liberationist critics choose to dance with their modernist partners. This situation inevitably entails clashes among rival gods, and also the responsibilities and negotiations made necessary by critical practice of a less totalizing mien.

---

28. For these contrasts in styles and substance, which should be taken as a loosely drawn map rather than rigidly defined topography, see Hassan, 91.

29. See, e.g., Edgar V. McKnight, *Post-Modern Use of the Bible: The Emergence of Reader-Oriented Criticism* (Nashville: Abingdon, 1988); Robert Fowler, "Postmodern Biblical Criticism," *Forum* 5 (1989): 3-30; Stephen Moore, *Mark and Luke in Poststructuralist Perspectives: Jesus Begins to Write* (New Haven: Yale University, 1992); David Jobling and Stephen Moore, eds., "Poststructuralism as Exegesis," *Semeia* 54 (1992).

I see this development as a happy one for scholarship, though unsettling for many. I am uncertain as to how it will work itself out among the consumers of theological products in churches and synagogues where negotiating the absolutisms of faith often proves a strange and difficult process. In any case, this shift toward contestatory diversity played out on leveled fields, at least in North America, seems almost inevitable, and peculiarly coherent with a strain of practical and critical pluralism deeply rooted in our social experience. William James, among others, gave it philosophical expression:

> Pragmatically interpreted, pluralism or the doctrine that it [the universe] is many means only that the sundry parts of reality *may be externally related.* Everything you can think of, however vast or inclusive, has on the pluralistic view a genuinely "external" environment of some sort or amount. Things are "with" one another in many ways, but nothing includes everything, or dominates over everything. The word "and" trails along after every sentence. Something always escapes. "Ever not quite" has to be said of the best attempts made anywhere in the universe at attaining all-inclusiveness. The pluralistic world is thus more like a federal republic than like an empire or a kingdom. . . .[30]

Our times do not encourage great prophets. But perhaps the day is coming, and lo! it approaches (maybe), when biblical theology, as indeed biblical criticism, might become more and more resigned to, if not at ease with, such Jamesian "manyness-in-oneness."

30. William James, *A Pluralistic Universe,* in *The Works of Henry James,* ed. Frederick Burkhardt (Cambridge: Harvard University, 1977), 145-46.

Yahweh's Compassion and Ecotheology

ELMER A. MARTENS

A biblical theology of environment commonly begins with creation. Another legitimate procedure, however, is to dip into a prophetic tradition and from that vantage point develop the Old Testament's word about the environment. A strategic insight on environment pertains to Yahweh's compassion. When the theme of compassion is probed, one is soon in the realm of Yahweh's justice (מִשְׁפָּט), which in turn is integral to the kingdom of God. This essay follows this chain of connectedness as a way of articulating an Old Testament position on environment.[1]

Compassion

The message of the Old Testament and especially of the prophets has often been explicated in the context of salvation history.[2] Center stage in this approach is God's relationship to his people together with traditions such as exodus, Sinai, covenant, Yahweh war, royal theology, messianism, and the salvation and judgment of God's people, past, present, and future. That the prophets, however, do

---

1. This essay is dedicated with esteem to Professor Rolf P. Knierim, from whose teaching has come to me large insight and a deep passion to discern the ways of Yahweh. My essay is a footnote to Knierim's essays: "Cosmos and History in Israel's Theology," *HBT* 3 (1981): 59-123, and to his "The Task of Old Testament Theology," *HBT* 6,1 (1984): 25-57. The latter proposes that theologians give greater attention to the Old Testament's emphasis on the structure of the world.

2. E.g., G. von Rad, *Old Testament Theology*, 2 vols. (New York: Harper and Row, 1962, 1965).

not work exclusively with the God-Israel theme is evident from the oracles against the nations, which are found in all three of the major prophets, not to mention the books of Obadiah and Nahum, which are devoted totally to nations outside Israel. A third theme — nature, environment, ecology — surfaces from time to time, not only in wisdom and legal material but in the prophetic corpus. Exclusive attention to salvation history easily blinds one to the perspectives the Old Testament gives on other matters, such as environment, clearly a current agenda.[3]

The book of Jonah may seem an unlikely starting point for an ecotheology, but with the *dramatis personae* so largely drawn from the realm of nature — fish, water, wind, worm, gourd, and animals — the book is in a position to instruct on "natural theology." And it does, both obliquely and directly. The animals enter the fast, by proclamation of the king, and are draped with sack-cloth in a gesture of repentance (Jon 3:7-9). This leads H. W. Wolff to comment: "Behind this [cattle and sheep fasting] stands the certainty, seen ever more clearly today, that the decisions made by mankind, whether they be for evil or for good, also draw dumb creatures into the ensuing disaster or salvation."[4] But more directly the final, somewhat enigmatic sentence bears directly and theo-logically on environmental concerns: "And should I not be concerned about Nineveh, that great city, in which there are more than a hundred and twenty thousand persons who do not know their right hand from their left, and also many animals?" (Jon 4:11 NRSV).

The final episode of a withering gourd and the dialogue about "concern" (חוס, pity) surrounding it must be factored into the theological thrust of the book.[5] The word חוס means "to make the eyes flow."[6] Jonah was moved to tears

---

3. The dimensions of the degradation of the physical environment are well publicized. For details see *National Geographic* (December 1988) and *Time* (January 2, 1989); Matthew Fox, *The Coming of the Cosmic Christ* (San Francisco: Harper and Row, 1988); Calvin De Witt, *The Environment and the Christian* (Grand Rapids: Baker, 1991); cf. "Tropical forests are disappearing 50% faster than a decade ago. Annually the Earth loses forests equal to areas of Austria, Denmark and the Netherlands combined" (*Wall Street Journal*, September 9, 1991, 1). For a negative assessment on the current surge of environmental concerns, see R. J. Bidinotto, "Environmentalism: Freedom's Foe for the '90's," *Freeman* 40 (1990): 409-20.

4. Hans Walter Wolff, "Jonah: The Messenger Who Obeys," *Theology and Mission* 3 (1976): 92.

5. Leslie Allen states, "Obviously the question in 4:11 is the climax of the book and the key to its understanding." *The Books of Joel, Obadiah, Jonah, and Micah*, NICOT (Grand Rapids: Eerdmans, 1976), 189. Cf. "It is through this final question that the writer drives home with telling impact the principal teaching for which he has written his story" (George Landes, "Jonah a Mašal?" in *Israelite Wisdom: Theological and Literary Essays in Honor of Samuel Terrien*, ed. John G. Gammie, Walter A. Brueggemann, W. Lee Humphreys, and James M. Ward [Missoula: Scholars, 1978], 148).

6. Cf. "The construction with *'ayin* ('eye') may preserve a more original sense: 'the eye overflows' (undoubtedly with tears) concerning (*'al*) a person or thing" (S. Wagner, "Ḥus" in *TDOT*, ed. G. J. Botterweck and H. Ringgren, vol. 4 [Grand Rapids: Eerdmans, 1980], 271).

over the disappearance of the bush for which he did not labor. His tears (also for himself, now without shade), notes Ceresko, establish "compassion" as a legitimate reason for saving a creature from destruction.[7] God's question, which ends the dialogue as well as the book, is whether God is entitled to show compassion to a great city, including its animals, upon which, as is implied, he has expended labor. "People and animals, whoever they may be, call forth God's compassion. At this point God does not even make repentance a qualification for divine compassion."[8] Freedman suggests God may be admitting that Nineveh's repentance cannot be trusted.[9] Yet God looks with concern and pity ("compassion," NASB) on the city with its people and its animals and averts the threatened judgment. The penultimate term in the book, בהמה (livestock), is linked with the 120,000 and reminds the reader of the earlier reference to the animals draped in sackcloth (3:7, 8). There as here, the interlocking of the destiny of both האדם and הבהמה is affirmed. H. G. May remarks, "It [the author's purpose] is to teach that the whole world, including Gentile peoples, symbolized by the people of Nineveh, even little children — and animals — are the object of God's compassion."[10] To Israel, sometimes smug while basking in God's favor, the message of the book of Jonah is that God's benevolence is universal, that it is for all people, yes, for animals too. God's stance toward the nonhuman world is also one of pity. That God does relent, and does so for reasons of compassion, is rich in implications for an audience living with a prophesied fate for themselves and their city. That God does relent for reasons of compassion on the Ninevites and their livestock has implications for a perspective on ecotheology.

To begin with, Jonah has the advantage of observing God's compassion, not as an abstract attribute, but operative in a given place. From our starting

7. Anthony J. Ceresko, "Jonah," *The New Jerome Biblical Commentary* (Englewood Cliffs: Prentice Hall, 1990), 584.

8. Eugene Roop, *Jonah* (Scottdale: Herald Press, forthcoming).

9. David Noel Freedman, "Did God Play a Dirty Trick on Jonah at the End?" *Bible Review* 6 (1990): 26-31; quote, 31.

10. Herbert G. May, "Aspects of the Imagery of World Dominion and World State in the Old Testament," in *Essays in Old Testament Ethics,* ed. J. L. Crenshaw (New York: KTAV, 1974), 57-76, here 60. Cf. Leslie Allen: "The book of Jonah is challenging its audience to face up to the unwelcome truth of God's sovereign compassion for foreigners and beasts" (190). R. E. Clements challenges this consensus, showing among other things that ill feeling between Israel and the Ninevites was not an issue in the book. At issue was the change of mind on the part of God — a change that Jonah found difficult to handle. "The theme of Jonah is the possibility of man's repentance, and its purpose is to show that where this occurs among men then it elicits a related change of purpose on the part of God" (R. E. Clements, "The Purpose of the Book of Jonah," *Congress Volume, Edinburgh, 1974,* VTSup 28 [Leiden: Brill, 1975], 28). But even this formulation of the book's message, though offering a fresh nuance, is premised on God's compassion. Other purposes for the book have been proposed: an apologetic aim of justifying unfulfilled prophecies, a contrast of the ways of man with the ways of God, a missionary tract, and a statement about deliverance (Allen, 189-90).

point with the micro-picture of Nineveh's animals, we may move toward the Old Testament's macro-picture, as given, e.g., in Hosea and Isaiah. To move to Hosea 2 is to move from God's concern for one urban center, Nineveh, almost directly to God's compassion expressed cosmologically. The language recalls the post-flood covenant making, which is not with Noah as much as it is with *all* living beings (Gen 9:1-10, 12, 15, 17), "I will make for you a covenant on that day with the wild animals, the birds of the air, and the creeping things of the ground; and I will abolish the bow, the sword, and war from the land; and I will make you lie down in safety" (Hos 2:18 NRSV).[11]

Since the discussion turns on covenant making between God and Israel, it is often thought that the consequence of such a covenant is the harmony that is then established between the animal and human world. In a provocative article Dianne Bergant challenges such a conclusion. She points first to the structure of Hos 2:18-21 (Eng. 2:16-19):

18	(16)	marital theme
	20	(18)	creation theme
21	(19)	marital theme

By its position, the creation theme is highlighted. The covenant with the animals is not one which addresses hostility,[12] but in the tradition of the post-flood covenant, the focus is on a harmony in the pristine state. Bergant notes that the language of *bow* and *sword* and the language of war are suited to the ancient Near Eastern mythology of conflict at creation (cf. Ps 74:13-14; Isa 27:1; 51:9; Ps 89:10f.). Hanging the bow in the sky (cf. Gen 9) is a way of saying that the conflict has ended. Order has been established and, as after creation, a time of rest has been ushered in. This eschatological covenant with its overtones to the creation account is not dependent on the fidelity of Israel. Therefore this covenant is not historical but cosmic. Moreover, the cosmic harmony about which it speaks is constitutive of the covenant. "The imagery here recalls the primordial covenant with all of creation, a covenant that exalted nature's intrinsic value and not simply its instrumental value." Bergant concludes that Hosea 2 rules out anthropomorphic imperialism, a view which sees nature as "there" primarily for the benefit of humankind.[13] Nature has its own value.

Isaiah furnishes a further example of divine attention to the restoration of the world of nature. The oracles of eschatological salvation not infrequently include mention of animals. Perhaps most striking among these is Isa 11:6:

---

11. The MT reads: "I will make for them a covenant." The "them" is possibly a reference to children. Francis I. Andersen and David N. Freedman, *Hosea*, AB 24 (Garden City: Doubleday, 1980), 121f.

12. Hans Walter Wolff, *Hosea*, Hermeneia (Philadelphia: Fortress, 1974), 51.

13. Dianne Bergant, "Restoration and Re-creation in Hosea 2" (forthcoming).

The wolf shall live with the lamb,
    the leopard shall lie down with the kid,
the calf and the lion and the fatling together. . . .
The cow and the bear shall graze,
    their young shall lie down together;
and the lion shall eat straw like the ox. (NRSV)

In a future day transformation will also come to the animal world. "They will not hurt or destroy on all my holy mountain" (Isa 11:9 NRSV; cf. 65:25; 35:9). Violence, which to this day is rocking the world, including the natural world, will have been terminated. Similarly, the natural order of plant life will be renewed in the future day of salvation. The desert will blossom. Upon the wilderness will be bestowed the glory of Lebanon. Reeds, grass, and rushes shall flourish where earlier there was parched ground (Isa 35:1-7; cf. 55:12-13). The word about God's care for the cows in Nineveh becomes a window through which one can see God's concern for, and future blessing upon, the whole world of nature.

True, the window may at first seem small, but the view widens: God's compassion on animal creatures is explicit in eschatological texts; it is also visible in narrative, didactic, and hymnic materials. The command to tend the garden (Gen 2:15) is expressive of God's compassion and concern for the whole world. The promise of "no more flood" is a promise of preservation to his creatures by a God who has power to give life but also to destroy life (Gen 9:11).[14] The Torah instructs that a farmer who plows his field and comes upon a bird's nest, either on the ground or in the tree, must spare the mother bird (Deut 22:6-7). The implicit principle is that reproduction and fecundity must be safeguarded. In today's terms: a species must not be allowed to become extinct.[15] Oxen who thresh shall be cared for (Deut 25:4) in accordance with the principle, "A righteous man cares for the needs of his animal" (Prov 12:10 NIV). Thus Torah touches, even if not extensively, on responsibility to bird and beast.

The psalmist identifies God's down-to-earth compassion. "You save humans and animals alike, O Lord" (Ps 36:7 [Eng. 36:6]). God's compassion (רחמים) "is over all that he has made" (Ps 145:9 NRSV). God's care is directly

---

14. The formulation is essentially that by C. Westermann, *Creation* (London: SPCK, 1974), 22.

15. Jewish rabbis noted that this command to preserve the mother bird is one of two commandments to which a promise of reward, namely well-being and longevity, is attached. The other is Exod 20:12. H. C. Brichto, "Kin, Cult, Land, and After-life — A Biblical Complex," *HUCA* 44 (1973): 1-54. I owe this reference to L. Frizzell, "Humanity and Nature according to the Jewish Scriptures," a paper read at the SBL annual meeting, 1990. Commentators generally see in the stipulation of Deut 22:6-7, as in Deut 22:4, a call for humaneness. For a contrary view, cf. C. M. Carmichael, *The Laws of Deuteronomy* (Ithaca: Cornell University, 1974).

for trees and animals (Ps 104:14-16). These have intrinsic worth without any reference to human desires or needs.

In brief, God's compassion toward the animal and inanimate world is already visible at creation, is further made explicit in the commandments, is celebrated in the Psalms, and is especially notable in the eschatological texts. We can agree with Matthew Fox, "True redemption is always about compassion. . . ." Fox's emphasis on compassion draws heavily on earlier mystics, e.g., Meister Eckhart, who stated, "The first outburst of everything God does, is compassion."[16]

Compassion and Justice

But to maintain God's compassion for the material world, clearly one strand in biblical traditions, is to fly headlong into data which at first glance deny the thesis. God destroys plant and animal life and gives divine commands for the annihilation of peoples together with their cattle.

Of God's destructive acts against the physical environment, the flood is the most obvious example (Gen 6–9). Extensive destruction of animal life also figures in the oracles of judgment depicting the day of the Lord. The grasshoppers described by Joel ruin vines, fig trees, pomegranate trees, palm trees, and apple trees (Joel 1:7, 12). Because there is no pasture, beasts groan and cattle are restless; their survival is threatened (Joel 1:18, 20). God's announcements of judgment seem contrary to his compassion for living things. "I will utterly sweep away everything from the face of the earth, says the Lord. I will sweep away humans and animals; I will sweep away the birds of the air and the fish of the sea" (Zeph 1:2-3a NRSV).[17] Creation will be unmade. How are such statements to be reconciled with God's compassion on Nineveh's beasts?

In addition, God's commands seem to belie concern for creatures. Three biblical instances mandate wholesale destruction of livestock. One relates to exterminating apostasy within Israel (Deut 13:15). Another instance involves Saul, who through Samuel is ordered to destroy the Amalekites, including their "ox and sheep, camel and donkey" (1 Sam 15:3b NRSV). Saul flinches. God makes an issue of Saul's sparing the livestock, and Saul forfeits his kingdom. Similarly, in Joshua's conquest of Canaan the report reads, "Then they devoted

16. Fox, 32, 56. Fox's overall argument is flawed, however, not only by a problematic definition of the "cosmic Christ," but by a use of the mystics and history which Rosemary Ruether (*The Catholic World* 233 [1990]: 168-72) claims lacks discernment and depth, and hence credibility.

17. M. DeRoche ("Zephaniah and the 'Sweeping' of Creation," *VT* 30 [1980]: 104-9) has noted how the ordering of the list here and elsewhere (Hos 4:30) is in the reverse order of creation (Gen 1).

to destruction by the edge of the sword all in the city, both men and women, young and old, oxen, sheep, and donkeys" (Josh 6:21 NRSV).[18] At other times, as at Ai, the livestock were spared (Josh 8:2, 27; cf. 11:14).

The dissonance one feels in moving from the Jonah text, which stresses God's compassion, to the Joshua text, which seems to leave little room for compassion, arises in part because of an expectation about God's consistency. Contradictory assertions about God are unsettling. One reply to the perceived contradiction is to shift from God to Israel and to fault Israel, who drew the improper conclusion that since there was an enemy in the path of God's intention, the answer, attributed to God as his will, was to fight the enemy.[19]

A better approach is that offered by biblical theology, which is not under constraint to systematize such statements into a logically rigid, consistent whole. Assertions both about God's compassion for his creatures and his commands on occasion for their destruction need to stand. While the tension must be allowed to remain, one may nevertheless reflect on the tension, and offer some assessment of it.

Initially it can be defined as a tension between God's justice and God's compassion. The tension is obvious in the book of Jonah. In Jonah's understanding of justice, God should destroy the Ninevites. For all the violence Assyria perpetrated on Israel, was it fair for God to spare Nineveh? The demand for people to receive their just deserts runs deep in the human psyche. Compassion and justice, so it appears, are at odds.

The prophets wrestle with the tension, not so much a tension between God's justice and God's compassion as between God's anger and his compassion. That God's anger is against evil is without debate. While he may relent on occasion, there are instances when his anger will not turn back (Amos 1:3, 6, 9, 13; 2:1).[20] Frequently there are explicit expressions about bringing destruction without a show of pity (Jer 13:14; Ezek 5:11; 7:4, 9; 8:18; 9:10). At still other times wrath, though deserved, is not the last word.

The prophet Hosea shows clearly that compassion triumphs over wrath. With retribution as the standard, Hosea would have every reason as an individual to deal severely with Gomer. Instead he takes her back (Hos 3). Similarly Israel's waywardness, indeed her rebellion against God (Hos 11:7), is ample reason for the arm of punishment to swing swiftly into action. But God agonizes over the situation. "How can I give you up, Ephraim?" (11:8 NRSV). God's maternal care is kindled. The decision is, "I will not execute my fierce anger; I

18. For a monograph devoted to Joshua 6 see L. Schwienhorst, *Die Eroberung Jerichos* (Stuttgart: Katholisches Bibelwerk, 1986).

19. Vernard Eller, *War and Peace from Genesis to Revelation* (Scottdale: Herald Press, 1981), 59.

20. Cf. R. Knierim, "'I Will Not Cause It to Return' in Amos 1 and 2," *Canon and Authority: Essays in Old Testament Religion and Theology*, ed. G. Coats (Philadelphia: Fortress, 1977), 163-75.

will not again destroy Ephraim; for I am God and no mortal, the Holy One in your midst, and I will not come in wrath." Helen Schüngel-Straumann notes the maternal dimensions of the chapter. She proposes the meaning "I am God and not male (שׁיא)." "Yahweh rejects *male* behavior for himself, but not (genuine) human behavior!"[21] God's wrathful actions against evil are not denied. But Hosea in a most magnificent theological assertion affirms that compassion is in the end more determining than wrath.

Jeremiah, who often follows Hosea's lead, and whose book is fairly dominated by references to God's anger, echoes the episode in Hosea.[22] Ephraim, who has been disciplined, seeks God's favor. God replies:

"Though I often speak against him,
  I still remember him.
Therefore my heart yearns for him;
  I have great compassion [רחם] for him," declares the Lord.
                                              (Jer 31:20b-c NIV)

William Holladay comments, "The emotion of Yahweh over Ephraim is overwhelming: every time he speaks or even thinks of Ephraim, he is overpowered by affection, so that he cannot help showing compassion (רחם) on him."[23] It is not that wrath is always rescinded, yet it may be followed by mercy. God promises to uproot the evil nations surrounding Israel. "And after I have plucked them up, I will again have compassion [רחם] on them, and I will bring them again to their heritage and to their land, everyone of them" (Jer 12:15 NRSV). Likewise Israel felt the impact of God's anger against her for her sin when temple and city were destroyed in 587 B.C.E. But God was grieved over the devastation which had been inflicted (42:10), and declared following the wreckage, "I will show you compassion [רחם] . . ." (42:12 NIV). This sequel of wrath followed by compassion is put into something of a principle by Isaiah: "Though in anger I struck you, in favor I will show you compassion [רחם]" (Isa 60:10b NIV).

Indeed, Isaiah, no less than Hosea and Jeremiah, addresses the tension between divine wrath and divine compassion and, like them, does so in the context of a story. Isaiah cites the flood as illustrative of the operation of both

---

21. Helen Schüngel-Straumann, "God as Mother in Hosea 11," *TD* 34,1 (1987): 3-8, citing p. 6. See now Siegfried Kreuzer, "Gott als Mutter in Hosea 11?" *TQ* 169,2 (1989): 123-32.

22. The term אף is used in Jeremiah more than in other books — 24 times (e.g., 2:35; 15:14; 33:5). Of the 125 occurrences of חמה, 17 are found in Jeremiah. In the book 42 different verses or passages mention or elaborate God's anger.

23. W. L. Holladay, *Jeremiah*, vol. 2 (Minneapolis: Fortress, 1989), 192. Holladay offers a full discussion on whether the first line (v. 20b) should be rendered "speak about him" or "speak against him." He thinks that the ambiguity could be part of Jeremiah's intention.

wrath and compassion. Floods are not the everyday rule, but the exception, for God spoke his "Never again" (Gen 9:11). Isaiah emphasizes the "Never again":

> This is like the days of Noah to me:
>> Just as I swore that the waters of Noah
>> would never again go over the earth,
> so I have sworn that I will not be angry with you
>> and will not rebuke you. (Isa 54:9 NRSV)

The flood becomes a paradigm for dealing with the ambivalence raised by God's anger against evil and his compassion both for people and for the physical world. Isaiah leaves no doubt that in this polarity of wrath and compassion (if such it is), God's compassion is the last word:

> In overflowing wrath for a moment
>> I hid my face from you,
> but with everlasting love I will have compassion [רחם] on you,
>> says the LORD, your Redeemer. . . .
> For the mountains may depart
>> and the hills be removed,
> but my steadfast love shall not depart from you,
>> and my covenant of peace shall not be removed,
>> says the LORD, who has compassion [רחם] on you. (Isa 54:8, 10 NRSV)

C. Westermann sees in verses 7-8 the climax of the poem and comments, "Here we have the heart of the matter, the basic factor in Deutero-Isaiah's proclamation — with God himself and in God himself the change has already taken place, and therefore everything must alter."[24] In God's activity compassion is preeminent.

One answer, then, to the tension posed in comparing Jonah (where God's compassion results in sparing livestock and people) and Joshua (where God's wrath calls for the destruction of livestock) is that God's compassion must be understood as the more definitive of God's ways. Jonah's statement "I knew that you are a gracious and compassionate [רחם] God" (4:2 NIV) echoes other such credos (cf. Joel 2:13; Exod 34:6). Knierim has advocated that the function of biblical theology is to adjudicate between the theologies in the Old Testament.[25] Clearly, especially if the New Testament is taken into account, the conclusion must be that though wrath appears, shall we say in light print, compassion is written in extrabold print.

But there is a second answer to the puzzle of both God's compassion and his anger, the latter popularly interpreted as God's justice. That answer is that

24. C. Westermann, *Isaiah 40–66*, OTL (London: SCM, 1969), 274.
25. Knierim, "Task of Old Testament Theology," 25-57.

in an understanding of biblical justice, divine compassion is not to be pitted against justice. Instead, justice, correctly understood, entails compassion.

Evidence for this integral linkage of compassion and justice is unambiguous, both in doctrinaire assertions and in practical directives. Isaiah, after detailing the obstinacy of Israel along with the divinely ordered consequences (Isa 30:8-17), explains:

> Yet the Lord longs to be gracious to you;
>   he rises to show you compassion [רחם].
> For [כי] the Lord is a God of justice. . . . (30:18 NIV)

With the telltale conjunction כי, the writer not only links divine compassion and justice but explains that divine compassion emerges and evolves from justice (משפט). That justice issues in compassion becomes clear when it is understood that justice (משפט) is a basic term incorporating honorable relations as defined by the kind of God Yahweh is. The Old Testament underscores both the importance of משפט and elucidates its meaning. Righteousness and justice (משפט) are the foundation of God's throne (Ps 89:14). "I the Lord love justice [משפט]" (Isa 61:8 NRSV). *Mišpāṭ* is the opposite of caprice, vacillation, inconsistency. It is constancy in rendering a decision, a decision characterized by righteous criteria. *Mišpāṭ* (justice) goes beyond dealing fairly to dealing with others by taking all factors, not only the legal ones, into account.

Moreover, the directives both to Israel generally and to her rulers particularly emphasize that compassionate treatment of others is what is entailed in justice. Zechariah admonishes:

> Administer true justice [משפט];
>   show mercy [חסד] and compassion [רחמים] to one another.
> Do not oppress the widow or the fatherless,
>   the alien or the poor. (Zech 7:9-10 NIV)

One might think of the injunctions serially and thus not necessarily related. However, the commands within this text seem nested in each other. Thus the directive not to oppress the widow is an explication of the command to show compassion, just as the command to show compassion is in apposition to the command to do justice. Jeremiah repeated similar directives which reiterate that compassion is an expression of justice. The command to those who sit on David's throne was to "Act with justice and righteousness." This directive is immediately followed by its explication: "deliver from the hand of the oppressor anyone who has been robbed" (22:3a + b NRSV; cf. 21:12a and Ps 72:1 with 72:12-13). That is, royal administration of justice does not have the retribution of the oppressor as its first goal; rather, the primary concern is to offer active help and show concern (compassion) for the victim.

In biblical thinking divine compassion cannot be set over against divine justice, nor can compassion be divorced from justice. Instead, compassion is subsumed as definitive of justice. Put the other way, the doing of justice entails extending compassion. So, to return to the subject of God sparing animals and people at Nineveh, God's compassionate move is not contrary to his justice, but instead is expressive of his justice.

Compassion, Justice, and the Kingdom of God

In considering God's stance toward nature as expounded in the Jonah story, we are put in touch with God's compassion for his creatures. But compassion, as has been shown, is integral to something more overarching, namely, justice. The exercise of justice, while incumbent on all of God's people, is specifically demanded from Israel's rulers, the kings. If we ask why this is so, we are pushed one stage further in the move from the micro- to the macro-picture and find ourselves up against the reality of the kingdom of God.

Justice, which by biblical definition incorporates compassion, is a hallmark of God's rule. Psalm 82 forcefully makes this point, once more not in abstract philosophical terms, but against the background of an ancient story, perhaps a myth or a vision rooted in Canaanite tradition.[26] God presides in the heavenly council and dispenses מִשְׁפָּט among the "gods."[27] God's evaluation of these "gods" is based on their treatment of oppressors and oppressed. The "gods" "miss the mark" because they have defended the unjust, shown partiality to the wicked, and failed to rescue the weak and the needy. While it is true that "The rottenness of the Old Order is described as bringing on its own destruction,"[28]

26. Peter F. Höffken, however, argues for an Israelite and late origin. "Werden und Vergehen der Götter: Ein Beitrag zur Auslegung von Psalm 82," *TZ* 39 (1983): 129-37. Franz Joseph Stendebach ("Glaube and Ethos: Überlegungen zu Ps. 82," in *Freude an der Weissung des Herrn*, hrsg. v. Ernst Haag und Frank-Lothar Hossfell [Stuttgart: Katholisches Bibelwerk, 1987], 425-40) modifies O. Loretz's view that in Psalm 82 there is a "Cananite short story" (vv. 1-4, 6-7) by suggesting that in the seventh century in Judah a story about the conflict among deities was constructed (cf. Baal and Mot in Ugaritic lore) which in the exilic/postexilic period was expanded (vv. 5, 8) and which, like the prophets' message, measures Israel's faith according to a social ethic.

27. An interpretation favoring "gods" understood within a polytheistic tradition may be preferable to the view that "gods" are human judges. Herbert Niehr ("Götter oder Menschen — eine falsche Alternative: Bemerkungen zu Ps. 82," *ZAW* 99 [1987]: 94-98), who reviews the relevant arguments, concludes that it is not necessary to choose between the two possibilities. Transactions of the gods are analogous to human transactions: verses 1 and 6f point to the heavenly transactions; verses 2-4 focus on the earthly. A foundational study is H. W. Juengling, *Der Tod der Götter*, SBS 38 (Stuttgart: KBW, 1968).

28. Cyrus H. Gordon, "History of Religion in Psalm 82," in *Biblical and Near Eastern Studies*, ed. Gary A. Tuttle (Grand Rapids: Eerdmans, 1978), 130.

the text leaves no doubt about Yahweh's direct intervention. The "gods" are deposed in no uncertain terms:

I say, "You are gods . . .
nevertheless, you shall die like mortals . . ." (Ps 82:6-7 NRSV)

The closing statement of this psalm clearly puts the episode into kingdom-of-God terms: "Rise up, O God, judge the earth; / for all the nations belong to you!" (Ps 82:8 NRSV). The message is pointed. In the heavenly realms God rules with מֹשְׁפֹט. The poet, himself passionate for justice, implores God to dispense justice "on earth as in heaven." Divine rule, whether in heaven or on earth, will have justice, defined here as including concern for the weak and oppressed, as its standard.[29]

The prophets also wed the themes of God's rule, justice, and compassion. These are the themes that are sounded in the announcements about Israel's return from the exile, but also in the larger cosmic revamping that shall characterize the day of the Lord. That justice, including compassion for the poor and the languishing, is God's *modus operandi* for kingdom rule is amply illustrated, among other ways, by his action toward an exiled Israel facing extinction. Isaiah put it bluntly: "But the LORD will have compassion [רחם] on Jacob . . . and will settle them in their own land" (Isa 14:1). The link between Yahweh's compassion and Israel's restoration is frequent (Jer 42:12; Isa 63:7-8; Zech 10:6).

If Yahweh's rule of justice with compassion is a marked reason for hope for the helpless exiles, it also figures in the restoration of the helpless non-human environment in "the day of the LORD." The prophets depict the day of the Lord as the day of God's decisive rule in which the world of nature will be transformed. The book of Hosea, where one is never far from the theme of compassion, announces a day when God will inaugurate a covenant that will involve wild animals, birds of the air, and creeping things (Hos 2:20 [Eng. 2:18]). This reversal of conditions resulting in harmony for the animal world will come about as a consequence of Yahweh's righteousness, justice, steadfast love, and compassion (רחמים) (Hos 2:21 [Eng. 2:19]). Also on that day, as the following oracle announces, the inanimate world shall be reordered. God will respond (in compassion!) to the heavens, and the heavens will respond (ענה) to the earth, and fertility of the ground will result (Hos 2:24 [Eng. 2:22]). The verb ענה can mean "to sing antiphonally." "But it can also mean 'speak up' and 'sing' with connotations both of acting by divine decree and creating cosmically harmonious 'music of the skies.'"[30] The two stanzas are themati-

---

29. The writer recalls the impact on him of a forceful sermon on Psalm 82 delivered by Prof. R. Knierim on a Sunday morning in a Methodist church in Claremont, California.
30. Douglas Stuart, *Hosea-Jonah*, WBC (Waco: Word, 1987), 60.

cally in parallel and illustrate the focus on a transformed world of nature arising from Yahweh's rule.[31]

Stanza A (Hos 2:18-22 [Eng. 2:16-20])	Stanza B (Hos 2:23-25 [Eng. 2:21-23])
Environment	Environment
A focus on the earth (v. 20 [Eng. 18])	A focus on the cosmos (v. 23 [Eng. 21])
Harmony among earth's creatures	Harmony between heaven and earth
Outcome: security	Outcome: abundant production
Spirituality	Spirituality
A reversal; single metaphor	A reversal; multiple metaphors
(v. 18 [Eng. 16])	(v. 25 [Eng. 23])
Response:	Response:
You are my Husband (v. 18 [Eng. 16])	You are my God (v. 25 [Eng. 23])[32]

In the book of Joel, where the subject is the day of the Lord, oracles are addressed to the soil (inanimate) and animals (animate).

> Do not fear, O soil;
>> be glad and rejoice,
>>> for the LORD has done great things!
> Do not fear, you animals of the field,
>> for the pastures of the wilderness are green;
> the tree bears its fruit,
>> the fig tree and vine give their full yield. (Joel 2:21-22 NRSV)

These oracles are headlined by a statement about God's jealousy for his land and his pity (חסד) for his people (2:18). To be sure, God's pity is for his people, but it is not restricted to humans; it extends to the created order.[33]

This approach to environmental concerns, which derives from the person of Yahweh, specifically God's compassion, represents a theological springboard quite different from customary and overworked approaches which stress do-

---

31. This interpretation regards "in that day" (v. 18) as resumptive, contra Dianne Bergant. Arguments for the resumptive usage are (1) that in Hebrew "In that day" (v. 20) is not in the initial position as in verses 18 and 23; (2) that verse 20 does not have the fuller "nĕ'um Yahweh" found in verses 18, 23; and (3) that the inclusion, an allusion to covenant in verse 22c (cf. v. 18), signals that the first "In that day . . ." oracle ends with verse 20.

32. An enlarged discussion may be found in this writer's article "Spirituality and Environment in Hosea," ACTS Theological Journal. Cf. William A. Dyrness, "Environmental Ethics and the Covenant of Hosea 2," Studies in Old Testament Theology, ed. Robert L. Hubbard, Robert K. Johnston, and Robert P. Meye (Dallas: Word, 1992), 263-78.

33. The New Testament aspect of the kingdom of God as it bears on environmental concerns is developed by Gordon Zerbe, "The Meaning of the Kingdom of God for the Stewardship of Creation," The Environment and the Christian, ed. Calvin B. De Witt (Grand Rapids: Baker, 1991), 73-92.

minion-having or stewardship. A key text for dominion theology is Gen 1:28. Even when רדה is qualified by Yahweh's criteria for "rule" (e.g., Ps 72),[34] the nuance of "taking charge" is hardly avoidable. The motif of stewardship is drawn from Gen 2:15. As often noted, "to till" (עבד) is to be understood as "serve," and "keep" (שמר) is "to exercise watchful care." Stewardship, however, popularly evokes ideas of management and profit. Besides, stewardship blesses the status quo, the situation which obtains following the fall and hardly that which God intends.[35] Both approaches — dominion-having and stewardship — are in the last analysis anthropocentric, as M. Fox and H. Paul Santmire rightly note.[36] Aside from the question whether the stewardship motif is informed anthropologically or theologically, we may, following R. Knierim's proposal that it is the function of biblical theology to adjudicate theologies,[37] ask about the relative dominance of the biblical tradition of "stewardship" vis-à-vis the compassion motif. While mention is made of "stewardship" of land in Gen 2:15 and may be echoed in legislation about the sabbatical and jubilee years (Lev 25), it is overshadowed as a motif by Yahweh's compassion.

Even when concepts such as covenant or sabbath are invoked as a warrant for Christian responsibility for the environment, one does not depart far from the anthropocentric approach.[38] The theocentric approach by contrast is driven by a protracted consideration of the "I AM."

To arrive at a biblical perspective on environment we began with the account in the book of Jonah which culminates in God's compassion as the reason for sparing the city, including the animals. The problematic which God's action created in the light of the deserved punishment was analyzed with the help of the prophetic literature and yielded two conclusions: (1) compassion triumphs over wrath; and (2) compassion is integral to a biblical understanding of justice. Justice, in turn, is foundational to God's rule (kingdom of God). It

---

34. Loren Wilkinson, *Earth Keeping: Christian Stewardship of Natural Resources* (Grand Rapids: Eerdmans, 1980); Wesley Granberg-Michaelson, ed., *Tending the Garden* (Grand Rapids: Eerdmans, 1987); Douglas J. Hall, *The Steward: A Biblical Symbol Come of Age*, rev. ed. (Grand Rapids: Eerdmans, 1990).

35. Issa J. Khalil opts instead for a transfiguration-of-nature approach. "For the Transfiguration of Nature: Ecology and Theology," *Epiphany* 10 (1990): 19-36.

36. M. Fox, *The Coming of the Cosmic Christ*. H. Paul Santmire, discussing the ecological reading of biblical theology, distinguishes between an anthropocentric approach to nature (citing G. von Rad and G. E. Wright) and a theocentric-ecological approach (citing C. Westermann and W. Brueggemann). *The Travail of Nature* (Philadelphia: Fortress, 1985), chap. 10.

37. Knierim, "Task of Old Testament Theology," 25-57.

38. Wesley Granberg-Michaelson, *Ecology and Life: Accepting Our Environmental Responsibility* (Waco: Word, 1988); cf. "Covenant and Creation," in *Liberating Life*, ed. Charles Birch, William Eakin, and J. B. McDaniel (Maryknoll: Orbis, 1990), 27-36. Cf. Carol S. Robb and Carl J. Casebold, eds., *Covenant for a New Creation: Ethics, Religion, and Public Policy* (Maryknoll: Orbis, 1991).

is finally in Yahweh's compassion that an ecotheology must be grounded. For Christians the reality of Yahweh is the decisive reality by which life is governed. So also their stance toward the world of the physical environment is determined by their understanding of who Yahweh is — a God of compassion who rules justly over all. With this understanding, Christians come to the environmental problem with sensitivity and work toward its rehabilitation and transformation with Yahweh-like compassion.

It is out of such a theology, one forged by an understanding of Yahweh as compassionate and whose rule is simultaneously one of justice, that the Christian is governed in his/her stance to the environment. Children of God's kingdom are called in both Testaments to emulate and, indeed, to be characterized by that which characterizes Yahweh their king. Jesus put it succinctly: "Be compassionate as your Creator in heaven is compassionate" (Luke 6:36 JB). It has been rightly said, "If we are to be earthkeepers according to God's way, we will first have to become Earth lovers."[39] The motivation of compassion, modeled after God's own compassion/justice, is for people of Christian faith a basic, defensible, and energizing motivation in the care and rehabilitation of the physical environment.

---

39. Mary Evelyn Jegen, *Sojourners*, February-March 1990, 17.

Israel and the Nations in Isaiah 40–55

ROY F. MELUGIN

I. Introduction

Is Israel accorded special favor and privilege in Yahweh's eyes? Are the foreign nations less favored simply because Israel is the chosen? Or are the nations just as much the object of Yahweh's concern and care as Israel? Is Israel the chosen given a special responsibility to the nations so that Yahweh's blessing may be experienced as fully by Gentiles as by Israel?

Exegesis of various biblical texts would show a diversity of theological perspectives on this issue. Indeed, a study which was exclusively exegetical would clearly reveal that the Bible is by no means univocal with regard to this matter. If one is concerned about biblical *theology*, however, the answer is not immediately so evident. Is biblical theology simply a catalogue of the various theologies in the Bible? Or does it involve a comparison of various canonical witnesses?

If one embraces the latter alternative, what does one do with diverse and contradictory theologies within the canon? One might argue, along with Brevard Childs, that the various witnesses should not be harmonized; each should be allowed to be heard on its own.[1] As long as the different theologies enrich one another and do not fundamentally clash, appropriating the different theologies is not problematic. But what if the theologies are fundamentally incompatible? Should we determine which theologies are more relevant to particular situations in which *we* find ourselves? Should we choose texts whose theologies are more readily adaptable to the particular contexts in which we find ourselves than the theologies of other biblical texts? Surely there is much wisdom here: what is appropriate in one situation is not necessarily what is called for in another.

---

1. B. S. Childs, *Biblical Theology in Crisis* (Philadelphia: Westminster, 1970), 111.

Moreover, the Bible itself frequently displays the re-using of earlier "canonical" traditions in new settings. Thus we should proceed from the conviction that biblical traditions are "adaptable to life" and should be appropriated in a dynamic way so that they can speak to situations here and now.[2]

Still more, however, must be said. Although communities of faith in the present must surely consider which texts are relevant to particular situations they must face, they also need to determine how to *evaluate* the various biblical traditions theologically, so that they may be applied judiciously and not capriciously. It is at this point that the theological writing of Rolf Knierim is especially illuminating, for he argues the necessity of evaluating which biblical claims are theologically more basic and fundamental.[3] If one is concerned, for example, with the theological significance of being God's chosen people, Knierim would have us inquire as to the nature of the relationships between the elect and other peoples in the world. Since various biblical texts give different answers, Knierim would have us ask whether God created the world for the sake of the elect or whether the elect were chosen for the sake of the world.[4] We cannot escape theological evaluation on this issue and on many others, for the Bible itself frequently confronts us with a multiplicity of theological perspectives.

Many texts in the Hebrew Bible deal with the relationships between Israel and the nations. But the perspectives are not univocal. Gentile nations are sometimes treated as enemies to be defeated. In the holy war traditions in Deuteronomy and Joshua, for instance, the assumption is that Yahweh has promised Palestine to Israel and that its native inhabitants are to be defeated and wiped out. The attitude toward Gentiles is quite different in Amos or Jonah.

If inquiries about chosenness were merely theoretical and of antiquarian interest alone, the topic would be interesting but safe. But the question is existential: How should the Scriptures inform the difficult issues of the Middle East? How should the Scriptures be used to assess relationships between those of Christian faith and those who stand outside the Christian tradition? Biblical texts must be evaluated as precedents to be applied to problems concerning such relationships. What benefits should Israel enjoy? What obligations to Palestinians should they have? What stances should Christians take toward non-Christians? Are they persons primarily to be evangelized? Or are there other, perhaps more important, obligations? Biblical texts must surely be applied. But different texts have different theologies. Thus their theologies must be assessed and evaluated, as precedents to be evaluated and applied.

2. J. A. Sanders, *From Sacred Story to Sacred Text: Canon as Paradigm* (Philadelphia: Fortress, 1987), 9-39. See also Sanders's article, "Hermeneutics," in *IDBSup*, 402-7 (esp. pp. 405-7).

3. Knierim, "Cosmos and History in Israel's Theology," *HBT* 3 (1981): 59-123; "The Task of Old Testament Theology," *HBT* 6,1 (1984): 25-57. See especially the latter essay (pp. 33-35).

4. Knierim, "Cosmos and History," 101; Knierim, "Task of Old Testament Theology," 40.

II. Exegetical Overview

Isaiah 40–55 is a good place to begin, for relationships between Israel and the nations are at the core of its concerns. It is indeed not infrequently said to be a "high-water mark" in the Hebrew Bible's understanding of the status of Gentiles in Yahweh's saving purposes. Such a claim obviously involves a value judgment. But is this value judgment justified? Is it a value judgment which should be more discriminatingly expressed? How well does Deutero-Isaiah's theology meet standards of justice articulated in a number of biblical texts? How adequate is its creation theology in shaping an appropriate theology about the relationships between Israel and the nations? What are the benefits and the limitations of the Deutero-Isaianic theology of Yahweh's glory in the assessment of its theology about Israel and the nations? What should be made of its theology of suffering?

A. Isa 40:1-11, in introducing chapters 40–55, sets the stage for the text's portrayal of the future of Israel and the nations in Yahweh's judging and saving purposes.[5] The opening instruction to comfort Jerusalem (40:1-2) makes clear that she had been punished for her iniquity but that the time of punishment was now ended. Next follow imperatives concerning preparation of a highway in the wilderness (vv. 3-5). A new exodus is to take place with a journey on an obstacle-free highway.[6] The result will be that "all flesh" will see Yahweh's glory. All this will happen because of the power of the divine word: "For the mouth of Yahweh has spoken."

In verses 6-8 someone is commissioned to "cry out." Whether one should read with MT ("and he said") or LXX and possibly Qumran ("and I said") is not certain. If one reads with MT, the "he" who responds to Yahweh might be a member of the heavenly council. Or if one reads "and I said," the speaker might be the prophet or Israel personified. In any event, there is a commission to proclaim the *word* of Yahweh, which can be relied upon to "stand forever."[7]

Once the commissioning in verses 6-8 has taken place, the bearer of glad tidings is instructed to deliver the good news of Yahweh's victory (vv. 9-11).[8] Yahweh comes to rule (v. 10) and to function as shepherd to a flock (v. 11). The message-bearer announces in advance of the king's victorious return (1) the victory that has been achieved and (2) the character of the king's rule in the future.

---

5. See, e.g., J. Muilenburg, *Interpreter's Bible*, vol. 5 (New York and Nashville: Abingdon, 1956), 422.

6. C. Stuhlmueller, *Creative Redemption in Deutero-Isaiah*, AnBib 43 (Rome: Pontifical Biblical Institute, 1970), 66, 74-86; R. Melugin, *The Formation of Isaiah 40–55*, BZAW 141 (Berlin and New York: de Gruyter, 1976), 85.

7. See C. R. Seitz, "The Divine Council: Temporal Transition and New Prophecy in the Book of Isaiah," *JBL* 109 (1990): 229-47.

8. Seitz, 245.

Isa 40:1-11 as a whole proclaims comfort to a Jerusalem that has suffered for her sins, a new exodus brought forth by the mouth of Yahweh, the commissioning of a message-bearer, and instructions to a tidings-bringer as to what to do and say. The object of deliverance is Jerusalem; it is she who will be the beneficiary of the new exodus. Yet the result of Jerusalem's deliverance and Yahweh's rule is the revelation of God's glory (v. 5). And the manifestation of Yahweh's glory has worldwide significance: it is beheld, not only by Israel, but by "all flesh." The salvation of Jerusalem is not an end in itself; it leads to the recognition of Yahweh's glory by *all* flesh.

Yahweh's glory will be seen by all because Yahweh has spoken. Yahweh's word is the creative force which brings about Jerusalem's deliverance and the rule of God. "All flesh" is grass; humans, like grass which withers, fade. If "all flesh" are to see God's glory, they will do so because Yahweh's word does not wither but "stands" forever in creative power.

B. With Isa 40:12-31 the text shifts immediately to disputation about Yahweh over against the nations and their gods.[9] Are there rivals to Yahweh? No! the text maintains. Who has measured the waters? Who marked off the heavens? With whom did Yahweh consult? Did Yahweh depend on any other for knowing the path of justice or for having understanding? Obviously not. Thus the nations are like nothing — like a drop from a bucket or dust from the scales. Moreover, Yahweh cannot be compared to any likeness (vv. 18-19). An idol is made from the hardiest of woods so that it will not rot, and erected by human skill so that it will not fall over. How unlike Yahweh, who sits about the earth's circle and stretches out the heavens! What is the idol, who must be fashioned and created by humans, in contrast with Yahweh, who brings even princes to nought (vv. 21-24)? To whom then may Yahweh, who created the heavenly hosts, be compared (vv. 25-26)?

Thus Israel need not complain that their "way" is hid from Yahweh, that their case *(mišpāṭ)* has been ignored (vv. 27-31).[10] Yahweh is creator of the ends of the earth; Yahweh does not grow weary or faint. And those who wait on Yahweh will be strengthened, so that they too will not be weary or faint.

Isa 40:1-11 proclaims that "all flesh" will see God's glory made manifest in the exodus. Verses 12-31 extend the claims of 1-11 by focusing on the incomparability of Yahweh. The assertions about Yahweh's glory and kingship (vv. 5, 10) could not stand if the nations and their gods were comparable to Yahweh; Israel's way would remain hidden (v. 27) were Yahweh not creator of the ends of the earth. The assertions of Yahweh's victorious rule and the recog-

---

9. C. Westermann, *Isaiah 40–66*, OTL (Philadelphia: Westminster, 1969), 48; Melugin, 31-36, 90-93.

10. The language about Israel's "way" in Isa 40:27 should be read in the light of the instructions in Isa 40:3-5.

nition of God's glory by all are thereby undergirded by the arguments of Yahweh's incomparability as creator and lord of creation.

C. In Isa 41:1–42:13 the glory of Yahweh over against the gods is an overarching theme. The nations are summoned to trial to answer questions as to which god "stirred up" Cyrus (41:1-7).[11] Might not some other gods be responsible? No, says the text. Had any god besides Yahweh "called the generations"? And, once the nations saw Yahweh's power, would they not desperately engage in mutual help to fashion idols which can be kept from toppling over by being fastened down with nails? What is at stake here is the powerlessness of the gods.

Then the text contrasts the nations' desperate "strengthening" of one another in the manufacture of idols (41:5-7) with the oracle in which Yahweh "strengthens" the chosen people Israel (41:8-13, esp. v. 10).[12] How the trembling nations (vv. 5-7) contrast with the Israel who becomes a powerful threshing sledge (vv. 15-16)! How the gods who must be made and secured by humans contrast with Yahweh, who drives away the humans who contend against Israel (vv. 11-12)!

The exodus/creation theme returns in Isa 41:17-20. Yahweh creates an oasis in the desert, presumably for Israel's sustenance on the journey back from captivity. Yahweh does this, not as an end in itself, but so that the creative hand of Yahweh can be known: "that they may see and know . . . that the hand of Yahweh has done this, that the Holy One of Israel has created it." Though it is unclear just *who* is to "see" (Israel? all flesh?), it is evident that the purpose of the deity's action is that *Yahweh* may be known as creator.

A second trial speech (41:21-29) shows the gods to be nothing.[13] To qualify as gods, they must do good or bad, that humans may be dismayed (v. 23); and, most important, they must be able to speak and have their words come to pass (vv. 22-23). As in 40:5, where the manifestation of Yahweh's glory is the result of the word Yahweh has spoken, so in 41:21-29 a true god must speak event-creating words. Yahweh spoke to Zion, while the gods were silent; therefore they are nothing (41:25-29).

---

11. For studies of the genres of the trial in Isaiah 40–55, see, e.g., the following works: J. Begrich, *Studien zu Deuterojesaja* (München: Kaiser, 1963), 26-48; E. von Waldow, "Anlass und Hintergund der Verkundigung des Deuterojesja" (Dissertation, Bonn, 1953), 37-46, and *Der traditionsgeschichtliche Hintergrund der prophetischen Gerichtsreden*, BZAW 85 (Berlin: Töpelmann, 1963); H. J. Boecker, *Redeformen des Rechtslebens in Alten Testament*, WMANT 14 (Neukirchen-Vluyn: Neukirchener, 1964); C. Westermann, "Sprache und Struktur der Prophetie Deuterojesajas," in *Forschung am Alten Testament: gesammelte Studien* (München: Kaiser, 1964), 133-44; A. Schoors, *I am God Your Saviour,* VTSup 24 (Leiden: Brill, 1973), 176-245; Melugin, 45-63.

12. Melugin, 96.

13. Westermann, *Isaiah 40–66,* 82-83; H. C. Spykerboer, *The Structure and Composition of Deutero-Isaiah* (Meppel: Krips, 1976), 73; Melugin, 98; K. Elliger, *Deuterojesaja,* vol. 1, BKAT 11 (Neukirchen-Vluyn: Neukirchener, 1978), 177.

Then Yahweh presents the servant (42:1-4) — undoubtedly the servant Israel. The servant's task is to bring justice and torah to the nations. He is to be a light to the nations (42:5-9). The servant has been "chosen" and "called" to his task because Yahweh is unwilling to share glory with other gods (42:8).

To sum up: In Isa 41:1–42:13 Israel *gets* salvation from Yahweh (41:8-20) and *gives* justice and light to the nations (42:1-9).[14] None of this happens for its own sake. Instead Israel is delivered that *Yahweh* may be known as creator (41:20); the servant is called to bring light to the nations that *Yahweh's* glory may not be given to another god. And with good reason: compared with Yahweh the gods are nothing (41:1-7, 21-29).

D. The theme of the glorification of Yahweh and the polemic against idols continues in Isa 42:14–44:23.[15] Yahweh's leading the blind in a new exodus (42:14-17; 43:1-7, 16-21) and the summoning of the blind to testify on Yahweh's behalf (43:8-13) are subordinate to the wider theme of the glory of Yahweh and the corresponding polemic against the gods. The first unit's exodus theme of Yahweh's leading the blind in a "way" not known to them (42:14-17) proclaims that those who worship graven and molten images will be "turned back" and "put to shame" (v. 17). The reader might surmise, with good reason, that those who trust in images are largely, if not entirely, foreign nations. Yet the text is not explicit about this. Even if the devotees of images are largely Gentiles, shame comes upon them because they worship images, not because they are foreigners.

As the composition continues to discuss Yahweh's dealing with the blind (42:18-25; 43:8-13) and with the divine promises of a new exodus (43:1-7),[16] the concern for God's glory and the denigration of the gods remain central. Isa 42:18-25, in showing that Yahweh was willing to punish Israel (vv. 21-25), attributes to Yahweh a "magnifying" and "glorifying" of Torah "for his righteousness' sake" (v. 21). Indeed, the punishment of Israel seems to have taken place *for the sake of* Yahweh's righteousness and glory. Furthermore, the exodus-like journey through waters by the created and redeemed Israel (43:1-2), the ransom of Israel (43:3-4), and the return of Israel's scattered offspring (43:5-6) take place because Israel was created for Yahweh's glory (43:7). Finally, in the trial speech of 43:8-13,[17] blind and deaf Israel, summoned to court together with foreign peoples to demonstrate whether Yahweh or the gods can show the "former things," testify on Yahweh's behalf both for their own sake (v. 10) and that their testimony might show that only Yahweh can deliver (vv. 11-13). These three units (42:18-25; 43:1-7; 43:8-13), taken together, describe Yahweh as acting for the sake of the divine glory and righteousness. For that reason disobedient

---

14. Melugin, "The Servant, God's Call, and the Structure of Isaiah 40–48," *Society of Biblical Literature 1991 Seminar Papers* (Atlanta: Scholars, 1991), 26.

15. Isa 42:17; 43:8-13; 44:6-20.

16. Melugin, "Structure of Isaiah 40–48," 27.

17. Westermann, *Isaiah 40–66*, 120; Melugin, *Formation of Isaiah 40–55*, 110.

Israel is punished; for the sake of Yahweh's glory Israel, God's creation, is brought through waters, and their offspring are brought home "from the ends of the earth." For Yahweh's sake Israel testifies in the law court that only Yahweh can deliver.

Even after language about deliverance of the blind and deaf is left behind, a theology of deliverance of Israel for Yahweh's own sake persists.[18] Though Yahweh defeats Babylon for Israel's sake (43:14-15), the exodus-like new creation in the desert (43:16-21) takes place on behalf of a chosen people whom Yahweh formed "that they might declare my praise" (43:21). Even then, Israel did not call upon Yahweh (43:22-28). But Yahweh nonetheless blotted out their sins *for Yahweh's own sake* (v. 25).

As Isa 42:14–44:23 draws closer to its end, the polemic against the gods moves once again to the center. In yet another trial speech (44:6-8)[19] Yahweh claims to be the first and last. Indeed, there is no god but Yahweh, for no other god can speak from beforehand the things to come. And Israel can bear witness to this! Therefore, all who make idols are nothing (44:9-20); the gods are nothing but the product of human artifice — made of leftover wood after humans have cooked food and warmed themselves by the fire. How ironic it is to bow down and worship what one has made of leftover wood!

Finally, Israel is exhorted to "remember" that Yahweh will not forget them, that God will sweep away their sins (44:21-22). They are then summoned to praise Yahweh, who has "redeemed" Israel, through whom Yahweh will be "glorified" (v. 23). The association of Israel's redemption and Yahweh's glorification in Isa 44:23 mirrors the connection between them throughout 42:14–44:23. As we have seen, Israel is the recipient of Yahweh's deliverance; Yahweh acts indeed for Israel's own sake. But even what God does in the way of saving and judging Israel is performed *primarily* for Yahweh's sake — for the sake of the divine glory. Israel's salvation is not an end in itself; Israel is created and redeemed for Yahweh's glory. And those who worship idols come to shame, not because they are Israel's enemies, but rather because the gods whom the worshipers have made can be contrasted with Yahweh, who creates by the divine word.

E. In Isa 44:24–48:22 the recognition of Yahweh as God alone and the polemic against idolatry continue to play a central role, but this time in the context of the commissioning of Cyrus and all that accompanies his conquests. The composition begins by proclaiming that Yahweh, redeemer of Israel and creator of all things, calls Cyrus so that Jerusalem and its temple will be rebuilt (44:24-28). The commissioning of Cyrus proper (45:1-7) proclaims that Cyrus

18. Melugin, *Formation of Isaiah 40–55*, 114.

19. Boecker, 160ff.; G. Tucker, "Witnesses and 'Dates' in Israelite Contracts," *CBQ* 28 (1966): 42-45; Westermann, *Isaiah 40–66*, 138-39; Melugin, *Formation of Isaiah 40–55*, 118-19.

will be a conqueror so that Cyrus himself may know that Yahweh commissions him (v. 3), that Yahweh's purposes "for Jacob's sake" may be fulfilled (v. 4), and that all humans — from east to west — may know that there is no god besides Yahweh (vv. 6-7).

Cyrus acts on Israel's behalf, not simply for Israel's benefit as an end in itself, but so that all humans may know that there is no god other than Yahweh. Indeed, the language of Cyrus's commissioning (45:1-7) and a closely related disputation (45:9-13) lead into texts which portray foreigners turning to Yahweh as God (45:14-17, 22-25) and depict idol worshipers as those who "pray to a god who cannot save" (45:18-21, esp. v. 20). Foreigners come over in chains, bringing their wealth to Zion (note the feminine singular pronouns) and confessing that God is with Zion alone and that only the God of Israel is savior (45:14-17). The defeat of foreign nations (v. 14) and Yahweh's salvation of Israel (v. 17) are two essential ingredients of the nations' recognition that Yahweh alone is God. The trial speech which follows (45:18-21) calls to trial a remnant of the nations — persons who carry idols and pray to a god who cannot save. They are told to present the case for their gods, while Yahweh alone claims to be God and savior (v. 21). Thereupon Yahweh exhorts the nations ("the ends of the earth") to "turn to me and be saved" (v. 22). The nations whose gods have been shown to be impotent (vv. 18-21) receive a divine word which will not return empty until every knee bows and every tongue swears to Yahweh (v. 23). As in 45:14-17, the nations confess Yahweh as God, and it will be said that there is "righteousness and strength" only in Yahweh. Furthermore, the nations recognize that "in Yahweh all the offspring of Israel have victory and glory" (v. 25). Both Israel and the nations experience salvation from Yahweh, and the gods are shown to be without power.[20] And, most important, the ends of the earth bend the knee before Yahweh, whose power becomes evident in the triumph and glory of Israel.

Isaiah 46 continues the polemic against the gods by means of satire. Idols loaded on animals cannot save but must be carried by others (vv. 1-2), while Yahweh carries Israel from birth to old age (vv. 3-4). Next comes a contrast of Yahweh with idols, who are fashioned by humans, carried by humans, and lack the power to move and to answer or save (vv. 5-7).[21] By contrast, Yahweh's word has the force to accomplish its purpose (vv. 8-11), so that the salvation and glory of Yahweh will be established in Zion/Israel (vv. 12-13).

The song mocking the virgin daughter Babylon (Isa 47) condemns her for her lack of mercy on Yahweh's chosen people (v. 6) and for godlike pretensions in her claim, "I am and there is no one besides me" (vv. 8, 10).[22] Both

---

20. Spykerboer, 143.
21. Spykerboer, 147; Melugin, *Formation of Isaiah 40–55*, 133.
22. Spykerboer, 155; Melugin, *Formation of Isaiah 40–55*, 136.

result from failure to recognize and glorify Yahweh and from neglecting to treat God's chosen people with mercy.

Isaiah 48 closes this compositional unit with a disputation (vv. 1-11) in which Yahweh is said to have prevented Israel from giving credit to an idol (v. 5).[23] Indeed, Yahweh's anger was deferred for the sake of Yahweh's own glory (vv. 9-11). It is *Yahweh* the creator whose purpose is expressed in the actions of Cyrus against Babylon (vv. 12-15); no god besides Yahweh is responsible for Cyrus.

To sum up: All that has been said about Cyrus and his victories throughout Isa 44:24–48:22 represents triumphs undertaken for the sake of God's glory. Salvation and judgment of both Israel and the nations occur so that all may confess Yahweh's name and that no other god or godlike pretender (the virgin Babylon) can obtain the glory due Yahweh.

F. With Isa 49:1-13 the text maintains continuity with what precedes but also introduces something fundamentally new. As Christopher Seitz has argued,[24] the commissioning in the heavenly council (40:1-8) anticipates the servant's own response to the call (48:16b; 49:1-6). Indeed, as I proposed elsewhere,[25] Isa 40:12–48:22 is a complex composition which leads from the commissioning in the heavenly council into the servant's acceptance of his commission. When the servant speaks in 49:1-6, he reports that he had been called so that Yahweh could be glorified in him (49:3). The claim in Isaiah 40–48 that Israel was chosen and saved for the sake of Yahweh's glory is reaffirmed here. Also restated is Yahweh's intent to bring salvation to the nations (49:6). Moreover, the text asserts once more that foreigners (kings) will "see," "arise," and "bow down," not for their own benefit, but *for Yahweh's sake* (49:7). What is new is the nations' recognition of Yahweh through that deity's redemption of an Israel who is "despised" and "abhorred." Such a theme begins to emerge at this point in Isaiah 40–55, only to be developed more fully in Isa 52:13–53:12.

Israel's suffering is not, however, the finale. Yahweh gives Israel a covenant to establish the land and to give as inheritances places which had been desolate (49:8). The text envisions prisoners brought forth and led in the "way" as the exiles travel home from afar (49:8-12), with the result that Yahweh's people are "comforted" (49:13). The Israel depicted in 49:7 is thus an Israel whose suffering comes to an end through their being comforted and brought home from exile.

G. As the Zion-Jerusalem section of the text (chaps. 49–54)[26] opens with 49:14-26, once more Yahweh promises that the chosen people will be returned from exile, so that "all flesh" may know Yahweh as Zion's savior (49:26). The

23. Begrich, 169-70; Melugin, *Formation of Isaiah 40–55*, 39-41.

24. Seitz, 245-46.

25. Melugin, "Structure of Isaiah 40–48," 24-30.

26. E. Hessler, "Gott der Schöpfer: Ein Beitrag zur Komposition und Theologie Deuterojesajas" (Dissertation, Greifswald, 1961), 82; Melugin, *Formation of Isaiah 40–55*, 85, 148-52.

mother Zion's children will return in such large numbers that the land will be unable to contain them (49:14-21). Moreover, Yahweh turns the tables so that nations' kings and queens will no longer oppress but will instead become foster fathers and nursing mothers, bowing down and licking the feet of Jerusalemites, *so that* Zion will know Yahweh and understand that those who wait on Yahweh will not be put to shame (49:22-23). Furthermore, Yahweh will rescue the children of Zion from the tyrant and will make oppressors eat their own flesh and drink their own blood, so that "all flesh" will know Yahweh as Jerusalem's savior and redeemer (49:24-26). Thus the return of the mother Zion's children takes place not only for Zion's sake but also that "all flesh" will know Yahweh as savior of Jerusalem.

H. In Isa 50:1-3 it becomes evident once again that the judgment and salvation of Jerusalem is the result of Yahweh's power. In apparent opposition to those who said that Yahweh had divorced Jerusalem or had been forced to sell her to creditors, Yahweh claims that she was sold because of her iniquities. No one had forced Yahweh to send her away. Furthermore, against those who contended that Yahweh's hand is too short to save, the text asserts that Yahweh's rebuke has power to dry up the sea, make rivers into a desert, clothe the skies with darkness. What additional power could Yahweh possibly need?

Now that these expectations of doubt have been answered, the servant of Yahweh can utter a psalm of confidence (50:4-9).[27] As in 42:1-4, the servant is said to be faithful; he did not rebel (v. 5). And in his constancy he does not turn back from his task under the pressure of tormenters (vv. 5-6). As in 49:7 the servant's shame is not the last word. Whoever contends against him will not prevail (vv. 7-9). Those who do not "fear Yahweh and obey the voice of his servant" indeed suffer condemnation (vv. 10-11).

I. In Isa 51:1–52:12, Yahweh delivers Zion. Yahweh's people are called to look to Abraham their father and Sarah their mother, for Yahweh will "comfort Zion" and make her barren wastes into Eden-like gardens (51:1-3). The deliverance of Yahweh's own people is not, however, isolated from the destiny of foreigners. Salvation of Yahweh's chosen is connected with the nations' receiving light; Yahweh's torah and justice go forth as a "light to the peoples," and Yahweh's salvation involves the incorporation of the peoples into Yahweh's rule (51:4-6).

Isa 51:1–52:12 focuses especially on the deliverance of Jerusalem. Yahweh's arm is called from sleep and summoned to dry up the sea so that Yahweh's "redeemed" and "ransomed" may return to Zion with singing and joy (51:9-11). Jerusalem, once forced by oppressors to drink the "cup of staggering," will experience a reversal of fortunes; her tormentors will have to drink that deadly cup (51:17-23). The uncircumcised and the unclean will no longer enter the

---

27. O. Kaiser, *Der königliche Knecht*, FRLANT 70 (Göttingen: Vandenhoeck & Ruprecht, 1959), 67-69; Westermann, *Isaiah 40–66*, 226; Melugin, *Formation of Isaiah 40–55*, 72.

holy city of Jerusalem; she is to loosen the bonds on her neck (52:1-2). Jerusalem's deliverance takes place, not simply for her own sake, but that the nations can "see" the salvation of Yahweh (52:7-10). Runners who bring glad tidings of Yahweh's victory declare to Zion, "your God rules." Yahweh returns to Zion as victor; God's holy arm was bared before the eyes of the nations that they might see the power of Yahweh the savior.

To sum up: Isa 51:1–52:12 speaks mostly of the deliverance of Jerusalem and of the defeat of their oppressors. But the salvation of Zion is not an end in itself. Not only does deliverance come to Jerusalem, but light is given to the nations as well (51:4). And the nations' recognition of Yahweh as savior remains, as elsewhere, the goal of Yahweh's deliverance of Jerusalem (52:10). Recognition of *Yahweh*, then, continues to be the fundamental purpose behind the redemption of Zion by their God.

J. In Isa 52:13–53:12,[28] Yahweh's servant (presumably Israel) prospers, as elsewhere in Isaiah 40–55 Israel is saved. Yahweh announces the servant's exaltation (52:13). And the nations experience surprise, for they "see" in his exaltation what they have not beforehand been told and "hear" what they have not previously understood (52:15). They are surprised because they did not expect one so marred to be raised up (52:12; cf. 49:7). Indeed, the nations' kings confess that the servant had been made to suffer for *their* iniquities (53:4-6). For the first time in Isaiah 40–55 it becomes clear that the servant's suffering is a vehicle for the nations' healing. It has admittedly been said repeatedly that all flesh will come to know Yahweh through victorious restoration of Israel. Moreover, the text had affirmed more than once that Yahweh intends "light" and "salvation" for the nations. But only in Isa 52:13–53:12 does it become manifest that the nations see in the servant's suffering the means by which they are made whole.

The nations apparently do not recognize the role of the servant in their healing until they see his exaltation. Although it was "by his stripes" that they were healed, they knew it not until they saw him raised high. Just as elsewhere in Isaiah 40–55 the nations know Yahweh as savior when they see Yahweh's deliverance of Israel, so also here they recognize the servant's healing significance only when Yahweh exalts him. Without his exaltation, they would have understood nothing beyond the insight that he was "smitten by God and afflicted" (53:4).

K. Isaiah 54–55 returns to an emphasis on Jerusalem's salvation. The mother who was once bereft of children must enlarge her tent to make room for a multitude of returning children (54:1-3). This woman, once cast off and put to shame, will soon forget her humiliation and remember her widowhood no more, for Yahweh her husband will take her back with great compassion

---

28. Begrich, 62-65; Westermann, *Isaiah 40–66*, 256-58; Melugin, *Formation of Isaiah 40–55*, 73-74.

(54:4-8). Yahweh had forsaken his bride for a brief moment (54:7, 8), but that time is now past. Yahweh will no longer be angry (54:9) but will inaugurate a "covenant of peace" which shall not be removed (54:9, 10). Prosperity will abound (54:11, 12, 13), and oppression and terror will disappear (54:14). No enemy shall prevail, for God's people will be vindicated (54:15, 16, 17).

The promises to Yahweh's own people once again do not stand alone without hopeful language about the nations. An offer of a banquet, yea, an offer of life and an everlasting Davidic covenant, involves a promise that foreign nations shall come to Israel (55:1-5) for the sake of Yahweh who glorifies Israel (55:5b). Isaiah 55 closes with an exhortation to seek Yahweh, whose ways and thoughts are higher than those of humans (55:6-13). Yahweh's word, it is said, will go forth to accomplish what Yahweh purposes and will not return empty (55:11). Just as at the beginning (40:1-11) Yahweh's word would create deliverance for Israel so that "all flesh" might see Yahweh's glory, so Isaiah 40–55 closes with a reaffirmation of Yahweh's powerful word.

III. Theological Analysis

A. Recognition of Yahweh's glory is the central purpose of the divine activity as portrayed in Isaiah 40–55. Admittedly, Yahweh's promised deliverance of Israel is of great importance, as is God's judgment and salvation of the nations. But Yahweh judges and saves for a reason: that all flesh will know that Yahweh is God. It is indeed not Yahweh's intent to share glory with another god. Yahweh's actions toward Israel and the nations are thus subservient to the more basic purpose of universal recognition of Yahweh as God. Divine compassion toward Israel is not the fundamental basis for Israel's salvation, nor is hatred or love for the nations the motivation for Yahweh's actions toward them. Yahweh saves Israel so that all nations will recognize Yahweh as God (Isa 45:6, 23; 49:23, 26); the ends of the earth are to be saved so that *every* tongue will confess Yahweh (45:23).

The awareness that Yahweh alone is God is closely tied to affirmations of Yahweh as creator. Creation is sometimes connected with the portrayal of a new exodus (43:16-21; cf. also 41:17-20). It is indeed frequently difficult to distinguish creation from exodus in Isaiah 40–55. Moreover, creation is sometimes portrayed as creation of Israel and thus not easily separable from Israel's election and redemption (43:1, 7; 44:1, 2).[29]

Although, in the texts just mentioned, creation is not said to be creation of the world, Yahweh's sovereignty is clearly implied. Yahweh, who makes a way in the sea and defeats chariot and horse (43:16, 17), creates an oasis in the

29. Stuhlmueller, 64, 66-73, 110-15, 125-31.

wilderness to sustain the chosen people (vv. 19, 20, 21). In Isa 43:1-7, Yahweh's creation of Israel leads to Yahweh's presence when they walk through fire and water (v. 2), to Yahweh's giving others in ransom for Israel (vv. 3, 4), and to Yahweh's bringing home Israel's scattered exiles (vv. 5, 6).

In other texts, Yahweh's creation of the *world* is discussed to demonstrate that Yahweh alone is God (40:18-24, 25-26; 42:5-9; 45:18-25). Only Yahweh can stretch out the heavens (40:22), compared to the idol which must be fashioned by humans (40:19, 20). Yahweh, creator of heavens and earth (45:18), is contrasted with wooden idols which must be carried (45:20). In Yahweh's acts of creation the nations behold Yahweh's lordship and thus turn to Yahweh to be saved (45:22).

B. There is much to be said for the theological claims found in Isaiah 40–55, for the recognition of Yahweh's universal lordship is its most central affirmation. An important issue is indeed at stake: Why is Yahweh to be recognized and worshiped? Because those who are saved by Yahweh benefit by what Yahweh has done? Or is Yahweh to be worshiped for Yahweh's own sake? Biblical theology must take with utmost seriousness the claim that Yahweh is to be worshiped, not simply because our own interests are met by Yahweh (cf. Job 1:9), but rather for Yahweh's own glory's sake. The danger of regarding Yahweh as an instrument to be used for our own purposes scarcely needs elaboration. History is littered with that kind of faith and its consequences.

At the same time, a theology in which God's glory is the central aim of worship can easily fail to attend to questions of justice. If one focuses too narrowly upon the glorification of God, insufficient attention may be paid to the equity accorded to elect and nonelect. Indeed, this very limitation characterizes Isaiah 40–55. Although Israel and the nations are both objects of Yahweh's salvation, Israel appears to be a more substantial beneficiary in the new creation/exodus than the nations. And how this apparent inequity squares with biblical traditions which affirm God's justice is not adequately addressed in Isaiah 40–55.

Some might argue that the nations fare better than I have been willing to concede. Admittedly, the nations are to be given justice and Torah (Isa 42:1, 4); salvation is to reach the ends of the earth (45:22; 49:6); the servant suffers that the nations might be healed (53:5). Still, the nations are to be severely punished at the time of Israel's deliverance. The nations become Israel's slaves; their wealth becomes Israel's; they come over in chains and lick the dust (45:14-17; 49:22-26). When the "ends of the earth" are saved and swear by Yahweh's name (45:22-25), special emphasis is given to the triumph of Israel (45:25). Even when the nations are saved, it seems, they are not relieved of their burden as Israel's servants. Isaiah 40–55 has taken only a limited step beyond a traditional Jerusalemite theology in which the nations are merely servants of Israel, and in particular, Israel's king (cf. Pss 2; 72:8-11), with the result that in Deutero-Isaiah the nations not only bow down before Yahweh and Israel but are also said to be given salvation. Precisely how salvation and servitude are related is not made clear, however. Isaiah 40–55 leaves these tensions unresolved.

Traditions in which justice is connected with Yahweh's creation and lordship of the world tend to promote a theology in which the nations are treated with equity.[30] In Psalm 96 Yahweh the creator is contrasted with the gods of the peoples (vv. 4-5), but the peoples are judged with equity (vv. 10, 13) without mention of special privilege for Israel (see also Ps 113). Admittedly, the belief that justice and righteousness are the foundations of Yahweh's throne (Ps 97:2) can stand side by side with assertions that worshipers of images (foreigners?) will be put to shame (97:7); a strong connection between justice and creation of the world (Ps 33:4-7) does not always rule out statements that Yahweh brings the counsel of the nations to nought or gives special blessings to Yahweh's chosen nation (Ps 33:10-12). A strong tie between justice and Yahweh's universal lordship nonetheless opens the door for greater potential awareness of questions of equity in the relationship between Israel and the nations.

Traditions in Genesis serve as an excellent example of what I mean. The Genesis narrative begins with God's creation of the world and the blessing of the humans whom God created (Gen 1). Indeed, God's purposive acts of blessing and cursing in Genesis 1–11 are directed toward persons related to the human race as a whole rather than Israelites. And when a special people are called into being through the commissioning of Abraham (Gen 12:1-3), they are not themselves alone recipients of blessing but are said to be a means by which all the families of the earth are to be blessed. Moreover, Abraham's becoming a nation through whom all nations are blessed is not unrelated to Yahweh's purposes for justice: Yahweh tells Abraham of his plans concerning Sodom and Gomorrah because Abraham has been called to be an agent of blessing for all nations and is expected to keep God's way by "doing righteousness and justice" (Gen 18:17-19). Now this Abraham whom Yahweh calls to be just holds *Yahweh* accountable to be just in dealing with the Gentile cities of Sodom and Gomorrah (Gen 18:24, 25). Furthermore, when Sarah goes into the harem of Abimelech (Gen 20), there is considerable reflection as to whether injustice might have been done to this Gentile king: Was Abimelech not innocent? Had he not taken Sarah because both Abraham and Sarah had told him that Sarah was Abraham's sister? To sum up: In Genesis Yahweh chooses Israel for the sake of the world. Through Abraham and his descendants all the families of the earth are to be blessed. Through Abraham, Yahweh's chosen, justice is to come to the Gentiles.

In view of the foregoing discussion, the precedents in Isaiah 40–55 concerning the relationships between Israel and the nations cannot legitimately be

30. Knierim, "Cosmos and History," 95-97.

called the "high-water mark" in biblical testimony on this subject. To be sure, Yahweh is portrayed as creator and lord of all. Yahweh judges and saves both Israel and the nations. Neither Israel nor the nations can use Yahweh as instrument for their own purposes, for both are judged and saved for the sake of Yahweh's glory. Moreover, the claim that the nations find healing through the suffering of Yahweh's servant is a profound insight worthy of much reflection. Nevertheless, the representation of the relationships between Israel and the nations in Genesis deals with the issue of justice in those relationships more adequately than does Deutero-Isaiah. Genesis expresses more explicitly and clearly than Isaiah 40–55 that Israel was chosen for the sake of the *world* and that justice for Gentiles is central to the purposes of Yahweh the creator and universal lord.

C. This essay is deeply indebted to Rolf Knierim, both for his recognition that the Bible contains multiple theologies which must be evaluated and for his insight that Yahweh's relationships with Israel must be understood in the context of the divine purposes for all creation. My thrust is nonetheless somewhat different: Knierim seems to be interested in developing a systematic biblical theology,[31] whereas my concerns are more with what might be called "occasional theology." I am more interested in the occasions or uses to which biblical texts are put than I am in constructing a theological system. I am concerned about how biblical texts might be applied as precedents to authorize behavior in communities of faith on particular occasions or settings.

This is scarcely the place to articulate a full-fledged *use* theory of Scripture together with a theoretical discussion of the nature and function of precedents. Instead I must close with a few brief remarks about the application of Isaiah 40–55 as precedent: (1) The Christian community has long read the suffering servant texts as precedent to shed light on Jesus' suffering for the sake of others. This is quite legitimate, but other possibilities might be explored as well. What if we were to focus on the suffering of a chosen *people* for the sake of other peoples? Could not Isaiah 53 be applied as a precedent for comprehending the death of six million Jews at the hands of Gentile oppressors? Or for understanding how the persecution of an entire black population might be a vessel for the healing of their white persecutors? (2) The inadequacy of Deutero-Isaiah's theology of justice concerning the relationship of Israel and the nations might profitably be considered in the examination of the present-day crisis in the Middle East. Surely, if Scripture is to be mined for precedents, the book of Genesis provides a better precedent than Deutero-Isaiah on this topic because of (a) its clear portrayal of Israel's call to be a blessing to Gentiles and (b) its insistence that Israel seek justice for Gentiles.

In sum: We must become theological evaluators of biblical traditions. We must not only interpret them, but we must also judge them and apply them in

31. Knierim, "Task of Old Testament Theology," 44, 45.

ever new and different situations. Like judges who must in diverse circumstances apply common law afresh,[32] we must take upon ourselves the courage to decide and the skills to apply our sacred precedents in intellectually and existentially responsible ways. I salute Rolf Knierim for having so capably challenged us to take up this task.

32. I am indebted to my Austin College colleague, James H. Ware, Jr., for this insight.

Reflections on a Critical Biblical Theology

ROLAND E. MURPHY, O.CARM.

The scholar honored by this volume is both a biblical theologian and an exponent of historical-critical methodology, as his many publications testify. It is in the spirit of the dialogue that one can always expect from him that this paper is offered in homage.[1] Historical criticism in biblical studies has received a generous share of criticism.[2] While most biblical scholars still practice it, various hermeneutical moves have tended to dethrone it: structuralism, liberation, feminist, reader-response, canonical shape, a purely literary or rhetorical interpretation, etc. The criticisms have been frequently off the mark, in the sense that they are demanding from historical criticism results it is not designed to yield. It is to be admitted that this approach has its own bias, thus laboring under the burden of any other methodology. It can never attain its goal; it can only approximate the precise historical past which it searches out. It is poisoned, as it were, at the outset by the inherent limitations of the questions it puts to the text. Admittedly too, the approach has begotten exaggerations. The strategy of

1. The first draft of this paper was presented initially in the process theology session (with Professor Knierim present) at the 1986 annual meeting of the Society of Biblical Literature, in response to the observations of John J. Collins, now published as "Is a Critical Biblical Theology Possible?" in *The Hebrew Bible and Its Interpreters,* ed. W. H. Propp et al., Biblical and Judaic Studies from the University of California, San Diego 1 (Winona Lake: Eisenbrauns, 1990), 1-17. Professor Collins has dealt with this subject also in "Old Testament Theology," in *The Biblical Heritage in Modern Catholic Scholarship,* ed. J. Collins and J. D. Crossan (Wilmington: Michael Glazier, 1986), 11-33. See also his "Biblical Theology and the History of Israelite Religion," in *Back to the Sources: Biblical and Near Eastern Studies,* ed. J. J. Collins and J. Healey (Dublin: Glendale, 1989), 1632.

2. For a balanced judgment, see W. Vogels, "Les limites de la méthode historico-critique," *LTP* 36 (1980): 173-94.

canonical shape is appealing precisely because of the innumerable hypotheses put forth in the name of historical criticism; a holistic approach is judged better than historical uncertainties.[3]

Despite the dissatisfaction, however, historical criticism still prevails, if only because it provides a level of common discussion of texts among scholars of various hues. Indeed, the issue to which this paper addresses itself is the applicability of the methodology of historical criticism to biblical theology. Recently J. Collins has raised the question of possibility: Is a critical biblical theology even possible?[4] He has sketched the growth of the thinking behind historical-critical methodology from J. Gabler to our own time. In particular, E. Troeltsch and W. Wrede laid down a stringent methodology. The three principles of Troeltsch are the key to the problem; the second (law of analogy) and the third (autonomy) need not be discussed in detail here. It may be said that Troeltsch exaggerated "the almighty power of analogy," but the law itself has pertinence. Autonomy (no one can mandate the conclusions for a scholar) is true, but not unlimited. It is limited by the fallibility and docility of individual scholars and by "assured conclusions." Responsibility to others is another factor that bears upon the results of scholarship. Whether one speaks of responsibility in the academic or the religious world, an obligation to the truth exists. The possibility of dissent has to be affirmed, but the limits of dissent are not easily defined. It is the first principle of Troeltsch that provides the stoutest challenge to biblical theology. This maintains that historical methodology can never attain more than probability, that the conclusions it yields are subject to revision — or, what amounts to the same thing, they are simply reversible. Hence Collins asks about the implications of accepting historical criticism as a basis for biblical theology.

The crux of the problem lies in the essential irreversibility of certain facts which a biblical theologian accepts as "historical," or real, on the one hand, and on the other hand, the ever open-ended, reversible character that is intrinsic to historical methodology. The issue is not that the Bible or biblical theology *interprets* certain events such as exodus or resurrection as acts of God that are beyond the reach of historical methodology. Theology accepts such interpretation as its business, the meaning of which it has to deal with. Rather, the crux is that the position of biblical theology seems to rule out a priori that any historical evidence can be found that is contrary to the historicity of such events, i.e., that they ever happened. The historicity of a foundational event (e.g., Did Jesus rise from the dead? Did a group of Hebrews come from Egypt into Canaan?) is the main issue. If a faith community cannot tolerate such reversibility, the historical method is not for it. It is not playing according to the rules

---

3. Cf. B. Childs, *Introduction to the Old Testament as Scripture* (Philadelphia: Fortress, 1979).

4. See the various writings mentioned in n. 1 above.

266

elaborated by Troeltsch and others. The role of faith is simply to believe, even when the historical method pulls out its rational underpinning. What, then, is left for biblical theology to do?

After presenting arguments indicating that a critical biblical theology is not possible in the Troeltschian mode, Professor Collins describes his vision of biblical theology:

> The answer evidently depends on the model of theology we are willing to accept. Historical criticism, consistently understood, is not compatible with a confessional theology that is committed to specific doctrines on the basis of faith. It is, however, quite compatible with theology understood as an open-ended and critical inquiry into the meaning and function of God-language. Biblical theology on this model is not a self-sufficient discipline, but is a subdiscipline that has a contribution to make to the broader subject of theology. The main contribution of the biblical theologian is to clarify the genre of the biblical material in the broad sense of the way in which it should be read and the expectations that are appropriate to it.[5]

This view can also be fittingly paired with the following quotation:

> It is my thesis that there is a legitimate enterprise that goes beyond the simple description of what was thought and believed (*à la* Wrede), while stopping short of the "projection of faith into facts" that was characteristic of neoorthodoxy. Theological language is an integral part of the biblical material, and should not be simply bypassed in the interests of secular interpretation. We can only ask that the methods we endorse in historical and literary research be applied consistently also to the theological problems.[6]

I am not sure of the implications of a position that lies between Wrede and neoorthodoxy. Who would want to be caught between those two choices? But I would want to argue that biblical theology is more than a study of God-language or a classification of biblical literary genres. Such studies are preliminary and helpful to biblical theology, but they do not constitute its heart. What, then, is biblical theology, and when is it critical?

Perhaps a neutral statement would be the following: biblical theology is a synthesis of biblical data about God, humans, and the world, according to biblical categories. It proceeds along both a diachronic and synchronic plane, aware of historical development within the Bible and exposing the data accordingly. This definition is basically a simple one that is applicable to the Old Testament alone and to the New Testament alone. It is even pertinent to the combined Testaments, but obviously in this case the assessing of continuities

5. Collins, "Is a Critical Biblical Theology Possible," 14.
6. Ibid., 15.

and discontinuities from a faith perspective would play a principal role. In this paper, our focus is on the Old Testament alone, and on the possibility of a critical Old Testament theology.

The difficult term in the description given above is "synthesis," i.e., the organization or systematization of the material. The history of attempts to write a theology of the Old Testament demonstrates that this can be carried out in many different ways, and with rather inconclusive results. One need merely recall the contrast between the approaches of W. Eichrodt and G. von Rad as an example. Thus far, no fixed synthesis has been agreed upon. I do not mean to deny the utility of the various studies of Old Testament theology that have been published by W. Zimmerli, C. Westermann, and S. Terrien, to name but a few. These approaches are stimulating in themselves, and they illuminate many biblical insights into reality, but they fail to capture a compelling unified theology. Indeed, there is reason to doubt whether any one principle of systematization will ever succeed, or even whether it is desirable. The option of a neat synthesis is the recognition of the pluralism of the Old Testament with its various theologies (e.g., historical systematizations made along the way by the Deuteronomist, or the Chronicler, etc.). It seems better to recognize that the Old Testament provides *many* varied insights into God and reality, and they are not subject to neat conceptual unity. These insights are the richer for their diversity and their resistance to being submerged into a supposed higher unity.

The "unity" of the Bible has long been a topic of investigation. Especially among German theologians the discussion has turned on the identification of the *Mitte,* or center, of the Old Testament. It is worth observing that there is a set of terms that appears in the theorizing about this topic. Writers characterize something as "basic": the basic event or thought or dimension or structure.[7] But the most recent work concerning the unity of the Old Testament wisely prescinds from conceptual unity and views the unity of the Hebrew Bible by analyzing the process of its formation and honoring various trends working in this process.[8] Ultimately, the failure of the search for the "center" is shown by the admission that "God" is the center.[9] This is true, but it is also meaningless as far as a conceptual unity, a *Grundstruktur,* is concerned. God is at the center of everything, but this is not the result of a systematic theological analysis of the Bible.

---

7. For example, there are about five compound nouns using the word "Grund-" in the work of H. D. Preuss, *Theologie des Alten Testaments,* Bd. 1 (Stuttgart: Kohlhammer, 1991), 28: "Grundgeschehen," "Grundhandeln," etc.

8. Cf. D. N. Freedman, *The Unity of the Hebrew Bible* (Ann Arbor: University of Michigan, 1991).

9. Cf. G. F. Hasel, *Old Testament Theology: Basic Issues in the Current Debate,* 4th ed. (Grand Rapids: Eerdmans, 1991), 139-71, esp. 168; also H. G. Reventlow, *Hauptprobleme der alttestamentlichen Theologie im 20. Jahrhundert* (Darmstadt: Wissenschaftliche Buchgesellschaft, 1983); ET, *Problems of Old Testament Theology in the Twentieth Century* (Philadelphia: Fortress, 1986), 125-33, 139-71.

At this point we must return to consider the "critical" aspect most biblical theologians would probably claim for their discipline. The following points should be scored:

1. Historical criticism is not only basically compatible with biblical theology, but indeed indispensable to it. This is not a denial of the many tensions and unanswered questions within the biblical material. But a diachronic aspect is needed in order to avoid a simplistic presentation of data, otherwise a theological construal (say, of the Chronicler's thought) tends to become speculative and abstract, if not downright wrong. Historical criticism will have its own weaknesses, such as a tendency to reconstruction without adequate basis, but this is a risk worth taking in view of a quest for knowledge, and the existence of peers that are ready to correct the mistakes of others. For example, today the early history of Israel is indeed a problem. Was it by military conquest, infiltration, or a peasant revolt that Canaan was taken over? Honest historical investigation has made it impossible to answer this with any certainty. This is better than a shortsighted view that would bypass the historical difficulties with mindless indifference. Historical reconstruction is mutable, but uncertainty is a small price to pay for the scholarly effort to get behind the biblical text, to understand better the biblical sources. The biblical theologian should be unwilling to abandon a methodology that eliminates a simplistic understanding of the exodus or the Sinai events. As regards the New Testament, historical criticism has prevented the blindness that a systematic presentation of the incarnation formula, God-Man, can produce. Emphasis on Christ's divinity can cloud over the limitations of the Jesus who really existed. In the area of Christology the study of the titles of Christ and of the work of Christ has been immensely enriching; a more exact view of what the incarnation meant to the primitive church is made possible. The rigorous use of historical criticism is completely necessary for a biblical theology that is worthy of respect.

2. What is to be said about the Troeltschian principle of reversibility? Is this applicable to the theological investigation of the foundational events such as the exodus or the resurrection of Christ? No, these are the "givens," on which theology is built. They are communicated through the preaching of the community, and developed by biblical theology. They are not events that are recoverable or reversible by means of critical biblical theology. They belong to another area of investigation.

It is the function of foundational theology (or the old-time "apologetics," which does not arouse much enthusiasm) to address the reversibility problem. The historicity of foundational events (which will certainly be small in number) is as it were a distraction to biblical theologians; at least it is certainly not their prime concern. It is possible to admit that certainty about the manner of the exodus, of the development of Israelite monotheism, is not at hand. But this does not mean that critical methodology has shown that there is no historical basis for an exodus from Egypt. The debate on this

issue belongs to the historians, who have to operate according to the principles of their science.

From the point of view of the New Testament, the recent study of John
Meier may be cited.[10] It illustrates historical criticism at work in an area that
has been repeatedly marked by reversibility of results. Meier proceeds to examine with a fine-tooth comb all that can be known about the historical Christ,
prescinding from a faith position. This is not only perfectly legitimate, but
necessary in the search for truth. But it is not biblical theology; it is a basis, an
aid, for enlightened biblical theology.

To summarize, historical criticism functions in two ways at least: (1) its
main contribution is to provide the groundwork or basis for the understanding
of biblical data in history, whether it is the development of Israel's relationship
with the Lord, or the teaching of Jesus as this is reflected in the Gospels and
other New Testament writings. (2) It may create problems of historicity which
are properly beyond the competence of theologians. Thus far, the problems
have not been severe enough to eliminate the theological enterprise.

Pertinent to this discussion is the relationship of the biblical theologian
to a community of faith. Some would claim that a personal stance of faith is
necessary to be a biblical theologian, if he or she is to be considered different
from an historian of religion.[11] This is not to deny empathy with the biblical
material to the historian or "outsider." Scholarly integrity has its proper role,
and if exercised by a person without faith, its findings can be identical with
those of a theologian with faith. On the other hand, without impugning integrity, one can recognize a certain predisposition in a person of faith to accept a
conclusion that is in harmony with his or her broader beliefs.

However, the biblical theologian who operates within a community of
faith may have difficulty in negotiating certain results of historical criticism.
One example would be the authorship of the Pentateuch. (The historicity of
Moses would be a separate problem.) It is clear from the arduous studies of
this century that there are several traditions behind the Pentateuch or Torah,
and that it did not receive its final form until about the exile or thereafter. It
may not be possible to adhere to the neat picture of J, E, D, and P, which has

---

10. J. P. Meier, *A Marginal Jew*, Anchor Bible Reference Library (New York: Doubleday,
1991).

11. Cf. R. de Vaux, "Is it Possible to Write a 'Theology of the Old Testament'?" in *The
Bible and the Ancient Near East* (Garden City: Doubleday, 1971), 49-62, esp. 56-62. The verdict
of B. Vawter is relevant to the question under discussion: "Historical criticism, it seems to
me, can mainly offer interesting suggestions, the value of which should not be minimized;
but it can offer no final solution. And thus we must reluctantly conclude that its findings,
in any positive sense, are usually of far more interest to the biblical scholar in his capacity
as student of Near Eastern culture and religion than as biblical theologian." Cf. B. Vawter,
"History and Kerygma in the Old Testament," in *The Path of Wisdom* (Wilmington: Michael
Glazier, 1986), 89-110; the quotation is from 101-2.

been postulated, but it is certain that the various traditions in the Torah are to be dated in their present form well after the time of Moses. It is impossible, historically, to go beyond this and to ferret out the traditions formed or written in a Mosaic period. This would seem to pose a problem for those whose theological views of the Bible (already fixed in advance by some aspect of faith) would not tolerate this interpretation of the Pentateuch.

It will be helpful for the common study of biblical theology to approach it from the point of view of Jewish scholars. The late M. Goshen-Gottstein recognized the ecumenical reality of historical criticism, which brought scholars from all over the world to study the Old Testament. But he also chided the academic guild for not going forward into theological questions.[12] He remarked that "Old Testament theology has not bothered hitherto to devise a method of inquiry so as to ask questions that might help us detect the structure" (a reference to the "overall structure of primary and secondary issues" within the Bible).[13] But he regarded this enterprise as "a matter of strict scholarly methodology, which should be acceptable without denominational restriction." He found something to praise in the works of W. Eichrodt and G. von Rad, despite the inevitable Christian presuppositions that mark their works. He agreed with their threefold concern: (1) to describe the Bible on its own terms; (2) to be responsible to critical biblical scholarship, thus participating in the ongoing academic enterprise; (3) to interpret from within a community of faith (an inevitable bias for Jew and Christian alike). To this, Jewish scholars must create their own alternative position. Goshen-Gottstein had taught Tanak theology for several years, without yet reaching the presentation at which he aimed. But the hints he gave suggest many challenges to all biblical theologians: the treatment of the law, the land, the sabbath, the *miṣwôt*, not to mention sacrifice, temple, and so forth — subjects that do not loom large in Old Testament theologies written by Christian scholars. Overall, he welcomed historical criticism, but it is also under the guidance of certain presuppositions about the Tanak which are to be frankly indicated. These are the invariable "givens" that are derived from the faith of the interpreter, but which do not vitiate the practice of historical criticism.

Although he has written at least two books that illustrate biblical theology at its best,[14] J. D. Levenson seems to be ambivalent, if not simply opposed, to

12. Cf. M. L. Goshen-Gottstein, "Christianity, Judaism, and Modern Bible Study," in *Congress Volume, Edinburgh, 1974*, VTSup 28 (Leiden: Brill, 1975), 69-88.

13. Cf. his Tanak theology: "The Religion of the Old Testament and the Place of Jewish Biblical Theology," in *Ancient Israelite Religion: Essays in Honor of Frank Moore Cross*, ed. P. Miller et al. (Philadelphia: Fortress, 1987), 617-44; the quotations are from 633, and see also 624-25.

14. *Sinai and Zion: An Entry into the Jewish Bible* (Minneapolis: Winston, 1985); *Creation and the Persistence of Evil: The Jewish Drama of Divine Omnipotence* (San Francisco: Harper and Row, 1988).

any role for historical methodology in biblical theology. He regards historical criticism as inimical to both the Jewish and Christian traditions which honor the literature as Scripture. The historical context and the literary (or canonical) context are irreconcilables which simply cannot be made to agree: "the price of recovering the historical context of sacred books has been the loss of the literary contexts that undergird the traditions that claim to be based upon them."[15] In another study quite germane to the topic of this paper he denies the validity of biblical theology, at least as it has been practiced by W. Eichrodt, G. von Rad, and others (whose presuppositions about the New Testament inevitably distort their treatment of the Old). Such theology can be *only* historical, but neither Jewish nor Christian: "the 'personal stance' of a faithful contemporary Jew does not allow for the isolation of the Jewish Bible *(Tanakh)* from the larger tradition. Such an isolation is possible on historical grounds, but not on personal, existential grounds."[16] If I understand Levenson correctly, he is unwilling to allow biblical theology to stand alone, separate from the total theological stance of the interpreters. In other words, he does the same kind of thing in the Judaic tradition that a Christian who draws on sources apart from the Bible does in a "systematic" theology. Such a position seems to characterize his view of the Mosaic authorship of the Pentateuch. He maintains that "although in historicocritical [sic] discourse, the notion of Mosaic authorship of the Pentateuch is indefensible, the underlying ideas of the unity and divinity of the Torah must remain relevant considerations for Jewish theologians. . . ."[17] He employs the eighth principle of Maimonides (to the effect that the Torah is from heaven rather than from Sinai) to affirm the unity and divinity of the Torah. "The corollary is that the faithful Jew may now conduct historical inquiry freely, without the need to allow old dogmatic formulations to predetermine the results. In short, historical research poses no threat to the religious life so long as it restricts itself to the reconstruction of the past and avoids prescription of present practice."

But this problem is precisely the kind of difficulty posed by Prof. Collins for biblical theology. Can one simply set aside the assured results of historical criticism as having no effect on one's theological understanding of the Bible? Levenson cannot agree with N. Sarna's attempt to interpret the Torah in the light of modern historical criticism. He finds that modern efforts simply decompose the unity of the Bible, and thus undo the "simultaneity" or holistic un-

15. Cf. Levenson, "The Hebrew Bible, The Old Testament, and Historical Criticism," in *The Future of Biblical Studies,* ed. R. Friedman and H. G. M. Williamson (Atlanta: Scholars, 1987), 19-59; the quotation is from 22.

16. Cf. Levenson, "Why Jews Are Not Interested in Biblical Theology," in *Judaic Perspectives on Ancient Israel,* ed. J. Neusner et al. (Philadelphia: Fortress, 1987), 281-307; the quotation is from 285.

17. Cf. Levenson, "The Eighth Principle of Judaism and the Literary Simultaneity of Scripture," *JR* 68 (1988): 205-25; the quotations are from 208 and 219.

derstanding of Scripture. It appears that he cannot admit the time-conditioned character of Scripture, and he favors a synchronic approach over the diachronic. The result is that on the one hand he grants the insights of historical criticism into the Torah, but on the other, these cannot be applied to, or utilized in, interpreting the Torah for modern life. "For to Maimonides and his Tannaitic sources, the doctrine that the Torah is from heaven requires that equal divine status be accorded every verse. . . . For the observant Jew, this is not an abstract point of theology." But here is the rub: can "literary simultaneity" override the valid conclusions drawn by historical methodology? Is a theological conclusion that is *contradictory* to the available historical context of either Testament a valid conclusion? What measure of revision is possible?

It is also possible that biblical interpreters fail to acknowledge that the Bible does contain divine words in the clothing of human words, that there are limitations to the way in which the divine mystery is to be found in the human-ness of biblical expression. This aspect of the Bible is something that Christian fundamentalists and many enthusiastic supporters of *sola scriptura* are unwilling to grant. The biblical understanding of YHWH as a warrior god is a case in point.[18] The valiant efforts to salvage this biblical datum with its theological implications have hardly met with success within biblical theology. Perhaps the only solution is to recognize it as a time-conditioned quality of the Word, and not viable theologically. This does not deny that Israel understood YHWH as warrior god, but it does question its validity for theology today. Is it any more viable than Israel's belief in Sheol?

In the discussion of biblical theology, many issues come to be passed over, or fall between the cracks. One of them is the distinction between *Weltan-schauung* and theology. To what extent are they separable in the Old Testament? Several examples can be given. Is the "heavenly court" concept (e.g., Job 1–2) properly theology? Or is it on a par with the various elements of the *Chaoskampf,* the mythical backdrop to creation/salvation themes in the Bible? Is the deed/consequence theory *(Tat-Ergehen Zusammenhang)* so ardently espoused by K. Koch and H. D. Preuss merely a part of the ancient Near Eastern world-view, or does it have theological import?[19] Are theological concepts such as omniscience applicable in Old Testament theology in view of the portrayal of

18. Cf. N. Lohfink's discussion, "Der 'heilige Krieg' und der 'Bann' in der Bibel," *Internationale katholische Zeitschrift* 18,2 (1989): 104-12, also translated into English in *TD* 38,2 (1991): 109-14. Ultimately Lohfink recognizes that this image of God in the Old Testa-ment is ambivalent, but is not simply to be explained away.

19. K. Koch, "Gibt es ein Vergeltungsdogma im Alten Testament?" *ZTK* 52 (1955): 1-42; H. D. Preuss, *Einführung in die alttestamentliche Weisheitsliteratur* (Stuttgart: Kohlham-mer, 1987). Perhaps the real question is this: was there a time-conditioned theory that existed along with the view of direct divine agency (Isa 45:7)?; cf. R. E. Murphy, *The Tree of Life: An Exploration of Biblical Wisdom Literature,* Anchor Bible Reference Library (New York: Dou-bleday, 1990), 116-17.

YHWH and Satan in Job 1–2.[20] How is the apparent changeability of God to be reconciled with the traditional understanding of the unchanging God of later tradition? To what extent is apocalyptic expressed in a key all its own, but from which theological substance can be drawn? Should not a critical biblical theology, given its possibility, answer these questions?

20. Cf. D. N. Freedman, "The Book of Job," in *The Hebrew Bible and Its Interpreters,* 33-51.

Problems in a Theology of (Only) the Old Testament

WOLFHART PANNENBERG

The task of a theology of the Old Testament may be the most difficult one that arises within the field of biblical exegesis. In his article of 1984 on this subject, Rolf Knierim questioned the various ways this task had been dealt with until now. He emphasized the pluralism of theologies within the Old Testament canon, and he raised doubts about the usefulness of many of the notions that have been proposed to conceptualize the basic theme that the different theologies in the biblical writings have in common, but he also questioned the use of tradition history as a clue to the unity of the Old Testament, because it rather seems to be responsible for the emergence of an ever richer plurality of theologies in the biblical literature.

In examining the foundations of that discipline, one should also pay attention to its origins in the history of modern theology. The existence of a discipline such as Old Testament theology cannot or should not be taken for granted. Its establishment was rather recent, and there were peculiar reasons behind it.

The demand for a "biblical" theology arose in the eighteenth century. It was intended as an alternative to the Protestant dogmatics of that time and was nourished by the new emphasis of pietism on the Scriptures as the norm and basis of Protestant theology. But as early as with J. A. Ernesti (1761) the historical character of biblical theology was also emphasized, and that led to the distinction between a biblical theology of the New Testament and that of the Old.[1] The separate treatment of the two biblical theologies was postulated by J. S. Semler since 1771 and was subsequently established on the assumption

---

1. See the treatment of this development in my book, *Theology and the Philosophy of Science* (Philadelphia: Westminster, 1976), 355ff., 371ff., and 381ff.

that the New Testament is the document of a different religion than the Old Testament.[2] This assumption, of course, contradicted the traditional Christian use of the Law and the Prophets as prophetic witnesses to the advent of Jesus Christ. The separation of New Testament theology from Old Testament theology by reason of the argument that the Old Testament belongs to a different religion, i.e., Judaism, may appear as awkward today. But nevertheless it underlies the separate treatment of the two biblical theologies to the present day. When this fact is pondered, one understands why in recent decades not a few biblical exegetes, including Hartmut Gese of Tübingen, have demanded a renewed "biblical" theology comprising the theologies of both Testaments.

If one does not want to accept that option, some argument is needed. An obvious reason could be that the documents of Jewish faith in the God of Israel should first be treated and interpreted in their own right lest specifically Christian concerns and assumptions are prematurely (and in unhistorical fashion) read into the Old Testament writings. But then, why stop at the limits of the Old Testament canon, and why choose the rabbinic canon rather than the Alexandrian for limiting the number of writings to which a theology of the Old Testament is related? Why not include the wisdom literature and apocalyptic writings until the end of the first century, i.e., until the watershed of Titus's conquest of Jerusalem and the temple? Why not also include, then, the message of Jesus as a Jewish phenomenon? It seems hard to imagine a purely historical reason for limiting the literary basis of theological reflection and presentation to the rabbinic canon of the biblical writings. One might respond: "We take the Old Testament in the form in which it was handed down by tradition." But how — short of inspiration[3] — can one justify this on grounds of historical judgment?

Within the framework of Christian theology it is possible to imagine a theological reason for treating the Old Testament — even within the limits of the rabbinic canon — independently with regard to its theology: that could be done precisely for the reason of checking the claim of Jesus' proclamation to be faithful to the God of the Jewish tradition as expressed in the Hebrew Bible. This claim was at the heart of the controversies that Jesus' proclamation and activity provoked, and in order to judge the correctness of that claim there is required a treatment of the canonic Jewish writings taken as a unified entity concerning their theological witness. Such a rationale for a theology of the Old Testament would have its basis, however, in a specifically Christian concern. Would that not entail that the resulting way of looking at the Old Testament writings would also be colored from the outset by a Christian point

---

2. Ibid., 383.

3. In this connection I do not want to put too much weight upon Knierim's remark: "We all affirm that the entire Old Testament is revealed, word of God, inspired" (*HBT* 6,1 [1984]: 33). Quotations from this article will henceforth be given in the text by page numbers.

of view? Even if distorting the historical meaning of what the biblical writings have to tell by themselves is avoided, the identification of the basic theme they supposedly have in common might still be determined by a Christian point of view.

I wonder whether this is not the case in the proposal of Rolf Knierim. After having rejected — among other options — the possibility of considering "the notion of Yahweh's oneness and exclusivity" as a unifying basis of the Old Testament's theology, because this notion "does not explain the nature of Yahwehism's pluralism" (31), Knierim proposes to take "the most universal extent of Yahweh's dominion" to represent "the most fundamental criterion and, hence, the most fundamental priority" (42). Knierim argues quite persuasively for the basic importance of Israel's God being "first of all God of all reality and of all humanity: without the critical notion of universality, the affirmation of Yahweh's oneness and exclusivity does not substantiate the affirmation of his true deity" (42). In my judgment, this is a fully convincing statement. But I cannot help asking myself whether in the course of Israel's history such a statement was always possible, or whether it is related to a particular point in the course of that history. It seems hardly possible to imagine it in the early development of that history, before David, and even in the course of the following centuries the universal and exclusive claim of Yahweh seems to have been in dispute. Not before Second Isaiah was it proclaimed that Yahweh is not only demanding to be worshiped exclusively by his people, but that he also exists as the one and only God, other gods being mere products of human imagination and art. With Second Isaiah as well as with certain psalms of that period and with the priestly report of creation, it is certainly true that Yahweh is "Israel's God because he is first of all God of all reality and of all humanity" (42). But was that always clear before? There are traces in the Old Testament traditions that though Yahweh was considered the only God of Israel, it was also assumed that there existed other gods beside him. His identity with the creator of heaven and earth has been considered as a consequence — a disputed consequence for a long time — of his claim to exclusive worship rather than the other way round.

Now Second Isaiah certainly emerges as a figure of major importance, when one looks back from the New Testament to the history of prophetic traditions. Jesus could argue from belief in the creator God as if that — and not the covenant with the people of Israel — was the overriding concern in Jewish faith in God. Such a way of proclaiming God could hardly have been possible in Judaism without Second Isaiah. The same is true with the subordination of the issues of law, justice, and righteousness — essential as they have been in all forms of Jewish spirituality — to the cosmological concern for Yahweh as creator of the world. Jesus' proclamation of God's kingdom to come certainly differed from Second Isaiah in its eschatological color and setting. Nevertheless, there is such a strong link that it could be said that reading the entire Old Testament from the perspective of Second Isaiah's conception of God the creator is tantamount to producing a Christian reading of it.

However, does not precisely at this point the pluralism of theological conceptions within the chorus of Old Testament writings disturbingly get in our way? It is not clear, then, how the universality of Yahweh's dominion could explain "the nature of Yahwehism's pluralism" (31). If the conception of that universal dominion is only developing in the preexilic history of Israel and fully emerges in Second Isaiah, are we not back to tradition history as the "holistic process" (26), where all the different conceptions are related to each other? Undoubtedly, Rolf Knierim is right that the tradition process as such does not provide a substantive unity. It is too formal a category, after all. We would still have a tradition history, where as a result of that process the substantial content of the tradition is beginning to break apart or disappear in the plurality of interpretations and adaptations. But on the other hand, there is no substantial issue exempt from historical change and pluralization. That applies even to Israel's idea of God and of his dominion. Nevertheless, it has to be admitted that the issue of Yahweh's dominion was a driving motive, perhaps even *the* driving motive in the course of that tradition history, a motive producing the plurality of theologies in the Old Testament writings as well as a trajectory that unifies them all. In this sense, then, one may accept Knierim's argument that an examination of the pluralism of theologies within the Old Testament "must focus on the substantive issues addressed" in those theologies "rather than on that tradition history or the canon as the substantive issue" (28). One may also agree with his contention that Yahweh's universal dominion is the most fundamental issue to be considered here: not in the sense of a conception to be found everywhere in the Old Testament writings, but rather as a motive developing in the tradition history of ancient Israel and even forming the driving force in its process. The tradition-historical outlook and the quest for God's dominion as providing the driving motive in the process of that history may be considered correlative principles in accounting for the structure and content of that particular tradition history and for the theological content of the Old Testament writings. The nature of this driving motive was variously articulated along the way and perhaps came to definitive expression first in Second Isaiah's proclamation of Israel's God being the only true God, finally perhaps in Jesus' proclamation of the dawning kingdom of God as the one concern that demands priority over everything else. But in the beginnings of Israel's religious history this issue seems to have been only implicit in the exclusivism of Yahweh's zealous claim for undivided devotion and worship.

If Knierim's project can be rephrased in such a way, I strongly concur with his claim that the concern for this issue is identical with the concern for the true deity of Israel's God and thus explains the various forms of witnessing to his unique divinity over against the competing claims of other gods. In this way, then, the applicability of this type of theological interpretation to other ancient

Near Eastern religions (50) and their tradition history is also plausible. For in each process of religious tradition the adherents of a particular god (or of a particular system of gods) have to argue for the truly divine reality of the god or gods they worship. In the course of their histories, there may be periods when within a given religious culture the claims of their gods are virtually beyond dispute. But there will always be other periods when those claims are challenged by competing gods either within a religious culture or from the outside, in situations of cultural encounter. In these cases changes in religious conceptions as well as in cultic institutions and rituals will always occur in order to meet those challenges and to extend, if possible, the "competence" of a given god in demonstrating himself (or herself) master of the segment of reality to which he or she is related.[4] The case of Israel's God, then, is a special one in that he claims universal competence and exclusive attention in worship. But this case is by no means without analogies.

Furthermore, the fact that the special character of the biblical God took shape in the course of Israel's tradition history — culminating in Second Isaiah or, even later, in Jesus' proclamation of the kingdom of the Father — and did not enter the scene of that history in its beginning in fully accomplished form, this fact is in need of being dealt with itself in theological terms, in terms of a divine economy or design. It cannot be merely extrinsic to the issue of God's universal dominion that his deity has become apparent not before a certain point in history. It is at this point that the idea of revelation is inescapable in theological discourse and will presumably prove so even in a theological inter-pretation of Israel's religious history and of the documents arising from it.

In his article on the task of Old Testament theology, Knierim rejected the idea that categories like word of God, revelation, etc., could provide a basis for solving the theological problem of the Old Testament (47). In a certain sense, I think he is right in this. The reality of the biblical God cannot be secured a priori by using one of these categories. Rather, one has to let oneself be involved in the struggle of the biblical authors themselves in arguing for the divine majesty of the God of Israel. But then, the idea of "Yahweh's universal dominion in justice and righteousness" (46) cannot be taken for granted either. Taken in itself, that idea is no more than a claim. To treat it theologically, however, means to consider it as real — not just a human idea, but divine reality. How does the theologian of the Old Testament get to advocate the reality of the God to whom that claim refers? It is not enough to declare that to be a presupposition of the whole enterprise, for that was precisely the function of the traditional use of categories like revelation, inspiration, word of God. Rather, if in the argument

---

4. This idea of accounting for the changes in religious history in a strictly theological way has been developed and recommended in several of my writings, notably in *Theology and the Philosophy of Science*, 300, 310ff., 364ff., and, more recently, in my *Systematic Theology*, vol. 1 (Grand Rapids: Eerdmans, 1991), 151-71.

of the Old Testament writings themselves the divine reality of Yahweh is at stake, the issue cannot be considered settled from the outset. And precisely its not being settled could account for the pluralism of theological conceptions. When we ask: "How do we know about Yahweh's universal dominion in justice and righteousness as a reality?" the category of revelation (indicating that this is God's own doing) seems inevitable. But such revelation does not occur in the beginning. Revelatory experiences seem to have had a more or less provisional character in Israel's history rather than settling once and for all the question of Yahweh's divine reality. On the other hand, revelation in the sense of a definitive decision of that issue seems to have become increasingly a matter of the eschatological future — be it in the sense of some immediate future or of a more distant one.[5]

A theology of the Old Testament need not and should not be done on a confessional basis. Its arguments should proceed according to standards of unprejudiced scholarship. Nevertheless, a confessional perspective may be unavoidable and become evident in the resulting picture. According to the unsettled dispute between Jewish and Christian ways of using and interpreting these writings, different emphases are to be expected to emerge in questions like whether the universal kingdom of God is to be considered an implication or extension of his covenant with Israel, or, as in the case of Knierim's proposal, the other way round. But the theology of the Old Testament may also function as a basis for promoting dialogue between Jews and Christians, because contrary to a widespread opinion it is not in the first place the person of Jesus, but the way he proclaimed the God of the Old Testament that is at stake in the continuing dispute between Christians and Jews.

---

5. See my treatment of the issue of revelation in my *Systematic Theology*, vol. 1, 198-214, but also Jörg Jeremias's book on the kingdom of God in the Psalms (*Das Königtum Gottes in den Psalmen: Israels Begegnung mit dem kanaanäischen Mythos in den Jahwe-König-Psalmen*, FRLANT 141 [Göttingen: Vandenhoeck & Ruprecht, 1987]).

Meat Eating and the Hebrew Bible

STEPHEN A. REED

Individuals and groups advocating "animal liberation" and "animal rights" have become increasingly vocal and active in the last decades of the twentieth century. One advocate for animal rights, Andrew Linzey, states that "Whatever else animal rights means it cannot mean that we can go on consuming their flesh, destroying their habitats, wearing their dead skins and inflicting suffering."[1] Animal rights activists have been presenting a critique of many people in their societies whom they claim are treating animals inhumanely.[2] Such claims should be taken seriously and addressed.[3]

The above quotation suggests that philosophical views about the nature of animals and about the relationship between humans and animals have ethical implications. If indeed animals have rights, then they ought to be treated in certain ways and not in others. In an analogous way one can argue that theological views about the nature of animals and about the relationship between humans and animals have ethical implications as well.

It is worthwhile to study biblical views related to animals first of all because the Bible has greatly shaped the thinking of many people in the modern world

1. Andrew Linzey, "Do Animals Have Rights?" *Christian Century,* October 9, 1991, 909.
2. Three prominent works favoring this movement are Peter Singer, *Animal Liberation: Towards an End to Man's Inhumanity to Animals* (London: Jonathon Cape, 1976); Stephen R. L. Clark, *The Moral Status of Animals* (Oxford: Clarendon Press, 1977); Tom Regan, *The Case for Animal Rights* (London: Routledge and Kegan Paul, 1984).
3. Keith Tester presents a sociological analysis of the animal rights movement in England in *Animals and Society: The Humanity of Animal Rights* (London and New York: Routledge, 1991). Lisa Mighetto presents a history of American attitudes toward wildlife during the last century in *Wild Animals and American Environmental Ethics* (Tucson: University of Arizona Press, 1991).

and secondly because many people still find the Bible useful in reflecting about how they should act in today's world.[4]

One could investigate a number of issues related to the relationship of animals and humans in the Bible. First, one could analyze the everyday realities of animal husbandry in ancient Israel.[5] Second, one could consider the various ways in which language regarding animals is used symbolically by the Israelites.[6] Third, one could analyze Israelite views concerning animals and their relationship to humans.

Ethical statements concerning how humans should treat animals are not directly addressed in the Bible. Many of the environmental concerns of today were not problems during biblical times. Still, an analysis of the everyday relationship of humans and animals, the symbolic usage of language regarding animals, and theological reflections upon the nature of animals and their relationship to humans can provide a framework for making ethical proposals.

In this paper one particular topic related to this issue will be briefly discussed: humans eating the flesh of animals. There are a number of themes and texts in the Bible which might provide guidance concerning whether humans should eat the meat of animals.

Rolf Knierim has provided a framework for analyzing, organizing, and critiquing the diverse messages found within the Bible which pertain to an issue like the human treatment of animals.[7] The proposed method helps one account for and explain the diversity present within the Bible.

Theology deals with the relationship between Yahweh or God and various modes of reality. One of these modes is God's relationship to the food supply of life forms. This includes provision for the sustenance of life for all members of the plant and animal kingdom. Texts can be found in the Hebrew Bible which refer to God's provision of food for each of the three basic realms which Knierim has suggested for the divine activity: nature, human communities, and individuals.[8] Texts related to God's provision of food for all would encompass all three of these realms.

This paper will survey the texts in the Hebrew Bible which indicate the

4. Theological/religious views concerning the treatment of animals can be found in Wesley Granberg-Michaelson, ed., *Tending the Garden: Essays on the Gospel and the Earth* (Grand Rapids: Eerdmans, 1987); Charles Birch, William Eakin, and Jay B. McDaniel, eds., *Liberating Life: Contemporary Approaches to Ecological Theology* (Maryknoll: Orbis, 1990); Lewis G. Regenstein, *Replenish the Earth: A History of Organized Religion's Treatment of Animals and Nature — Including the Bible's Message of Conservation and Kindness toward Animals* (New York: Crossroad, 1991).

5. F. S. Bodenheimer, *Animals and Man in Bible Lands* (Leiden: Brill, 1960).

6. See Howard Eilberg-Schwartz, *The Savage in Judaism: An Anthropology of Israelite Religion and Ancient Judaism* (Bloomington and Indianapolis: Indiana University Press, 1990).

7. Rolf Knierim, "The Task of Old Testament Theology," *HBT* 6,1 (1984): 25-57.

8. Ibid., 38-39.

relationship between God and the food supply of life forms.[9] In the first section the similarities among humans and animals concerning the food supply will be examined. In the second section an examination of conflicting views related to the food supply will be addressed. Finally, ethical implications concerning whether and how humans should treat animals as food will be discussed.[10]

I. Similarities among Humans and Animals concerning Food Supply

A. Shared Experience of Need to Eat

Eating and drinking are essential activities of living creatures which are necessary to meet the needs of hunger and thirst. After living beings eat and drink, the desired result is being filled and satisfied. This basic hunger/thirst cycle must be repeated over and over throughout the lifetime of living beings. This cycle helps to define the nature of living beings. Living creatures become hungry and thirsty, they seek food and drink, they eat and drink, and they experience satisfaction.[11]

Many of the terms related to eating, drinking, and satisfaction are used for both animal and human alike. Animals, like humans, participate in the hunger/thirst cycle.[12]

B. Shared Experience of Food Shortages

Having enough food and drink is not guaranteed. Animals need to seek out their food and drink. Humans devote a great deal of time to the production, distribution, preparation, and consumption of food.

The dependency upon the divine provision of food was not usually construed like the dependency of a baby at its mother's breast. Normally, human

9. In my dissertation "Food in the Psalms" (Dissertation, Claremont Graduate School, 1986), I treated in detail many more aspects related to food in the book of the Psalms. Reflections in this paper arise in part from this work.

10. Strictly speaking this is not part of theology but of ethics. Knierim does not state how he perceives the relationship between theology and ethics. Possibly ethics falls under the discipline of hermeneutics. It would be useful to have a separate article on "The Task of Old Testament Ethics" which would also discuss the relationship between theology and ethics.

11. Reed, "Food in the Psalms," 495.

12. Ibid., 225. For animals see: Pss 34:11 (Eng. 34:10); 59:16 (Eng. 59:15); 78:45; 80:14 (Eng. 80:13); 104:11; 105:35. For all living creatures see: Pss 104:27-28; 145:15-16. Some of these references of animals eating are used metaphorically.

beings have to labor for their food from the ground, and animals have to seek out and find food. Since fruitful land, human and animal fertility, and productive labor were considered to be the result of divine blessing, Yahweh was involved with the production of food.

Times of famine, when sufficient food was not available, were all too frequent for a variety of reasons in Israel/Palestine. Scott states:

> Since rainfall in Palestine is marginal and irregular, crop failure through drought (Hag 1:10-11), blight, or locusts (Amos 4:9); loss of cattle and herds (1 Kings 18:5); and the ravaging of the land in warfare (Isa 1:7; 3:1, 7) quickly led to starvation.[13]

Since food resources were limited, this led to competition for these resources. While there is competition between various animal groups, considerable attention in the Hebrew Bible is given to competition between humans. Numerous texts in the Hebrew Bible indicate that some have control of the food resources and are well fed while others do not have control of the food resources and are hungry. There is competition between societies as well as within societies for these resources.

C. Shared Experience of Divine Dependence

Some texts indicate that God provides food for all living creatures (Pss 104:27; 136:25; 145:15, 16). In other texts all animals are fed (Ps 147:9), and drink is given to wild animals (Ps 104:11). Reference is made to the feeding of particular animals such as the lion (Job 38:39; Ps 104:21) and birds such as the young ravens (Job 38:41; Ps 147:9). There are also texts which indicate that God waters vegetation and causes it to grow (Ps 104:13-14).

In the Genesis creation stories God provides food for living creatures. In Psalms 104, 145, and 147 sustenance is related to Yahweh's creative activity and is viewed as his continuing activity carried out on behalf of his creatures. Yahweh's provision of food is based upon his initial creation of a world which can supply food and his continuing control of this world in order that it will continue to supply food. In Psalms 104 and 145 Yahweh's creative and sustaining activities are perceived as divine acts of kingship.[14]

Every creature is dependent upon Yahweh's continual sustenance. Non-speaking creatures, which cannot express words of request or thanks, exemplify the kind of trust which humans ought to have. All creatures look to Yahweh for food (Pss 104:27; 145:15). The young ravens call to Yahweh for food (Ps 147:9).

13. R. B. Y. Scott, "Famine," *IDB*, 241.
14. Reed, 459-60.

The lions seek food from God (Ps 104:21). The beasts of the field pant for God (Joel 1:20). It would seem that beasts would be panting for water and not for God. Here, however, they are personified as looking to God in order that he will provide water. Joel indicates that he along with the animals is crying out to God for relief during an intense drought. These texts show how creatures recognize their dependence upon Yahweh for their food.

II. Conflicting Views Related to the Food Supply

A. Universal Statements Have Exceptions

Sometimes the food of one creature encompasses taking the life of another. Animals and humans live from the life of vegetation. Carnivores live by eating other animals. The lives of individual plants and animals are sacrificed on behalf of the continued life of other life forms. How can one understand the apparent contradiction between the universal provision of food for all and the provision of food for some which means the loss of life for others?

Vegetation is granted to humans and animals as food according to Gen 1:29-30. Adam is given permission to eat from every tree of the garden except the tree of the knowledge of good and evil in Gen 2:16-17. Eating vegetation or fruit of vegetation would not necessarily imply the death of vegetation, but it might.

Carnivores must eat meat to live, which means that other life forms must die. Reference to God's giving food to the lions (Job 38:39-40; Ps 104:21) implies that this is ordained by God.

Humans are omnivores who can eat vegetation and meat but can live as vegetarians. Many humans, however, prefer meat when they have the opportunity. Marvin Harris, in a chapter entitled "Meat Hunger," indicates how prevalent hunger for meat is among humans and shows that meat is nutritionally very important for the human diet.[15] He notes that "animal foods contain essential proteins, minerals, and vitamins in concentrated form."[16] While it is sometimes possible to substitute plant foods for such essentials, this can be quite costly, particularly when one considers the implications of doing this globally. Human hunger for meat, however, goes beyond dietary needs, as Nick Fiddes points out.[17]

On what basis are some animals justified in taking the lives of other

15. Marvin Harris, *Good to Eat: Riddles of Food and Culture* (New York: Simon and Schuster, 1985), 19-46.

16. Ibid., 45.

17. Nick Fiddes, *Meat: A Natural Symbol* (London and New York: Routledge, 1991).

animals and thus depriving them of the right to eat and live? Human experience shows that some are fed and some are not. Ps 104:27-30 is aware of this and offers no reason for Yahweh's selective treatment of living beings. Some he chooses to feed and let live, and some he chooses not to feed and let die. He chooses some to be fed and some to be food. Norman Habel indicates concerning Job 38:1–40:5 that "In a world where paradox and incongruity are integral to its design, there is no simplistic answer to the problem of innocent suffering. The baby eagle survives because another young creature dies."[18]

God's universal provision of food seems to be relativized by the fact that the lives of individual humans are valued more highly than the lives of individual plants and animals, the lives of individual animals are valued more highly than the lives of individual plants, and the lives of some animals are valued more highly than others. Even in the context of a creation hymn like Psalm 104, which speaks of a universal provision of food for all, there is mention of the lion being fed (v. 21), which means that some creature loses its life. This reflects what is known about the food chain. Members higher up on the chain eat members below them.

Humans are particularly interested in food for themselves and for their domestic animals. There is conflict between animals and humans for food even if animals are not eaten. The practice of agriculture competes with animals for food. Animals are displaced from lands where they graze so that farmers can plant crops. Animals are kept out of planted fields. Farmers protect their livestock from predators.

B. Ideal-Real; Urzeit, Present, Endzeit; Regulated Life–Unregulated Life

1. Reality of Treatment of Animals in Israel

Agriculture in Israel shared the three classical Mediterranean components which had been established by the third millennium: "grain farming, horticulture and sheep-goat pastoralism."[19] Hunting and gathering sometimes supplemented these agricultural methods. Meat was an important part of the diet of the Israelites. Many texts of the Hebrew Bible refer to the eating of meat by humans, and there is no indication that there is anything wrong with such behavior. Meat was too expensive for most people to eat regularly but was reserved for special feasts. Animal fat was valued very highly, and linguistic terminology was used metaphorically for abundance and fertility (Pss 63:6 [Eng. 63:5]; 36:9 [Eng.

18. Norman Habel, *The Book of Job: A Commentary*, OTL (Philadelphia: Westminster, 1981), 534.

19. Lawrence Stager, *IDBSup*, "Agriculture," 13.

36:8]; 65:12 [Eng. 65:11]; Job 36:16). Meat was eaten at festivals (1 Kgs 1:25) as well as at special times of hospitality (Gen 18:8).

Numerous texts in the Hebrew Bible refer to this basic agricultural economy of Israel and raise no questions of the rightness or wrongness of it. In such a society vegetarianism would be quite unexpected. Daniel's refusal to eat meat in the court of a foreign king (Dan 1:8-17) was not because he considered eating meat generally unethical.

2. Urzeit *and* Endzeit

Ideals for human behavior are sometimes indicated in statements concerning creation *(Urzeit)* and statements about the eschatological future *(Endzeit)*. Often depictions of the *Urzeit* and *Endzeit* bear a resemblance to one another.

According to the Priestly source humans were given permission to eat vegetation at creation (Gen 1:29-30), while permission to eat meat was only granted after the flood (Gen 9:2-3).[20] In Psalm 104 and perhaps Psalm 8 the nature of human food is probably vegetarian.

A number of scholars have argued that according to the priestly view the granting of meat to humans was a concession to their weak nature.[21] Edwin Firmage points out, however, that one might argue that "by being allowed to eat meat humans were thought to have been granted access to what had previously been God's exclusive reserve. . . ."[22] He also notes that along with the permission to eat animals, animals now fear humans. The relationship between animals and humans has changed from creation. He further comments that

> There is indeed something awe-inspiring in the act of eating animal flesh, for in doing so man takes life — a right that God jealously guards. Man's diet therefore comes to resemble God's at the same time that he is given a measure of divine power in the right to take animal life with impunity.[23]

Nick Fiddes in his analysis of the symbolism of meat argues that eating meat "tangibly represents human control of the natural world. Consuming the muscle flesh of other highly evolved animals is a potent statement of our supreme power."[24]

In the future promised in the prophets there will be harmony among creatures so that even carnivores like lions will not eat meat. Indeed, the bear

---

20. Claus Westermann, *Genesis 1–11: A Commentary* (Minneapolis: Augsburg, 1984), 159, 462-63.

21. See appendix 5 of E. Firmage, "The Biblical Dietary Laws and the Concept of Holiness," in *Studies in the Pentateuch,* ed. J. A. Emerton (Leiden: Brill, 1990), 203-4.

22. Ibid., 196.

23. Ibid., 196-97.

24. Fiddes, 2.

will graze with the cow, and the lion will eat straw like the ox (Isa 11:7). This is a depiction of the world at peace. Competition for food would be eliminated.

While wild animals are frequently used metaphorically in the Hebrew Bible for the enemies of Israel,[25] wild animals were a real threat at least to children as well as livestock. Some narrative texts indicate that animals were a threat to domestic animals as well as humans (1 Sam 17:34-37; 2 Kgs 17:25-26). Wild animals might also devour crops.

Depictions of cursed life often included the presence of wild animals — "I will let loose wild animals against you, and they shall bereave you of your children and destroy your livestock; they shall make you few in number, and your roads shall be deserted" (Lev 26:22 NRSV) — and depictions of the blessed life included safety from such animals (Lev 26:6). In prophetic literature depictions of disaster included the presence of wild animals (Jer 15:3; Ezek 5:17; 14:21; 33:27; Hos 2:14 [Eng. 2:12]; Deut 32:24) and mention of humans becoming prey to scavengers (Deut 28:26; Isa 18:6).

Depictions of future salvation include a covenant between humans and life forms which will lead to peace.[26] Wild animals will no longer threaten people (Hos 2:20 [Eng. 2:18]). As a result of the coming of the royal messiah in Isaiah 11, there will be peace and tranquillity among natural enemies. Predator and prey will live peacefully together. Small children will be safe from wild animals. "They will not hurt or destroy on all my holy mountain" (Isa 11:9 NRSV).

In some eschatological depictions meat is still a part of the human diet. In Ezekiel 47 after the life-giving stream flows out of the temple into the Dead Sea, fish will serve as food. The eschatological feast Yahweh will prepare for the nations on Mount Zion includes wine and the fat of animals (Isa 25:6). Jesus' parable of the wedding feast also involves the slaughtering of animals (Matt 22:1-14).

Depictions of the future remain quite anthropocentric. While there is a concern that humans be safe from other predators, it is not clear that other animals will be safe from humans. However, the covenant made between the humans and other creatures in Hos 2:20 (Eng. 2:18) may imply that even humans will no longer kill animals.

A further question related to passages of the eschatological future is whether they are meant to be ideals for which humans should strive or whether they are meant to be implemented by God. While humans can choose to be vegetarians, carnivores cannot. Unless carnivores are killed, domesticated, or placed in zoos, it is unlikely that such a world can be implemented by humans.

---

25. Othmar Keel, *The Symbolism of the Biblical World: Ancient Near Eastern Iconography and the Book of the Psalms* (New York: Seabury, 1978), 78-109.

26. See Donald E. Gowan, *Eschatology in the Old Testament* (Philadelphia: Fortress, 1986).

A world which refuses to allow carnivores to eat meat deprives carnivores of their right to live according to their nature.

3. Regulated Life–Unregulated Life

Many passages in the Hebrew Bible make no mention of any regulations placed upon humans about what kinds of foods they should eat. Certainly, as we shall see, in the priestly material a fairly elaborate dietary system is developed. It is not clear, however, how old such a system actually was and how widely it was actually practiced.

According to the biblical story the very first prohibition given to humans by God in the Bible was the prohibition of eating from the tree of the knowledge of good and evil (Gen 2:17). While this action may be interpreted symbolically as a limitation imposed upon humans by the deity, it is not incidental that the prohibition refers to the basic and mundane activity of eating. It is also important that this prohibition is found in the Yahwist source, which is understood by many scholars to be the oldest source of the Pentateuch. Its presence also indicates that it was not only the priests who were interested in the eating habits of people.

Many societies have certain food preferences and avoidances. There are many reasons why people eat some foods and abstain from others. Jean Bottéro states: "The choices of foods and their preparation have always been dependent on each society's natural resources, economy, and the likes and dislikes of its members."[27] The wealthier members of a society generally have more choices than the poor.

Marvin Harris argues that material factors are most decisive for shaping eating practices. Religious or ideological perceptions function to solidify and reinforce reasonable cultural practices: "religions gain strength when they help people make decisions which are in accord with preexisting useful practices, but which are not so completely self-evident as to exclude doubts and temptations."[28]

In contrast to Mary Douglas, who contends that the Israelites did not eat pork because the pig was a taxonomic anomaly,[29] Harris argues that the pig was not as well adapted to the Palestinian climate and ecology as ruminants such as cows, sheep, and goats. The religious taboo on pork helped ensure that cheaper forms of meat would be raised.

Jacob Milgrom contends that the purpose of the dietary laws is "to allow man to satiate his lust for animal flesh — and yet not be dehumanized in the process."[30] Such laws are intended to teach the Israelites reverence for life.

---

27. Jean Bottéro, "The Cuisine of Ancient Mesopotamia," *BA* 48,1 (1985): 36.
28. Harris, 77.
29. Mary Douglas, *Purity and Danger: An Analysis of Concepts of Pollution and Taboo* (New York: Praeger, 1966).
30. Jacob Milgrom, "The Biblical Diet Laws as an Ethical System," *Int* 17 (1963): 288.

The Bible has evolved a system of dietary restrictions which teaches the Jew to have reverence for life by (1) reducing his choice of flesh to a few animals, (2) limiting the slaughter of even these permitted animals to the most humane way and by the few who can qualify, and (3) prohibiting the consumption of the blood, as acknowledgement that bringing death to living beings is a concession of God's grace and not a privilege.[31]

Firmage points out that although the dietary laws restrict the range of animals eaten, they do not restrict the number of permitted animals that may be eaten.[32] It would be possible to kill a large number of the permitted animals. Milgrom responds that as a practical matter little meat was slaughtered because meat was too expensive to be eaten very frequently.[33] While this answer makes sense for the poor, some of the wealthy evidently could afford quite a lot of meat. Note Solomon's daily provisions for his household: "Solomon's provision for one day was thirty cors of choice flour, and sixty cors of meal, ten fat oxen, and twenty pasture-fed cattle, one hundred sheep, besides deer, gazelles, roebucks, and fatted fowl" (1 Kgs 4:22-23 NRSV [Heb. 5:2-3]). While it is hard to take the report of Solomon's sacrificing of 22,000 oxen and 120,000 sheep literally, there is no concern that the slaughter of many animals is immoral (1 Kgs 8:62-63).

A second and related question pertains to why so many blood sacrifices are required of humans in their cultic practice if life is so precious. As Milgrom himself states: "How then could God have circumscribed Israel's access to the animal world but permitted, indeed mandated, interminable holocausts of animals for himself?"[34] The answer he proposes is "the supernal realm runs by different rules than the earthly realm."[35] Still, if humans are to imitate the deity at least in some ways, it would seem that here the deity sets a bad example for humans. It is difficult to avoid the possibility that this God is as hungry for meat as most humans.

Another question relates to whether the priests were indeed disinterested theologians largely motivated by ethical concerns. Some of the restrictions they advocated required their assistance and thus ensured a portion of meat for themselves. Thus they stood to benefit from the particular restrictions for slaughtering meat and the need for meat sacrifices. One is suspicious of those

---

31. Ibid., 293; cf. Jacob Milgrom, *Leviticus 1–16: A New Translation with Introduction and Commentary*, AB 3 (New York: Doubleday, 1991), 735.

32. Firmage, 195 n. 24; cf. also David Wright, "Observations on the Ethical Foundations of the Biblical Dietary Laws: A Response to Jacob Milgrom," in *Religion and Law: Biblical, Jewish, and Islamic Perspectives*, ed. E. B. Firmage et al. (Winona Lake: Eisenbrauns, 1989), 195.

33. Milgrom, *Leviticus 1–16*, 735.

34. Ibid.

35. Ibid.

who say, "Bring your filthy lucre to the Lord's house where it can be used for the Lord's work."

There were evidently some priests who fell prey to greed. Note the prophet's rebuke of Eli and his sons.

> Why then look with greedy eye at my sacrifices and my offerings that I commanded, and honor your sons more than me by fattening yourselves on the choicest parts of every offering of my people Israel? (1 Sam 2:29 NRSV; cf. 1 Sam 2:12-17)

Surprisingly, vegetarianism is not directly taught or commanded, even though it seems that one might draw that implication if such an ethical concern was so prominent among the priestly theologians. Instead of advocating vegetarianism the priests develop a fairly elaborate system of food prohibitions which provide humans with a regulated diet that is ordained by God. Those who follow such a regimen do so out of obedience to God. Such a practice is a way of submitting to the authority of God.

Regulations concerning the eating habits of humans are found particularly in the priestly materials. Certain prohibitions (such as the prohibition against eating blood) seem to be old in Israel and to predate the priestly literature (1 Sam 14:31-35). Even if the reasons for such prohibitions are not clear, there are restrictions placed upon humans in terms of what they eat. Even though humans have dominion over animals, this does not mean they are free to eat anything they please.

The Priestly writer contends that the blood prohibition applies to all human beings, whereas the other food prohibitions apply to Israel alone. According to Milgrom, the blood prohibition in Gen 9:4 contains two parts: "Man must abstain from blood: human blood must not be shed and animal blood must not be ingested."[36] This occurs in the context of permission granted to humans to eat the meat of animals. The Priestly writer considers that this blood prohibition is universal and should apply to all. While most Jewish dietary practices were abandoned by early Christians, the prohibition of blood was not (Acts 15:20).

III. Ethical Implications

Biblical views concerning the nature of animals and the relationship of animals to humans do not lead directly to ethical norms for people. It seems valid to propose ethical principles and perhaps even practices which would be consistent

---

36. Milgrom, *Leviticus 1–16*, 705.

with the biblical tradition. It is a further step, a hermeneutical one, which would ask about the relevance of such statements for today.

It is also quite possible for different interpreters to derive different ethical principles from the same texts. While the proposed "implications" are admittedly subjective, they can point to some principles which may inform present-day treatment of animals.

A. Dependency upon God for Food

Living beings are Yahweh's creatures. Not only did Yahweh make creatures which need to eat and drink to survive, but he also created a world which could produce food for them. Yahweh's continued activity in this world as sustainer ensured that the world would provide food. Living beings are dependent upon Yahweh for their origin and for their continued existence. Each bite of food and each drink of water are in essence a gift from Yahweh which gives humans and animals a further lease on life.[37] Animals and humans share this basic nature.

Even the dumb animals know to cry to God for drink and food. Animals are personified, sometimes to serve as an object lesson for humans. In Isa 1:3 "The ox knows its owner, and the donkey its master's crib; but Israel does not know, my people do not understand" (NRSV). Here domestic animals are used to teach the Israelites that they should recognize God as their provider, turn to God to supply their needs, and give thanks for food and life.

In Job 38:41 the young of the raven call out to God (cf. also Ps 147:9). This reference to ravens is probably because of the popular belief that ravens neglected their young.[38] God provides for even the most helpless of creatures. One might argue from the lesser to the greater (as in Matt 6:26) that if God cares even about animals (or birds), he will care much more about humans.

B. Humans Can Bring Harm to Animals

During disasters humans, animals, and plants lack food and may die. The cause of "natural" disasters is not always addressed, but according to biblical thinking humans can disrupt the created world and therefore bring calamity not only upon themselves but also upon animals and plants. The flood story is a paradigmatic case of this. Only a small remnant of animals is preserved.

Humans by their actions can affect the world of nature. They can bring

---

37. Reed, 497.

38. Robert Gordis, *The Book of God and Man: A Study of Job* (Chicago, 1965), 454; A. A. Anderson, *The Book of Psalms: Volume II: 73–150* (Grand Rapids: Eerdmans; London: Marshall, Morgan and Scott, 1981), 946.

drought that affects animal and plant life. Because of their ability to rule over creation, they have the potential to twist severely the created world. The drastic possibilities have become fully recognized only in modern times.

C. Humans Can Provide Care for Animals

There are few direct statements in the Bible which exhort humans to share food with other creatures or to be concerned about the preservation of vegetation. Still, one may derive some ethical insights for the treatment of the world from the theology of creation.

God cares about his creatures. When God indicates his concern about the destruction of Nineveh to Jonah, he mentions the presence of many animals as well as humans (Jon 4:11). Since the lives of animals are important to God, they ought to be important for humans as well. The world was created to support life. Humans are most important to God, but animals are also important. Humans must take care not to violate God's created order. As stewards they ought to care responsibly for this world.

If Yahweh has provided the means of sustenance for all creatures, humans should not distort this created order by depriving creatures of food. Since food is a gift, it should not be abused or considered only as personal property.

Humans should not be complacent when others are hungry. Humans ought to provide food for those who have none since it is God's desire that all receive food. Concern ought to extend also to the provision of food for animals and the preservation of plant life.

Humans are beginning to recognize that even their own survival depends upon the entire ecosystem, which is very fragile. Failure to be concerned about the sustenance of all life forms may lead ultimately to the lack of means for the preservation even of human life.

D. Should People Eat Animal Flesh?

For the most part the Hebrew Bible is clear that meat is highly desirable as food and that people eat a lot of it if they have the opportunity. A mixture of animal husbandry and rainfall agriculture was the basic means for the Israelites to procure food from their environment.

Sacrifices of animals were offered to God upon the altar as God's "food."[39] According to the priestly tradition, humans were also granted permission to eat meat after the flood.

---

39. Menahem Haran, *Temples and Temple Service in Ancient Israel* (Winona Lake: Eisenbrauns, 1985), 219; cf. also 216-29.

Life belonged to God, and so to take life, humans and animals needed permission. Such permission was granted, but this did not mean that humans should forget that life is precious and belongs to God. Permission to eat meat was not meant to give humans the power to do anything they pleased with animals.

There were restrictions given by God to humans concerning what they could and could not eat. All humans were to refrain from eating blood, and the Israelites were to restrict their diets to certain animals. The restraints were understood to remind humans that life belonged to God. Humans ought not to take life, even animal life, casually.

In the light of the extinction of many species today, one might well wonder if humans have maintained a reverence for life which is firmly rooted in the Bible. Some Jewish believers keep the dietary laws to remind them of the reverence of life. Some may decide that vegetarianism may make a much stronger message and impact about their respect for other life forms. Many will continue to eat meat with no qualms of conscience.

Humans ought to pause when they casually take the lives of animals for their food. Americans consume much meat, just as they consume other natural resources in large quantities. In the light of limited resources in the world and the fact that these resources are not equally distributed to all people in our world, Americans should reflect upon their consumption patterns. What we eat and how much we eat are not simply matters of personal preference. They are ethical concerns.

The Ninth Day: To Say "Creation" in Genesis 1:1–11:26

STAN RUMMEL

During my years as a student at Claremont, one of the ongoing discussions among the various constituencies involved in the study of religion raised the question of whether it is possible to listen, without presuppositions, to a text. For his part in this discussion, Prof. Knierim argued that a sense of method can allow interpreters to clarify their own presuppositions and distinguish them from those of the text. I have found that to be a valuable lesson, and offer the following considerations by way of congratulations to Prof. Knierim on this occasion.

If we would say "creation" *along with* Gen 1:1–11:26 in its present form, should we not first inquire into our own presuppositions and be willing to question them?[1] The presuppositions that pose the greatest hindrance to the process of listening to ancient texts are those that stem from some ethnocentric bias — whether the bias is simply the unconsidered imposition of anachronistic categories in translating the language and ideas of the text, or whether it is a genuine belief that a coherent interpretation of the text requires the text to speak in categories that are of concern to us and which fit comfortably into our frame of reference.

One outstanding feature of our frame of reference is its belief that linear modes of thought are more valuable than other modes, such as circular or spiral.[2]

---

1. Perhaps the first presupposition to question here is that Gen 1:1–11:26 is a unit. This presupposition rests on the distinction of Gen 1:1–11:26 from the patriarchal cycles that follow and the belief that תולדות-formulas are introductory. Note that Claus Westermann, *Genesis 1–11: A Commentary* (Minneapolis: Augsburg, 1984), takes 1:1–11:26 as the basic unit.

2. This may be the most enduring appeal of the documentary hypothesis. One of its convenient features is that most nonlinear phenomena in a work such as Genesis (e.g., the stories in the first two chapters, the use of "Yahweh" and "Elohim," or the count of the animals at the end of chap. 6 and the start of chap. 7) can be explained away as deriving from different

When applied to Gen 1:1–11:26, this belief supports three presuppositions. First, in the larger context of the narrative with which the Bible opens, Gen 1:1–11:26 can be best understood through the categories of "history"/"science" (because they provide the primary voices of our linear orientation). Second, the overall aim of this historical/scientific presentation is to present some plan(s), or model(s), of "salvation." The essential message of the text — that is, the message we as modern readers most urgently need to hear — centers on its contribution to the subject of salvation. Third, the statements of the text regarding "creation" function as a prologue to the message of salvation that follows.

Remarkably, these linear presuppositions have led to two diametrically opposed views of what it means to say "creation" in Gen 1:1–11:26.

The first linear view could be called the "historical" view, a relatively modern category[3] increasingly applied to the study of ancient Mediterranean literature. In listening to Gen 1:1–11:26, this perspective found one of its most outstanding exponents in Gerhard von Rad. According to von Rad, we should understand the opening chapters of the Bible as a "primeval history." The thrust of this history becomes apparent in Genesis 10, where "Israel broke resolutely with myth. . . . when Israel looked back, she found herself always merely one member of the historical nations.[4] . . . Whatever peculiar experiences she was to have at God's hands would come to her quite unmythologically, and within the realm of history."[5] History, as a category, stands over against myth, and with myth, creation. In pursuing this vision, Claus Westermann speaks of the "Primeval Story" rather than the "Primeval History," but argues that "What is peculiar to the biblical primeval story is that it links the account of the primeval period with history. . . . The whole of the primeval story is thereby completely freed from the realm of myth."[6] It would seem that, according to this linear view, one should say "creation" in Gen 1:1–11:26 rather hurriedly in order to get to the more significant category of "history."

At the other extreme stands a linear vantage point that could be called "creationist." For those who listen in this way, "creation" also should be said only

---

sources. This allows modern readers to minimize confrontation with the logic of the text in its present form.

3. See R. G. Collingwood, *The Idea of History* (Oxford: Clarendon, 1944).

4. The use of "nation" is an anachronism dignified by its constant repetition among biblical scholars. The nation-state as a fundamental political unit did not emerge until the Peace of Westphalia in 1648. The birth of this new system marked the beginning of a new epoch in world political affairs. Both within and among nations, new principles of organization replaced those that had previously existed. See Leo Gross, "The Peace of Westphalia, 1648-1948," in *International Law in the Twentieth Century*, ed. Leo Gross (New York: Appleton-Century-Crofts, 1969), 25-46. This seminal article appears repeatedly in collections on international law.

5. Gerhard von Rad, *Old Testament Theology*, vol. 1, *The Theology of Israel's Historical Traditions* (Edinburgh: Oliver and Boyd, 1962), 162.

6. Westermann, 65.

at the start of Gen 1:1–11:26. According to Donald DeYoung, a representative exponent of this view, "Scripture teaches that the entire universe was created in six literal days by an infinite, miracle-working God."[7] This point is tied to a "scientific"-theological agenda that involves locating God above time, denying any form of physical or biological evolution, promoting "faith in the Scriptures," and helping people "com[e] to Christ."[8] It also limits the scope of human "history" to approximately ten thousand years. And how persuasive this view has become! According to a Gallup poll conducted 21-24 November 1991, 47 percent of all "Americans" believe that "God created man pretty much in his present form at one time within the last 10,000 years."[9] It would seem that, according to this linear view, one should say "creation" in Gen 1:1–11:26 rather hurriedly in order to get to further "scientific" facts as they emerge in the narrative sequence.[10]

The messages the two camps hear when they listen to Gen 1:1–11:26 are radically different, but the presuppositions that allow them to hear their messages are essentially the same. History or science, as we define the category, provides the matrix of ideas that allows us to listen to the text. Then the text can answer the theological questions we put to it. The answers in both cases depend on understanding the text as a linear statement that breaks free of the realm of myth.

There is an old question about the opening chapters of Genesis. Students in introductory courses always seem to ask it. They ask it because it jumps out of the text when the text is read as a linear sequence. *Where did Cain and Abel get their wives?*[11] Wherever these wives came from, they did not emerge from

---

7. Donald DeYoung, "The Fingerprint of God?" *Associates for Biblical Research Newsletter* 22/4 (July-August 1991): 1. That creationist thinkers attach their basic theses to the story which happens to appear first in the Bible, while ignoring contradictory fragments scattered throughout the Bible, illustrates the force of linear thought in modern life.

8. DeYoung, "The Fingerprint of God?" At the end of his article, he notes that "Beyond scientific questions, certain theological ideas are of even greater concern." Creationism is a program of biblical theology.

9. Reported in *U.S. News and World Report* 111/26 (23 December 1991): 59. When Rolf Knierim, in stressing the importance of discourse about creation to the task of Old Testament theology, states that "the history of biblical theology has lost contact with natural science virtually totally" ("The Task of Old Testament Theology," *HBT* 6,1 [1984]: 39), he reflects the fact that the agendas of the historical and creationist camps are so different that a constructive dialogue seems nearly impossible. Creationist theology constantly appeals to what Knierim refers to as "natural science."

10. The next major group of "scientific" facts appears in the flood story, but creationists are also interested in "man's early history" — an interest that centers around "Adam" and the genealogies; see DeYoung, "The Fingerprint of God?"

11. For "serious" biblical scholars, a question like this — along with creationist theology — might just seem frivolous. I work at a small school in Fort Worth, Texas, i.e., in the southern part of what is informally called the United States "Bible Belt." I believe that anyone who understands the demographics of Protestant Christianity in the United States will appreciate the fact that such questions — and the theological agendas they reflect — stand at the center of my concerns when I talk with students about the Bible.

a linear perspective in the narrative as it stands. We can treat this and other similar problems as trivialities to be dispensed with so we can get to the "real" message of the text. Or we could try to listen to the text in a different way — a way that is less oriented to linear concerns.

Suppose we were at least temporarily to abandon our presupposition that "linear is better," for fear that it might be an ethnocentric overlay on the biblical perspective. How would we then proceed to ask what it means to say "creation" in Gen 1:1–11:26?

As a first step, we could try to achieve some conceptual clarity about the idea of "creation" expressed in Gen 1:1–11:26. If, as I will argue, the idea of creation provides the basic organizational principle of the entire unit, an assessment of its overall structure and intention would then be possible.

The way we say "creation" in Gen 1:1–11:26 as a whole is shaped by our translation-understanding of the initial unit in 1:1–2:3, and particularly by 1:1-2. These two verses establish an ideology of (and a program for!) creation that counters — and often offends — our modern sensibilities.

In Western culture, we have presuppositions about the meaning of "creation" that are central to whatever collective spiritual enterprise still exists. That is, the fundamental theologies (at least, in the traditional sense) of Judaism, Christianity, and Islam are grounded on an understanding that "creation" signifies creation-from-nothing. A decade and a half ago, Gerhard May studied the origins of this notion.[12]

According to May, the earliest known attestation of the idea of creation-from-nothing is found in 2 Macc 7:28: "I beg you, my child, to look at the heaven and the earth and see everything that is in them, and recognize that God did not make them out of things that existed. And in the same way the human race came into being" (NRSV). This is not a theoretical discourse about the nature of creation, but a parenetical entreaty from a mother to her child about God's power in a situation where that power is not evident. The intention of the parenesis is to encourage the child to remain true to the Mosaic "law" in the face of both bribes and threats. It works. The child "died in his integrity, putting his whole trust in the Lord" (v. 40).

If this text, situated in Hellenistic Judaism of the early first century B.C.E., provides the earliest evidence we have for the origins of creation-from-nothing thinking, that thinking soon turned in a more theoretical direction, spread widely in the Hellenistic world, became centered in early Christianity because of the challenge of gnostic ideas, and was resolved by the start of the third century C.E. When we look, with May's help, at the contours of that discussion

---

12. Gerhard May, *Schöpfung aus dem Nichts: Die Entstehung der Lehre von der Creatio ex Nihilo*, Arbeiten zur Kirchengeschichte 48 (Berlin: de Gruyter, 1978); see especially pp. 183-84 for a summary of his overall argument, and pp. 6-8 on 2 Macc 7:28. I am grateful to Fred Tiffany, a fellow student at Claremont, for bringing this work to my attention in 1984.

and its resolution, we can see that "creation-from-nothing" is the answer to a question that occurs in a dualistic framework of thought. The question may be generalized as: is evil as powerful as good? Or: was creation the result of a struggle by God against evil? The idea of creation-from-nothing offers the only satisfactory basis for a firm no to both forms of the question.[13]

Creation-from-nothing is also the basis for another answer to a similar question of fundamental concern to Western religious thought since Hellenistic times. This second answer is "monotheism," an elusive concept composed of at least three statements:

1. There is only one deity.
2. This deity created everything else from nothing (so evil does not have the same power as good).
3. God rules the creation with justice (so evil does not have the same status as good).

For us, the term "monotheism" provides a linguistic symbol to represent these three ideas.[14] It cannot legitimately be reduced to its etymological meaning of "one god."

If our concepts of "creation" and the related category "monotheism" have their origins in Hellenistic Judaism and early Christianity, we need to abandon them in order to say "creation" in Gen 1:1–11:26.[15] Procedurally, we need to find the concept(s) of creation available to the Hebrews, and on that basis listen to Genesis. The information for this is readily available.

Westermann, e.g., describes four models of creation known in the world of the Hebrews: (1) creation by (a succession of) births, (2) creation as the result of a struggle or victory, (3) creation by an action, and (4) creation by a saying.[16] These categories are not mutually exclusive. The last two emphasize techniques of creation, while the first two specify modes of creation. The first mode is theogonic, and the second mode is cosmogonic. Neither

13. Note that "cosmogonic" views of creation can be construed to answer the latter form of the question in the affirmative, while answering the first form negatively. Only when the questions are set in the dualistic context in which they arose will the answers necessarily be the same.

14. See, e.g., Ronald Clements, "Monotheism," in *The Westminster Dictionary of Christian Theology*, ed. Alan Richardson and John Bowden (Philadelphia: Westminster, 1983), 381-82. The third idea embraces the category of "ethical monotheism."

15. Even if the concept of monotheism is arbitrarily reduced to the first and third ideas (cf. Knierim, "Task of Old Testament Theology"), it still poses a significant block in our efforts to listen to Gen 1:1–11:26. At one level, this block is illustrated by the famous plural pronouns in 1:26. The cosmology implicit in these chapters raises other questions. Who are the "sons of the gods" in 6:2? More generally, how can we be certain that Yahweh and Elohim are always the same god at each level of the tradition?

16. Westermann, 26-41.

mode concerns creation-from-nothing. Neither mode refers to absolute beginnings.[17]

In turning to Gen 1:1-2, then, we start with the two modes of creation discourse available to the Hebrews. If verse 1 should not be understood as a reference to an absolute beginning,[18] and if it does not refer to creation-from-nothing,[19] it must describe a circumstance on which the narrative in 1:3–2:3 builds — on the basis of either a theogonic or cosmogonic view of creation.[20] That Genesis could make use of cosmogonic ideas is a position that finds abundant support within the Hebrew Bible, when it is examined in light of the extrabiblical evidence known to us.

In 1965, Loren R. Mack-Fisher pointed to evidence from Ugarit confirming that cosmogonic creation is narrated through a cluster of motifs which include:

1. Conflict-victory
2. Kingship
3. Order
4. Palace
5. Banquet[21]

Since then, numerous scholars have supported and expanded the thesis, finding dozens of texts in the Hebrew Bible which display this cluster, filling it with a variety of contents.[22]

The relationship of this discovery to our understanding of how to say "creation" in Gen 1:1–2:3 is indirect. The texts show that cosmogonic ideas were

17. The idea of an absolute beginning can reasonably be associated with creation-from-nothing. The most powerful image of beginnings in theogonies is that of a watery chaos, and the most powerful image of beginnings in cosmogonies is that of conflict among the deities. In Western culture there is no language available to speak of "ultimate origins."

18. This general conclusion is also supported on syntactical and lexicographical grounds; see William R. Lane, "The Initiation of Creation," *VT* 13 (1963): 63-73, who surveyed the issues and concluded that the translation "In the beginning God created . . ." is not likely.

19. See Lane, 73. Westermann, 93, asks: ". . . is Gen 1 speaking of *creatio ex nihilo?*" He concludes (pp. 108-10) that the category itself is irrelevant to Genesis, and that verse 1 is an "introductory resume" composed by P (see pp. 93-102). Yet his translation feeds the very presuppositions he argues against: "In the beginning God created the heavens and the earth."

20. This is true if we are willing to limit our understanding of the text to what the Hebrews might have presupposed. The ongoing power of theological presuppositions is illustrated by the NRSV translation of Gen 1:1: "In the beginning when God created [note: or *when God began to create* or *In the beginning God created*] the heavens and the earth." Something for everyone!

21. Loren R. Mack-Fisher, "From Chaos to Cosmos," *Encounter* 26/2 (spring 1965): 183-97; see also "Creation at Ugarit and in the Old Testament," *VT* 15 (1965): 313-24.

22. See Stan Rummel, "Narrative Structures in the Ugaritic Texts," in *Ras Shamra Parallels: The Texts from Ugarit and the Hebrew Bible*, vol. 3, pp. 233-84, ed. Stan Rummel, AnOr 51 (Rome: Pontifical Biblical Institute, 1981), for bibliography and discussion of texts.

widespread in the Hebrew Bible. They also reveal what we might call a cosmogonic "ideology": creation is the creation of order from chaos, and conflict lies at the core of the creative process.[23] Both of these affirmations must be made in order to speak of cosmogonic creation, and they answer two related questions: how should "we" understand the circumstances *in which "we" live?* and what is the role of conflict in the circumstances *in which "we" live?* The final clause in each question is of crucial importance in understanding cosmogonic ideology. It is a practical means of coming to terms with the "world" as humans experience it, not a theoretical or abstract exposition of the nature of reality.[24]

Gen 1:1–2:3 deals only with the first question: how should "we" understand the circumstances in which "we" live? It offers the cosmogonic solution: "we" should understand our circumstances to grow out of a fundamental orderliness. The reference in verse 2 to "waters," the basic symbol of chaos in cosmogonic narratives, strengthens the cosmogonic connotations involved in such a claim and — along with verse 1 — establishes the circumstances on which the ordering process described in 1:3-31 is based.[25] This is, in a literal sense, the creation of order from chaos. But Gen 1:1–2:3 does not present a complete view of creation. It does not describe the world of ordinary human experience. The ironic characterization "very good" in 1:31 immediately follows the description of an earth whose living inhabitants are all vegetarians and is followed by the ambiguous statement in 2:2 that Elohim "finished" this world. More importantly, Gen 1:1–2:3 bypasses the cosmogonic issue of conflict entirely — and at precisely the point where the issue is often treated: at the cosmic level of a conflict within the pantheon.[26] There is no battle among deities here.

23. This already suggests that we must say "creation" beyond Gen 2:3.

24. In cosmogonic narratives, the practical intention is demonstrated by the motifs of palace and banquet, which correspond — at the human level — to temple and cult. Mack-Fisher has demonstrated that both the palace of the deity in the heavens and the temple of the deity on earth are microcosms (see "The Temple Quarter," *JSS* 8 [1963]: 34-41; and "From Chaos to Cosmos," 185-86). We need also to recognize that temple and palace are mirror images of each other.

25. Syntactically, there is no reason to understand the "days" in Genesis 1 as a sequence. The initial phrase of each unit ("Elohim said" in vv. 3, 6, 9, 14, 20, and 24) bears the same syntactical relationship to verses 1-2. As a whole verses 3-31 explicate verses 1-2, and 2:1-3 provides a conclusion.

26. Cosmogonic ideology must deal with conflict. However, a literal transfer of motifs from one narrative to the next is not necessary (see Rummel, "Narrative Structures"). The results of such an expectation have been illustrated by Dennis J. McCarthy, S.J., " 'Creation' Motifs in Ancient Hebrew Poetry," *CBQ* 29/3 (1967): 87-100, 393-406. Working explicitly from the historical-theological perspective generated by linear presuppositions, McCarthy not only denied a cosmogonic point of view to Genesis because it is not literally tied to a "*Chaoskampf*"; he argued that we should not ask about creation at all from these texts, because they do not speak of absolute origins. The consideration of conflict that will appear in the sequence beginning in Gen 2:4 is discounted by McCarthy because its implications are "political and social" (i.e., historical) in nature. Even disregarding the ethnocentrism

To say "creation" in Gen 1:1–11:26, we must continue past 2:3. With this in mind, Mack-Fisher translates Gen 1:1-2 as follows:

> When Elohim *first* began to form the heavens and the earth, the earth was devastation and desolation, darkness was over [the] deep, the wind of Elohim was storming over the waters.[27] (italics mine)

There is more to come! However, before moving beyond Gen 2:3, we need to consider the other great category of discourse about creation available to the Hebrews: theogony. For this consideration, the presuppositions available to the Hebrews may be illustrated by examining the *Enuma Elish*.[28]

The *Enuma Elish* presents a dynamic cosmogony in which Marduk, the chief god of the city of Babylon during the first part of the second millennium, defeats Tiamat, the "deep." In Gen 1:2, the use of תהום, "deep," without the definite article, provides an evident allusion to the Mesopotamian narrative.[29] If this allusion is understood as a cosmogonic reference, it adds some depth to our understanding of the idea of order in Genesis, since the word translated by Mack-Fisher as "form" in Gen 1:1 signifies forming by means of cutting (that is, sculpting) — as Marduk forms the cosmos by cutting up Tiamat in the *Enuma Elish*. It also reminds us that conflict must be discussed.

Yet the allusion not only invokes cosmogonic ideology. It invokes theogonic ideology as well. In the first twenty lines of the *Enuma Elish*, Tiamat is portrayed as the goddess who, with the "marital" help of Apsu (another image of water), "gives birth" to all that will be. If cosmogonic ideology provides answers to questions of world order and the role of conflict in that order, theogonic ideology provides a practical answer to the question of origins. This answer invokes the metaphor of "parenting."[30]

At the beginning of Genesis there is Tehom, and there is Elohim. Whatever the use of "Elohim" ultimately denotes here, its connotations can hardly fail to

---

inherent in this view, why should each example of cosmogonic ideology not reflect particular concerns and develop the ideology in a unique way?

27. This and subsequent translations from Genesis are based on a work in process by Loren R. Mack-Fisher and used with the permission of the author. His complete translation of Genesis will appear in a new series called the Scholars Bible. The first volume of the series is already in print: Daryl D. Schmidt, *The Gospel of Mark* (Sonoma, Calif.: Polebridge, 1990).

28. See especially Thorkild Jacobsen, *The Treasures of Darkness: A History of Mesopotamian Religion* (New Haven: Yale University, 1976), 165-91.

29. We may never know precisely what תהום in Gen 1:2 is meant to denote, but its connotations can be explored as part of the thought-world of the Hebrews.

30. Jacobsen, 145-64, treats parenting as a second-millennium metaphor apart from the *Enuma Elish*. This seems partly due to his interest in exploring the rise of "personal religion" as a separate topic and partly due to the force of the "theomachy" that begins in line 21 of the first tablet of the *Enuma Elish* (see p. 170), which replaces the parenting motif with a conflict motif.

include the El known to us from the Ugaritic texts as "father of the deities," "creator of creatures," and "father of man" *('ab 'adm).*[31] Elohim does not mate with Tehom, as the cosmogonic motif of "forming/sculpting" supplants the theogonic motif of "giving birth"; yet in 1:26-27 the relationship between Elohim and humans is described in intimate terms, while a like relationship between Elohim and other, unnamed deities is implied. "Let *us* make human beings [אדם] in *our* image" (italics mine), says Elohim; and "Elohim formed the human beings [האדם] in his image." This is not just the Divine Sculptor speaking and acting; it is the Divine Parent.

The parent-child type of relationship adumbrated in 1:26-27 is developed somewhat more fully in 2:7, where Yahweh-Elohim blows the "breath of life" into the nostrils of the human, who becomes a "living being" — an epithet attributed also to the animals in 1:30 and 2:19. In 5:1 and 5:3, just as Elohim formed human beings "in the likeness of Elohim," so Adam fathered a son "in his likeness." In 6:2 and 6:4 there are explicit references to the "sons of *the* elohim," who mate with the "daughters of the human beings."

Such examples could be multiplied, and we could speculate about the psychology of the relationships established as the narrative proceeds, but the essential thought process should be confirmed at this point. For Genesis, an orderly world is provided by a divine figure who functions in a parental manner, and family relationships provide a fundamental metaphor by which the order of the world is assessed. In using theogonic categories to express their understanding of the world, the Hebrews were no less original than when they used cosmogonic categories. We need not expect a literal transfer of motifs deriving from an explicit understanding of deity in terms of pantheon. Nevertheless, to say "creation" in Gen 1:1–11:26 is to speak of God as "parent" — and, in this frame of thought, genealogies become important. Indeed, a sense of genealogical relationships establishes one strategy by which the perspectives in the book of Genesis as a whole are united. The individual human figures must fit into a genealogical pattern whose starting point is God.[32] It should come as no surprise that the second strategy which unites the book of Genesis — the תולדות-formulas in 2:4; 5:1; 6:9; 10:1; 11:10, 27; 25:12, 19; 36:1; 37:2 — also appeals to the imagery of "birth." The "stories" (Mack-Fisher's translation) of Genesis are, in the broad sense of the word-field of ילד, birth stories.

A grasp of theogonic presuppositions might help us understand what it

---

31. See Frank Moore Cross, *Canaanite Myth and Hebrew Epic: Essays in the History of the Religion of Israel* (Cambridge: Harvard University Press, 1973), 15.

32. We tend to view the momentum of genealogies that mention people as linear while treating genealogies that mention deities as time-less. This distinction exemplifies a "history" versus "myth" ethnocentrism. The precise functions of the genealogies and genealogical relationships asserted in Genesis may well be complex. Our interest here is limited to what it means to say "creation." Within the boundaries set by this concern, the sequence of relationships is of minor importance compared to the assertion of such relationships.

means to say "creation" in Gen 1:1–11:26 in yet one other way. In his discussion of the *Enuma Elish,* Jacobsen contrasts the "potential" world of the theogony with the "actual" world brought about by the cosmogony.[33] This contrast confirms what we have already seen in our study of cosmogonic ideology: to say "creation" in Gen 1:1–11:26, we must go beyond 2:3. In Gen 2:4 we encounter another "day" (ביום) of creation, an eighth day, that — along with the תולדות-formula at the start of the verse — both connects and differentiates the following narrative from Gen 1:1–2:3.

"These are the stories of the heavens and the earth since their formation. On another day when Yahweh-Elohim was about to make earth and heaven . . ." (Gen 2:4). The subject — heavens and earth — introduced in 1:1 is now to be explored further. The new "day" of creation reveals the logic of this exploration. It is not linear: no peg exists on which to hang an "eighth" day of creation. Rather, this "eighth" day functions to remind us that we must say "creation" in the following material, too. We have seen that theogonic ideology is developed in chapters 2–6. We have also observed that the second great cosmogonic question has yet to be answered: what is the role of conflict in the circumstances *in which "we" live?*

To come to terms with the cosmogonic motif of conflict as it is developed in Genesis, we need to focus on the basic language symbol used to connect and differentiate 1:1–2:3 from the following material. This symbol is the "adam" introduced in 1:26-27 and reiterated in 2:5: "there was no adam to till the ground." Precisely here — at the most fundamental point of connection — the most radical point of differentiation occurs. The "humans," formed on the sixth and climactic day of the opening narrative, distinguished by sex but not by number, metamorphose into a single "human" with no name. He is just "the adam."[34]

But what an adam! This human and then the other individual humans who follow become the focal point of the narrative. At the center stands the human-divine relationship. The story in Gen 1:1–2:3 is subordinated as one perspective on what we can now call the "adam-world." The exploration of conflict in Genesis must derive from the human-divine relationship. This narrative strategy alone precludes the text from detailing a cosmic conflict between the deity and the forces of chaos. That conflict must occur in the heavens, while the decision in Genesis is to focus on the earth. Does this mean that the writers of the text did not believe in a cosmic battle among deities? We have no way of knowing. What we can know is that the conflict motif as used in Genesis describes an uneasy, ambiguous,

---

33. Jacobsen, 169.

34. See Loren R. Mack-Fisher, "The Man with No Name," *The Fourth R* 3/2 (March 1990): 11-12. In Gen 4:25, this individual human will be named "Adam," as in 5:1a and 5:3. Yet the interplay among multiple levels of meaning is not lost: in 5:1b-2, which in part echoes 1:27-28, the "humans" (adam) are formed male and female. The two texts move apart when the blessing is given. In 1:28, the blessing is cited; in 2:2, the male and female are given the name "Adam."

parent-child relationship between humans and the deity. Expectations deriving from the treatment of the conflict motif as a cosmic event are disappointed: there is no victory to be won, as in a cosmic battle. As presented in Genesis, the orders of physical reality do not result from a cosmic conflict.

The earthly conflict described in Genesis occurs, first of all, between the deity and humans. From this conflict order derives: not the order of the cosmos but the order of society. The social order that results from the conflict between (Yahweh-)Elohim and the adam in the garden (2:4–3:24) involves pain, labor, weeds, and death. In 4:1-24, this order is specified further as a result of the conflict between "Yahweh" and Cain. Cain, the wanderer, settles down (v. 16). From his progenitive efforts — a creative interweaving of the cosmogonic motif of conflict with the theogonic motif of parenting! — the city is built (17), those who "dwell with tents and herds" are "fathered" (20), as are all who "are skilled with lyre and pipe" (21), copper and iron are crafted (22), and vengeance becomes part of the social order (23-24; cf. 14-15). To say "creation" in these texts is to say that certain basic orders of society depend for their existence on conflict. The garden story extends the fundamental divine-human conflict to a human-"ground" conflict (3:17-18), while the Cain story extends the conflict to a human-human level (4:8-9, 23-24). To say "creation" here is not to say that conflict is bad so much as to say it is necessary: the conflicts that are narrated may be resolved (not won!) with curses (as in 3:14, 17; 4:11), but there are gifts, too (the clothing in 3:21, the "mark" in 4:15).

Beginning in 4:25, the theogonic motif of parenting dominates the text through 6:4. As employed in the text, the parenting motif reminds us that to say "creation" in Gen 1:1–11:26, we must go beyond 6:4. Gen 4:25–5:32 constitutes a unit built around a list organized as a genealogy. In 4:25-26 is a thematic statement about progeniture that takes us back to the central human figure, "Adam." This is followed in 5:1a by an expanded תולדות-formula that picks up the thematic statement, which is immediately linked to "Elohim" (through the cosmogonic motif of "forming") in 5:1b-2, and developed in 5:3-32 via a genealogy which connects Adam to Noah and his sons. In 5:28-29 we encounter a Lamech who plays a considerably different role than the Lamech of 4:23-24. If the Lamech of chapter 4 represents the principle of vengeance that is part of the (ongoing) social order of the adam-world, the Lamech of chapter 5 fathers Noah, who will become the human centerpoint of 6:5–11:26. Lamech's speech in 5:29 underlines the need to include the "Noah-world" when saying "creation" in Gen 1:1–11:26:

> This one [Noah] will comfort us from our work,
> And from the toil of our hands,
> From the ground that Yahweh cursed.

In referring back to the Yahweh-curse in 3:17, Lamech's speech informs us that the ordering process is not yet complete. The adam-world must be connected to the Noah-world. As if to reinforce this point, Gen 6:1-4 concludes the description of the adam-world by once again connecting that world with the Noah-world. I cite Mack-Fisher's translation in full:

> When the human beings began to multiply upon the face of the ground, and daughters were born to them, the sons of the gods saw that the daughters of the human beings were beautiful, they took for themselves wives from any of those they chose. Yahweh said:
> "My spirit can not be bottled up in human beings forever
> In as much as they are flesh.
> Their days will be a hundred and twenty years."
> The Nephilim were on earth in those days and afterwards, for the sons of the gods did mate with the daughters of the human beings; they bore [children] to them. They were the heroes of old, the men of renown.

"In those days and afterwards. . . ." There is yet one more day, a ninth day, of creation to consider: "Yahweh saw how great was the evil of the human beings [האדם] on the earth, and how every form of the thoughts of their minds was only evil all of the day [כל־היום]" (6:5). To gain some insight into what it means to say "creation" as we move from the adam-world of human-divine beings into the Noah-world, we will turn to one of the more famous "heroes of old," whose story is recounted in the *Gilgamesh Epic*. The following rendition of selected "high points" from the epic-cycle will provide a basis for discussion.[35]

GILGAMESH AND ENKIDU

Tablet 1

Gilgamesh, King of Uruk, experienced everything
    in all the countries of the world;
He rebuilt the city-wall of Uruk
    and the holy place "Eanna" for the sky-god Anu.
Two-thirds of him was divine; he was like a wild bull.
One day, the men of Uruk complained to the deities:
    "Gilgamesh is the greatest fighter in the world,
    but he pushes us too hard.
    His arrogance is limitless in the night and in the day."
So the deities summoned the goddess Aruru:
    "You created this wild bull; now create his image.
    Let them contend with each other, that Uruk might have peace."
Aruru took a pinch of mud
    and threw the valiant Enkidu into the desert.

---

35. See Jacobsen, 193-219, for a fuller translation and discussion.

The mighty Enkidu knew nothing of civilization.
He lived with the wild animals.
One day, a trapper saw Enkidu tearing up his traps;
and he told Gilgamesh, who replied:
"Take a prostitute to the desert. Let her lure Enkidu.
Then the wild animals will run away from him."
After seven nights of love, the prostitute said to Enkidu:
"You are like a god. Why live with the wild animals?
Let me take you to Uruk,
where Gilgamesh lords it over the men like a wild bull.
Maybe you could challenge him and take over."

Tablet 2

When Enkidu met Gilgamesh, they fought like wild bulls
until Gilgamesh sank to one knee in defeat,
and he turned his back.
Yet Enkidu said:
"The goddess Ninsuna, strong as a wild bull, gave birth to you.
She raised your head above those of other men.
You are the true king!"

Tablet 3

Gilgamesh embraced Enkidu, and they became friends.

THE FIRST QUEST

One day, Enkidu's eyes filled with tears.
Gilgamesh looked into his eyes and asked,
"What's wrong, my friend?"
Enkidu replied, "My desert-strength has turned to city-weakness."
Gilgamesh said, "There is evil in all the land,
caused by Huwawa, the giant monster who lives in the forest.
We must go to the cedar forest in the west and kill him."
Enkidu pleaded with Gilgamesh:
"Once I saw the monster in the distant forest.
When he roars, the floodstorm comes;
His mouth is filled with fire — his breath means death."
Gilgamesh chided Enkidu:
"My friend, what human could rise to heaven and live forever?
Our days are numbered — our achievements like a breath of wind.
Already, you are afraid to die. What happened to your courage?

If I fall, I will have lasting fame.
Later generations will say:
'Gilgamesh went down fighting the terrible Huwawa.'"

Tablet 5

Finally, they reached the cedar forest
    where mighty Huwawa lived.
    He came out of his house of cedar,
    and looked at Gilgamesh with death in his eyes.
But Gilgamesh summoned the sun-god Shamash
    to send the scorching winds,
    and Huwawa's eyes filled with tears.
Huwawa said, "Let me live, Gilgamesh, and I will be your slave."
Gilgamesh felt sorry for him and asked Enkidu,
    "Shouldn't we let him live?"
Enkidu replied,
    "The tallest man who has no judgment will fall to death."
Then Gilgamesh and Enkidu drew their swords,
    and the guardian of the cedars lay dead on the ground,
        slain by Enkidu.

THE SECOND QUEST

Tablet 7

The earth-god Enlil,
    who had made Huwawa guardian of the cedars,
    Became enraged and said, "Enkidu must die."
Then Enkidu became ill and his eyes filled with tears:
    "I die not like one fallen in battle,
    but as one cursed and ashamed."

Tablet 8

Gilgamesh said, "What sleep is this that has taken you?
    You are in the dark and cannot hear me."
Then Gilgamesh touched Enkidu's heart, but it did not beat.

Tablet 9

Gilgamesh cried out,
    "Will I not die like Enkidu? I am afraid.
    I must go to my ancestor Utanapishtim,
    who joined the council of the deities and became immortal."

Tablet 10

Finally, Gilgamesh arrived at the Waters of Death,
   and met Urshanabi, the boatman of Utanapishtim.
So Urshanabi took Gilgamesh to Utanapishtim.

Tablet 11

Utanapishtim said to Gilgamesh:
   "I will tell you a secret known only to the deities . . .
   [*at this point the story of the great flood is told*].
   Afterward, Enlil blessed me:
      'Utanapishtim shall be like the deities'.
   But who will gather the deities for you,
      that you might find the life you search for?"
Gilgamesh said, "What can I do? Where shall I go?
   Wherever I look, I see death."
Utanapishtim answered,
   "At the bottom of the great sea is a thorny plant.
   Eat it when you grow old, and you will return to childhood."
So Gilgamesh tied stones to his feet and got the plant,
   though it stung his hand.
   He said, "I will share with all the old men
   this plant called 'Old Man Becomes A Child'."
And he started back for Uruk with Urshanabi.
After one day's journey,
   Gilgamesh saw a cool pond and went to bathe.
   But deep in the pond was a snake that sniffed the sweet flower.
   The snake rose out of the water and ate the plant.
   Immediately it shed its old skin and returned to the pond.
Gilgamesh sat down and cried, "Is this what I worked for?
   I gained nothing — but at least the snake is happy."
When they arrived in Uruk, Gilgamesh said to Urshanabi:
   "Walk on the city-wall. Examine it closely.
   Is it not made of the finest bricks,
   as though the seven sages before the flood
      laid its foundations?
   One part of the whole is city, one part is orchards,
   one part is fields; and there is the temple-precinct.
   Three parts and the temple-precinct make up Uruk."

In both the *Gilgamesh Epic* and Genesis, the story of the great flood is told as a creation account with cosmogonic overtones.[36] In both settings the

---

36. The cosmogonic ideology is that order results from conflict. In terms of classifi-

flood is presented as a unique, turning-point event that defines the orders of creation. From chaos, manifested as water, comes order and new beginnings. The new beginnings limit the potential of the created order, while affirming its fundamental validity. Gilgamesh learns that he cannot achieve the immortal status of his ancestor, the flood-hero Utanapishtim. The world of Gilgamesh (and Enkidu, his counterpart) has been defined by the flood as a world of the city and civilization. This is a world in which Enkidu, the man of the desert, ultimately cannot survive. It is the Utanapishtim-world. Gilgamesh must finally return to his own starting point, the city and its responsibilities.

Although the specific agenda of the *Gilgamesh Epic* is considerably different from that of Genesis, a comparison of similar themes reveals what we should expect: the pre- or post-flood setting of themes is of minor interest. The event of the flood in itself, as the destruction of one sector (the "living beings") of an existing world order, presupposes a certain linear continuity. But this continuity remains undeveloped. The flood is part of the essential ordering process. Gilgamesh, the two-thirds divine man, provides the analogue of the Nephilim of Gen 6:4, who appear before the flood; as the king of Uruk, he also provides the analogue of the post-flood rulers of Genesis 10. The serpent robs Gilgamesh of immortality in the Utanapishtim-world, but in Genesis the analogous event occurs in the adam-world.[37] The city life affirmed by Gilgamesh is established in Genesis in the adam-world (4:17).

Within Gen 1:1–11:26, there is a strong interest in connecting specific phenomena of the adam- and Noah-worlds. As the "wind of Elohim" stormed over the waters in 1:2, so Elohim "made a wind move upon the earth" in 8:1. This circumstance leads to physical order, detailed as a process of formation in 1:3-31, stated as a cosmic cycle in 8:22: "Throughout all the days of the earth, Sowing and reaping, Cold and heat, Summer and winter, Day and night, They shall not cease." As with the humans in 1:28, so Elohim blesses Noah and his sons in 9:1-2 with fruitfulness and control over other living beings. The social principle of blood vengeance adumbrated in 4:23-24 is reconfigured by Elohim in 9:5-6. As the adam, and Cain after him, must become "tillers of the ground" (3:23; 4:2), so Noah "became a farmer" in 9:20. As the city is built in 4:17, so the Noah-world is characterized by cities (e.g., 10:11-12; 11:4).

Yet, the Noah-world does not simply mirror the adam-world. The Noah-

---

cation, it would seem reasonable to categorize cosmogonic stories into two basic types: the achievement of order through a battle with the forces of chaos (divine-divine conflict) and the achievement of order using chaos as material (often with divine-human conflict). Flood stories would then fit in the second category.

37. In 3:4 the serpent promises the woman immortality, and in 3:22 "Yahweh-Elohim" negates the possibility. This negation is so severe that even Noah, the flood-hero, cannot aspire to such a status: he must be the new adam, not the new Utanapishtim. The treatment of the motif of immortality in the *Gilgamesh Epic* and in Genesis provides yet another example of the unique ways in which different cultures dealt with the same subject matter.

world literally marks a new day in creation. The evil thoughts of humans "all of the day" provide the reason for "Yahweh's" decision to blot out the living beings from the creation (6:5-7). After the flood, in 8:21, "Yahweh considered, 'Never again will I despise the ground because of the humans, since the formations in the minds of humans are evil from their youth. Never again will I destroy all life as I did.'" It is striking that the reason given for the decision is also the reason given never to repeat the decision, but even more striking is the connection with Lamech's announcement in 5:29 that with his son Noah there would be "comfort" from the ground that Yahweh cursed. The issues of creation come to a focus in Noah. The subject is the evil of human beings.

In the *Gilgamesh Epic* evil is located outside of the city and its life, with the monster Huwawa in the western forest. In Genesis, the evil is located wherever humans reside — in the country (9:20-27) and within the city (11:1-9). The covenant between Yahweh/Elohim and Noah (see 8:20–9:17) largely reaffirms the physical order of the adam-world[38] and ignores the problem of human evil which provides the narrative matrix for the covenant. However, beginning in 9:20 the problem of human evil is directly addressed, first by Noah (9:25-27) and then by "Yahweh" (11:6-9). The net result for social order is detailed in chapter 10. Humans are organized in diverse (political) units, such as cities and kingdoms; and they are divided by various ethnic categories, such as clans and languages. That this social order is given a negative cast in terms of human-human conflict (chap. 9) and human-divine conflict (chap. 11) represents a departure from the type of thinking reflected in the Gilgamesh tradition and a new contribution to what it means to say "creation." To say "creation" in Genesis is to speak of an orderly society.

To this point, we have argued that to say "creation" in Gen 1:1–11:26, we must say the whole text. This whole is divided into two parts, which we have characterized as the adam-world and the Noah-world. The claims in Genesis about the meaning of creation are complex, and they are found in the interrelationships of the two parts. The parts present not so much a sequence of events as a collage of events, sometimes cast as narratives/speeches, sometimes cast as lists. To reduce the claims to a series of propositions (such as the fundamental orderliness of the physical world and society, the parental role of deity, the grounding of human existence in conflict, or the fact of human evil) for the purpose of theological discussion is dangerous because it cuts them loose from the presuppositions that give them life and simplifies the process of substituting other claims (such as absolute beginnings, creation-from-nothing, or monotheism) based on different presuppositions. This danger is enhanced if the propositions are further detached from what we can determine of the original intentions of the texts in which they are generated. Although our understanding of the significance of biblical texts may not be limited to their original inten-

---

38. Note, however, the revision in 9:3-4 of the vegetarian diet prescribed in 1:29-30.

tions, it seems worthwhile to raise this question in the context of ancient institutions and presuppositions. Who was generating the type of material found in Gen 1:1–11:26 and why?

In 1973 Loren R. Mack-Fisher, building on the work of Cyrus H. Gordon, initiated an argument that the genre of the book of Genesis as a whole is "royal epic," and the setting of this epic is the Davidic monarchy.[39] That royal institutions provide one matrix for discourse about creation may be illustrated by the following rendition of the prologue of the Hammurapi Stele.

1)   When the deities of old[40]
     who allot the destinies of the world,
  Gave the rule of human beings to Marduk,
     set him over all other deities,
5)   made Babylon the foremost city-state in all the earth
     and the capital of an everlasting kingdom,
     with foundations laid strong as those of heaven and earth,
  At that time I, Hammurapi,
     the pious, god-fearing prince,
10)   was called forth by name for the welfare of the people:
  To cause justice to appear in the world,
     to destroy the evil and the wicked
     so that the strong should not oppress the weak,
     and to rise like Shamash to give light to the land.
15)   I, Hammurapi the shepherd,
     have gathered abundance and plenty,
     have stormed the four quarters of the world,
     have magnified the fame of Babylon,
     and have elated the mind of Marduk my lord.
20)   To me has been given the authority,
     and I have been faithful to Shamash.
  I am like a god among kings,
     endued with knowledge and wisdom.
  I have provided plentiful offerings for the deities
25)   and built their temples.
  I am pure of mind,
     and the deities listen to my prayers.

---

39. Loren R. Mack-Fisher, "The Patriarchal Cycles," in *Orient and Occident: Essays Presented to Cyrus H. Gordon on the Occasion of His Sixty-Fifth Birthday,* ed. Harry A. Hoffner, Jr., AOAT 22 (Kevelaer: Butzon & Bercker), 59-65. For a discussion of this suggestion, see Rummel, 284-95. In recent years, Mack-Fisher has collected much additional evidence, particularly in regard to burial rituals, birth, and blessing. Publication of this evidence is expected in the near future.

40. See Jacobsen, 188-90, for the deities named at this point of the prologue and their political significance.

I am the wise ruler
who bears the responsibility of government,
30)   who has attained the source of wisdom,
   who has enlarged the kingdom,
   and who has established pure sacrifices for ever.
I am first of all kings;
   I have conquered all peoples.
35) I am the shepherd of the people
   who causes the truth to appear,
   guiding my flock rightly.
I am the pious prince,
   deep in prayer to the great deities.
40) I am the mighty king, the sun of Babylon,
   who causes light to appear in the land,
   who brings all the world to obedience.
I am the favorite of the deities.
When Marduk commanded me
45)   to establish justice for the people of the land
   and to provide orderly government,
I set forth truth and justice throughout the land,
   and caused the people to prosper.

In the opening section, Marduk's installation as king is related according to a different scenario than that of the *Enuma Elish*. Here, as in Genesis, there is no cosmic battle. There is cosmogonic ideology, cast in the language of political propaganda. Marduk's rise to kingship is connected to Babylon's rise to prominence, and the foundations of that "everlasting kingdom" (l. 6) are cosmic in nature (l. 7).[41] In this context, Hammurapi is "called forth by name" (l. 10) to provide order for the people of the "world." The order provided by Hammurapi is identified as a struggle against human evil, set in the context of the king's responsibility to provide justice, as represented by the god Shamash (ll. 11-14). In the second section (ll. 15-39), the motifs of conflict, order, and kingship are connected to the motifs of temple and cult, as Hammurapi identifies himself as the one responsible for maintaining the correct ceremonies. The consequences for the role of Hammurapi as the nexus between heaven and earth are restated in the third section (ll. 40-48).

The prologue of the Hammurapi Stele demonstrates the royal use of the cosmogonic cluster of motifs. To say "creation" is to speak of leadership.[42] In

---

41. Compare the conception of the city-wall expressed in Gilgamesh's closing speech to Urshanabi in the rendition given above: a good wall, like a good city or kingdom, must be established on the orders of the cosmos itself.

42. Note Jacobsen's argument that the primary theme of the *Enuma Elish* itself is political (pp. 183-90).

this context, names become very important.[43] Hammurapi must be called forth by name. From Elohim's naming the elements of the cosmos in Genesis 1, to Yahweh-Elohim's assignment for the human of naming all the other living beings (2:19-20), to the human's calling forth the name of his wife (3:20), and on through 11:26, Genesis is prepossessed with the significance of naming and calling forth the name. In view of the Hammurapi Stele, we can argue that the intention of Gen 1:1–11:26 is to affirm the necessity of the one "right" leader for society — the leader whose rule is grounded on cosmic origins and order. The validation of this "leadership principle" in Gen 1:1–11:26 continues through the patriarchal cycles and into the Moses story. At Sinai, Moses becomes a new Hammurapi, mediating between the deity and the people, producing a written prescription for an orderly society.

The view that the primary intention of Gen 1:1–11:26 is to legitimize the rule of a king is necessarily speculative. The writers of Genesis were considerably more subtle than the writers of the Hammurapi Stele! Yet, in assessing the presuppositions the Hebrews might have held concerning creation, we have seen hints — from the *Enuma Elish,* from the *Gilgamesh Epic,* and from the Hammurapi Stele — that the institution of monarchy could not exist apart from an explicit view of creation and its significance for human life. Less speculative is the notion that the intention of Gen 1:1–11:26 must be discovered within the institutions of ancient Israel as those institutions are unveiled by our growing knowledge of the ancient world. To say "creation" in Gen 1:1–11:26 is not to make an abstract statement. To say "creation" has some purpose — and that purpose seems quite unlikely to coincide with our current presuppositions. The concept of creation as we have defined it for two millennia in Western culture may have grown so powerful that it will inevitably crowd out all other views. For this reason, after learning that to say "creation" in Gen 1:1–11:26 is to speak of the whole, we might conclude it would be better not to say "creation" at all.[44]

43. In his forthcoming work, Mack-Fisher will discuss the significance of "calling forth the name" in detail.

44. Aside from the concession to ethnocentrism this would make (cf. McCarthy, " 'Creation' Motifs"), it is difficult to find a descriptive category if we abandon the word "creation." In a note to his translation of Gen 1:1, Mack-Fisher explains that he uses "form" instead of "create" because the term "create" carries with it "just too much baggage," and because "form" conveys the appropriate image of God the sculptor.

The Task of Text Criticism

JAMES A. SANDERS

Two almost simultaneous events which occurred during the Jewish-Arab War (Israel's War of Independence), just before the middle of the century, have caused reassessment of the concept and role of text criticism in the study of the Old/First Testament. As the reassessment has progressed it has become clear to an increasing number of scholars that text criticism is in a period of transition from what it largely has been the past two centuries to a new concept and method.

The Dead Sea Scrolls first came to light in war-torn Palestine about the same time efforts were being made to rescue the oldest, and some say the finest, product of the Tiberian Masoretes from a fire caused by the same conflict in the synagogue in Aleppo.[1] The two recoveries brought dramatic focus to bear on the Masoretic phenomenon, the one providing primary evidence of the beginnings of the process of stabilization of the text of the Hebrew Bible, and the other offering primary evidence of the magnificent end of that process. It would be difficult to overestimate the importance of either for the perception of the history of transmission of the text of the Hebrew Bible — the foundation of any concept or theory of text criticism.

Text criticism, since the formulations of its task by Johann David Michaelis in the mid–eighteenth century, had been understood to be a part of exegesis of the text in the sense that one can better judge which reading to choose if one knows first what the fuller context is about. There can be no doubt that the observation is true. But the practice developed to the point, by the time of Julius Wellhausen's work on Samuel in the mid–nineteenth century, that text criticism was not limited to choice among available "variants" but was obligated to

---

1. See I. Ben-Zvi, "The Codex of Ben Asher," *Textus* 1 (1960): 1-16; and M. Goshen-Gottstein, "The Authenticity of the Aleppo Codex," *Textus* 1 (1960): 17-58.

include conjecture in the conviction that it was possible to reconstruct *Urtexte* of much of the biblical text.[2] By the middle of this century there was little debate about the principal task of text criticism; it was to reconstruct a text as close to what may be perceived as "the original" as possible. The fact that H. S. Nyberg in 1935 called for a return to the MT, as the only solid base for philological and exegetic interpretation, hardly stemmed the tide of understanding of what text criticism was meant to do; his call has drawn more attention during the second half of the century than it did earlier.[3]

The recovery of Aleppensis, along with the scrolls, launched the Hebrew University Bible Project (HUBP) headed by Moshe Goshen-Gottstein. The latter had become convinced that the vocalization, punctuation, and *massorot* of the Aleppo Codex were the work of Aaron ben Asher himself, the son of Moshe ben Aaron and the fifth generation of the famous Tiberian family who brought the Masoretic phenomenon to its finest expression; this much is affirmed in a colophon, now lost, written not by Aaron but by someone a century later.[4] Goshen-Gottstein also believed that Aleppensis was the codex approved by Maimonides himself. It took five generations of the ben Asher family to write the entire Bible in one codex; Moses completed the prophetic corpus in 895 (Codex Cairensis of the prophets) and Aaron, his son, the whole Bible in 915, the date of Aleppensis.

Eight centuries earlier the consonants of most of what is now called the Hebrew Bible had been stabilized in a process that took about a century but was especially intense in the period between the two Jewish revolts. By the beginning of the second century of the common era the Masoretic phenomenon had been launched; prior to that the Hebrew text existed in variants. That observation is undoubtedly the most relevant for text criticism after forty years of study of the Dead Sea Scrolls. What can be seen happening to the consonantal text of the Bible through study of the Dead Sea Scrolls is the beginning of a process that would culminate in the achievement of the ben Asher family and school; the two ends of the process came to light in the middle decades of this century. The stabilization of the consonantal text provided the *ketiv* of the Bible; the Masoretic phenomenon would provide the *qere. Miqra* requires both.

The tendency in text criticism to value the consonants more highly than the vowels came to full expression in Luther's work of translating the Hebrew Bible, beginning in 1523, influenced in part by Elias Levita, who believed that the work of the Tiberian Masoretes had little historical value.[5] Luther's belief

---

2. *Der Text der Bücher Samuelis untersucht* (Göttingen: Vandenhoeck & Ruprecht, 1871).

3. *Studien zum Hoseabuche: Zugleich ein Beitrag zur Klärung des Problems der alttestamentarischen Textkritik* (Uppsala: Almqvist & Wiksels, 1935).

4. Israel Yevin, *Introduction to the Tiberian Masorah*, Masoretic Studies 5 (Missoula: Scholars Press, 1980); Ben-Zvi, 13-15.

5. *Massoret ha-Massoret* (1538); see Richard Simon, *Histoire critique du Vieux Testament* (Rotterdam, 1685; reprint, Geneva: Slatkine Reprints, 1971), 132.

in *sola scriptura,* supported by his text-critical hermeneutic of *Res et Argumentum,* made it very clear that Christian students of the Hebrew Bible should modify vowel points, accents, constructions, and meanings, in fact, anything outside Hebrew grammar itself, and thus turn it away from Jewish interpretations toward accord with the gospel of Jesus Christ. Cappel in the seventeenth century and Houbigant in the eighteenth, among others, argued that the vowel points had been invented five hundred years after Christ and that the danger in ignoring them would be contained by close attention to literary context. By 1697 Clericus argued for the validity of conjecture, without the support of manuscripts or versions, in reconstructing the text.

Buxtorf, father and son, along with some Calvinists, disagreed, but by the time of Johann H. Michaelis's *Biblia Hebraica* of 1720, and certainly by the time of Johann David Michaelis's *Orientalische und Exegetische Bibliothek* of 1771-73, the path text criticism would take was largely set.[6] It was a part, albeit an essential part, of exegesis, a point circumspect text critics do not dispute. But text criticism became a subservient partner in that the consonants commanded great respect and the work of the Masoretes very little. A hermeneutic of suspicion toward the contributions of the Masoretes was deemed fair, in the light of the need, almost universally felt, to construct a history of formation of the text — a point Spinoza had made in 1670 that met with almost universal recognition.[7] The next centuries until the middle of the twentieth would see a tendency to reconstruct texts, even compose eclectic texts, in order not to follow Luther's hermeneutic but to press a text back as close to a supposed "original" as possible, so that the history of the formation of the text would be as clear as possible. Critical scholarship and fundamentalism had an area of common interest, the *ipsissima verba* of the original contributors to the text, albeit for different reasons. And yet they both exhibit Western cultural tendencies to seek individuals as sources or vehicles of truth.[8] Behind both is a view of authority tacitly or openly held.

In 1969 the United Bible Societies (UBS) translations department, headed by Eugene Nida, formed a team to work on the text of the Old/First Testament to be called the Hebrew Old Testament Text Project (HOTTP). The reason he

---

6. D. Barthélemy, *Critique textuelle de l'Ancien Testament (CTAT)* vol. 1, OBO 50/1 (Fribourg: Éditions Universitaires, 1982), *10-*40; J. Sanders, "Hebrew Bible *and* Old Testament: Textual Criticism in Service of Biblical Studies," *Hebrew Bible or Old Testament,* ed. R. Brooks and J. Collins (Notre Dame, 1990), 41-68, esp. 45-57.

7. Whether Spinoza was cited, credited, or ignored because of his heretical standing: *Tractatus Theologico-Politicus,* eds. G. Gawlick and F. Niewöhner, Opera. Werke lateinisch und deutsch 1 (Darmstadt, 1979).

8. See J. Sanders, "Communities and Canon," in *Oxford Study Bible of the Revised English Bible* (Oxford, 1992), 91*-100*; and Sanders, "Introduction: Why the Pseudepigrapha?" in *The Pseudepigrapha and Early Biblical Interpretation,* ed. James H. Charlesworth and Craig A. Evans (Sheffield: JSOT Press, 1993), 13-19.

did so was to provide guidance to the numerous teams of translators supported by the UBS throughout the world in their use of the Hebrew text (BHK, then BHS). Whenever a textual difficulty surfaced, most of the teams would turn to the modern Western Bible translations in the languages of former (or continuing) colonists to find a solution. In effect, they translated into their receptor languages what they found in the Revised Standard Version, *La Bible de Jerusalem (première édition)* (BJ1), *Die Revidierte Lutherbible,* the New English Bible, and *La Traduction Oecuménique de la Bible* (TOB). If they looked at only one such, they simply translated what they found there rather than struggle with the Hebrew text. But often they would consult more than one such translation, and that was when they cried for help. Nida wanted to provide the kind of textual assistance which would replace the tendency to find solutions in Western translations of German, French, and English culture; he had already done the same for the New Testament when in 1955 he had launched the Greek New Testament Project.

It was clear to the HOTTP committee that the principal problem lay in the developed concept and practice of text criticism.[9] Most of the 5,000 passages assigned to the team by the UBS translations department contained the kinds of textual characteristics which permitted text critics to offer varying and often opposing readings which then surfaced in the translations consulted. The RSV and the TOB were clearly the most sober with regard to trying to understand the MT, but for different reasons. The RSV translators in the second quarter of the century had been under considerable restraints to maintain the formal equivalence character of the KJV as a translation of the MT; the TOB represented a conscious new effort, over against the BJ1, to take the MT seriously. The NEB had the most outright conjectures and stood with BJ1 as an exponent of the trajectory of text criticism that had developed since the late seventeenth century.

It was interesting that these translations representing the fruits of text

---

9. See, e.g., Ralph Klein, *Textual Criticism of the Old Testament: From the Septuagint to Qumran,* Guides to Biblical Scholarship (Philadelphia: Fortress, 1974), 62-84, where regret is expressed that the BHK apparatus fails to "cite all synonymous readings or all the evidence for shorter or longer readings" (62). Klein is right to cite Orlinsky's many observations that the BHK apparatuses (still the case in BHS) are replete with errors; but the HOTTP found in its work that genetically related witnesses are often cited in support of what the editor had chosen as preferred readings, instead of indicating that some of the cited versions really depended on an earlier version, such as the Old Greek, and, like the translations of many current UBS national committees, were not independent witnesses as the apparatus might lead the student to believe. We also found that the apparatus as constructed was essentially a defense of how the editor had arranged the text (with innovative spacing) to support an exegetic position already arrived at. These are reasons Barthélemy in the introduction to volume 3 of *CTAT,* OBO 50/3 (Fribourg: Éditions Universitaires, 1992), calls for two distinct apparatuses, a Reconstructive Textual Critique and a Genetic Textual Analysis, one quite separate from the other (see the introduction, and especially the conclusions to it, pp. ccxxviii-ccxxxviii).

criticism so long in development should appear just after the middle of the twentieth century, and the recovery of the scrolls and Aleppensis. The NRSV (1990) has in part abandoned its heritage of the KJV/RSV line of sober, formal equivalence translation of the MT. Because the regnant concept of text criticism in this country is still that of creating eclectic texts that attempt to reconstruct supposed "originals," the NRSV translation committee in part reflects that position; where a LXX reading appears to have support of a Qumran manuscript an innovative, eclectic text based on them was often translated. But the HOTTP committee did not have the NRSV as part of its assignment, and through the third volume of its published results does not include the NRSV in its considerations. Whereas the NRSV in the translation of some books moves in the direction of facile emendation of the MT, and even conjectures, the revisions of the other translations, especially the third edition of the BJ and the REB (a revision of the NEB), move in the direction of more sober evaluation of the MT.

What is the task of text criticism? Numerous attempts have recently been made to answer the question in the light of recent developments. It is not difficult to find agreement on a goal such as "establishing the critically most responsible text" by sound critical method.[10] It is when one attempts to locate the stage of development and transmission of the text at which one should aim the establishment of the "critically most responsible text" that one is confronted with varying concepts. The older concept of aiming for a "primitive text" as close to an "original" as possible by constructing an eclectic text where necessary still finds many adherents.[11] The clearest or simplest alternative position is that of aiming to establish the "final" canonical text based on the MT.[12] The meaning

---

10. The study by Martin Jan Mulder, "The Transmission of the Biblical Text," in *Mikra: Text, Translation, Reading, and Interpretation of the Hebrew Bible in Ancient Judaism and Early Christianity*, ed. M. J. Mulder (Philadelphia: Fortress, 1988), 87-132, is an excellent overview and classification of all the chores involved in doing text criticism. See the programmatic introduction to *CTAT*, vol. 3, i-vi, for precise procedures.

11. See P. Kyle McCarter, Jr., *Textual Criticism: Recovering the Text of the Hebrew Bible*, Guides to Biblical Scholarship (Philadelphia: Fortress, 1986), 12; note what McCarter calls "common fallacies," 13-18.

12. Some recent studies which discuss the current "aims" of various text critics in targeting the stage of development of the text include F. E. Deist, *Witnesses to the Old Testament* (Pretoria: Orion, 1988), 1-9; Albert Frey's review of *CTAT*, vol. 1, in *Revue de théologie et de philosophie* 117 (1985): 197-207; Hermann-Josef Stipp, "Das Verhältnis von Textkritik und Literarkritik in neueren alttestamentlich Veröffentlichungen," *BZ* (n.f.) 34 (1990): 16-37; and Bruce K. Waltke, "Aims of Old Testament Textual Criticism," *WTJ* 51 (1989): 93-108. Deist's formulations are perhaps more suited to dialogues within the Dutch Reformed Church than to general use, but they are clear and informative, especially his discussion of how one's epistemology probably determines which "aim" one adopts (pp. 160-63), where he writes (162, top), "Scholarly criticism should not be intended to demolish opposing opinions or to verify a private perceptional bias, but to detect error in the opposing or differing view in order to *better* [emphasis his] that view." Waltke's discussion seems

of the term "original" depends on the author using it and the context in which it is used. There are those who apparently think it possible and worth the effort to pierce back to autographs.[13] The term is used by Emanuel Tov in what he calls a "moderate" sense.

> At the end of the process of composition of the biblical books stood at least one entity (a tradition or single copy) which was completed at the literary level. Possibly at one point parallel compositions were created as well, but they are not evidenced, and in any event, textual criticism takes into consideration only the literary composition that has been accepted as authoritative in Judaism. Even if we assume a very complicated literary development, at some time that process was ended. At the end of that process stood a finished literary product which at the same time stood at the beginning of a process of copying and textual transmission. During the textual transmission many complicated changes occurred which make it almost impossible for us to reconstruct the original form that stood at the beginning of the textual transmission. However, these difficulties do not refute the correctness of the assumption. All the textual witnesses — except for those that are based on an earlier literary stage of the book — had developed from this textual entity (tradition or single copy). This entity forms the textual source aimed at by textual criticism, even if that aim can be accomplished in some details only. Reference to the originality of details in the texts pertains to this entity and not to an earlier or later literary stage. Its date differs from book to book and usually cannot be determined. For textual criticism this entity thus forms the "original" text, though in a moderate formulation, since it was preceded by oral and written stages.[14]

If the word "original" continues to have a valid function in text criticism, it is probably in the meaning Tov ascribes to it. But it should be noted that Tov insists on the assumption in text-critical work of an original text, despite the distinctly parallel texts of Proverbs, Exodus 35–40, and others. (For Tov, LXX Jeremiah is not a parallel text but the "first edition" of which MT Jeremiah is a deuteronomistic expansion.) Others, such as Goshen-Gottstein, Shemaryahu Talmon, Moshe Greenberg, Stanley Walters, and Dominique Barthélemy — each with differing nuances, to be sure — assume a multiplicity of texts, or of parallel texts. The temptation is to think of Tov as agreeing with de LaGarde, and the others with Kahle, insofar as their opposing theories concerning the LXX apply generally also to the Hebrew text tradition, but it has been shown

---

designed to support a Protestant conservative view, but the article reflects recent discussion. Frey and Stipp offer helpful analyses.

13. G. Thomas Tanselle, "The Editorial Problem of Final Authorial Intentions" (1976), reprinted in Tanselle, *Selected Studies in Bibliography* (Charlottesville: University Press of Virginia, 1979), 314 (see Waltke, 93 n. 1).

14. Emanuel Tov, "The Original Shape of the Biblical Text," VTSup 43 (1991): 355-56.

time and again that to base or initiate one's thinking about the task of text criticism on a choice between de LaGarde and Kahle is to revert to a dilemma that can be misleading.

A major problem for all text critics stems from the difficulty in distinguishing a text's literary development and its textual transmission, where the one ceases and the other begins. In a very fine review of the positions of various text critics on the difficulty, Hermann-Josef Stipp concludes nonetheless, "Textkritik analysiert Daten der Textüberlieferung, Literarkritik solche der Textbeschaffenheit."[15] He adds that so-called "Konjekturalkritik" belongs in the realm of literary criticism, ranging himself with Barthélemy and the HOTTP, as well as the HUBP, against B. Albrektson.[16] The reason the boundary between the two disciplines for any given biblical text or book is difficult to locate is that written transmission of the biblical books started before the process of literary growth was complete; hence some early manuscripts witness to a period when the text was still being formulated.[17] It is in this sense that text criticism cannot totally escape involvement in exegesis; the boundary between literary criticism and text criticism on many biblical texts remains elusive. But such an admission does not give license to return to the old practice of text criticism where the latter is subservient to exegesis and made to serve the modern critic's concept of what a given text ought to have said.

The other boundary equally elusive is the stage at which the text-critical enterprise should aim. It has become quite current to say that that stage should be the beginnings of a text's recognition as canonical. Tov puts it well.

> The reconstruction of the "original" composition at the textual level depends among other things upon a certain view of the content of the composition that was accepted as authoritative (canonical) in Judaism. The Bible contains the holy writings of the Jewish people, and the decisions that were made within that religious community determine to a great extent also the approach of the learned world towards that text. . . . One has to take into consideration the authoritative status given to the consonantal text by Judaism at an earlier stage [than the Ben Asher text], not with regard to small details, but regarding the scope of the literary composition. . . . As for the LXX, the canonical conception reflected in it differs from that of the MT; it pertains mainly to literary criticism and not to textual criticism. . . . [LXX Jeremiah] reflects elements from the process of the growth of the book . . . it has to be disregarded in this discussion. One should disregard also other elements that apparently are later than the compositions found in the MT. For either during

---

15. Stipp, 37.

16. B. Albrektson, "Difficilior lectio probabilior: A Rule of Textual Criticism and Its Use in Old Testament Studies," *Oudtestamentische Studiën* 21 (1981): 5-18.

17. E. Tov, *The Text-Critical Use of the Septuagint in Biblical Research,* Jerusalem Biblical Studies 3 (Jerusalem: Simon, 1981), 294.

or after the process of canonization some books continued to develop on a literary level, such as Daniel, Esther and Psalms. . . . [They] will be disregarded in the reconstruction of the "original" text defined here, since [they do] not pertain to the literary compositions that have been accepted as authoritative by the Jewish community.[18]

Barthélemy and the HOTTP, recognizing early on the validity of the position Tov has recently outlined, chose to aim reconstruction of the text at a different period in the canonical process, namely, at the earliest stage discernible when the text in question functioned as sacred scripture and was distributed sufficiently widely within an identity group that held that text as sacred. At one point this was described as the period of "accepted texts," that is, when a text was accepted by some discrete community or communities within Judaism to function canonically. This is different from understanding canon as *norma normata*, a closed list of books forming a canon, a "final form" of the text.[19] It is derived from understanding canon as *norma normans*, when a discrete text was diffused sufficiently within a historically and sociologically identifiable Jewish community to function canonically, in much the same manner that early traditions were widely recognized in some portion of ancient Israel or Judah as authoritative and functioned in oral recitation canonically. Martin Jan Mulder expresses the point well.

> The reader is referred to the Hebrew Old Testament Project of Barthélemy and others, instigated by the United Bible Society, in which besides the methods of textual and literary criticism used in the BHK and BHS and the purely informative textual criticism as reproduced in the HUBP, a form of textual criticism based on the history of interpretation is applied. The text which was regarded as "sacred scripture" during the period in which the OT canon came into being, is thought to be attainable in its original form. This period lasted from approximately the fourth to the first century BCE.[20]

The introduction to *Critique textuelle de l'Ancient Testament*, volume 3, states very clearly the task of text criticism as perceived by the HOTTP committee.[21] Review of the five modern translations revealed that the thrust of text criticism as practiced since the eighteenth century, and especially since the beginning of the twentieth when BHK1 was first published, had reduced text

18. Tov, "Original Shape," 357.
19. Brevard Childs argues that the task of text criticism is that of establishing the final form of the text (*Introduction to the Old Testament as Scripture* [Philadelphia: Fortress, 1979], 96-106), a position similar to those who subscribe to the Reformation ideal of *sola scriptura* (so Deist, 4-7).
20. Mulder, 99 n. 43.
21. *Critique textuelle de l'Ancient Testament*, vol. 3, OBO 50/3 (Fribourg: Éditions Universitaires, 1992).

criticism to subservience to literary criticism. The committee decided to aim its work at the stage a biblical book was held to function canonically in certain identifiable Jewish communities. It ruled out conjectures, based on literary criticism, which have no support in the ancient witnesses. It was understood that when a composition reached the status of sacred scripture, that of functioning canonically, it had as a distinctive characteristic that it would need to address those communities in different time/space parameters, and so would be subject to textual modifications for applicability, clarity, and relevance. It had reached the status of being "adaptable for life."[22] But when that text or book became canonical scripture it would have been distributed in authentic editions in numerous communities, the nonauthentic having fallen, or falling, into disuse. Modifications were now limited to attribution of *tiqqunê sopherîm* in some passages, the *qere/ketiv* phenomenon, *sebirîm*, etc., or in translations where translational hermeneutics played an essential role as they would once the text was firmly established.

The stabilization process for the Torah/Pentateuch was achieved quite early, conceivably as early as the time of Ezra, at least in bulk. The stabilization for the rest of the Tanak would be achieved by the beginning of the Second Jewish Revolt, symbolized by the assembly at Jabne. The Greek Minor Prophets Scroll from Nahal Hever provided the data for describing the stabilization process.[23] So much for the consonantal text. But a true *Miqra* needs a *qere* as well as a *ketiv*. Of the various efforts at encoding a full *qere* (vowels and punctuation) the Tiberian proved itself the most thorough and complete, not the Babylonian or the Palestinian. It took five generations of the ben Asher family to write the entire Bible in one codex. The stabilization that began in late Early Judaism, especially in the second half of the first century B.C.E., came to fruition in the classical Tiberian MT with its four major characteristics: the consonantal text with carefully placed columns and spaces in the text (*la mise en page* — text units, arrangement of the great canticles, *petuhot*, *setumot*, etc.); vocalization system; accentuation systems; and the Masorah. The Masorah's principal function was to protect the unusual, especially the single readings, anomalies, and seeming discrepancies in the text, from being harmonized or eliminated in the scribal transmission process. There is no other literature on earth that has been transmitted with such care for every detail.[24] There are a few Syriac New Testament manuscripts which have a few scribal, marginal notes, but even they are rare.

22. See Sanders, *From Sacred Story to Sacred Text* (Philadelphia: Fortress, 1987), 9-39.
23. The thesis of D. Barthélemy in his *Devaniers d'Aquila*, VTSup 10 (Leiden: Brill, 1963), fully affirmed by the editors of 8HevXIIgr in *The Greek Minor Prophets Scroll from Nahal Hever*, DJD 8 (Oxford: Clarendon, 1990); see Sanders, "Stability and Fluidity in Text and Canon," in *Tradition of the Text*, ed. G. Norton and S. Pisano, OBO 109 (Fribourg: Universitätsverlag, 1991), 203-17.
24. See Sanders *From Sacred Story*, 125-51.

Aleppensis clearly was the "first completed edition" realized by the Tiberian Masoretes.[25] In the course of the some twenty-five years of work on the HOTTP it has become clear that the work of the Masoretes is more reliable, proved by many detailed tests, than the consonantal text which was first prepared by a professional scribe, Solomon ben Buya'a in the case of Aleppensis, before the Masorete(s) inserted their system.[26]

A critical edition of the text should be centered in the base text chosen. Since Aleppensis lacks significant portions of the text, decisions must be made about which consonantal text to use as textual base; the HOTTP uses L because it is the oldest complete Hebrew Bible in existence, but also recommends the Pentateuch of Damascus for the Torah, Cairensis for the Prophets, and L for the Writings, with careful reference to A where extant. Witnesses should be distinguished along two lines. According to the history of transmission of the text used, they may be divided into pre- and extra-Masoretic, proto-Masoretic, and Masoretic.[27] They should also be classified into text-types so that, e.g., versions that depend on the Greek would not be listed as true variants. These would be treated in a separate "genetic textual analysis" (see n. 9).

25. Malachi Beit-Arié, former librarian of the Hebrew University and the National Jewish Archives in Jerusalem, has with a team from Israel begun, since the summer of 1990 (see n. 26 below), the first truly systematic searches and study of the Firkovitch I and II and Antonin Collections in the Saltykov-Shchedrin National Public Library in Leningrad/St. Petersburg. Along with the small collection at the Institute of Oriental Studies, Leningrad has, it is now estimated, about 17,000 Hebrew manuscripts, most of which have never been studied or even properly catalogued. Beit-Arié claims that these new "discoveries" will, among other things, considerably expand our knowledge of the history of the Masoretic movement. See "Exhuming the Hebrew Secrets of St. Petersburg," *Jerusalem Post International Edition,* week ending October 12, 1991, p. 1.

26. This conclusion runs counter to most text-critical practice since Luther/Levita, but must now be reckoned with. On colopha, see Ben-Zvi, 3-16. On the issue of whether the ben Asher family was rabbanite or Qaraite, the high probability is that they were rabbanite but learned a great deal from the reverence and care for the text Qaraites practiced in Palestine, even in Tiberias; see the summary judgment in this regard in *CTAT* 3, xvi-xvii. The colophon of Leningradensis indicates that the scribe and Masorete, Shemuel ben Jacob, were the same. The Ancient Biblical Manuscript Center fielded a photographic team to the Saltykov-Shchedrin State Public Library in the spring of 1990 (see n. 25 above) to photograph L afresh and intends to publish a facsimile edition in due course.

27. The pre-Masoretic would include the Qumran manuscripts, the Samaritan Pentateuch, and the Old Greek; the proto-Masoretic would include manuscripts from the caves of the Second Revolt, especially the Greek Minor Prophets Scroll (see n. 23), the Hexaplaric versions (Aquila, Theodotion, Symmachus, and Quinta), the Vulgate, the Peshitta where influenced by the Greek and the Targum; the Masoretic would include the great manuscripts A, C, and L, the Ben Asher/Ben Naftali differences, lemmas in the Judaeo-Arabic exegetes, lexicographers, and grammarians of the tenth century, New York Ms JTS Luzki 232, Oriental manuscripts in Babylonian and Palestinian traditions, the Ben Hayyim edition, Norzi, some Sephardic or Yemenite manuscripts, and Paris BN hébr 1-3, BL Arundel Or 16, BL Add 21161 and Berlin Or fol 1213.

The task of text criticism can be formulated succinctly as the quest for true variants. The method employed for locating textual accidents should be carefully devised and applied.[28] Most so-called variant readings can be dismissed as facilitating or harmonizing, like most of the suggestions for emendation in the apparatuses of BHK1-3 and BHS.[29] When it has been determined that a genuine variant has been located, and no amount of testing permits dismissing it, the question arises as to how to view it and how to treat it. It is because there are a number of genuine variants text critics cannot dismiss that an increasing number of critics speak, against Tov, of a multiplicity of texts, or different "pristine" texts in the fourth- to first-century-B.C.E. time frame. Goshen-Gottstein spoke of a mainstream and many rivulets.[30] Tov sets the sixth to fifth century B.C.E. period as the stage of development at which text criticism should aim, since he views the "equally valid readings" all text critics find in the prestabilization period as having been created in the second (fluid or prestabilization) stage of the development of the biblical text; for him even though such readings are of equal value, nonetheless "one of them was original."[31] What is not yet clear is the method by which Tov feels he can legitimately locate his "moderate original" text.

In the meantime text criticism in its new configuration attempts, after the most stringent tests have been applied, to identify true variants, as opposed to pseudo-variants. Rigorous text-critical praxis demands defending both or all opposing readings as carefully as possible before dismissing one or the other as

---

28. See the fifteen factors characterizing such accidents in each "avant-propos" to *The Preliminary and Interim Report on the Hebrew Old Testament Text Project*, vols. 1-5 (London: United Bible Society, 1972-80), and to *CTAT*, vols. 1-3 (Fribourg: Éditions Universitaires, 1982-).

29. On the place of comparative philology in text-critical work see Yohanan Muffs, "Two Comparative Lexical Studies," The Gaster Festschrift, *JANES* 5 (1973): 296: "Only after new meanings emerge naturally from the context of one language should comparative material be brought into the picture." See also Sh. Talmon, "The Comparative Method in Biblical Interpretation," VTSup 29 (Leiden: Brill, 1978), 343-47, and Talmon, "Emendations of Biblical Texts on the Basis of Ugaritic Parallels," *Scripta Hierosolymitana* 31, ed. S. Japhet (1986): 279-300; see also J. Sanders, "The Dead Sea Scrolls and Biblical Studies," in *Sha'arei Talmon: Studies in the Bible, Qumran, and the Ancient Near East Presented to Shemaryahu Talmon*, ed. M. Fishbane, E. Tov, and W. Fields (Winona Lake: Eisenbrauns, 1992), 333.

30. M. Goshen-Gottstein, *The Book of Isaiah: Sample Edition with Introduction* (Jerusalem: Magnes, 1965), 17. The introduction to the Sample Edition, fully explaining Goshen-Gottstein's understanding of the task of text criticism, continued to serve as introduction to the two subsequent fascicles (1975, 1981), which include only Isaiah 1–44. Goshen-Gottstein's untimely death in August of 1991 leaves the foreseeable future of the Hebrew University Bible Project in the secure grasp of Shemaryahu Talmon, who has finished the volume on Jeremiah and is completing the third fascicle of Isaiah (chaps. 44–66) for publication in 1993-94.

31. Tov, "Original Shape," 354-55, and E. Tov, *Textual Criticism of the Hebrew Bible* (Minneapolis: Fortress, 1992), 164-80.

pseudo-variant or as "corrupt." Often the HOTTP committee found that what scholarship had tagged "corrupt" in the MT made perfectly good sense to the medieval, especially Judeo-Arabic, grammarians and commentators, and suited the context perfectly well. "Corrupt" is a misleading judgment against a reading that is not given a real chance but is facilely dismissed in favor of an exegetically favored reading.

What should be done with true variants once located? Here is where the proposal of a truly pluriform Bible is pertinent. Some true variants are single words or short phrases. Most modern translations already give alternate readings in the margin, so that most current Bibles are already to that extent pluriform. The translation here envisaged would make sure that the text of the translation reflected the base text-type, the classical Tiberian text, with genuine variants and their sources in the margin. But instead of giving a single word or so in the margin, where the true variant gives the larger passage a different complexion or even a different concept lying behind the text, a truly pluriform Bible would offer in the margin a translation of the "variant" passage as fully as need be to see that the conceptuality of what the text was doing is truly different — even where only one word differs but makes a conceptual difference to the larger unit.

Then there are the larger units, increasingly recognized, sometimes called genuine parallels, which are simply very different in concept from that of the MT. Stipp offers a list, as does Eugene Ulrich.[32] If they are truly genuine variant understandings of the larger unit, the pluriform Bible would offer the two translations side by side in parallel columns of text and not put the "variant" in the margin. To put it in the margin indicates that a choice has been made about the "more genuine" one, which is the position of both Ulrich and Tov; and in some instances that may be indicated. Many current translations put Hebrew Esther in the biblical text and the full Greek Esther in the Apocrypha, which is itself a kind of margin indicating a decision about the priority of the Hebrew; but at least it is now being given in full and not, following Jerome, as addenda. Other examples are the parallel between the deuteronomistic history and that of the Chronicler, the four Gospels in the Second/New Testament, and numerous others actually within the canons of discrete identity communities.

Those would be decisions of translators. Text criticism has as its principal task locating and identifying for the translator and the student of the Bible those true variants, large or small, that survive the rigorous tests of current text-critical practice. This would eliminate eclectic texts that claim to press back toward some undefined original, but which are nothing but the product of imagination

---

32. Stipp, 19; Ulrich in "Double Literary Editions of Biblical Narratives and Reflections on Determining the Form to Be Translated," *Perspectives on the Hebrew Bible*, ed. J. Crenshaw (Macon, Ga.: Mercer Press, 1988), 101-16.

of a particular generation of scholarship. A pluriform Bible would honor the integrity of those ancient believing communities which had a different book of Samuel, or Joshua or Judges, or Exodus 35–40, or Proverbs or Ezekiel, or whatever text, small or large, which text criticism is finally constrained to designate as a "true variant."[33]

33. The surest way of determining a true variant parallel text is the method of structure analysis developed by the scholar whose work we honor in this volume. It should be applied to both (or all) parallel literary units following the accentuation of each text — for the MT the Masoretic *ṭe'amîm*. But for the LXX one should be careful not to be influenced, as the Göttingen LXX unfortunately is, by the later Hebrew verse and other unit divisions, but by the early commentaries of the Greek Fathers to see how the LXX was read prior to the MT; see *CTAT* 3, cxiv-cxx and ccxxxvii, and the work of the team producing *La Bible d'Alexandrie*, ed. M. Harl (Paris: Cerf, 1986-).

Beobachtungen zur Sachbewegung vorexilischer Gerichtsprophetie

ODIL HANNES STECK

In seinem Beitrag »The Task of Old Testament Theology«[1] hat der verehrte Jubilar eine eindrucksvolle Perspektive aufgewiesen, wie eine Theologie des Alten Testaments zu erarbeiten sei, die sich dem Zusammenbestand einer Vielzahl von Theologien in diesem Buche stellt und über eine bloße Beschreibung dieser Pluralität ebenso hinausschreitet wie über deren faktische Eliminierung im Rückzug auf eine holistische Sicht des sogenannten Endtextes des Kanons und auf die scheinbar einheitliche Rezeption im Neuen Testament. Soll die Vielstimmigkeit des Alten Testaments wirklich erhalten bleiben und gleichwohl als höhere Einheit wahrgenommen werden können, bedarf es umgreifender Sachkriterien, die Verschiedenes vergleichbar und als Elemente eines Ganzen sichtbar machen — einer systematischen Hinsicht also. Als grundlegende Perspektive wird von Knierim für eine Theologie des Alten Testaments »Yahweh's relationship to reality in justice and righteousness« vorgeschlagen.[2] Es ist in unserem kleinen Beitrag nicht der Raum, diesen Vorschlag als solchen zu diskutieren. Gegenstand unseres Beitrags ist vielmehr eine gewichtige alttestamentliche Thematik, die in dieser Metaebene eingeschlossen ist — die prophetische Gerichtsankündigung. Zur gegebenen Vielfalt und Sachbewegung dieser Thematik vor allem in der vorexilischen Prophetie sollen im Folgenden Beobachtungen vorgeführt werden.

1. *HBT* 6,1 (1984) 25-57.
2. AaO 33ff, besonders 41ff, Zitat: 41. Knierim verweist in diesem Zusammenhang selbst (56 Anm. 11) auf H. H. Schmid; vgl. auch dessen Beiträge in H. H. Schmid, *Altorientalische Welt in der alttestamentlichen Theologie* (Zürich: Theologischer Verlag, 1974); Ders., "Gerechtigkeit und Glaube — Genesis 15,1-6 und sein biblisch-theologischer Kontext," *EvT* 40 (1980) 396-420, und zur Diskussion J. Halbe, "»Altorientalisches Weltordnungsdenken« und alttestamentliche Theologie," *ZTK* 76 (1979) 381-418.

Zunächst ein Wort zur Terminologie. Die Ankündigung negativen Ergehens, die Propheten über Einzelpersonen, Menschengruppen, das Gottesvolk
im ganzen im Norden wie im Süden, über fremde Könige, Städte und Völker
aussprechen, als Ankündigung von »Gericht« zu bezeichnen, hat den Nachteil,
daß diese Bezeichnung forensisch-juristische Assoziationen weckt, die der
prophetischen Sicht dieses Geschehens nicht unbedingt eigen sind,[3] wenngleich
jedenfalls in der Spätzeit des Alten Testaments derartige Vorstellungen auftreten
können, wie beispielsweise Jes 65,6; Mal 3,5 (.16?); Dan 7,10 zeigen.[4] Die
Bezeichnung hat aber im Deutschen gegenüber »Unheilsprophezeiung« o.ä. den
Vorteil, auszudrücken, daß es sich bei diesem Geschehen um Konsequenz, Folge,
Ahndung bestehender, aufgedeckter Schuld handelt, von Jahwe mittels des
prophetischen Wortes aufgewiesen und wirksam in Gang gesetzt.

Hinsichtlich dieser prophetischen Ankündigung negativen Ergehens sind im
Alten Testament Wandlungen festzustellen; also auch hier erst mit der Zeit gewor-
dene Pluralität und Komplexität, von der hebräischen Bibel als höherer literarischer
Einheit umschlossen. Welche *Sachbewegung* läßt das Alte Testament in den Wandlungen dieser Thematik erkennen? Man kann eine Sachbewegung, wie uns scheint,
in drei im wesentlichen aufeinanderfolgende Konstellationen fassen; eine vierte
schließlich bedeutet der umfassende Eintritt solcher Ankündigungen.

I

Nicht nur idealtypisch, sondern auch zeitlich steht *am Anfang* folgende Konstellation prophetischer Gerichtsankündigung: Der Prophet deckt eine gesche-
hene Untat auf und sagt dem Täter die unausweichliche Straffolge dessen zu;
Adressat ist ein einzelner, genauer der einzelne schlechthin im Gottesvolk —
der König. Wesentlich ist, daß sich dieser Vorgang nur auf den Schuldigen, den
König selbst und allenfalls dessen Familie, Dynastie richtet; Land und Volk im
ganzen sind zwar gegebenenfalls mitbetroffen, aber selber nicht Adressat von
Anklage und Gericht; sie bleiben offenbar im Status der Zuwendung Jahwes.
Die zeitlich und — trotz gegenteiliger Auffassung in der jüngsten Forschung —
auch überlieferungsgeschichtlich ältesten Beispiele bieten Logien in Prophe-
tenerzählungen aus dem Nordreich; 1 Kön 21,17-19 und 2 Kön 1,15f seien als
Beispiele genannt. In der Folgezeit bleibt der Aspekt königlichen Unheils bei
Amos, Hosea, sowie knapp, aber radikal auch bei Jesaja und wieder verstärkt in
der letzten Zeit vor dem Untergang des Königreiches Juda bei Jeremia und

---

3. Vgl. dazu K. Koch, *Was ist Formgeschichte? Methoden der Bibelexegese*, 4th ed.
(Neukirchen-Vluyn: Neukirchener Verlag, 1981) 235f.258ff.
4. S. ferner späte Verwendungen von *špṭ* q./ni., vgl. HALAT 1500f und K. Seybold,
"Gericht Gottes, I. Altes Testament," TRE XII (1984) 460-466, dort 461.

Ezechiel zwar durchaus virulent; zu erwähnen sind in diesem Zusammenhang vor allem noch Jes 7,*10-17 und in anderer Sprachform Ez 17. Es fällt jedoch auf, wie sehr seit Amos die Konstellation den König anredender prophetischer Gerichtsankündigung zurücktritt. Daß es neben dieser Konstellation Gerichtsankündigungen an den König ohne ausdrückliche Tataufdeckung gibt und andererseits mahnende, warnende Worte an den König mit lediglich möglichen Unheilsfolgen im Falle der Fehlentscheidung wie vergleichbar in den Mari-Briefen und im Wen-Amun-Reisebericht, muß uns hier nicht näher beschäftigen.

II

Eine *zweite,* im ganzen jüngere, neben Nachwirkungen der ersten in der überlieferung nun dominierende Konstellation vorexilischer Gerichtsprophetie unterscheidet sich von der ersten zunächst dadurch, daß der Kreis der Betroffenen über Person und Haus des Königs hinausgeht. Vor allem aber unterscheidet sie sich dadurch, daß Straffolge von Frevel nicht erst für die Zukunft angekündigt, sondern, wenn auch in verschiedenen Stadien, vom Propheten bereits in aktuellem Vollzug wahrgenommen wird; Ausgangspunkt gerichtsprophetischen Wirkens ist hier also nicht die Wahrnehmung einer Freveltat bzw. eines diesbezüglichen Jahweworts, sondern die Wahrnehmung einer Unheilslage, die als Straffolge gesehen ist. Diese Konstellation tritt in dreifacher Gestalt auf.

(1) Die Bevölkerung wird von einer nationalen Notlage militärischer oder anderer Art betroffen, die sich zu Katastrophe und Untergang des Volkes auswachsen könnte. In dieser Lage erfolgt auf Befragung oder durch spontan prophetisches Auftreten ein Vorgang, der das Geschehen auf die Untat von *Frevlern in* der Bevölkerung zurückführt, diesen Frevlern die unausweichliche Straffolge ihrer Untat freilegt, für die übrige Bevölkerung die nationale Notlage fürbittend aber zum Stehen bringt und in einen wieder positiven Status quo ante für das also gereinigte Gottesvolk wendet. J. Jeremias hat das Sachprofil dieses Vorgangs in seinem Buch *Kultprophetie und Gerichtsverkündigung in der späten Königszeit Israels* eindrucksvoll aus den Texten erhoben und von dem der klassischen spontanen Gerichtsprophetie der sogenannten Schriftprophetie unterschieden.[5] Zu der schwierigen Frage, ob es sich dabei um ein institu-

5. (WMANT 35: Neukirchen-Vluyn: Neukirchener Verlag, 1970) zusammenfassend 176ff; vgl. sein Beispiel Habakuk, ebd. 108ff. Zum Problem prophetischer Fürbitte, die bei den Schriftpropheten alles andere als durchgängig belegt ist, was aber auch mit überlieferungsdominanz und Aufzeichnung der dritten Konstellation zusammenhängen könnte, die die Schriftpropheten schließlich prägt, vgl. jetzt S. E. Balentine, "The Prophet as Intercessor: A Reassessment," *JBL* 103 (1984) 161-173. Eine wichtige Rolle für die zweite Konstellation bei den Schriftpropheten spielen deshalb vor allem deren Mahnworte, die wir im

tionelles Wirken von Kultpropheten am Heiligtum handelt, können wir hier nicht Stellung nehmen;[6] ein Zusammenhang mit dem Phänomen von Prophetie auf Befragen in Notlagen liegt nahe, und für eine Vernetzung dieser ersten Gestalt mit entsprechenden alttestamentlichen Sachverhalten in anderen Textbereichen ist wichtig, daß sich Analoges in Klageliturgien des Psalters findet.[7]

(2) Auch gemäß der zweiten Gestalt steht die Bevölkerung bereits inmitten der Erfahrung einer nationalen Notlage, die für das Gottesvolk katastrophal werden könnte, im Unterschied zu (1) wird daraus aber von der Bevölkerung oder vom Propheten auf den Schuldstatus *des Volkes im ganzen* zurückgeschlossen. Die Untat des ganzen Volkes also wird aufgedeckt, doch kann durch kollektives Sündenbekenntnis mit entsprechender Verhaltensänderung und auf Vergebung Jahwes gerichtete, prophetische Fürbitte hin erwirkt werden, daß das Äußerste abgewendet und das von Jahwe bereits in Gang gesetzte Unheil zum Stehen und Aufhören gebracht wird. Jer 14,1-12 ist auf die beschriebene Intention der Bevölkerung gesehen hierfür ein Beispiel, die Kernüberlieferung von Jes 22,1-14 ein weiteres.

(3) Besonders wichtig ist die (2) in vielem ähnliche, dritte Gestalt dieser Konstellation, weil sie auch für die klassischen Gerichtspropheten mehr als weithin angenommen in Betracht kommt, obwohl sie in den aufgezeichneten Texten freilich nur noch als die verweigerte oder verspielte Möglichkeit erscheint, die inzwischen durch die Botschaft unabwendbaren Gerichts abgelöst ist. Bezeichnend für diese dritte Gestalt ist, daß im Unterschied zu Gestalt (1) und (2) nicht eine Anfangsphase göttlichen Gerichts in der Erfahrung des Volkes schon gegeben ist, die sich zur Katastrophe auswachsen könnte, sondern daß der göttlich beschlossene Untergang des Volkes als solchen, die Vollverwirklichung totalen Gerichts am Volk also, bereits den Ausgangspunkt des Vorgangs bildet, dieses katastrophale Gericht sich aber *erst* noch im Status der *prophetischen Wahrnehmung* befindet, mögen Anzeichen dessen bereits erlebbar sein oder nicht. Treten Gestalt (1) und (2) zwischen gegebene Erfahrung von Anfängen des Gerichts und auch bei Jahwe noch ausstehender Vollverwirklichung, so ist der Ort von Gestalt (3) zwischen der prophetischen Wahrnehmung und dem Erfahrungseintritt des Wahrgenommenen als des vernichtenden Gerichts über das Gottesvolk; das Mahnwort Jes 28,22, in G. Warmuths Untersuchung

---

Unterschied zu G. Warmuths Untersuchung (*Das Mahnwort* [Beiträge zur biblischen Exegese und Theologie 1, Frankfurt und Bern: Lang, 1976]) zum Nennwert nehmen, aber für eine frühere Phase des Wirkens dieser Propheten.

6. Vgl. zur Frage außer der genannten Untersuchung von Jeremias jüngst z.B. H. Utzschneider, *Hosea, Prophet vor dem Ende* (OBO 31; Fribourg: Universitätsverlag/Göttingen: Vandenhoeck & Ruprecht, 1980; D. L. Petersen, *The Roles of Israel's Prophets* (JSOTSup 17; Sheffield: JSOT, 1981); jüngst unter Einschluß des Problems der Rolle der vorexilischen Schriftpropheten und der Intention ihres Wirkens W. Groß, "Prophet gegen Institution im alten Israel?," *TQ* 171 (1991) 15-30.

7. Vgl. dazu Jeremias, aaO 110ff.

wenig überzeugend besprochen, wäre, gegenüber seinem literarischen Kontext für sich gesehen, eines von zahlreichen Beispielen für diese Konstellation. Die Abwendung dieses Eintretens wird auch hier noch als möglich angesehen; sie wird angestrebt in der Fürbitte des mit so fürchterlichem Wissen begabten Propheten zur Abwendung der Vollstreckung der Straffolge und/oder infolge prophetisch aufgedecktem Schuldstatus durch prophetisch angemahnte Verhaltensänderung, durch Sinneswandel der Betroffenen — des Königs, bestimmter Frevlergruppen und des Volkes im ganzen, bevor es endgültig zu spät ist. Man hat allen Anlaß zur Annahme, daß es jedenfalls bei einigen der klassischen Gerichtspropheten eine Phase ihres Wirkens vor der aufgezeichneten und uns im Kern von Prophetenbüchern überlieferten gab, die von dieser Gestalt (3) geprägt war. Sei es, daß die Propheten selbst unmittelbar zunächst in diesem Sinne wirksam waren, sei es, daß sie von offiziellen Organen solches Wirken hin auf eine Verhaltensänderung gemäß dem Modell hinter Jer 14,1ff erwarteten und ihre definitive und unausweichliche Gerichtsbotschaft erst laut werden ließen, als diese Möglichkeit verweigert wurde — von Jahwe oder von den unwilligen Betroffenen, die von Einsicht in die schreckliche Lage nichts wissen wollen. Als diese Verweigerung eingetreten ist, wie es prophetischer Sicht aus Verhalten der Betroffenen und/oder Erfahrungseintritt umfassender Straffolge ablesbar oder in einer erneuten Jahwebotschaft kundgegeben ist, beherrscht die schließlich geäußerte, unausweichliche Gerichtsbotschaft, die sich bis auf das Volk als Volk erstreckt, das Feld der überlieferten, in Ansehung ihres Effekts aufgezeichneten Botschaft der vorexilischen Schriftprophetie völlig; folglich kann der Einfluß von Gestalt (3) in einer früheren Phase des Wirkens der Schriftpropheten hinter der Brechung durch die jüngere Phase und erst recht durch die Verschriftung nur noch mehr oder minder erschlossen werden. Aber wichtige Textanhalte gibt es; es sind zB. die folgenden: der Sachablauf der Amos-Visionen im Rückblick; der Text Jes 6 im Rückblick, in dem mit 6,9-11 ein Vorgang gemäß Gestalt (3) ausdrücklich ausgeschlossen werden soll;[8] Jes 7,3-9 (und Jes 8,1-4?) in der ursprünglichen Situation[9] im Unterschied zur Rückblickperspektive der aufgezeichneten »Denkschrift« Jes *6-8; weiter Jes 9,12; 28,12; 30,15-17; auch für Jeremia wird noch eine vorangehende Phase

---

8. Zum Text Jes 6, dem R. Knierim eine wichtige Untersuchung gewidmet hat ("The Vocation of Isaiah," *VT* 18 [1968] 47-68), vgl. O. H. Steck, "Wahrnehmungen Gottes im Alten Testament," *Gesammelte Studien* (TBü 70; München: Kaiser, 1982) 149-70. Dem anderssinnigen Verständnis von 6,9f zB. bei O. Keel ("Rechttun oder Annahme des Gerichts?" *BZ* 21 [1977] 200-218, dort 209 Anm.37); R. Kilian ("Der Verstockungsauftrag Jesajas," *Bausteine biblischer Theologie: Festgabe für G. J. Botterweck zum 60. Geburtstag dargebracht von seinen Schülern* [BBB 50; Köln/Bonn: Hanstein, 1977] 209-25); H. Niehr ("Zur Intention von Jes 6,1-9," *BN* 21 [1983] 59-65) oder A. Schenker ("Gerichtsverkündigung und Verblendung bei den vorexilischen Propheten," *RB* 93 [1986] 563-580, dort 568ff) kann ich aus Gründen des Aussagegefüges dieses von vornherein für die »Denkschrift« Jes *6-8 verfaßten Textes nicht zustimmen.

9. Vgl. dazu Steck, "Wahrnehmungen," 171-86, 187-203.

sichtbar, in der er angesichts des Zornes Jahwes dafür eingetreten ist, daß das prophetisch wahrgenommene Gericht in seinem Eintritt abgewendet wird (18,20; vgl. 3,22b-25); vgl. auch in Ezechiel die Spur 9,8-11; 22,30. — Ist dieser Befund richtig gesehen, dann ist er in mehrfacher Hinsicht bemerkenswert. Zum einen: Diese Sicht prophetischen Wirkens angesichts wahrgenommenen Gerichts über das Gottesvolk ist, wenngleich keineswegs identisch, so doch in Sachbeziehung zu der stereotypen Funktion, die der Deuteronomismus den vorexilischen Propheten zugewiesen hat — die Rolle der Mahner und Warner des Volkes im Horizont der Segens- und Fluch-Aussagen des Dtn, damit der mögliche Eintritt solcher Fluchfolgen abgewendet werde — 2 Kön 17,13 und Aussagen in der C-Schicht des Jeremiabuches (25,3-11; 26,1-6; 35,12-17) sind hier zu nennen; man bedenke in diesem Zusammenhang aber auch Rückblicke wie Jes 9,7ff und Am 4,6-13. Auch die prophetische Funktion des Spähers (Ez 33,1ff; vgl. Jer 6,17) ist im Rahmen von Gestalt (3) der zweiten Konstellation zu sehen. Zum anderen: Die klassischen Gerichtspropheten seit Amos sind zumindest teilweise offenbar nicht von Anfang an Künder des unabwendbaren Gerichts Jahwes über das Gottesvolk als Volk gewesen. Voran geht vielmehr eine Phase, in der sie angesichts allererst wahrgenommenen, drohenden Gerichts gleichsam Alarm schlagen, auf Sinnesänderung der Betroffenen durch Schuldaufweis und/oder Kundgabe des Wahrgenommenen hinwirken, um den Eintritt des Untergangs noch abzuwenden. Diese frühere, hinter einer jüngeren und vollends hinter der Aufzeichnung prophetischer Logien liegende Phase könnte demnach ein gewisser Anhalt für die Auffassung einiger Forscher sein, die Intention prophetischer Gerichtsankündigung sei die Umkehr zur Vermeidung des Gerichts gewesen;[10] einfach als »Umkehrpredigt« sollte man das Wirken der Schriftpropheten selbst in dieser Phase jedoch nicht bezeichnen; der Begriff wird der Komplexität der Konstellation nicht gerecht und übersieht, daß im Grunde äußerste Betroffenheit von einem bereits wahrgenommenen, kommenden Gericht angemahnt wird. Diese frühere Phase wird im Wirken der vorexilischen Schriftpropheten freilich überholt und in die Retrospektive gedrängt durch die spätere, das überlieferte und im Zuge der Erstverschriftung aufgezeichnete Wirken dieser Gestalten völlig dominierende, wonach die Schriftpropheten schließlich nur noch unabwendbares Gericht und damit das Ende des Gottesvolkes als Volk, auch wenn es Menschen als einzelne überleben, zu künden hatten. Auch für die ältere Phase gemäß Gestalt (3) ist deutlich, daß anders als in den genannten Elia-Belegen nicht die Wahrnehmung von Frevel

---

10. Vgl. die Position von G. Fohrer, verdienstvoll vorgeführt und mit der von W. H. Schmidt verglichen in der Arbeit von L. Markert und G. Wanke, "Die Propheteninterpretation," *KD* 22 (1976) 191-220, dort 192f, 195ff, und neuerdings die Anm.8 genannten Aufsätze von Keel und Schenker. Hinsichtlich der jüngeren und resultativ aufgezeichneten Phase der Gerichtsankündigung der vorexilischen Schriftpropheten und deren Intention halten wir die u.a. von H. W. Wolff und W. H. Schmidt vertretene Sicht für die, die allein dem Textbefund gerechtzuwerden vermag.

bei König, Bevölkerungsgruppen oder Volksganzem der Auslöser gerichtsprophetischen Wirkens war, sondern der zweiten Konstellation im ganzen entsprechend die Wahrnehmung von Gericht;[11] die Amos-Visionen oder Jes 6 sind dafür markante Beispiele. Zum dritten: Welch grundstürzende Wende die Gerichtsbotschaft der vorexilischen Schriftpropheten gegen Israel in der dominant überlieferten zweiten Phase ihres Wirkens war, ergibt sich nicht nur aus dem Inhalt — der Ansage unausweichlicher Katastrophe über das Volk als ganzes, sondern profiliert sich gegebenenfalls an dem Umstand, daß die dritte Gestalt der zweiten Konstellation in ihrem Wirken vorherging. Doch dann wird aus dem wahrgenommenen Gericht, das noch nicht unaufhaltsam bis zum Untergang des Volkes eintreten muß, nun ein unausweichliches, in dem Jahwe diesen Untergang vollstreckt. Damit sind wir im Verlauf der Sachbewegung bei der dritten Konstellation angelangt.

III

Die *dritte* Konstellation betrifft — gegebenenfalls als eine zweite Phase des Wirkens — das Spezificum der vorexilischen Gerichtspropheten, wie es zur Weiterüberlieferung gelangt ist: die mit Frevelgeschehen ausdrücklich oder nicht korrelierte Ansage unausweichlich und unabwendbar kommenden Jahwegerichts nicht über einen, einige, viele, sondern über das Gottesvolk als solches und im ganzen. Wie in den beiden vorangehenden Konstellationen ist das Gericht auch hier Jahwes Handeln, der darin vorgängigen Frevel ahndet und konsequent zu dessen Folgen bringt. Und wie in Gestalt (2) und (3) der zweiten Konstellation ist das Gericht über das Volk schon im Gange, sei es, daß seine Anfänge schon allgemein erlebbar sind (2), sei es, daß es zur Gänze bei Jahwe schon vorgesehen ist, sich als solches aber allererst im Status der prophetischen Wahrnehmung befindet (3). Neu aber ist, daß Jahwe nun Fürbitte abweist, Vergebung verweigert, so daß für prophetische Wahrnehmung das

---

11. Dem entspricht, daß der Schuldaufweis der vorexilischen Schriftpropheten, der sich auf Rechts- und Sozialvergehen innerhalb des Volkes, auf außenpolitisch-militärische Vergehen und auf Vergehen direkt an Jahwes Gottheit beziehen kann, aktuell und situationell sogar während des Wirkens ein und desselben Propheten wechseln kann; die jeweils aktuell-präsentische Gestalt des Frevels wird in Korrespondenz zur Gerichtsankündigung namhaft gemacht! An den Gerichts-formulierungen fällt auf, wie facettenreich, unkonventionell sie formuliert und nicht zuletzt wie wenig sie mit konkreten und zeitgeschichtlichen Einzelereignissen verknüpft sind; sie koinzidieren alle darin, daß sie in verschiedenen Hinsichten den Zusammenbruch, das Ende Israels und Judas als Volk ankündigen — wie, durch wen, wann genau, kann in der Schwebe bleiben; daß eine Anzahl Menschen übrigbleibt und mit dem Leben davonkommt, ist nicht mehr Volk, sondern Rest, der die Totalität des Gerichts über das Gottesvolk anzeigt.

Gericht in die Phase definitiver Unabwendbarkeit gelangt ist. Die Wende, die sich hier vollzogen hat, wäre auf ihre Gründe hin erneut zu befragen. Sie spiegelt sich als solche schon in den Reaktionen prophetischen Erschreckens über solche Wahrnehmung (vgl. vor allem Jer 4,19-26; 8,18-23; 14,17f; 15,5, vgl. 13,17), abgründig und haderend gegenüber Jahwe zum Ausdruck gebracht in Jeremias Konfessionen (15,10.15ff; 20,14-18), in Entsetzensrufen des betroffenen Volkes (Jer 8,14b-15.19aβ.20; 10,19f), ja sogar Jahwes selbst (Jer 12,7ff);[12] vgl. auch die Spiegelungen dieser Wende in Jes 1,2f; 8,11; Hos 11,1-9.11; Ez 2,1–3,2. Ausdruck dieser Wende ist offenbar auch, daß die Gerichtsankündigungen bezüglich des Volkes vielfach eine Sprachgestalt aufweisen, derzufolge vom betroffenen Volk nicht anredend, sondern in 3.p. gesprochen wird — die Gerichtsbotschaft ergeht nicht zu den Betroffenen, sondern über sie, die das Hören verweigern; mit ihnen ist nicht mehr zu reden, weil nun auch Jahwe die Beziehung abgebrochen hat; zeitlich wie sachlich handelt es sich um resultative Formulierungen. Nur für den Propheten selbst bleibt die direkte Kommunikation mit Jahwe erhalten (vgl. Jes 6; 7,13 (meinen Gott); 8,11-15 als Anrede an Jesaja und die Seinen gegenüber 6,9-11; 8,6-8a.11-15 bezüglich des auf der resultativen Ebene nicht mehr angeredeten Volkes). Die »Denkschrift« Jesajas Jes *6-8 in dem von uns vorgeschlagenen Sinne,[13] an dem wir trotz neuer Einsprüche literarkritischer oder anderer Art[14] festhalten, macht in ihrem resultativen Gepräge die genannte Wende selbst zum Thema und damit eine Bewegung und Wandlung ausdrücklich, die in der vorexilischen Schriftprophetie über Jesaja hinaus auch sonst in Betracht zu ziehen ist, wenn man den Weg von der selektierenden, reduzierenden, konzentrierenden Erstaufzeichnung der Logien zurückgeht zu gebotenen Rekonstruktionen der Phase von deren mündlicher Äußerung und noch weiter zurück zu der nur noch aus Relikten erschließbaren, vorangehenden Phase prophetischen Wirkens, das noch auf Abwendung des bereits aufgezeigten Gerichts hinarbeitete.

Für das Verständnis der nachgezeichneten Sachbewegung ist wesentlich,

---

12. Vgl. zu diesen Texten Jeremias, aaO 162.

13. Vgl. dazu "Wahrnehmungen," 149-203.

14. Vgl. neuere, uns sehr fragwürdige Bemühungen vor allem um Jes 7,1-17 und zur Frage der »Denkschrift« die überaus einfache Argumentation, mit der H. Graf Reventlow ("Das Ende der sog. »Denkschrift« Jesajas," *BN* 38,39 [1987] 62-67) die Annahme einer ursprünglichen, literarischen Größe des hochkomplexen Textes Jes *6-8 zu Fall bringen will. daß der vorliegende Fremdbericht in Jes 7 keine so sichere Argumentationsbasis abgibt, wird sichtbar, wenn man sich die Frage nach der Redaktionsgeschichte von Protojesaja nicht erspart, die überarbeitung in 7,1f und die bewußte Gegenüberstellung Ahas/Hiskia bedenkt. Bezüglich der Ausgrenzung eines ursprünglichen Bestandes der »Denkschrift« erhebt Stuart A. Irvine (*Isaiah, Ahaz and the Syro-Ephraimitic Crisis* [SBLDS 123; Atlanta: Scholars, 1990] 120ff, besonders 126ff) den Vorwurf, es werde in Zirkelschlüssen argumentiert; doch ist angesichts der Komplexität des vorliegenden Textes von Jes 6–9 der Suche nach stilistischer und sachlicher Kohärenz mehr Beachtung zu schenken; eine diachrone Sicht der Entstehung der Textfolge erscheint dann unausweichlich.

daß ähnlich wie das Wort Jahwes so auch das von Jahwe vorgesehene Gericht prophetisch in verschiedenen Geschehensstadien erfaßt wird: als anfänglich bereits eingetretenes und so allgemein erfahrbares, aber bei Jahwe noch aufzuhaltendes; als vollumfänglich vom Propheten wahrgenommener Untergang des Gottesvolkes und parallel dazu der von Fremdvölkern, der aber als solcher möglicherweise noch abwendbar erscheint, in einer späteren Wahrnehmungsphase dann aber als definitiv unabwendbarer gewiß ist.

IV

Eine *vierte* Konstellation schließlich ist die, da dieser erwartete Untergang in das Stadium der Erfahrungsrealität getreten ist — für Israel im Norden noch in vorexilischer Zeit, für Juda und damit das Gottesvolk zur Gänze durch Nebukadnezar. Nach ihrem Eintritt erhalten in der exilisch-nachexilischen Zeit diese bezeichnenderweise gleichwohl weiterüberlieferten und damit auch das Gottesvolk jüngerer Zeit in seine Geschichte mit Jahwe einbindenden, definitiven Gerichtsankündigungen der vorexilischen Schriftpropheten eine neue Funktion. Sie erhellen auf Jahwe als Ursprung bezogen die Erfahrungsrealität nationaler Katastrophe, die im Rahmen prophetischer wie im Rahmen deuteronomistischer Tradition als andauernd und weiterwirkend erlebt wird, und zwar andauernd oder weiterwirkend bis zum umfassenden Eintritt nunmehr als bevorstehend geweissagter bzw. in deuteronomistischer Segensperspektive ohne zeitliche Festlegung vorgewiesener Heilswende. Sie dienen jetzt der Orientierung und Mahnung, damit diese Heilswende kommt und nicht länger verzieht, und sie dienen der theologischen Wahrnehmung entsprechender Gerichtsschläge der jüngeren Zeit, die sprachlich und sachlich wie 587 v.Chr. gesehen werden. Doch müssen wir es hierzu statt weiterer Ausführungen bei diesen Andeutungen belassen.

Unser Beitrag lädt ein, einmal zusammen und in einem Sachzusammenhang zu sehen, was unter der Wucht des Neuen, das bei den vor-exilischen Schriftpropheten hervortritt, gern getrennt betrachtet wird. Die skizzierte Zusammenschau könnte Folgen haben für die Frage nach Wirkungsphasen dieser Propheten, nach Wandlungen dieser Propheten in der Wahrnehmung des Jahwegerichts gegen das Gottesvolk, die die Komplexität der aufgezeichneten Botschaft erklärlicher und die Streitfrage der Intention der Gerichtsaussagen durch ein Nacheinander beantworten, und die skizzierte Zusammenschau könnte nicht zuletzt Folgen haben für die sachliche Vergleichbarkeit von Gerichtskonzeptionen prophetischer Tradition und deren pädagogisierend-retrospektiven Rezeption in deutero-nomistischer Umkehr-Tradition, aber auch der Tradition der Psalmen. Eine kleine Vorarbeit also für die Dynamik und Bewegung, die es in Knierims Kriterium, von dem wir ausgegangen waren, zu bewahren gilt, getreu dem theologischen Vorbild, das in der Bildung von Nebiim samt Psalmen unter Bewahrung des gesamten überlieferten Textbestands als maßgeblicher Orientierungsgröße für Israel in hellenistischer Zeit sichtbar wird.[15] Schon in diesem quasi kanonischen Rahmen haben die Ankündigungen umfassenden Gerichts über das Gottesvolk durch die vorexilischen Schriftpropheten einer nachgeborenen Hörer- und Leserschaft nicht mehr unmittelbar gegolten, sondern waren aufgehoben in Heilsperspektiven, die Jahwe seither dem Volk eröffnet hat. Für Christen tut sich ein weiterer Sinn und damit das für sie Bleibende dieser Gerichtsaussagen auf. Post Christum natum sind diese Aussagen keinem Menschenkreis mehr aktuell-kerygmatisch entgegenzuschleudern; die 'Stunde des Amos' ist auch theologisch eine historische Stunde. Die Aussagen decken aber christologisch auf, was Christus am Karfreitag auf sich genommen hat, und sie decken in anthropologischem, ethischem Horizont nach wie vor Verhalten ohne Sinn und Zukunft auf — freilich ohne den Täter, dem das Evangelium angeboten ist, zu verwerfen. Die Aussagen haben schließlich erneute Realität in dem Geschehen enthüllter Sinnlosigkeit, das Spättexte des Alten Israel ebenso wie das Neue Testament als weltweites Endgericht über jeden nach den Werken vorweisen; doch der Richter ist Christus.

---

15. Vgl. dazu O. H. Steck, *Der Abschluß der Prophetie im Alten Testament. Ein Versuch zur Frage der Vorgeschichte des Kanons* (BThSt 17; Neukirchen-Vluyn: Neukirchener Verlag, 1991).

"The Place Which Yahweh Your God Will Choose" in Deuteronomy

YOSHIHIDE SUZUKI

In the book of Deuteronomy, the central sanctuary is always designated by the formula "the place which Yahweh your God will choose." Interestingly the proper names of the sanctuary, such as "Jerusalem," "Bethel," "Shechem," etc., are not used at all. Naturally, it is explained that the formula presupposes the artistic literary setting in which Moses left his testament to the Israelites beyond the Jordan (Deut 1:1; 31:1, 9; 34:1ff.).[1] Because of this reference to the unnamed sanctuary, however, the clarification of the origin of the deuteronomic legal corpus becomes one of the major disputes in Old Testament studies.[2]

Due to the fact that the central sanctuary is not specified with the name "Jerusalem," some scholars were inclined to seek the origin of the deuteronomic legal corpus not in Judah, but in the northern kingdom.[3] They assumed that it was compiled in northern Israel and brought to the south after the fall of Samaria,[4]

---

1. Cf. G. von Rad, *Das fünfte Buch Mose: Deuteronomium,* ATD 8 (Göttingen: Vandenhoeck & Ruprecht, 1964), 16. Regarding the genre of testament, see E. von Nordheim, *Die Lehre der Alten I: Das Testament als Literaturgattung im Judentum der hellenistisch-römischen Zeit,* ALGHJ 13,1 (Leiden: Brill, 1980).

2. See S. Loersch, *Das Deuteronomium und seine Deutungen: Ein forschungsgeschichtlicher Überblick,* SBS 22 (Stuttgart: KBW, 1967); N. Lohfink, *Das Hauptgebot: Eine Untersuchung literarischer Einleitungsfragen zu Dtn 5-11,* AnBib 20 (Romae: Pontificio Instituto Biblico, 1963); H. D. Preuss, *Deuteronomium,* ErFor 164 (Darmstadt: Wissenschaftliche Buchgesellschaft, 1982).

3. See A. Alt, "Die Heimat des Deuteronomiums," *Kleine Schriften zur Geschichte des Volkes Israel,* Bd. 2 (München: C. H. Beck'sche, 1964), 250-75; von Rad, *Deuteronomium;* idem, "Deuteronomium-Studien," *Gesammelte Studien zum Alten Testament,* Bd. 2, TBü 48 (München: Kaiser, 1973), 109-53.

4. See E. W. Nicholson's argument in his *Deuteronomy and Tradition* (Philadelphia: Fortress, 1967).

338

where it was found in the temple of Jerusalem and used by King Josiah for his religious reformation (2 Kgs 22:8-13; 2 Chr 34:14-21). Recently not a few counter-arguments were voiced, claiming that the deuteronomic law was codified originally in Judah.[5] Some have argued that it was codified under the reign of King Josiah at the royal court in Jerusalem.[6] Regardless of the position one takes, the reason the proper name of the sanctuary was not specified in the code remains unexplained.

In this article, a theological struggle over the pedigree of the Jerusalem priesthood will be used to exemplify the pluralism of the theology[7] of one religious institution in the Old Testament. The deuteronomic name theology will show us the struggle over the charismatic nature of religious institutions. This investigation finds its place also as part of the task of Old Testament theology.

I

Needless to say, the formula "the place which Yahweh your God will choose" is not only an allusion to a sanctuary in general. This notion must also reflect particular thought(s) about the sanctuary. While the book of Deuteronomy does not specify the proper name of the place chosen by Yahweh, several variations of the formula (found in Deut 12:14 and many other passages) unfold the essential connection of the divine name to the central sanctuary.[8] Thus, the problem is specified as follows: why was the name of the place not identified in Deuteronomy?

1. Central Sanctuary without Its Proper Name

The interpretations put to the deuteronomic formula not only suggest an idea of the consecration of the place by the name of Yahweh; they also indicate an

---

5. O. Bächli, *Israel und Völker. Eine Studie zum Deuteronomium,* ATANT 41 (Zürich: Zwingli, 1962); M. Weinfeld, *Deuteronomy and Deuteronomic School* (Oxford: Clarendon, 1972); idem, *Deuteronomy 1–11: A New Translation with Introduction and Commentary,* AB 5 (New York: Doubleday, 1991).

6. Y. Suzuki, "The 'Numeruswechsel' in Deuteronomy" (Dissertation, Claremont Graduate School, 1982); idem, "Deut. 6:4-5: Perspectives as a Statement of Nationalism and of Identity of Confession," *AJBI* 9 (1983): 65-87; cf. M. Sekine, "Beobachtungen zu der josianischen Reform," *VT* 22 (1972): 361-68.

7. R. Knierim, "The Task of Old Testament Theology," *HBT* 6,1 (1984): 25-57.

8. See H. Seebass, "בחר *bāchar,*" in *TDOT,* vol. 2, 73-87. Regarding the notion "Yahweh will choose in one of your tribes" in Deut 12:14, see Th. Oestreicher, *Das Deuteronomische Grundgesetz,* BFCT 27,4 (Gütersloh: Bertelsmann, 1923). His argument that it should be translated as "in irgend einer deiner Stamme" is not convincing (104ff.); contra W. Staerk, *Das Problem des Deuteronomiums; Ein Beitrag zur neusten Pentateuchkritik,* BFCT 29 (Gütersloh: Bertelsmann, 1924), 26ff., and A. C. Welch, *The Code of Deuteronomy: A New Theory of Its Origin* (New York: G. H. Doran; London: J. Clark, 1924), 48ff.

interesting feature in that its ideology is not based on any cult traditions, nor does it depend on its historical glory or the charisma fixed to the place. The formula, such as in Deut 12:21, represents the deuteronomic theology of the sanctuary associated with the name of Yahweh (cf. Exod 20:24). However, it is amazing that the name of the sanctuary is not specified, while the name of Yahweh is the essential part of the formula. It is quite clear that the interrelation of the two factors is not substantial but heuristic.

It is necessary to indicate that the compiler(s) must have self-consciously referred to the place without its proper name. Thus, the formula itself must be a farsighted scheme based on a deep ideology and/or theology concerning the central sanctuary. Although the close relation between the deuteronomic legal corpus, which was believed to be found in the temple of Jerusalem, and the reformation movement by King Josiah is widely accepted, it is not properly interpreted as long as the most important sanctuary in Israel is left unnamed.

Nevertheless, the central sanctuary was crucial for King Josiah to fulfill the centralization of entire religious institutions into a single Yahweh sanctuary by illegalizing the others, so that Yahweh sanctuaries at the local city were abolished together with all other pagan shrines. Did King Josiah take it for granted that Jerusalem was the place which Yahweh the God of Israel chose, when he carried out his reformation program based on the deuteronomic legal corpus newly found in the Jerusalem temple?

2. Origin of the Legal Corpus in Judah

In view of its peculiar thought of eliminating other holy places and consecrating the single place as the authentic Yahweh sanctuary, it seems much more reasonable to assume that the deuteronomic legal corpus was compiled (at least) in Judah rather than seeking its origin in the northern kingdom.

Several factors lead to such a judgment. First of all, it must be noted that the northern kingdom would accrue little benefit by restricting the sanctuaries to a single place in the wide territory. Without a doubt, the plural sanctuaries must have supported the national interests of the northern kingdom (1 Kgs 12:26-30). In addition to that, one must consider the religious circumstances in the northern kingdom. Each regime of northern Israel would have a strong motivation to build as many sanctuaries as possible because of the heavy influence of the Baal cult (1 Kgs 16:32-34; 2 Kgs 16:3-4; Hos 4:13; 8:11). Traditionally each regime sought the religious benefit due to the economic prosperity at the shrines.

Due to these factors alone, one may safely suppose that the idea of the centralization of holy places did not come from the northern kingdom, despite the fact that plural sanctuaries existed in Judah, such as the ones founded at Gilgal and Beersheba. Why not?

3. King Josiah and His Policy of Reformation

Equally important in our judgment are the many positive aspects which make the hypothesis that the deuteronomic legal corpus was originally compiled not in Israel but in Judah reasonable.[9] There seem to be not a few evidences for a positive relationship between an official intention of codifying the legal standard and the policy of reformation carried out by King Josiah. For instance, his political purpose could be represented by the policy of reforming the body of administration. Indeed, the nature of his policy is not summarized with the category of "the religious reformation" by and large, since King Josiah seems to have reorganized not only the religious institutions, but also the military institution, the administration of justice, and the system of the national economy. Interestingly, a new structure of the entire administration is obviously recognized in the deuteronomic legal corpus. Its format is extracted by the composition analysis of the corpus as a whole.[10]

Whichever of the several options concerning the origin of the deuteronomic legal corpus one may choose, it is appropriate to inquire about a causal relationship regardless of whether King Josiah had the legal corpus utilized or compiled. Such an official codification of legal materials does not exist in the Old Testament apart from the Covenant Code. In addition, the latter does not include any aspect of reorganizing the structure of state administration as a whole. There must be a historical cause for the systematic codification of the legal corpus in Deuteronomy.

The major cause must be sought in the historical factor of King Josiah's military campaign. Due to the fact that Josiah as a king of Judah made a military campaign to the Assyrian territory which originally belonged to former Israel and succeeded in recovering the huge territory[11] as in the period of David and Solomon, King Josiah's close advisers might have believed that the glory of the house of David was being revived.[12] Indeed, King Josiah's successful campaign gave a decisive impetus to his government officials to reorganize the structure of the administration as a whole. This should be explained by the necessity that his royal court inevitably started a new policy to dominate the wide territory newly recovered, especially to control the land of the former Israelite kingdom.[13]

9. This does not mean to exclude the traces of religious traditions originated in northern Israel in Deuteronomy.

10. See Y. Suzuki, "Deuteronomic Reformation in View of the Centralization of the Administration of Justice," *AJBI* 13 (1987): 22-58.

11. See Alt, "Judas Gaue unter Josia," *Kleine Schriften*, Bd. 2, 276-88.

12. E.g., see M. Noth's indication in his *The History of Israel* (New York: Harper and Brothers, 1958), "In the absence of a king in Israel, the way was clear for an attempt to enforce the old claim of the house of David to rule once more over the State of Israel and thereby to restore the former dual monarchy of David and Solomon in Judah and Israel" (272).

13. See Y. Aharoni and M. Avi-Yona, *The Macmillan Bible Atlas* (New York: Macmillan, 1978), #158.

4. Occupation Policy and Necessity of New Administration Body

There is no doubt about the historical circumstances into which the royal court of King Josiah had been thrown. They must have faced the serious problem that the occupied territory was populated no longer by the people of Yahweh but by pagan worshipers. Those people had nothing to do with the Israelite culture or Yahweh religion. Therefore, strategic concerns required King Josiah and his government to institute nothing less than a comprehensive reorganization. There is little doubt that King Josiah and his government officials rebuilt a new structure to rule the population of the occupied land (Deut 20:11), such as organizing a new system of the administration of justice (Deut 16:18; 17:8ff.; 19:15ff.), eliminating pagan shrines and priests (Deut 18:9-14) and pagan custom from all the territory (Deut 22:5, 9-11; 23:18; 25:4), and proclaiming the purification of cult (Deut 13:2ff.; 17:2-5). As a matter of fact, King Josiah inevitably introduced a brand-new plan for ruling the large, newly annexed population; i.e., the socioreligious education of the population of the occupied territory.

Thus, the category of "religious reformation" does not adequately represent King Josiah's policy by and large. For instance, King Josiah and his officials are supposed, sooner or later, to recruit new officials, of whom as many as possible were sent to the local cities (Deut 16:18); they rebuilt a new military force to hold a wide territory, constituted a standing army next to the draft (Deut 20:5-8, 9; 23:10ff.),[14] and reinforced the scale of the economic structure (Deut 14:22ff., 28ff.; 22:9ff.; 23:20ff., 25; 24:10ff., 14ff., 19ff.).

Regarding the national economy of the occupied land, it must be noted that the traditional idea of "the land of inheritance" had vanished with the fall of Samaria. The policy for the national economy of the occupied land must have been especially pragmatic for the royal court of King Josiah. In fact, the huge amount of agricultural products from the newly annexed territory was incorporated into the economic structure of the government of Judah.[15]

5. Occupation Policy and a Unified Legal Standard

It is widely believed that the notion of the central sanctuary in the deuteronomic legal corpus had a decisive impact on King Josiah's reformation. However, the

14. Cf. E. Junge, *Der Wiederaufbau Heerwesens des Reiches Juda unter Josia*, WMANT 4,23 (Stuttgart: Kohlhammer, 1937).

15. A Hebrew ostracon found at Meṣad Ḥashavyahu must be referred to here. A petition written on the ostracon shows that a duty of crop was burdened on the people of occupied land. Regarding its historical significance, see S. Talmon, "The New Hebrew Letter from the Seventh Century B.C. in Historical Perspective," *BASOR* 176 (1964): 29-38; and Y. Suzuki, "A Hebrew Ostracon from Meṣad Hashavyahu: A Form-Critical Reinvestigation," *AJBI* 8 (1982): 3-49.

most important thing is that King Josiah and his government officials should have felt it inevitable to declare the legitimate legal standard to the new population of the occupied land by the name of Yahweh. One should be aware that such a proclamation of the legal standard was neither meaningful nor significant to the original people of Judah.

To rule the wide territory newly recovered seems to be the major reason King Josiah and his administration of justice[16] compiled the legal code. King Hammurapi of Babylon had done the same thing. King Hammurapi had the legal code compiled and written on stone at the latest stage of his reign. There was an administrative necessity for King Hammurapi and his royal court to proclaim the authentic legal standard all over the country, where heterogeneous cultural and legal traditions were alive.[17] The most important factor for our argument is that the Code of Hammurapi was compiled as the ultimate symbol of the unified legal standard. In other words, the codification of the legal materials was accomplished in conjunction with the reformation of the administration of justice. In short, all the legal materials that originated in Sumer, Akkad, Eshnunna, Assyria, and Mari were revised and fitted to the Babylonian standard. This is a unification of the legal standard.

In fact, King Josiah and his royal court must have chosen a policy, similar to Hammurapi's, of unification and of centralization of the administration of justice for the sake of ruling his territory. King Josiah legitimized the central sanctuary alone as authentic and illegalized the others. This is also regarded as a part of his policy of centralization of religious administration. More precisely, he had the legal standard codified for his administrative purpose.

Furthermore, according to the present author's view, the report of discovery of the legal corpus, "the Book of the Torah," in the temple of Jerusalem (2 Kgs 22:8; 2 Chr 34:14) must represent a farsighted political strategy to give the deuteronomic legal corpus ultimate authenticity. Its effect must have been enormous indeed. This seems to be an outstanding way to make the legal corpus divine. The codification work might be hidden from the eyes of antireformation groups until its official public debut. Needless to say, this strategy must be effective for the Zadokites.

---

16. Contra G. C. Macholz, "Zur Geschichte der Justizorganisation in Juda," *ZAW* 84 (1972): 314-40. Concerning the positive argument of centralization of the administration of justice under King Josiah, see K. W. Whitelam, *The Just King: Monarchical Judicial Authority in Ancient Israel*, JSOTSup 12 (Sheffield: JSOT, 1979); H. Niehr, *Rechtsprechung in Israel: Untersuchungen zur Geschichte der Gerichtsorganisation im Alten Testament*, SBS 130 (Stuttgart: KBW, 1987); see also my article, "Deuteronomic Reformation"; idem, "A New Aspect on Occupation Policy by King Josiah: Assimilation and Codification in View of Yahwism," *AJBI* 18 (1992): 31-61.

17. See H. J. Boecker, *Recht und Gesetz im Alten Testament und im Alten Orient*, Neukirchener Studienbücher 10 (Neukirchen-Vluyn: Neukirchener, 1976), 66.

6. Unnamed Central Sanctuary

Despite the fact that the Jerusalem temple had functioned as the central sanctuary under the reign of King Josiah, he did not specify the name of the sanctuary in order to help institute the political and administrative changes. Indeed, he must have had the chance to proclaim the name of the central sanctuary officially "Jerusalem," or to make an order that revised the legal expression of the central sanctuary without any difficulty.

If our understanding on this matter is correct, the issue is again focused on the crucial point: why the name of Jerusalem was not adopted in the process of the compilation of the legal corpus, and/or why the central sanctuary was not identified directly and officially with the Jerusalem temple by King Josiah. Those who make any statement on this issue, such as claiming that King Josiah simply utilized the deuteronomic legal corpus found in the temple of Jerusalem (2 Kgs 22:8-13; 2 Chr 34:14-21), are also supposed to explain the actual reason why King Josiah failed to have the code revised and to specify the name of the place chosen by Yahweh, "Jerusalem," in the process of reformation. So, the question remains open.

II

Now we assume that the deuteronomic reference to the central sanctuary must reflect such a serious and essential problem that the name of the place should not be obviously specified. It is not totally unreasonable to suggest that the naming of the place could jeopardize King Josiah's policy of reorganizing the administration as a whole and alter the nature of the reformation itself. The same problem must exist for the deuteronomic compiler(s) if they were to legitimize the Jerusalem temple with the name of Yahweh without examining its supreme authority, which would recall religious traditions kept by the Zadokite priesthood. Specifically, no particular reasons would be conceivable for their avoidance of vocalizing the name of the place chosen by Yahweh that would be free of serious ideological and theological problems.

Since the name Jerusalem is used in a deuteronomistic context (Josh 9:27 is an exception), it is clear that the historical situation concerning the central sanctuary was drastically changed by the destruction of Judah and the fall of Jerusalem. In other words, the reference to the sanctuary need no longer be an allusion in the exilic age. In fact, the Deuteronomist simply specified the city and her temple with the proper name "Jerusalem" (1 Kgs 11:13, 32, 36; 14:21; 2 Kgs 21:7; 23:27), mainly because of the deportation of the Zadokite priests from Jerusalem.

Regarding this change of attitude toward the central sanctuary, a clear difference with regard to the name of the place can be recognized between the deuteronomic understanding of the central sanctuary and the deuteronomistic interpretation of it. For the Deuteronomist, a certain theological tension was totally wiped out because of the destruction of the Jerusalem temple. This difference of historical situation is beyond our suspicion.

1. Struggle Hidden behind the Codification

Now the question must be stated once again to clear the issue. What were the major ideological and theological tensions hidden behind the deuteronomic formula that did not identify the sanctuary by its proper name? If our view of this matter is correct, one may be allowed to combine the issue of the literary setting of Moses' testament beyond the Jordan with religious and institutional factors attached to the temple of Jerusalem. It is a historical issue over the charisma of the priestly group.

According to the present author's view, the formula "the place which Yahweh your God will choose" was adopted intentionally by the deuteronomic compiler(s) in order to make a firm declaration over the central sanctuary against the religious traditions kept by the Zadokite group at Jerusalem.[18] In fact, the reference to the central sanctuary is stated carefully by the formula based on deep ideological and theological perspectives. Because it manifests the necessity of the renovation of the traditional basis of the temple of Jerusalem by means of the charismatic legitimacy of Mosaic Yahwism, the deuteronomic formula is a strong statement against admitting any continuity of the religious traditions carried by the Zadokite group since the pre-Israelite age. The deuteronomic setting of the composition of the legal corpus indicates this: just before the crossing of the Jordan, Moses tells the Israelites the place of the central sanctuary will be elected by Yahweh for a dwelling place for the divine name. Why was this setting inevitable for the codification? Why does this setting suggest a critical approach to the charisma kept by the Jerusalem priesthood?

2. Charisma of the Pedigree of the Zadokites

It was certainly acknowledged by the deuteronomic compiler(s) that the religious traditions of the city of Jerusalem had nothing to do with the Yahweh religion before the occupation of the city by King David (2 Sam 5:6ff.; 15:24ff.). So, if the authority of the temple was legitimized by the name of Yahweh in the

---

18. W. Dietrich is right in insisting "Gewiß, aber erst, nachdem diese von allem Jebusitischen gründlich gereinigt worden war." See his *Israel und Kanaan*, SBS 94 (Stuttgart: KBW, 1979), 110.

reign of King Josiah, then the ongoing tradition might be authorized as a whole without any examination of the traditionalism of the cult, i.e., the cult theology and the offering technique, and of the priesthood of Zadokite pedigree (1 Kgs 1:38ff.; 4:4; 6:1ff.).

The deuteronomic compiler(s) seemed to have realized the problem that the religious traditions kept by the Jerusalem group of priests consisted of not a few impure elements of cult tradition originating from the pagan altar of the Jebusites.[19] If that sort of religious and institutional continuity of cult tradition were acceptable as it had been, then there should have been no necessity for the deuteronomic compiler(s) either to avoid specifying the place of the central sanctuary with its proper name, "Jerusalem," or to reform its religious institution.

If so, the literary setting of the Mosaic speech beyond the Jordan should not be inevitable for the codification, too. However, the composition of the deuteronomic legal corpus indicates a different perspective. The artistic literary setting of the Mosaic testament beyond the Jordan was indispensable for the codification.

3. Struggle over the Name of the Authentic Yahweh Priest

It is true that King Josiah had eliminated Yahweh sanctuaries in local cities and centralized the religious institutions. However, it is doubtful that he authorized the name of the Zadokites as the authentic lineage for Yahweh priests. According to the deuteronomic legal standard, King Josiah should have changed the name of the Zadokite pedigree to "the Levite" (Deut 18:1ff.), insofar as he wanted to promote the reorganization of the religious administration.

III

Setting a hypothesis opposite to the deuteronomic presentation of the central sanctuary is valuable for clarifying the issue. If the place of the central sanctuary should be identified with the proper name "Jerusalem," if Jerusalem should be legitimized without any legal setting of Mosaic speech at all, then what would be the theoretical consequences? What would be derived from the legal verification of Jerusalem as the only place chosen by Yahweh? There must be a revelation crisis on the charisma of the Jerusalem temple.[20]

19. Regarding the argument on the theology of the name of God, see T. N. D. Mettinger, *In Search of God* (Philadelphia: Fortress, 1988).
20. Regarding the problem of revelation crisis in the Old Testament, see R. Knierim, "Offenbarung im Alten Testament," *Probleme biblischer Theologie: Gerhard von Rad zum 70. Geburtstag*, hg. von H. W. Wolff (München: Kaiser, 1971), 206-35.

1. Theoretical Consequences of Identifying Jerusalem

The theoretical implications of the opposite assumption mentioned above are clear: (1) The charisma of the Jerusalem temple would become the single authentic source prior to any other religious and institutional authorities, because it would become the only place elected directly by Yahweh for the dwelling place of the divine name. Then their other bearers of Yahwism might lose their legitimacy in the history of Israel in the promised land. This would deprive the Levite of authenticity as a Yahweh priest, and might affect Moses' prestige. (2) The temple itself would bear the charisma, which might confirm the spiritual and cultural supremacy of Jerusalem because of Yahweh's name. Then the history of Jerusalem would be authorized by itself together with the Zadokite priesthood. In short, the charisma of Jerusalem would become a dogmatic ideology no one could ever reform; it might become an idol in the heart (Ezek 14:3ff.). (3) The theology of the holy place would be firmly established by means of exclusive verification by the divine name. Then a direct election by Yahweh might be firmly combined only with the Jerusalem temple (Jer 7:4). If so, other Yahweh traditions concerning election, such as the exodus traditions recognized at Gilgal, would lose their religious dignity.[21] In other words, it would produce a glorification of the history of Jerusalem alone, a glorification of the Jebusites' tradition prior to the Mosaic prestige and to the exodus traditions.

It is necessary to indicate that the deuteronomic theology of the name of Yahweh must have been associated with the problem of the legitimacy of Yahwism. Despite the strong tradition of Jerusalem since King David, the deuteronomic compiler(s) knew the legal effect that naming the chosen place would produce: a decisive legitimacy for an exclusive ideology of the Jerusalem temple over any other religious and administrative institutions. It might jeopardize Mosaic authority and Levitical authority as well. Therefore, the deuteronomic literary setting must be indispensable for the compiler(s) and King Josiah as well.

2. Political Compromise between Two Groups

We must admit that some may raise a question, claiming that centralizing authority into Jerusalem might be beneficial for King Josiah in achieving his reformation. However, it is exactly what the king did not expect to materialize, because that sort of supreme dignity under the name of Yahweh the God of Israel would create a dogmatic authority mixed with the traditionalism of the lineage of the Jerusalem priesthood.

One must be cautious and assume that the reform of the religious institution was carried out with the helpful assistance of the Zadokites. As far as the

---

21. See E. Otto, *Das Mazzotfest in Gilgal*, BWANT 7,7 (Stuttgart: Kohlhammer, 1975).

347

deuteronomic instruction is concerned, the Zadokite priests must have been disinclined to be fully obedient to the Mosaic order, since the deuteronomic legal corpus insists that the Yahweh priests are to be called "the Levite the priest" (Deut 18:1, 7; 21:5). It is doubtful that the Zadokites accepted the name "the Levite" as the authentic Yahweh priest[22] without any compromise under the critical situation that its justification is legitimized in the legal code (cf. 2 Kgs 22:8).

Under such historical circumstances, how did King Josiah perform his reorganization program? It is worth noting that King Josiah utilized the Levites, the Yahweh priests who lost their jobs at the local sanctuaries due to King Josiah's policy of centralization of the religious institutions. Josiah summoned them to the royal court at Jerusalem and newly appointed them as officials,[23] the judges and the officers (Deut 16:18ff.; 17:8ff.; 19:17ff.). On the other hand, King Josiah gave the Zadokites an exclusive religious responsibility at the central sanctuary (Deut 12:13ff.) for the purpose of keeping a balance of power at Jerusalem.

Our theoretical assumption on this matter is that while the Levites had acquired the authentic name of Yahweh priest as well as priority in the administration of justice, the Zadokites enjoyed the substantial benefit of offerings from all over the country (Deut 12:13; 14:24-26). This must be a compromise policy mediated by King Josiah and his advisers, for it might have been quite difficult to achieve the reorganization of the religious institutions without any resolution of a struggle between two groups. Even if this compromise should have been mediated by King Josiah's leadership, however, one must be aware that it could be fulfilled without depending on the Mosaic prestige at all. Why was the Mosaic prestige necessary?

3. Priority of Constitutional Authority to Any Prestige

In fact, there was a more complicated problem than the political compromise between two groups. A clue to understanding the nature of the problem is found in the deuteronomic instruction on the Yahweh cult at the central sanctuary,

22. Concerning the history of priesthood, see A. H. J. Gunneweg, *Leviten und Priester,* FRLANT 89 (Göttingen: Vandenhoeck & Ruprecht, 1965); and A. Cody, *A History of Old Testament Priesthood,* AnBib 35 (Rome: Pontifical Biblical Institute, 1969). Regarding the pedigree of the Jerusalem priesthood, one must recognize that there were several groups. Each group might stem from a religious tradition at Jerusalem (1 Kgs 9:24; 11:1-8; 14:21, 31; 2 Kgs 11:1-3; 16:1-4, 10-16; 21:3-7, 19-22).

23. See M. Sekine. See his article, "Shinmeiki to sono eikyou" (Japanese) *Seisho-gakuronshu* ("Deuteronomy and Its Influence," *AJBI*); and my Japanese book, *Shinmeiki no bunkengakutekikenkyu* (*A Philological Study of Deuteronomy* [Tokyo: Board of Publications of the United Church of Christ in Japan, 1987]). See also a review by K.-H. Walkenhorst, "Neueste Deuteronomiumforschung in Japan," *BZ* (1989): 81-92.

which simply prescribes the treatment of blood (Deut 12:16, 23-24, 27). Amazingly its instruction is just a minimum requirement in view of the Yahweh cult.

Is it really a requirement of reformation? This question leads to the issue of legal authority. Why was the constitutional authority, which was the basis of codifying various legal materials, indispensable for King Josiah and his close advisers?

It is noteworthy that even the shortest instruction for the Yahweh altar of the central sanctuary would have placed a legal restriction on the Zadokites. Once it was legalized, it would bind the priesthood under the Mosaic authority by the name of Yahweh. Whatever should be necessary for the sake of the national interests, the legal restriction would authorize King Josiah and his royal court to intervene and restrain any activities of a Zadokite group at the altar and temple economy in the name of Yahweh, the God of Israel. Codification gives the royal court of King Josiah the national jurisdiction by the name of Yahweh to control the administration as a whole.

IV

One may be allowed to ask if the deuteronomic compiler(s) left any room for a traditional source of authority, such as the charisma of the royal lineage of the house of King David (2 Sam 7), the traditionalism of the Zadokite pedigree, or other aristocratic and military lineages (2 Sam 15:18) grounded in the rich soil of the city Jerusalem.

1. Reformation by the National Project in Unity

There were undeniable factors of Canaanite origin among those military and religious pedigrees. Nevertheless, none of their charismatic traditions are verified by the name of Yahweh prior to the constitutional authority in the deuteronomic legal corpus (Deut 7:2b-4, 6; 8:11-18).

A clear example is sufficient for an appreciation of the spirit of this constitutional authority: the king is placed under Mosaic instruction (Deut 17:14ff.). The aim is not simply to state a limitation of kingship in general, but specifically to proclaim officially that even the king himself should be subject to the constitutional authority.[24] The most important factor of this instruction is that the source

---

24. According to Deut 17:16f., the king "must not acquire more horses for himself. And he must not acquire many wives for himself; also silver and gold he must not acquire in great quantity for himself." This is a statement that the king must not make a military buildup, form an alliance with many countries, and enrich himself on his own judgment

of the constitutional authority is Yahweh alone (Deut 6:4-5). This means that the codification of a unified legal standard is nothing but a proclamation of supreme legitimacy to any competing charismatic authority or traditionalism of any kind. For the sake of this constitutional authorization of the Mosaic tradition, King Josiah's reformation — by reorganizing the administration — is supposed to be completed by the codification project. And this codification led by King Josiah must be a national project performed in unity. For that purpose, it is meaningful that the king himself is always obedient to the code officially.

2. Codification and Mosaic Tradition

Indeed, the codification of the legal standard must have been indispensable for King Josiah to achieve his goal. There was no room for compromise with any traditional authority originating from the Canaanite soil of the culture (Deut 7:1-4; 20:16-17). Therefore, one can agree that the deuteronomic legal corpus was originally compiled under the leadership of King Josiah to accomplish the reorganization of administration as a whole. The codification of Mosaic instruction was aimed at establishing nothing but the legal standard of the name of Yahweh. In addition, the process of codification suggests that there was a powerful antireformation group or sect in Jerusalem. In fact, the formula of the central sanctuary, "the place which Yahweh your God will choose," represents a strategy of "reformation," a policy of indomitable attitude to build a new structure of the nation — not by any traditional authority but only by Mosaic Yahwism.

3. Death of King Josiah and Reaction by the Jerusalem Sect

Considering the reorganization strategy promoted by King Josiah, it is natural that his death caused the end of the reformation. That meant also the end of the occupation policy. The legal standard had lost its ability to control the political balance of power at Jerusalem. Those who supported King Josiah's reformation movement were purged out of the royal court. In fact, it is known that there was a serious struggle at Jerusalem (2 Kgs 24:4) after the death of Josiah. The Zadokites may have recovered their prestige and seized full authority at Jerusalem as long as the sanctuary existed under the notion of "the God of Israel," despite the fact that the name of Yahweh was forsaken.

---

apart from national interest, namely, apart from the administration. These instructions ask the king to make a proper distinction between public and private matters and not to confuse them in making any political judgment.

Regarding the theological struggle hidden behind the deuteronomic formula of the central sanctuary, the change to the opposite direction in the political and religious attitude under the reign of King Jehoiakim would verify our interpretation about the historical circumstances of the origin of the deuteronomic legal corpus.

<h1 style="text-align:center">V</h1>

Finally, the theological significance of the deuteronomic formula "the place which Yahweh your God will choose" can be treated as a task of Old Testament theology. This deuteronomic theology of the name of Yahweh associated with divine election manifests a historical problem with a specific political and religious background, although its theological dimension is not limited to the administrative perspective alone.

First of all, it reveals Yahweh's unrestricted decision of election. Even though the deuteronomic formula indicates the central sanctuary as the dwelling place of the divine name, the allusion to the unnamed place is not identified with any substantial reality in Deuteronomy.[25] It may be related to the effect of the artistic literary setting of the Mosaic testament beyond the Jordan.

Indeed, the character of the election of the unnamed place is represented by the historical retrospection in the Mosaic speech beyond the Jordan. In other words, its theological function was already beyond contemporaneity in the codification process under King Josiah. Because of the peculiarity included in the codification, one would appreciate the metahistorical nature of the formula that wears the character of the ultimate freedom of Yahweh's election. So, the issue of the deuteronomic formula is nothing but the matter of divine revelation, which is always left open for a new divine election. As a matter of fact, "the place which Yahweh your God will choose" does not always mean the location of the sanctuary per se, since the formula does not fix the actual place.

One must not overlook the spiritual tension between the divine freedom and the historical reality associated with the temple of Jerusalem. Since the formula is simply a proclamation of the divine will through Moses, it suggests an everlasting theological significance regardless of its substantial framework. It is worth calling attention to a new theological dimension of Yahweh revelation which Deuteronomy has opened.[26]

---

25. Cf. R. de Vaux, "Le lieu que Yahvé a choisi pour y établir son nom," *Das ferne und nahe Wort. Festschrift Leonard Rost zur Vollendung seines 70. Lebensjahres*, hg. von F. Maass, BZAW 105 (Berlin: Töpelmann 1967), 219-28. De Vaux seems to appreciate the name theology in view of Yahweh's ownership of the sanctuary by indicating its deuteronomistic origin.

26. See O. Kaiser, *Einleitung in das Alte Testament. Eine Einführung in ihre Ergebnisse und Probleme* (Gütersloh: Gerd Mohn, 1969), 112.

The notion of the deuteronomic formula may include not only the earthly place but also a heavenly place (John 14:2-3). Interestingly, the place which Yahweh will choose is specified by a new concept of "heavenly Jerusalem" (Heb 12:22; Rev 3:12; 21:2, 10). The formula itself allows room for the pluralism of confessions concerning the place which Yahweh will choose, however, only under the view of Yahweh's transcendent freedom of election. In fact, the formula functions as a vessel to carry the divine will beyond the historical framework.

Tanak versus Old Testament: Concerning the Foundation for a Jewish Theology of the Bible

MARVIN A. SWEENEY

I

The years since World War II have proven to be an extremely dynamic period for Judaism and Jewish thought. The destruction of European Judaism and the uprooting of Middle Eastern Jewry, the birth of the state of Israel, the emergence of the American Jewish community as the leading center for diaspora Jewish life, and the current redemption of Russian and Ethiopian Jewry together constitute fundamental changes that present challenges to Jewish thinkers grappling with the meaning and directions of Jewish life. One aspect of these momentous changes has been the emergence of Jewish scholarship in the modern secular university, including not only areas that might once have been described as of nearly exclusive Jewish interest, such as talmudic studies or Zionist thought, but also areas that Christians have viewed as fundamental to their own interests, such as the study of the Bible or systematic theology. The result has been increasing interaction and dialogue between Jewish and Christian thinkers that is marked by a new willingness to understand the other and to explore common ground.

Yet with respect to biblical studies, there are important differences in the approach to the subject matter, despite the acceptance of modern historical and literary methodologies which strive for scientific objectivity by both Christian and Jewish scholars. For the Christian Bible scholar, whose training is grounded in the theological disciplines, the fundamental paradigm for biblical scholarship is generally that of biblical theology, or more specifically Old Testament theology for those whose concern is the Hebrew Bible. As such, Old Testament theology embodies the attempt to systematize the religious ideas of the Hebrew Bible, so that such systematization might serve as a basis for examining the Hebrew Bible in relation to the larger structure of Christian thought. For the Jewish Bible scholar, grounded in a tradition of close textual study, the fundamental paradigm tends to be philological analysis and historical reconstruction. Insofar as Jewish Bible scholars attempt a systematic evaluation of the Bible, it tends to be in the form of a history of the religion of the Bible rather than a systematic theology of the Bible.[1]

The reasons for this difference are not hard to fathom. Old Testament theology emerged less than two hundred years ago with the work of G. L. Bauer and W. M. L. de Wette on the biblical theology of the Old and New Testaments.[2] These studies in turn were prompted by the inaugural lecture in 1787 by Johann Philipp Gabler that called for the establishment of biblical theology as a discipline separate from that of dogmatic theology.[3] Although Gabler defined biblical theology as an historical discipline, its purpose was to clarify the theology of the Bible in and of itself as a preparation for dogmatics.[4] Thus at its very foundation, Old Testament theology was defined as a Christian theological discipline and as such served the Protestant dictum *sola scriptura,* insofar as biblical theology would serve as the basis for dogmatics. Despite the pervading concern for scientific objectivity among Christian biblical scholars, Old Testament theology is still understood in many quarters as an explicitly Christian theological discipline.[5]

It is because Old Testament theology is defined as a Christian theological discipline that Jews are hesitant to participate in the field. At present, only a handful of works have been published by Jewish scholars, including those by Moshe Goshen-Gottstein,[6] Abraham Joshua Heschel,[7] Jon Leven-

---

1. E.g., Yehezkel Kaufmann, *History of the Religion of Israel* (Hebrew) (Tel Aviv: Bialik Institute-Dvir, 5720/1959); idem, *The Religion of Israel from Its Beginnings to the Babylonian Exile* (Chicago: University of Chicago, 1960). For a recent study of Kaufmann's life and thought, see Thomas Krapf, *Yehezkel Kaufmann: Ein Lebens- und Erkenntnisweg zur Theologie der Hebräischen Bibel,* Studien zu Kirche und Israel 11 (Berlin: Institut Kirche und Judentum, 1990).

2. Cf. H. Graf Reventlow, *Problems of Old Testament Theology in the Twentieth Century* (London: SCM, 1985), 4. For full discussions of the development of the fields of biblical and Old Testament theology, see Gerhard Hasel, *Old Testament Theology: Basic Issues in the Current Debate,* 3rd ed. (Grand Rapids: Eerdmans, 1987); John H. Hayes and Frederick Prussner, *Old Testament Theology: Its History and Development* (Atlanta: John Knox, 1985); Reventlow, *Problems of Old Testament Theology;* idem, *Problems of Biblical Theology in the Twentieth Century* (Philadelphia: Fortress, 1986).

3. Reventlow, *Problems of Old Testament Theology,* 3.

4. Reventlow, *Problems of Old Testament Theology,* 4.

5. E.g., B. S. Childs, *Old Testament Theology in a Canonical Context* (London: SCM, 1985), 1-19.

6. M. H. Goshen-Gottstein, "Christianity, Judaism and Modern Bible Study," in *Congress Volume, Edinburgh, 1974,* VTSup 28 (Leiden: Brill, 1975), 69-88; idem, "Jewish Biblical Theology and the Science of the Religion of the Bible" (Hebrew), *Tarbiz* 50 (1980-81): 37-64; idem, "Tanakh Theology: The Religion of the Old Testament and the Place of Jewish Biblical Theology," *Ancient Israelite Religion: Essays in Honor of Frank Moore Cross,* ed. P. D. Miller, Jr., P. D. Hanson, and S. D. McBride (Philadelphia: Fortress, 1987), 617-44.

7. A. J. Heschel, *The Prophets* (New York: Harper and Row, 1962).

son,[8] and Mattitiahu Tsevat.[9] Levenson points to a number of specific factors for such hesitancy, including the anti-Semitism prevalent in many classic works of the field, the Protestant character of the undertaking, the long tradition of systematic theology in Christianity that is lacking in Judaism, and the role that the context of the New Testament plays in defining the issues and perspectives of Old Testament theology.[10] But Levenson well recognizes, as evidenced by his substantial contributions to the field, that biblical theology need not be defined as an exclusively Christian discipline. Rather, the newly found place of Jewish scholars in the field of modern biblical studies represents an opportunity to appropriate the Bible for Jewish theology as well. Such an enterprise enables Jewish thinkers to enter the discourse of the modern Western world on the meaning and significance of the Bible. It thereby contributes to a fruitful Jewish-Christian dialogue which has been engaged since the end of World War II, enhancing the mutual understanding which is fostered by such dialogue.[11] More importantly, the discipline of biblical theology provides an opportunity to define a systematic understanding of the Bible for Jews. This was not possible during the long years when Jews and Judaism were excluded from Western academic scholarship. But in an age of increasing secularization and, for Jews in the diaspora, assimilation, biblical theology serves the purposes of the larger field of Jewish theology in defining, in a positive and systematic fashion, what Jews stand for and how the Bible relates to that self-understanding.[12]

8. J. D. Levenson, "The Temple and the World," *JR* 64 (1984): 275-98; idem, *Sinai and Zion: An Entry into the Jewish Bible* (Minneapolis: Winston, 1985); idem, "Why Jews Are Not Interested in Biblical Theology," *Judaic Perspectives on Ancient Israel*, ed. J. Neusner, B. A. Levine, and E. S. Frerichs (Philadelphia: Fortress, 1987), 281-307; idem, *Creation and the Persistence of Evil: The Jewish Drama of Divine Omnipotence* (San Francisco: Harper and Row, 1988); idem, "Theological Consensus or Historical Evasion? Jews and Christians in Biblical Studies," *Hebrew Bible or Old Testament? Studying the Bible in Judaism and Christianity*, ed. Roger Brooks and John J. Collins (Notre Dame: University of Notre Dame, 1990), 109-45.

9. M. Tsevat, "Theology of the Old Testament — A Jewish View," *HBT* 8 (1986): 33-49.

10. See Levenson, "Why Jews Are Not Interested in Biblical Theology," 281-307.

11. For a recent example which illustrates the fruitfulness of such dialogue, see the essays contained in *Hebrew Bible or Old Testament?* and *Scripture in the Jewish and Christian Traditions: Authority, Interpretation, Relevance*, ed. F. Greenspahn (Nashville: Abingdon, 1982).

12. For a review of the current state of Jewish theology, see D. Novack, "Jewish Theology," *Modern Judaism* 10 (1990): 311-23. For a review of Jewish theological discussion in America, see R. G. Goldy, *The Emergence of Jewish Theology in America* (Bloomington: Indiana University Press, 1990).

II

For the most part, modern biblical scholarship is characterized by a self-conscious sense of objectivity. That is to say, modern biblical scholars attempt by and large to interpret the Bible on its own terms, by identifying the intentions of the Bible's authors in relation to their respective ancient historical settings, without imposing upon them the theology or beliefs of later times. The extent to which such objectivity is achieved, or even if it is possible, can be debated. Nevertheless, the attempts by modern scholars to read the Bible on the terms offered by its authors are essential to arrive at a full and accurate understanding of what the Bible attempts to say.

In attempting to delineate the meaning or theology of the Bible, however, the modern interpreter must be fully aware of what he or she means when speaking about the Bible. The modern concern with uncovering the intentions of the Bible's authors in relation to their historical and social settings has produced a plethora of fine studies on the components of the Bible, including individual books (e.g., Jeremiah, Proverbs), larger groupings of books (e.g., deuteronomistic history), and literary units within books or larger groupings of books (e.g., Second Isaiah, Priestly source). Although such studies are essential to the task of biblical theology[13] insofar as they identify the message or theology of the component parts of the Bible, they do not confront the question of what constitutes the Bible as a whole. That is to say, how are the component messages and theologies of the Bible organized and arranged in the final form of the Bible as a whole?

The difficulties of defining a central organizing principle for the Bible are well known.[14] But the individual messages and theologies of the Bible are presented to the communities that accept them as sacred scripture in the form of one Bible, and that Bible constitutes the context in which its component messages and theologies are interpreted. What then do we mean by Bible? If we are to address the question of the meaning of the Bible, we must therefore not only address the question of the meanings of its component parts, we must also address the question of the meaning of the whole, which selects, organizes, and presents the component parts, whatever that whole might be. In other words, we must address the basic form-critical question to the Bible as a whole: What is the form of the Bible, including its structure, genre, setting, and intent?

This question is complicated because the form of the Bible varies from community to community, not only between Judaism and Christianity, but also within the various forms of Christianity. Apart from the question of the original intention of the authors, the selection and ordering of books and the structure of the canon itself often has a bearing on how the Bible is understood. What

---

13. R. Knierim, "The Task of Old Testament Theology," *HBT* 6,1 (1984): 25-57.
14. See Reventlow, *Problems of Old Testament Theology*, 125-33.

does it mean, for example, when the Roman Catholic Church accepts as sacred scripture 1 Maccabees, which grants the Hasmonean dynasty the right to rule forever "until a trustworthy prophet should arise" (1 Macc 14:27-45, esp. v. 41), whereas 1 Maccabees does not even appear in the Jewish Bible because Rabbinic Judaism regarded the legitimacy of the Hasmonean dynasty with suspicion? What does it mean when the prophetic books, which contain statements pertaining to Israel's role as a light unto the nations and to the need for a new covenant, appear immediately before the New Testament in Christian forms of the canon, whereas in the Jewish form of the Bible they appear before the Ketubim, which relate the establishment of a Temple- and Torah-based Jewish community in the period of Ezra and Nehemiah? Although these questions have nothing to do with the intentions of the authors who wrote the works that now comprise the Bible, they have much to do with the perceptions and intentions of those who assembled the component parts and thereby created the various forms of the Bible that serve as sacred scripture for their respective communities. In this respect, they reveal the different understandings of the Bible in each community and point to the reasons why the message or messages of the Bible are regarded as sacred scripture.[15]

The significance of the fact that the Bible appears in different forms is generally overlooked. Although scholars are well aware of the multiplicity of forms, the focus on the intention of the Bible's authors results in a situation in which the components of the Bible serve as the basis for discussion of its theological meaning but the overall form of the Bible and the distinctive nature of its various forms are often ignored.[16] Werner Lemke's recent call for Jews to participate in the field of Old Testament theology illustrates the point.[17] Lemke argues correctly that the anti-Jewish attitudes present in prior works and the lack of a strong tradition of systematic theology in Jewish thought do not preclude Jewish participation in the field. But Lemke's contention that the designation of the field as Old Testament theology should pose no problem to Jewish participation misses an essential point. Although he is correct to maintain that the New Testament should not influence the interpretation of the Old

---

15. For discussion of the function of sacred scripture in religious communities, see J. A. Sanders, *Torah and Canon* (Philadelphia: Fortress, 1972); idem, "Adaptable for Life: The Nature and Function of Canon," *Magnalia Dei/The Mighty Acts of God: In Memorium G. E. Wright,* ed. F. M. Cross, Jr., et al. (Garden City: Doubleday, 1976), 531-60; idem, *Canon and Community: A Guide to Canonical Criticism* (Philadelphia: Fortress, 1984).

16. For exceptions to this perspective, see J. A. Sanders, *Torah and Canon;* R. E. Murphy, "Old Testament/Tanakh — Canon and Interpretation," *Hebrew Bible or Old Testament?* 11-29. Note also D. Barthélemy, "La place de la Septante dans l'Église," *Études d'Histoire du Texte de l'ancien Testament,* OBO 21 (Fribourg: Éditions universitaires, 1978), 111-26, who maintains that the Septuagint should form the canonical scripture of the Roman Catholic Church due to its historical role in defining the Christian Bible.

17. Werner E. Lemke, "Is Old Testament Theology an Essentially Christian Discipline?" *HBT* 11 (1989): 59-71.

Testament, his statement that the documents of the Jewish canon also happen to be part of the Christian canon of scripture is true only insofar as the Old Testament includes the individual books of the Jewish canon. But as various studies by Sundberg have shown, the early church did not appropriate the Bible of Judaism or even an Alexandrian Jewish canon per se.[18] Rather, the early church admitted closed collections of the Law and the Prophets, together with an undefined body of literature that included the "Writings" as well as the deuterocanonical and apocryphal works. Although Sundberg's assumption that the Jewish canon was closed at Yavneh has been proved to be erroneous,[19] his discussion of the various forms of the Old Testament that appeared in the early church demonstrates that both the selection of books and their order and arrangement were quite fluid. As Sundberg states, "the OT of the early church was distinctly a Christian canon."[20]

The reason for this difference lies not in the selection of books but in the respective structures of the Old Testament and of the Tanak. Although the present four-part form of the Christian Old Testament, including the Pentateuch, Historical Books, Wisdom and Poetic Books, and the Prophets, is relatively late,[21] the fact remains that the Christian Old Testament is not equivalent to the three-part Jewish Tanak, even if one excludes the deuterocanonical books of the Roman Catholic canon. Despite the fact that the respective structures of the Old Testament and the Tanak are not the product of the authors whose works are found in each form of the Bible, the theological significance of this observation must not be overlooked. The different forms of the Old Testament and Tanak derive from and contribute to the distinctive worldview of each tradition, including its distinctive understanding of the Bible. It is important to acknowledge that not only are the individual books and literary works that constitute the Bible the products of sometimes long processes of tradition history and literary formation, so also are the final forms of the Bible the

18. A. C. Sundberg, "The 'Old Testament': A Christian Canon," *CBQ* 30 (1968): 143-55; idem, "The Old Testament of the Early Church (A Study in Canon)," *HTR* 51 (1958): 205-26; idem, *The Old Testament of the Early Church*, HTS 20 (Cambridge: Harvard, 1964); idem, "A Symposium on the Canon of Scripture: 2. The Protestant Old Testament Canon: Should It Be Reexamined?" *CBQ* 28 (1966): 194-203.

19. J. P. Lewis, "What Do We Mean by Jabneh?" *JBR* 32 (1964): 127-32; cf. R. T. Beckwith, *The Old Testament Canon of the New Testament Church and Its Background in Early Judaism* (Grand Rapids: Eerdmans, 1986).

20. Sundberg, "The 'Old Testament': A Christian Canon," 155. Sundberg's understanding of the development of a vague Palestinian-Alexandrian canon has been questioned (cf. Beckwith, *Old Testament Canon of the New Testament Church*, 382-408). Nevertheless, his observation that the Old Testament represents a Christian canon must be upheld. Whether the present Christian Old Testament originated in a Christian context can be debated; nonetheless the early Greek Christian manuscripts demonstrate that the current order of books functioned as the definitive Christian Old Testament canon.

21. Beckwith, *Old Testament Canon of the New Testament Church*, 181.

products of long processes of formation that reflect the perspectives of the tradents who selected the books and organized them into the respective forms of the Bible. In short, we are not dealing with one Bible, with respect to the Old Testament and the Tanak, but with multiple forms of the Bible that are theologically significant in their respective community settings.[22]

The balance of this paper will attempt to demonstrate the significance of these structural differences. It will maintain that the Christian Bible, comprising the Old Testament and the New Testament, is organized according to an historical perspective that posits a progressive movement through history toward an ideal of eschatological redemption in the messianic age. The Christian Bible organizes the books of the Old Testament (and the New) in an order that presents a linear progression through stages in human history. As such, it posits movement and change from a less than ideal circumstance, the disruption of the cosmos because of human sin, to an ideal circumstance, human salvation in the restored cosmos of the eschaton. The ideal cosmos is presented as the presupposition and culmination of the historical process; that is, it stands outside or beyond history as its goal. The organization of the Jewish Tanak, on the other hand, is also influenced by historical considerations. But it posits an ideal state at the outset, in which the establishment of the Temple in the land of Israel and the observance of Mosaic Torah complete the creation of the world. The Tanak is organized to portray the disruption of that ideal during the period of the monarchy and its restoration in the postexilic era. As such the rebuilding of the Temple in Jerusalem and the restoration of the Jewish community centered around the Temple and Mosaic Torah constitute the potential for the realization of an ideal cosmos within history, once the purification of the community is completed by the full implementation of Mosaic Torah.

III

The Old Testament is part of the larger structure of the Christian canon which contains two basic divisions: the Old Testament and the New Testament. This division is theologically significant in that it reflects Christianity's view of the periodization in world history caused by the revelation of Jesus as the Christ. The Old Testament reflects the period of the Mosaic covenant in which God established a special relationship with Israel within the larger context of world history. The New Testament represents the period of the revelation of Jesus whereby the old Mosaic covenant is superseded or fulfilled by the new relationship between God and humanity at large.

Yet within this basic structure, the Christian canon varies among the

22. Cf. Sanders, *Canon and Community*, 1-20.

various forms of Christianity with regard to the selection of books included within the canon and their arrangement or order. This is especially true in the early periods of church history when the Christian canon shows a great deal of fluidity, as an examination of various canon lists and early manuscripts demonstrates.[23] Although both portions of the Christian canon were so affected, the Old Testament shows the greater degree of fluidity. As the early church or churches tried to define their relationship to Judaism and Jewish scripture, they frequently varied in their selection of Old Testament books.[24]

Nevertheless, it is clear that three basic genres of Jewish scripture entered the Old Testament canon of the early church: narrative, poetic, and prophetic.[25] It is also clear that despite the variation of early periods, the Western church traditions, including both Roman Catholic and Protestant, have settled on a standardized selection and order of books, with the exception of the deuterocanonical or apocryphal books. The result is a four-part structure for the Old Testament which includes the Pentateuch, the Historical Books, the Poetic and Wisdom Books, and the Prophetic Books. Although this structure (and the order of the books therein) appears to have been set only after the widespread use of printed Bibles in the Western world,[26] it is based on the order of books in the Latin Vulgate, and prior to that, the order of various Greek traditions. As such, the order reflects the generic character of the books admitted into the Christian canon, allowing for a distinction between the Pentateuch and the following narrative books, due to the traditional designation of the Pentateuch as a distinct block of scripture.

This four-part structure reflects not only the generic character of the literature that comprises the Christian Old Testament; it also reflects the historical perspective of the canon as a whole, insofar as the four sections together represent a progressive movement of history from the past, through the present, and into the future.[27] The Pentateuch presents the distant past insofar as it presents the origins or foundation of the world and of Israel. The Historical

---

23. For a thorough review of the canon lists of early Christianity, see Sundberg, *Old Testament of the Early Church*, 51-79. Cf. Beckwith, *Old Testament Canon of the New Testament Church*, 182-98.

24. Sundberg, *Old Testament of the Early Church*, 81-103, 129-69.

25. G. W. Anderson, "Canonical and Non-Canonical," in *From the Beginnings to Jerome*, ed. P. R. Ackroyd and C. F. Evans, Cambridge History of the Bible, vol. 1 (Cambridge, Eng.: Cambridge University Press, 1970), 136-37.

26. Beckwith, *Old Testament Canon of the New Testament Church*, 181.

27. The use of a principle of "salvation history" for organizing the books of the Old Testament appears as early as the second century in the works of Justin Martyr (cf. H. von Campenhausen, *The Formation of the Christian Bible* [London: Adam and Charles Black, 1972], 97-102). For more recent applications of the "salvation history" model, see G. von Rad, *Old Testament Theology*, 2 vols. (New York: Harper and Row, 1962-65), and C. Westermann, *Elements of Old Testament Theology* (Atlanta: John Knox, 1982) (cf. Reventlow, *Problems of Old Testament Theology*, 59-124).

Books present the more recent past insofar as they present the history of Israel from the time of the conquest under Joshua through the Persian period as represented by Ezra-Nehemiah and the book of Esther. The Poetic and Wisdom Books present the concerns of the present, that is, the timeless concerns of the human spirit as it is reflected in the religiosity of the Psalms, the sensuality of the Song of Solomon, or the intellectual speculation of the Wisdom Books. Finally, the Prophetic Books focus on the future as envisioned by the prophets of the Old Testament. Given their position in the Christian canon, they naturally point to the New Testament as the fulfillment of their visions of the future and thereby contribute to the overall perspective of the whole. As such, the four sections of the Old Testament serve the overall perspective of historical periodization evident in the larger two-part structure of Old Testament and New Testament, in that they subdivide the pre-Christian period into component parts that reflect on the past, the present, and the future of Mosaic revelation.

Each of these sections may be considered in greater detail. The theological intention of the Pentateuch as a component of the Christian Old Testament is determined fundamentally by its focus on the distant past, i.e., on the foundations or origins of the world and of the people of Israel centered around the Mosaic covenant. The intention is further specified by the literary structure of the work. Although the Pentateuch is arranged in five books — Genesis, Exodus, Leviticus, Numbers, and Deuteronomy — these five books do not constitute the Pentateuch's literary structure, nor do they demonstrate its theological intent. As Knierim's analysis of the literary structure of the Pentateuch demonstrates,[28] the Pentateuch comprises two major portions: the introduction to the Moses story in the book of Genesis and the Moses story itself in the books of Exodus, Leviticus, Numbers, and Deuteronomy.

The book of Genesis serves as an introduction to the Moses story insofar as it presents world history and the early history of Israel prior to the Mosaic period as a prelude to the Mosaic period and the revelation at Sinai. Genesis begins with a focus on all creation and humanity in general but increasingly narrows its focus to the people of Israel as YHWH's partner in covenant relationship. Cross's examination of the Priestly source demonstrates that the structure of Genesis is determined by a series of ten statements, based on the formula "these are the generations of XX."[29] Following the creation account in Gen 1:1–2:3, these formulas introduce the successive stages in the history of the world and of Israel prior to the Mosaic period. But they also function as the major indicator of the increasingly narrow focus of the narrative. Thus, "these are the generations of Noah" in Gen 10:1 introduces a narrative block which

28. Rolf Knierim, "The Composition of the Pentateuch," *Society of Biblical Literature 1985 Seminar Papers,* ed. Kent Richards (Atlanta: Scholars, 1985), 393-415.
29. Frank M. Cross, Jr., "The Priestly Work," *Canaanite Myth and Hebrew Epic: Essays in the History of the Religion of Israel* (Cambridge: Harvard, 1973), 293-325, esp. 301-7.

traces the history of the Semites; "these are the generations of Shem" in Gen 11:10 narrows the focus to Terah and Abram; "these are the generations of Terah" in Gen 11:27 narrows the focus to Abram and Isaac, and so on. Other instances of the formula introduce sections that trace the generations of characters who are eliminated from the narrative as its focus narrows. Thus after Ishmael is denied a role in the covenant, Gen 25:12, "these are the generations of Ishmael," traces his genealogy, and Gen 36:1, "these are the generations of Esau," traces the genealogy of Jacob's twin brother, who is likewise excluded from the covenant relationship. The final instance of the formula "these are the generations of Jacob" in Gen 37:2 introduces the narrative that focuses on the twelve sons of Jacob, the ancestors of the twelve tribes of Israel. In this manner, Genesis places the origins of Israel in the context of world history and thereby prepares for Israel's experience of the exodus and revelation at Sinai during the subsequent Mosaic period. The Moses story constitutes the primary concern of the Pentateuch insofar as it focuses attention here as the larger of the Pentateuch's two structural parts. It thereby presents the Mosaic period as the culmination of world history.[30] This perspective is reinforced by the observation that language employed in the account of YHWH's completion of creation in Gen 2:1-3 and that employed for the completion of the tabernacle in Exodus 39–40 are quite similar.[31] From this observation, scholars have concluded that the erection of the wilderness tabernacle, which serves as the paradigm for the Jerusalem Temple, is presented as a human parallel to YHWH's creation of the world.[32] Such a parallel not only points to the role of the Temple as the center or navel of the universe in ancient Israel's worldview,[33] it also points to the role that the Sinai revelation plays, in conjunction with the wilderness tabernacle, as a step in the process of completing or perfecting the world at large that YHWH began in Gen 1:1–2:3.

Within the Moses story, two major units appear which present its two major events or concerns. Exod 1:1–Num 10:10 traces the journey from Egypt to Sinai, including the narrative of the exodus, and culminates in the revelation of the Mosaic covenant at Sinai. Num 10:11–Deut 34:12 traces the journey from Sinai to Moab and culminates in Moses' repetition of the entire covenant prior

---

30. Knierim, "Composition of the Pentateuch," 394-96.

31. See Martin Buber, *Die Schrift und Ihre Verdeutschung* (Berlin: Schocken, 1936), 39ff.

32. J. Blenkinsopp, *Prophecy and Canon: A Contribution to the Study of Jewish Origins* (Notre Dame: University of Notre Dame, 1977), 59-69; idem, "The Composition of P," *CBQ* 38 (1976): 275-92; M. Fishbane, *Text and Texture: Close Readings of Selected Biblical Texts* (New York: Schocken, 1979), 3-16.

33. M. Weinfeld, "Sabbath, Temple and the Enthronement of the Lord: The Problem of the Sitz im Leben of Genesis 1:1–2:3," *Mélanges bibliques et orientaux en l'honneur de M. Henri Cazelles*, AOAT 212 (Kevelaer: Butzon & Bercker; Neukirchen-Vluyn: Neukirchener, 1981), 501-12; Levenson, "Temple and the World," 275-98; idem, *Sinai and Zion*, 111-45.

to Israel's entry into the promised land. In this respect, the Pentateuch's interest in presenting the Mosaic covenant as the foundation for Israel's existence is clear. Furthermore, the fact that the Mosaic covenant is presented in the context of human history and creation at large indicates the Pentateuch's intent to present the Mosaic covenant as the significant event of human history up to that point. When viewed in relation to the rest of the Christian Old Testament canon, the Mosaic covenant becomes the foundation for the subsequent history of Israel and humanity at large.

Like the Pentateuch, the Historical Books — Joshua, Judges, Ruth, 1-2 Samuel, 1-2 Kings, 1-2 Chronicles, Ezra-Nehemiah, and Esther — focus on the past. They differ from the Pentateuch in that they are not concerned with the origins or foundation of Israel and the world, but with the history of the people of Israel from the conquest of the land of Canaan under Joshua until the time of the postexilic period when the remnant of the people of Israel found themselves under Persian rule. As such, the Historical Books of the Old Testament canon present the history of Israel as one of failure. Following the entry into the promised land, Joshua, Judges, Ruth, Samuel, and Kings present Israel's history as one of sin and rebellion against YHWH. Although the Temple, conceived as the center of the universe and the symbol of YHWH's creation, is erected during the reign of Solomon, subsequent periods see the breakup of the people into the separate kingdoms of Israel and Judah, the destruction of the kingdom of Israel by the Assyrians due to its apostasy, and the exile of Judah and destruction of the Jerusalem Temple by the Babylonians for similar reasons. Likewise, Chronicles and Ezra-Nehemiah present the history of the people of Judah as one of failure due to particularization, in that they do not establish the Temple as the center of creation. Although Chronicles and Ezra-Nehemiah focus on Judah as an observant community centered around the Temple in Jerusalem, the observance of Torah introduced by Ezra results in the expulsion of Gentiles from the community. Thus the original goal of the Pentateuch, which presents the Mosaic covenant as the culmination of creation, is not realized in that all humanity is unable to take part. This impression is reinforced by the inclusion of the book of Esther as the concluding book of this section. Here, a diaspora Jewish community is presented as wreaking vengeance on Gentile oppressors. In the context of the Historical Books and the larger structure of the Christian canon, this suggests that God's intention in revealing the Torah to Israel has not been realized because of the increasing separation of the Jewish community from the Gentiles.

Unlike the Pentateuch and Historical Books, the Poetic and Wisdom Books do not focus on the past but on the timeless or ahistorical issues of the human spirit, religiosity, and intellect. The present order of these books — including Job, Psalms, Proverbs, Ecclesiastes, and the Song of Solomon — presents these concerns according to a logical progression that highlights the difficulties of understanding God and divine purpose in the universe but maintains the hope of relating to God just the same. Thus, Job presents YHWH's role as creator at the foundation of the world in order to satisfy Job's desire to understand the moral principles by which the world operates. The book of Psalms in all its diversity expresses human longing for God, sometimes through a sense of threat and estrangement, sometimes through praise and an experience of deliverance or divine majesty. Proverbs presents wisdom as the foundation of the universe, but in light of the Historical Books, it is clear that this principle is not fully realized. Ecclesiastes expresses pessimism at ever finding full satisfaction outside the limits of human existence, concluding that one must enjoy the vanity of human life because the grave is the only reward. But finally, the Song of Songs, always interpreted metaphorically in terms of the relationship between YHWH and Israel, holds out hope that humans can know God.

The Prophetic Books — including Isaiah, Jeremiah, Ezekiel, Daniel, and the Twelve — focus on the future. In the context of the Christian Old Testament canon, they presuppose the failure of the past, but they also build upon the longing of the human spirit for God and point to salvation in the eschaton. Thus Isaiah begins with the eschatological scenario of the nations streaming to Zion to hear YHWH's Torah, then points to the role of Israel as the "light to the nations," and concludes with a portrayal of "a new heaven and earth" or new creation in which the nations will acknowledge YHWH's glory together with Israel. Jeremiah condemns the apostasy of Judah as a prelude to presenting a new covenant in which the Torah of YHWH is inscribed upon the heart. Ezekiel presents a vision of YHWH's abandonment of a polluted Jerusalem so that the city can be consumed like a sacrificial offering and the people cleansed prior to a vision of a renewed Temple at the center of a new Garden of Eden. Daniel posits an eschatological redemption of the righteous as the culmination of the progression of human history through the various earthly empires that dominate the world prior to the revelation of God's kingdom. Finally, the Twelve Minor Prophets focus on the judgment of Israel and Judah prior to an eschatological scenario of a restored Temple, a Davidic messiah, and divine judgment against the wicked of the nations.

When viewed in relation to the New Testament, it is clear that the structure of the Old Testament is designed to rehearse the failure of Israel and the Mosaic covenant to achieve God's purposes for the world, to point to the continued need by humans for God, and to project an eschatological scenario of salvation for the righteous that will be fulfilled in the revelation of Jesus as the Christ. It is striking that the structure of the New Testament canon is parallel to that of the Old. The Gospels treat the foundations of Christian revelation by presenting the life, crucifixion, and significance of Jesus as the Christ. Matthew focuses on Jesus as the fulfillment of Judaism, Mark on the eschatological significance of Jesus in relation to the destruction of the Second Temple, Luke on Jesus' role in bringing God to the Gentiles, and John on Jesus' role as the principle or logos of creation. The book of Acts likewise treats the early history of the Christian church but presents it in terms of its success in reaching Rome, the seat of world power at the time, rather than as a failure. The Epistles focus on the timeless concerns of the human spirit and the significance of Jesus as the Christ for meeting the needs of humans in the early church. Finally, Revelation turns to the future with an eschatological scenario for the second coming of Christ for the redemption of the world and the judgment of evil. Like the Old Testament, the structure of the New Testament is oriented to presenting a progression through history, the goal of which is the ultimate redemption and the realization of God's salvation for the entire world. As such, the New Testament presents the revelation of Jesus Christ as the stage following the Mosaic covenant and the revelation to Israel.

IV

In contrast to the Christian Old Testament, the Tanak is complete in and of itself insofar as it does not constitute a component of a larger body of scripture. Although rabbinic literature builds upon the Tanak, the relationship is not analogous to that of the New Testament and the Old Testament in that rabbinic literature does not present itself as the historical successor to or theological fulfillment of the Tanak.[34] Much of rabbinic literature, such as the Midrashim and Targumim, consists of commentaries on or translations of biblical books that can hardly constitute canonical books like those of the Tanak. The two Talmuds are organized according to basic categories of halakhic concern that are designed to implement the principles of halakhah or expound upon the narratives found within the Tanak. As such, the Talmuds do not constitute canonical scripture as the New Testament does in the context of the Christian Bible but function more or less as commentary upon the Tanak like the Midrashim and Targumim.

The basic structure of the Tanak includes three sections: the Torah or "Instruction"; the Nebi'im or "Prophets," including both the "Former Prophets" and the "Latter Prophets"; and the Ketubim or "Writings." This division is frequently explained in terms of the historical sequence in which each section was recognized as authoritative, but more recent research suggests a different explanation.[35] The Torah serves as the fundamental basis for Jewish scripture,

---

34. Cf. Levenson, "Why Jews Are Not Interested in Biblical Theology," 286-87.

35. For full discussions of the formation of the Jewish canon, see Sid Leiman, *The Canonization of Hebrew Scripture: The Talmudic and Midrashic Evidence* (Hamden, Conn.: Connecticut Academy of Arts and Sciences/Archon, 1976); Roger T. Beckwith, *Old Testament Canon of the New Testament Church,* 1985; idem, "Formation of the Hebrew Bible," *Mikra: Text, Translation, Reading, and Interpretation of the Hebrew Bible in Ancient Judaism and Early Christianity,* ed. M. J. Mulder, CRINT 2/1 (Assen: Van Gorcum; Philadelphia: Fortress, 1988), 39-86.

and the Prophets and Writings both serve as literature that is read in conjunction with the Torah as a means to provide a broader perspective on and interpretation of the Torah text. The difference between the two is that the Prophets are read publicly and the Writings are not.[36]

The structural organization of the Tanak is heavily influenced by historical considerations insofar as each section contains historical narrative that presents successive stages in the Tanak's account of the history of ancient Israel. But the structure of the Tanak does not present a fundamental change in the stages in human history equivalent to that marked by the revelation of Jesus in the Christian Bible. Rather, the Tanak presents an ideal system of national and community organization and self-understanding based on the Temple and Mosaic Torah that is disrupted during the course of the monarchical period, only to be restored in the time of Ezra and Nehemiah. Although historical factors influence the Tanak's structure, the Temple and Torah, symbolizing the ideal pattern of national and community organization and self-understanding, play the dominant role.

Each section may now be considered in greater detail. The Torah is essentially identical to the Pentateuch of the Old Testament and contains the books of Genesis, Exodus, Leviticus, Numbers, and Deuteronomy. Like the Pentateuch of the Christian Old Testament, it functions as the foundation for the Tanak in that it presents the creation of the world and the account of the relationship between God and Israel. As such, it presents the same historical progression evident in the Christian Old Testament. The Mosaic story and revelation at Sinai are the central concerns of the Torah. Likewise, the account of the ancestral age in Genesis places the Mosaic story and Sinai revelation in the context of world history and presents them as its culmination. Consequently, the Mosaic covenant constitutes the ideal means for establishing a relationship between God and humanity.

But the absence of historical periodization analogous to that created by the inclusion of the New Testament in the Christian Bible indicates that no new ideal relationship between God and humanity supersedes or replaces that established by the Mosaic covenant. Rather, the Mosaic covenant remains the ideal basis for a relationship between God and humanity throughout the entire Tanak. Consequently, the stage of human history inaugurated by the Mosaic covenant continues throughout the entire Tanak, and most importantly, it does not come to an end.

It is important to note the presence of large quantities of material in the Torah that presupposes a cyclical view of national life rather than a linear view of historical progression. The essential content of YHWH's promise to Abraham, for

36. Beckwith, *Old Testament Canon of the New Testament Church*, 144-49. For a review of the discussion of the early synagogue lectionary practices, see C. Perrot, "The Reading of the Bible in the Ancient Synagogue," *Mikra*, 137-59.

example, is that he will possess the land of Canaan and become the father of a great people who will populate the land.[37] Furthermore, as noted above, the construction of the wilderness tabernacle in Exodus 39–40, representing the role of the Jerusalem Temple in later Israelite/Judean society, is presented as the human equivalent to God's completion of creation in Gen 1:1–2:3. Insofar as the tabernacle serves as the basis for the balance of the Sinai revelation in the Torah, including the laws of sacrifice and holiness in Leviticus and cultic community organization in Numbers 1–10, it points to the role that the Temple will play as the holy center for the land and people promised to Abraham. The tabernacle, or Temple, serves as the basis for continuous revelation in the midst of the people and thereby provides legitimation for the rules or laws of community organization presented in the context of the Mosaic revelation.[38]

The Mosaic covenant constitutes the basis for ancient Israel's national and religious life. That the Mosaic covenant presupposes a continuing state of national or community existence is evident from the nature of the laws for community organization contained within the Torah. It is well known that the Torah contains a mixture of civil and criminal law on the one hand, as exemplified by the Covenant Code of Exodus 21–23 or large segments of the deuteronomic code, and cultic law on the other, such as the sacrificial laws of Leviticus 1–16 or the Holiness Code of Leviticus 17–26. But the perspective of the Torah presupposes that the entire system of law and community organization is to be implemented once the Israelites establish themselves in the land. Variations of the formula "when you enter the land that YHWH your God is giving to you" indicate an expectation of continuous national life in the land.[39] Furthermore, although the festival system often commemorates historical events, such as the exodus from Egypt at Passover, it is oriented to celebrate the seasonal cycles of the agricultural year; that is, Passover celebrates the beginning of the grain harvest, Shavuot its conclusion, and Sukkot the harvest of the vintage.

Perhaps the clearest example of an interest in subsuming linear historical perspective to the cyclical pattern of agricultural life appears in Deuteronomy 26.[40] When the Israelite farmer presents his firstfruits offerings at the Temple,

37. On the centrality of the land of Israel as the basis for the covenant between God and Israel, see H. Orlinsky, "The Biblical Concept of the Land of Israel: Cornerstone of the Covenant between God and Israel," *The Land of Israel: Jewish Perspectives*, ed. L. A. Hoffman (Notre Dame: University of Notre Dame, 1986), 27-64.

38. Cf. Knierim, "Composition of the Pentateuch," 404-6. Note that Levenson, *Creation and the Persistence of Evil*, demonstrates that the continual renewal of creation rather than the idea of *creatio ex nihilo* stands as a central principle of biblical thought. The Temple, as the central symbol for YHWH's order in the world, therefore serves as the source for the renewal of creation in the cosmos and order in Israelite life.

39. E.g., Exod 34:12; Lev 14:34; 19:23; 23:10; 25:2; Num 14:30; 15:2; 15:18; 34:2; Deut 17:14; 18:9; 26:1.

40. I am indebted to the honoree of this Festschrift for raising the issues discussed here during the course of my doctoral qualifying examinations in March 1981.

he is to recite YHWH's acts of deliverance on behalf of his ancestors, "My father was a wandering Aramaean. . . ." Von Rad identified this text as a primary example of the historical credo by which Israel established its self-identity in terms of YHWH's actions on behalf of the people throughout history.[41] Historical consciousness plays a role in establishing Israel's self-identity in this text, but it is more important to note the agricultural context in which this identification occurs. Although the motivation to present the offering stems from historical memory, the relationship itself between Israel and YHWH is constituted by the annual presentation of offerings by the people and the continuing bestowal of agricultural produce by YHWH. The relationship is no longer constituted in terms of linear historical progression but on a cyclical pattern of seasonal change and natural renewal. It is not intended to end or change in any significant way but to continue indefinitely as the ideal state of relationship between YHWH and Israel. Even the concluding sections of blessings and curses are included not to point to the end of the relationship but to insure its continuation.

One might legitimately ask why there is a need to continue scripture beyond the Torah. After all, the Torah presents an ideal scenario for the relationship between God and Israel, in which Israel would serve as the holy center for the world at large. But Israel's historical experience reenters the picture at this point, in that the succeeding sections of the Tanak point to the disruption of this ideal in the Prophets and the potential for the implementation of this ideal in the Writings.

The second major section of the Tanak, the Nebi'im or "Prophets," contains two subdivisions: the "Former Prophets" (Nebi'im Rishonim), including the books of Joshua, Judges, Samuel, and Kings; and the "Latter Prophets" (Nebi'im Aharonim), including the books of Isaiah, Jeremiah, Ezekiel, and the Twelve Minor Prophets. Both sections focus on Israel's existence in the land as an independent nation and the significance of the loss of that status as a result of the Babylonian exile. Because both sections explain the exile as the result of Israel's failure to implement the provisions of the covenant with YHWH, the Prophets present this period as a disruption of the Mosaic ideal as portrayed in the Torah.

The Former Prophets are entirely narrative in form and present the history of Israel in the land from the time of the conquest under Joshua to the period of the Babylonian exile when King Jehoiachin is finally released from prison during the reign of Evil-Merodach. This block of literature has been identified as the deuteronomistic history, and it has been the subject of numerous studies concerned with defining its intent in relation to the historical settings of its literary composition. Although it is impossible to rehearse this entire discussion,

---

41. G. von Rad, "The Form Critical Problem of the Hexateuch," *The Problem of the Hexateuch and Other Essays* (New York: McGraw; London: Oliver and Boyd, 1966), 1-78.

it is possible to make some general observations. The final form of this history is designed to explain the Babylonian exile as a judgment brought by YHWH for Israel's failure to implement the terms of its covenant with YHWH. Specifically, it points to two major factors: the continued presence and influence of Canaanites who are left in the land after the time of Joshua, and the monarchy, which is identified as an institution characteristic of the Gentiles. The monarchy, including those of the northern kingdom of Israel as well as the Davidic dynasty of Judah, is presented as the primary source of Israel's apostasy in that the monarchs are generally portrayed as leading the people in the abandonment of YHWH by polluting the Temple with pagan worship and establishing pagan altars throughout the land.

This perspective is quite clear when one surveys the books of the Former Prophets. Joshua portrays the conquest of Canaan as an ideal fulfillment of YHWH's promise that Israel would possess the land of Canaan. The book portrays YHWH's miraculous intervention in the war and the complete defeat of the Canaanite inhabitants prior to Israel's renewal of the covenant at Shechem. But in Judges, the situation changes in that many Canaanite enclaves are allowed to remain despite YHWH's commands to the contrary. These enclaves become a source of cultic apostasy and punishment for Israel in a continuing cycle of apostasy, punishment, repentance, and deliverance in the period of the judges. By the end of the book, Israel's situation has deteriorated to the point of civil war, and kingship emerges as the only solution to the people's problems. Samuel presents the rise of kingship in Israel, first through the failed monarchy of Saul and then through the successful monarchy of David. David is noteworthy for his establishment of Jerusalem as the site of the Temple, thus presenting the potential for the fulfillment of the Mosaic ideal. But his inability to control his family, and especially his affair and subsequent marriage to Bathsheba, wife of Uriah the Hittite, mar the potential of the Davidic dynasty to realize the Mosaic ideal. Once Solomon, the son of David and Bathsheba, attains the throne in the book of Kings, the Davidic dynasty is presented as the primary cause of the country's problems, including continuing cultic apostasy and the division of the kingdom into northern Israel and southern Judah. The eventual destruction of the northern kingdom is blamed on its kings, who are uniformly condemned for following Jeroboam's example in rejecting the Jerusalem Temple. With only a few exceptions, the Davidic monarchs are likewise condemned for apostasy and the corruption of the Temple. Ultimately, they are blamed for bringing about the Babylonian exile. In sum, the Davidic dynasty is presented as a major cause of the country's downfall and failure to implement the Mosaic ideal.

The same situation prevails in the Latter Prophets. These books are not presented as narrative history but as the prophetic critique of Israel's and Judah's rejection of YHWH together with their projections of YHWH's punishment of the people as a prelude to YHWH's restoration of Jerusalem and the Temple as the holy center of the land. Thus, Isaiah begins with a vision of the nations streaming to the site of the Jerusalem Temple and ends with a portrayal of the new heaven and earth as the result of YHWH's punishment of Israel and the nations. Jeremiah's announcement of judgment against the people and the Temple precedes his announcement of a new covenant in which YHWH's Torah will be inscribed on the heart. Ezekiel presents the destruction of Jerusalem and the Temple as a purifying sacrifice which precedes his portrayal of a new Eden-like Temple at the center of a restored land that waters the entire world. The Twelve Minor Prophets likewise begin with Israel's harlotry but conclude with projections of the defeat of evil in the world as YHWH returns to the Temple in Jerusalem. Again, the Latter Prophets present Israel's experience in the land as one of failure to implement YHWH's covenant, but they project that such implementation will take place once the land and people are purified through the punishment of exile and return.

The Writings — Ruth, Psalms, Job, Proverbs, Qohelet, Song of Solomon, Lamentations, Daniel, Esther, Ezra-Nehemiah, and Chronicles — constitute the final major section of the Tanak. They are frequently viewed as a loose collection of diverse genres that entered the canon at a late stage when the preceding sections were closed. With minor exceptions, the arrangement of the books generally follows generic lines, with the nonnarrative books presented according to the order of their descending sizes and the narrative books presented according to their historical order.[42] Because of the prevailing view that they constitute a literary and theological grab bag, the Writings are frequently neglected as a coherent block of scripture. But recent research into the structure and arrangement of this section has begun to focus on the Writings as a block of canonical literature that emphasizes the implementation of the ideal of Mosaic Torah in the world at large.[43]

The hymnic and wisdom books play an important role in relation to the implementation of the Mosaic ideal, especially as it is expressed in the establishment of the Jerusalem Temple. The Psalms constitute the Temple hymnbook which frequently celebrates YHWH's role as creator of the world and points to the role of the Temple as the center of that creation. Job focuses on God's role as creator of the world, and Proverbs emphasizes the role of Wisdom or Torah as the foundation of the world that YHWH created. Finally, each of the Five Megillot or Scrolls is associated with a different festival of the liturgical year. Altogether, these books emphasize the interrelationship of the Temple as the center of the created world and YHWH's Torah or Wisdom as the foun-

---

42. Beckwith, *Old Testament Canon of the New Testament Church*, 154-65.

43. E.g., Donn F. Morgan, *Between Text and Community: The "Writings" in Canonical Interpretation* (Minneapolis: Fortress, 1990); cf. Charles Vernoff, "The Contemporary Study of Religion and the Academic Teaching of Judaism," *Methodology in the Academic Teaching of Judaism*, ed. Zev Garber (Lanham, Md.: UPA, 1986), 15-40, esp. 29-32.

dation on which that world was created, thereby emphasizing the need for humans to align themselves with the principles of Torah by means of the Temple.

The narrative books place the implementation of this ideal in historical perspective. Ruth emphasizes the role of the faithful Gentile who becomes the ancestress of David, and thus this book provides a worldwide perspective for the Writings. Daniel is set in the period of Babylonian exile but projects YHWH's intervention in the world to destroy evil and reinstitute the righteous elect of God. Esther emphasizes the protection of the Jewish people in the diaspora, despite the absence of God from the narrative. Ezra-Nehemiah portrays the return of the people to the land and the restoration of the Temple. Insofar as these books present the postexilic community in compliance with Torah,[44] they present the potential full implementation of Mosaic Torah in a Jewish community centered on the Temple. It is no accident that the books of Chronicles conclude the Writings, in that they present David and the Davidic dynasty in ideal terms as the founders, builders, and caretakers of the Temple, fulfilling the role that the Chronicler apparently felt YHWH had intended. Inasmuch as Judah, Benjamin, and Levi are portrayed as the true Israel following the elimination of the disloyal northern tribes, the Chronicler's history is intended as a presentation of the model for the restored postexilic Jewish community, centered on the Temple and Torah. As such, the restored Jewish community represents the potential for the implementation of the Mosaic ideal as represented in the Torah. The fact that Chronicles begins with a genealogy that starts with Adam and continues through the Davidic dynasty only reinforces this perspective.

V

In conclusion, the above analysis points to two distinctive readings of the Hebrew Bible, determined by the respective canonical arrangement of the biblical books in Judaism and Christianity. Although both traditions are based in the same scriptural books, their respective understandings of these books point to very different views of the Bible, the course and meaning of world history, and the significance of God's relationship with humanity and the world of creation. Although some might argue that these differences point to fundamental and irreconcilable differences between the two traditions, it is important to keep in mind that it is essential for each tradition to recognize and accept the reality of different points of view as a basis for establishing any meaningful

44. Cf. Tamara Cohn Eskenazi, *In an Age of Prose: A Literary Approach to Ezra-Nehemiah*, SBLMS 36 (Atlanta: Scholars, 1988).

dialogue. Although well intentioned, attempts to find a common Jewish-Christian reading of the Hebrew Bible run the risk of assimilating the distinctive identities of either or both traditions. True dialogue can take place only when both traditions can speak on the basis of their unique understanding of scripture, and acknowledge the legitimacy of their differences.[45]

45. This is a revised version of a lecture presented at Brown University on April 3, 1991, and a seminar paper presented at the University of Miami Religious Studies Colloquium on December 4, 1991. I would like to thank Prof. Ernest Frerichs, director of the Judaic Studies Program at Brown, for his kind invitation to present this paper. In addition, I would like to thank Prof. Alan Avery-Peck, Dr. Herbert Baumgard, Prof. David Carr, Mr. Herbert Chauser, Prof. Wendell Dietrich, Prof. Zev Garber, Dr. David Kling, Prof. Jon Levenson, Dr. Jodi Magness, Ms. Joan Ruland, Prof. Stephen Sapp, and Prof. Christopher Seitz for their comments and encouragement in connection with the preparation of this study. Naturally, these individuals are not to be held accountable for the ideas expressed here.

Sin and "Judgment" in the Prophets

GENE M. TUCKER

The Old Testament prophets, especially the preexilic prophets and those we read about in the books of Kings, were preoccupied with sin and judgment — or so we have been taught. It is not fundamentally incorrect to say that these voices in ancient Israel generally proclaimed divine judgment — Yahweh's intervention — against their people because of various sins and crimes.

But is that the whole story of the prophetic understanding of the relationship between acts and consequences? Is it always or necessarily the case that a third party — Yahweh speaking through the prophet — first judges particular acts to be sins or crimes and then intervenes to impose the consequences — punishment — as more-or-less legal sanctions?[1] Are the disastrous effects of sinful actions always seen as legal sanctions imposed by Yahweh?

1. Here the definition of law developed by Leopold Pospisil is useful (Leopold J. Pospisil, *The Ethnology of Law*, 2nd ed. [Menlo Park, Calif.: Cummings, 1978]). He defines law not in terms of a single feature but by means of a set of four attributes, all of which must be present for a phenomenon to be called legal rather than, e.g., religious or political. These characteristics are authority, intention of universal application, obligation, and sanction. A decision has legal authority if it is accepted by the parties to a dispute or can be forced on them, and it requires a person or persons with powers of enforcement. A legal decision is distinguished from an ad hoc political pronouncement in that the authority intends for it to apply to all similar cases, at least within the particular group. Sometimes this intention of universal application is recognized by an appeal to precedent. Obligation, from the *obligatio* of Roman law, is that part of a legal decision which "defines the rights of the entitled and the duties of the obligated parties" (46), and must concern living persons and not, e.g., the dead or the gods. Finally, real but not necessarily physical sanctions are necessary for a matter to be considered law. Pospisil defines a legal sanction "either as a negative device — withdrawing rewards or favors that would have been granted if the law had not been violated — or as a positive measure for inflicting some painful experience, physical or psychological"

Such a juridical interpretation of the prophets in general and of Israelite religion in general is common among historians of religion as well as theologians. In a recent comparative study of sin and sanction in Israel and Mesopotamia, K. van der Toorn argues that in both cultures the "temple of morality [was] firmly grounded in the authority of the gods. . . . Calamities are conceived as divinely contrived punishments. . . ."[2]

It seems obvious on the face of it that the juridical language of crime and punishment, and with it the metaphor of Yahweh as judge, is not sufficient to account for all perspectives on the relationship between actions and consequences in the prophetic literature, wrongful actions and baleful consequences in particular. It would be surprising if that were so, given the wide diversity of perspectives over a long period of time. However, one of our problems is the lack of a vocabulary and a syntax for describing, analyzing, and accounting for nonjuridical perspectives. In a study of ancient religions in general, J. Gwyn Griffiths acknowledges that "In several areas, notably in Egypt and Israel, it is shown that punishment in this life is sometimes presented as a fate that man brings upon himself rather than as one imposed by God, though always against a moral background derived from religion. More often, however, God himself is regarded as the intervening judge, who may also apportion rewards."[3] However, this nonjuridical perspective — this "fate that man brings upon himself" — is hardly touched.

Without a doubt some prophetic texts present problems for the conventional legal reading of the relationship between acts and consequences in the prophetic literature. An example of the kind of text that evokes this question is Hos 8:7a:

For they sow the wind,
  and they shall reap the whirlwind.

That is hardly juridical thinking, nor does it speak of Yahweh's intervention.

One possibility, and the one we mean to investigate here, is that there was another view or preunderstanding, what could be called a dynamistic view of acts and consequences. The meaning of such language needs to be explored more fully, but generally I mean by "dynamistic" a point of view that sees actions

---

(51). It is a model such as this that stands behind the typical juridical interpretation of the relationship between wrongful acts and consequences in the prophets in particular. See Gene M. Tucker, "The Law in the Eighth Century Prophets," in *Canon, Theology, and Old Testament Interpretation: Essays in Honor of Brevard S. Childs*, ed. Gene M. Tucker, David L. Petersen, and Robert R. Wilson (Philadelphia: Fortress, 1988), 201-16.

2. K. van der Toorn, *Sin and Sanction in Israel and Mesopotamia: A Comparative Study*, Studia Semitica Neerlandica 22 (Assen: Van Gorcum, 1985), 56.

3. J. Gwyn Griffiths, *The Divine Verdict: A Study of Divine Judgement in the Ancient Religions*, Studies in the History of Religions [Supplements to *Numen*] 52 (Leiden: Brill, 1991), xiii.

— whether good or bad — as entailing or setting into motion their con-sequences. The term "dynamistic" is not entirely satisfactory, but it will have to serve until a more precise vocabulary can be developed.[4] I certainly do not mean to suggest the existence of a theory or philosophical system that explains the universe in terms of force or energy. At the very least, actions or events themselves are viewed in some contexts as portentous.

But more than that, I intend to demonstrate that although the juridical metaphor — with juridical language and thinking — was widely used in the prophetic literature (and likely by the prophets themselves) and reflects an understanding of Yahweh as the just king and judge (instead of an arbitrary one, i.e., one whose behavior is inconsistent with any set of theological or ideological principles), prophetic literature and most likely the prophets them-selves also share an understanding of reality as one in which justice is built in, in which actions entail their consequences. Such an understanding or preunder-standing of the matrix of reality may — for lack of a better term — be called a dynamistic perspective.

At first glance that kind of thinking might appear strange or primitive or possibly even magical. But when one thinks about it, such a point of view turns out not to be so alien after all. Human experience regularly confirms that foolish or careless or antisocial actions lead to disastrous results — at least some of the time. If you put your hand in the fire you will be burned, and without the need for intervention, divine or otherwise. The idea that acts have their consequences, that they set effects into motion, is the foundation for all historical interpreta-tion as well as any serious planning for the future. Of course, it is not always easy to anticipate which actions will produce which effects. What is distinctive in the literature before us, of course, and does not necessarily correspond to general human experience is the moral dimension, namely, that actions regarded as immoral entail or set into motion evil consequences. It is, to be sure, a major step from recognizing actions as careless or foolish to identifying them as criminal or sinful.

At the very least we can show that the prophetic understanding of the relationship between wrong actions and consequences cannot be reduced to a juridical pattern or understanding. But we hope to go further by beginning to identify a dynamistic perspective as well, and then relating that to the broadly juridical interpretation of actions and of history in the prophets.

The results of an inquiry into this question are potentially far-reaching,

---

4. This perspective is not unlike Max Weber's "karmic" thinking in contrast to legal. See his *The Sociology of Religion* (Boston: Beacon Press, 1956) and the introduction to the volume by Talcott Parsons. For Weber this distinction was related to his fundamental under-standing that religions arose and continued to function in societies to deal with the problem of evil and suffering, that religions were theodicies. He saw two basically different approaches, the legal of Israel, Islam, and the West, and the karmic of India and the East. (See also the allusion to a doctrine of karma in India and early China in Griffiths, xiii.)

both for biblical theology and for the interpretation of Israelite religion. If the relationship between sin and its effects is an exclusively juridical understanding, then, obviously, Yahweh is best seen as a judge. There are significant implications for the biblical understanding of history: Are all effects seen to be set into motion by divine intervention? Is all history caused by Yahweh's reactions to human actions? An extreme form of a dynamistic idea, on the other hand, would see the power that sets consequences into motion either in the cosmos itself or in individual actions. Among other matters, the inquiry has implications for how the biblical tradition — or the prophetic literature in particular — accounts for evil and suffering in the world.

If the perspective is not entirely juridical or legal, then translators of the Bible have done general readers a disservice at many points. From the time of the Septuagint[5] through the King James and into the present time, translators have tended to stress the juridical understanding when faced with some unusual idioms. A typical example is the reading of Amos 3:1-2 (NRSV; and similar in AV):

> You only have I known of all the families of the earth;
>   therefore I will punish you for all your iniquities.

This is clearly a misreading or overinterpretation based on the assumption that the pattern is a legal one. "Punish" is not in the text, nor is the "for" that on the one hand links the alleged punishment to the sins and on the other hand establishes a distinction between "iniquities" and punishment. One could read the second line more literally, "therefore I will visit all your sins upon you," that is, insure that you do not escape your sins. Idioms formed with this particular verb, *pāqad,* generally are interpreted legally by translators. I doubt that the translators read the Hebrew in this way because they were legalists. It seems more likely that they failed to recognize something because it appeared too foreign to their perspectives. More on this expression later.

In order to place the question into its context, and to avoid exaggerating the extent of nonjuridical assumptions in the prophets, I propose to take up the question in three stages: (1) the possibility of a "dynamistic" perspective in the Old Testament generally, (2) the typical characteristics of prophetic speech and thought concerning sin and punishment, and (3) particular prophetic texts that do not fit a juridical model.

---

5. It was K. Koch who recognized that the Septuagint introduced a great deal of legal vocabulary into the reading of the Old Testament. See K. Koch, "Gibt es ein Vergeltungsdogma im Alten Testament," *ZTK* 52 (1955): 1-42, esp. 37-39. His conclusions have been summarized by Robert L. Hubbard, "Dynamistic and Legal Processes in Psalm 7," *ZAW* 94 (1982): 267. See the helpful and sensitive discussion of this issue in Antony F. Campbell, *The Study Companion to Old Testament Literature: An Approach to the Writings of Pre-Exilic and Exilic Israel* (Wilmington, Del.: Michael Glazier, 1989), 414-27.

I. Dynamistic Thinking in the Old Testament

The modern debate on this question — the possibility of the power of actions to set into motion their consequences as an alternative to juridical patterns — was initiated more than thirty years ago by Klaus Koch.[6] One finds, of course, similar interpretations of ancient Israel's worldview in older works such as those of Johannes Pedersen,[7] who focused upon the psychic power of the soul as well as the force of the curse, and some historians of religion who saw in the Old Testament vestiges of primitive magical notions. But Koch brought the matter into the discussion by interpreting Israel's worldview in terms of *Tatsphären-denken* — sphere of action thinking, the idea that there is a continuity of acts and consequences. "In Koch's view, an act surrounds an individual with a powersphere which effects the advent of the appropriate consequence without any outside intervention ('die schicksalwirkender Tatsphäre')."[8]

Koch argued that there is no doctrine of retribution in the Old Testament; that is, that there is no judicial norm or set of rules concerning punishment that, e.g., provides the basis for the judgments announced by the prophets. To cite Patrick D. Miller's summary of his position:

> The judgment is not independent of the crime or sin. Rather it is rooted directly in the sin in a relationship of deed and its consequence. The evil that one does comes back upon the sinner even as the good comes upon the righteous. There is a connection between the deed and its results. One may speak of the fate one creates for oneself out of one's actions ("menschlicher Tat entspringendes Schicksal"). . . . Some of the technical vocabulary of "retribution" also conveys the *Tun-Ergehen* connection, e.g. *šillēm, pāqad, hēšîb*, and many words can represent both a sin and its punishment (e.g. *raʿ, ʿāwōn*). Yahweh is actively involved in the process. He is the one who makes the connection. That is, Yahweh links a deed back to the doer. He sets the deed in power so that the negative fate comes out of the negative deed and vice versa.[9]

Given all of the explicit references to Yahweh's actions, it would have been impossible for Koch to deny any divine role in this process. "In his view the Old Testament allots to God the role of confirming or triggering off the natural results of a human action; it does not ascribe to Him interventions that would introduce a foreign element into the normal course of events."[10]

---

6. Koch, 1-42.
7. J. Pedersen, *Israel: Its Life and Culture* (London: Oxford University; Copenhagen: Branner og Korch, 1926). See, e.g., 411-52.
8. Hubbard, 267. Koch was influenced by K. Hj. Falgren, *Sedaka, nahestehende und entgehengesetzte Begriffe im Alten Testament* (Uppsala: Almqvist & Wiksell, 1932).
9. Patrick D. Miller, *Sin and Judgment in the Prophets*, SBLMS (Chico, Calif.: Scholars, 1982), 5.
10. Van der Toorn, 53-54.

Although Koch's proposal stimulated a number of scholars to investigate aspects of such a possibility in various Old Testament traditions,[11] no scholar, so far as I can determine, found his extreme position acceptable,[12] and many rejected it out of hand. Typical of the rejections was that of Horst, who argued that what Koch identified was a primitive way of thinking that had been overcome very early by Yahwistic legal thought.[13] A moderating position was that of Rolf Knierim in his extensive investigation of the Hebrew words for sin. With regard to the understanding of sin, he argued that "the legal and the Tatsphäre — sphere of act — categories were so interwoven in the Old Testament as to represent one and the same thing."[14]

It would be a serious mistake to write off Koch's proposal entirely. Because he seems to reduce Old Testament thinking to this frame of reference is no reason to throw the baby out with the bathwater. There certainly are dimensions of Old Testament thought that reflect a dynamistic point of view.

Something akin to such thinking has long been acknowledged in various understandings of retribution, as in Deuteronomy and in wisdom literature. To be sure, Deuteronomy and the deuteronomistic history speak explicitly in juridical — that is to say, covenant legal — terms: Israel sins and Yahweh punishes, as in the cycle in Judges. But what of the blessings and the curses? Does Yahweh have to set the effects of the curses into motion, or has the structure of reality been established by the covenant: If you sin then the curses are effective? Israel's actions will set them into force. In fact, the history of Israel under the kings is interpreted as a history of Yahweh's holding back the effects of those curses until the very end.

Proverbial wisdom is rich in the language of the virtually inevitable connection between acts and consequences, particularly foolish or immoral actions, and not all of it is in terms of suffering as punishment for evil deeds.

> Whoever digs a pit falls into it,
>   and whoever rolls a stone, it rolls back on him. (Prov 26:27)

> Can fire be carried in the bosom
>   without burning one's clothes?
> Or can one walk on hot coals
>   without scorching the feet? (Prov 6:27-28)

11. See the bibliography and summary by Hubbard, 267.

12. Gerhard von Rad seems to have accepted more of Koch's interpretation than other scholars did.

13. F. Horst, "Recht und Religion im Bereich des Alten Testaments," *EvT* 16 (1956): 49-75; reprinted in K. Koch, ed., *Um das Prinzip der Vergeltung in Religion und Recht des Alten Testaments* (Darmstadt: Wissenschaftliche Buchgesellschaft, 1972). See also Hubbard, 267.

14. Hubbard, 268. R. Knierim, *Die Hauptbegriffe für Sünde im Alten Testament* (Gütersloh: Gütersloher Verlagshaus Gerd Mohn, 1965), 73-112.

And who could challenge the following:

> A little sleep, a little slumber,
>   a little folding of the hands to rest,
> and poverty will come upon you like a robber,
>   and want like an armed man. (Prov 24:33-34)

There is no need for the actions — or, here, the inactivity — to be weighed in the balance and for judgment to be meted out. As surely as night follows day, laziness leads to poverty.[15]

The Hebrew vocabulary in many respects is not as juridical as it may appear. Gerhard von Rad has pointed out that the Hebrew Bible does not even have a word for "punishment" as such. "The words עון and חטאת can denote the evil act: but they can also denote its evil result, and therefore punishment, because the two things are basically the same." With reference to bloodguiltiness he agrees with Koch concerning "a sphere of action which creates fate." "Murder initiates a baneful process which, before overtaking the murderer himself, first of all brings his community into the gravest danger."[16] Moreover, one can incur bloodguilt — "his blood is on his head" — even without malice aforethought, for manslaughter or even accidental death (see Deut 22:8) sets the dangerous process into motion. Thus the event is more significant than the individual motivations behind it.

And consider the sequence of events in the primeval and paradigmatic story of sin and its consequences in the Bible, the Yahwistic account of creation and the "fall" in Genesis 2–3. There is, to be sure, a fundamentally legal pattern of crime and punishment in that the first pair violate the divine instructions and Yahweh exercises judgment. But the punishment, the more-or-less legal sanction, does not come until the very end of the story, when Adam and Eve are driven from the garden and forbidden to return. Most interesting and revealing here is everything that has transpired between the action itself — eating of the forbidden tree — and this punishment. As soon as the man and the woman eat of the fruit their eyes are opened and they know they are naked (3:7). The act leads directly to loss of innocence and to shame. Next, when they hear Yahweh walking in the garden in the cool of the day, they hide themselves (3:8), and when confronted by Yahweh they acknowledge that they were afraid. Thus the act is seen to produce guilt and fear. When accused, the parties quickly blame one another and finally even Yahweh himself (3:12-13), for the man says to Yahweh that it was the woman "whom *you* gave to me" who is responsible.

---

15. On the wisdom perspective see G. von Rad, *Wisdom in Israel* (Nashville: Abingdon, 1972), 128. He also cites Prov 11:21; 12:7; and 15:6.

16. Von Rad, *Theology of the Old Testament*, vol. 1 (New York: Harper and Row, 1962), 385. He cites Josh 2:19; Judg 9:24; 2 Sam 1:16; Deut 21:8. Disaster could be averted (שוב השיב); cf. 2 Sam 16:8; 1 Kgs 2:5, 31ff.

Though committed in common, the crime produces estrangement. The penultimate step before pronouncement of punishment is the divine curses, which then set into motion painful conditions for human existence. To the Yahwist and those who share his cultural matrix, sins lead to or entail their own negative results.

The wide range of biblical taboos concerning ritual purity and defilement certainly must be seen as evidence of a dynamistic perspective. Impurity is viewed as virtually "automatic" — one becomes unclean by certain actions, such as coming into contact with a corpse or the carcass of an unclean animal, or by having a certain skin disease or touching one who does (see Lev 11–15). The dangerous results of such actions have nothing to do with the intentions or motivations of the affected party.[17] That is because impurity is contagious — one becomes unclean by coming into contact with something or someone who is unclean. Significantly, certain actions *render* one unclean; the defilement is no "punishment" in the sense that it is imposed from without, either by God or the community. The legal process of fact-finding and sanctions or purification rituals comes afterward, as in the diagnosis of leprosy, and in the prescription of rituals to cleanse the one who has become unclean, that is, to break the power of the defiling act or condition. Moreover, viewed from the perspective of cultural anthropology and the history of religions, the distinction between clean and unclean is arbitrary; that is, there is not necessarily a "rational" explanation for determining which actions would render one unclean.[18]

II. The Prophets on Sin and Punishment: Typical Patterns

Having established that dynamistic perspectives are reflected in various parts of the Old Testament, we turn now to the prophetic literature. In order to keep the matter in perspective, we should consider first the typical or dominant patterns of prophetic language and thought concerning the relationship between immoral actions and human suffering.

How one understands the prophetic role or office has a distinct bearing on the question of the prophetic perspective on sin and its effects.[19] Although they were critics of their societies, they neither called for reform as such nor did they — as the nineteenth-century scholars argued — introduce any new laws or

17. On the related question of inadvertent or unconscious sins, see J. Milgrom, "The Cultic שגגה and Its Influence in Psalms and Job," *JQR* 58 (1967/68): 115-25.

18. On this issue see Mary Douglas, *Purity and Danger: An Analysis of Pollution and Taboo* (Harmondsworth: Penguin Books, 1970).

19. See Gene M. Tucker, "The Role of the Prophets and the Role of the Church," *Quarterly Review* 1 (1981): 5-22; reprinted in *Prophecy in Israel,* ed. David L. Petersen (Philadelphia: Fortress, 1987), 159-74.

morality. Rather, they held their people accountable to ancient traditions.[20] They did not predict the future but announced it, and only rarely called for repentance. The distinctive prophetic role in ancient Israel, as revealed by an analysis of what they said and how they said it, was to function as one who proclaimed the word of Yahweh — divine revelation — concerning the future. "Prophecy" was an institution — or more likely, several institutions — in ancient Israel. The prophets viewed themselves as designated by divine vocation, and in doing so stepped into a traditional — that is to say, institutionalized — mode of behavior.

The prophets announced the word of God for the future, and in both negative and positive terms. It is clear that there are a great many texts in which the prophets, in announcing that negative future, drew a logical relationship between sin and punishment, making it clear that the offenses of individuals or of the people as a whole are the reasons for Yahweh's direct intervention against them. These are the so-called basic forms of prophetic speech (Westermann), often identified as judgment speeches or, somewhat more neutrally, prophecies of punishment. Such addresses may be said to reflect a juridical understanding or perspective, if not — as Westermann proposed — roots in the ordinary legal procedures of ancient Israel. This most typical form of prophetic speech may be illustrated with an example from the book of Amos:

> Hear this word, you cows of Bashan,
> who are in the mountain of Samaria,
> who oppress the poor, who crush the needy,
> who say to their husbands, "Bring, that we may drink!"
> The Lord God has sworn by his holiness
> that, behold, the days are coming upon you,
> when they shall take you away with hooks,
> even the last of you with fishhooks.
> And you shall go out through the breaches,
> everyone straight before her;
> and you shall be cast forth into Harmon,
> says the Lord. (4:1-3)

This short, self-contained prophetic speech, addressed to the wealthy women of the capital city, contains the three elements typical of prophecies. *First*, there is an indictment of the addressees, here a particular group but more often the nation as a whole. The indictment, giving the reasons for punishment, is twofold: social injustice — oppression of the poor and needy — and arrogance, pride, and self-satisfaction. The *second* element is an announcement of punishment as judgment for those crimes. Typical of Amos and other early

---

20. Gene M. Tucker, "The Law in the Eighth Century Prophets," in *Canon, Theology, and Old Testament Interpretation*, ed. Gene M. Tucker, David L. Petersen, and Robert R. Wilson (Philadelphia: Fortress, 1988), 201-16.

prophets, that judgment is to be a military disaster, the destruction of the city and the nation. Those who survive the siege will be carried off as captives. The *third* element is the important transition between the other two. It identifies the words as a message from God: "the Lord God has sworn. . . ." Similarly the entire speech concludes with an oracle formula, "says the Lord."

Although the prophets could speak in other ways, this form of address is both typically and distinctively prophetic. Significantly, they do not *predict* but *announce* the future, as if one posted the time and place of a meeting on a bulletin board. Furthermore, since that announcement is the very word of God, it has the power to set those events into motion (see Amos 1:2). The word is taken to be reformative. Although a dramatic idea, it is not strange in the Hebrew scriptures. In Genesis 1, God said . . . and it was. In his original call, Jeremiah is empowered with the word of the Lord: Touching the prophet's mouth Yahweh says, "Behold, I have put my words in your mouth. See, I have set you this day over nations and over kingdoms, to pluck up and to break down, to destroy and to overthrow, to build and to plant" (Jer 1:9-10). The prophet is one who speaks for God, announcing what God is about to do. Moreover, both prophet and hearers feared and respected the power of that word to set events into motion.

Analysis of the early prophetic literature in particular[21] confirms the typicality of this pattern. Claus Westermann,[22] whose work on this subject has been highly influential, perhaps accounts for one extreme with regard to the juridical pattern. He sees this so-called basic form of prophetic speech as rooted in actual legal procedure, and hence uses the terms "judgment speech" and "announcement of judgment." This goes too far. (Westermann depended heavily on accounts of prophets in the books of Kings. Thus Westermann's reconstruction may give us more information about the deuteronomistic understanding of prophecy than it does about prophetic speech itself.) It is better to be somewhat more neutral. We have attempted to modify Westermann's understanding with the category "announcement of punishment" to indicate that the pattern does not necessarily presume a formal juridical background.[23]

---

21. Gene M. Tucker, "Prophetic Speech," *Int* 32 (1978): 31-45; reprinted in *Interpreting the Prophets*, ed. James Luther Mays and Paul J. Achtemeier (Philadelphia: Fortress, 1987), 27-40.

22. Claus Westermann, *Basic Forms of Prophetic Speech* (Philadelphia: Westminster, 1967). German original, *Grundformen prophetischer Rede* (München: Kaiser, 1960).

23. Others such as Harvey and Huffmon have seen a specifically religious understanding and institutional background here, in the ריב, or covenant lawsuit of the prophets. See H. B. Huffmon, "The Covenant Lawsuit in the Prophets," *JBL* 78 (1959): 285-95; J. Harvey, *Le plaidoyer prophétique contre Israël après la rupture de l'alliance* (Bruges and Montréal: Desclée de Brouwer; Éditions Bellarmin, 1967). But at most this category applies to a very few texts, and the specific institutional background — a cultic service in which the prophet functioned to indict the people in terms of violations of the covenant — cannot be reconstructed with certainty. In any case, this cannot explain the prophetic role and message as a whole.

At the other extreme stands Koch, who denies this legal pattern on the basis of his "act-consequence" or dynamistic understanding of Israelite thought. What Westermann and others call "announcements of judgment" he calls, simply, "prophecies of disaster."[24] He alleged that the "prophecy" usually was formulated passively, thus reducing the sense of divine intervention. However, statistical analysis of the eighth-century prophets shows that he was incorrect. Although some of what Koch identifies as prophecies are expressed passively, most are in fact active forms of the verbs, and generally indicating the future.[25] The identification of particular human actions as sinful, and the drawing of logical connections between these actions and the announcement of punishment effected by Yahweh's intervention — these are typical patterns of prophetic speech and thought.

III. Dynamistic Thought in the Prophets

There are, however, numerous examples of speeches attributed to the prophets that do not fit this more-or-less juridical mold, cases in which the disaster is characterized as following from the action without reference to Yahweh's intervention, or where the lines between "sin," "guilt," and "punishment" are difficult if not impossible to establish. The general interpretation of the prophets as pronouncing Yahweh's intervention to punish is not fundamentally wrong, it is just incomplete.

There are, to begin with, a great many instances in which the prophets see the punishment as corresponding to the sin, and express that correlation in striking rhetorical patterns,[26] where a relationship between acts and consequences is presented ironically:

> If you are willing and obedient,
>> you shall *eat* the good of the land.
> But if you refuse and rebel,
>> you shall *be eaten* by the sword. . . . (Isa 1:19-20)

In this warning, the consequences of both obedient and disobedient behavior are formulated passively; that is, there is no reference to divine judgment. Isa 5:8-10 is similar: Those who join house to house and field to field will be left alone, and finally without a place to live.

24. K. Koch, *The Growth of the Biblical Tradition: The Form-Critical Method* (New York: Charles Scribner's Sons, 1969), 210-20.
25. Tucker, "Prophetic Speech."
26. P. D. Miller (*Sin and Judgment in the Prophets,* 7-95) has analyzed in some detail the pattern of the correspondence of sin and judgment throughout the prophetic literature and in other parts of the Old Testament as well.

One can, however, go further in many instances and recognize that the crime seems actually to sow the seeds for its own punishment, or to set the disastrous effects into motion. That appears to be the force of Hos 8:7: "For they sow the wind, and they shall reap the whirlwind." One cannot deny that the prophets and their audiences were familiar with principles of cause and effect, as Amos 3:3-8 shows ("Do two walk together unless they have made an appointment?" etc.), and they could apply that principle to sin and its effects.

"On one occasion," as von Rad points out, "Jeremiah describes the disaster which Yahweh will bring upon the people as 'fruit of their endeavors' (Jer 6.19). It is her own wickedness that Yahweh pours out on Jerusalem (Jer 14.16)." He goes on to characterize the perspective reflected here and in similar passages as an "ontological definition of good and evil."[27] Likewise the image of growth may be used for good deeds, as in Hos 10:12:

> Sow for yourselves righteousness,
>> reap the fruits of steadfast love . . .
>> [or better, "reap according to steadfast love"].

The admonition includes a reference to divine intervention:

> for it is the time to seek Yahweh,
>> that he may come and rain righteousness upon you.

But what follows these lines concerns the past behavior of the people, and the relationship between sins and their effects is not a legal one, or at least not necessarily so:

> You have plowed wickedness,
>> you have reaped injustice,
>> you have eaten the fruit of lies.

Moreover, the longer description of the coming disaster (vv. 14-15) is stated passively. (See also Jer 2:3.)

Similar to metaphors of seed and fruit for the relationship between behavior and consequences is Isa 3:9:

> Woe to them!
>> For they have brought evil upon themselves.

Is this just rhetoric, used as an argument that people receive what they deserve, or possibly by the accuser as self-vindication? In effect, "You brought it upon yourselves. . . . You asked for it." Certainly the language is rhetorical in the formal sense that it seeks to present a convincing case. But in order to be

---

27. Von Rad, *Wisdom in Israel*, 128.

effective — or to be considered effective — any rhetoric must make contact with what the speaker and the audience consider to be reality. Thus behind this and similar expressions stands a point of view, an assumption, that there is justice built into the very structure of reality.

We alluded earlier to the tendency of translators sometimes to read ambiguous texts juridically, as in Amos 3:2, where *ʾepqōd ʾălêkem ʾet kol-ʾăwōnōtêkem* has been read "punish you for all your iniquities." This idiom formed with the verb *pāqad* is common in the prophets, as in Hos 1:4, which should not read "I will punish the house of Jehu for the blood of Jezreel" but "I will visit (or bring) the blood of Jezreel upon the house of Jehu." To be sure, Yahweh promises to intervene; not, however, to impose a sanction distinct from the crime, but to see that the crime comes upon, confronts, and has *its* effects upon the criminal. The text also alludes to the deep understanding of bloodguilt, stressing the continuity of deed and consequence.[28]

Likewise it is often difficult if not impossible to distinguish clearly between sin, guilt, and "punishment." The same Hebrew term may refer to more than one of these concepts, as in Hos 5:5:

> Ephraim and Israel shall stumble in his guilt [*baʿăwōnô;* BHS[mg]];
> Judah also shall stumble with them.

Here *ʿāwōn* could legitimately be understood either as "sin" or "guilt" (NJPSV reads "sin").

There is that particularly enigmatic phrase in the sequence of announcements of punishment against the foreign nations in Amos 1–2. In every case the accusation begins, in the typical translation:

> For three transgressions of X,
> and for four, I will not revoke the punishment.

Again, no word for "punishment" appears. The Hebrew is *lōʾ ʾăšîbennû*, literally, "I will not cause it to return." Both the antecedent of the pronominal suffix *-nû* and the meaning of the verb *šwb* are unclear and uncertain. In an especially careful analysis, Rolf Knierim concluded that the expression alludes to a tradition about the anger of Yahweh, sent out in punishment or judgment, but that this anger could be recalled, revoked to end the punishment. To say that he will not cause it to return means that Yahweh will not hold back his anger but will allow it to burn.[29] Knierim has argued that the antecedent of "it" in "I will not cause it to return or come back" is Yahweh's burning anger or

---

28. See also Hos 4:9; 8:13; Jer 23:1-2; Zeph 1:12.

29. R. Knierim, " 'I Will Not Cause It to Return' in Amos 1–2," in *Canon and Authority: Essays in Old Testament Religion and Theology,* ed. G. W. Coats and B. O. Long (Philadelphia: Fortress, 1977), 163-75.

wrath. That interpretation is not unreasonable. It is equally plausible, however, since everything hinges upon the unclear pronoun, that "it" refers to the consequences of the criminal acts just described. Thus *lōʾ ʾăšîbennû* means that Yahweh will allow the actions — the crimes — to have their consequences. What he will not turn back, or interfere with, is the expected effects of the nations' crimes. The fact that *šwb* parallels *pāqad* in Hos 4:9 lends further support to this possibility:

> I will punish them for their ways,
> and repay them for their deeds. (NRSV)

Or better:

> I will visit his ways upon him,
> and return upon him his deeds.

There are a great many instances in the prophetic literature as well as elsewhere in which the verb *pāqad* followed by "iniquities" (*ʿāwōnôt*) or "deeds" typically is translated and interpreted as "to punish," but the meaning is problematic (Exod 20:5; 32:34; 1 Sam 15:2; Isa 10:12; Jer 6:15; 15:15; 49:8; 50:31; Pss 8:5; 59:6). The subject is Yahweh, usually in the first person, the object is "sins," "iniquities," or "deeds," followed by a prepositional phrase beginning with *ʿal:* "I will visit their sins upon X" (or in the case of Exod 20:5, upon their descendants). Since Yahweh is actively involved in making the connection between the deeds and the consequences, the perspective is not strictly dynamistic. But neither is the perspective strictly juridical, since there are no sanctions distinct from the violations; rather, the sins or deeds themselves are laid upon the violators.

We may consider one final prophetic address in which the relationship between sins and results — that is, sanctions if one understands the text legally and "effects" if it is viewed dynamistically — is open to question. A striking sequence of events is described or announced in Hos 4:1-3 — described if the verbs are read in the present tense or announced if they are seen to be future. This is not a matter that can be resolved on strictly grammatical grounds, although most translations read the present tense throughout.

> There is no faithfulness or loyalty,
>   and no knowledge of God in the land.
> Swearing, lying, and murder,
>   and stealing and adultery break out;
>   bloodshed follows bloodshed.
> Therefore the land mourns,
>   and all who live in it languish;
> together with the wild animals

and the birds of the air,
even the fish of the sea are perishing. (NRSV)

The continuity of events, which seems to be one of cause and effect, makes it difficult if not impossible to distinguish between sin and "judgment." First there is the apparently human failure of commitment and faithfulness to Yahweh at the deepest level. The effect of that failure is specific crimes against the neighbor, resulting in a situation of bloody violence. But these "effects" are themselves sins, violations of five of the prohibitions of the Decalogue. Finally, the earth and all of its inhabitants — human beings as well as creatures of field, air, and sea — suffer and in the end disappear. Obviously the very cosmos already is affected by the effects of human sinfulness. That corresponds to the act-consequence perspective described by Klaus Koch, and that is how Hans Walter Wolff saw it.[30]

Remarkably, however, this speech is set into an explicitly juridical context. It is introduced as a covenant lawsuit:

Hear the word of Yahweh, O people of Israel;
for Yahweh has a lawsuit [*rib*, "indictment against" — NRSV] with the inhabitants of the land.

If the acts already have and will continue to have their consequences, then why do these words need to be said at all, and by the voice of God? Why does the prophet not simply let it be, let the acts go forth to do their evil? Part of the answer is the human need to account for circumstances, specifically, to make disaster rational and comprehensible within a larger scheme of thought. Above all, the goal is to make sense of experience, and to understand not only the past but also the future. In this case, why does the land mourn? Thus it is not surprising that the dynamistic perspective is brought into the sphere of the dominant legal pattern. A text that starts out or ends up speaking of Yahweh's intervention to punish may include an allusion to something like a dynamistic view. But that act-consequence viewpoint is not entirely obliterated, so the two strands are intertwined.

With regard to the understanding of sin and its effects in the Old Testament generally, Rolf Knierim concluded that the legal and the *Tatsphäre* categories were so interwoven as to represent one and the same thing.[31] That goes too far, since to speak of strands implies that there is more than one perspective. Since there is more than one perspective, we need to recognize the color and texture of that other strand — the dynamistic — and when possible sort out its relationship to the dominant — the juridical — thread. We have only made a beginning here.

30. H. W. Wolff, *Hosea* (Philadelphia: Fortress, 1974), 68. See also Miller, 9-11.
31. Knierim, *Hauptbegriffe für Sünde*, 73-112, and see Hubbard's summary, 267-68.

Such dynamistic thinking is not necessarily a more primitive point of view. It may be linked in some way with a particular social-institutional facet or even some historical horizon, but there is not yet sufficient evidence to be specific. Most likely, the juridical metaphor — related as it is to specific interpretations of the will and ways of God — is the theological/reflective dimension. The alternative dynamistic understanding, although not more "primitive" or magical, is the less self-consciously reflective point of view. It represents an alternative way of making sense — of rationalizing — the relationship between wrong actions and baleful results. Consequently, our biblical theological models should not be limited to juridical images.

Gottes Handeln und Gottes Reden im Alten Testament

CLAUS WESTERMANN

Vorwort

Lieber Herr Kollege Knierim!

Mein Beitrag zu der Festschrift zu Ihrem 65. Geburtstag soll, da ich einmal einer Ihrer Lehrer war, die Form eines Briefes haben. Ich gratuliere Ihnen zu Ihrem Jubiläum und wünsche Ihnen Kraft und Gelingen zu Ihrem weiteren Wirken.

Ich erinnere mich eines Gespräches, das ich mit Ihnen führte im Zusammenhang des Abschlusses Ihrer Promotionsarbeit. Auf den letzten Seiten Ihres Manuskriptes hatten Sie gesagt, das Ziel Ihrer Untersuchung der Begriffe für Sünde im AT müsse eigentlich eine Hamartiologie, eine systematische Lehre von der Sünde sein. Ich erinnere mich noch genau daran (es war vor etwa 30 Jahren), wie ich versuchte, Ihnen klarzumachen, die historisch-kritische Untersuchung eines Begriffes (oder Begriffsfeldes) könne keinesfalls ihre Krönung in einer Hamartiologie haben. Es schien mir damals, daß meine Argumente Sie doch ein wenig zum Nachdenken gebracht hätten. Ihr Entwurf zu einer AT-Theologie,[1] den ich jetzt sehr gründlich studiert habe, hat mir gezeigt, daß ich Sie nicht habe überzeugen können, sondern daß Sie auf dem Weg geblieben sind, der zu einer abstrakten Systematik hinstrebt.

In meinem Beitrag zu Ihrer Festschrift versuche ich, das Gespräch von damals noch einmal aufzunehmen. Meine Gründe werden Sie jetzt so wenig überzeugen wie damals; aber vielleicht kann ich Ihnen einen Dienst damit erweisen, daß ich Ihnen einige Hinweise für ein nochmaliges Durchdenken des Entwurfes gebe.

---

1. Rolf P. Knierim, "The Task of Old Testament Theology," *HBT* 6 (1984): 25-57.

Originalität kann man Ihrem Entwurf nicht absprechen; es lohnt auf jeden Fall, sich mit ihm auseinanderzusetzen.

Schöpfung

Darin, daß es ein schwerer Fehler war, der Schöpfung in der bisherigen Theologie des Alten Testaments eine nur geringe oder untergeordnete Bedeutung (z.B. als Prolog der Heilsgeschichte) zuzuerkennen, stimme ich Ihnen zu, ebenso darin, daß die Schöpfung im Reden von Gott im Alten Testament eine grundlegende Bedeutung hat, die sich durch das ganze AT hindurch erkennen läßt. Dem stimmen auch die drei Stellungnahmen von W. Harrelson, R. E. Murphy und W. S. Towner zu.[2]

Umso mehr erstaunt es mich, daß Sie der Flut überhaupt keine Bedeutung zuerkennen, ja, sie nicht einmal erwähnen. Das wäre nicht möglich, wenn erkannt wäre, daß Genesis 1–11, die Urgeschichte, einen Zusammenhang bildet, in dem Schöpfung und Flut zueinander gehören, und zwar komplementär: sie ergänzen sich wechselseitig.[3] Die von Gott erschaffene Welt und Menschheit bleibt in seiner Hand; er kann sie wieder zurücknehmen. Ein Zeichen dafür ist, daß auf die Schöpfung die Sintflut folgt, die ebenso wie die Schöpfung einen universalen Charakter und eine universale Bedeutung hat. Es ist unzutreffend und exegetisch nicht haltbar, allein der vom Kontext abgeschnittenen Schöpfung einen universalen Charakter zuzuerkennen; er kommt dem Urgeschehen Gen 1–11 im ganzen zu. Die Sintflut folgt auf die Schöpfung als ein Zeichen dafür, daß es in der von Gott geschaffenen Welt Katastrophen gibt, kosmische und menschheitliche Katastrophen. Redet man von der Schöpfung, ohne daß auf diese dunkle Seite hingewiesen wird, dann ist das nicht die Schöpfung, von der das AT spricht. Das Bedrohtsein der Schöpfung, das in der Urgeschichte so deutlich und so großartig in der universalen Dimension dargestellt wird, zieht sich von da in den verschiedenen Bereichen durch das ganze Alte Testament.

Dazu gehört ein weiterer Aspekt. Sie geben in starken Worten der Schöpfung als Anfang eine überragende Bedeutung für das Reden von Gott im AT. Schöpfung ist Anfang. Aber vom Ende reden Sie nicht. Das wendet auch W. Harrelson S. 61, 63 ein. Die Apokalyptik hat für das AT eine hohe Bedeutung, und

2. Walter Harrelson, "The Limited Task of Old Testament Theology," *HBT* 6 (1984): 59-64; Roland E. Murphy, "A Response to 'The Task of Old Testament Theology,'" *HBT* 6 (1984): 65-71; W. Sibley Towner, "Is Old Testament Theology Equal to Its Task? A Response to a Paper by Rolf P. Knierim," *HBT* 6 (1984): 73-80.

3. Claus Westermann, *Genesis 1–11,* BKAT 1/1 (Neukirchen-Vluyn: Neukirchener Verlag, 1974); *Genesis 1–11: A Commentary,* trans. John J. Scullion, S.J. (Minneapolis: Augsburg, 1984).

in ihr hat das Wirken Gottes den gleichen universalen Charakter wie der Anfang; ihr geht die prophetische Gerichtsankündigung voraus. Wenn beides in Ihrem Entwurf nicht vorkommt, ist der Grund dafür wahrscheinlich, daß für Sie die zeitliche Erstreckung keine Rolle spielt, daß sie für eine Systematik gar nicht existiert.

Zwischen Anfang und Ende ist das Wirken Gottes ebenfalls von Gegensätzen bestimmt, z.B. in der Geschichte des Volkes Israel von Aufstieg und Sturz, von Heilsankündigung und Gerichtsankündigung. Im Leben des einzelnen Menschen ebenso: die Polarität von Geburt und Tod, vorkommend in Freude und Leid, wie sie in den Lobpsalmen und in den Klagepsalmen zu Wort kommen; beides wird als Wirken Gottes erfahren:

"Der Herr tötet und macht lebendig,
    er führt in die Hölle und wieder heraus" (1 Sam 2:6).

Einen tiefsinnigen Ausdruck hat dieses Daseinsverständnis in Qoh 3 gefunden, dem Text, auf den auch W. S. Towner (S. 76) hinweist:

"Alles hat seine Zeit
    und jedes Ding unter dem Himmel hat seine Stunde,
Weinen hat seine Zeit und Lachen hat seine Zeit. . . ."

Aber natürlich: in einer Systematik kann es einen solchen polaren Rhythmus nicht geben, weil es keine zeitliche Erstreckung gibt, oder weil sie irrelevant ist, weder vom Anfang zum Ende der Welt noch von der Geburt eines Menschen bis hin zu seinem Tod. Diese wunderbare Bewegtheit des Schöpferwirkens haben Sie in zeitlose statische Begriffe umgewandelt und die Bewegtheit damit zum Erstarren gebracht. Wenn das ganze AT von einem Grundbegriff her verstanden werden soll, verliert es etwas, was zu seinen Wesensmerkmalen gehört: den Reichtum und die Vielfalt; es wird immer nur eines, immer dasselbe gesagt. Sprachlich zeichnet sich das ab in der Monotonie Ihres Schlußteils, in dem die gleichen Sätze immer wiederkehren.

In Gen 1–11 begründet die Erschaffung der Welt und der Menschheit nicht einen Status, der dann immer so bleibt. Vielmehr geht die Schöpfung bruchlos über in ein Geschehen, von dem Gen 1–11 berichtet. Ich stimme Ihnen darin zu, daß die Schöpfung, das Wirken des Schöpfers sich über alle drei Bereiche bis in die Gegenwart erstreckt;[4] aber das ist nur möglich in einer Geschehensfolge; es ist nicht in statischen Begriffen festzulegen. Ich will das in zwei Linien nur andeuten.

Stimmt man dem zu, daß in Gen 1–11 Schöpfung und Flut zusammengehören, so ergibt sich, daß auch das rettende Wirken Gottes schon hier im universalen Horizont begegnet. Das Ziel der Fluterzählung ist der Bericht von

---

4. Diese drei Bereiche sind die gleichen wie in vielen anderen Theologien des AT.

einer Errettung; ein Rest wird gerettet. Der Herr des Universums ist der Retter. Von diesem universalen Horizont aus geht das Reden vom rettenden Gott durch die ganze Bibel des Alten und Neuen Testaments, und zwar in allen drei Bereichen. Das Wirken Gottes, das sich der Leidenden erbarmt, reicht vom Anfang bis zum Ende und vom Kleinsten bis zum Größten.

Sie werden vielleicht sagen, dies sei enthalten in "justice and righteousness." Das trifft nicht zu. Das Erbarmen Gottes mit den Leidenden ist ein Akt; es ist nicht ein Zustand oder eine Eigenart. Ich war darüber erschrocken, daß das Wort "Erbarmen" in ihrem ganzen Entwurf nicht vorkommt, vgl. auch R. E. Murphy, S. 67. Meinen Sie, das, was der 113. oder 103. Psalm vom Erbarmen Gottes mit den Leidenden sagt, habe keine Bedeutung für das Reden von Gott im AT?

Dazu die andere Linie: Erst gegen Ende Ihres Entwurfes kommen Sie S. 39f auf die Beziehung Jahwes zu seiner Schöpfung zu sprechen. Ich stimme Ihnen zu, wenn Sie die schlimme Einseitigkeit der abendländischen Theologie ablehnen, die sich allein geistesgeschichtlich orientiert hat, aber den Kontakt mit den Naturwissenschaften ganz verloren hat. Ich habe das auch in mehreren meiner Schriften nachdrücklich gesagt.[5]

Sie fragen dann (S. 39) mit berichtigendem Pathos: "The question involves . . . also [the aspect] of our earth and its natural life . . . including the provision of water, fertility and food for the sustenance of the living. When has anybody bothered to include in an Old Testament theology a . . . chapter on a subject as trivial as a theology of food?" Wenn Sie gestatten: ich. I have bothered. In meiner *Theologie des Alten Testaments in Grundzügen* [6] Teil III: *"Der segnende Gott und die Schöpfung," und ausführlicher: Der Segen in der Bibel und im Handeln der Kirche.*[7]

Das ist die andere Linie von der Schöpfung her: Der Schöpfer segnet seine Geschöpfe (Gen 1), gibt ihnen Fruchtbarkeit und Nahrung. Da es Ihnen ausreicht, nur allgemein und abstrakt von Beziehungen Gottes zur Realität zu sprechen, können Sie das segnende Handeln Gottes nicht in den Blick bekommen. Der Segen Gottes spielt aber im AT wie im NT (aber mehr im AT) eine sehr gewichtige Rolle, und es ist ja Ihre Meinung, daß eine "theology of food" notwendig sei. Sie sprechen zwar an einigen Stellen von "sustenance" (Erhaltung), aber das ist der dogmatische, statische Begriff, nicht der biblische, lebendige.[8]

---

5. "Schöpfung und Evolution," in *Evolution und Gottesglaube: Ein Lese- und Arbeitsbuch zum Gespräch zwischen Naturwissenschaft und Theologie*, hg. W. Böhme (Göttingen: Vandenhoeck und Ruprecht, 1988), 240-50.

6. Göttingen: Vandenhoeck & Ruprecht, 1978; *Elements of Old Testament Theology*, trans. D. W. Stott (Atlanta: John Knox, 1982).

7. München: Kaiser, 1968; Blessing in the Bible and the Life of the Church, trans. K. R. Crim (Philadelphia: Fortress, 1978).

8. F. W. Golka, "God Who Blesses," *Theology* 83.692 (1980): 83-91.

Wenn das Alte Testament von Gott spricht, dann spricht es von der ersten bis zur letzten Seite von einem vielfältigen, vielgestaltigen Handeln und Reden Gottes. Dann ist es doch wohl dem Alten Testament gemäß, wenn eine Theologie des Alten Testaments von diesem Handeln und Reden ausgeht.

Das Handeln Gottes

Von einem Handeln und Reden Gottes spricht das erste Kapitel der Bibel. Von einem Handeln verbunden mit einem Reden Gottes spricht das AT in seiner Mitte (Rettung am Schilfmeer und Sinai). Von einem Handeln mit einem Reden verbunden sprechen die Prophetenbücher und sprechen die Geschichtsbücher und auch die Apokalypsen am Ende. Was das AT von Gott sagt, ist vom Anfang bis zum Ende vom Handeln und Reden Gottes bestimmt. Das kann verschieden erklärt werden; aber ohne das bestünde das Alte Testament nicht. Eine Theologie des Alten Testaments, die diesen Tatbestand nicht beachtet oder ihn bestreitet, kann nicht wiedergeben, was das AT von Gott sagt.

Das Reden Gottes

Die Geschichte der Prophetie ist vom Anfang bis zum Ende bestimmt vom Reden Gottes. Am Anfang steht der Auftrag Gottes an den Propheten, wie in Jes 6. Man kann diesen Auftrag, also das Reden Gottes zum Propheten, verschieden erklären; aber wie immer man es erklärt, wir kennen das Phänomen Prophetie nicht anders als von einem Auftrag Gottes an den Propheten bestimmt. Das wird durch die prophetischen Redeformen objektiv bezeugt. — Es genügt dieses eine Beispiel des Redens Gottes im Alten Testament. In Ihrem Entwurf einer Theologie des Alten Testaments kommt die Prophetie nicht vor.

Wenn eine Theologie des AT dem Reden Gottes in vielerlei Gestalt durch das ganze AT hindurch keine wesentliche Bedeutung zuerkennt, kann sie nicht beanspruchen wiederzugeben, was das AT von Gott sagt.

Sie mögen als ungerecht empfinden, daß ich an mehreren Stellen darauf hinweise, daß in Ihrem Entwurf fehlt, was dem AT selbst sehr wesentlich ist. Sie werden dagegen einwenden, daß in einem kurzen Entwurf nicht alles gesagt werden kann. Ich würde diese Hinweise auf das Fehlende zurückziehen, wenn Ihr Entwurf zeigen würde, welches seine Textgrundlage ist, d.h. welche großen Textkomplexe des AT — die Geschichtsbücher, die Propheten, die Psalmen, die Gesetzeskomplexe — dem Aufbau Ihres Entwurfes zugrundeliegen und in welchem Zusammenhang.

Zu den Hauptzügen des Entwurfes

Ich gebe eine kurze Skizze des Aufbaus: Der Entwurf hat drei Hauptteile: I. Das Problem (23), II. Die Kriterien (31), III. Schluß (46).

I. Hauptteil: Das Problem

Teil I ist gegliedert: A. in die Formulierung des Problems: Das AT enthält eine Pluralität von Theologien, B. einen kurzen Blick auf die Geschichte der Disziplin: die bisherigen Versuche ganzheitlicher Perspektiven, C. geht es um die Untersuchung der Beziehungen der einzelnen Theologien zueinander; dabei muß nach der "Sache" gefragt werden, D. sind alle Forscher zwar einig in der Bejahung der Einzigkeit Jahwes, unterscheiden sich aber in deren Erklärung.

II. Hauptteil: Die Kriterien

Es gilt die Basis zu finden, auf der die AT-Theologien zu konzeptualisieren sind. A: Ungeeignet sind acht bisherige Versuche.

B: Positive Kriterien, die Frage nach Prioritäten. Alle Kriterien aus Zeit, Entstehung, literarischem Genus und Redeformen sind für die Frage nach Prioritäten irrelevant; nur solche Kriterien kommen in Frage, bei denen Prioritäten unter den theologischen Argumenten selbst gefunden werden können. Zu den notwendigen Beziehungen gehören die qualitativen Begriffe in Worten wie Schöpfung, Erwählung. Dazu der quantitative Aspekt, die Bereiche der Wirklichkeit, die Welt, die Völker, die Individuen. Dieser quantitative Aspekt beherrscht alle anderen.

Die bisherige Theologie des AT war so mit der Geschichte beschäftigt, daß die Schöpfung dagegen abfiel. Sie verlor den Kontakt mit den Naturwissenschaften. Dabei geht es nicht nur um die Schöpfung als solche, sondern auch um Fruchtbarkeit, Wasser, Nahrung zur Erhaltung des Lebens. Die Geschichte hängt von der Schöpfung ab; diese ist die Basis für die drei Bereiche. Jahwe ist der Gott der Menschen und der Menschengeschichte, weil er der Gott der Schöpfung ist. Der quantitative Aspekt hat daher den Vorrang vor dem qualitativen.

C: Die Aufgabe der AT-Theologie ist eine zweifache: Sie muß die Beziehung zwischen Jahwe und seiner Welt untersuchen, und zwar wechselseitig. Die zweite Aufgabe: Sie muß die individuellen Theologien im Licht der Beziehungen Jahwes zur Wirklichkeit sehen.

III. Hauptteil: Schluß

Die zwei heuristischen Leitlinien, dazu einige Unterschei-
dungen in 11 Punkten, darunter Oberflächenstrukturen und Tiefen-
strukturen.

Pluralität der Theologien und ihre Summa

Ihr Entwurf beginnt mit dem Satz: "Das Alte Testament enthält eine Pluralität
von Theologien." Was Sie genau mit Theologien meinen, sagen Sie nicht. Einmal
sind es "theologische Positionen," einmal ist an ein ganzes literarisches Werk
gedacht, wie die Priesterschrift, manchmal nur an kleine Texte oder an Begriffe,
z.B. "Theologie der Befreiung." Deswegen ist es schwierig, darauf einzugehen.
Dazu kommt, daß Sie von einer Pluralität von Theologien reden, als handle es
sich nur um ein Nebeneinander; sie sind aber in der Mehrzahl nacheinander
entstanden und erhalten ihren Sinn aus der zeitlichen Folge. Auch müßte man,
wenn man aus dieser Pluralität Schlüsse ziehen will, zunächst klären, worin sie
verschieden sind und worin sie übereinstimmen. Sie hatten den ansprechenden
Gedanken, die Vertreter dieser Theologien in Jerusalem zu einer Konferenz
zusammenkommen zu lassen, um ihre verschiedenen theologischen Positionen
zu diskutieren. Auf jeden Fall werden sie dabei zuerst Gott gedankt haben, daß
er sie auf ihrem Weg behütet hat, dazu ihn um Segen und Gelingen für das
Zusammenkommen gebeten haben. Ich will damit andeuten: Für die, die da
zusammenkamen, war das ihnen allen Gemeinsame stärker als das, worin sie
verschiedener Meinung waren. Das Wirken des Schöpfers war den Vertretern
der verschiedenen theologischen Positionen ganz gewiß ein gemeinsames Anliegen. Dieser Tatbestand des verbindenden Gemeinsamen wird durch den abstrakten Begriff einer "Pluralität von Theologien" verdunkelt.

Die verschiedenen theologischen Positionen wollen Sie dann in der Weise
miteinander in Verbindung bringen, daß Sie sie nach ihrer theologischen Bedeutung werten und unterscheiden und nach solcher Werteskala eine Hierarchie
der verschiedenartigen Theologien aufbauen, die alle nach ihrer Spitze hin
orientiert sind. Diese Spitze ist eine theologische Summa oder ein leitendes
Prinzip, nach dem alle anderen ausgerichtet werden müssen. Dieses oberste
Prinzip ist "Yahweh's universal dominion in justice and righteousness" (S. 49).
Hierzu fragt W. Harrelson S. 60 mit Recht: "must one have a single, controlling
concept?"

Um dieses Programm durchzuführen, müssen Sie das ganze AT "conceptualize," also begrifflich gestalten, und diese Begriffe müssen dann in Beziehung zueinander gebracht werden. An diesem Punkt muß ich widersprechen.
Wer das ganze AT in Begriffe fassen will, nimmt ihm damit seine Eigenart.
Das AT besteht nicht aus einer Summe von Begriffen; es ist auf gar keinen Fall

eine in Gedanken und Begriffe gefaßte Ganzheit. Sie reden in diesem Zusammenhang von einer Ontologie, die dem AT eingeprägt sei. Damit geben Sie zu, daß Sie das AT von Grundbegriffen des griechischen Denkens und der abendländischen Philosophie her deuten wollen. Diese Konzeption ist dem AT fremd. S. 37-38 führen Sie ein Beispiel der Hierarchiebildung aus Prioritäten an: "The theology of liberation is no independent theology in the Old Testament. It is a sub-chapter of a dominant theology in the service of which it stands: the theology of justice and righteousness" (S. 38). Das ist eine bloße Behauptung. Sie hat im AT selbst keinerlei Grundlage.

Das Haupt der Hierarchie

Die Spitze der Hierarchie begründen Sie damit (S. 42), daß der Begriff der universalen Wirklichkeit, der sich aus dem Begriff der Schöpfung und Weltherrschaft ergibt, das Kriterium für die Anerkennung Jahwes als universaler Gott und für seine wahre Gottheit sei. Mit anderen Worten: Der Begriff der Universalität ergibt sich aus dem Begriff der Weltherrschaft Jahwes. Sie haben damit betont, daß es Ihnen bei der Spitze der Hierarchie um einen Begriff geht, der sich auch aus anderen Begriffen ergibt. Das mag eine interessante begriffliche Konstruktion sein; aber was hat sie mit der Wirklichkeit zu tun? Dazu mit Recht W. S. Towner (S. 76): "the universal hegemony of Yahweh can be imaged in radically different ways. . . . Psalm 148 . . . Eccl 3:1-9."

Sehr wichtig ist Ihnen, daß bei der Bestimmung der Relationen der quantitative Aspekt den Vorrang vor dem qualitativen hat. In diesem Zusammenhang führen Sie als ein Argument an, daß Gottes universale Herrschaft den Vorrang haben muß, weil die Geschichte der Menschheit und die Geschichte Israels die Schöpfung voraussetzen. Diesem Argument stimme ich zu. Und ich halte es für ein sehr wichtiges Argument, das in der bisherigen Theologie des AT nicht genügend berücksichtigt worden ist, wie Sie mit Recht sagen. Nur kann es für Ihre Hierarchie von Theologien keine Bedeutung haben, weil es sich in dieser ja um gedankliche, begriffliche Priorität handelt, während die grundlegende Voraussetzung der Schöpfung für alles andere eine zeitliche ist: Die Schöpfung ist Geschehendes, von dem alles Geschehende ausgeht, begründet im Wirken des Schöpfers. Gegen Ihre Anwendung des Arguments spricht aber auch ein geschichtlicher Tatbestand: Israel ist Jahwe zuerst als seinem Retter begegnet; das Reden vom Schöpfer und seiner Schöpfung ist erst später hinzugekommen.

Jahwe und die Wirklichkeit

Sie sprechen öfter (z.B. S. 38) von der Beziehung zwischen Jahwe und der Wirklichkeit. Aber eine Beziehung zwischen Gott und der Wirklichkeit abgesehen von der Schöpfung kommt im AT nicht vor. Der abstrakte Begriff "reality" soll hier wohl alle drei Bereiche dieser Beziehung umfassen. Die Beziehung Gottes zu diesen drei Bereichen ist aber derart verschieden, daß eine abstrakte Zusammenfassung dafür nicht ausreicht.

Darüber hinaus ist der Begriff in der Anwendung, die er hier erfährt, nicht eindeutig. Er hat vom lateinischen her in den europäischen Sprachen eine zweifache Bedeutung: reality als Vorhandensein und reality als Geschehendes (lateinisch *res* = Ding, Sache und *res* = Geschehen, wie in *res gestae*). Wenn das nicht geklärt ist, bleibt eine Unklarheit, die sich durch den ganzen Entwurf zieht. Da Ihr Entwurf auf eine geschichtslose Systematik zielt, ist anzunehmen, daß Sie reality als Vorhandensein verstehen.

Jahwes universale Herrschaft in Recht und Gerechtigkeit

Diesen Satz erklären Sie zum Haupt der Hierarchie der Theologien des AT. Ein Begriff, der vor allen anderen den Vorrang hat, auf den die anderen alle bezogen werden müssen, S. 34: "ein Aspekt, der alle anderen beherrscht."

Das Wort Herrschaft, dominium, bezeichnet das Wirken eines Herrschers. Gott der Schöpfer ist der Herr der ganzen Schöpfung (oder Welt oder reality). Das Wort bezeichnet also das Wirken einer Person. Das gibt es aber nur in einer Zeitfolge.

Sie haben Ihre Aufgabe in einer "Konzeptualisierung" dessen gesehen, was das AT von Gott sagt. Hier stößt diese Bemühung an eine Grenze. Eine nur gedankliche universale Herrschaft Gottes ist ein Widerspruch in sich. Die Schwierigkeit scheint mir darin zu liegen, daß der Unterbau der Pyramide Ihrer Systematik gedanklich begrifflicher Art ist und auf ihre Spitze ein personaler Vorgang, der der Herrschaft, gesetzt wird. Hier zeigt sich besonders die Problematik dieses ganzen Unternehmens.

Die Wechselseitigkeit der Beziehung

Gegen Ende Ihres Entwurfs betonen Sie ausdrücklich die Wechselseitigkeit der Beziehung zwischen Gott und der Wirklichkeit, zwischen Gott und der Welt. S. 44: "Die AT-Theologie muß die Beziehung zwischen Jahwe und seiner Welt untersuchen. Dabei ist zu unterscheiden zwischen Jahwes Beziehung zur Welt und der Beziehung der Welt zu Jahwe." Ganz ähnlich S. 51-52: "Both, the Old and the New Testament . . . must be interpreted in view of what can be discerned in either testament and in the Jewish tradition as God's universal dominion over his world and the world's response to this dominion."

Wenn Sie von einer Antwort (response) reden, können doch wohl nur Bestandteile der Welt und der Menschheit gemeint sein. Das aber ist notwendig ein Geschehen in der Zeit. Ausübung des Dominium und Reaktion (response) darauf können nicht gleichzeitig sein. Zu Anfang, bei der Abweisung der Ihrer Meinung nach falschen Konzeptionen einer AT-Theologie (S. 32), haben Sie ein solches Wechselgeschehen ausdrücklich als unsachgemäß abgelehnt, denn es hat ja in einer Systematik, die ihrem Wesen nach zeitlos ist, keinen Ort; sie hat es mit begrifflichen Wertungen zu tun.

Von der Wechselseitigkeit sprechen Sie in einem sehr allgemeinen Ausdruck: "The world's response to this dominion." Im AT reagiert die Welt als ganze (abgesehen von der Schöpfung) nie, wohl aber die Himmel (Ps 19); der Wind gehorcht seinem Befehl und die Sterne, die Kreaturen in der Aufzählung des 148. Psalms oder das Gotteslob im Gottesdienst. Es gibt diese Antwort immer nur partiell, immer nur in bestimmten, festen Zusammenhängen: Mit dieser Einschränkung halte auch ich die Antwort der Schöpfung auf das Wirken des Schöpfers für einen wichtigen Bestandteil der AT-Theologie.

Die Beziehung des Menschen zu Gott, die Reaktion des Menschen auf Gottes Handeln und Reden, auf seine Herrschaftsausübung tritt in Ihrem Entwurf ganz zurück. Sie geben zwar eine sehr kurze Zusammenfassung auf S. 35, aber die zeigt nur, daß Ihnen die Beziehung des Menschen zu Gott unwichtig ist. Der Glaube an Gott hat in Ihrem Entwurf keinen Platz; Hoffnung gibt es auch nicht, weil es ja ein geschichtsloser Entwurf ist. Auch das Vertrauen zu Gott, von dem die Psalmen sprechen, kommt nicht vor. Die Beziehung des Menschen zu Gott bleibt ein leerer Begriff.

Eins fiel mir besonders auf: Die wechselseitige Beziehung von Gott und Mensch erfährt im AT ihre beherrschende Ausprägung im Gottesdienst, im Kult. Auch der Kult wird nicht erwähnt. Wie ist es zu verstehen, daß zu Ihrem Entwurf einer AT-Theologie die Wechselseitigkeit der Beziehung zwischen Gott und Mensch gehört, der Ort aber, an dem sie sich vollzieht, der Kult, nicht einmal erwähnt wird? Ich kann mir das nur so erklären, daß Sie mit der Wechselseitigkeit etwas nur Gedankliches meinen, etwas Gedachtes, das mit der Wirklichkeit nichts zu tun hat. Aber den Kult kann man nicht "konzeptualisieren."

Gottes Heiligkeit

Es ist logisch, daß, weil in Ihrem Entwurf der Kult nicht vorkommt, auch Gottes Heiligkeit nicht begegnet. Auch wenn Sie vielleicht sagen, das komme erst in der Einzelausführung, so ändert das nichts daran, daß das Heilige in dem Grundgerüst Ihres Entwurfs fehlt; Gottes Heiligkeit hat in ihm keine Funktion. Dem das Universum Beherrschenden kommt Heiligkeit nicht zu.

Die Heiligkeit Gottes, ein allgemein religiöses Phänomen, hat im AT die besondere Bedeutung, daß in ihm Kult und Prophetie zusammenkommen. Die Heiligkeit Gottes verbindet Gottesdienst und Geschichte, vor allem in dem Bericht von der Berufung Jesajas, aber nicht nur hier. Jahwe ist "der Heilige

Israels." Insofern hat die Heiligkeit Gottes eine für das ganze AT zentrale Bedeutung. Der Entwurf einer AT-Theologie, in der der Kult, die Heiligkeit Gottes
und die Prophetie keinen Ort haben, ist für mich schwer vorstellbar.

Die universale Herrschaft Gottes zwischen Anfang und Ende

Wie ist es mit der universalen Herrschaft Gottes in der Völkergeschichte? In der
Urgeschichte handelt Gott an der ganzen Welt, eingeschlossen die Völkergeschichte. So wird es aber nur in der Urgeschichte und deren Nachklängen,
z.B. in den Psalmen, gesagt. Mit Gen 12 beginnt ein Wirken Gottes, das es immer
nur mit einem bestimmten, begrenzten Bereich zu tun hat. Erst wieder in der
Apokalyptik begegnet ein Wirken Gottes am ganzen Kosmos. Dazwischen
begegnet das Wirken Gottes in den drei Bereichen jeweils besonders; in der
Mitte steht das Handeln Gottes an seinem Volk in einer kontinuierlichen
Geschichte, darauf bezogen das Wirken in den anderen Bereichen. Dieses aber
auf einen einzigen Begriff zu bringen oder es einem beherrschenden Begriff
unterzuordnen, ist nicht möglich. Denn es ist ein so vielfältiges, so viele Bereiche
der Wirklichkeit einbeziehendes Wirken; und gerade diese Eigenart des Wirkens
Gottes würde zerstört, wollte man es einem einzigen Begriff unterordnen. Ich
nenne nur eines: Alle Formen menschlicher Gemeinschaften sind in den Verlauf
der Geschichte Gottes mit seinem Volk einbezogen, dazu das menschliche Leben
in allen seinen Phasen, von der Geburt bis zum Tod; wie sollte man das alles
auf einen Nenner bringen!

Und auch hier ist eine polare Entsprechung zu beachten. Von dem, was
außerhalb des vom AT Berichteten zwischen Gott und seiner Schöpfung
geschieht, erfahren wir nichts. Wie seine universale Herrschaft zwischen Anfang
und Ende sich im einzelnen auf der Erde, im Kosmos, in der Menschheits-
geschichte, im Leben der unzähligen Einzelnen vollzieht, davon sagt uns die
Bibel nichts. Von seinem Wirken unter anderen Völkern wird nur da etwas
gesagt, wo es das Wechselverhältnis zu Israel berührt, alles andere bleibt im
Dunkel. Wenn dies in einer AT-Theologie nicht ausdrücklich gesagt wird, und
daß uns die Herrschaft Gottes über das Universum verborgen ist, dann bleibt
der Satz von Gottes universaler Herrschaft eine Leerformel; sie sagt dann gar
nichts.

"In Recht und Gerechtigkeit"

W. Harrelson sagt zu diesem zweiten Teil des das Ganze bestimmenden Leit-
satzes (S. 62): "justice and righteousness . . . need to be identified as to their
precise meanings," and R. E. Murphy meint dasselbe, wenn er sagt (S. 66): "I
wonder if 'in justice and righteousnes [sic]' . . . is not somewhat redundant."

Dazu fragt W. S. Towner (S. 75): "Do not justice and righteousness mean quite startlingly different things in different contexts?"

Diese Sätze deuten es schon an: Es ist höchst merkwürdig, daß Sie zu diesem Zusatz in Ihrem Entwurf fast nichts sagen, obwohl er doch eine allumfassende Bedeutung haben soll; daß dagegen der Satz von der universalen Weltherrschaft Jahwes alles Gewicht hat? Die Stellungnahmen zeigen, daß er einige wichtige Fragen aufwirft. Ihr Satz S. 43: "I have already suggested that the notions of justice and righteousness seem to be governing the other qualitative notions" ist da wenig hilfreich. R. E. Murphy führt das weiter (S. 65): "the 'criterion': the universal dominion of Yahweh in justice and righteousness . . . cuts across the three essential realms . . . is neither proved nor illustrated." Dem stimme ich zu. Die Psalmen, das Hiobbuch und die Threni bringen die bitteren Klagen derer vor, die in dem, was ihnen geschieht, Gottes Gerechtigkeit nicht mehr erkennen können. Wenn in dem Leitsatz der weiteste Horizont der Herrschaftsausübung Gottes als eine Herrschaft in "Recht und Gerechtigkeit" bezeichnet wird, wird im persönlichen Leben des Einzelnen, in der Geschichte des Gottesvolkes und darüber hinaus in der Geschichte der Völker und aller Kreatur diese wirklich in allem als eine Herrschaft in Recht und Gerechtigkeit erfahren (so auch Murphy)? Kann das so allgemein und so summarisch gesagt werden, etwa angesichts der schrecklichen Leiden und Qualen der Kinder und ihrer Eltern bei der Eroberung Jerusalems, die die Threni so ergreifend schildern?

Wenn die Leidenschaft der universalen Herrschaftsausübung Gottes verschwiegen wird, wenn von der Schöpfung gesprochen wird, ohne daß gesagt wird, daß ihr die Flut folgt, dann fehlt ein entscheidender Aspekt dessen, was die Bibel von der universalen Weltherrschaft Gottes sagt, und sie entspricht nicht der Wirklichkeit. Man wundert sich dann auch nicht mehr darüber, daß vom Erbarmen Gottes mit den Leidenden nichts gesagt wird.

Zur Sprache

Oberflächenstruktur und Tiefenstruktur

Bei der Näherbestimmung der Kriterien sagen Sie (S. 33): "Die Kriterien hängen davon ab, was gesagt ist, nicht wie, früh oder spät; keine Redegattung, ob Erzählungstext, Gesetzestext oder Hymnos hat einen Vorrang; eine Form kann in andere umgewandelt werden. Sie alle treffen nicht das Herz der theologischen Substanz." Oder (S. 48): "Die Basis sind die entscheidenden theologischen Argumente selbst, gleichgültig wo, wann, wie und vom wem sie ausgedrückt sind." Und dazu (S. 47): ". . . noch gibt es irgendwelche Texte, kleine oder große, die nur die Oberflächen-struktur wiedergeben . . . und nicht auch eine begriffliche

Tiefen-struktur." Dies ist ausgesprochen idealistisch gedacht und gesagt. Diese Auffassung, daß es nicht auf die äußere Form, sondern den tieferen Sinngehalt (depth-structure) ankomme, und daß für die Erkenntnis dieses tieferen Sinngehalts die äußere Form irrelevant sei, findet man in den Bibelauslegungen des 19. und des angehenden 20. Jahrhunderts sehr häufig; es ist hier weit verbreitete Überzeugung.

Wenn die geschichtlichen Situationen, aus denen Worte und größere Zusammenhänge im AT entstanden sind (d.h. also z.B., ob der Ruf "Tröstet, tröstet mein Volk!" im 8. Jahrhundert oder im Exil gesprochen wurde), und wenn für die Erkenntnis ihres tieferen Sinngehalts die Formen, aus denen diese Worte erwuchsen (z.B. die Form einer prophetischen Gerichtsankündigung) keine Bedeutung mehr haben, dann ist damit die Grundlage der geschichtlichen und der formgeschichtlichen Auslegung verlassen. Ich habe das früher anders von Ihnen gehört.

Die Sprache der Auslegung

Es ist eine alte, bewährte Regel der Auslegung jeglicher Art, daß die Sprache der Auslegung der Sprache des Textes, den sie auslegt, möglichst nahe bleibt, so daß der Text bei der Auslegung mitsprechen kann. Das gilt insofern auch für das Erarbeiten einer AT-Theologie, als sie sich ja auch auf einen Text bezieht.

Nun ist es eine Eigenart des Alten Testaments, daß es mehr konkret als abstrakt redet, daß es mehr von Verben als von Nomina bestimmt ist. Dieser Wirklichkeitsnähe des AT sollte die Auslegung entsprechen. Mir scheint bei Ihnen von Fachtermini bestimmtes Reden zu überwiegen, so daß der Eindruck einer dem AT sehr fernen Sprache entsteht.

Das beginnt schon mit dem Wort System, Systematik. Das Wort ist dem Reden und dem Denken des AT fremd. Das ist auch die Meinung von R. E. Murphy (S. 68): "Systematization is then born in a post-biblical era." Man kann zwar von einzelnen systematischen Zügen im AT reden, aber keines der Bücher des AT als Ganzes ist System oder Systematik. R. E. Murphy (S. 69): "In systematization a guiding idea, which is never used as a guide within the Old Testament, is imposed upon the material in order to arrive at 'biblical theology' as a unitary concept." G. von Rad: "Das Alte Testament erzählt eine Geschichte." Aus einer Geschichte kann man keine Systematik machen. Andererseits steht es bei diesem Wort fest, daß es ein dem griechischen Denken erwachsener Begriff ist und daß er seine stärkste Ausprägung in der auf Aristoteles beruhenden Dogmatik des Mittelalters in ihren großen Systemen erhalten hat. Wodurch ist dann die Umprägung des AT in eine Systematik legitimiert?

Sie haben dafür als einen Grund die Bemühung angegeben, eine Brücke herzustellen zwischen der Exegese und dem Fach Systematik-Dogmatik. Diese

Bemühung ist als solche respektabel, ich fürchte aber, daß Sie damit zu spät kommen. Wenn man ein wenig beobachtet, was heute in diesem Fach vor sich geht, so bemerkt man eine grundlegende Wandlung. Die systematischen Fächer (auch die Ethik) wenden sich heute zusehends mehr von den altkirchlich-mittelalterlichen Denkstrukturen, also von der klassischen Dogmatik ab und bemühen sich um ein theologisches Reden, an dem mitzuarbeiten auch der christlichen Kirche und ihrer Theologie aufgegeben ist.[9] Die aus dem griechischen Denken erwachsenen Denkmodelle treten dabei Schritt für Schritt zurück. Wenn Sie also eine Brücke von der Auslegung des AT zur Systematik bauen wollen, dann wird es gut sein, darauf zu achten, ob denn auf der anderen Seite die alten Pfeiler noch stehen.

Ein weiteres Beispiel ist "spirituality." S. 35 sagen Sie: "The Old Testament's theologies are expressions of Israel's Yahweh-spirituality," und dann: "This spirituality reflects an anthropology." W. Harrelson bemerkt hierzu (S. 63): "The term 'Yahweh-spirituality' sets my teeth on edge"; mir geht es nicht anders.

Ein weiteres Beispiel ist Ihr Gebrauch des Wortes "Semantik" (S. 46). Hierzu R. E. Murphy (S. 67): "I don't think I understand the significance of the word 'semantic.'" Das Wort Semantik gehört in die Sprachwissenschaft. Die Semantik fragt nach Bedeutungen; sie hat keinen normativen Charakter (S. 43: "semantische Hierarchie"). Mit einer Hierarchie, die von einem Oberbegriff beherrscht wird und mit Prioritäten arbeitet, die festgestellt werden sollen, hat sie nichts zu tun.

Bei den Aufzählungen einzelner Wörter (S. 31f, 36, 37, 47) ist mir auch manches unklar geblieben. Die Aufzählung (S. 37) leiten Sie ein: "The qualitative modalities of Yahweh's relationship to reality are reflected in words . . . such as creation. . . ." Bezeichnen Sie hier die Schöpfung als eine qualitative Modalität von Jahwes Beziehung zur Wirklichkeit? S. 47: "Categories such as the Word of God, Revelation, Yahweh's Presence . . . provide no basis for solving the theological problem of the Old Testament. . . ." Was ist das theologische Problem des Alten Testaments? Wenn Sie (S. 47) fortfahren: "They have their place in the interpretation of Israel's theological anthropology," meinen Sie wirklich, daß "Wort Gottes" und "Offenbarung" in die Anthropologie gehören? Das klingt mir doch sehr nach Feuerbach.

Abschließend ist zur Sprache noch ein anderer Gesichtspunkt anzumerken. Dieser Entwurf wird für die jungen Kirchen außerhalb von den U.S.A. und Europa kaum Bedeutung haben können. Wenn diese, um zu erfahren, was das Alte Testament von Gott sagt, sich erst in das griechische Denken einarbeiten und sich eine übermäßige Fülle methodischer Begriffe auf der Basis der griechischen und lateinischen Sprache verständlich machen und übersetzen müssen, wird man sie kaum davon überzeugen können, daß das

9. Hierzu E. Schüßler Fiorenza, "The Ethics of Interpretation: De-Centering Biblical Scholarship," *JBL* 107 (1988): 3-17.

wirklich notwendig ist, um zu verstehen, was das Alte Testament von Gott sagt.[10]

Zum Schluß möchte ich noch einmal darauf hiweisen, daß ich ebenso wie die drei Stellungnahmen an einem Hauptpunkt Ihrem Entwurf zustimme: daß dem, was das AT vom Schöpfer und von der Schöpfung sagt, eine sehr viel höhere und weiterreichende Bedeutung zuerkannt werden muß, als das in der bisherigen Theologie des AT gesehen und anerkannt worden ist. Von diesem Gemeinsamen sollte die weitere Diskussion ausgehen.

Mit guten Wünschen
C. WESTERMANN

---

10. Hierzu E. Gerstenberger, "Der Realitätsbezug alttestamentlicher Exegese," *Congress Volume: Salamanca 1983*, ed. J. A. Emerton, VTSup 36 (Leiden: E. J. Brill, 1985), 132-44.